Student Book, **Foundation 1**

Approved by AQA

NEW GCSE MATHS
AQA Modular

Matches the 2010 GCSE Specification

Brian Speed • **Keith Gordon** • **Kevin Evans** • **Trevor Senior**

CONTENTS

CORE

UNIT 1: Statistics and Number

UNIT 2: Number and Algebra

INTRODUCTION

Welcome to Collins New GCSE Maths for AQA Modular Foundation Book 1. The first part of this book covers all the Core content you need for your Unit 1 and Unit 2 exams. The second part covers the content that is specific for Unit 1 and Unit 2, divided into separate sections.

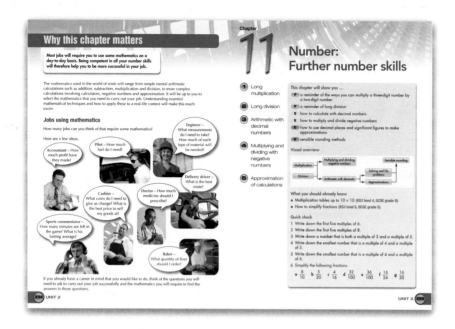

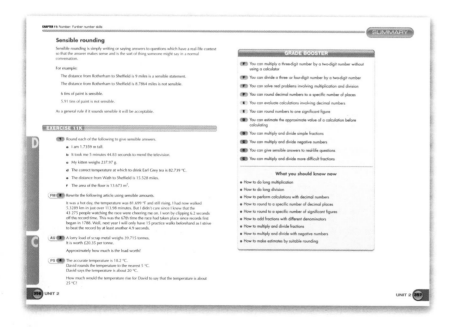

Why this chapter matters

Find out why each chapter is important through the history of maths, seeing how maths links to other subjects and cultures, and how maths is related to real life.

Chapter overviews

Look ahead to see what maths you will be doing and how you can build on what you already know.

Colour-coded grades

Know what target grade you are working at and track your progress with the colour-coded grade panels at the side of the page.

Use of calculators

Questions when you must or could use your calculator are marked with an 🖩 icon. Explanations involving calculators are based on the *Casio fx-83ES*.

Grade booster

Review what you have learnt and how to get to the next grade with the Grade booster at the end of each chapter.

Worked examples

Understand the topic before you start the exercise by reading the examples in blue boxes. These take you through questions step by step.

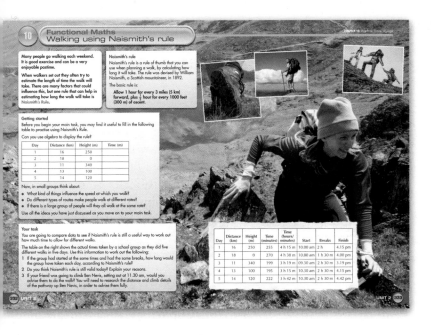

Functional maths

Practise functional maths skills to see how people use maths in everyday life. Look out for practice questions marked FM.

There are also extra functional maths and problem-solving activities at the end of every chapter to build and apply your skills.

New Assessment Objectives

Practise new parts of the curriculum (Assessment Objectives AO2 and AO3) with questions that assess your understanding marked AU and questions that test if you can solve problems marked PS. You will also practise some questions that involve several steps and where you have to choose which method to use; these also test AO2. There are also plenty of straightforward questions (AO1) that test if you can do the maths.

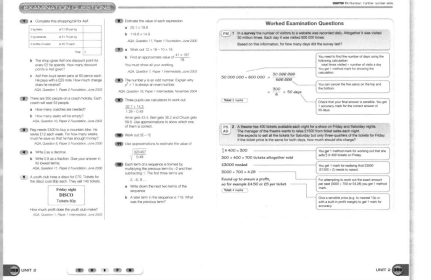

Exam practice

Prepare for your exams with past exam questions and detailed worked exam questions with examiner comments to help you score maximum marks.

Quality of Written Communication (QWC)

Practise using accurate mathematical vocabulary and writing logical answers to questions to ensure you get your QWC (Quality of Written Communication) marks in the exams. The Glossary and worked exam questions will help you with this.

Why this chapter matters

Thousands of years ago, many different civilisations developed different number systems. Most of these ways of counting were based on the number 10 (decimal numbers), simply because humans have 10 fingers and 10 toes.

The Egyptian number system (from about 3000BC) used different symbols to represent 1, 10, 100, 1000 and so on.

So the number 23 would be written: ∩∩ |||

The Chinese number system used sticks.

1	2	3	4	5	6	7	8	9

10	20	30	40	50	60	70	80	90

So, the number 23 would be written: ☰ |||

The Roman number system is still used today, often on clocks, and is based on the numbers five and ten.

I	V	X	L	C	D	M
1	5	10	50	100	500	1000

So, the number 23 would be written: XXIII

The system we use today is called the **Hindu-Arabic system** and uses the symbols 0, 1, 2, 3, 4, 5, 6, 7, 8 and 9. This has been widely used since about 900AD.

This system provides an almost universal 'language' of maths that has allowed us to make sense of the world around us and communicate ideas to others, even when their spoken language may differ from ours.

Decimal number	Egyptian symbol	
1 =	│	staff
10 =	∩	heel bone
100 =	☉	piece of rope
1000 =	⚘	flower
10 000 =	⌇	pointing finger
100 000 =	⤸	tadpole
1 000 000 =	⚇	man

Here you can see the Roman numerals for 1–12 on a clock face.

Roman numerals also appear on Big Ben.

1

Number:
Basic number

This chapter will show you ...

to **G** **F** how to use basic number skills without a calculator

Visual overview

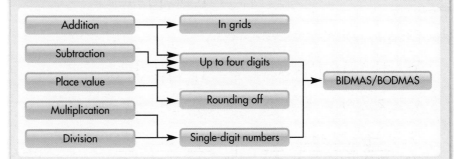

What you should already know

- Multiplication tables up to 10×10 (**KS3 level 4, GSCE grade G**)
- Addition and subtraction of numbers less than 20 (**KS3 level 2, GSCE grade G**)
- Simple multiplication and division (**KS3 level 3, GSCE grade G**)
- How to multiply numbers by 10 and 100 (**KS3 level 3, GSCE grade G**)

Quick check

How quickly can you complete these?

1 4×6	2 3×7	3 5×8	4 9×2
5 6×7	6 $13 + 14$	7 $15 + 15$	8 $18 - 12$
9 $19 - 7$	10 $11 - 6$	11 $50 \div 5$	12 $48 \div 6$
13 $35 \div 7$	14 $42 \div 6$	15 $36 \div 9$	16 8×10
17 9×100	18 3×10	19 14×100	20 17×10

Adding with grids

This section will show you how to:
- add and subtract single-digit numbers in a grid
- use row and column totals to find missing numbers in a grid

Key words
add
column
grid
row

ACTIVITY

Adding with grids

You need a set of cards marked 0 to 9.

| 0 | 1 | 2 | 3 | 4 | 5 | 6 | 7 | 8 | 9 |

Shuffle the cards and lay them out in a three by three **grid**. You will have one card left over.

3	5	0
7	6	4
8	2	9

Copy your grid onto a piece of paper. Then **add** up the numbers in each **row** and each **column** and write down their totals. Finally, find the grand total and write it in the box at the bottom right.

3	5	0	8
7	6	4	17
8	2	9	19
18	13	13	44

Look out for things that help. For example:
- in the first column, 3 + 7 make 10 and 10 + 8 = 18
- in the last column, 9 + 4 = 9 + 1 + 3 = 10 + 3 = 13

Reshuffle the cards, lay them out again and copy the new grid. Copy the new grid again on a fresh sheet of paper, leaving out some of the numbers.

4	5	8
0	2	6
9	1	7

4	5	8	17
0	2	6	8
9	1	7	17
13	8	21	42

4	☐	8	17
☐	2	☐	8
9	☐	7	☐
☐	8	21	42

Pass this last grid to a friend to work out the missing numbers. You can make it quite hard because you are using only the numbers from 0 to 9. Remember: once a number has been used, it *cannot* be used again in that grid.

FM Functional Maths **AU** (AO2) Assessing Understanding **PS** (AO3) Problem Solving

Example Find the numbers missing from this grid.

□	□	9	17
□	2	□	11
8	□	□	□
19	3	17	□

Clues The two numbers missing from the second column must add up to 1, so they must be 0 and 1. The two numbers missing from the first column add up to 11, so they could be 7 and 4 or 6 and 5. Now, 6 or 5 won't work with 0 or 1 to give 17 across the top row. That means it has to be:

7	1	9	17
4	2	□	11
8	0	□	□
19	3	17	□

giving

7	1	9	17
4	2	5	11
8	0	3	11
19	3	17	39

as the answer.

You can use your cards to try out your ideas.

EXERCISE 1A

1 Find the row and column totals for each of these grids.

a
1	3	7	□
9	2	8	□
6	5	4	□
□	□	□	□

b
0	6	7	□
8	1	4	□
9	5	3	□
□	□	□	□

c
0	8	7	□
1	6	2	□
9	3	4	□
□	□	□	□

d
2	4	6	□
3	5	7	□
8	9	1	□
□	□	□	□

e
5	9	3	□
6	1	8	□
2	7	4	□
□	□	□	□

f
0	8	3	□
7	2	4	□
1	6	5	□
□	□	□	□

g
9	4	8	□
7	0	5	□
1	6	3	□
□	□	□	□

h
0	8	6	□
7	1	4	□
5	9	2	□
□	□	□	□

i
1	8	7	□
6	2	5	□
0	9	3	□
□	□	□	□

FM 2 **a** Adam has two £10 notes, one £5 note and eight £1 coins in his pocket. Does he have enough money to buy a shirt costing £32?

b Belinda puts some plants into pots. There are six roses, eight sunflowers and nine lilies. How many plants altogether does she put into pots?

AU 3 Here is a list of numbers.

$$4 \quad 5 \quad 7 \quad 8 \quad 11 \quad 12$$

a From the list write down **two** numbers that add up to 18.

b From the list work out the largest total that can be made using **three** numbers.

c From the list work out the largest **even** total that can be made using **three** numbers.

PS 4 What number could be being described?

'It is bigger than three'

'It is less than 10'

'It is an even number'

5 Find the numbers missing from each of these grids. Remember: the numbers missing from each grid must be chosen from 0 to 9 without any repeats.

a

1	7	□	16
□	3	6	9
5	□	2	11
6	14	16	36

b

1	□	3	6
□	5	4	15
7	8	□	24
14	15	16	35

c

9	3	□	18
4	□	5	9
□	2	8	11
14	5	19	38

d

□	□	□	16
2	□	4	13
8	5	0	13
19	13	10	42

e

2	□	6	17
□	1	□	□
5	□	8	13
11	□	17	38

f

1	□	□	16
□	2	4	12
□	9	3	□
12	□	15	□

g

0	2	□	3
9	□	□	□
□	4	5	17
17	□	13	42

h

□	□	3	4
□	7	4	□
9	6	□	20
18	□	12	□

i

□	□	4	10
□	2	□	□
8	□	□	15
15	□	□	36

PS 6 Find **three different** numbers that add up to 36.

PS 7 Find **two different odd** numbers that add up to 24.

Multiplication tables check

This section will show you how to:
- recall and use your knowledge of multiplication tables

Key words
multiplication
multiplication tables
sign
times table

ACTIVITY

Special table facts

You need a sheet of squared paper.

Start by writing in the easy multiplication tables (or **times tables**). These are the 1 ×, 2 ×, 5 ×, 9 × and 10 × tables.

Now draw up a 10 by 10 table square before you go any further. (Time yourself doing this and see if you can get faster.)

Once you have a complete tables square, shade out all the **multiplications** that you already know. You should be left with something like the square on the right.

×	1	2	3	4	5	6	7	8	9	10
1										
2										
3			9	12		18	21	24		
4			12	16		24	28	32		
5										
6			18	24		36	42	48		
7			21	28		42	49	56		
8			24	32		48	56	64		
9										
10										

Now cross out **one** of each pair that have the same answer, such as 3 × 4 and 4 × 3. This leaves you with:

×	1	2	3	4	5	6	7	8	9	10
1										
2										
3			9							
4			12	16						
5										
6			18	24		36				
7			21	28		42	49			
8			24	32		48	56	64		
9										
10										

Now there are just 15 table facts. Do learn them.

The rest are easy tables, so you should know all of them. But keep practising!

EXERCISE 1B

G

1 Write down the answer to each of the following without looking at the multiplication square.

a 4 × 5	**b** 7 × 3	**c** 6 × 4	**d** 3 × 5	**e** 8 × 2
f 3 × 4	**g** 5 × 2	**h** 6 × 7	**i** 3 × 8	**j** 9 × 2
k 5 × 6	**l** 4 × 7	**m** 3 × 6	**n** 8 × 7	**o** 5 × 5
p 5 × 9	**q** 3 × 9	**r** 6 × 5	**s** 7 × 7	**t** 4 × 6
u 6 × 6	**v** 7 × 5	**w** 4 × 8	**x** 4 × 9	**y** 6 × 8

(FM) **z** Matt works for 6 hours each day and is paid £8 an hour.

He is saving for a bike that costs £75.

Will he have enough after two days?

Show how you worked out your answer.

2 Write down the answer to each of the following without looking at the multiplication square.

a 10 ÷ 2	**b** 28 ÷ 7	**c** 36 ÷ 6	**d** 30 ÷ 5	**e** 15 ÷ 3
f 20 ÷ 5	**g** 21 ÷ 3	**h** 24 ÷ 4	**i** 16 ÷ 8	**j** 12 ÷ 4
k 42 ÷ 6	**l** 24 ÷ 3	**m** 18 ÷ 2	**n** 25 ÷ 5	**o** 48 ÷ 6
p 36 ÷ 4	**q** 32 ÷ 8	**r** 35 ÷ 5	**s** 49 ÷ 7	**t** 27 ÷ 3
u 45 ÷ 9	**v** 16 ÷ 4	**w** 40 ÷ 8	**x** 63 ÷ 9	**y** 54 ÷ 9

(FM) **z** Viki works for 7 hours and is paid £42. She wants to save £60 to buy two tickets to the ballet.

How many hours will she need to work in order to save enough?

3 Write down the answer to each of the following. Look carefully at the **signs**, because they are a mixture of ×, +, – and ÷ .

a 5 + 7	**b** 20 – 5	**c** 3 × 7	**d** 5 + 8	**e** 24 ÷ 3
f 15 – 8	**g** 6 + 8	**h** 27 ÷ 9	**i** 6 × 5	**j** 36 ÷ 6
k 7 × 5	**l** 15 ÷ 3	**m** 24 – 8	**n** 28 ÷ 4	**o** 7 + 9
p 9 + 6	**q** 36 – 9	**r** 30 ÷ 5	**s** 8 + 7	**t** 4 × 6
u 8 × 5	**v** 42 ÷ 7	**w** 8 + 9	**x** 9 × 8	**y** 54 – 8

(FM) **z** Ahmed works for 3 hours and is paid £11 an hour. Ben works for 4 hours and is paid £8 an hour. Who is paid more?

AU 4 Here are four single-digit number cards.

| 5 | 8 | 3 | 6 |

The cards are used for making calculations. Complete the following.

a | 3 | 5 | + | ... | ... | = 121

b | 8 | 3 | − | ... | ... | = 27

c | ... | ... | 8 | + | ... | = 364

5 Write down the answer to each of the following.

a 3×10 **b** 5×10 **c** 8×10 **d** 10×10 **e** 12×10

f 18×10 **g** 24×10 **h** 4×100 **i** 7×100 **j** 9×100

k 10×100 **l** 14×100 **m** 24×100 **n** 72×100 **o** 100×100

p $20 \div 10$ **q** $70 \div 10$ **r** $90 \div 10$ **s** $170 \div 10$ **t** $300 \div 10$

u $300 \div 100$ **v** $800 \div 100$ **w** $1200 \div 100$ **x** $2900 \div 100$ **y** $5000 \div 100$

PS 6 a Two numbers when multiplied together give an answer of 24. One of the numbers is odd and greater than one. What is the other number?

b One whole number is divided by another whole number and gives an answer of 90. One of the numbers is 10. What is the other number?

PS 7 Consecutive numbers are numbers that are next to each other, for example 2 and 3.

Phil says that when two consecutive numbers are multiplied together the answer is always even.

Show, with two different examples, that this is true.

PS 8 Jenna says that when you multiply three consecutive numbers together you always get a number in the six times table, for example $2 \times 3 \times 4 = 24 = 4 \times 6$

Show, with two different examples, that this is true.

Order of operations and BIDMAS/BODMAS

This section will show you how to:
- work out the answers to a problem with a number of different mathematical operations

Key words
brackets
operation
order

Suppose you have to work out the answer to $4 + 5 \times 2$. You may say the answer is 18, but the correct answer is 14.

There is an **order** of **operations** which you *must* follow when working out calculations like this. The $\times$ is always done *before* the $+$.

In $4 + 5 \times 2$ this gives $4 + 10 = 14$.

Now suppose you have to work out the answer to $(3 + 2) \times (9 - 5)$. The correct answer is 20.

You have probably realised that the parts in the **brackets** have to be done *first*, giving $5 \times 4 = 20$.

So, how do you work out a problem such as $9 \div 3 + 4 \times 2$?

To answer questions like this, you *must* follow the BIDMAS (or BODMAS) rule. This tells you the order in which you *must* do the operations.

B	Brackets	**B**	Brackets
I	Indices (Powers)	**O**	pOwers
D	Division	**D**	Division
M	Multiplication	**M**	Multiplication
A	Addition	**A**	Addition
S	Subtraction	**S**	Subtraction

For example, to work out $9 \div 3 + 4 \times 2$:

First divide:	$9 \div 3 = 3$	giving	$3 + 4 \times 2$
Then multiply:	$4 \times 2 = 8$	giving	$3 + 8$
Then add:	$3 + 8 = 11$		

And to work out $60 - 5 \times 3^2 + (4 \times 2)$:

First, work out the brackets:	$(4 \times 2) = 8$	giving	$60 - 5 \times 3^2 + 8$
Then the index (power):	$3^2 = 9$	giving	$60 - 5 \times 9 + 8$
Then multiply:	$5 \times 9 = 45$	giving	$60 - 45 + 8$
Then add:	$60 + 8 = 68$	giving	$68 - 45$
Finally, subtract:	$68 - 45 = 23$		

ACTIVITY

Dice with BIDMAS/BODMAS

You need a sheet of squared paper and three dice.

Draw a five by five grid and write the numbers from 1 to 25 in the spaces.

The numbers can be in *any order*.

14	13	18	7	24
15	1	16	17	6
23	8	2	12	5
3	22	4	10	19
25	21	9	20	11

Now throw three dice. Record the score on each one.

Use these numbers to make up a number problem.

You must use all three numbers, and you must not put them together to make a number (such as making 136 with the three dice shown above). For example, with 1, 3 and 6 you could make:

$$1 + 3 + 6 = 10 \qquad 3 \times 6 + 1 = 19 \qquad (1 + 3) \times 6 = 24$$
$$6 \div 3 + 1 = 3 \qquad 6 + 3 - 1 = 8 \qquad 6 \div (3 \times 1) = 2$$

and so on. The answer to the problem must be from 1 to 25. Remember to use **BIDMAS/BODMAS**.

You have to make only one problem with each set of numbers.

When you have made a problem, cross the answer off the grid and throw the dice again. Make up a problem with the next three numbers and cross that answer off the grid. Throw the dice again and so on.

The first person to make a line of five numbers across, down or diagonally is the winner.

You must write down each problem and its answer so that they can be checked.

Just put a line through each number on the grid, as you use it. Do not cross it out so that it cannot be read, otherwise your problem and its answer cannot be checked.

This might be a typical game.

14	13	18	7	24
15	1	16	17	6
23	8	2	12	5
3	22	4	10	19
25	21	9	20	11

First set (1, 3, 6) $6 \times 3 \times 1 = 18$

Second set (2, 4, 4) $4 \times 4 - 2 = 14$

Third set (3, 5, 1) $(3 - 1) \times 5 = 10$

Fourth set (3, 3, 4) $(3 + 3) \times 4 = 24$

Fifth set (1, 2, 6) $6 \times 2 - 1 = 11$

Sixth set (5, 4, 6) $(6 + 4) \div 5 = 2$

Seventh set (4, 4, 2) $2 - (4 \div 4) = 1$

EXERCISE 1C

1 Work out each of these.

a $2 \times 3 + 5 =$ **b** $6 \div 3 + 4 =$ **c** $5 + 7 - 2 =$

d $4 \times 6 \div 2 =$ **e** $2 \times 8 - 5 =$ **f** $3 \times 4 + 1 =$

g $3 \times 4 - 1 =$ **h** $3 \times 4 \div 1 =$ **i** $12 \div 2 + 6 =$

j $12 \div 6 + 2 =$ **k** $3 + 5 \times 2 =$ **l** $12 - 3 \times 3 =$

2 Work out each of the following. Remember: first work out the bracket.

a $2 \times (3 + 5) =$ **b** $6 \div (2 + 1) =$ **c** $(5 + 7) - 2 =$

d $5 + (7 - 2) =$ **e** $3 \times (4 \div 2) =$ **f** $3 \times (4 + 2) =$

g $2 \times (8 - 5) =$ **h** $3 \times (4 + 1) =$ **i** $3 \times (4 - 1) =$

j $3 \times (4 \div 1) =$ **k** $12 \div (2 + 2) =$ **l** $(12 \div 2) + 2 =$

3 Copy each of these and put a loop round the part that you do first. Then work out the answer. The first one has been done for you.

a $\boxed{3 \times 3} - 2 = 7$ **b** $3 + 2 \times 4 =$ **c** $9 \div 3 - 2 =$

d $9 - 4 \div 2 =$ **e** $5 \times 2 + 3 =$ **f** $5 + 2 \times 3 =$

g $10 \div 5 - 2 =$ **h** $10 - 4 \div 2 =$ **i** $4 \times 6 - 7 =$

j $7 + 4 \times 6 =$ **k** $6 \div 3 + 7 =$ **l** $7 + 6 \div 2 =$

4 Work out each of these.

a $6 \times 6 + 2 =$ **b** $6 \times (6 + 2) =$ **c** $6 \div 6 + 2 =$

d $12 \div (4 + 2) =$ **e** $12 \div 4 + 2 =$ **f** $2 \times (3 + 4) =$

g $2 \times 3 + 4 =$ **h** $2 \times (4 - 3) =$ **i** $2 \times 4 - 3 =$

j $17 + 5 - 3 =$ **k** $17 - 5 + 3 =$ **l** $17 - 5 \times 3 =$

m $3 \times 5 + 5 =$ **n** $6 \times 2 + 7 =$ **o** $6 \times (2 + 7) =$

p $12 \div 3 + 3 =$ **q** $12 \div (3 + 3) =$ **r** $14 - 7 \times 1 =$

s $(14 - 7) \times 1 =$ **t** $2 + 6 \times 6 =$ **u** $(2 + 5) \times 6 =$

v $12 - 6 \div 3 =$ **w** $(12 - 6) \div 3 =$ **x** $15 - (5 \times 1) =$

y $(15 - 5) \times 1 =$ **z** $8 \times 9 \div 3 =$

5 Copy each of these and then put in brackets where necessary to make each answer true.

a $3 \times 4 + 1 = 15$ **b** $6 \div 2 + 1 = 4$ **c** $6 \div 2 + 1 = 2$

d $4 + 4 \div 4 = 5$ **e** $4 + 4 \div 4 = 2$ **f** $16 - 4 \div 3 = 4$

g $3 \times 4 + 1 = 13$ **h** $16 - 6 \div 3 = 14$ **i** $20 - 10 \div 2 = 5$

j $20 - 10 \div 2 = 15$ **k** $3 \times 5 + 5 = 30$ **l** $6 \times 4 + 2 = 36$

m $15 - 5 \times 2 = 20$ **n** $4 \times 7 - 2 = 20$ **o** $12 \div 3 + 3 = 2$

p $12 \div 3 + 3 = 7$ **q** $24 \div 8 - 2 = 1$ **r** $24 \div 8 - 2 = 4$

6 Three dice are thrown. They give scores of three, one and four.

A class makes the following questions with the numbers. Work them out.

a $3 + 4 + 1 =$ **b** $3 + 4 - 1 =$ **c** $4 + 3 - 1 =$

d $4 \times 3 + 1 =$ **e** $4 \times 3 - 1 =$ **f** $(4 - 1) \times 3 =$

g $4 \times 3 \times 1 =$ **h** $(3 - 1) \times 4 =$ **i** $(4 + 1) \times 3 =$

j $4 \times (3 + 1) =$ **k** $1 \times (4 - 3) =$ **l** $4 + 1 \times 3 =$

AU 7 Jack says that $5 + 6 \times 7$ is equal to 77.

Is he correct?

Explain your answer.

AU 8 This is Micha's homework.

Copy the questions where she has made mistakes and work out the correct answers.

a $2 + 3 \times 4 =$ $\boxed{20}$ **b** $8 - 4 \div 4 =$ $\boxed{7}$ **c** $6 + 3 \times 2 =$ $\boxed{12}$

d $7 - 1 \times 5 =$ $\boxed{30}$ **e** $2 \times 7 + 2 =$ $\boxed{16}$ **f** $9 - 3 \times 3 =$ $\boxed{18}$

9 Three different dice give scores of 2, 3, 5. Add ÷, ×, + or – signs to make each calculation work.

a $2 \quad 3 \quad 5 = 11$ **b** $2 \quad 3 \quad 5 = 16$ **c** $2 \quad 3 \quad 5 = 17$

d $5 \quad 3 \quad 2 = 4$ **e** $5 \quad 3 \quad 2 = 13$ **f** $5 \quad 3 \quad 2 = 30$

AU 10 Which is smaller

$4 + 5 \times 3$ or $(4 + 5) \times 3$?

Show your working.

PS 11 Here is a list of numbers, some signs and one pair of brackets.

$2 \quad 5 \quad 6 \quad 18 \quad - \quad \times \quad = \quad (\quad)$

Use **all** of them to make a correct calculation.

PS 12 Here is a list of numbers, some signs and one pair of brackets.

$3 \quad 4 \quad 5 \quad 8 \quad - \quad \div \quad = \quad (\quad)$

Use **all** of them to make a correct calculation.

FM 13 Jeremy has a piece of pipe that is 10 m long.

He wants to use his calculator to work out how much pipe will be left when he cuts off three pieces, each of length 1.5 m.

Which calculations would give him the correct answer?

$10 - 3 \times 1.5$ $\qquad\qquad$ $10 - 1.5 + 1.5 + 1.5$ $\qquad\qquad$ $10 - 1.5 - 1.5 - 1.5$

Place value and ordering numbers

This section will show you how to:
- identify the value of any digit in a number

Key words
digit
order
place value

The ordinary counting system uses **place value**, which means that the value of a **digit** depends upon its place in the number.

In the number 5348

the 5 stands for five thousands or 5000

the 3 stands for three hundreds or 300

the 4 stands for four tens or 40

the 8 stands for eight units or 8

You write and say this number as:

five thousand, three hundred and forty-eight

In the number 4 073 520

the 4 stands for four millions or 4 000 000

the 73 stands for 73 thousands or 73 000

the 5 stands for five hundreds or 500

the 2 stands for two tens or 20

You write and say this number as:

four million, seventy-three thousand, five hundred and twenty

Note the use of narrow spaces between groups of three digits, starting from the right. All whole and mixed numbers with five or more digits are spaced in this way.

EXAMPLE 1

Put these numbers in **order**, putting the smallest first.

7031   3071   3701   7103   7130   1730

Look at the thousands column first and then each of the other columns in turn. The correct order is:

1730   3071   3701   7031   7103   7130

EXERCISE 1D

1 Write the value of each underlined digit.

a 3<u>4</u>1	**b** 47<u>5</u>	**c** <u>1</u>86	**d** 2<u>9</u>8	**e** <u>8</u>3
f 83<u>9</u>	**g** 23<u>8</u>0	**h** 1<u>5</u>07	**i** 653<u>0</u>	**j** 2<u>5</u> 436
k 29 <u>0</u>54	**l** 18 25<u>4</u>	**m** 4<u>3</u>08	**n** 52 9<u>9</u>4	**o** <u>8</u>3 205

2 Copy each of these sentences, writing the numbers in words.

a The last Olympic Games in Greece had only 43 events and 200 competitors.

b The last Olympic Games in Britain had 136 events and 4099 competitors.

c The last Olympic Games in the USA had 271 events and 10 744 competitors.

3 Write each of the following numbers in words.

a 5 600 000   **b** 4 075 200   **c** 3 007 950   **d** 2 000 782

4 Write each of the following numbers in numerals or digits.

a Eight million, two hundred thousand and fifty-eight

b Nine million, four hundred and six thousand, one hundred and seven

c One million, five hundred and two

d Two million, seventy-six thousand and forty

5 Write these numbers in order, putting the *smallest* first.

a 21, 48, 23, 9, 15, 56, 85, 54

b 310, 86, 219, 25, 501, 62, 400, 151

c 357, 740, 2053, 888, 4366, 97, 368

6 Write these numbers in order, putting the *largest* first.

a 52, 23, 95, 34, 73, 7, 25, 89

b 65, 2, 174, 401, 80, 700, 18, 117

c 762, 2034, 395, 6227, 89, 3928, 59, 480

7 Copy each sentence and fill in the missing word, *smaller* or *larger*.

a 7 is …… than 5

b 34 is …… than 29

c 89 is …… than 98

d 97 is …… than 79

e 308 is …… than 299

f 561 is …… than 605

g 870 is …… than 807

h 4275 is …… than 4527

i 782 is …… than 827

FM 8 An estate agent advertises the following houses.

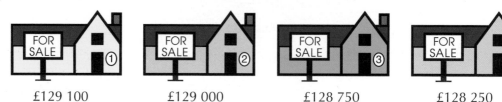

| £129 100 | £129 000 | £128 750 | £128 250 |

a Which house is the cheapest?

b Which house is the most expensive?

c George has just enough money to buy the cheapest house. How much more money would he need to buy the most expensive house?

PS 9 a Write as many three-digit numbers as you can, using the digits 3, 6 and 8. (Only use each digit once in each number.)

b Which of your numbers is the smallest?

c Which of your numbers is the largest?

PS 10 Using each of the digits 0, 4 and 8 only once in each number, write as many different three-digit numbers as you can. (Do not start any number with 0.) Write your numbers down in order, smallest first.

PS 11 Write down in order of size, smallest first, all the two-digit numbers that can be made using 3, 5 and 8. (Each digit can be repeated.)

AU 12 Using each of the digits 0, 4, 5 and 7, make a four-digit odd number greater than seven thousand.

13 Nick has these number cards

a Copy the blank calculation below and insert numbers into the boxes to make the largest possible total.

b Copy the blank calculation below and insert numbers into the boxes to make the smallest possible difference.

Rounding

This section will show you how to:
- round a number

Key words
approximation
rounded down
rounded up

You use rounded information all the time. Look at the examples on the right. All of these statements use rounded information. Each actual figure is either above or below the **approximation** shown here. But if the rounding is done correctly, you can find out what the maximum and the minimum figures really are. For example, if you know that the number of matches in the packet is rounded to the nearest 10, and it states that there are 30 matches in a packet:

- the smallest figure **rounded up** to 30 is 25, and
- the largest figure **rounded down** to 30 is 34 (because 35 would be rounded up to 40).

So, there could actually be from 25 to 34 matches in the packet.

What about the number of runners in the marathon? If you know that the number 23 000 is rounded to the nearest 1000:

- the smallest figure rounded up to 23 000 is 22 500, and
- the largest figure rounded down to 23 000 is 23 499 (because 23 500 would be rounded up to 24 000).

So, there could actually be from 22 500 to 23 499 people in the marathon.

EXERCISE 1E

1 Round each of these numbers to the nearest 10.

a 24	**b** 57	**c** 78	**d** 54	**e** 96
f 21	**g** 88	**h** 66	**i** 14	**j** 26
k 29	**l** 51	**m** 77	**n** 49	**o** 94
p 35	**q** 65	**r** 15	**s** 102	**t** 107

2 Round each of these numbers to the nearest 100.

a 240	**b** 570	**c** 780	**d** 504	**e** 967
f 112	**g** 645	**h** 358	**i** 998	**j** 1050
k 299	**l** 511	**m** 777	**n** 512	**o** 940
p 350	**q** 650	**r** 750	**s** 1020	**t** 1070

3 On the shelf of a sweetshop there are three jars like the ones below.

Jar 1   Jar 2   Jar 3

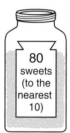

80 sweets (to the nearest 10)   120 sweets (to the nearest 10)   190 sweets (to the nearest 10)

Look at each of the numbers below and write down which jar it could be describing. (For example, 76 sweets could be in jar 1.)

a 78 sweets	**b** 119 sweets	**c** 84 sweets	**d** 75 sweets
e 186 sweets	**f** 122 sweets	**g** 194 sweets	**h** 115 sweets
i 81 sweets	**j** 79 sweets	**k** 192 sweets	**l** 124 sweets

m Which of these numbers of sweets *could not* be in jar 1: 74, 84, 81, 76?

n Which of these numbers of sweets *could not* be in jar 2: 124, 126, 120, 115?

o Which of these numbers of sweets *could not* be in jar 3: 194, 184, 191, 189?

4 Round each of these numbers to the nearest 1000.

a 2400	**b** 5700	**c** 7806	**d** 5040	**e** 9670
f 1120	**g** 6450	**h** 3499	**i** 9098	**j** 1500
k 2990	**l** 5110	**m** 7777	**n** 5020	**o** 9400
p 3500	**q** 6500	**r** 7500	**s** 1020	**t** 1770

5 Round each of these numbers to the nearest 10.

a 234	**b** 567	**c** 718	**d** 524	**e** 906
f 231	**g** 878	**h** 626	**i** 114	**j** 296
k 279	**l** 541	**m** 767	**n** 501	**o** 942
p 375	**q** 625	**r** 345	**s** 1012	**t** 1074

AU 6

<table>
<tr><td>

Welcome to Elsecar
Population 800
(to the nearest 100)

</td><td>

Welcome to Hoyland
Population 1200
(to the nearest 100)

</td><td>

Welcome to Jump
Population 600
(to the nearest 100)

</td></tr>
</table>

Which of these sentences could be true and which must be false?

a There are 789 people living in Elsecar.　**b** There are 1278 people living in Hoyland.

c There are 550 people living in Jump.　**d** There are 843 people living in Elsecar.

e There are 1205 people living in Hoyland.　**f** There are 650 people living in Jump.

FM 7 A sign maker is asked to create a sign similar to those shown in question 6 for Swinton, which has a population of 1385.

Make a diagram of the sign he should paint.

FM 8 These were the numbers of spectators in the crowds at nine Premier Division games on a weekend in May 2005.

Aston Villa v Man City	39 645
Blackburn v Fulham	18 991
Chelsea v Charlton	42 065
C. Palace v Southampton	26 066
Everton v Newcastle	40 438
Man.Utd v West Brom	67 827
Middlesbrough v Tottenham	34 766
Norwich v Birmingham	25 477
Portsmouth v Bolton	20 188

a Which match had the largest crowd?

b Which had the smallest crowd?

c Round all the numbers to the nearest 1000.

d Round all the numbers to the nearest 100.

9 Give these cooking times to the nearest 5 minutes.

a 34 min　**b** 57 min　**c** 14 min　**d** 51 min　**e** 8 min

f 13 min　**g** 44 min　**h** 32.5 min　**i** 3 min　**j** 50 s

PS 10 Matthew and Viki are playing a game with whole numbers.

a What is the smallest number Matthew could be thinking of?

I am thinking of a number. Rounded to the nearest 10 it is 380.

I am thinking of a different number. Rounded to the nearest 100 it is 400.

b Is Viki's number smaller than Matthew's? How many possible answers are there?

PS
AU **11** The number of adults attending a comedy show is 80 to the nearest 10.

The number of children attending is 50 to the nearest 10.

Katie says that 130 adults and children attended the comedy show.

Give an example to show that she may **not** be correct.

This section will show you how to:
- add and subtract numbers with more than one digit

Key words

addition
column
digit
subtract

Addition

There are three things to remember when you are adding two whole numbers.

- The answer will always be larger than the bigger number.

- Always add the units **column** first.

- When the total of the **digits** in a column is more than nine, you have to carry a digit into the next column on the left, as shown in Example 2. It is important to write down the carried digit, otherwise you may forget to include it in the **addition**.

EXAMPLE 2

Add: **a** 167 + 25   **b** 2296 + 1173

$$
\begin{array}{r}
\mathbf{a} \quad 167 \\
+ \ 25 \\
\hline
192 \\
\hline
{\scriptstyle 1}
\end{array}
\qquad
\begin{array}{r}
\mathbf{b} \quad 2296 \\
+ \ 1173 \\
\hline
3469 \\
\hline
{\scriptstyle 1}
\end{array}
$$

Subtraction

These are four things to remember when you are subtracting one whole number from another.

- The bigger number must always be written down first.

- The answer will always be smaller than the bigger number.

- Always **subtract** the units column first.

- When you have to take a bigger digit from a smaller digit in a column, you must 'borrow' a 10 by taking one from the column to the left and putting it with the smaller digit, as shown in Example 3.

EXAMPLE 3

Subtract: **a** 874 − 215   **b** 300 − 163

$$
\begin{array}{r}
\mathbf{a} \quad 8\,{}^{6}7{}^{1}4 \\
- \ 215 \\
\hline
659
\end{array}
\qquad
\begin{array}{r}
\mathbf{b} \quad {}^{2}3\,{}^{9}\emptyset\,{}^{1}0 \\
- \ 163 \\
\hline
137
\end{array}
$$

EXERCISE 1F

1 Copy and work out each of these additions.

a	b	c	d	e
365	95	4872	317	287
+ 348	+ 56	+ 1509	416	+ 335
			+ 235	

f	g	h	i	j
483	4676	438	175	562
+ 832	+ 3584	147	+ 276	93
		+ 233		+ 197

2 Copy and complete each of these additions.

a 128 + 518	**b** 563 + 85 + 178	**c** 3086 + 58 + 674
d 347 + 408	**e** 85 + 1852 + 659	**f** 759 + 43 + 89
g 257 + 93	**h** 605 + 26 + 2135	**i** 56 + 8407 + 395
j 89 + 752	**k** 6143 + 557 + 131	**l** 2593 + 45 + 4378
m 719 + 284	**n** 545 + 3838 + 67	**o** 5213 + 658 + 4073

3 Copy and complete each of these subtractions.

a	b	c	d	e
637	908	954	572	732
− 187	− 345	− 472	− 158	− 447

f	g	h	i	j
673	602	638	650	580
− 187	− 358	− 354	− 317	− 364

k	l	m	n	o
6254	8043	8432	8034	5375
− 3362	− 3626	− 4665	− 3947	− 3547

4 Copy and complete each of these subtractions.

a 354 − 226	**b** 285 − 256	**c** 663 − 329
d 506 − 328	**e** 654 − 377	**f** 733 − 448
g 592 − 257	**h** 753 − 354	**i** 6705 − 2673
j 8021 − 3256	**k** 7002 − 3207	**l** 8700 − 3263

FM 5 The distance from Cardiff to London is 152 miles.
The distance from London to Edinburgh is 406 miles.

a How far is it to travel from London to Cardiff and then from Cardiff to Edinburgh?

b How much further is it to travel from London to Edinburgh than from Cardiff to London?

G

AU 6 Jon is checking the addition of two numbers.

His answer is 843.

One of the numbers is 591.

What should the other number be?

7 Copy each of these additions and fill in the missing digits.

a
```
   5 3
+ 2 □
  □ 9
```

b
```
  □ 7
+ 3 □
  8 4
```

c
```
   4 5
+ □ □
   9 3
```

d
```
   4 □ 7
+ □ 5 □
   9 3 6
```

e
```
  □ 1 8
+ 2 5 □
  8 □ 7
```

f
```
   5 4 □
+ □ □ 6
   8 2 2
```

g
```
   4 6 9
+ □ □ □
   7 3 5
```

h
```
  □ □ □
+ 3 4 8
  8 0 7
```

i
```
  □ 4 □
+ 3 3 7
  7 □ 5
```

j
```
   3 5 7 8
+ □ □ □ □
   8 0 7 6
```

F

AU 8 Lisa is checking the subtraction: 614 − 258.

Explain how you know that her answer of 444 is incorrect without working out the whole calculation.

9 Copy each of these subtractions and fill in the missing digits.

a
```
   7 4
− 2 □
  □ 1
```

b
```
  □ 7
− 3 □
  5 4
```

c
```
   8 5
− □ □
   2 7
```

d
```
   6 7 □
− □ □ 3
   1 3 5
```

e
```
  □ 1 4
− 2 5 □
  3 □ 7
```

f
```
   5 4 □
− □ □ 6
   3 2 5
```

g
```
   4 6 2
− □ □ □
   1 8 5
```

h
```
  □ □ □
− 2 4 7
  3 0 9
```

i
```
  □ 4 □
− 5 5 8
  2 □ 5
```

j
```
   8 0 7 6
− □ □ □ □
   6 1 8 7
```

PS 10 A two-digit number is subtracted from a three-digit number.

The answer is 154.

Work out one pair of possible values for the numbers.

Multiplying and dividing by single-digit numbers

This section will show you how to:
* multiply and divide by a single-digit number

Key words
division
multiplication

Multiplication

There are two things to remember when you are multiplying two whole numbers.

* The bigger number must always be written down first.

* The answer will always be larger than the bigger number.

EXAMPLE 4

a Multiply 231 by 4.

$$\begin{array}{r} 213 \\ \times \quad 4 \\ \hline 852 \\ \scriptstyle 1 \end{array}$$

b Multiply 543 by 6.

$$\begin{array}{r} 543 \\ \times \quad 6 \\ \hline 3258 \\ \scriptstyle 2\,1 \end{array}$$

Note that in part **a** the first multiplication, 3 × 4, gives 12. So, you need to carry a digit into the next column on the left, as in the case of addition. Similar actions are carried out in part **b**.

Division

There are two things to remember when you are dividing one whole number by another whole number:

* The answer will always be smaller than the bigger number.

* Division starts at the *left-hand side*.

EXAMPLE 5

a Divide 417 by 3.

417 ÷ 3 is set out as:

$$3\overline{)4^1 1^2 7} \quad = 139$$

b Divide 508 by 4.

508 ÷ 4 is set out as:

$$4\overline{)5^1 0^2 8} \quad = 127$$

This is how the division was done in part **a**:

* First, divide 3 into 4 to get 1 and remainder 1. Note where to put the 1 and the remainder 1.

* Then, divide 3 into 11 to get 3 and remainder 2. Note where to put the 3 and the remainder 2.

* Finally, divide 3 into 27 to get 9 with no remainder, giving the answer 139.

A similar process takes place in part **b**.

EXERCISE 1G

1 Copy and work out each of the following multiplications.

a 14	**b** 13	**c** 17	**d** 19	**e** 18
× 4	× 5	× 3	× 2	× 6

f 23	**g** 34	**h** 42	**i** 53	**j** 85
× 5	× 6	× 7	× 4	× 5

k 50	**l** 200	**m** 320	**n** 340	**o** 253
× 3	× 4	× 3	× 4	× 6

2 Calculate each of the following multiplications by setting the work out in columns.

a 42×7 **b** 74×5 **c** 48×6

d 208×4 **e** 309×7 **f** 630×4

g 548×3 **h** 643×5 **i** 8×375

j 6×442 **k** 7×528 **l** 235×8

m 6043×9 **n** 5×4387 **o** 9×5432

3 Calculate each of the following divisions.

a $438 \div 2$ **b** $634 \div 2$ **c** $945 \div 3$

d $636 \div 6$ **e** $297 \div 3$ **f** $847 \div 7$

g $756 \div 3$ **h** $846 \div 6$ **i** $576 \div 4$

j $344 \div 4$ **k** $441 \div 7$ **l** $5818 \div 2$

m $3744 \div 9$ **n** $2008 \div 8$ **o** $7704 \div 6$

AU 4 Dean, Sean and Andy are doing a charity cycle ride from Huddersfield to Southend. The distance from Huddersfield to Southend is 235 miles.

a How many miles do all three travel altogether?

b Dean is sponsored £6 per mile.
Sean is sponsored £5 per mile.
Andy is sponsored £4 per mile.

How much money do they raise altogether?

FM 5 The 235-mile charity cycle ride in question 4 is planned to take five days.

    a What is the least number of miles each cyclist has to cover each day?

    b The cyclists travel 60 miles on the first day and 50 miles on the second day.

       Fill in a copy of the plan for the remaining days so they complete the ride on time. Each day the number of miles covered has to be fewer than for the previous day.

	Mileage
Day 3	
Day 4	
Day 5	

6 By doing a suitable multiplication, answer each of these questions.

    a How many days are there in 17 weeks?

    b How many hours are there in four days?

    c Eggs are packed in boxes of six. How many eggs are there in 24 boxes?

    d Joe bought five boxes of matches. Each box contained 42 matches. How many matches did Joe buy altogether?

    e A box of Tulip Sweets holds 35 sweets. How many sweets are there in six boxes?

7 By doing a suitable division, answer each of these questions.

    a How many weeks are there in 91 days?

    b How long will it take me to save £111, if I save £3 a week?

    c A rope, 215 m long, is cut into five equal pieces. How long is each piece?

    d Granny has a bottle of 144 tablets. How many days will they last if she takes four each day?

    e I share a box of 360 sweets among eight children. How many sweets will each child get?

PS 8 Here is part of the 38 times table.

×1	×2	×3	×4	×5
38	76	114	152	190

Show how you can use this table to work out

    a 9×38 **b** 52×38 **c** 105×38.

Letter sets

Find the next letters in these sequences.

a O, T, T, F, F, ...   **b** T, F, S, E, T, ...

Valued letters

In the three additions below, each letter stands for a single numeral. But a letter may not necessarily stand for the same numeral when it is used in more than one sum.

a   O N E
        + O N E
        ———————
          T W O

b   T W O
          + T W O
          ———————
            F O U R

c   F O U R
          + F I V E
          ———————
            N I N E

Write down each addition in numbers.

Four fours

Write number sentences to give answers from 1 to 10, using only four fours and any number of the operations +, −, × and ÷ . For example:

$1 = (4 + 4) \div (4 + 4)$ $2 = (4 \times 4) \div (4 + 4)$

Heinz 57

Pick any number in the grid on the right. Circle the number and cross out all the other numbers in the row and column containing the number you have chosen. Now circle another number that is not crossed out and cross out all the other numbers in the row and column containing this number. Repeat until you have five numbers circled. Add these numbers together. What do you get? Now do it again but start with a different number.

19	8	11	25	7
12	1	4	18	0
16	5	8	22	4
21	10	13	27	9
14	3	6	20	2

Magic squares

This is a magic square. Add the numbers in any row, column or diagonal. The answer is *always* 15.

8	1	6
3	5	7
4	9	2

Now try to complete this magic square using every number from 1 to 16.

1		14	
	6		9
8		11	
	3		16

GRADE BOOSTER

G You can add columns and rows in grids

G You know the multiplication tables up to 10×10

G You can use BIDMAS/BODMAS to work out calculations in the correct order

G You can identify the value of digits in different places

G You can round numbers to the nearest 10 and 100

G You can add and subtract numbers with up to four digits

G You can multiply numbers by a single-digit number

F You can solve problems involving multiplication and division by a single-digit number

What you should know now

- How to use BIDMAS/BODMAS
- How to put numbers in order
- How to round to the nearest 10, 100, 1000
- How to solve simple problems in context, using the four operations of addition, subtraction, multiplication and division

1 **a** **i** Write down the number sixty-three thousand, five hundred and seven in figures.

ii Write down sixty-three thousand, five hundred and seven correct to the nearest thousand.

b **i** Write down 10 780 in words.

ii Write down 10 780 correct to the nearest 100.

2 Ben has four cards, each with a number written on it.

| 3 | 7 | 2 | 9 |

Ben puts all four cards on the floor to make a number.

a **i** What is the smallest number Ben can make?

ii What is the largest number Ben can make?

b Ben uses all the cards to make a true statement.

 × =

What is this true statement?

c Another card is needed to show the answer to the question 3729 × 10.
What number should be on this other card?

3 The size of the crowd at a football match is given as 43 600 to the nearest hundred.

a What is the lowest number of people that could be in the crowd?

b What is the largest number of people that could be in the crowd?

4 For each of the following, write down whether it is true or false and give a reason for your answer.

a $9 \times 8 \times 4 = 8 \times 4 \times 9$

b $36 \div 9 = 9 \div 36$

c $6 \times 3 + 5 \times 3 = 11 \times 3$

5 Mount Everest is 8848 metres high.
Mount Snowdon is 1085 metres high.

How much higher is Mount Everest than Mount Snowdon?

Give your answer to the nearest 10 metres.

6 It costs £7 per person to visit a show.

a 215 people attend the show on Monday. How much do they pay altogether?

b On Tuesday the takings were £1372. How many fewer people attended on Tuesday than on Monday?

7 **a** Write ten thousand in figures. (1)

b Write 1010 in words. (1)

c Round 2634 to the nearest thousand. (1)

d What is the value of the digit 8 in 9875? (1)

e Work out $7249 + 2163 - 5075$ (1)

(Total 5 marks)

AQA, June 2009, Module 3 Foundation, Question 1

8 The table shows the number of candidates who sat a GCSE Mathematics examination.

Tier	Foundation	Intermediate	Higher
Number of candidates	30 338	65 306	29 581

a Which tier had the greatest number of candidates? (1)

b Write 30 338 in words. (1)

c Write 29 581 to the nearest thousand. (1)

(Total 3 marks)

AQA, June 2007, Paper 1 Foundation, Question 2

9 Write the number 15382

a to the nearest 10 (1)

b to the nearest 100. (1)

(Total 2 marks)

AQA, June 2008, Paper 1 Foundation, Question 2

10 Put brackets into these calculations to make them true.

a $2 \times 3^2 + 6 = 42$

b $2 \times 3^2 + 6 = 30$

11 The following are two students' attempts at working out $3 + 5^2 - 2$.

Adam: $3 + 5^2 - 2 = 3 + 10 - 2 = 13 - 2 = 11$

Bekki: $3 + 5^2 - 2 = 8^2 - 2 = 64 - 2 = 62$

a Each student has made one mistake. Explain what this is for each of them.

b Work out the correct answer to $3 + 5^2 - 2$.

Worked Examination Questions

1 Here are four number cards, showing the number 2745.

| 2 | 7 | 4 | 5 |

Using all four cards, write down:

a the largest possible number

b the smallest possible number

c the missing numbers from this problem.

☐ 7 × 2 = ☐ ☐

a 7542

1 mark

> Start with the largest number as the thousands digits, use the next largest as the hundreds digit and so on. This is worth 1 mark.

b 2457

1 mark

> Start with the smallest number as the thousands digits, use the next smallest as the hundreds digit and so on. Note the answer is the reverse of the answer to part **a**. This is worth 1 mark.

c 27 × 2 = 54

2 marks

Total: 4 marks

> There are three numbers left, 2, 5, 4. The 2 must go into the first box and then you can work out that 2 × 27 is 54.
> You get 1 mark for identifying the units digit of the answer as 4 and 2 marks if the whole answer is correct.

FM **2** I want to buy a burger, a portion of chips and a bottle of cola for my lunch. I have the following coins in my pocket: £1, 50p, 50p, 20p, 20p, 10p, 2p, 2p, 1p.

a Do I have enough money?

b What about if I replace the chips with beans?

Price List	
Burger	£1.20
Chips	90p
Beans	50p
Cola	60p

a Total cost for a burger, chips and a cola = £2.70.

Total of coins in my pocket = £2.55

No, as £2.70 > £2.55

3 marks

> This is a question in which you could be assessed on your quality of written communication, so set out your answer clearly.

> Show the total cost of the meal and the total of the coins in your pocket. This is worth 2 marks.

b Beans are 40p cheaper and £2.30 < £2.55.

So, I could afford this.

1 mark

> It is important to show a clear conclusion. Do not just say 'No'. Use the numbers to back up your answer. This is worth 1 mark.

> Explain clearly why you could afford this meal. This is worth 1 mark.

Total: 4 marks

You are planning to go on an activity holiday in Wales with a group of friends.
You are arriving late on Sunday evening and will be staying all week until the end of Friday.
You have chosen the area that you are staying in because there are lots of activities available and you want to make sure that everyone in the group can find something that they will enjoy on the holiday.

Your task

Work in groups of three or four.

Decide what the different interests in your group are and work together to make a timetable of activities that addresses all of these interests. You will need to make sure that everyone has the time to do all of the things that they would like to do.

You must then work out how much the holiday is going to cost for each of you.

Getting started

Use the following points to get you started:

● On your own, decide the activities you would like to do. You don't have to do everything.

● As a group, think of the questions you are going to ask as you do this task to find out the information that you will need.

● Think about how you might keep track of all the information that you need.

● Decide on how you will work out the cost for each member of your group.

Windsurfing Half-day £59 Full day £79	**Paragliding** Half-day £99 for 1 person £189 for 2 people	**Quadbikes** £21 per hour Race Event (2 hours) £100 for three or four people	**Horse riding** Half-day (Mondays, Wednesdays and Fridays) £32
Fishing Trip Half-day £18 per person	**Coast jumping** 2 hours £85 per group of up to 4 people	**Kayaking** Half-day £29 Full Day £49	**Raft racing** Half-day £60 per team (minimum 2 people)
Diving 3 hours £38 per person	**Spa** 2 hours £24 for 1 person £40 for 2 people	**Shopping Trip** Half-day £60 budget	**Steam train up mountain** 2 hours £5.60 per person (10% discount for groups of 4)

Why this chapter matters

The word 'fraction' comes from the Latin word *fractus*, meaning broken. Just think of when you fracture an arm or leg – you have cracked (or broken) it into parts.

We use fractions to break things – from measurements to shapes – into parts.

Chapter 1 (page 6) showed how there used to be several different number systems, developed by many different ancient civilisations. Each of these civilisations developed their own way of expressing fractions. Most of these fraction systems died out, but one – the Arabic system – directly led to the fractions that we use today.

The Babylonians – the first fractions

Fractions can be traced back to the Babylonians, in around 1800BC. This civilisation in Mesopotamia (modern day Iraq) was the first to develop a sensible way to represent a fraction.

Their fractions were based on the number 60 as was its whole number system. However, its number symbols could not accurately represent the fractions and the fractions had no symbol to show that they were fractions rather than standard numbers. This made their system of fractions very complicated.

Egyptian fractions

The Egyptians (around 1000BC) were known to use fractions but generally these were unit fractions (fractions with a numerator of 1), for example, $\frac{1}{2}, \frac{1}{3}, \frac{1}{4}$.

The Egyptians used this symbol to represent the "one":

Then, using the number symbols shown in Chapter 1, they made their fractions:

$$\frac{\bigcirc}{|||} = \frac{1}{3}$$

They also had special symbols for $\frac{1}{2}, \frac{2}{3},$ and $\frac{3}{4}$.

$$\smile = \frac{1}{2} \qquad \leftthreetimes = \frac{2}{3} \qquad \curlywedge = \frac{3}{4}$$

Greek fractions

The Greeks also used unit fractions but the way they wrote them led to confusion. They had symbols for numbers, for example, the number 2 was β (beta) and to make the fraction $\frac{1}{2}$ they added a dash so $\frac{1}{2} = β'$.

Number	Symbol	Fraction	Symbol
2	β (beta)	$\frac{1}{2}$	β'
3	γ (gamma)	$\frac{1}{3}$	γ'
4	δ (delta)	$\frac{1}{4}$	δ'

Fractions in India

In India, around 500AD a system called *brahmi* was devised using symbols for the numbers. Fractions were written as a symbol above a symbol but without a line as used now.

Brahmi symbols

1	2	3	4	5	6	7	8	9
—	=	≡	+	ʰ	⅌	?	ৎ	?

So $\frac{5}{9}$ was written as:

ʰ
?

Arabic fractions

The Arabs, probably around 1200AD, built on the number system – including the fractions – developed by the Indians. It was in Arabia that the line was first introduced into fractions – sometimes drawn horizontally and sometimes slanting – leading to the clear fractions that we use today.

$$\frac{3}{4} \qquad \frac{1}{8} \qquad \frac{1}{2} \qquad \frac{2}{3} \qquad \frac{1}{4} \qquad \frac{5}{10}$$

Number: Fractions

1. Recognise a fraction of a shape
2. Adding and subtracting simple fractions
3. Recognise equivalent fractions, using diagrams
4. Equivalent fractions and simplifying fractions by cancelling
5. Improper fractions and mixed numbers
6. Adding and subtracting fractions with the same denominator
7. Finding a fraction of a quantity
8. Multiplying and dividing fractions
9. One quantity as a fraction of another
10. Rational numbers and reciprocals

This chapter will show you ...

- **G** **C** how to add, subtract, multiply, divide and order simple fractions
- **G** how to cancel fractions
- **F** how to convert an improper fraction to a mixed number (and vice versa)
- **F** how to calculate a fraction of a quantity
- **C** how to calculate a reciprocal
- **C** how to recognise a terminating and a recurring decimal fraction

Visual overview

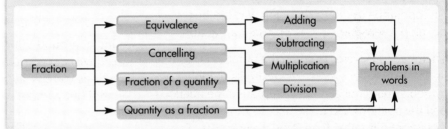

What you should already know

- Multiplication tables up to 10×10 **(KS3 level 4, GCSE grade G)**
- What a fraction is **(KS3 level 3, GCSE grade G)**

Quick check

How quickly can you calculate these?

1 2×4	**2** 5×3	**3** 5×2	**4** 6×3
5 2×7	**6** 4×5	**7** 3×8	**8** 4×6
9 9×2	**10** 3×7	**11** half of 10	**12** half of 12
13 half of 16	**14** half of 8	**15** half of 20	**16** a third of 9
17 a third of 15	**18** a quarter of 12	**19** a fifth of 10	**20** a fifth of 20

Recognise a fraction of a shape

This section will show you how to:
- recognise what fraction of a shape has been shaded
- shade a given simple fraction of a shape

Key words
fraction
shape

A **fraction** is a part of a whole. The top number is called the **numerator**. The bottom number is called the **denominator**. So, for example, $\frac{3}{4}$ means you divide a whole into four portions and take three of them.

It really does help if you know the multiplication tables up to 10×10. They will be tested in the non-calculator paper, so you need to be confident about tables and numbers.

EXERCISE 2A

1 What **fraction** is shaded in each **shape** in these diagrams?

FM Functional Maths **AU** (AO2) Assessing Understanding **PS** (AO3) Problem Solving

2 Draw diagrams as in question 1 to show these fractions.

a $\dfrac{3}{4}$ b $\dfrac{2}{3}$ c $\dfrac{1}{5}$ d $\dfrac{5}{8}$ e $\dfrac{1}{6}$ f $\dfrac{8}{9}$

g $\dfrac{1}{9}$ h $\dfrac{1}{10}$ i $\dfrac{4}{5}$ j $\dfrac{2}{7}$ k $\dfrac{3}{8}$ l $\dfrac{5}{6}$

3 A farmer decides to divide up a field into two parts so that one part is twice as big as the other part.

Make two copies of the grid and show two different ways that she can do this.

Shade the smaller area in each case.

PS 4 Look again at the diagrams in question 1.

For each question, decide which diagram, if any, has the greater proportion shaded.

a a and g   b b and i   c b and l   d e and j

e k and o   f e and m   g g and k   h e and i

AU 5 Three fractions are shown on the grids below.

A   **B**   **C**

The fraction in grid A is the odd one out because it does not have a denominator of 9.

Give reasons as to why the fractions in grid B and grid C could be the odd one out.

FM 6 A field is divided up into six allotments, numbered 1 to 6.

Each allotment is the same shape and size.

The owners want to sell potatoes at market and decide that they need to plant half the field with potatoes to meet demand.

1	2
3	4
5	6

Potatoes are planted in half of allotment 4 and all of allotments 3 and 6. There are no potatoes in allotments 1 and 5.

The owner of allotment 2 agrees to plant some potatoes so that half the field will be potatoes.

What fraction of her allotment needs to be potatoes?

Adding and subtracting simple fractions

This section will show you how to:
- add and subtract two fractions with the same denominator

Key words
denominator
numerator

Fractions that have the same **denominator** (bottom number) can easily be added or subtracted.

EXAMPLE 1

Work out $\dfrac{3}{10} + \dfrac{4}{10}$

Add the **numerators** (top numbers). The bottom number stays the same.

$\dfrac{3}{10} + \dfrac{4}{10} = \dfrac{7}{10}$

Work out $\dfrac{7}{8} - \dfrac{2}{8}$

Subtract the **numerators** (top numbers). The bottom number stays the same.

$\dfrac{7}{8} - \dfrac{2}{8} = \dfrac{5}{8}$

EXERCISE 2B

1 Calculate each of the following.

a $\dfrac{1}{4} + \dfrac{2}{4}$ **b** $\dfrac{1}{8} + \dfrac{3}{8}$ **c** $\dfrac{2}{5} + \dfrac{1}{5}$ **d** $\dfrac{3}{10} + \dfrac{5}{10}$

e $\dfrac{1}{3} + \dfrac{1}{3}$ **f** $\dfrac{2}{7} + \dfrac{3}{7}$ **g** $\dfrac{2}{9} + \dfrac{5}{9}$ **h** $\dfrac{1}{6} + \dfrac{4}{6}$

i $\dfrac{3}{5} + \dfrac{1}{5}$ **j** $\dfrac{5}{8} + \dfrac{2}{8}$ **k** $\dfrac{2}{10} + \dfrac{3}{10}$ **l** $\dfrac{4}{7} + \dfrac{1}{7}$

m $\dfrac{3}{5} + \dfrac{1}{5}$ **n** $\dfrac{2}{6} + \dfrac{3}{6}$ **o** $\dfrac{4}{9} + \dfrac{1}{9}$ **p** $\dfrac{2}{11} + \dfrac{5}{11}$

2 Calculate each of the following.

a $\dfrac{3}{4} - \dfrac{1}{4}$ **b** $\dfrac{4}{5} - \dfrac{1}{5}$ **c** $\dfrac{7}{8} - \dfrac{4}{8}$ **d** $\dfrac{8}{10} - \dfrac{5}{10}$

e $\dfrac{2}{3} - \dfrac{1}{3}$ **f** $\dfrac{5}{6} - \dfrac{1}{6}$ **g** $\dfrac{5}{7} - \dfrac{2}{7}$ **h** $\dfrac{7}{9} - \dfrac{2}{9}$

i $\dfrac{3}{5} - \dfrac{2}{5}$ **j** $\dfrac{4}{7} - \dfrac{1}{7}$ **k** $\dfrac{8}{9} - \dfrac{5}{9}$ **l** $\dfrac{9}{10} - \dfrac{3}{10}$

m $\dfrac{4}{6} - \dfrac{1}{6}$ **n** $\dfrac{5}{8} - \dfrac{3}{8}$ **o** $\dfrac{7}{11} - \dfrac{5}{11}$ **p** $\dfrac{7}{10} - \dfrac{3}{10}$

AU 3 Copy and shade the diagrams to show the working for this question and then write down the answer.

$$\frac{1}{2} \qquad + \qquad \frac{1}{3} \qquad = \qquad ......$$

AU 4 **a** Draw a diagram to show $\frac{2}{4}$.   **b** Show on your diagram that $\frac{2}{4} = \frac{1}{2}$.

c Use the above information to write down the answers to these.

i $\frac{1}{4} + \frac{1}{2}$ **ii** $\frac{3}{4} - \frac{1}{2}$

AU 5 **a** Draw a diagram to show $\frac{5}{10}$.   **b** Show on your diagram that $\frac{5}{10} = \frac{1}{2}$.

c Use the above information to write down the answers to these.

i $\frac{1}{2} + \frac{1}{10}$ **ii** $\frac{1}{2} + \frac{3}{10}$ **iii** $\frac{1}{2} + \frac{2}{10}$

PS 6 On an egg tray there are 30 eggs.

Four-fifths of the eggs are removed.
Half of these eggs are now put back on the tray.

What fraction of the 30 eggs is now on the tray?

PS 7 An aeroplane can carry 240 passengers when full.

On a flight it is exactly half full. Two-thirds of the passengers are male. What fraction of the seats are occupied by females?

PS 8 In a class of 32 students, three-quarters walk to school.

Of the remainder, half come by car.

What fraction of the class comes by car?

FM 9 On a train there are two carriages, each with 180 seats.

The train operator estimates that 1 in every 20 people will buy a snack on the journey.

They carry 30 snacks.

a Will they have enough snacks for two journeys if the train is full?

b What fraction of the snacks will be used on the first journey if the train is full?

Recognise equivalent fractions, using diagrams

This section will show you how to:
- recognise equivalent fractions, using diagrams

Key words
equivalent
equivalent fractions

ACTIVITY

Making eighths

You need lots of squared paper and a pair of scissors.

Draw three rectangles, each 4 cm by 2 cm, on squared paper.

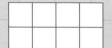

Each small square is called an *eighth* or $\frac{1}{8}$.

Cut one of the rectangles into halves, another into quarters and the last one into eighths.

You can see that the strip equal to one half takes up 4 squares, so:

$$\frac{1}{2} = \frac{4}{8}$$

These are called **equivalent fractions**.

1 Use the strips to write down the following fractions as eighths.

  a $\dfrac{1}{4}$ **b** $\dfrac{3}{4}$

2 Use the strips to work out the following problems. Leave your answers as eighths.

  a $\dfrac{1}{4} + \dfrac{3}{8}$ **b** $\dfrac{3}{4} + \dfrac{1}{8}$ **c** $\dfrac{3}{8} + \dfrac{1}{2}$

  d $\dfrac{1}{4} + \dfrac{1}{2}$ **e** $\dfrac{1}{8} + \dfrac{1}{8}$ **f** $\dfrac{1}{8} + \dfrac{1}{4}$

  g $\dfrac{3}{8} + \dfrac{3}{4}$ **h** $\dfrac{3}{4} + \dfrac{1}{2}$

Making twenty-fourths

You need lots of squared paper and a pair of scissors.

Draw four rectangles, each 6 cm by 4 cm,
on squared paper.

Each small square is called a *twenty-fourth* or $\frac{1}{24}$.
Cut one of the rectangles into quarters, another
into sixths, another into thirds and the remaining one
into eighths.

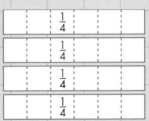

You can see that the strip equal to a quarter
takes up six squares, so:

$$\frac{1}{4} = \frac{6}{24}$$

This is another example of equivalent fractions.

This idea is used to add fractions together.
For example:

$$\frac{1}{4} + \frac{1}{6}$$

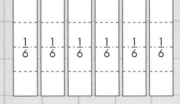

can be changed into:

$$\frac{6}{24} + \frac{4}{24} = \frac{10}{24}$$

EXERCISE 2C

1 Use the strips from the activity to write down each of these fractions as twenty-fourths.

a $\frac{1}{6}$

b $\frac{1}{3}$

c $\frac{1}{8}$

d $\frac{2}{3}$

e $\frac{5}{6}$

f $\frac{3}{4}$

g $\frac{3}{8}$

h $\frac{5}{8}$

i $\frac{7}{8}$

j $\frac{1}{2}$

2 Use the strips from the activity to write down the answer to each of the following problems. Write each answer in twenty-fourths.

a $\frac{1}{3}+\frac{1}{8}$

b $\frac{1}{8}+\frac{1}{4}$

c $\frac{1}{6}+\frac{1}{8}$

d $\frac{2}{3}+\frac{1}{8}$

e $\frac{5}{8}+\frac{1}{3}$

f $\frac{1}{8}+\frac{5}{6}$

g $\frac{1}{2}+\frac{3}{8}$

h $\frac{1}{6}+\frac{3}{4}$

i $\frac{5}{8}+\frac{1}{6}$

j $\frac{1}{3}+\frac{5}{8}$

3 Draw three rectangles, each 5 cm by 4 cm. Cut one into quarters, another into fifths and the last into tenths.

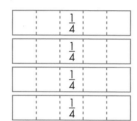
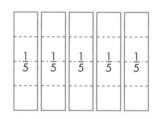
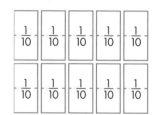

Use the strips to find the equivalent fraction, in twentieths, to each of the following.

a $\frac{1}{4}$

b $\frac{1}{5}$

c $\frac{3}{4}$

d $\frac{4}{5}$

e $\frac{1}{10}$

f $\frac{1}{2}$

g $\frac{3}{5}$

h $\frac{2}{5}$

i $\frac{7}{10}$

j $\frac{3}{10}$

4 Use the strips from question 3 to write down the answer to each of the following.

a $\frac{1}{4}+\frac{1}{5}$

b $\frac{3}{5}+\frac{1}{10}$

c $\frac{3}{10}+\frac{1}{4}$

d $\frac{3}{4}+\frac{1}{5}$

e $\frac{7}{10}+\frac{1}{4}$

PS 5 Use the strips from the activity to decide which fraction in each set of three, if any, is the odd one out.

a $\frac{6}{24}, \frac{2}{6}, \frac{2}{8}$

b $\frac{6}{8}, \frac{2}{3}, \frac{3}{4}$

c $\frac{1}{2}, \frac{4}{8}, \frac{3}{6}$

d $\frac{2}{3}, \frac{4}{6}, \frac{6}{8}$

AU 6 Here is a multiplication table.

×	2	3	4	5
2	4	6	8	10
5	10	15	20	25

The table can be used to pick out equivalent fractions.

For example, $\dfrac{2}{5} = \dfrac{6}{15}$.

a Use the table to write down three more fractions that are equivalent to $\dfrac{2}{5}$.

b Extend this table to write down a different fraction that is equivalent to $\dfrac{2}{5}$.

AU 7 a Complete this multiplication table.

×	2	3	4	5
3				
4				

b Use this table to write down four fractions that are equivalent to $\dfrac{3}{4}$.

8 You will need lots of squared paper and a pair of scissors.
Draw three rectangles on squared paper, each 6 cm by 2 cm.

a Write down the fraction of a rectangle that each small square represents.

b Use your own choice of strips to write down the answer to each of the following.

i $\dfrac{1}{2} + \dfrac{1}{12}$ **ii** $\dfrac{5}{12} + \dfrac{1}{3}$ **iii** $\dfrac{1}{12} + \dfrac{5}{6}$ **iv** $\dfrac{2}{3} + \dfrac{1}{12}$ **v** $\dfrac{1}{3} + \dfrac{1}{4}$

Equivalent fractions and simplifying fractions by cancelling

This section will show you how to:
- create equivalent fractions
- simplify fractions by cancelling

Key words
cancel
denominator
lowest terms
numerator
simplest form
simplify

Equivalent fractions are two or more fractions that represent the same part of a whole.

EXAMPLE 2

Complete the following.

a $\dfrac{3}{4} \longrightarrow \dfrac{\times 4}{\times 4} = \dfrac{\square}{16}$ b $\dfrac{2}{5} = \dfrac{\square}{15}$

a Multiplying the **numerator** by 4 gives 12. This means $\dfrac{12}{16}$ is an equivalent fraction to $\dfrac{3}{4}$.

b To change the **denominator** from 5 to 15, you multiply by 3. Do the same thing to the numerator, which gives $2 \times 3 = 6$. So, $\dfrac{2}{5} = \dfrac{6}{15}$.

The fraction $\dfrac{3}{4}$, in Example 2a, is in its **lowest terms** or **simplest form**.

This means that the only number that is a factor of both the numerator and denominator is 1.

EXAMPLE 3

Write these fractions in their simplest forms.

a $\dfrac{15}{35}$ b $\dfrac{24}{54}$

a Here is one reason why you need to know the multiplication tables. What is the biggest number that has both 15 and 35 in its multiplication table? You should know that this is the five times table. So, divide both the numerator and denominator by 5.

$$\dfrac{15}{35} = \dfrac{15 \div 5}{35 \div 5} = \dfrac{3}{7}$$

You can say that you have '**cancelled** by five'.

b The biggest number that has both 24 and 54 in its multiplication table is 6. So, divide both the numerator and denominator by 6.

$$\dfrac{24}{54} = \dfrac{24 \div 6}{54 \div 6} = \dfrac{4}{9}$$

Here, you have 'cancelled by six'.

You have **simplified** the fractions to write them in their lowest terms.

EXAMPLE 4

Put the following fractions in order, with the smallest first.

$$\frac{5}{6}, \frac{2}{3}, \frac{3}{4}$$

First write each fraction with the same denominator by using equivalent fractions.

$$\frac{5}{6} = \frac{10}{12}$$

$$\frac{2}{3} = \frac{4}{6} = \frac{6}{9} = \frac{8}{12}$$

$$\frac{3}{4} = \frac{6}{8} = \frac{9}{12}$$

This shows that $\frac{5}{6} = \frac{10}{12}$, $\frac{2}{3} = \frac{8}{12}$ and $\frac{3}{4} = \frac{9}{12}$.

In order, the fractions are:

$$\frac{2}{3}, \frac{3}{4}, \frac{5}{6}$$

EXERCISE 2D

1 Copy and complete the following.

a $\dfrac{2}{5} \longrightarrow \dfrac{\times 4}{\times 4} = \dfrac{\square}{20}$

b $\dfrac{1}{4} \longrightarrow \dfrac{\times 3}{\times 3} = \dfrac{\square}{12}$

c $\dfrac{3}{8} \longrightarrow \dfrac{\times 5}{\times 5} = \dfrac{\square}{40}$

d $\dfrac{4}{5} \longrightarrow \dfrac{\times 3}{\times 3} = \dfrac{\square}{15}$

e $\dfrac{5}{6} \longrightarrow \dfrac{\times 3}{\times 3} = \dfrac{\square}{18}$

f $\dfrac{3}{7} \longrightarrow \dfrac{\times 4}{\times 4} = \dfrac{\square}{28}$

g $\dfrac{3}{10} \longrightarrow \dfrac{\times \square}{\times 2} = \dfrac{\square}{20}$

h $\dfrac{1}{3} \longrightarrow \dfrac{\times \square}{\times \square} = \dfrac{\square}{9}$

i $\dfrac{3}{5} \longrightarrow \dfrac{\times \square}{\times \square} = \dfrac{\square}{20}$

j $\dfrac{2}{3} \longrightarrow \dfrac{\times \square}{\times \square} = \dfrac{\square}{18}$

k $\dfrac{3}{4} \longrightarrow \dfrac{\times \square}{\times \square} = \dfrac{\square}{12}$

l $\dfrac{5}{8} \longrightarrow \dfrac{\times \square}{\times \square} = \dfrac{\square}{40}$

m $\dfrac{7}{10} \longrightarrow \dfrac{\times \square}{\times \square} = \dfrac{\square}{20}$

n $\dfrac{1}{6} \longrightarrow \dfrac{\times \square}{\times \square} = \dfrac{4}{\square}$

o $\dfrac{3}{8} \longrightarrow \dfrac{\times \square}{\times \square} = \dfrac{15}{\square}$

G

2 Copy and complete the following.

a $\dfrac{1}{2} = \dfrac{2}{\square} = \dfrac{3}{\square} = \dfrac{\square}{8} = \dfrac{\square}{10} = \dfrac{6}{\square}$

b $\dfrac{1}{3} = \dfrac{2}{\square} = \dfrac{3}{\square} = \dfrac{\square}{12} = \dfrac{\square}{15} = \dfrac{6}{\square}$

c $\dfrac{3}{4} = \dfrac{6}{\square} = \dfrac{9}{\square} = \dfrac{\square}{16} = \dfrac{\square}{20} = \dfrac{18}{\square}$

d $\dfrac{2}{5} = \dfrac{4}{\square} = \dfrac{6}{\square} = \dfrac{\square}{20} = \dfrac{\square}{25} = \dfrac{12}{\square}$

e $\dfrac{3}{7} = \dfrac{6}{\square} = \dfrac{9}{\square} = \dfrac{\square}{28} = \dfrac{\square}{35} = \dfrac{18}{\square}$

3 Copy and complete the following.

a $\dfrac{10}{15} = \dfrac{10 \div 5}{15 \div 5} = \dfrac{\square}{\square}$

b $\dfrac{12}{15} = \dfrac{12 \div 3}{15 \div 3} = \dfrac{\square}{\square}$

c $\dfrac{20}{28} = \dfrac{20 \div 4}{28 \div 4} = \dfrac{\square}{\square}$

d $\dfrac{12}{18} = \dfrac{12 \div \square}{\square \div \square} = \dfrac{\square}{\square}$

e $\dfrac{15}{25} = \dfrac{15 \div 5}{\square \div \square} = \dfrac{\square}{\square}$

f $\dfrac{21}{30} = \dfrac{21 \div \square}{\square \div \square} = \dfrac{\square}{\square}$

FM 4 A shop manager is working out how much space to use for different items on a shelf.

The shelf has six equal sections.

He puts baked beans on three sections, tomatoes on two sections and spaghetti on one section.

a Baked beans are in boxes of 48 tins.
Each section of shelf holds 500 tins.
How many boxes will be needed to fill the baked bean sections?

b What fraction of the shelf has baked beans on it?
Give your answer in its simplest form.

c What fraction of the shelf does not have spaghetti on it?
Give your answer in its simplest form.

5 Cancel each of these fractions to its simplest form.

a $\dfrac{4}{6}$ b $\dfrac{5}{15}$ c $\dfrac{12}{18}$ d $\dfrac{6}{8}$ e $\dfrac{3}{9}$

f $\dfrac{5}{10}$ g $\dfrac{14}{16}$ h $\dfrac{28}{35}$ i $\dfrac{10}{20}$ j $\dfrac{4}{16}$

k $\dfrac{12}{15}$ l $\dfrac{15}{21}$ m $\dfrac{25}{35}$ n $\dfrac{14}{21}$ o $\dfrac{8}{20}$

p $\dfrac{10}{25}$ q $\dfrac{7}{21}$ r $\dfrac{42}{60}$ s $\dfrac{50}{200}$ t $\dfrac{18}{12}$

u $\dfrac{6}{9}$ v $\dfrac{18}{27}$ w $\dfrac{36}{48}$ x $\dfrac{21}{14}$ y $\dfrac{42}{12}$

6 Put the fractions in each set in order, with the smallest first.

a $\dfrac{1}{2}, \dfrac{5}{6}, \dfrac{2}{3}$

b $\dfrac{3}{4}, \dfrac{1}{2}, \dfrac{5}{8}$

c $\dfrac{7}{10}, \dfrac{2}{5}, \dfrac{1}{2}$

d $\dfrac{2}{3}, \dfrac{3}{4}, \dfrac{7}{12}$

e $\dfrac{1}{6}, \dfrac{1}{3}, \dfrac{1}{4}$

f $\dfrac{9}{10}, \dfrac{3}{4}, \dfrac{4}{5}$

g $\dfrac{4}{5}, \dfrac{7}{10}, \dfrac{5}{6}$

h $\dfrac{1}{3}, \dfrac{2}{5}, \dfrac{3}{10}$

AU 7 Here are four unit fractions.

$$\dfrac{1}{2} \qquad \dfrac{1}{3} \qquad \dfrac{1}{4} \qquad \dfrac{1}{5}$$

a Which two of these fractions have a sum of $\dfrac{7}{12}$?

Show clearly how you work out your answer.

b Which fraction is the biggest?
Explain your answer.

PS 8 **a** Use the fact that $2 \times 2 \times 2 \times 2 \times 2 = 32$ to cancel the fraction $\dfrac{64}{320}$ to its lowest terms.

b Use the fact that $7 \times 11 \times 13 = 1001$ to cancel the fraction $\dfrac{13}{1001}$ to its simplest form.

PS 9 What fraction of each of these grids is shaded?

        a   **b**   **c**

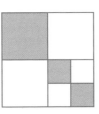
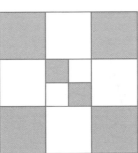
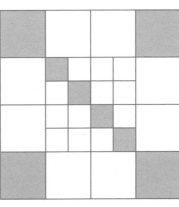

Improper fractions and mixed numbers

This section will show you how to:
- change improper fractions into mixed numbers
- change mixed numbers into improper fractions

Key words

improper fraction
mixed number
proper fraction
top-heavy

A fraction with the numerator (top number) smaller than the denominator (bottom number) is called a **proper fraction**. An example of a proper fraction is $\frac{4}{5}$.

An **improper fraction** has a bigger numerator (top number) than the denominator (bottom number). An example of an improper fraction is $\frac{9}{5}$. It is sometimes called a **top-heavy** fraction.

A **mixed number** is made up of a whole number and a proper fraction. An example of a mixed number is $1\frac{3}{4}$.

EXAMPLE 5

Convert $\frac{14}{5}$ into a mixed number.

$\frac{14}{5}$ means $14 \div 5$.

Dividing 14 by 5 gives 2 with a remainder of 4 (5 fits into 14 two times, with $\frac{4}{5}$ left over).

This means that there are 2 whole ones and $\frac{4}{5}$ left over.

So, $\frac{14}{5} = \frac{5}{5} + \frac{5}{5} + \frac{4}{5}$

$= 2\frac{4}{5}$

EXAMPLE 6

Convert $3\frac{1}{4}$ into an improper fraction.

Each whole one is four-quarters.

So, 3 whole ones = 12 quarters $\left(\frac{4}{4} + \frac{4}{4} + \frac{4}{4} \right)$

This means that $3\frac{1}{4} = \frac{12}{4} + \frac{1}{4} = \frac{13}{4}$

Using a calculator with improper fractions

Check that your calculator has a fraction key.

To key in a fraction press [a b/c] .

Input the fraction so that it looks like this: $\frac{9}{5}$ or [9] [⌐] [5] .

Now press the equals key [=] so that the fraction displays in the answer part of the screen.

Pressing shift and the key S [⌐] D will convert the fraction to a mixed number.

[1] [⌐] [4] [⌐] [5]

This is the mixed number $1\frac{4}{5}$.

Pressing the equals sign again will convert the mixed number back to an improper fraction.

- Can you see a way of converting an improper fraction to a mixed number without using a calculator?

- Test your idea. Then use your calculator to check it.

Using a calculator to convert mixed numbers to improper fractions

To input a mixed number, press the shift key first and then the fraction key [a b/c] .

Pressing the equals sign will convert the mixed number to an improper fraction.

- Now key in at least ten improper fractions and convert them to mixed numbers.

- Remember to press the equals sign to change the mixed numbers back to improper fractions.

- Now try inputting at least 10 mixed numbers and converting them to improper fractions.

- Look at your results. Can you see a way of converting a mixed number to an improper fraction without using a calculator?

- Test your idea. Then use your calculator to check it.

EXERCISE 2E

F

1 Change each of these improper fractions into a mixed number.

a $\frac{7}{3}$ b $\frac{8}{3}$ c $\frac{9}{4}$ d $\frac{10}{7}$ e $\frac{12}{5}$ f $\frac{7}{5}$

g $\frac{13}{5}$ h $\frac{15}{4}$ i $\frac{10}{3}$ j $\frac{15}{7}$ k $\frac{17}{6}$ l $\frac{18}{5}$

m $\frac{19}{4}$ n $\frac{22}{7}$ o $\frac{14}{11}$ p $\frac{12}{11}$ q $\frac{28}{5}$ r $\frac{19}{7}$

s $\frac{40}{7}$ t $\frac{42}{5}$ u $\frac{21}{10}$ v $\frac{5}{2}$ w $\frac{5}{3}$ x $\frac{25}{8}$

y $\frac{23}{10}$ z $\frac{23}{11}$

2 Change each of these mixed numbers into an improper fraction.

a $3\frac{1}{3}$ b $5\frac{5}{6}$ c $1\frac{4}{5}$ d $5\frac{2}{7}$ e $4\frac{1}{10}$ f $5\frac{2}{3}$

g $2\frac{1}{2}$ h $3\frac{1}{4}$ i $7\frac{1}{6}$ j $3\frac{5}{8}$ k $6\frac{1}{3}$ l $9\frac{8}{9}$

m $11\frac{4}{5}$ n $3\frac{1}{5}$ o $4\frac{3}{8}$ p $3\frac{1}{9}$ q $5\frac{1}{5}$ r $2\frac{3}{4}$

s $4\frac{2}{7}$ t $8\frac{1}{6}$ u $2\frac{8}{9}$ v $6\frac{1}{6}$ w $12\frac{1}{5}$ x $1\frac{5}{8}$

y $7\frac{1}{10}$ z $8\frac{1}{9}$

3 Check your answers to questions 1 and 2, using the fraction buttons on your calculator.

AU **4** Which of these improper fractions has the largest value?

$\frac{27}{4}$ $\frac{31}{5}$ $\frac{13}{2}$

Show your working to justify your answer.

PS **5** Find a mixed number that is greater than $\frac{85}{11}$ but smaller than $\frac{79}{10}$.

PS 6 Find a mixed number that is greater than $5\frac{9}{11}$ but smaller than $5\frac{7}{8}$.

PS 7 Here is a list of numbers.

4	9	16	25

Using one of these numbers for the numerator and one for the denominator, find an improper fraction with a value between two and three.

2.6 Adding and subtracting fractions with the same denominator

This section will show you how to:
- add and subtract two fractions with the same denominator, then simplify the result
- solve problems in words

Key words
improper fraction
lowest terms
mixed number
proper fraction
simplest form

When you add two fractions with the same denominator, you get one of the following:

- a **proper fraction** that cannot be simplified, for example:

$$\frac{1}{5} + \frac{2}{5} = \frac{3}{5}$$

- a proper fraction that can be simplified to its **lowest terms** or **simplest form**, for example:

$$\frac{1}{8} + \frac{3}{8} = \frac{4}{8} = \frac{1}{2}$$

- an **improper fraction** that cannot be simplified, so it is converted to a **mixed number**, for example:

$$\frac{6}{7} + \frac{2}{7} = \frac{8}{7} = 1\frac{1}{7}$$

- an improper fraction that can be simplified before it is converted to a mixed number, for example:

$$\frac{5}{8} + \frac{7}{8} = \frac{12}{8} = \frac{3}{2} = 1\frac{1}{2}$$

When you subtract two fractions with the same denominator, you get one of the following:

- a proper fraction that cannot be simplified, for example:

$$\frac{3}{5} - \frac{1}{5} = \frac{2}{5}$$

- a proper fraction that can be simplified, for example:

$$\frac{1}{2} - \frac{1}{10} = \frac{5}{10} - \frac{1}{10} = \frac{4}{10} = \frac{2}{5}$$

Note You must *always* simplify fractions by cancelling if possible.

EXAMPLE 7

In a box of chocolates, a quarter are truffles, half are orange creams and the rest are mints. What fraction are mints?

Truffles and orange creams together are $\frac{1}{4} + \frac{1}{2} = \frac{3}{4}$ of the box.

Take the whole box as 1. So, mints are $1 - \frac{3}{4} = \frac{1}{4}$ of the box.

EXERCISE 2F

1 Copy and complete each of these additions.

a $\frac{3}{7} + \frac{2}{7}$ b $\frac{5}{9} + \frac{2}{9}$ c $\frac{3}{5} + \frac{1}{5}$ d $\frac{3}{7} + \frac{3}{7}$

e $\frac{1}{11} + \frac{6}{11}$ f $\frac{4}{9} + \frac{3}{9}$ g $\frac{3}{13} + \frac{7}{13}$ h $\frac{2}{11} + \frac{8}{11}$

2 Copy and complete each of these subtractions.

a $\frac{4}{7} - \frac{1}{7}$ b $\frac{5}{9} - \frac{4}{9}$ c $\frac{7}{11} - \frac{3}{11}$ d $\frac{9}{13} - \frac{2}{13}$

e $\frac{6}{7} - \frac{2}{7}$ f $\frac{3}{5} - \frac{2}{5}$ g $\frac{8}{9} - \frac{4}{9}$ h $\frac{5}{11} - \frac{2}{11}$

3 Copy and complete each of these additions.

a $\frac{5}{8} + \frac{1}{8}$ b $\frac{3}{10} + \frac{1}{10}$ c $\frac{2}{9} + \frac{4}{9}$ d $\frac{1}{4} + \frac{1}{4}$

e $\frac{3}{10} + \frac{3}{10}$ f $\frac{5}{12} + \frac{1}{12}$ g $\frac{3}{16} + \frac{5}{16}$ h $\frac{7}{16} + \frac{3}{16}$

4 Copy and complete each of these subtractions.

a $\dfrac{7}{8} - \dfrac{3}{8}$ b $\dfrac{7}{10} - \dfrac{3}{10}$ c $\dfrac{5}{6} - \dfrac{1}{6}$ d $\dfrac{9}{10} - \dfrac{1}{10}$

e $\dfrac{7}{12} - \dfrac{1}{12}$ f $\dfrac{5}{8} - \dfrac{3}{8}$ g $\dfrac{9}{16} - \dfrac{7}{16}$ h $\dfrac{7}{18} - \dfrac{1}{18}$

5 Copy and complete each of these additions. Use equivalent fractions to make the denominators the same.

a $\dfrac{1}{2} + \dfrac{7}{10}$ b $\dfrac{1}{2} + \dfrac{5}{8}$ c $\dfrac{3}{4} + \dfrac{3}{8}$ d $\dfrac{3}{4} + \dfrac{7}{8}$

e $\dfrac{1}{2} + \dfrac{7}{8}$ f $\dfrac{1}{3} + \dfrac{5}{6}$ g $\dfrac{5}{6} + \dfrac{2}{3}$ h $\dfrac{3}{4} + \dfrac{1}{2}$

6 Copy and complete each of these additions.

a $\dfrac{3}{8} + \dfrac{7}{8}$ b $\dfrac{3}{4} + \dfrac{3}{4}$ c $\dfrac{2}{5} + \dfrac{3}{5}$ d $\dfrac{7}{10} + \dfrac{9}{10}$

e $\dfrac{5}{8} + \dfrac{5}{8}$ f $\dfrac{7}{16} + \dfrac{15}{16}$ g $\dfrac{5}{12} + \dfrac{11}{12}$ h $\dfrac{11}{16} + \dfrac{7}{16}$

7 Copy and complete each of these subtractions. Use equivalent fractions to make the denominators the same.

a $\dfrac{7}{8} - \dfrac{1}{4}$ b $\dfrac{7}{10} - \dfrac{1}{5}$ c $\dfrac{3}{4} - \dfrac{1}{2}$ d $\dfrac{5}{8} - \dfrac{1}{4}$

e $\dfrac{1}{2} - \dfrac{1}{4}$ f $\dfrac{7}{8} - \dfrac{1}{2}$ g $\dfrac{9}{10} - \dfrac{1}{2}$ h $\dfrac{11}{16} - \dfrac{3}{8}$

8 At a recent Premiership football match, $\frac{7}{8}$ of the crowd were home supporters. What fraction of the crowd were not home supporters?

PS 9 After Emma had taken a slice of cake, $\frac{3}{4}$ of the cake was left. Ayesha then had $\frac{1}{2}$ of what was left.

Who had more cake?

FM 10 Three friends share two pizzas. Each pizza is cut into six equal slices. What fraction of a pizza did each friend get?

11 In a box of old CDs from a jumble sale, $\frac{1}{4}$ of them were rock music, $\frac{3}{8}$ of them were pop music and the rest were classical. What fraction of the CDs were classical?

PS 12 In a car park, $\frac{1}{5}$ of the cars were German makes. Half of the rest were Japanese makes. What fraction of the cars were Japanese makes?

E

(PS) **13** A fruit drink consists of $\frac{1}{2}$ orange juice, $\frac{1}{8}$ lemon juice and the rest is pineapple juice. What fraction of the drink is pineapple juice?

14 In a hockey team, $\frac{2}{11}$ of the team are French, $\frac{2}{11}$ are Italian, $\frac{3}{11}$ are Scottish and the rest are English. What fraction of the team is English?

15 In a packet of biscuits, $\frac{1}{6}$ are digestives, $\frac{2}{3}$ are Bourbons and the rest are Jammy Dodgers. What fraction are jammy dodgers?

(FM) **16** Jide pays $\frac{1}{4}$ of his wages in tax and $\frac{1}{8}$ of his wages in National Insurance. What fraction of his wages does he take home?

(AU) **17** Sally and Paul each buy a pizza.

Sally cuts hers into eight equal pieces and eats five.

Paul cuts his into six equal pieces and eats four.

Who eats the most pizza? Explain your answer.

2.7 Finding a fraction of a quantity

This section will show you how to:
- find a fraction of a given quantity

Key words
fraction
quantity

To do this, you simply multiply the **fraction** by the **quantity**, for example, $\frac{1}{2}$ of 30 is the same as $\frac{1}{2} \times 30$.

Remember: In mathematics 'of' is interpreted as $\times$.

For example, two lots of three is the same as 2×3.

EXAMPLE 8

Find $\frac{3}{4}$ of £196.

First, find $\frac{1}{4}$ by dividing by 4. Then find $\frac{3}{4}$ by multiplying your answer by 3:

$$196 \div 4 = 49 \quad \text{then} \quad 49 \times 3 = 147$$

The answer is £147.

Of course, you can use your calculator to do this problem by either:

- pressing the sequence: **1** **9** **6** **÷** **4** **×** **3** **=**

- or using the **a b/c** key: **3** **a b/c** **4** **×** **1** **9** **6** **=**

EXERCISE 2G

1 Calculate each of these.

   a $\frac{3}{5}$ of 30   **b** $\frac{2}{7}$ of 35   **c** $\frac{3}{8}$ of 48   **d** $\frac{7}{10}$ of 40

   e $\frac{5}{6}$ of 18   **f** $\frac{3}{4}$ of 24   **g** $\frac{4}{5}$ of 60   **h** $\frac{5}{8}$ of 72

2 Calculate each of these quantities.

   a $\frac{3}{4}$ of £2400   **b** $\frac{2}{5}$ of 320 grams   **c** $\frac{5}{8}$ of 256 kilograms

   d $\frac{2}{3}$ of £174   **e** $\frac{5}{6}$ of 78 litres   **f** $\frac{3}{4}$ of 120 minutes

   g $\frac{4}{5}$ of 365 days   **h** $\frac{7}{8}$ of 24 hours   **i** $\frac{3}{4}$ of 1 day

   j $\frac{5}{9}$ of 4266 miles

3 In each case, find out which is the larger number.

   a $\frac{2}{5}$ of 60 or $\frac{5}{8}$ of 40   **b** $\frac{3}{4}$ of 280 or $\frac{7}{10}$ of 290

   c $\frac{2}{3}$ of 78 or $\frac{4}{5}$ of 70   **d** $\frac{5}{6}$ of 72 or $\frac{11}{12}$ of 60

   e $\frac{4}{9}$ of 126 or $\frac{3}{5}$ of 95   **f** $\frac{3}{4}$ of 340 or $\frac{2}{3}$ of 381

4 A director receives $\frac{2}{15}$ of his firm's profits. The firm made a profit of £45 600 in one year. How much did the director receive?

5 A woman left £84 000 in her will.

She left $\frac{3}{8}$ of the money to charity.

How much did she leave to charity?

AU 6 In the season 2008/2009, the attendance at Huddersfield Town versus Leeds United was 20 928. Of this crowd, $\frac{3}{8}$ were female. How many were male?

7 Two-thirds of a person's weight is water. Paul weighs 78 kg. How much of his body weight is water?

8 **a** Information from the first census in Singapore suggests that then $\frac{2}{25}$ of the population were Indian. The total population was 10 700. How many people were Indian?

b By 1990 the population of Singapore had grown to 3 002 800. Only $\frac{1}{16}$ of this population were Indian. How many Indians were living in Singapore in 1990?

9 Mark normally earns £500 a week. One week he is given a bonus of $\frac{1}{10}$ of his wage.

a Find $\frac{1}{10}$ of £500.

b How much does he earn altogether for this week?

10 The contents of a standard box of cereals weigh 720 g. A new larger box holds $\frac{1}{4}$ more than the standard box.

a Find $\frac{1}{4}$ of 720 g.

b How much do the contents of the new box of cereals weigh?

FM 11 The price of a new TV costing £360 is reduced by $\frac{1}{3}$ in a sale.

a Find $\frac{1}{3}$ of £360.

b How much does the TV cost in the sale?

FM 12 A car is advertised at Lion Autos at £9000 including extras but with a special offer of one-fifth off this price.

The same car is advertised at Tiger Motors for £6000 but the extras add one-quarter to this price.

Which garage is the cheaper?

FM 13 A jar of instant coffee normally contains 200 g and costs £2.

There are two special offers on a jar of coffee.

    Offer A: $\frac{1}{4}$ extra for the same price.

    Offer B: Same weight for $\frac{3}{4}$ of the original price.

Which offer is the best value?

This section will show you how to:
- multiply a fraction by a fraction

Key words
denominator
multiply
numerator

What is $\frac{1}{2}$ of $\frac{1}{4}$?   The diagram shows the answer is $\frac{1}{8}$.

In mathematics, you always write $\frac{1}{2}$ of $\frac{1}{4}$ as $\frac{1}{2} \times \frac{1}{4}$

So you know that $\frac{1}{2} \times \frac{1}{4} = \frac{1}{8}$

To **multiply** fractions, you multiply the **numerators** together and you multiply the **denominators** together.

EXAMPLE 9

Work out $\frac{1}{4}$ of $\frac{2}{5}$.

$$\frac{1}{4} \times \frac{2}{5} = \frac{1 \times 2}{4 \times 5} = \frac{2}{20} = \frac{1}{10}$$

Dividing fractions

Look at the problem $3 \div \frac{3}{4}$. This is like asking, 'How many $\frac{3}{4}$s are there in 3?' Look at the diagram.

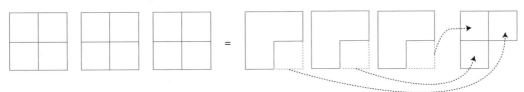

Each of the three whole shapes is divided into quarters. What is the total number of quarters divided by 3? Can you see that you could fit the four shapes on the right-hand side of the = sign into the three shapes on the left-hand side?

i.e. $3 \div \frac{3}{4} = 4$ or $3 \div \frac{3}{4} = 3 \times \frac{4}{3} = \frac{3 \times 4}{3} = \frac{12}{3} = 4$

So, to divide by a fraction, you turn the fraction upside down (finding its reciprocal), and then multiply.

E

EXERCISE 2H

1 Work out each of these multiplications.

a $\frac{1}{2} \times \frac{1}{3}$ **b** $\frac{1}{4} \times \frac{1}{5}$ **c** $\frac{1}{3} \times \frac{2}{3}$ **d** $\frac{1}{4} \times \frac{2}{3}$

e $\frac{1}{3} \times \frac{3}{4}$ **f** $\frac{2}{3} \times \frac{3}{5}$ **g** $\frac{3}{4} \times \frac{2}{3}$ **h** $\frac{5}{6} \times \frac{3}{5}$

i $\frac{2}{7} \times \frac{3}{4}$ **j** $\frac{5}{6} \times \frac{7}{8}$ **k** $\frac{4}{5} \times \frac{2}{3}$ **l** $\frac{3}{4} \times \frac{7}{8}$

FM **2** A farmer is converting a field into sheep pens. He divides the field in half and then divides each half into three equal parts.

     a Each pen can hold 20 sheep.

        The farmer already has 95 sheep.

        How many more sheep should he buy in order to fill the pens?

     b What fraction of the field does each sheep pen take up?

D

PS **3** There are 7.5 million people living in London. One-eighth of these are over 65. Of the over-65s, three-fifths are women.

How many women over 65 live in London?

PS **4** Alec eats $\frac{1}{4}$ of a cake.

Ben eats $\frac{1}{3}$ of what is left.

Callum eats $\frac{1}{2}$ of what is left.

Dec gets the final piece.

Who got the most cake?

C

5 Evaluate the following, giving your answer as a mixed number where possible.

a $\frac{1}{4} \div \frac{1}{3}$ **b** $\frac{2}{5} \div \frac{2}{7}$ **c** $\frac{4}{5} \div \frac{3}{4}$ **d** $\frac{3}{7} \div \frac{2}{5}$

e $5 \div 1\frac{1}{4}$ **f** $6 \div 1\frac{1}{2}$ **g** $7\frac{1}{2} \div 1\frac{1}{2}$ **h** $3 \div 1\frac{3}{4}$

6 A grain merchant has only thirteen and a half tonnes in stock. He has several customers who are ordering three-quarters of a tonne. How many customers can he supply?

7 Evaluate the following, giving your answer as a mixed number where possible.

a $2\frac{2}{9} \times 2\frac{1}{10} \times \frac{16}{35}$ **b** $3\frac{1}{5} \times 2\frac{1}{2} \times 4\frac{3}{4}$

c $1\frac{1}{4} \times 1\frac{2}{7} \times 1\frac{1}{6}$ **d** $\frac{18}{25} \times \frac{15}{26} \div 2\frac{2}{5}$

One quantity as a fraction of another

This section will show you how to:
● express one quantity as a fraction of another

Key words
fraction
quantity

You may often be asked to give one amount or **quantity** as a **fraction** of another.

EXAMPLE 10

Write £5 as a fraction of £20.

As a fraction this is written $\frac{5}{20}$. This cancels to $\frac{1}{4}$.

So £5 is one-quarter of £20.

EXERCISE 2I

1 In each of the following, write the first quantity as a fraction of the second.

  a 2 cm, 6 cm   **b** 4 kg, 20 kg

  c £8, £20   **d** 5 hours, 24 hours

  e 12 days, 30 days   **f** 50p, £3

  g 4 days, 2 weeks   **h** 40 minutes, 2 hours

2 In a form of 30 pupils, 18 are boys. What fraction of the form are boys?

3 During March, it rained on 12 days. For what fraction of the month did it rain?

4 Reka wins £120 in a competition and puts £50 into her bank account. What fraction of her winnings does she keep to spend?

FM 5 Jon earns £90 and saves £30 of it.

Matt earns £100 and saves £35 of it.

Who is saving the greater proportion of their earnings?

AU 6 In two tests Isobel gets 13 out of 20 and 16 out of 25. Which is the better mark?

Explain your answer.

Rational numbers and reciprocals

This section will show you how to:
- recognise rational numbers, reciprocals, terminating decimals and recurring decimals
- convert terminal decimals to fractions
- convert fractions to recurring decimals
- find reciprocals of numbers or fractions

Key words
rational number
reciprocal
recurring decimal
terminating decimal

Rational numbers

A **rational number** is a number that can be written as a fraction, for example, $\frac{1}{4}$ or $\frac{10}{3}$.

When a fraction is converted to a decimal it will be either:

- a **terminating decimal** or

- a **recurring decimal**

A terminating decimal has a finite number of digits. For example, $\frac{1}{4} = 0.25$, $\frac{1}{8} = 0.125$.

A recurring decimal has a digit, or block of digits, that repeat. For example, $\frac{1}{3} = 0.3333 \ldots$, $\frac{2}{11} = 0.181818 \ldots$

Recurring digits can be shown by putting a dot over the first and last digit of the group that repeats.

0.3333 … becomes 0.$\dot{3}$

0.181818 … becomes 0.$\dot{1}\dot{8}$

0.123123123 … becomes 0.$\dot{1}2\dot{3}$

0.58333 becomes 0.58$\dot{3}$

0.6181818 … becomes 0.6$\dot{1}\dot{8}$

0.4123123123 … become 0.4$\dot{1}2\dot{3}$

Converting fractions into recurring decimals

A fraction that does not convert to a terminating decimal will give a recurring decimal. You may already know that $\frac{1}{3} = 0.333 \ldots = 0.\dot{3}$ This means that the 3s go on for ever and the decimal never ends.

To convert the fraction, you can usually use a calculator to divide the numerator by the denominator.

Note that calculators round off the last digit so it may not always be a true recurring decimal in the display.

Use a calculator to check the following recurring decimals.

$$\frac{2}{11} = 0.181\,818\ldots = 0.1\dot{8}$$

$$\frac{4}{15} = 0.2666\ldots = 0.2\dot{6}$$

$$\frac{8}{13} = 0.615\,384\,615\,384\,6\ldots = 0.\dot{6}15\,38\dot{4}$$

Converting terminal decimals into fractions

To convert a terminating decimal to a fraction, take the decimal number as the numerator. Then the denominator is 10, 100, 1000 and so on, depending on the number of decimal places. Because a terminating decimal has a specific number of decimal places, you can use place value to work out exactly where the numerator and the denominator end. For example,

- $0.7 = \dfrac{7}{10}$

- $0.23 = \dfrac{23}{100}$

- $0.045 = \dfrac{45}{1000} = \dfrac{9}{200}$

- $2.34 = \dfrac{234}{100} = \dfrac{117}{50} = 2\dfrac{17}{50}$

- $0.625 = \dfrac{625}{1000} = \dfrac{5}{8}$

Finding reciprocals of numbers or fractions

The **reciprocal** of any number is one divided by the number.

For example: the reciprocal of 2 is $1 \div 2 = \frac{1}{2} = 0.5$

the reciprocal of 0.25 is $1 \div 0.25 = 4$.

You can find the reciprocal of a fraction by swapping the numerator and the denominator.

For example: the reciprocal of $\frac{2}{3}$ is $\frac{3}{2}$

the reciprocal of $\frac{7}{4}$ is $\frac{4}{7}$.

EXERCISE 2J

1 Write each of these fractions as a decimal. Give them as terminating decimals or recurring decimals, as appropriate.

a $\frac{1}{2}$　　b $\frac{1}{3}$　　c $\frac{1}{4}$　　d $\frac{1}{5}$　　e $\frac{1}{6}$

f $\frac{1}{7}$　　g $\frac{1}{8}$　　h $\frac{1}{9}$　　i $\frac{1}{10}$　　j $\frac{1}{13}$

AU 2 There are several patterns to be found in recurring decimals. For example:

$$\frac{1}{7} = 0.142\,857\,142\,857\,142\,857\,142\,857\ldots$$

$$\frac{2}{7} = 0.285\,714\,285\,714\,285\,714\,285\,714\ldots$$

$$\frac{3}{7} = 0.428\,571\,428\,571\,428\,571\,428\,571\ldots$$

and so on.

a Write down the decimals for each of the following to 24 decimal places.

i $\frac{4}{7}$　　　　ii $\frac{5}{7}$　　　　iii $\frac{6}{7}$

b What do you notice?

PS 3
AU　a Work out　　i $1 \div 2.5$　　ii $1 \div 5$　　iii $1 \div 10$

b The sequence 2.5, 5, 10, … is formed by doubling each term to find the next term.

Using your answers to part **a**, explain how you can find the answers to $1 \div 20$ and $1 \div 40$ without using your calculator.

AU 4 Work out the ninths, $\frac{1}{9}, \frac{2}{9}, \frac{3}{9}$, and so on up to $\frac{8}{9}$, as recurring decimals.

Describe any patterns that you notice.

AU 5 Work out the elevenths, $\frac{1}{11}, \frac{2}{11}, \frac{3}{11}$, and so on up to $\frac{10}{11}$, as recurring decimals.

Describe any patterns that you notice.

6 Write each of these fractions as a decimal. Use your results to write the list in order of size, smallest first.

$$\frac{4}{9} \qquad \frac{5}{11} \qquad \frac{3}{7} \qquad \frac{9}{22} \qquad \frac{16}{37} \qquad \frac{6}{13}$$

7 Write the following list of fractions in order of size, smallest first.

$$\frac{19}{60} \qquad \frac{7}{24} \qquad \frac{3}{10} \qquad \frac{2}{5} \qquad \frac{5}{12}$$

8 Convert each of these terminating decimals to a fraction.

a 0.125   **b** 0.34   **c** 0.725   **d** 0.3125

e 0.89   **f** 0.05   **g** 2.35   **h** 0.218 75

9 Use a calculator to work out the reciprocal of each of the following.

a 12   **b** 16   **c** 20   **d** 25   **e** 50

10 Write down the reciprocal of each of the following fractions.

a $\frac{3}{4}$ **b** $\frac{5}{6}$ **c** $\frac{2}{5}$

d $\frac{7}{10}$ **e** $\frac{11}{20}$ **f** $\frac{4}{15}$

11 a Write the fractions and their reciprocals in question 9 as decimals. Write them as terminating decimals or recurring decimals, as appropriate.

b Is it always true that a terminating decimal has a reciprocal that is a recurring decimal?

12 Multiply each of the fractions in question 9 by its reciprocal.

What result do you get every time?

AU 13 Explain why zero has no reciprocal.

PS 14 a Work out the reciprocal of the reciprocal of 10.

b Work out the reciprocal of the reciprocal of 2.

c What do you notice?

AU 15 x and y are two positive numbers.
If x is less than y, which statement below is true?

The reciprocal of x is less than the reciprocal of y.
The reciprocal of x is greater than the reciprocal of y.
It is impossible to tell.

Give an example to support your answer.

GRADE BOOSTER

G You can state the fraction of a shape that is shaded

G You can shade in a fraction of a shape

G You can add and subtract simple fractions

G You know how to identify equivalent fractions

G You can simplify fractions by cancelling (when possible)

G You can put simple fractions into order of size

F You can change improper fractions to mixed numbers

F You can find a fraction of a quantity

F You can change mixed numbers to improper fractions

F You can solve fraction problems expressed in words

E You can add more difficult fractions

E You can compare two fractions of quantities

E You can multiply a fraction by a fraction

D You can write a quantity as a fraction of another quantity

C You can divide a fraction by a fraction

C You can convert a terminating decimal to a fraction

C You can convert a fraction to a decimal

C You can work out the reciprocal of a number

What you should know now

- How to recognise and draw fractions of shapes
- How to add, subtract, multiply and cancel simple fractions without using a calculator
- How to work out equivalent fractions
- How to convert an improper fraction to a mixed number (and the other way)
- How to calculate a fraction of a quantity
- How to solve simple practical problems using fractions
- How to work out reciprocals and decimals from fractions
- How to add, multiply and divide fractions with different denominators

1 Work out:

$$\frac{7}{10} - \frac{2}{5}$$

2 a What fraction of this shape is shaded? (1)

b Shade $\frac{2}{3}$ of this square. (1)

c Which **two** of these fractions are **not** equal to $\frac{2}{3}$? (2)

$$\frac{4}{6} \qquad \frac{8}{9} \qquad \frac{14}{21} \qquad \frac{22}{32} \qquad \frac{30}{45}$$

(Total 4 marks)

AQA, November 2008, Module 5, Paper 2 Foundation,
Question 2

3 Here are three fractions.

$$\frac{1}{3} \qquad \frac{7}{10} \qquad \frac{1}{5}$$

Write each fraction in the correct box on the number line below. (2)

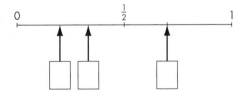

(Total 2 marks)

AQA, June 2007, Paper 1 Foundation, Question 11

4 The land area of a farm is 385 acres. One-fifth of the land is used to grow barley. How many acres is this?

5 A gardener plants a vegetable plot with potatoes, onions and carrots.

He plants $\frac{1}{8}$ with carrots.

He plants $\frac{3}{8}$ with onions.

What fraction does he plant with potatoes?

6 When a cross is carved from a piece of wood, $\frac{4}{5}$ of the wood is cut away. The original block weighs 215 grams. What weight of wood is cut off?

7 Two-fifths of the price of a book goes to the bookshop. A book cost £12. How much goes to the bookshop?

8 Find $\frac{3}{5}$ of 45 kg.

9 There are 175 pupils in Year 10 at a school.

a $\frac{2}{5}$ of these pupils own a dog.

How many pupils in Year 10 own a dog? (2)

b Alice says that exactly half of the Year 10 pupils are boys.

Explain why Alice must be wrong. (1)

c The number of pupils in Year 10 is $\frac{1}{8}$ of the total number of pupils in the school.

Work out the total number of pupils in the school. (2)

(Total 5 marks)

AQA, November 2008, Module 3 Foundation, Question 4

10 In a field there are 40 animals.

a Three out of every ten of the animals are sheep.

How many animals are sheep? (2)

b Connie says $\frac{2}{3}$ of the animals are cows.

Explain why Connie must be wrong. (1)

(Total 3 marks)

AQA, March 2007, Module 3 Foundation, Question 4

11 **a** Work out

$$\frac{3}{5} - \frac{2}{7}$$ (2)

b Use your answer to part (a) to write down the answer to

$$1\frac{3}{5} - \frac{2}{7}$$ (1)

(Total 3 marks)

AQA, June 2008, Module 3 Foundation, Question 19

12 David, Gareth and Kerry share out the contents of a jar of 600 sweets.

David receives $\frac{1}{4}$ of the sweets.

Gareth receives $\frac{5}{8}$ of the sweets.

What fraction of the sweets are left in the jar for Kerry? (4)

(Total 4 marks)

AQA, March 2007, Module 3 Foundation, Question 7

13 Calculate:

$$1\frac{3}{8} + 2\frac{1}{2}$$

14 Packets of Wheetix used to contain 550 grams of cereal. New packets contain one-fifth more. How much does a new packet contain?

15 The size of a packet of cereal is increased by one-fifth.

The new size is later reduced by one-fifth.

Is the new packet smaller, the same size or larger than the original packet?

Explain clearly how you work out your answer.

16 **a** Write down the reciprocal of:

i 5   **ii** $\frac{4}{5}$

b $\frac{1}{9} = 0.1111\ldots$

$\frac{2}{9} = 0.2222\ldots$

Using this information, or otherwise, write down the following fractions as recurring decimals.

i $\frac{5}{9}$ **ii** $\frac{2}{3}$

17 **a** Write down the reciprocal of 1.25.

b Zoe says that the reciprocal of a number is always smaller than the number. Give an example to show that Zoe is wrong.

Worked Examination Questions

1 Fred gets 3 pints of milk delivered on Saturday.

He uses $\frac{5}{8}$ of a pint a day.

On which day will he run out of milk?

$3 \div \frac{5}{8}$ ——————————— You get 1 method mark for identifying this as a division problem.

$= 4.8$ or $4\frac{4}{5}$ ——————————— Use your calculator to work this out. This is worth 1 mark.

The milk runs out on Wednesday. ——————

Total: 3 marks

Count 5 days on from Saturday. The correct answer receives 1 mark.

PS **2** There are 900 students in a college.

$\frac{1}{10}$ are under 16.

$\frac{1}{4}$ are over 18.

What fraction of the students are neither under 16 nor over 18?

First method:

$\frac{1}{10}$ of $900 = \frac{1}{10} \times 900$ ——————— 1 method mark is available for identifying a method to work out the number under 16 or over 18.

$\frac{1}{4}$ of $900 = \frac{1}{4} \times 900$

$= 90$ and 225 ——————————— You get 1 mark for obtaining both of these answers.

$900 - 90 - 225 = 585$ ——————

$\frac{585}{900}$ or $\frac{13}{20}$ ——————

You get 1 mark for attempting to work out the number of people.

You get 1 accuracy mark for the correct answer.

Second method:

$\frac{1}{10} + \frac{1}{4}$ ——————————— 1 method mark is available for identifying the valid method of adding the given fractions.

$\frac{2}{20} + \frac{5}{20}$ ——————————— You get 1 method mark for getting a common denominator.

$\frac{7}{20}$ ——————————— You get 1 mark for correctly getting the fraction under 16 and over 18.

$\frac{13}{20}$ ——————————— You get 1 mark for the correct answer.

Total: 4 marks

During World War I, soldiers were often faced with very difficult circumstances. For long periods of time, they would live in trenches that were wet, dirty, and full of rats and disease. During periods either just before or during a big battle, food was also scarce.

Getting started

Think about the following questions.

- What are ounces and gills?
- With a partner, work out the metric equivalents of a soldier's rations.
- How much would each soldier receive each week?

Is there any other information that you need to be able to complete your task? Where might you be able to find this information?

Below is a list of what each soldier might be expected to receive each day.

20 oz bread

3 oz cheese

$\frac{5}{8}$ oz tea

4 oz jam

8 oz fresh vegetables

$\frac{1}{3}$ oz chocolate

$\frac{1}{2}$ gill rum

Current supplies

$\frac{3}{4}$ ton bread

300 lb cheese

100 lb tea

355 lb jam

$\frac{1}{2}$ ton fresh vegetables

30 lb chocolate

20 gallons rum

Your task

The logistics corps faced one of the biggest challenges of the war. They were in charge of making sure that the soldiers in the trenches got the food they were entitled to. Imagine you were working in the logistics corps.

Using the information below, decide if you have everything you need to supply the 200 troops on your part of the front line for the next week. If you have shortages, decide how you are going to ration what you have.

Then, write a letter to the field commander, ordering your supplies, so that you have everything you need for the following week.

Life is full of pairs: up and down, hot and cold, left and right, light and dark, rough and smooth, to name a few. One pairing that is particularly relevant to maths is positive and negative.

You are already familiar with positive numbers, including where they appear in real life and how to carry out calculations with them. However, sometimes we need to use a set of numbers in addition to the positive counting numbers. This set of numbers is known as the negative numbers. Here are some examples of where you might encounter negative numbers.

A negative number on a bank statement will show by how much you are overdrawn (or, how much money you have spent above what you have in your bank account).

On the temperature scale of degrees Celsius zero is known as 'freezing point'. In many places – even in the UK! – temperatures fall below freezing point. At this stage we need negative numbers to represent the temperature.

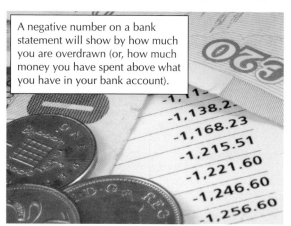

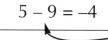

Jet pilots experience g-forces when their aircraft accelerates or decelerates quickly. Negative g-forces can be felt when an object accelerates downwards very quickly and they are represented by negative numbers. These negative forces are responsible for the feeling of weightlessness that you have on rollercoasters!

$$5 - 9 = -4$$

When a bigger number is taken from a smaller one, the result is a negative number.

In lifts, negative numbers are used to represent floors below ground level. These are often called 'lower ground' floors.

Sea level can be given the value 'zero'. Mountains are described as being 'above sea level' and ocean floors as 'below sea level'. This means that when a submarine goes under the sea the depths that it reaches are given using negative numbers.

As you can see, negative numbers are just as important as positive numbers and you will encounter them in your everyday life.

3 Number: Negative numbers

1 Introduction to negative numbers

2 Everyday use of negative numbers

3 The number line

4 Arithmetic with negative numbers

This chapter will show you ...

- **G** how negative numbers are used in real life
- **G** what is meant by a negative number
- **G** how to use inequalities with negative numbers
- **F** how to do arithmetic with negative numbers

Visual overview

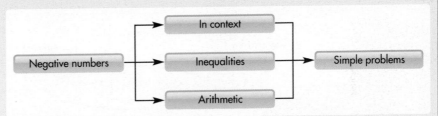

What you should already know

- What a negative number means (KS3 level 3, GCSE grade G)
- How to put numbers in order (KS3 level 3, GCSE grade G)

Quick check

Put the numbers in the following lists into order, smallest first.

1 8, 2, 5, 9, 1, 0, 4

2 14, 19, 11, 10, 17

3 51, 92, 24, 0, 32

4 87, 136, 12, 288, 56

5 5, 87, $\frac{1}{2}$, 100, 0, 50

Introduction to negative numbers

Negative numbers are numbers **below** zero. You meet **negative numbers** often in winter when the temperature falls below freezing (0 °C).

The diagram below shows a thermometer with negative temperatures. The temperature is −3 °C. This means the temperature is three degrees below zero.

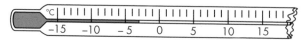

The number line below shows positive and negative numbers.

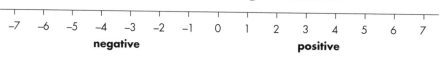

negative   positive

ACTIVITY

Seaport colliery

Top of winding gear 80 ft above ground

Ground / 400 ft

South drift / 310 ft

225 ft — Closed gate

150 ft — Collapsed tunnel

Zero level / 0 ft
−50 ft — North gate

A seam / −325 ft

B seam / −425 ft
−475 ft — Dead Man's seam

C seam / −550 ft
−600 ft — D seam

Bottom gate / −700 ft

This is a section through Seaport Colliery.

The height above sea (zero) level for each tunnel is shown. Note that some of the heights are given as negative numbers.

The ground is 400 ft above sea level.

Sea level

1 What is the **difference** in height between the following levels?

   a South drift and C seam

   b The ground and A seam

   c The closed gate and the collapsed tunnel

   d Zero level and Dead Man's seam

   e Ground level and the bottom gate

   f Collapsed tunnel and B seam

   g North gate and Dead Man's seam

FM Functional Maths   **AU** (AO2) Assessing Understanding   **PS** (AO3) Problem Solving

   h Zero level and the south drift

   i Zero level and the bottom gate

   j South drift and the bottom gate

2 How high above sea level is the top of the winding gear?

3 How high above the bottom gate is the top of the winding gear?

4 There are two pairs of tunnels that are 75 ft apart. Which two pairs are they?

5 How much cable does the engineman let out to get the cage from the south drift to D seam?

6 There are two pairs of tunnels that are 125 ft apart. Which two pairs are they?

7 Which two tunnels are 200 ft apart?

EXERCISE 3A

1 Write down the temperature for each thermometer.

a
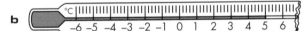

b
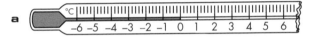

c
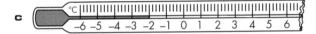

d
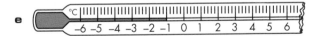

e

2
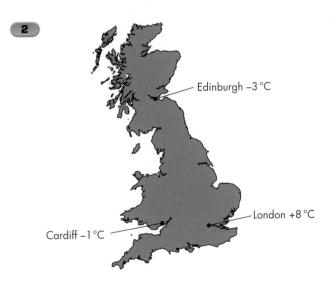

Edinburgh −3 °C

London +8 °C

Cardiff −1 °C

  a How much colder is it in Edinburgh than in London?

  b How much warmer is it in London than in Cardiff?

CORE 75

FM 3 The instructions on a bottle of de-icer say that it will stop water freezing down to –12 °C. The temperature is –4 °C.

How many more degrees does the temperature need to fall before the de-icer stops working?

FM 4 Chris Boddington, the famous explorer, is leading a joint expedition to the Andes mountains and cave system. The climbers establish camps at the various places shown and the cavers find the various caves shown.

To help him move supplies about, Chris needs a chart of the differences between the heights of the camps and caves. Help him by copying the chart below into your book and filling it in. (Some of the boxes have been done for you.)

Everyday use of negative numbers

This section will show you how to:
- use positive and negative numbers in everyday life

Key words
above/below
after/before
credit/debit
negative number/
    positive number
profit/loss

There are many other situations where **negative numbers** are used. Here are three examples.

- When +15 m means 15 metres **above** sea level, then –15 m means 15 metres **below** sea level.
- When +2 h means 2 hours **after** midday, then –2 h means 2 hours **before** midday.
- When +£60 means a **profit** of £60, then –£60 means a **loss** of £60.

You also meet negative numbers on graphs, and you may already have plotted coordinates with negative numbers.

On bank statements and bills a negative number means you owe money. A **positive number** means they owe you money.

A **debit** is when you pay money out of your account.

A **credit** is when you pay money into your account.

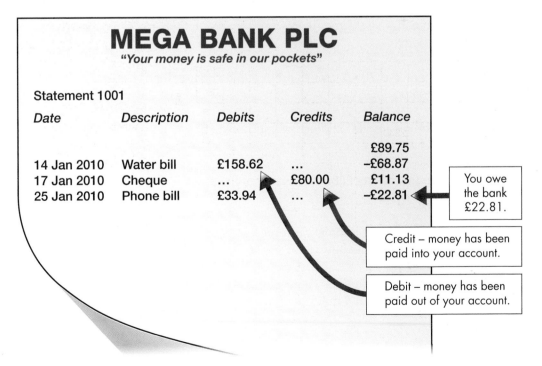

MEGA BANK PLC
"Your money is safe in our pockets"

Statement 1001

Date	Description	Debits	Credits	Balance
				£89.75
14 Jan 2010	Water bill	£158.62	...	–£68.87
17 Jan 2010	Cheque	...	£80.00	£11.13
25 Jan 2010	Phone bill	£33.94	...	–£22.81

You owe the bank £22.81.

Credit – money has been paid into your account.

Debit – money has been paid out of your account.

EXERCISE 3B

Copy and complete each of the following.

1 If +£5 means a profit of five pounds, then ...... means a loss of five pounds.

2 If +£9 means a profit of nine pounds, then a loss of £9 is ....

3 If −£4 means a loss of four pounds, then +£4 means a ...... of four pounds.

4 If +200 m means 200 metres above sea level, then ...... means 200 metres below sea level.

5 If +50 m means fifty metres above sea level, then fifty metres below sea level is written ....

6 If −100 m means one hundred metres below sea level, then +100 m means one hundred metres ...... sea level.

7 If +3 h means three hours after midday, then ...... means three hours before midday.

8 If +5 h means 5 hours after midday, then ...... means 5 hours before midday.

9 If −6 h means six hours before midday, then +6 h means six hours ...... midday.

10 If +2 °C means two degrees above freezing point, then ...... means two degrees below freezing point.

11 If +8 °C means eight degrees above freezing point, then ...... means eight degrees below freezing point.

12 If −5 °C means five degrees below freezing point, then +5 °C means five degrees ...... freezing point.

13 If +70 km means 70 kilometres north of the equator, then ...... means 70 kilometres south of the equator.

14 If +200 km means 200 kilometres north of the equator, then 200 kilometres south of the equator is written ....

15 If −50 km means fifty kilometres south of the equator, then +50 km means fifty kilometres ...... of the equator.

16 If 10 minutes before midnight is represented by −10 minutes, then five minutes after midnight is represented by ....

17 If a car moving forwards at 10 miles per hour is represented by +10 mph, then a car moving backwards at 5 miles per hour is represented by ....

18 In an office building, the third floor above ground level is represented by +3. So, the second floor below ground level is represented by ....

FM 19

> # MEGA BANK PLC
> *"Your money is safe in our pockets"*
>
> Statement 2010
>
> | Date | Description | Debits | Credits | Balance |
> |------|-------------|--------|---------|---------|
> | | | | | £320.45 |
> | 20 Sept 2009 | Gas bill | £410.17 | ... | –£89.72 |
> | 23 Sept 2009 | Cheque | ... | £140.00 | £50.28 |
> | 25 Sept 2009 | Mobile phone bill | £63.48 | ... | –£13.20 |

  a What does –£89.72 mean?

  b What is a debit?

  c What is a credit?

20 The temperature on three days in Moscow was –7 °C, –5 °C and –11 °C.

  a Which temperature is the lowest?

  b What is the difference in temperature between the coldest and the warmest days?

21 **a** Which is the smallest number in the cloud?

  b Which is the largest number in the cloud?

  c What is the difference between the smallest and largest numbers in the cloud?

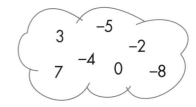

PS 22 Sydney the snail is at the bottom of a 10-foot well.

Each day he climbs 2 feet up the wall of the well.

Each night he slides 1 foot back down the wall of the well.

How many days does it take Sydney to reach the top of the well?

AU 23 A thermostat is set at 16 °C.

The temperature in a room at 1.00 am is –2 °C.

The temperature rises two degrees every 6 minutes.

At what time is the temperature on the thermostat reached?

The number line

This section will show you how to:

- use a number line to represent negative numbers
- use inequalities with negative numbers

Look at the **number line**.

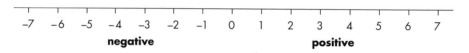

Notice that the **negative** numbers are to the left of 0 and the **positive** numbers are to the right of 0.

Numbers to the right of any number on the number line are always bigger than that number.

Numbers to the left of any number on the number line are always smaller than that number.

So, for example, you can see from a number line that:

2 is *smaller* than 5 because 2 is to the *left* of 5.

You can write this as 2 < 5.

−3 is *smaller* than 2 because −3 is to the *left* of 2.

You can write this as −3 < 2.

7 is *bigger* than 3 because 7 is to the *right* of 3.

You can write this as 7 > 3.

−1 is *bigger* than −4 because −1 is to the *right* of −4.

You can write this as −1 > −4.

Reminder   The **inequality** signs:

< means 'is **less than**'

> means 'is **greater than**' or 'is **more than**'

EXERCISE 3C

1 Copy and complete each of the following by putting a suitable number in the box.

a ☐ is smaller than 3   **b** ☐ is smaller than 1   **c** ☐ is smaller than –3

d ☐ is smaller than –7   **e** –5 is smaller than ☐   **f** –1 is smaller than ☐

g 3 is smaller than ☐   **h** –2 is smaller than ☐   **i** ☐ is smaller than 0

j –4 is smaller than ☐   **k** ☐ is smaller than –8   **l** –7 is smaller than ☐

2 Copy and complete each of the following by putting a suitable number in the box.

a ☐ is bigger than –3   **b** ☐ is bigger than 1   **c** ☐ is bigger than –2

d ☐ is bigger than –1   **e** –1 is bigger than ☐   **f** –8 is bigger than ☐

g 1 is bigger than ☐   **h** –5 is bigger than ☐   **i** ☐ is bigger than –5

j 2 is bigger than ☐   **k** ☐ is bigger than –4   **l** –2 is bigger than ☐

3 Copy each of these and put the correct phrase in each space.

a –1 3   **b** 3 2   **c** –4 ...... –1

d –5 ...... –4   **e** 1 ...... –6   **f** –3 0

g –2 ...... –1   **h** 2 ...... –3   **i** 5 ...... –6

j 3 4   **k** –7 ...... –5   **l** –2 ...... –4

4

$$-1 \quad -\frac{3}{4} \quad -\frac{1}{2} \quad -\frac{1}{4} \quad 0 \quad \frac{1}{4} \quad \frac{1}{2} \quad \frac{3}{4} \quad 1$$

Copy each of these and put the correct phrase in each space.

a $\frac{1}{4}$ ...... $\frac{3}{4}$ **b** $-\frac{1}{2}$ 0   **c** $-\frac{3}{4}$ ...... $\frac{3}{4}$

d $\frac{1}{4}$ ...... $-\frac{1}{2}$ **e** –1 ...... $\frac{3}{4}$ **f** $\frac{1}{2}$ 1

5 In each case below, copy the statement and put the correct symbol, either < or >, in the box.

a 3 ☐ 5   **b** –2 ☐ –5   **c** –4 ☐ 3   **d** 5 ☐ 9

e –3 ☐ 2   **f** 4 ☐ –3   **g** –1 ☐ 0   **h** 6 ☐ –4

i 2 ☐ –3   **j** 0 ☐ –2   **k** –5 ☐ –4   **l** 1 ☐ 3

m –6 ☐ –7   **n** 2 ☐ –3   **o** –1 ☐ 1   **p** 4 ☐ 0

G

PS 6 Copy these number lines and fill in the missing numbers.

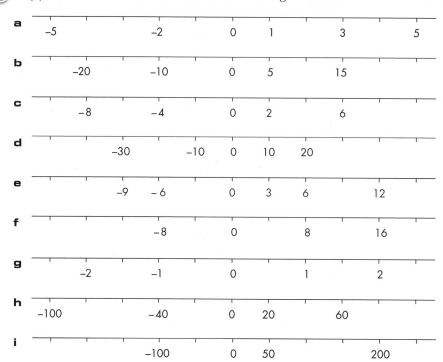

FM 7 Here are some temperatures.

2 °C   –2 °C   –4 °C   6 °C

Copy and complete the weather report, using these temperatures.

> The hottest place today is Barnsley with a temperature of _____, while in Eastbourne a ground frost has left the temperature just below zero at _____. In Bristol it is even colder at _____. Finally, in Tenby the temperature is just above freezing at _____.

AU 8 Here are some numbers.

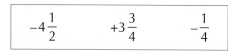

$$-4\frac{1}{2} \qquad +3\frac{3}{4} \qquad -\frac{1}{4}$$

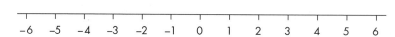

| –6 | –5 | –4 | –3 | –2 | –1 | 0 | 1 | 2 | 3 | 4 | 5 | 6 |

Copy the number line and mark the numbers on it.

Arithmetic with negative numbers

This section will show you how to:

- add and subtract positive and negative numbers to or from both positive and negative numbers

Key words
add
subtract

Adding and subtracting positive numbers

These two operations can be illustrated on a thermometer scale.

- **Adding** a positive number moves the marker *up* the thermometer scale. For example,

  $-2 + 6 = 4$

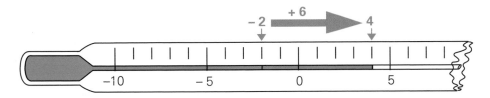

- **Subtracting** a positive number moves the marker *down* the thermometer scale. For example,

  $3 - 5 = -2$

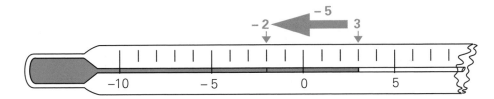

EXAMPLE 1

The temperature at midnight was 2 °C but then it fell by five degrees. What was the new temperature?

Falling five degrees means the calculation is $2 - 5$, which is equal to -3. So, the new temperature is -3 °C.

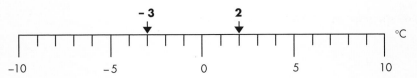

EXAMPLE 2

The temperature is −4 °C. It then falls by five degrees. What is the new temperature?

Falling five degrees means the calculation is −4 − 5, which is equal to −9. So, the new temperature is −9 °C.

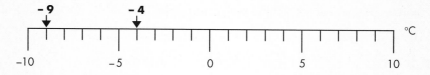

EXERCISE 3D

1 Use a thermometer scale to find the answer to each of the following.

a $2° − 4° =$	**b** $4° − 7° =$	**c** $3° − 5° =$	**d** $1° − 4° =$
e $6° − 8° =$	**f** $5° − 8° =$	**g** $−2 + 5 =$	**h** $−1 + 4 =$
i $−4 + 3 =$	**j** $−6 + 5 =$	**k** $−3 + 5 =$	**l** $−5 + 2 =$
m $−1 − 3 =$	**n** $−2 − 4 =$	**o** $−5 − 1 =$	**p** $3 − 4 =$
q $2 − 7 =$	**r** $1 − 5 =$	**s** $−3 + 7 =$	**t** $5 − 6 =$
u $−2 − 3 =$	**v** $2 − 6 =$	**w** $−8 + 3 =$	**x** $4 − 9 =$

2 Answer each of the following *without* the help of a thermometer scale.

a $5 − 9 =$	**b** $3 − 7 =$	**c** $−2 − 8 =$	**d** $−5 + 7 =$
e $−1 + 9 =$	**f** $4 − 9 =$	**g** $−10 + 12 =$	**h** $−15 + 20 =$
i $23 − 30 =$	**j** $30 − 42 =$	**k** $−12 + 25 =$	**l** $−30 + 55 =$
m $−10 − 22 =$	**n** $−13 − 17 =$	**o** $45 − 50 =$	**p** $17 − 25 =$
q $18 − 30 =$	**r** $−25 + 35 =$	**s** $−23 − 13 =$	**t** $31 − 45 =$
u $−24 + 65 =$	**v** $−19 + 31 =$	**w** $25 − 65 =$	**x** $199 − 300 =$

3 Work out each of the following.

a $8 + 3 − 5 =$	**b** $−2 + 3 − 6 =$	**c** $−1 + 3 + 4 =$
d $−2 − 3 + 4 =$	**e** $−1 + 1 − 2 =$	**f** $−4 + 5 − 7 =$
g $−3 + 4 − 7 =$	**h** $1 + 3 − 6 =$	**i** $8 − 7 + 2 =$
j $−5 − 7 + 12 =$	**k** $−4 + 5 − 8 =$	**l** $−4 + 6 − 8 =$
m $103 − 102 + 7 =$	**n** $−1 + 4 − 2 =$	**o** $−6 + 9 − 12 =$
p $−3 − 3 − 3 =$	**q** $−3 + 4 − 6 =$	**r** $−102 + 45 − 23 =$
s $8 − 10 − 5 =$	**t** $9 − 12 + 2 =$	**u** $99 − 100 − 46 =$

4 Use a calculator to check your answers to questions 1 to 3.

AU 5 At 5 am the temperature in London was −4 °C.

At 11 am the temperature was 3 °C.

a By how many degrees did the temperature rise?

b The temperature in Brighton was two degrees lower than in London at 5 am
What was the temperature is Brighton at 5 am?

PS 6 Here are five numbers.

    4   7   8   2   5

a Use two of the numbers to make a calculation with an answer of −6.

b Use three of the numbers to make a calculation with an answer of −1.

c Use four of the numbers to make a calculation with an answer of −18.

d Use all five of the numbers to make a calculation with an answer of −12.

FM 7 A submarine is 1600 feet below sea level.

A radar system can detect submarines down to 900 feet below sea level.

To safely avoid detection, the submarine captain keeps the submarine 200 feet below the level of detection.

How many feet can the submarine climb to be safe from detection?

Adding and subtracting negative numbers

To *subtract a negative number* …

    … treat the − − as a +

For example: $4 - (-2) = 4 + 2 = 6$

To *add a negative number* …

    … treat the + − as a −

For example: $3 + (-5) = 3 - 5 = -2$

Using your calculator

Calculations involving negative numbers can be done by using the **(−)** key.

EXAMPLE 3

Work out −3 + 7.

Press **(−)** **3** **+** **7** **=**

The answer should be 4.

EXAMPLE 4

Work out $-6 - (-2)$.

Press (−) 6 − (−) 2 =

The answer should be -4.

EXERCISE 3E

F

1 Answer each of the following. Check your answers on a calculator.

a $2 - (-4) =$	**b** $4 - (-3) =$	**c** $3 - (-5) =$	**d** $5 - (-1) =$
e $6 - (-2) =$	**f** $8 - (-2) =$	**g** $-1 - (-3) =$	**h** $-4 - (-1) =$
i $-2 - (-3) =$	**j** $-5 - (-7) =$	**k** $-3 - (-2) =$	**l** $-8 - (-1) =$
m $4 + (-2) =$	**n** $2 + (-5) =$	**o** $3 + (-2) =$	**p** $1 + (-6) =$
q $5 + (-2) =$	**r** $4 + (-8) =$	**s** $-2 + (-1) =$	**t** $-6 + (-2) =$
u $-7 + (-3) =$	**v** $-2 + (-7) =$	**w** $-1 + (-3) =$	**x** $-7 + (-2) =$

2 Write down the answer to each of the following, then check your answers on a calculator.

a $-3 - 5 =$	**b** $-2 - 8 =$	**c** $-5 - 6 =$	**d** $6 - 9 =$
e $5 - 3 =$	**f** $3 - 8 =$	**g** $-4 + 5 =$	**h** $-3 + 7 =$
i $-2 + 9 =$	**j** $-6 + -2 =$	**k** $-1 + -4 =$	**l** $-8 + -3 =$
m $5 - -6 =$	**n** $3 - -3 =$	**o** $6 - -2 =$	**p** $3 - -5 =$
q $-5 - -3 =$	**r** $-2 - -1 =$	**s** $-4 - 5 =$	**t** $2 - 7 =$
u $-3 + 8 =$	**v** $-4 + - 5 =$	**w** $1 - -7 =$	**x** $-5 - -5 =$

3 The temperature at midnight was 4 °C. Find the temperature if it *fell* by:

a 1 degree **b** 4 degrees **c** 7 degrees

d 9 degrees **e** 15 degrees

4 What is the *difference* between the following temperatures?

a 4 °C and −6 °C

b −2 °C and −9 °C

c −3 °C and 6 °C

5 Rewrite the following list, putting the numbers in order of size, lowest first.

1   −5   3   −6   −9   8   −1   2

6 Write down the answers to each of the following, then check your answers on a calculator.

a $2 - 5 =$ **b** $7 - 11 =$ **c** $4 - 6 =$

d $8 - 15 =$ **e** $9 - 23 =$ **f** $-2 - 4 =$

g $-5 - 7 =$ **h** $-1 - 9 =$ **i** $-4 + 8 =$

j $-9 + 5 =$ **k** $9 - -5 =$ **l** $8 - -3 =$

m $-8 - -4 =$ **n** $-3 - -2 =$ **o** $-7 + -3 =$

p $-9 + 4 =$ **q** $-6 + 3 =$ **r** $-1 + 6 =$

s $-9 - -5 =$ **t** $9 - 17 =$

7 Find what you have to *add to* 5 to get:

a 7   **b** 2   **c** 0

d -2 **e** -5 **f** -15

8 Find what you have to *subtract from* 4 to get:

a 2   **b** 0   **c** 5

d 9   **e** 15   **f** -4

9 Find what you have to *add to* -5 to get:

a 8   **b** -3 **c** 0

d -1 **e** 6   **f** -7

10 Find what you have to *subtract from* -3 to get:

a 7   **b** 2   **c** -1

d -7 **e** -10 **f** 1

AU 11 Write down *ten* different addition sums that give the answer 1.

AU 12 Write down *ten* different subtraction calculations that give the answer 1. There must be *one negative number* in each calculation.

13 Use a calculator to work out each of these.

a $-7 + -3 - -5 =$ **b** $6 + 7 - 7 =$ **c** $-3 + -4 - -7 =$

d $-1 - 3 - -6 =$ **e** $8 - -7 + -2 =$ **f** $-5 - 7 - -12 =$

g $-4 + 5 - 7 =$ **h** $-4 + -6 - -8 =$ **i** $103 - -102 - -7 =$

j $-1 + 4 - -2 =$ **k** $6 - -9 - 12 =$ **l** $-3 - -3 - -3 =$

m $-45 + -56 - -34 =$ **n** $-3 + 4 - -6 =$ **o** $102 + -45 - 32 =$

F

14 Give the outputs of each of these function machines.

a $-4, -3, -2, -1, 0$ → $[+3]$ → ?, ?, ?, ?, ?

b $-4, -3, -2, -1, 0$ → $[-2]$ → ?, ?, ?, ?, ?

c $-4, -3, -2, -1, 0$ → $[+1]$ → ?, ?, ?, ?, ?

d $-4, -3, -2, -1, 0$ → $[-4]$ → ?, ?, ?, ?, ?

e $-4, -3, -2, -1, 0$ → $[-5]$ → ?, ?, ?, ?, ?

f $-4, -3, -2, -1, 0$ → $[+7]$ → ?, ?, ?, ?, ?

g $-10, -9, -8, -7, -6$ → $[-2]$ → ?, ?, ?, ?, ?

h $-10, -9, -8, -7, -6$ → $[-6]$ → ?, ?, ?, ?, ?

i $-5, -4, -3, -2, -1, 0$ → $[+3]$ → ?, ?, ?, ?, ?, ? → $[-2]$ → ?, ?, ?, ?, ?, ?

j $-5, -4, -3, -2, -1, 0$ → $[-7]$ → ?, ?, ?, ?, ?, ? → $[-2]$ → ?, ?, ?, ?, ?, ?

k $-5, -4, -3, -2, -1, 0$ → $[+3]$ → ?, ?, ?, ?, ?, ? → $[+2]$ → ?, ?, ?, ?, ?, ?

l $-3, -2, -1, 0, 1, 2, 3$ → $[-5]$ → ?, ?, ?, ?, ?, ? → $[+3]$ → ?, ?, ?, ?, ?, ?

m $-3, -2, -1, 0, 1, 2, 3$ → $[-7]$ → ?, ?, ?, ?, ?, ? → $[+9]$ → ?, ?, ?, ?, ?, ?

n $-3, -2, -1, 0, 1, 2, 3$ → $[+6]$ → ?, ?, ?, ?, ?, ? → $[-8]$ → ?, ?, ?, ?, ?, ?

15 What numbers are missing from the boxes to make the number sentences true?

a $2 + -6 = \square$

b $4 + \square = 7$

c $-4 + \square = 0$

d $5 + \square = -1$

e $3 + 4 = \square$

f $\square - -5 = 7$

g $\square - 5 = 2$

h $6 + \square = 0$

i $\square - -5 = -2$

j $2 + -2 = \square$

k $\square - 2 = -2$

l $-2 + -4 = \square$

m $2 + 3 + \square = -2$

n $-2 + -3 + -4 = \square$

o $\square - 5 = -1$

p $\square - 8 = -8$

q $-4 + 2 + \square = 3$

r $-5 + 5 = \square$

s $7 - -3 = \square$

t $\square - -5 = 0$

u $3 - \square = 0$

v $-3 - \square = 0$

w $-6 + -3 = \square$

x $\square - 3 - -2 = -1$

y $\square - 1 = -4$

z $7 - \square = 10$

AU 16 You have the following cards.

a Which card should you choose to make the answer to the following sum as large as possible? What is the answer?

+6 + ▢ = ...

b Which card should you choose to make the answer to part **a** as small as possible? What is the answer?

c Which card should you choose to make the answer to the following subtraction as large as possible? What is the answer?

+6 − ▢ = ...

d Which card should you choose to make the answer to part **c** as small as possible? What is the answer?

AU 17 You have the following cards.

−9 −7 −5 −4 0 +1 +2 +4 +7

a Which cards should you choose to make the answer to the following calculation as large as possible? What is the answer?

+5 + ▢ − ▢ = ...

b Which cards should you choose to make the answer to part **a** as small as possible? What is the answer?

c Which cards should you choose to make the answer to the following number sentence zero? Give all possible answers.

▢ + ▢ = 0

FM 18
AU The thermometer in a car is inaccurate by up to two degrees.
An ice alert warning comes on at 3 °C, according to the thermometer temperature.
If the actual temperature is 2 °C, will the alert come on?
Explain how you decide.

PS 19 Two numbers have a sum of 5.
One of the numbers is negative.
The other number is even.
What are the two numbers if the even number is as large as possible?

Negative magic squares

Make your own magic square with negative numbers. You need nine small square cards and two pens or pencils of different colours.

This is perhaps the best known magic square.

8	3	4
1	5	9
6	7	2

But magic squares can be made from many different sets of numbers, as shown by this second square.

This square is now used to show you how to make a magic square with negative numbers. But the method works with any magic square. So, if you can find one of your own, use it!

- Arrange the nine cards in a square and write on them the numbers of the magic square. Picture **a** below.

- Rearrange the cards in order, lowest number first, to form another square. Picture **b** below.

- Keeping the cards in order, turn them over so that the blank side of each card is face up. Picture **c** below.

a

8	13	6
7	9	11
12	5	10

b

5	6	7
8	9	10
11	12	13

c

- Now use a different coloured pen to avoid confusion.

- Choose any number (say four) for the top left-hand corner of the square. Picture **d** below.

- Choose another number (say three) and subtract it from each number in the first row to get the next number. Picture **e** below.

- Now choose a third number (say two) and subtract it from each number in the top row to make the second row, and then again from each number in the second row. Picture **f** below.

d

4		

e

4	1	−2

f

4	1	−2
2	−1	−4
0	−3	−6

- Turn the cards over. Picture **g**.
- Rearrange the cards into the original magic square. Picture **h**.
- Turn them over again. Picture **i**.

g

5	6	7
8	9	10
11	12	13

h

8	13	6
7	9	11
12	5	10

i

2	–6	1
–2	–1	0
–3	4	–4

You should have a **magic square of negative numbers**.

Try it on any square. It works even with squares bigger than 3 × 3. Try it on this 4 × 4 square.

2	13	9	14
16	7	11	4
15	8	12	3
5	10	6	17

EXERCISE 3F

PS Copy and complete each of these magic squares. In each case, write down the 'magic number'.

1

–1		
–5	–4	–3
		–7

2

	–4	3
		–2
	4	–1

3

–6	–5	–4
		–10

4

2		
	–4	
–7	6	–8

5

		–9
–3	–6	–9

6

		–1
	–7	
–13		–12

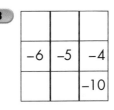

7

–4		
–8		–6
–9		

8

2	1	–3
	0	

9

–2		
	–5	
–7		–8

10

–8			–14
–8	–9		
		–4	–5
1	–10	–12	–5

11

–7		2	–16
	–8		
–11	–3	0	–2
		–13	–1

GRADE BOOSTER

G You can use negative numbers in context

G You can use < for less than and > for greater than

F You can add positive and negative numbers to positive and negative numbers

F You can subtract positive and negative numbers from positive and negative numbers

E You can solve problems involving simple negative numbers

What you should know now

- How to order positive and negative numbers
- How to add and subtract positive and negative numbers
- How to use negative numbers in practical situations
- How to use a calculator when working with negative numbers

1 Write down the number that is

a 100 more than 2480 (1)   **b** 10 less than 305 (1)

c 1 more than –5 (1)

(Total 3 marks)

AQA, March 2008, Module 3 Foundation, Question 11

2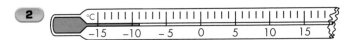

a What temperature is shown on the thermometer?

b One winter morning, the temperature went up from –3 °C to 2 °C.
By how many degrees did the temperature rise?

c In the afternoon, the temperature fell by six degrees from 2 °C.
What was the temperature at the end of the afternoon?

3 These maps show the maximum and minimum temperatures in five towns during January 2006.

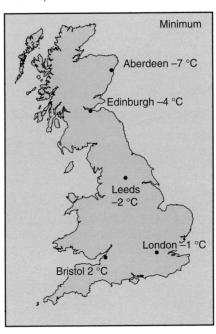
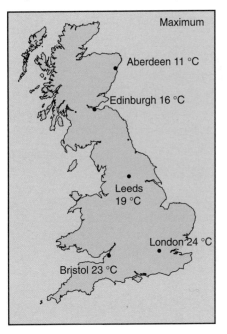

a Which place had the lowest minimum temperature?

b How much lower was the minimum temperature in Edinburgh than in Bristol?

c Which two places had a difference of 21 degrees between the minimum and maximum temperatures?

d Which place had the lowest difference between the minimum and maximum temperatures and what was this difference?

4 The diagram shows a number line with the number $2\frac{1}{4}$ marked.

Copy the number line and mark the following numbers on it.

a $-1\frac{1}{2}$ **b** $\frac{3}{4}$ **c** $-\frac{1}{3}$

5 The temperatures on three days round Christmas are 2 °C, –5 °C and –1 °C.

  a Write down these temperatures, in order, with the lowest first.

  b What is the difference in temperature between the coldest and the hottest days?

 6 At 3 pm the temperature in Sheffield was 3 °C. According to the weather forecast, the temperature at midnight was predicted as –5 °C.

  a By how many degrees was the temperature predicted to fall?

  b In fact, the temperature at midnight was two degrees lower than forecast. What was the temperature that night?

7 **a** At 7 pm the temperature was 3°.

    At midnight, the temperature had fallen by 5°C.

    What was the temperature at midnight? (1)

  b At 2 am the temperature was –4°C.

    By midday the temperature had risen by 10°C.

    What was the temerature at midday? (1)

    (Total 2 marks)

AQA, June 2005, Module 3 Foundation, Question 11

8 **a** The temperatures in a number of towns in Turkey on one day in December were

    11°C   –15°C   –7°C   –4°C
    2°C   12°C   –3°C

    i Write down the coldest of these temperatures. (1)

    ii Write down the warmest of these temperatures. (1)

  b The temperature in Istanbul at 4 pm was 1°C.

    At midnight this temperature had fallen by 7°C.

    What was the temperature at midnight? (1)

    (Total 3 marks)

AQA, November 2005, Module 3 Foundation, Question 3

9 The temperature at midnight was recorded at a weather station in Scotland during a week in February.

Five of these temperatures are shown in the table.

Day	Mon	Tue	Wed	Thu	Fri	Sat	Sun
Temperature (°C)	2	–4		–1	–4	–8	

  a Which of these five temperatures was the warmest? (1)

  b On Wednesday the temperature at midnight was 3 degrees lower than that recorded on Tuesday.

    What was the temperature at midnight on Wednesday? (1)

  c On Sunday the temperature at midnight was 5 degrees higher than that recorded on Saturday.

    What was the temperature at midnight on Sunday? (1)

    (Total 3 marks)

AQA, March 2006, Module 3 Foundation, Question 15

10 Oxygen turns to liquid at –58 °C. Carbon dioxide turns to liquid at –86 °C.

  a What is the difference between these two temperatures?

  b In each of the statements below, write a possible temperature. Remember that a temperature below –273 °C is not possible.

    i At ......°C, oxygen is a gas.

    ii At ...... °C, carbon dioxide is a liquid.

Worked Examination Questions

AU **1** The number $2\frac{1}{2}$ is halfway between 1 and 4.

What number is halfway between:

a −8 and −1   **b** $\frac{1}{4}$ and $1\frac{1}{4}$?

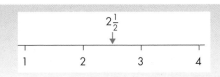

a The number halfway between −8 and −1 is $-4\frac{1}{2}$.

1 mark

The hint in the question is to sketch the numbers on a number line.

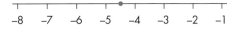

Just by counting from each end you can find the middle value. You get 1 mark for the correct answer.

b The number halfway between $\frac{1}{4}$ and $1\frac{1}{4}$ is $\frac{3}{4}$.

1 mark

Total: 2 marks

Sketch the number line and mark on the quarters.

Count from each end to identify the middle value to get 1 mark.

2 The table shows the temperatures in four cities.

  a Write down the lowest temperature.
  b Work out the difference in temperature between Birmingham and London.
  c Three hours later the temperature in Manchester had risen by two degrees. Work out the new temperature in Manchester.

Birmingham	5 °C
London	−1 °C
Manchester	−3 °C
Exeter	1 °C

a Lowest temperature is −3 °C in Manchester

1 mark

From lowest to highest the temperatures are −3 °C, −1 °C, 1 °C, 5 °C.
You get 1 mark for the correct answer.

b 6 degrees

1 mark

Find the difference between temperatures in Birmingham (5°C) and London (−1 °C).
You get 1 mark for independent workings.

c −1 °C

1 mark

Total: 3 marks

You get 1 mark for independent workings for the correct calculation −3 °C + 2 °C.

FM **3** Maisie has £103.48 in her bank account.

On 11th December 2009 she takes £20 out of a cash machine and uses her debit card to pay for petrol that costs £25.60.

	Transaction	Paid In	Paid Out	Balance
11/12/09	Carried forward			£103.48
11/12/09	Cash ATM		£20	
11/12/09	Sovereign garage		£25.60	
11/12/09	Hair n' Nails	£152.70		
11/12/09	Closing Balance			

On the same day her weekly wages of £152.70 are paid in. Fill in the statement to work out how much she has at the end of the day.

£83.48, £77.48, £230.58

Subtract any values in the 'Paid out' column and add any values in the 'Paid in' column. You get 1 mark for each correct answer.

Total: 3 marks

In some sports you are required to keep a score card as you play and each player is responsible for filling in their card. In some sports these cards are handed in at the end of the game for checking.

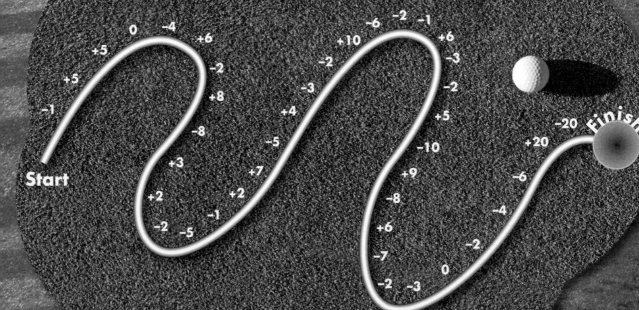

Your task

You are going to fill in a score card of your own but instead of positive numbers, your card will involve negative numbers.

How to play

- In groups of three or four, discuss the rules given below and check that you all understand how to play the game.
- Together, decide how many errors you can make before you are disqualified.

- Once you are sure of the rules, each player takes a score card and throws the dice. The person who rolls the highest number goes first.
- After all the players have reached the finish line, compare final scores.
- You should consider:
  - who has won
  - what the most popular scores in the game were
  - if there were some numbers that were better to roll than others.

Resources required

Coloured counters
A dice
Score cards

The rules

- Each player starts with 10 points.
- Each player must keep a record of their total but they must not reveal it to their opponents until the end of the game.

- In turn, players throw the dice and move their counter forward that number of spaces.
- Each time they land on a number they have to add it to their score.
- At the finish the player with the highest score wins.
- Other players have to check the winner's score card. Any errors should be corrected but too many errors can lead to a player being disqualified!

Score card

Number landed on	Running total
Start	+10

Why this chapter matters

You will have seen percentages in many places and situations.

Why use percentages?

Because:

- basic percentages are quite easy to understand

- they are a good way of comparing fractions

- percentages are used a lot in everyday life.

Who uses them?

Shops often have sales where they offer a certain percentage off their standard prices. By understanding percentages you will be able to quickly work out where the real bargains are.

Each month (or year) banks pay their customers interest on their savings. The interest rate the banks offer is expressed as a percentage. Also, banks charge interest on loans. Again, the rate of interest is also expressed as a percentage. With loans, banks add a percentage of the total money owed onto the debt each month so unless you pay off the loan, the money you owe will continue to get bigger.

Some salespeople, such as this car salesman, earn commission on every sale they make. Their commission is paid as a percentage of the retail price of every item they sell. Commission acts as an incentive to sell lots of items – all those percentages can add up to a lot of money!

The government will often use percentages to demonstrate changes in social and economic circumstances. For example, they may tell the public that 7% of the population of working age is unemployed or that value added tax (VAT) will be set at 17.5%.

You will have often received marks on a test in the form of a percentage.

Can you think of other examples? You will find several everyday uses in this chapter.

Number: Percentages and ratio

1 Equivalent percentages, fractions and decimals

2 Calculating a percentage of a quantity

3 Increasing or decreasing quantities by a percentage

4 Expressing one quantity as a percentage of another quantity

5 Ratio

This chapter will show you ...

- **G** what is meant by percentage
- **E** how to convert between decimals and fractions
- **E** what a ratio is
- **E** how to do calculations involving percentages
- **D** how to use your calculator to work out percentages by using a multiplier
- to **D** **C** how to divide an amount according to a given ratio
- **C** how to work out percentage increases and decreases

Visual overview

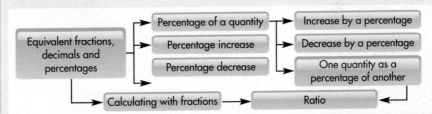

What you should already know

- Multiplication tables up to 10×10 (KS3 level 4, GCSE grade G)
- How to simplify fractions (KS3 level 5, GCSE grade G)
- How to calculate with fractions (KS3 level 5, GCSE grade F)
- How to multiply decimals by 100 (move the digits two places to the left) (KS3 level 5, GCSE grade G)
- How to divide decimals by 100 (move the digits two places to the right) (KS3 level 5, GCSE grade G)

Quick check

1 Simplify these fractions.

 a $\dfrac{12}{32}$ b $\dfrac{20}{45}$ c $\dfrac{28}{48}$ d $\dfrac{36}{60}$

2 Work out these amounts.

 a $\dfrac{2}{3}$ of 27 b $\dfrac{5}{8}$ of 32 c $\dfrac{1}{4} \times 76$ d $\dfrac{3}{5} \times 45$

3 Work out these amounts.

 a 12×100 b $34 \div 100$ c 0.23×100 d $4.7 \div 100$

Equivalent percentages, fractions and decimals

This section will show you how to:
- convert percentages to fractions and decimals and vice versa

Key words
decimal
decimal equivalents
fraction
percentage

100% means the *whole* of something. So if you want to, you can express *part* of the whole as a **percentage**.

Per cent means 'out of 100'.

So, any percentage can be converted to a **fraction** with denominator 100.

For example:

$32\% = \dfrac{32}{100}$ which can be simplified by cancelling to $\dfrac{8}{25}$

Also, any percentage can be converted to a **decimal** by dividing the percentage number by 100. This means moving the digits two places to the right.

For example:

$65\% = 65 \div 100 = 0.65$

Any decimal can be converted to a percentage by multiplying by 100%.

For example:

$0.43 = 0.43 \times 100\% = 43\%$

Any fraction can be converted to a percentage by making the denominator into 100 and taking the numerator as the percentage.

For example:

$\dfrac{2}{5} = \dfrac{40}{100} = 40\%$

Fractions can also be converted to percentages by dividing the numerator by the denominator and multiplying by 100%.

For example:

$\dfrac{2}{5} = 2 \div 5 \times 100\% = 40\%$

FM Functional Maths   **AU** (AO2) Assessing Understanding   **PS** (AO3) Problem Solving

Knowing the percentage and **decimal equivalents** of the common fractions is extremely useful. So, do try to learn them.

$\frac{1}{2} = 0.5 = 50\%$ $\qquad$ $\frac{1}{4} = 0.25 = 25\%$ $\qquad$ $\frac{3}{4} = 0.75 = 75\%$ $\qquad$ $\frac{1}{8} = 0.125 = 12.5\%$

$\frac{1}{10} = 0.1 = 10\%$ $\qquad$ $\frac{1}{5} = 0.2 = 20\%$ $\qquad$ $\frac{1}{3} = 0.33 = 33\frac{1}{3}\%$ $\qquad$ $\frac{2}{3} = 0.67 = 67\%$

The following table shows how to convert from one to the other.

Convert from percentage to:	
Decimal	**Fraction**
Divide the percentage by 100, for example $52\% = 52 \div 100$ $\quad = 0.52$	Make the percentage into a fraction with a denominator of 100 and simplify by cancelling down if possible, for example $52\% = \frac{52}{100} = \frac{13}{25}$

Convert from decimal to:	
Percentage	**Fraction**
Multiply the decimal by 100%, for example $0.65 = 0.65 \times 100\%$ $\quad = 65\%$	If the decimal has 1 decimal place put it over the denominator 10, if it has 2 decimal places put it over the denominator 100, etc. Then simplify by cancelling down if possible, for example $0.65 = \frac{65}{100} = \frac{13}{20}$

Convert from fraction to:	
Percentage	**Decimal**
If the denominator is a factor of 100 multiply numerator and denominator to make the denominator 100, then the numerator is the percentage, for example $\frac{3}{20} = \frac{15}{100} = 15\%$ or convert to a decimal and change the decimal to a percentage, for example $\frac{7}{8} = 7 \div 8 = 0.875 = 87.5\%$	Divide the numerator by the denominator, for example $\frac{9}{40} = 9 \div 40 = 0.225$

EXAMPLE 1

Convert the following to decimals: **a** 78% **b** 35% **c** $\frac{3}{25}$ **d** $\frac{7}{40}$.

a $78\% = 78 \div 100 = 0.78$ $\qquad\qquad$ **b** $35\% = 35 \div 100 = 0.35$

c $\frac{3}{25} = 3 \div 25 = 0.12$ $\qquad\qquad\quad$ **d** $\frac{7}{40} = 7 \div 40 = 0.175$

EXAMPLE 2

Convert the following to percentages: **a** 0.85 **b** 0.125 **c** $\frac{7}{20}$ **d** $\frac{3}{8}$.

a $0.85 = 0.85 \times 100\% = 85\%$ **b** $0.125 = 0.125 \times 100\% = 12.5\%$

c $\frac{7}{20} = \frac{35}{100} = 35\%$ **d** $\frac{3}{8} = 3 \div 8 \times 100\% = 0.375 \times 100\% = 37.5\%$

EXAMPLE 3

Convert the following to fractions: **a** 0.45 **b** 0.4 **c** 32% **d** 15%.

a $0.45 = \frac{45}{100} = \frac{9}{20}$ **b** $0.4 = \frac{4}{10} = \frac{2}{5}$

c $32\% = \frac{32}{100} = \frac{8}{25}$ **d** $15\% = \frac{15}{100} = \frac{3}{20}$

EXERCISE 4A

1 Write each percentage as a fraction in its simplest form.

   a 8%   **b** 50%   **c** 25%

   d 35%   **e** 90%   **f** 75%

2 Write each percentage as a decimal.

   a 27%   **b** 85%   **c** 13%

   d 6%   **e** 80%   **f** 32%

3 Write each decimal as a fraction in its simplest form.

   a 0.12   **b** 0.4   **c** 0.45

   d 0.68   **e** 0.25   **f** 0.625

4 Write each decimal as a percentage.

   a 0.29   **b** 0.55   **c** 0.03

   d 0.16   **e** 0.6   **f** 1.25

5 Write each fraction as a percentage.

   a $\frac{7}{25}$ **b** $\frac{3}{10}$ **c** $\frac{19}{20}$

   d $\frac{17}{50}$ **e** $\frac{11}{40}$ **f** $\frac{7}{8}$

6 Write each fraction as a decimal.

   a $\frac{9}{15}$ **b** $\frac{3}{40}$ **c** $\frac{19}{25}$

   d $\frac{5}{16}$ **e** $\frac{1}{20}$ **f** $\frac{1}{8}$

7 Of the 300 members of a social club 50% are men. How many members are women?

8 Gillian came home and told her dad that she got 100% of her spellings correct. She told her mum that there were 25 spellings to learn. How many spellings did Gillian get wrong?

9 Every year a school library likes to replace 1% of its books. One year the library had 2000 books. How many did it replace?

10 **a** If 23% of pupils go home for lunch, what percentage do not go home for lunch?

  b If 61% of the population takes part in the National Lottery, what percentage do not take part?

  c If 37% of members of a gym are males, what percentage of the members are females?

11 I calculated that 28% of my time is spent sleeping and 45% is spent working. How much time is left to spend doing something else?

12 In one country, 24.7% of the population is below the age of 16 and 13.8% of the population is aged over 65. How much of the population is aged from 16 to 65 inclusive?

13 Approximately what percentage of each bottle is filled with water?

a    **b**    **c**

PS 14 Helen made a cake for James. The amount of cake left each day is shown in the diagram.

What percentage has been eaten each day?

Monday   Tuesday   Wednesday   Thursday   Friday

15 Convert each fraction into a percentage.

  a $\frac{1}{5}$ **b** $\frac{1}{4}$ **c** $\frac{3}{4}$ **d** $\frac{9}{20}$ **e** $\frac{7}{50}$

  f $\frac{1}{2}$ **g** $\frac{3}{5}$ **h** $\frac{7}{40}$ **i** $\frac{11}{20}$ **j** $\frac{13}{10}$

16 Convert each fraction into a percentage. Give your answers to one decimal place.

  a $\frac{1}{3}$ **b** $\frac{1}{6}$ **c** $\frac{2}{3}$ **d** $\frac{5}{6}$ **e** $\frac{2}{7}$

  f $\frac{47}{60}$ **g** $\frac{31}{45}$ **h** $\frac{8}{9}$ **i** $\frac{73}{90}$ **j** $\frac{23}{110}$

17 Change each of these decimals into a percentage.

    a 0.07   **b** 0.8   **c** 0.66   **d** 0.25   **e** 0.545

    f 0.82   **g** 0.3   **h** 0.891   **i** 1.2   **j** 2.78

18 Chris scored 24 marks out of a possible 40 in a maths test.

    a Write this score as a fraction.

    b Write this score as a decimal.

    c Write this score as a percentage.

19 **a** Convert each of the following test scores into a percentage. Give each answer to the nearest whole number.

Subject	Result	Percentage
Mathematics	38 out of 60	
English	29 out of 35	
Science	27 out of 70	
History	56 out of 90	
Technology	58 out of 75	

    b If all the tests are of the same standard, which was the best result?

20 There were two students missing from my class of 30. What percentage of my class were away?

21 In one season, Paulo Di Canio had 110 shots at goal. He scored with 28 of these shots. What percentage of his shots resulted in goals?

22 Copy and complete the table.

Percentage	Decimal	Fraction
34%		
	0.85	
		$\frac{3}{40}$
45%		
	0.3	
		$\frac{2}{3}$
84%		
	0.45	
		$\frac{3}{8}$

FM 23 The manager of a garage wants to order 27 000 litres of fuel. A fuel tanker holds 30 000 litres when full. How much fuel should the manager order as a fraction or percentage of a full tanker load?

Calculating a percentage of a quantity

This section will show you how to:
- calculate a percentage of a quantity

Key words
multiplier
quantity

To calculate a percentage of a **quantity**, you multiply the quantity by the percentage. The percentage may be expressed as either a fraction or a decimal. When finding percentages without a calculator, base the calculation on 10% (or 1%) as these are easy to calculate.

EXAMPLE 4

Calculate: **a** 10% of 54 kg **b** 15% of 54 kg.

a 10% is $\frac{1}{10}$ so $\frac{1}{10}$ of 54 kg = 54 kg ÷ 10 = 5.4 kg

b 15% is 10% + 5% = 5.4 kg + 2.7 kg = 8.1 kg

EXAMPLE 5

Calculate 12% of £80.

10% of £80 is £8 and 1% of £80 is £0.80

12% = 10% + 1% + 1% = £8 + £0.80 + £0.80 = £9.60

Using a percentage multiplier

You have already seen that percentages and decimals are equivalent so it is easier, particularly when using a calculator, to express a percentage as a decimal and use this to do the calculation.

For example, 13% is a **multiplier** of 0.13, 20% a multiplier of 0.2 (or 0.20) and so on.

EXAMPLE 6

Calculate 45% of 160 cm.

45% = 0.45, so 45% of 160 = 0.45 × 160 = 72 cm

Find 52% of £460.

52% = 0.52

So, 0.52 × 460 = 239.2

This gives £239.20.

Remember to always write a money answer with 2 decimal places.

EXERCISE 4B

1 What multiplier is equivalent to a percentage of:

    a 88%   **b** 30%   **c** 25%   **d** 8%   **e** 115%?

2 What percentage is equivalent to a multiplier of:

    a 0.78   **b** 0.4   **c** 0.75   **d** 0.05   **e** 1.1?

3 Calculate the following.

a 15% of £300	**b** 6% of £105	**c** 23% of 560 kg
d 45% of 2.5 kg	**e** 12% of 9 hours	**f** 21% of 180 cm
g 4% of £3	**h** 35% of 8.4 m	**i** 95% of £8
j 11% of 308 minutes	**k** 20% of 680 kg	**l** 45% of £360

FM 4 The manager of a school canteen estimates that 40% of students will buy a school lunch. There are 1200 students in the school. She knows that her estimates are usually accurate to within 2%. Including this 2% figure, what is the greatest number of lunches she will have left over?

5 An estate agent charges 2% commission on every house he sells. How much commission will he earn on a house that he sells for £120 500?

6 A department store had 250 employees. During one week of a flu epidemic, 14% of the store's employees were absent.

    a What percentage of the employees went into work?

    b How many of the employees went into work?

7 It is thought that about 20% of fans at a rugby match are women. For a match at Twickenham there were 42 600 fans. How many of these do you think would be women?

8 At St Pancras railway station, in one week 350 trains arrived. Of these trains, 5% arrived early and 13% arrived late. How many arrived on time?

AU 9 For the FA Cup Final that was held at Wembley, each year the 90 000 tickets were split up as follows.

Each of the teams playing received 30% of the tickets.

The referees' association received 1% of the tickets.

The other 90 teams received 10% of the tickets among them.

The FA associates received 20% of the tickets among them.

The rest were for the special celebrities.

How many tickets went to each set of people?

FM 10 A school estimates that for a school play 60% of the students will attend. There are 1500 students in the school. The caretaker is told to put out one seat for each person expected to attend plus an extra 10% of that amount in case more attend. How many seats does he need to put out?

> **HINTS AND TIPS**
>
> It is not 70% of the number of students in the school.

11 A school had 850 pupils and the attendance record in the week before Christmas was:

Monday 96%   Tuesday 98%   Wednesday 100%   Thursday 94%   Friday 88%

How many pupils were present each day?

12 Calculate the following.

a 12.5% of £26

b 6.5% of 34 kg

c 26.8% of £2100

d 7.75% of £84

e 16.2% of 265 m

f 0.8% of £3000

13 Air consists of 80% nitrogen and 20% oxygen (by volume). A man's lungs have a capacity of 600 cm^3. How much of each gas will he have in his lungs when he has just taken a deep breath?

14 A factory estimates that 1.5% of all the garments it produces will have a fault in them. One week the factory produces 850 garments. How many are likely to have a fault?

15 An insurance firm sells house insurance and the annual premiums are usually set at 0.3% of the value of the house. What will be the annual premium for a house valued at £90 000?

PS 16 Average prices in a shop went up by 3% last year and 3% this year. Did the actual average price of items this year rise by more, the same amount, or less than last year?

Explain how you decided.

4.3 Increasing or decreasing quantities by a percentage

This section will show you how to:
- increase and decrease quantities by a percentage

Key word
multiplier

Increasing by a percentage

There are two methods for increasing a quantity by a percentage.

Method 1

Work out the increase and add it on to the original amount.

EXAMPLE 7

Increase £6 by 5%.

Work out 5% of £6: (5 ÷ 100) × 6 = £0.30

Add the £0.30 to the original amount: £6 + £0.30 = £6.30

Method 2

Use a **multiplier**. An increase of 6% is equivalent to the original 100% *plus* the extra 6%. This is a total of 106% and is equivalent to the multiplier 1.06

EXAMPLE 8

Increase £6.80 by 5%.

A 5% increase is a multiplier of 1.05

So £6.80 increased by 5% is 6.80 × 1.05 = £7.14

EXERCISE 4C

1 What multiplier is used to increase a quantity by:

    a 10%   **b** 3%   **c** 20%   **d** 7%   **e** 12%?

2 Increase each of the following by the given percentage. (Use any method you like.)

    a £60 by 4%   **b** 12 kg by 8%   **c** 450 g by 5%   **d** 545 m by 10%

    e £34 by 12%   **f** £75 by 20%   **g** 340 kg by 15%   **h** 670 cm by 23%

    i 130 g by 95%   **j** £82 by 75%   **k** 640 m by 15%   **l** £28 by 8%

3 Kevin, who was on a salary of £27 500, was given a pay rise of 7%. What is his new salary?

4 In 2005 the population of Melchester was 1 565 000. By 2010 it had increased by 8%. What was the population of Melchester in 2010?

AU 5 A small firm made the same pay increase of 5% for all its employees.

    a Calculate the new pay of each employee listed below. Each of their salaries before the increase is given.

      Bob, caretaker, £16 500   Jean, supervisor, £19 500
      Anne, tea lady, £17 300   Brian, manager, £25 300

    b Explain why the actual pay increases are different for each employee?

FM 6 A bank pays 7% interest on the money that each saver keeps in the bank for one year. Alison keeps £385 in this bank for one year. At the end of the year she wants to buy some furniture advertised for £550. She is offered a 10% discount on the furniture. If she uses all her savings, including interest, from the bank, how much more money will she need to buy the furniture?

7 In 1980 the number of cars on the roads of Sheffield was about 102 000. Since then it has increased by 90%. Approximately how many cars are there on the roads of Sheffield now?

8 An advertisement for a breakfast cereal states that a special offer packet contains 15% more cereal for the same price as a normal 500 g packet. How much breakfast cereal is there in a special offer packet?

9 A headteacher was proud to point out that, since he had arrived at the school, the number of students had increased by 35%. How many students are now in the school, if there were 680 when the headteacher started at the school?

10 At a school disco there are always about 20% more girls than boys. If there were 50 boys at a recent disco, how many girls were there?

FM 11 The Government adds a tax called VAT to the price of most goods in shops. At the moment, it is 17.5% on all electrical equipment.

Calculate the price of the following electrical equipment after VAT of 17.5% has been added.

Equipment	Pre-VAT price
TV set	£245
Microwave oven	£72
CD player	£115
Personal stereo	£29.50

PS 12 A television costs £400 before the VAT is added.

If the rate of VAT goes up from 15% to 20%, by how much will the cost of the television increase?

Decreasing by a percentage

There are two methods for decreasing a quantity by a percentage.

Method 1

Work out the decrease and subtract it from the original amount.

EXAMPLE 9

Decrease £8 by 4%.

Work out 4% of £8: $(4 \div 100) \times 8 = £0.32$

Subtract the £0.32 from the original amount: $£8 - £0.32 = £7.68$

Method 2

Use a multiplier. A 7% decrease is 7% less than the original 100% so it represents 100% − 7% = 93% of the original. This is a multiplier of 0.93

EXAMPLE 10

Decrease £8.60 by 5%.

A decrease of 5% is a multiplier of 0.95

So £8.60 decreased by 5% is 8.60 × 0.95 = £8.17

EXERCISE 4D

1 What multiplier is used to decrease a quantity by:

    a 8%   **b** 15%   **c** 25%   **d** 9%   **e** 12%?

2 Decrease each of the following by the given percentage. (Use any method you like.)

    a £10 by 6%   **b** 25 kg by 8%   **c** 236 g by 10%   **d** 350 m by 3%

    e £5 by 2%   **f** 45 m by 12%   **g** 860 m by 15%   **h** 96 g by 13%

    i 480 cm by 25%   **j** 180 minutes by 35%   **k** 86 kg by 5%   **l** £65 by 42%

3 A car valued at £6500 last year is now worth 15% less. What is its value now?

4 A new P-plan diet guarantees that you will lose 12% of your weight in the first month. How much should the following people weigh after one month on the diet?

    a Gillian, who started at 60 kg   **b** Peter, who started at 75 kg

    c Margaret, who started at 52 kg

FM 5 A motor insurance firm offers no-claims discounts off the full premium, as follows.

1 year no claim   15% discount off the full premium

2 years no claim   25% discount off the full premium

3 years no claim   45% discount off the full premium

4 years no claim   60% discount off the full premium

Mr Speed and his family are all offered motor insurance from this firm:

    Mr Speed has four years' no-claim discount and the full premium would be £440.

    Mrs Speed has one year's no-claim discount and the full premium would be £350.

    James has three years' no-claim discount and the full premium would be £620.

    John has two years' no-claim discount and the full premium would be £750.

Calculate the actual amount each member of the family has to pay for the motor insurance.

6 A large factory employed 640 people. It had to streamline its workforce and lose 30% of the workers. How big is the workforce now?

7 On the last day of the Christmas term, a school expects to have an absence rate of 6%. If the school population is 750 pupils, how many pupils will the school expect to see on the last day of the Christmas term?

8 A particular charity called *Young Ones* said that since the start of the National Lottery they have had a decrease of 45% in the amount of money raised by scratch cards. If before the Lottery the charity had an annual income of £34 500 from their scratch cards, how much do they collect now?

9 Most speedometers in cars have an error of about 5% from the true reading. When my speedometer says I am driving at 70 mph:

a what is the lowest speed I could be doing

b what is the highest speed I could be doing?

10 You are a member of a club that allows you to claim a 12% discount off any marked price in shops. What will you pay in total for the following goods?

Sweatshirt   £19

Track suit   £26

FM AU 11 **a** I read an advertisement in my local newspaper last week that stated: "By lagging your roof and hot water system you will use 18% less fuel." Since I was using an average of 640 units of gas a year, I thought I would lag my roof and my hot water system. How much gas would I expect to use now?

b I actually used 18% more gas than I expected to use.

Did I use less gas than last year, more gas than last year, or the same amount of gas as last year?

Show how you work out your answer.

PS 12 Shops add VAT to the basic price of goods to find the selling price that customers will be asked to pay. In a sale, a shop reduces the selling price by a certain percentage to set the sale price. Calculate the sale price of each of these items.

Item	Basic price	VAT rate	Sale discount	Sale price
TV	£220	17.5%	14%	
DVD player	£180	17.5%	20%	

AU PS 13 A shop advertises garden ornaments at £50 but with 10% off in a sale. It then advertises an extra 10% off the sale price.

Show that this is not a decrease in price of 20%.

This section will show you how to:

- express one quantity as a percentage of another
- work out percentage change

Key words

percentage change
percentage decrease
percentage increase
percentage loss
percentage profit

You can express one quantity as a percentage of another by setting up the first quantity as a fraction of the second, making sure that the *units of each are the same*. Then you convert the fraction into a percentage by multiplying by 100%.

EXAMPLE 11

Express £6 as a percentage of £40.

Set up the fraction and multiply by 100%.

$(6 \div 40) \times 100\% = 15\%$

EXAMPLE 12

Express 75 cm as a percentage of 2.5 m.

First, change 2.5 m to 250 cm to work in a common unit.

So the problem now becomes: Express 75 cm as a percentage of 250 cm.

Set up the fraction and multiply by 100%.

$(75 \div 250) \times 100\% = 30\%$

Percentage change

$$\text{Percentage change} = \frac{\text{change}}{\text{original amount}} \times 100\%$$

You can use this method to calculate **percentage profit (percentage increase)** or **percentage loss (percentage decrease)** in a financial transaction.

EXAMPLE 13

Jabeer buys a car for £1500 and sells it for £1800. What is Jabeer's percentage profit?

Jabeer's profit is £300.

$$\text{Percentage profit} = \frac{\text{profit}}{\text{original amount}} \times 100\%$$

$$= \frac{300}{1500} \times 100 = 20\%$$

Using a multiplier

Find the multiplier by dividing the change by the original quantity, then change the resulting decimal to a percentage.

EXAMPLE 14

Express 5 as a percentage of 40.

Set up the fraction or decimal: $5 \div 40 = 0.125$

Convert the decimal to a percentage: $0.125 = 12.5\%$

EXERCISE 4E

1. Express each of the following as a percentage. Give suitably rounded figures where necessary.

   a £5 of £20
   b £4 of £6.60
   c 241 kg of 520 kg

   d 3 hours of 1 day
   e 25 minutes of 1 hour
   f 12 m of 20 m

   g 125 g of 600 g
   h 12 minutes of 2 hours
   i 1 week of a year

   j 1 month of 1 year
   k 25 cm of 55 cm
   l 105 g of 1 kg

2. Liam went to school with his pocket money of £2.50. He spent 80p at the tuck shop. What percentage of his pocket money had he spent?

3. In Greece, there are 3 654 000 acres of agricultural land. Olives are grown on 237 000 acres of this land. What percentage of the agricultural land is used for olives?

4. During the wet year of 1981, it rained in Manchester on 123 days of the year. What percentage of days were wet?

D

5 Find the percentage profit on the following. Give your answers to one decimal place.

Item	Retail price (selling price)	Wholesale price (price the shop paid)
a CD player	£89.50	£60
b TV set	£345.50	£210
c Computer	£829.50	£750

6 Before Anton started to diet, he weighed 95 kg. He now weighs 78 kg. What percentage of his original weight has he lost?

7 In 2009 the Melchester County Council raised £14 870 000 in council tax. In 2010 it raised £15 597 000 in council tax. What was the percentage increase?

8 When Blackburn Rovers won the championship in 1995, they lost only four of their 42 league games. What percentage of games did they *not* lose?

AU 9 In the year 1900 Britain's imports were as follows.

British Commonwealth	£109 530 000
USA	£138 790 000
France	£53 620 000
Other countries	£221 140 000

a What percentage of the total imports came from each source? Give your answers to 1 decimal place.

b Add up your answers to part **a**. What do you notice? Explain your answer.

AU 10 Calum and Stacey take the same tests. Both tests are out of the same mark.

Here are their results.

	Test A	Test B
Calum	12	17
Stacey	14	20

Whose result has the greater percentage increase from test A to test B?

Show your working to explain your answer.

FM 11 A shopkeeper wants to make 40% profit on his total sales of three items of clothing.

Item	Wholesale price	Retail Price
Shirt	£15	£19.99
Trousers	£18	£24.99
Pair of socks	£1.50	£2

If he sells 5 shirts, 1 pair of trousers and 10 pairs of socks, will he achieve his target?

EXERCISE 4F

This exercise includes a mixture of percentage questions, which you should answer without using a calculator.

1 Copy and complete this table.

	Fraction	Decimal	Percentage
a	$\frac{3}{5}$		
b		0.7	
c			55%

2 Work out these amounts.

   a 15% of £68   **b** 12% of 400 kg   **c** 30% of £4.20

3 What percentage is:

   a 28 out of 50   **b** 17 out of 25   **c** 75 out of 200?

4 What is the result if:

   a 240 is increased by 15%   **b** 3600 is decreased by 11%?

5 **a** A paperboy's weekly wage went up from £10 to £12. What was the percentage increase in his wages?

   b The number of houses he has to deliver to increases from 60 to 78. What is the percentage increase in the number of houses he delivers to?

   c The newsagent then increased his new wage of £12 by 10%. What are the boy's wages now?

FM 6 The on-the-road price of a new car was £8000.

   a In the first year it depreciated in value by 20%. What was the value of the car at the end of the first year?

   b Trevor wants to buy this car when it is two years old. He has £5000 in savings. If it depreciates by a further 15% in the second year, will he be able to afford it?

AU 7
PS The members of a slimming club had a mean weight of 80 kg before they started dieting. After a month they calculated that they had lost an average of 12% in weight.

   a What was the average weight after the month?

   b One of the members realised she had misread the scale and she was 10 kg heavier than she thought. Which of these statements is true?

     i The mean weight loss will have decreased by more than 12%.

     ii The mean weight loss will have stayed at 12%.

     iii The mean weight loss will have decreased by less than 12%.

     iv There is not enough information to answer the question.

Ratio

This section will show you how to:
- simplify a ratio
- express a ratio as a fraction
- divide amounts according to ratios
- complete calculations from a given ratio and partial information

Key words

cancel

common unit

ratio

simplest form

A **ratio** is a way of comparing the sizes of two or more quantities.

A ratio can be expressed in a number of ways. For example, if Joy is five years old and James is 20 years old, the ratio of their ages is:

Joy's age : James's age

which is: 5 : 20

which simplifies to: 1 : 4   (dividing both sides by 5)

A ratio is usually given in one of these three ways.

Joy's age : James's age   or   5 : 20   or   1 : 4

Joy's age to James's age   or   5 to 20   or   1 to 4

$\dfrac{\text{Joy's age}}{\text{James's age}}$ or $\dfrac{5}{20}$ or $\dfrac{1}{4}$

Common units

When working with a ratio involving different units, *always convert them to a* **common unit**. A ratio can be simplified only when the units of each quantity are the *same*, because the ratio itself has no units. Once the units are the same, the ratio can be simplified or **cancelled**.

For example, the ratio of 125 g to 2 kg must be converted to the ratio of 125 g to 2000 g, so that you can simplify it.

125 : 2000

Divide both sides by 25:   5 : 80

Divide both sides by 5:   1 : 16   The ratio 125 : 2000 can be simplified to 1 : 16.

EXAMPLE 15

Express 25 minutes : 1 hour as a ratio in its simplest form.

The units must be the same, so change 1 hour into 60 minutes.

25 minutes : 1 hour = 25 minutes : 60 minutes

=   25 : 60   Cancel the units (minutes)

=   5 : 12   Divide both sides by 5

So, 25 minutes : 1 hour simplifies to 5 : 12

Ratios as fractions

A ratio in its **simplest form** can be expressed as portions of a quantity by expressing the whole numbers in the ratio as fractions with the same denominator (bottom number).

EXAMPLE 16

A garden is divided into lawn and shrubs in the ratio 3 : 2.

What fraction of the garden is covered by **a** lawn, **b** shrubs?

The denominator (bottom number) of the fraction comes from adding the number in the ratio (that is, 2 + 3 = 5).

a the lawn covers $\frac{3}{5}$ of the garden

b and the shrubs cover $\frac{2}{5}$ of the garden.

EXERCISE 4G

1 Express each of the following ratios in its simplest form.

a 6 : 18	**b** 15 : 20	**c** 16 : 24	**d** 24 : 36
e 20 to 50	**f** 12 to 30	**g** 25 to 40	**h** 125 to 30
i 15 : 10	**j** 32 : 12	**k** 28 to 12	**l** 100 to 40
m 0.5 to 3	**n** 1.5 to 4	**o** 2.5 to 1.5	**p** 3.2 to 4

2 Write each of the following ratios of quantities in its simplest form. (Remember to always express both parts in a common unit before you simplify.)

a £5 to £15	**b** £24 to £16	**c** 125 g to 300 g
d 40 minutes : 5 minutes	**e** 34 kg to 30 kg	**f** £2.50 to 70p
g 3 kg to 750 g	**h** 50 minutes to 1 hour	**i** 1 hour to 1 day
j 12 cm to 2.5 mm	**k** 1.25 kg : 500 g	**l** 75p : £3.50
m 4 weeks : 14 days	**n** 600 m: 2 km	**o** 465 mm : 3 m
p 15 hours : 1 day		

3 A length of wood is cut into two pieces in the ratio 3 : 7. What fraction of the original length is the longer piece?

4 Jack and Thomas find a bag of marbles that they share between them in the ratio of their ages. Jack is 10 years old and Thomas is 15 years old. What fraction of the marbles did Jack get?

5 Dave and Sue share a pizza in the ratio 2 : 3. They eat it all.

a What fraction of the pizza did Dave eat?

b What fraction of the pizza did Sue eat?

D

6 A camp site allocates space to caravans and tents in the ratio 7 : 3. What fraction of the total space is given to:

    a the caravans

    b the tents?

7 Two sisters, Amy and Katie, share a packet of sweets in the ratio of their ages. Amy is 15 and Katie is 10. What fraction of the sweets does each sister get?

8 The recipe for a fruit punch is 1.25 litres of fruit crush to 6.75 litres of lemonade. What fraction of the punch is each ingredient?

PS 9 Three cows, Gertrude, Gladys and Henrietta, produced milk in the ratio 2 : 3 : 4. Henrietta produced $1\frac{1}{2}$ litres more than Gladys. How much milk did the three cows produce altogether?

10 In a safari park at feeding time, the elephants, the lions and the chimpanzees are given food in the ratio 10 to 7 to 3. What fraction of the total food is given to:

    a the elephants   **b** the lions   **c** the chimpanzees?

11 Three brothers, James, John and Joseph, share a huge block of chocolate in the ratio of their ages. James is 20, John is 12 and Joseph is 8. What fraction of the bar of chocolate does each brother get?

12 The recipe for a pudding is 125 g of sugar, 150 g of flour, 100 g of margarine and 175 g of fruit. What fraction of the pudding is each ingredient?

C

PS 13 June wins three-quarters of her bowls matches. She loses the rest.

What is the ratio of wins to losses?

AU 14 Three brothers share some cash.
The ratio of Mark's and David's share is 1 : 2
The ratio of David's and Paul's share is 1 : 2

What is the ratio of Mark's share to Paul's share?

Dividing amounts in a given ratio

> ! This topic will be tested in Unit 2.

To divide an amount in a given ratio, you first look at the ratio to see how many parts there are altogether.

For example, 4 : 3 has 4 parts and 3 parts giving 7 parts altogether.

    7 parts is the whole amount.

    1 part can then be found by dividing the whole amount by 7.

    3 parts and 4 parts can then be worked out from 1 part.

EXAMPLE 17

Divide £28 in the ratio 4 : 3

4 + 3 = 7 parts altogether

So 7 parts = £28

Dividing by 7:

1 part = £4

4 parts = 4 × £4 = £16 and 3 parts = 3 × £4 = £12

So £28 divided in the ratio 4 : 3 = £16 : £12

To divide an amount in a given ratio you can also use fractions. You first express the whole numbers in the ratio as fractions with the same common denominator. Then you multiply the amount by each fraction.

EXAMPLE 18

Divide £40 between Peter and Hitan in the ratio 2 : 3

Changing the ratio to fractions gives:

Peter's share $= \dfrac{2}{(2+3)} = \dfrac{2}{5}$

Hitan's share $= \dfrac{3}{(2+3)} = \dfrac{3}{5}$

So Peter receives £40 × $\frac{2}{5}$ = £16 and Hitan receives £40 × $\frac{3}{5}$ = £24.

EXERCISE 4H

1 Divide the following amounts according to the given ratios.

a 400 g in the ratio 2 : 3

b 280 kg in the ratio 2 : 5

c 500 in the ratio 3 : 7

d 1 km in the ratio 19 : 1

e 5 hours in the ratio 7 : 5

f £100 in the ratio 2 : 3 : 5

g £240 in the ratio 3 : 5 : 12

h 600 g in the ratio 1 : 5 : 6

i £5 in the ratio 7 : 10 : 8

j 200 kg in the ratio 15 : 9 : 1

2 The ratio of female to male members of Lakeside Gardening Club is 7 : 3. The total number of members of the group is 250.

a How many members are female?

PS **b** What percentage of members are male?

3 A supermarket aims to stock branded goods and their own goods in the ratio 2 : 3. They stock 500 kg of breakfast cereal.

a What percentage of the cereal stock is branded?

b How much of the cereal stock is their own?

4 The Illinois Department of Health reported that, for the years 1981 to 1992 when they tested a total of 357 horses for rabies, the ratio of horses with rabies to those without was 1 : 16.

How many of these horses had rabies?

FM 5
AU

Being overweight increases the chances of an adult suffering from heart disease. A way to test whether an adult has an increased risk is shown below:

For women, there is increased risk when $W/H > 0.8$

For men, there is increased risk when $W/H > 1.0$

| W = waist measurement |
| H = hip measurement |

a Find whether the following people have an increased risk of heart disease.

Miss Mott: waist 26 inches, hips 35 inches

Mrs Wright: waist 32 inches, hips 37 inches

Mr Brennan: waist 32 inches, hips 34 inches

Ms Smith: waist 31 inches, hips 40 inches

Mr Kaye: waist 34 inches, hips 33 inches

b Give three examples of waist and hip measurements that would suggest no risk of heart disease for a man, but would suggest a risk for a woman.

6 Rewrite the following scales as ratios as simply as possible.

a 1 cm to 4 km	**b** 4 cm to 5 km	**c** 2 cm to 5 km
d 4 cm to 1 km	**e** 5 cm to 1 km	**f** 2.5 cm to 1 km
g 8 cm to 5 km	**h** 10 cm to 1 km	**i** 5 cm to 3 km

7 A map has a scale of 1 cm to 10 km.

a Rewrite the scale as a ratio in its simplest form.

b What is the actual length of a lake that is 4.7 cm long on the map?

c How long will a road be on the map if its actual length is 8 km?

HINTS AND TIPS

1 km = 1000 m
= 100 000 cm

8 A map has a scale of 2 cm to 5 km.

a Rewrite the scale as a ratio in its simplest form.

b How long is a path that measures 0.8 cm on the map?

c How long should a 12 km road be on the map?

9 The scale of a map is 5 cm to 1 km.

    a Rewrite the scale as a ratio in its simplest form.

    b How long is a wall that is shown as 2.7 cm on the map?

    c The distance between two points is 8 km; how far will this be on the map?

10 You can simplify a ratio by changing it into the form $1 : n$. For example, $5 : 7$ can be rewritten as

$$\frac{5}{5} : \frac{7}{5} = 1 : 1.4$$

Rewrite each of the following ratios in the form $1 : n$.

    a $5 : 8$ **b** $4 : 13$ **c** $8 : 9$

    d $25 : 36$ **e** $5 : 27$ **f** $12 : 18$

    g 5 hours : 1 day   **h** 4 hours : 1 week   **i** £4 : £5

Calculating with ratios when only part of the information is known

---

EXAMPLE 19

A fruit drink is made by mixing orange squash with water in the ratio 2 : 3
How much water needs to be added to 5 litres of orange squash to make the drink?

    2 parts is 5 litres

Dividing by 2:

    1 part is 2.5 litres

    3 parts = 2.5 litres × 3 = 7.5 litres

So 7.5 litres of water is needed to make the drink.

EXAMPLE 20

Two business partners, Lubna and Adama, divided their total profit in the ratio 3 : 5.
Lubna received £2100. How much did Adama get?

Lubna's £2100 was $\frac{3}{8}$ of the total profit. (Check that you know why.)
$\frac{1}{8}$ of the total profit = £2100 ÷ 3 = £700

So Adama's share, which was $\frac{5}{8}$, amounted to £700 × 5 = £3500.

EXERCISE 4I

1 Derek, aged 15, and Ricki, aged 10, shared all the conkers they found in the woods in the same ratio as their ages. Derek had 48 conkers.

a Simplify the ratio of their ages.

b How many conkers did Ricki have?

c How many conkers did they find altogether?

2 A blend of tea is made by mixing Lapsang with Assam in the ratio 3 : 5. I have a lot of Assam tea but only 600 g of Lapsang. How much Assam do I need to make the blend using all the Lapsang?

3 The ratio of male to female spectators at ice hockey games is 4 : 5. At the Steelers' last match, 4500 men watched the match. What was the total attendance at the game?

4 A teacher always arranged the content of each of his lessons to Year 10 as 'teaching' and 'practising learnt skills' in the ratio 2 : 3.

a If a lesson lasted 35 minutes, how much teaching would he do?

b If he decided to teach for 30 minutes, how long would the lesson be?

5 A 'good' children's book is supposed to have pictures and text in the ratio 17 : 8. In a book I have just looked at, the pictures occupy 23 pages.

a Approximately how many pages of text should this book have to be deemed a 'good' children's book?

b What percentage of a 'good' children's book will be text?

6 Three business partners, Kevin, John and Margaret, put money into a business in the ratio 3 : 4 : 5. They shared any profits in the same ratio. Last year, Margaret made £3400 out of the profits. How much did Kevin and John make last year?

7 **a** Iqra is making a drink from lemonade, orange and ginger ale in the ratio 40 : 9 : 1. If Iqra has only 4.5 litres of orange, how much of the other two ingredients does she need to make the drink?

b Another drink made from lemonade, orange and ginger ale uses the ratio 10 : 2 : 1.

Which drink has a larger proportion of ginger ale, Iqra's or this one? Show how you work out your answer.

PS 8 There is a group of boys and girls waiting for school buses. 25 girls get on the first bus. The ratio of boys to girls at the stop is now 3 : 2. 15 boys get on the second bus. There are now the same number of boys and girls at the bus stop. How many students altogether were originally at the bus stop?

PS 9 A jar contains 100 cc of a mixture of oil and water in the ratio 1 : 4. Enough oil is added to make the ratio of oil to water 1 : 2. How much water must be added to make the ratio of oil to water 1 : 3?

GRADE BOOSTER

G You can find equivalent fractions, decimals and percentages

E You can find simple percentages of a quantity

E You can find any percentages of a quantity

E You can convert fractions to decimals and decimals to fractions

E You can simplify ratios

D You can find a new quantity after an increase or decrease by a percentage and find one quantity as a percentage of another

C You can find a percentage change, for example percentage increase or percentage decrease

C You can solve problems using ratios

What you should know now

- How to find equivalent percentages, decimals and fractions
- How to calculate percentages, percentage increases and decreases
- How to calculate one quantity as a percentage of another
- How to divide any amount according to a given ratio
- How to complete calculations from a given ratio and partial information

1 Complete the table below.

Fraction	Decimal	Percentage
$\frac{1}{2}$	0.5	
	0.7	70%
$\frac{3}{100}$		3%

(Total 3 marks)

AQA, June 2005, Paper 1 Foundation, Question 2

2 **a** **i** Write $\frac{7}{16}$ as a decimal.

ii Write 27% as a decimal.

b Write these values in order of size, smallest first.

0.7 $\frac{6}{10}$ 65%   0.095

3 Mr and Mrs Jones are buying a tumble dryer that normally costs £250. They save 12% in a sale.

a What is 12% of £250?

b How much do they pay for the tumble dryer?

4 Which is the larger amount?

40% of £30 $\frac{3}{5}$ of £25

5 The price of a white fridge is £250.

A silver fridge costs 8% more than the white fridge.

Calculate the **extra** cost of the silver fridge. (2)

(Total 2 marks)

AQA, June 2005, Module 5, Paper 2 Foundation, Question 8

6 Mr Shaw's bill for new tyres is £120 plus VAT. VAT is charged at $17\frac{1}{2}$%.

What is his total bill?

7 Supermarkets often make 'Buy one, get one free' offers. What percentage saving is this?

10%, 50%, 100% or 200%

8 A school raises £660 from a sponsored walk.

a $\frac{1}{4}$ of the money is spent on books.

The rest of the money is spent on sports equipment.

How much money is spent on sports equipment? (2)

b The £660 was raised by teachers and pupils in the ratio 1 : 9

The pupils raised the greater amount of money.

How much money did the pupils raise? (2)

(Total 4 marks)

AQA, November 2006, Module 3 Foundation, Question 8

9 In 2006 the population of a town was 68 000.

By 2007 the population had decreased by 3.2%.

Work out the population of the town in 2007. (3)

(Total 3 marks)

AQA, March 2008, Module 3 Foundation, Question 8

10 Tom measured up a wall for ceramic tiles. He worked out that he needed 200 tiles, which he had seen advertised at 60p each.

a How much did Tom expect to pay for the 200 tiles?

b When he went to the store he decided to buy 10% more tiles than he needed, in case of breakages. Then he found that the price of the tiles had been reduced by 10%.

i How many tiles did he buy?

ii What was the new price per tile?

c Calculate the percentage saving of the actual cost over the expected cost.

11 A TV originally cost £300.

In a sale, its price was reduced by 20%, then this sale price was reduced by a further 10%.

Show why this is not a 30% reduction of the original price.

12 **a** Write 60% as a decimal. (1)

b Work out 38% of £146. (2)

c What percentage is £108 of £150? (2)

(Total 5 marks)

AQA, March 2006, Module 3 Foundation, Question 7

C   D   E   F   G

Worked Examination Questions

FM **1** The land area of a farm is 385 acres.

Two-fifths of the land is used to grow barley.

96 acres is pasture.

22% is used to keep livestock.

The rest is unused.

How many acres are unused?

$\frac{2}{5} \times 385 = 154$ ———— You will get 1 mark for setting up the calculation and 1 mark for the answer. You could also do this as 0.4×385.

$0.22 \times 385 = 84.7$ acres ———— You will get 1 mark for setting up the calculation and 1 mark for the answer.

$385 - 96 - 154 - 84.7 = 50.3$ or 50 acres ———— Work out the area by subtracting all the areas from 385. You will get 1 mark for this.

Total: 5 marks

PS
AU **2** David is mixing compost with soil.
He mixes 2 kg of compost with 1 kg of soil.

Kayren is also mixing compost with soil.
She mixes 3 kg of compost with 2 kg of soil.

Which mixture has the greater percentage of compost?
You **must** show your working.

David uses 2 kg of compost out of
3 kg altogether.

Percentage $= \frac{2}{3} \times 100\%$ ———— You will get 1 mark for method, used at least once.

$= 66.6\%$ or 67% ————

Kayren uses 3 kg of compost out of 5 kg altogether.

You will get 1 mark for accuracy of 66.6% (67%) or 60%.

Percentage $= \frac{3}{5} \times 100\%$

$= 60\%$ ————

So David's mixture has the greater percentage of compost.

You will get 1 mark for accuracy of the other percentage and stating David's mixture. Stating David's mixture without showing working scores no marks.

Total: 3 marks

Functional Maths
Conserving water

We use water every day: it is vital to our survival and important in making our lives more comfortable.

Ushma's use of water

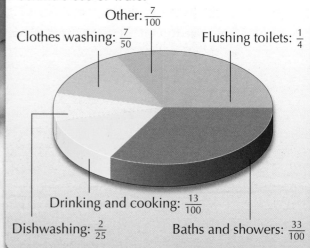

Other: $\frac{7}{100}$

Clothes washing: $\frac{7}{50}$

Flushing toilets: $\frac{1}{4}$

Drinking and cooking: $\frac{13}{100}$

Dishwashing: $\frac{2}{25}$

Baths and showers: $\frac{33}{100}$

Your task

Ushma has noticed that her water bill has increased over the last few months. The rates charged by the water company have not changed, so Ushma knows that she is paying more money because she is using more water. She is not only concerned that she is spending too much money on water: she is also worried about the impact that her increased water use is having on the environment.

1 Using the information opposite, write a report analysing Ushma's use of water.

In your report you should think about:

- the percentage of water that Ushma uses for different domestic activities
- the cost of each domestic activity that involves water
- where she could realistically reduce her water usage and by how much
- the impact that reducing her usage would have on her water bill
- what her total percentage decrease in water usage would be
- how best to represent your findings.

2 Seeing her water bill inspires Ushma to research how water is used on a global scale. The pie chart and table show the information she discovered.

What can Ushma tell from this information about water supplies throughout the world? Can she work out how reducing her water usage will impact on global water supplies?

Express your ideas as they might be seen in a newspaper.

Global usage of freshwater

Irrigation 70%

Domestic use 8%

Industry: 22%

Global distribution of water

Location	Volume (km^3)
Oceans	1 338 000 000
Ice	24 364 000
Groundwater	23 400 000
Lakes and reservoirs	176 400
Soil moisture	16 500
Water vapour	12 900
Rivers	2120
Swamp water	11 470

Handy hint

Use the internet to look up facts to do with water usage. How do water companies and global organisations represent their 'water facts'?

Handy hint

Water bills include a 'standing charge', which is a fixed amount paid by all customers regardless of how much water they have used. They also include a variable charge, which will change according to how much water the household has used.

Water utility bill

South UK Water

Account number 12349876001	Date: 15-03-2010
Bill period January – March 2010	Meter No. 367X93007

Bill summary	
Water supply standing charge	£35.80
Water supply	£301.10
Surface drainage	£39.78
Sewerage standing charge	£1.68
Sewerage	£321.45
Total	**£699.81**
Payment due by: 14 April 2010	

contact us at: www.south-ukwater.co.uk

Water utility bill

South UK Water

Account number 12349876001	Date: 15-12-2090
Bill period October – December 2009	Meter No. 367X93007

Bill summary	
Water supply standing charge	£35.80
Water supply	£258.00
Surface drainage	£39.78
Sewerage standing charge	£1.68
Sewerage	£294.48
Total	**£629.74**
Payment due by: 14 Jan 2010	

contact us at: www.south-ukwater.co.uk

Why this chapter matters

For centuries statistical graphs such as bar charts, line graphs and pictograms have been used in many different areas, from science to politics. They provide a way to represent, analyse and interpret information.

Developing statistical analysis

The development of statistical graphs was spurred on by:

- the need in the 17th and 18th centuries to base policies on demographic and economic data and for this information to be shared with a large number of people

- greater understanding of measures and numbers in the 19th century

- increasing interest in analysing and understanding social conditions in the 19th and 20th centuries.

Since the later part of the 20th century, statistical graphs have become an important way of analysing information, and computer-generated statistical graphs are seen every day on TV, in newspapers and in magazines.

Who invented statistical diagrams?

William Playfair was a Scottish engineer, who is thought to be the founder of representing statistics in a graphical way.

He invented three types of diagrams: in 1786 the line graph and bar chart, then in 1801 the pie chart (which you will come across in later chapters).

Florence Nightingale was born in 1820. She was very good at mathematics from an early age, becoming a pioneer in presenting information visually. She developed a form of the pie chart now known as the 'polar area diagram' or the 'Nightingale rose diagram', which was like a modern circular bar chart. It illustrated monthly patient deaths in military field hospitals. She called these diagrams 'coxcombs' and used them a great deal to present reports on the conditions of medical care in the Crimean War to Parliament and to civil servants who may not have fully understood traditional statistical reports.

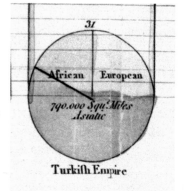

William Playfair pioneered charts and graphs such as this pie chart.

In 1859, Florence Nightingale was elected the first female member of the Royal Statistical Society.

This chapter introduces you to some of the most common forms of statistical representation. They fall into two groups: graphical diagrams, such as pictograms and bar charts; and quantitive diagrams, such as frequency tables and stem-and-leaf diagrams.

Florence Nightingale was a nurse and hospital reformer. She used charts and graphs in her work.

5

Statistics: Statistical representation

This chapter will show you ...

- **F** how to collect and organise data, and how to represent data on various types of diagram
- **F** to **D** how to draw diagrams for data, including line graphs for time series and frequency diagrams
- **G** to **D** how to draw conclusions from statistical diagrams
- **E** to **D** how to draw diagrams for discrete data, including stem-and-leaf diagrams

Visual overview

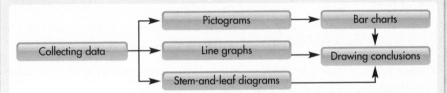

Collecting data → Pictograms → Bar charts
Collecting data → Line graphs → Drawing conclusions
Collecting data → Stem-and-leaf diagrams → Drawing conclusions

What you should already know

- How to use a tally for recording data **(KS3 level 3, GCSE grade G)**
- How to read information from charts and tables **(KS3 level 3, GCSE grade G)**

Quick check

Zoe works in a dress shop. She recorded the sizes of all the dresses sold during a week. The table shows the results.

Day	Size of dresses sold									
Monday	12	8	10	8	14	8	12	8	8	
Tuesday	10	10	8	12	14	16	8	12	14	16
Wednesday	16	8	12	10						
Thursday	12	8	8	10	12	14	16	12	8	
Friday	10	10	8	10	12	14	14	12	10	8
Saturday	10	8	8	12	10	12	8	10		

a Use a tallying method to make a table showing how many dresses of each size were sold in the week.

b Which dress size had the most sales?

Frequency diagrams

This section will show you how to:
● collect and represent discrete and grouped data using tally charts and frequency tables

Key words
class
class interval
data collection sheet
experiment
frequency
frequency table
grouped data
grouped frequency
   table
observation
sample
tally chart

Statistics is concerned with the collection and organisation of data, the representation of data on diagrams and the interpretation of data.

When you are collecting data for simple surveys, it is usual to use a **data collection sheet**, also called a **tally chart**. For example, data collection sheets are used to gather information on how people travel to work, how students spend their free time and the amount of time people spend watching TV.

It is easy to record the data by using tally marks, as shown in Example 1. Counting up the tally marks in each row of the chart gives the **frequency** of each category. By listing the frequencies in a column on the right-hand side of the chart, you can make a **frequency table** (see Example 1). Frequency tables are an important part of making statistical calculations, as you will see in Chapter 11.

EXAMPLE 1

Sandra wanted to find out about the ways in which students travelled to school. She carried out a survey. Her frequency table looked like this:

Method of travel	Tally	Frequency
Walk	Ա՜Ի Ա՜Ի Ա՜Ի Ա՜Ի Ա՜Ի III	28
Car	Ա՜Ի Ա՜Ի II	12
Bus	Ա՜Ի Ա՜Ի Ա՜Ի Ա՜Ի III	23
Bicycle	Ա՜Ի	5
Taxi	II	2

By adding together all the frequencies, you can see that 70 students took part in the survey. The frequencies also show you that more students travelled to school on foot than by any other method of transport.

FM Functional Maths   **AU** (AO2) Assessing Understanding   **PS** (AO3) Problem Solving

Three methods are used to collect data.

- **Taking a sample:** For example, to find out which 'soaps' students watch, you would need to take a sample from the whole school population by asking at random an equal number of boys and girls from each year group. In this case, a good sample size would be 50.

- **Observation:** For example, to find how many vehicles a day use a certain road, you would need to count and record the number of vehicles passing a point at different times of the day.

- **Experiment:** For example, to find out how often a six occurs when you throw a dice, you would need to throw the dice 50 times or more and record each score.

EXAMPLE 2

Andrew wanted to find out the most likely outcome when two coins are tossed. He carried out an experiment by tossing two coins 50 times. His frequency table looked like this.

Number of heads	Tally	Frequency
0	ⅣⅠ ⅣⅠ ⅠⅠ	12
1	ⅣⅠ ⅣⅠ ⅣⅠ ⅣⅠ ⅣⅠ ⅠⅠ	27
2	ⅣⅠ ⅣⅠ Ⅰ	11

From Andrew's table, you can see that a single head appeared the highest number of times.

Grouped data

Many surveys produce a lot of data that covers a wide range of values. In these cases, it is sensible to put the data into groups before attempting to compile a frequency table. These groups of data are called **classes** or **class intervals**.

Once the data has been grouped into classes, a **grouped frequency table** can be completed. The method is shown in Example 3.

EXAMPLE 3

These marks are for 36 students in a Year 10 mathematics examination.

31	49	52	79	40	29	66	71	73	19	51	47
81	67	40	52	20	84	65	73	60	54	60	59
25	89	21	91	84	77	18	37	55	41	72	38

a Construct a frequency table, using classes of 1–20, 21–40 and so on.

b What was the most frequent interval of marks?

a Draw the grid of the table shown below and put in the headings.

Next, list the classes, in order, in the column headed 'Marks'.

Using tally marks, indicate each student's score against the class to which it belongs. For example, 81, 84, 89 and 91 belong to the class 81–100, giving five tally marks, as shown below.

Finally, count the tally marks for each class and enter the result in the column headed 'Frequency'. The table is now complete.

Marks	Tally	Frequency
1–20	|||	3
21–40	⦀⦀ |||	8
41–60	⦀⦀ ⦀⦀		11
61–80	⦀⦀ ||||	9
81–100	⦀⦀	5

b From the grouped frequency table, you can see that the highest number of students obtained a mark in the 41–60 interval.

EXERCISE 5A

1 Philip kept a record of the number of goals scored by Burnley Rangers in the last 20 matches. These are his results:

0 1 1 0 2 0 1 3 2 1

0 1 0 3 2 1 0 2 1 1

a Draw a frequency table for his data.

b Which was the most frequent score?

c How many goals were scored in total for the 20 matches?

FM 2 Monica was doing a geography project on the weather. As part of her work, she kept a record of the daily midday temperatures in June.

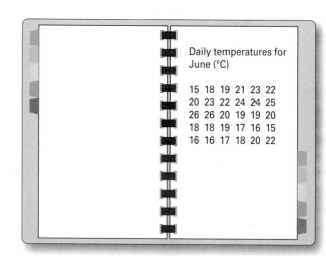

Daily temperatures for June (°C)

15 18 19 21 23 22
20 23 22 24 24 25
26 26 20 19 19 20
18 18 19 17 16 15
16 16 17 18 20 22

a Copy and complete the grouped frequency table for her data.

Temperature (°C)	Tally	Frequency
14–16		
17–19		
20–22		
23–25		
26–28		

b In which interval do the most temperatures lie?

c Describe what the weather was probably like throughout the month.

3 For the following surveys, decide whether the data should be collected by:

i sampling   **ii** observation   **iii** experiment.

a The number of people using a new superstore.

b How people will vote in a forthcoming election.

c The number of times a person scores double top in a game of darts.

d Where people go for their summer holidays.

e The frequency of a bus service on a particular route.

f The number of times a drawing pin lands point up when dropped.

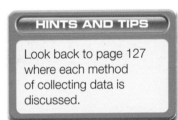

HINTS AND TIPS

Look back to page 127 where each method of collecting data is discussed.

4 In a game, Mitesh used a six-sided dice. He decided to keep a record of his scores to see whether the dice was fair. His scores were:

2 4 2 6 1 5 4 3 3 2 3 6 2 1 3

5 4 3 4 2 1 6 5 1 6 4 1 2 3 4

a Draw a frequency table for his data.

b How many throws did Mitesh have during the game?

c Do you think the dice was a fair one? Explain why.

5 The data shows the heights, in centimetres, of a sample of 32 Year 10 students.

172 158 160 175 180 167 159 180

167 166 178 184 179 156 165 166

184 175 170 165 164 172 154 186

167 172 170 181 157 165 152 164

a Draw a grouped frequency table for the data, using class intervals 151–155, 156–160, …

b In which interval do the most heights lie?

c Does this agree with a survey of the students in your class?

D

PS **6** Kathy used a stopwatch to time how long it took her rabbit to find food left in its hutch.

The following is her record in seconds.

7	30	14	27	8	31	8	28	10	41	51	37	15	21	37	16	38
23	20	9	11	55	9	33	8	35	45	35	25	25	49	23	43	55
45	8	13	9	39	12	57	16	37	26	32	19	48	29	37		

Find the best way to put this data into a frequency chart to illustrate the length of time it took the rabbit to find the food.

AU **7** David was doing a survey to find the ages of people at a football competition.

He said that he would make a frequency table with the regions 15–20, 20–25, 25–30.

Explain what difficulty David could have with these class divisions.

8 Conduct some surveys of your own choice and draw frequency tables for your data.

Double dice

This is an activity for two or more players. Each player needs two six-sided dice.

Each player throws their two dice together 100 times. For each throw, add together the two scores to get a total score.

What is the lowest total score anyone can get? What is the highest total score?

Everyone keeps a record of their 100 throws in a frequency table.

Compare your frequency table with someone else's and comment on what you notice. For example: Which scores appear the most often? What about 'doubles'?

How might this information be useful in games that use two dice?

Repeat the activity in one or more of the following ways.

- For each throw, multiply the score on one dice by the score on the other.
- Use two four-sided dice (tetrahedral dice), adding or multiplying the scores.
- Use two different-sided dice, adding or multiplying the scores.
- Use three or more dice, adding and/or multiplying the scores.

Statistical diagrams

This section will show you how to:
- show collected data as pictograms

Key words
key
pictograms
symbol

Data collected from a survey can be presented in pictorial or diagrammatic form to help people to understand it more quickly. You see plenty of examples of this in newspapers and magazines and on TV, where every type of visual aid is used to communicate statistical information.

Pictograms

A **pictogram** is a frequency table in which frequency is represented by a repeated **symbol**. The symbol itself usually represents a number of items, as Example 5 shows. However, sometimes it is more sensible to let a symbol represent just a single unit, as in Example 4. The **key** tells you how many items are represented by a symbol.

EXAMPLE 4

The pictogram shows the number of phone calls made by Mandy from her mobile phone during a week.

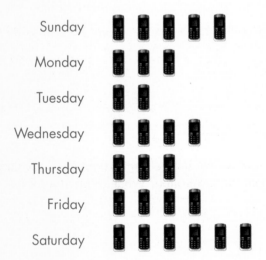

Key represents 1 call

How many calls did Mandy make in the week?

From the pictogram, you can see that Mandy made a total of 27 calls.

Although pictograms can have great visual impact (particularly as used in advertising) and are easy to understand, they have a serious drawback. Apart from a half, fractions of a symbol cannot usually be drawn accurately and so frequencies are often represented only approximately by symbols.

Examples 5 and 6 highlight this difficulty.

EXAMPLE 5

The pictogram shows the number of Year 10 students who were late for school during a week.

Key ♀ represents 5 students

How many students were late on:

a Monday

b Thursday?

Precisely how many students were late on Monday and Thursday respectively?

If you assume that each 'limb' of the symbol represents one student and its 'body' also represents one student, then the answers are:

a 19 students were late on Monday.

b 13 on Thursday.

EXAMPLE 6

This pictogram is used to show how many trains ran late in the course of one weekend.

Key 🚂 represents 10

Give a reason why the pictogram is difficult to read.

The last train of those representing the number of trains late on Sunday is drawn as a fraction of 10. However, we cannot easily make out what this fraction is specifically.

EXERCISE 5B

1 The frequency table shows the numbers of cars parked in a supermarket's car park at various times of the day. Draw a pictogram to illustrate the data. Use a key of 1 symbol = 5 cars.

Time	9 am	11 am	1 pm	3 pm	5 pm
Frequency	40	50	70	65	45

2 Mr Weeks, a milkman, kept a record of how many pints of milk he delivered to 10 flats on a particular morning. Draw a pictogram for the data. Use a key of 1 symbol = 1 pint.

Flat 1	Flat 2	Flat 3	Flat 4	Flat 5	Flat 6	Flat 7	Flat 8	Flat 9	Flat 10
2	3	1	2	4	3	2	1	5	1

3 The pictogram, taken from a Suntours brochure, shows the average daily hours of sunshine for five months in Tenerife.

   a Write down the average daily hours of sunshine for each month.

   b Which month had the most sunshine?

   c Give a reason why pictograms are useful in holiday brochures.

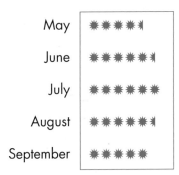

4 The pictogram shows the amounts of money collected by six students after they had completed a sponsored walk for charity.

   a Who raised the most money?

   b How much money was raised altogether by the six students?

   c Robert also took part in the walk and raised £32. Why would it be difficult to include him on the pictogram?

Anthony £ £ £ £ £
Ben £ £ £ £ £ £
Emma £ £ £ £ £
Leanne £ £ £ £
Reena £ £ £ £ £ £
Simon £ £ £ £ £ £ £

Key £ represents £5

FM 5 A newspaper showed the following pictogram about one of its team member's family and the number of emails they each received during one Sunday.

Key ⊠ represents 4 emails

		Frequency
Dad	⊠ ⊠ ⊠	
Mum	⊠ ▷	
Teenage son	⊠ ⊠ ⊠ ▷	
Teenage daughter		23
Young son		9

a How many emails did:

   i Dad receive

   ii Mum receive

   iii the teenage son receive?

b Copy and complete the pictogram.

c How many emails were received altogether?

PS 6 A survey was taken on the types of books read by students of a school.

	Frequency
Thriller	51
Romance	119
Science fiction	187
Historical	136

This information is to be put into a pictogram.

Design a pictogram to show this information with as few symbols as possible.

AU 7 A pictogram is to be made from this frequency table which shows the ways students travel to school.

Car	342
Bus	336
Walk	524

Explain why a key of four students to a symbol is not a good idea.

8 Draw pictograms of your own to show the following data.

a The number of hours for which you watched TV every evening last week.

b The magazines that students in your class read.

c The favourite colours of students in your class.

AU 9 A children's charity produces an advert to show how much money they have raised over the last two years.

Toys 4 Tots

We have doubled our income since 2008 to 2009

2008   2009

Why is the advert misleading?

This section will show you how to:
- draw bar charts to represent statistical data

Key words
axis
bar chart
class interval
dual bar chart

A **bar chart** consists of a series of bars or blocks of the *same* width, drawn either vertically or horizontally from an **axis**.

The heights or lengths of the bars always represent *frequencies*.

Sometimes, the bars are separated by narrow gaps of equal width, which makes the chart easier to read.

EXAMPLE 7

The grouped frequency table below shows the marks of 24 students in a test. Draw a bar chart for the data.

Marks	1–10	11–20	21–30	31–40	41–50
Frequency	2	3	5	8	6

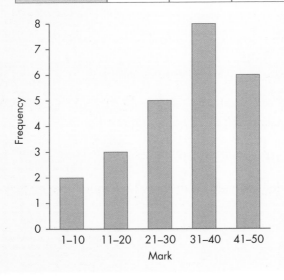

Note:

- Both axes are labelled.

- The **class intervals** are written under the middle of each bar.

- The bars are separated by equal spaces.

By using a **dual bar chart**, it is easy to compare two sets of related data, as Example 8 shows.

EXAMPLE 8

This dual bar chart shows the average daily maximum temperatures for England and Turkey over a five-month period.

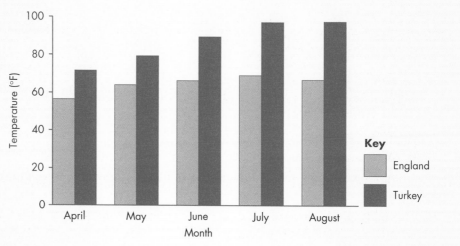

In which month was the difference between temperatures in England and Turkey the greatest?

The largest difference can be seen in August.

Note: You must always include a key to identify the two different sets of data.

EXERCISE 5C

1 For her survey on fitness, Maureen asked a sample of people, as they left a sports centre, which activity they had taken part in. She then drew a bar chart to show her data.

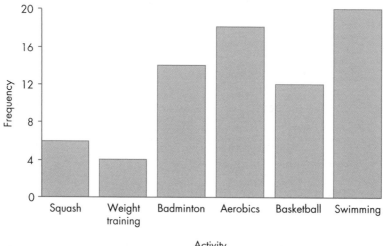

a Which was the most popular activity?

b How many people took part in Maureen's survey?

c Give a probable reason why fewer people took part in weight training than in any other activity.

d Is a sports centre a good place in which to do a survey on fitness? Explain why.

2 The frequency table below shows the levels achieved by 100 Year 10 students in their mock GCSE examinations.

Grade	F	E	D	C	B	A
Frequency	12	22	24	25	15	2

a Draw a suitable bar chart to illustrate the data.

b What fraction of the students achieved a grade C or grade B?

c Give one advantage of drawing a bar chart rather than a pictogram for this data.

3 This table shows the number of points Richard and Derek were each awarded in eight rounds of a general knowledge quiz.

Round	1	2	3	4	5	6	7	8
Richard	7	8	7	6	8	6	9	4
Derek	6	7	6	9	6	8	5	6

a Draw a dual bar chart to illustrate the data.

b Comment on how well each of them did in the quiz.

4 Kay did a survey on the time it took students in her form to get to school on a particular morning. She wrote down their times to the nearest minute.

15 23 36 45 8 20 34 15 27 49

10 60 5 48 30 18 21 2 12 56

49 33 17 44 50 35 46 24 11 34

a Draw a grouped frequency table for Kay's data, using class intervals 1–10, 11–20, …

b Draw a bar chart to illustrate the data.

c What conclusions can Kay draw from the bar chart?

5 This table shows the number of accidents at a dangerous crossroads over a six-year period.

Year	2000	2001	2002	2003	2004	2005
No. of accidents	6	8	7	9	6	4

a Draw a pictogram for the data.

b Draw a bar chart for the data.

AU c Which diagram would you use if you were going to write to your local council to suggest that traffic lights should be installed at the crossroads? Explain why.

F

AU 6 The diagram below shows the minimum and maximum temperatures, in degrees Celsius, for one day in August in five cities.

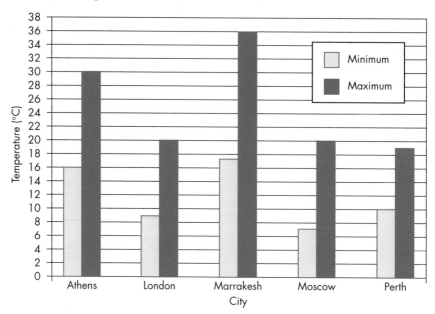

Chris says that the minimum temperature is always about half the maximum temperature for most cities.

Is Chris correct?

Give reasons to justify your answer.

AU 7 The bar chart shows the average daily temperatures, in degrees Celsius, in England and Scotland.

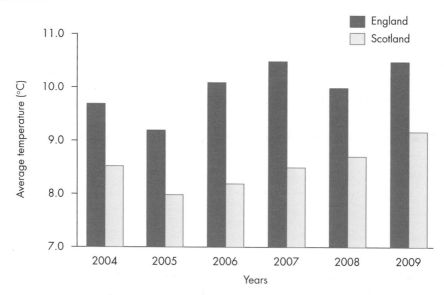

Derek says that the graph shows that the temperature in England is always more than double the temperature in Scotland.

Explain why Derek is wrong.

FM 8 Conduct a survey to find the colours of cars that pass your school or your home.

 a Draw pictograms and bar charts to illustrate your data.

 b Compare your results with someone else's in your class and comment on any conclusions you can draw concerning the colours of cars in your area.

FM 9 Choose a broadsheet newspaper, such as *The Times* or the *Guardian* and a tabloid newspaper, such as the *Sun* or the *Mirror*. Take a fairly long article from both papers, preferably on the same topic. Count the number of words in the first 50 sentences of each article.

 a For each article, draw a grouped frequency table for the number of words in each of the first 50 sentences.

 b Draw a dual bar chart for your data.

 c Do your results support the hypothesis that

 'Sentences in broadsheet newspapers are longer than the sentences in tabloid newspapers'?

FM 10
AU This is a composite bar chart showing the number of students absent from Year 10 in one week.

 a How many boys were absent on Tuesday?

 b How many girls were absent on Monday?

 c How many students were absent on Friday?

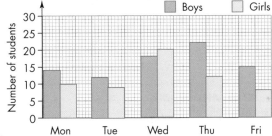

 d Compare how the numbers of absences change during the week, for both boys and girls.

5.4 Line graphs

This section will show you how to:	Key words
● draw a line graph to show trends in data	line graphs trends

Line graphs are usually used in statistics to show how data changes over a period of time. One such use is to indicate **trends**, for example, whether the Earth's temperature is increasing as the concentration of carbon dioxide builds up in the atmosphere, or whether a firm's profit margin is falling year-on-year.

Line graphs are best drawn on graph paper.

EXAMPLE 9

This line graph shows the outside temperature at a weather station, taken at hourly intervals. Estimate the temperature at 3.30 pm.

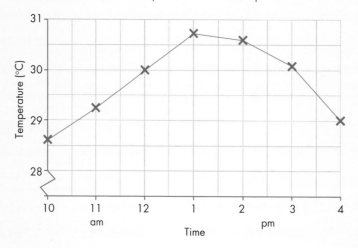

At 3.30 the temperature is approximately 29.5 °C.

Note: The temperature axis starts at 28 °C rather than 0 °C. This allows the use of a scale which makes it easy to plot the points and then to read the graph. The points are joined with lines so that the intermediate temperatures can be estimated for other times of the day.

EXAMPLE 10

This line graph shows the profit made each year by a company over a six-year period. Between which years did the company have the greatest increase in profits?

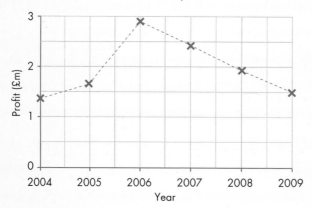

The greatest increase in profits was between 2005 and 2006.

For this graph, the values between the plotted points have no meaning because the profit of the company would have been calculated at the end of every year. In cases like this, the lines are often dashed. Although the trend appears to be that profits have fallen after 2006, it would not be sensible to predict what would happen after 2009.

EXERCISE 5D

1 This line graph shows the value of Spevadon shares on seven consecutive trading days.

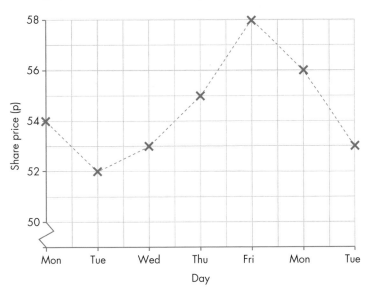

a On which day did the share price have its lowest value and what was that value?

b By how much did the share price rise from Wednesday to Thursday?

c Which day had the greatest rise in the share price from the previous day?

FM **d** Mr Hardy sold 500 shares on Friday. How much profit did he make if he originally bought the shares at 40p each?

2 The table shows the population of a town, rounded to the nearest thousand, after each census.

Year	1941	1951	1961	1971	1981	1991	2001
Population (1000s)	12	14	15	18	21	25	23

a Draw a line graph for the data.

b From your graph estimate the population in 1966.

c Between which two consecutive censuses did the population increase the most?

AU **d** Can you predict the population for 2011? Give a reason for your answer.

D

3 The number of ants in an ants' nest are counted at the end of each week.

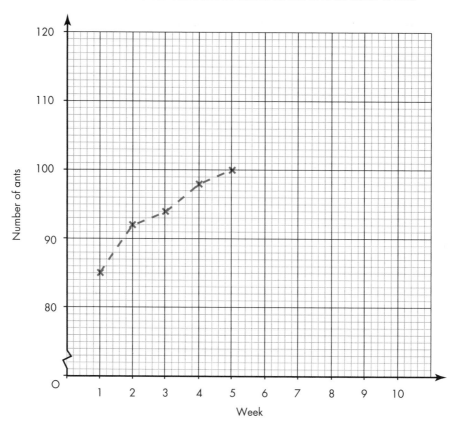

The graph shows the number of ants. At the end of week 5 the number is 100.

a At the end of week 6 the number is 104. At the end of week 10 the number is 120.

   i Copy the graph and plot these points on the graph.

   ii Complete the graph with straight lines.

b Use your graph to estimate the number of ants at the end of week 8.

FM 4 The table shows the estimated number of tourists worldwide.

Year	1970	1975	1980	1985	1990	1995	2000	2005
No. of tourists (millions)	100	150	220	280	290	320	340	380

a Draw a line graph for the data.

b Use your graph to estimate the number of tourists in 2010.

c Between which two consecutive years did tourism increase the most?

d Explain the trend in tourism. What reasons can you give to explain this trend?

D

5 The table shows the maximum and minimum daily temperatures for London over a week.

Day	Sunday	Monday	Tuesday	Wednesday	Thursday	Friday	Saturday
Maximum (°C)	12	14	16	15	16	14	10
Minimum (°C)	4	5	7	8	7	4	3

a Draw line graphs on the *same* axes to show the maximum and minimum temperatures.

b Find the smallest and greatest differences between the maximum and minimum temperatures.

PS 6 A puppy is weighed at the end of each week as shown in the table.

Week	1	2	3	4	5
Weight (g)	850	920	940	980	1000

Estimate how much the puppy would weigh after eight weeks.

AU 7 When plotting a graph to show the summer midday temperatures in Spain, Abbass decided to start his graph at the temperature 20 °C.

Explain why he might have done that.

ACTIVITY

Diagrams from the press

This is an activity for a group of two or more people. You will need a large selection of recent newspapers and magazines.

In a group, look through the newspapers and magazines.

Cut out any statistical diagrams and stick them on large sheets of coloured paper.

Underneath each diagram, explain what the diagram shows and how useful the diagram is in showing that information.

If any of the diagrams appears to be misleading, explain why.

You now have a lot of up-to-date statistics to display in your classroom.

Stem-and-leaf diagrams

This section will show you how to:
- draw and read information from an ordered stem-and-leaf diagram

Key words
discrete data
ordered data
raw data
unordered data

Raw data

If you were recording the ages of the first 20 people who line up at a bus stop in the morning, the **raw data** might look like this.

23, 13, 34, 44, 26, 12, 41, 31, 20, 18, 19, 31, 48, 32, 45, 14, 12, 27, 31, 19

This data is **unordered** and is difficult to read and analyse. When the data is **ordered**, it will look like this.

12, 12, 13, 14, 18, 19, 19, 20, 23, 26, 27, 31, 31, 31, 32, 34, 41, 44, 45, 48

This is easier to read and analyse.

Another method for displaying **discrete data** is a stem-and-leaf diagram. The tens digits will be the 'stem' and the units digits will be the 'leaves'.

Key 1 | 2 represents 12

1	2	2	3	4	8	9	9
2	0	3	6	7			
3	1	1	1	2	4		
4	1	4	5	8			

This is called an ordered stem-and-leaf diagram and gives a better idea of how the data is distributed.

A stem-and-leaf diagram should always have a key.

EXAMPLE 11

Put the following data into an ordered stem-and-leaf diagram.

45, 62, 58, 58, 61, 49, 61, 47, 52, 58, 48, 56, 65, 46, 54

a What is the largest value?

b What is the most common value?

c What is the difference between the largest and smallest values?

First decide on the stem and the leaf.

In this case, the tens digit will be the stem and the units digit will be the leaf.

Key 4 | 5 represents 45

```
4 | 5  6  7  8  9
5 | 2  4  6  8  8  8
6 | 1  1  2  5
```

a The largest value is 65.

b The most common value is 58 which occurs three times.

c The difference between the largest and the smallest is 65 − 45 = 20.

EXERCISE 5E

1 The following stem-and-leaf diagram shows the times taken for 15 students to complete a mathematical puzzle.

Key 1 | 7 represents 17 seconds

```
1 | 7  8  8  9
2 | 2  2  2  5  6  9
3 | 3  4  5  5  8
```

a What is the shortest time to complete the puzzle?

b What is the most common time to complete the puzzle?

c What is the difference between the longest time and the shortest time to complete the puzzle?

FM 2 This stem-and-leaf diagram shows the marks for the boys and girls in form 10E in a maths test.

Key Boys: 2 | 4 means 42 marks

Girls: 3 | 5 means 35 marks

> **HINTS AND TIPS**
>
> Read the boys' marks from right to left.

			Boys			Girls					
6	4	2	3	3	3	5	7	9			
9	9	6	2	4	4	2	2	3	8	8	8
7	6	6	6	5	5	1	1	5			

a What was the highest mark for the boys?

b What was the highest mark for the girls?

c What was the most common mark for the boys?

d What was the most common mark for the girls?

e What overall conclusions can you draw from this data?

3 The heights of 15 sunflowers were measured.

43 cm, 39 cm, 41 cm, 29 cm, 36 cm,

34 cm, 43 cm, 48 cm, 38 cm, 35 cm,

41 cm, 38 cm, 43 cm, 28 cm, 48 cm

a Show the results in an ordered stem-and-leaf diagram, using this key:

Key 4 | 3 represents 43 cm

b What was the largest height measured?

c What was the most common height measured?

d What is the difference between the largest and smallest heights measured?

4 A student records the number of text messages she receives each day for two weeks.

12, 18, 21, 9, 17, 23, 8, 2, 20, 13, 17, 22, 9, 9

a Show the results in an ordered stem-and-leaf diagram, using this key:

Key 1 | 2 represents 12 messages

b What was the largest number of text messages received in a day?

c What is the most common number of text messages received in a day?

AU 5 The number of matches in a set of boxes were each counted with the following results.

50, 52, 51, 53, 52, 51, 51, 53, 54, 55, 54, 52, 52, 51, 50, 53

Explain why a stem-and-leaf diagram is not a good way to represent this information.

GRADE BOOSTER

F You can draw and read information from bar charts, dual bar charts and pictograms

F You can work out the total frequency from a frequency table and compare data in bar charts

E You can read information from a stem-and-leaf diagram

D You can draw an ordered stem-and-leaf diagram

What you should know now

- How to draw frequency tables for grouped and ungrouped data
- How to draw and interpret pictograms, bar charts and line graphs
- How to read information from statistical diagrams, including stem-and-leaf diagrams

1 A shopkeeper records the type of person entering his shop on Monday morning as Man (M), Woman (W) or Child (C).

His results are

M M W C C W C C M W
C M C W M C W C W M
W C C M C W C W W C

a Complete the tally and frequency columns.
(2)

Type of person	Tally	Frequency
Man (M)		
Woman (W)		
Child (C)		

b What type of person was recorded most often? (1)

c The shopkeeper records similar data on Tuesday morning.

The bar chart shows his results.

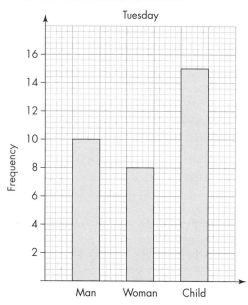

The shopkeeper says, "On Tuesday morning there were more children than adults entering my shop."

Is he correct?

You **must** show your working. (3)

(Total 6 marks)

AQA, November 2007, Module1 Foundation, Question 7

2 A school is raising money to buy sports equipment.

The pictogram shows the amount of money raised during some events.

Coffee morning	◯ ◖
Concert	◯ ◯ ◯ ◯
Jumble sale	◯ ◯ ◖
Sports day	◯

Key: ◯ represents £50

a Which event raised the most money? (1)

b How much money did the concert raise? (1)

c How much more money did the Jumble sale raise than the Sports day? (1)

d The school needs to raise £500 in total.

How much more money do they need to raise to meet their target? (3)

(Total 6 marks)

AQA, March 2009, Module 1 Foundation, Question 1

3 Children at a playgroup choose either milk or orange juice each lunchtime.

The table shows the choices for one week.

	Milk	Orange juice
Monday	17	8
Tuesday	20	10
Wednesday	10	16
Thursday	15	12
Friday	14	11

a Complete the dual bar chart to show this information. (3)

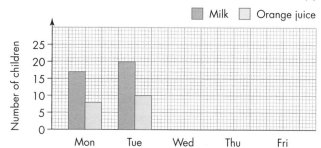

b Kieran says that milk is always more popular than orange juice.

Is he correct?

Give a reason for your answer. (1)

(Total 4 marks)

AQA, March 2009, Module 1 Foundation, Question 7

D E F

4 Mary is collecting data to show how much protein and fat are in some food products.

The table shows her results.

Product	Soup	Oven Chips	Corn Flakes	Yoghurt	Salad Cream
Amount of protein per 100 g	1 g	2 g	9 g	5 g	1 g
Amount of fat per 100 g	3 g	5 g	6 g	1 g	10 g

The bar chart shows some of the information above.

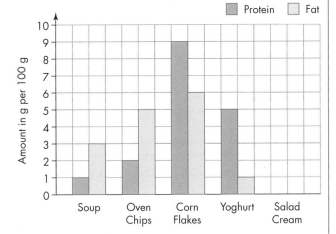

a Complete the bar chart for the Salad Cream. (2)

b Which product has the most protein per 100 g? (1)

c Which product has $2\frac{1}{2}$ times more fat than protein?

Explain your answer. (1)

(Total 4 marks)

AQA, May 2008, Paper 1 Foundation, Question 5

5 The bar chart shows the shoe sizes of boys and girls in Year 6 at a school.

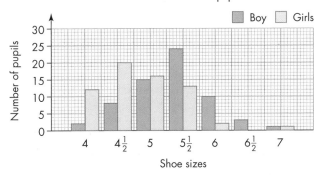

a How many girls have shoe size 4? (1)

b Which shoe size is the mode for the boys? (1)

c How many girls have a shoe size greater than 6? (1)

d How many more girls than boys have shoe size $4\frac{1}{2}$? (2)

(Total 5 marks)

AQA, March 2008, Module 1 Foundation, Question 1

6 The following dual bar chart appeared in a daily newspaper showing the numbers of people who attended swimming lessons at an international pool in Sheffield.

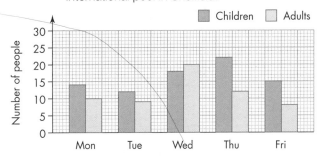

a How many children attended on Monday?

b On which day did most children attend?

c How many people attended the session on Friday?

d Calculate the total number of adults who attended these five sessions.

e Joe said, "Each session is attended by more children than adults."

Is he correct?

Give a reason for your answer.

7 The time series graph shows the number of students attending mathematics revision classes over a seven week period.

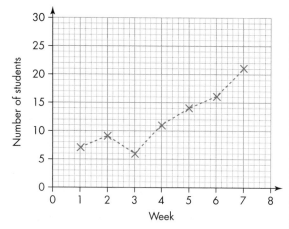

a In which week did the least number of students attend the class? (1)

b How many **more** students attended in week 7 than in week 1? (2)

c Give a possible reason why the attendance was highest in week 7. (1)

(Total 4 marks)

AQA, March 2009, Module 1 Foundation, Question 3

8 This graph appeared in a newspaper.

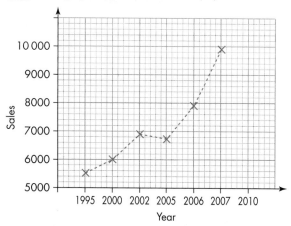

a Write down two reasons why this graph is misleading. (2)

(Total 2 marks)

AQA, March 2008, Module 1 Foundation, Question 2(a)

9 The graph shows the average weekly household income in the UK.

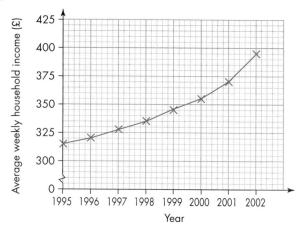

a By how much did the average weekly household income increase from 2000 to 2001? (1)

b Between which two years was there the largest annual increase in average weekly household income? (1)

(Total 2 marks)

AQA, March 2005, Module 1 Foundation, Question 4,

Worked Examination Questions

1 The temperature is recorded in 20 towns on one day.

  8 14 21 15   2 10 11 17   7 24

  23 18   5 11   4 20 18 23   4 19

Draw a **stem-and-leaf diagram** to represent these data.

Key 1 | 4 represents 14 ——————— Draw a basic stem-and-leaf diagram when the stem is the tens digits and the leaves are the units digits. Create a key, using any value for 1 method mark.

0	2	4	4	5	7	9
1	0	1	1	4	5	7	8	8	9
2	0	1	3	3	4

Now complete the stem-and-leaf diagram, keeping the data in order. You get 2 marks for accuracy and 1 mark if you make only one error.

Total: 3 marks

PS **2** Andrew was born on 27 March and had his weight recorded regularly as shown in the table.

Day	1	5	9	13	17
Weight (g)	4100	3800	4000	4500	4900

Estimate how much Andrew would weigh after 3 weeks.

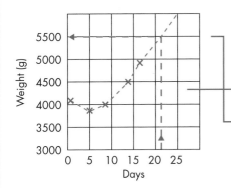

Use the table to draw the given points and plot a line graph.

Plot the points on a graph so that a prediction can be made by extending the graph. You get 1 mark for accuracy for this.

You get 1 method mark for showing 21 days (3 weeks) being read vertically to the extended graph.

You get 1 method mark for showing a horizontal reading from the graph to the weight.

Estimated weight is 5500 g ——— You get 1 mark for accuracy for an answer close to 5500 g.

Total: 4 marks

AU **3** When drawing a bar chart to show the summer midday temperatures in various capital cities of Europe, Joy decided to start her graph at the temperature 10 °C.

Explain why she might have done that.

The lowest temperature to be shown would be about 10 degrees and she wanted to emphasise the differences between the cities. ——— State a lowest temperature of 10 °C or just higher. This is worth 1 mark.

Suggest that she wanted to emphasise the differences. This is worth 1 mark.

Total: 2 marks

The weather often appears in the news headlines and a weather report is given regularly on the television. In this activity you are required to look at the data supplied in a weather report and interpret its meaning.

Your task

The type of information given on the map and in the table is found in most newspapers in the UK each day. The map gives a forecast of the weather for the day in several large towns, while the table summarises the weather on the previous day.

It is your task to use appropriate statistical diagrams and measures to summarise the data given in the map and table.

Then, you must write a report to describe fully the weather in the UK on Friday 21st April 2010. You should use your statistical analysis to support your descriptions.

Getting started

Look at the data provided in the table.

- Which cities had the most sun, which had the most rain and which were the warmest on this particular day?

- Is there any other information you can add?

Friday 21st April 2010

	Sun (hrs)	Rain (mm)	Max (°C)	Min (°C)	Daytime weather		Sun (hrs)	Rain (mm)	Max (°C)	Min (°C)	Daytime weather
Aberdeen	5	3	10	5	rain	**Leeds**	5	0	11	6	cloudy
Barnstaple	5	0	12	8	sunny	**Lincoln**	5	3	10	4	rain
Belfast	5	0	10	4	cloudy	**Liverpool**	5	1	12	6	mixed
Birmingham	5	0	11	5	sunny	**London**	5	2	13	6	rain
Bournemouth	5	0	12	6	sunny	**Manchester**	5	0	13	7	sunny
Bradford	5	1	10	5	rain	**Middlesbrough**	5	1	11	6	rain
Brighton	5	0	11	5	mixed	**Newcastle**	5	0	11	6	cloudy
Bristol	5	2	11	6	rain	**Newquay**	5	0	12	8	sunny
Cardiff	5	2	11	6	rain	**Nottingham**	5	0	12	6	cloudy
Carlisle	5	3	10	5	rain	**Oxford**	5	2	12	5	rain
Chester	5	3	10	4	rain	**Plymouth**	6	0	12	9	sunny
Eastbourne	5	0	9	5	windy	**Rhyl**	5	1	9	4	mixed
Edinburgh	5	0	9	5	cloudy	**Scunthorpe**	5	1	10	4	mixed
Falmouth	5	0	12	8	sunny	**Sheffield**	5	0	12	7	sunny
Glasgow	5	0	9	4	cloudy	**Shrewsbury**	5	0	9	4	windy
Grimsby	5	1	10	4	mixed	**Southampton**	5	0	12	6	sunny
Holyhead	5	0	8	3	windy	**Swindon**	5	1	11	5	mixed
Ipswich	5	1	11	6	mixed	**Weymouth**	5	0	12	6	sunny
Isle of Man	5	0	9	3	windy	**Windermere**	5	2	10	4	mixed
Isle of Wight	5	0	13	6	sunny	**York**	5	0	11	5	cloudy

Saturday 22nd April 2010

Why this chapter matters

Today, people always seem to be asking "Am I average?" But, how do we answer this question? The idea of an 'average' is not a modern one. History shows us that people have always been concerned with averages as the examples below demonstrate.

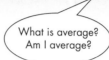

What is average? Am I average?

Mean in Ancient India

There is a story about Rtuparna who was born in India around 5000BC. He wanted to estimate the amount of fruit on a single tree. He counted how much fruit was on one branch, then estimated the number of branches on the tree. He multiplied the estimated number of branches by the counted fruit on one branch and was amazed that the total was very close to the actual counted number of fruit when it was picked.

This is seen as a first attempt at an arithmetic **mean**, because the one branch he chose would have been an average one representing all the branches. So the number of fruit on that branch would have been in the middle of the smallest and largest number of fruit on other branches on the tree.

Rtuparna may have been estimating the amount of fruit on a mango tree. These trees are common in India.

Mode in Ancient Greece

The Athenian army would have needed regular-sized bricks, as on this wall, to make their calculations accurate and useful.

This story comes from the Peloponnesian War in Ancient Greece (431–404BC). It is about a battle between the Peloponnesian League (led by Sparta) and the Delian League (led by Athens).

The Athenians had to get over the Peloponnesian Wall so they needed to work out the height of the wall. They did this by looking at the wall and counting the layers of bricks. This was done by hundreds of soldiers at the same time because many of them would get it wrong – but the majority would get it about right.

They then had to guess the height of one brick and so calculate the total height of the wall. They could then make ladders long enough to reach the top of the wall.

This is seen as an early use of the **mode**: the number of layers that occurred the most was deemed as the one most likely to be correct.

The other average that we use is the **median**, and there is no record of any use of this (which finds the middle value) being used until the early 17th century.

These ancient examples demonstrate that we do not always work out the average in the same way – we must choose a method that is appropriate to the situation. Bearing this in mind, how will you seek to answer the question "Am I average?"?

Statistics: Averages

This chapter will show you ...

- **F** how to calculate the mode, median, mean and range of small sets of discrete data
- **E** how to decide which is the best average for different types of data
- **D** how to calculate the mode, median, mean and range from frequency tables of discrete data
- **D** how to draw frequency polygons
- **C** how to use and recognise the modal class and calculate an estimate of the mean from frequency tables of grouped data

Visual overview

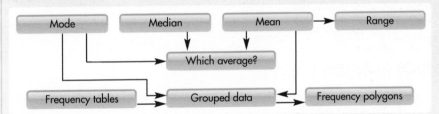

What you should already know

- How to collect and organise data **(KS3 level 4, GCSE grade F)**
- How to draw frequency tables **(KS3 level 4, GCSE grade F)**
- How to extract information from tables and diagrams **(KS3 level 4, GCSE grade F)**

Quick check

The marks for 15 students in a mathematics test are:

2, 3, 4, 5, 5, 6, 6, 6, 7, 7, 7, 7, 7, 8, 10

a What is the most common mark?

b What is the middle value in the list?

c Find the difference between the highest mark and the lowest mark.

d Find the total of all 15 marks.

Average is a term often used when describing or comparing sets of data, for example, the average rainfall in Britain, the average score of a batsman, an average weekly wage or the average mark in an examination.

In each of the above examples, you are representing the whole set of many values by just a single, 'typical' value, which is called the average.

The idea of an average is extremely useful, because it enables you to compare one set of data with another set by comparing just two values – their averages.

There are several ways of expressing an average, but the most commonly used averages are the **mode**, the **median** and the **mean**.

6.1 The mode

This section will show you how to:
● find the mode from lists of data and from frequency tables

Key words
frequency
modal class
modal value
mode

The **mode** is the value that occurs the most in a set of data. That is, it is the value with the highest **frequency**.

The mode is a useful average because it is very easy to find and it can be applied to non-numerical data (qualitative data). For example, you could find the modal style of skirts sold in a particular month.

EXAMPLE 1

Suhail scored the following number of goals in 12 school football matches:

1 2 1 0 1 0 0 1 2 1 0 2

What is the mode of his scores?

The number which occurs most often in this list is 1. So, the mode is 1.

You can also say that the modal score or **modal value** is 1.

EXAMPLE 2

Barbara asked her friends how many books they had each taken out of the school library during the previous month. Their responses were:

2 1 3 4 6 4 1 3 0 2 6 0

Find the mode.

Here, there is *no mode*, because no number occurs more than any of the others.

FM Functional Maths   **AU** (AO2) Assessing Understanding   **PS** (AO3) Problem Solving

EXERCISE 6A

1 Find the mode for each set of data.

HINTS AND TIPS

It helps to put the data in order or group all the same things together.

    a 3, 4, 7, 3, 2, 4, 5, 3, 4, 6, 8, 4, 2, 7

    b 47, 49, 45, 50, 47, 48, 51, 48, 51, 48, 52, 48

    c −1, 1, 0, −1, 2, −2, −2, −1, 0, 1, −1, 1, 0, −1, 2, −1, 2

    d $\frac{1}{2}, \frac{1}{4}, 1, \frac{1}{2}, \frac{3}{4}, \frac{1}{4}, 0, 1, \frac{3}{4}, \frac{1}{4}, 1, \frac{1}{4}, \frac{3}{4}, \frac{1}{4}, \frac{1}{2}$

    e 100, 10, 1000, 10, 100, 1000, 10, 1000, 100, 1000, 100, 10

    f 1.23, 3.21, 2.31, 3.21, 1.23, 3.12, 2.31, 1.32, 3.21, 2.31, 3.21

2 Find the modal category for each set of data.

    a red, green, red, amber, green, red, amber, green, red, amber

    b rain, sun, cloud, sun, rain, fog, snow, rain, fog, sun, snow, sun

    c α, γ, α, β, γ, α, α, γ, β, α, β, γ, β, β, α, β, γ, β

    d ❋, ☆, ★, ★, ☆, ❋, ★, ✩, ★, ✩, ✭, ❋, ✪, ✩, ★, ✭, ★, ✩

FM 3 Joan did a survey to find the shoe sizes of students in her class. The bar chart illustrates her data.

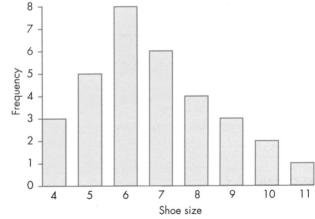

    a How many students are in Joan's class?

    b What is the modal shoe size?

    c Can you tell from the bar chart which are the boys or which are the girls in her class?

    d Joan then decided to draw a bar chart to show the shoe sizes of the boys and the girls separately. Do you think that the mode for the boys and the mode for the girls will be the same as the mode for the whole class? Explain your answer.

4 The frequency table shows the marks that Form 10MP obtained in a spelling test.

Mark	3	4	5	6	7	8	9	10
Frequency	1	2	6	5	5	4	3	4

    a Write down the mode for their marks.

AU **b** Do you think this is a typical mark for the form? Explain your answer.

5 The grouped frequency table shows the number of e-mails each household in Orchard Street received during one day.

No. of e-mails	0–4	5–9	10–14	15–19	20–24	25–29	30–34	35–39
Frequency	9	12	14	11	10	8	4	2

a Draw a bar chart to illustrate the data.

b How many households are there in Orchard Street?

c How many households received 20 or more e-mails?

AU d How many households did not receive any e-mails during the week? Explain your answer.

e Write down the modal class for the data in the table.

> **HINTS AND TIPS**
>
> You cannot find the mode of the data in a grouped frequency table. So, instead, you need to find the **modal class**, which is the class interval with the highest frequency.

6 Explain why the mode is often referred to as the 'shopkeeper's average'.

7 This table shows the colours of eyes of the students in form 11P.

	Blue	Brown	Green
Boys	4	8	1
Girls	8	5	2

a How many students are in form 11P?

b What is the modal eye colour for:

    i boys   ii girls   iii the whole form?

AU c After two students join the form the modal eye colour for the whole form is blue. Which of the following statements is true?

• Both students had green eyes.

• Both students had brown eyes.

• Both students had blue eyes.

• You cannot tell what their eye colours were.

AU 8 Here is a large set of raw data.

5 6 8 2 4 8 9 8 1 3 4 2 7 2 4 6 7 5 3 8

9 1 3 1 5 6 2 5 7 9 4 1 4 3 3 5 6 8 6 9

8 4 8 9 3 4 6 7 7 4 5 4 2 3 4 6 7 6 5 5

a What problems may occur if you attempted to find the mode by counting individual numbers?

b Explain a method that would make finding the mode more efficient and accurate.

c Use your method to find the mode of the data.

The median

This section will show you how to:	Key words
• find the median from a list of data, a table of data and a stem-and-leaf diagram	median middle value

The **median** is the **middle value** of a list of values when they are put in *order* of size, from lowest to highest.

The advantage of using the median as an average is that half the data-values are below the median value and half are above it. Therefore, the average is only slightly affected by the presence of any particularly high or low values that are not typical of the data as a whole.

EXAMPLE 3

Find the median for the following list of numbers:

2, 3, 5, 6, 1, 2, 3, 4, 5, 4, 6

Putting the list in numerical order gives:

1, 2, 2, 3, 3, **4**, 4, 5, 5, 6, 6

There are 11 numbers in the list, so the middle of the list is the 6th number. Therefore, the median is 4.

EXAMPLE 4

Find the median of the data shown in the frequency table.

Value	2	3	4	5	6	7
Frequency	2	4	6	7	8	3

First, add up the frequencies to find out how many pieces of data there are.

The total is 30 so the median value will be between the 15th and 16th values.

Now, add up the frequencies to give a running total, to find out where the 15th and 16th values are.

Value	2	3	4	5	6	7
Frequency	2	4	6	7	8	3
Total frequency	2	6	12	19	27	30

There are 12 data-values up to the value 4 and 19 up to the value 5.

Both the 15th and 16th values are 5, so the median is 5.

To find the median in a list of n values, written in order, use the rule:

$$\text{median} = \frac{n + 1}{2}\text{th value}$$

For a set of data that has a lot of values, it is sometimes more convenient and quicker to draw a stem-and-leaf diagram. Example 5 shows you how to do this.

EXAMPLE 5

The ages of 20 people attending a conference were as follows:

28, 34, 46, 23, 28, 34, 52, 61, 45, 34, 39, 50, 26, 44, 60, 53, 31, 25, 37, 48

Find the modal age and median age of the group.

Taking the tens to be the 'stem' and the units to be the 'leaves', draw the stem-and-leaf diagram as shown below.

```
2 | 3  5  6  8  8
3 | 1  4  4  4  7  9
4 | 4  5  6  8
5 | 0  2  3
6 | 0  1                    Key  2 | 3 represents 23 people
```

The most common value is 34, so the mode is 34.

There is an even number of values in this list, so the middle of the list is between the two central values, which are the 10th and 11th values. To find the central values count up 10 from the lowest value, 23, 25, 26, 28, 28, 31 … or *down* 10 from the highest value 61, 60, 53, 52, 50, 48 …

Therefore, the median is exactly midway between 37 and 39.

Hence, the median is 38.

EXERCISE 6B

1 Find the median for each set of data.

a 7, 6, 2, 3, 1, 9, 5, 4, 8

b 26, 34, 45, 28, 27, 38, 40, 24, 27, 33, 32, 41, 38

c 4, 12, 7, 6, 10, 5, 11, 8, 14, 3, 2, 9

d 12, 16, 12, 32, 28, 24, 20, 28, 24, 32, 36, 16

e 10, 6, 0, 5, 7, 13, 11, 14, 6, 13, 15, 1, 4, 15

f −1, −8, 5, −3, 0, 1, −2, 4, 0, 2, −4, −3, 2

g 5.5, 5.05, 5.15, 5.2, 5.3, 5.35, 5.08, 5.9, 5.25

HINTS AND TIPS

Remember to put the data in order before finding the median.

HINTS AND TIPS

If there is an even number of pieces of data, the median will be halfway between the two middle values.

2 A group of 15 sixth-formers had lunch in the school's cafeteria. Given below are the amounts that they spent.

£2.30, £2.20, £2, £2.50, £2.20, £3.50, £2.20, £2.25, £2.20, £2.30, £2.40, £2.20, £2.30, £2, £2.35

a Find the mode for the data.

b Find the median for the data.

AU **c** Which is the better average to use? Explain your answer.

3 **a** Find the median of 7, 4, 3, 8, 2, 6, 5, 2, 9, 8, 3.

b Without putting them in numerical order, write down the median for each of these sets.

   i 17, 14, 13, 18, 12, 16, 15, 12, 19, 18, 13

   ii 217, 214, 213, 218, 212, 216, 215, 212, 219, 218, 213

   iii 12, 9, 8, 13, 7, 11, 10, 7, 14, 13, 8

   iv 14, 8, 6, 16, 4, 12, 10, 4, 18, 16, 6

> ### HINTS AND TIPS
>
> Look for a connection between the original data and the new data. For example, in **i**, the numbers are each 10 more than those in part **a**.

4 Given below are the age, height and weight of each of the seven players in a netball team.

	Ella	Linda	Pat	Marion	Amina	Martha	Elisa
Age (yr)	13	15	12	11	11	15	14
Height (cm)	161	165	162	158	154	168	169
Weight (kg)	41	42	37	32	35	42	40

a Find the median age of the team. Which player has the median age?

b Find the median height of the team. Which player has the median height?

c Find the median weight of the team. Which player has the median weight?

AU **d** Who would you choose as the average player in the team? Give a reason for your answer.

F

5 The table shows the number of sandwiches sold in a corner shop over 25 days.

Sandwiches sold	10	11	12	13	14	15	16
Frequency	2	3	6	4	3	4	3

a What is the modal number of sandwiches sold?

b What is the median number of sandwiches sold?

6 The bar chart shows the marks that Mrs Woodhead gave her students for their first Functional Mathematics task.

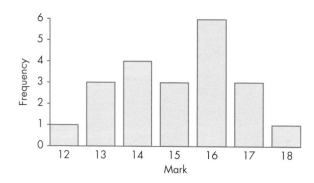

a How many students are there in Mrs Woodhead's class?

b What is the modal mark?

c Copy and complete this frequency table.

Mark	12	13	14	15	16	17	18
Frequency	1	3					

d What is the median mark?

E

PS **11** **a** Write down a list of nine numbers that has a median of 12.

b Write down a list of 10 numbers that has a median of 12.

c Write down a list of nine numbers that has a median of 12 and a mode of 8.

d Write down a list of 10 numbers that has a median of 12 and a mode of 8.

8 The following stem-and-leaf diagram shows the times taken for 15 students to complete a mathematical puzzle.

Key 1 | 7 represents 17 seconds

```
1 | 7   8   8   9
2 | 2   2   2   5   6   9
3 | 3   4   5   5   8
```

a What is the modal time taken to complete the puzzle?

b What is the median time taken to complete the puzzle?

9 The stem-and-leaf diagram shows the marks for 13 boys and 12 girls in form 7E in a science test.

> **Key** 2 | 3 represents 32 marks for boys
> 3 | 5 represents 35 marks for girls

			Boys		Girls					
	6	4	2	3	5	7	9			
	9	9	6	2	4	2	2	3	8	8	8
7	6	6	6	5	3	5	1	1	5	

a What was the modal mark for the boys?

b What was the modal mark for the girls?

c What was the median mark for the boys?

d What was the median mark for the girls?

FM e Who did better in the test, the boys or the girls? Give a reason for your answer.

PS 10 A list contains seven even numbers. The largest number is 24. The smallest number is half the largest. The mode is 14 and the median is 16. Two of the numbers add up to 42. What are the seven numbers?

11 The marks of 25 students in an English examination were as follows.

> 55, 63, 24, 47, 60, 45, 50, 89, 39, 47, 38, 42, 69, 73, 38, 47, 53, 64, 58, 71, 41, 48, 68, 64, 75

Draw a stem-and-leaf diagram to find the median.

PS 12 Look at this list of numbers.

> 4, 4, 5, 8, 10, 11, 12, 15, 15, 16, 20

a Add four numbers to make the median 12.

b Add six numbers to make the median 12.

c What is the least number of numbers to add that will make the median 4?

AU 13 Here are five payments.

> £3, £5, £8, £100, £3000

Explain why the median is not a good average to use in this set of payments.

6.3 The mean

This section will show you how to:
- calculate the mean of a set of data

Key words

average

mean

The **mean** of a set of data is the sum of all the values in the set divided by the total number of values in the set. That is:

$$\text{mean} = \frac{\text{sum of all values}}{\text{total number of values}}$$

This is what most people mean when they use the term '**average**'.

Another name for this average is the arithmetic **mean**.

The advantage of using the mean as an average is that it takes into account all the values in the set of data.

EXAMPLE 6

Find the mean of 4, 8, 7, 5, 9, 4, 8, 3.

Sum of all the values = 4 + 8 + 7 + 5 + 9 + 4 + 8 + 3 = 48

Total number of values = 8

Therefore, mean = $\frac{48}{8}$ = 6

EXAMPLE 7

The ages of 11 players in a football squad are:

21, 23, 20, 27, 25, 24, 25, 30, 21, 22, 28

What is the mean age of the squad?

Sum of all the ages = 266

Total number in squad = 11

Therefore, mean age = $\frac{266}{11}$ = 24.1818… = 24.2 (1 decimal place)

When the answer is not exact, it is usual to round the mean to 1 decimal place.

Using a calculator

If your calculator has a statistical mode, the mean of a set of numbers can be found by simply entering the numbers and then pressing the $\bar{x}$ key. On some calculators, the statistical mode is represented by SD.

EXAMPLE 8

The mean weight of eight members of a rowing crew is 89 kg. When the cox is included, the mean weight is 85 kg.

What is the weight of the cox?

The eight crew members have a total weight of 8 × 89 = 712 kg.

With the cox the total weight is 9 × 85 = 765 kg.

So the cox weighs 765 − 712 = 53 kg.

EXAMPLE 9

Find the mean of 2, 3, 7, 8 and 10.

First put your calculator into statistical mode.

Then press the following keys:

2 DATA 3 DATA 7 DATA 8 DATA 1 0 DATA $\bar{x}$

You should find that the mean is given by $\bar{x}$ = 6.

You can also find the number of data-values by pressing the n key.

Your calculator may use the following process for finding the mean.

Set up into statistics mode by keying:

MODE 2 (stat) 1 (1-var)

Enter the data 12, 16, 17 by keying:

1 2 = 1 6 = 1 7

Calculate the mean by keying:

AC SHIFT 1 (stat) 5 (var) 2 ($\bar{x}$) =

This gives: mean = 15

> **HINTS AND TIPS**
>
> It is generally more difficult to find the mean on a calculator by this method than simply adding up the data values and dividing. So don't use this method to find the mean unless you are very confident about using it.

EXERCISE 6C

1 Find, without the help of a calculator, the mean for each set of data.

    a 7, 8, 3, 6, 7, 3, 8, 5, 4, 9

    b 47, 3, 23, 19, 30, 22

    c 42, 53, 47, 41, 37, 55, 40, 39, 44, 52

    d 1.53, 1.51, 1.64, 1.55, 1.48, 1.62, 1.58, 1.65

    e 1, 2, 0, 2, 5, 3, 1, 0, 1, 2, 3, 4

2 Calculate the mean for each set of data, giving your answer correct to 1 decimal place. You may use your calculator.

    a 34, 56, 89, 34, 37, 56, 72, 60, 35, 66, 67

    b 235, 256, 345, 267, 398, 456, 376, 307, 282

    c 50, 70, 60, 50, 40, 80, 70, 60, 80, 40, 50, 40, 70

    d 43.2, 56.5, 40.5, 37.9, 44.8, 49.7, 38.1, 41.6, 51.4

    e 2, 3, 1, 0, 2, 5, 4, 3, 2, 0, 1, 3, 4, 5, 0, 3, 1, 2

FM 3 The table shows the marks that 10 students obtained in Mathematics, English and Science in their Year 10 examinations.

Student	Abigail	Brian	Chloe	David	Eric	Frances	Graham	Howard	Ingrid	Jane
Maths	45	56	47	77	82	39	78	32	92	62
English	54	55	59	69	66	49	60	56	88	44
Science	62	58	48	41	80	56	72	40	81	52

    a Work out the mean mark for Mathematics.

    b Work out the mean mark for English.

    c Work out the mean mark for Science.

    d Which student obtained marks closest to the mean in all three subjects?

    e How many students were above the average mark in all three subjects?

4 Heather kept a record of the amount of time she spent on her homework over 10 days:

    $\frac{1}{2}$ h, 20 min, 35 min, $\frac{1}{4}$ h, 1 h, $\frac{1}{2}$ h, $1\frac{1}{2}$ h, 40 min, $\frac{3}{4}$ h, 55 min

Calculate the mean time, in minutes, that Heather spent on her homework.

HINTS AND TIPS

Convert all times to minutes, for example, $\frac{1}{4}$ h = 15 minutes.

5 The weekly wages of 10 people working in an office are:

£350   £200   £180   £200   £350   £200   £240   £480   £300   £280

a Find the modal wage.

b Find the median wage.

c Calculate the mean wage.

d Which of the three averages best represents the office staff's wages? Give a reason for your answer.

HINTS AND TIPS

Remember that the mean can be distorted by extreme values.

6 The ages of five people in a group of walkers are 38, 28, 30, 42 and 37.

a Calculate the mean age of the group.

b Steve, who is 41, joins the group. Calculate the new mean age of the group.

7 a Calculate the mean of 3, 7, 5, 8, 4, 6, 7, 8, 9 and 3.

b Calculate the mean of 13, 17, 15, 18, 14, 16, 17, 18, 19 and 13. What do you notice?

c Write down, without calculating, the mean for each of the following sets of data.

  i   53, 57, 55, 58, 54, 56, 57, 58, 59, 53

  ii 103, 107, 105, 108, 104, 106, 107, 108, 109, 103

  iii 4, 8, 6, 9, 5, 7, 8, 9, 10, 4

HINTS AND TIPS

Look for a connection between the original data and the new data. For example in **i** the numbers are 50 more.

PS 8 Two families were in a competition.

Speed family		Roberts family	
Brian	aged 59	Frank	aged 64
Kath	aged 54	Marylin	aged 62
James	aged 34	David	aged 34
Helen	aged 34	James	aged 32
John	aged 30	Tom	aged 30
Joseph	aged 24	Helen	aged 30
Joy	aged 19	Evie	aged 16

Each family had to choose four members with a mean age of between 35 and 36.

Choose two teams, one from each family, that have this mean age between 35 and 36.

AU 9 Asif had an average batting score of 35 runs. He had scored 315 runs in nine games of cricket.

What is the least number of runs he needs to score in the next match if he is to get a higher average score?

10 The mean age of a group of eight walkers is 42. Joanne joins the group and the mean age changes to 40. How old is Joanne?

This section will show you how to:
- find the range of a set of data and compare different sets of data, using the mean and the range

Key words
consistency
range
spread

The **range** for a set of data is the highest value of the set minus the lowest value.

The range is *not* an average. It shows the **spread** of the data. It is, therefore, used when comparing two or more sets of similar data. You can also use it to comment on the **consistency** of two or more sets of data.

EXAMPLE 10

Rachel's marks in 10 mental arithmetic tests were 4, 4, 7, 6, 6, 5, 7, 6, 9 and 6.

Therefore, her mean mark is 60 ÷ 10 = 6 and the range is 9 − 4 = 5.

Adil's marks in the same tests were 6, 7, 6, 8, 5, 6, 5, 6, 5 and 6.

Therefore, his mean mark is 60 ÷ 10 = 6 and the range is 8 − 5 = 3.

Although the means are the same, Adil has a smaller range. This shows that Adil's results are more consistent.

EXERCISE 6D

1 Find the range for each set of data.

   a 3, 8, 7, 4, 5, 9, 10, 6, 7, 4

   b 62, 59, 81, 56, 70, 66, 82, 78, 62, 75

   c 1, 0, 4, 5, 3, 2, 5, 4, 2, 1, 0, 1, 4, 4

   d 3.5, 4.2, 5.5, 3.7, 3.2, 4.8, 5.6, 3.9, 5.5, 3.8

   e 2, −1, 0, 3, −1, −2, 1, −4, 2, 3, 0, 2, −2, 0, −3

G

2 The table shows the maximum and minimum temperatures at midday for five cities in England during a week in August.

	Birmingham	Leeds	London	Newcastle	Sheffield
Maximum temperature (°C)	28	25	26	27	24
Minimum temperature (°C)	23	22	24	20	21

a Write down the range of the temperatures for each city.

b What do the ranges tell you about the weather for England during the week?

FM 3 Over a three-week period, the school tuck shop took the following amounts.

	Monday	Tuesday	Wednesday	Thursday	Friday
Week 1	£32	£29	£36	£30	£28
Week 2	£34	£33	£25	£28	£20
Week 3	£35	£34	£31	£33	£32

a Calculate the mean amount taken each week.

b Find the range for each week.

c What can you say about the total amounts taken for each of the three weeks?

4 In a womens' golf tournament, the club chairperson had to choose either Sheila or Fay to play in the first round. In the previous eight rounds, their scores were as follows.

Sheila's scores: 75, 92, 80, 73, 72, 88, 86, 90

Fay's scores: 80, 87, 85, 76, 85, 79, 84, 88

a Calculate the mean score for each golfer.

b Find the range for each golfer.

AU c Which golfer would you choose to play in the tournament? Explain why.

HINTS AND TIPS

The best person to choose may not be the one with the biggest mean but could be the most consistent player.

5 Dan has a choice of two buses to get to school: Number 50 or Number 63. Over a month, he kept a record of the number of minutes each bus was late when it set off from his home bus stop.

No. 50: 4, 2, 0, 6, 4, 8, 8, 6, 3, 9

No. 63: 3, 4, 0, 10, 3, 5, 13, 1, 0, 1

a For each bus, calculate the mean number of minutes late.

b Find the range for each bus.

AU c Which bus would you advise Dan to catch? Give a reason for your answer.

E

PS **6** The table gives the ages and heights of 10 children.

Name	Age (years)	Height (cm)
Billy	9	121
Isaac	4	73
Lilla	8	93
Lewis	10	118
Evie	3	66
Andrew	6	82
Oliver	4	78
Beatrice	2	69
Isambard	9	87
Chloe	7	82

a Chloe is having a party. She wants to invite as many children as possible but does not want the range of ages to be more than 5. Who will she invite?

b This is a sign at a theme park:

You have to be taller than … cm

and

shorter than … cm to go on this ride

Isaac is the shortest person who can go on the ride and Isambard is the tallest.

What are the smallest and largest missing values on the sign?

AU **7** **a** The age range of a school quiz team is 20 years and the mean age is 34. Who would you expect to be in this team? Explain your answer.

b Another team has an average age of $15\frac{1}{2}$ and a range of 1. Who would you expect to be in this team? Explain your answer.

ACTIVITY

Your time is up

You are going to find out how good you are at estimating 1 minute.

You need a stopwatch and a calculator.

This is a group activity. One person in the group acts as a timekeeper, says 'Start' and starts the stopwatch.

When someone thinks 1 minute has passed, they say 'Stop', and the timekeeper writes down the actual time, in seconds, that has passed. The timekeeper should try to record everyone's estimate.

Repeat the activity, with every member of the group taking a turn as the timekeeper.

Collate all the times and, from the data, find the mean (to the nearest second) and the range.

- How close is the mean to 1 minute?

- Why is the range useful?

- What strategies did people use to estimate 1 minute?

Repeat the activity for estimating different times, for example, 30 seconds or 2 minutes.

Write a brief report on what you find out about people's ability to estimate time.

Which average to use

This section will show you how to:
- understand the advantages and disadvantages of each type of average and decide which one to use in different situations

Key words
appropriate
extreme values
representative

An average must be truly **representative** of a set of data. So, when you have to find an average, it is crucial to choose the **appropriate** type of average for this particular set of data.

If you use the wrong average, your results will be distorted and give misleading information.

This table, which compares the advantages and disadvantages of each type of average, will help you to make the correct decision.

	Mode	Median	Mean
Advantages	Very easy to find Not affected by **extreme values** Can be used for non-numerical data	Easy to find for ungrouped data Not affected by extreme values	Easy to find Uses all the values The total for a given number of values can be calculated from it
Disadvantages	Does not use all the values May not exist	Does not use all the values Often not understood	Extreme values can distort it Has to be calculated
Use for	Non-numerical data Finding the most likely value	Data with extreme values	Data with values that are spread in a balanced way

EXERCISE 6E

1 The ages of the members of a hockey team were:

29 26 21 24 26 28 35 23 29 28 29

a Give:

   i the modal age   **ii** the median age   **iii** the mean age.

b What is the range of the ages?

2 **a** For each set of data, find the mode, the median and the mean.

   i 6, 10, 3, 4, 3, 6, 2, 9, 3, 4   **ii** 6, 8, 6, 10, 6, 9, 6, 10, 6, 8

   iii 7, 4, 5, 3, 28, 8, 2, 4, 10, 9

AU **b** For each set of data, decide which average is the best one to use and give a reason.

3 A newsagent sold the following numbers of copies of *The Evening Star* on 12 consecutive evenings during a promotion exercise organised by the newspaper's publisher.

65 73 75 86 90 112 92 87 77 73 68 62

a Find the mode, the median and the mean for the sales.

AU **b** The newsagent had to report the average sale to the publisher after the promotion. Which of the three averages would you advise the newsagent to use? Explain why.

4 The mean age of a group of 10 young people was 15.

a What do all their ages add up to?

b What will be their mean age in five years' time?

5 **a** Find the median of each list below.

i 2, 4, 6, 7, 9

ii 12, 14, 16, 17, 19

iii 22, 24, 26, 27, 29

iv 52, 54, 56, 57, 59

v 92, 94, 96, 97, 99

b What do you notice about the lists and your answers?

c Use your answer above to help find the medians of the following lists.

i 132, 134, 136, 137, 139

ii 577, 576, 572, 574, 579

iii 431, 438, 439, 432, 435

iv 855, 859, 856, 851, 857

d Find the mean of each of the sets of numbers in part **a**.

AU **6** Decide which average you would use for each of the following. Give a reason for your answer.

a The average mark in an examination

b The average pocket money for a group of 16-year-old students

c The average shoe size for all the girls in Year 10

d The average height for all the artistes on tour with a circus

e The average hair colour for students in your school

f The average weight of all newborn babies in a hospital's maternity ward.

7 A pack of matches consisted of 12 boxes. The contents of each box were counted as:

34 31 29 35 33 30 31 28 29 35 32 31

On the box it stated 'Average contents 32 matches'. Is this correct?

8 A firm showed the annual salaries for its employees as:

Chairman	£83 000
Managing director	£65 000
Floor manager	£34 000
Skilled worker 1	£28 000
Skilled worker 2	£28 000
Machinist	£20 000
Computer engineer	£20 000
Secretary	£20 000
Office junior	£8 000

a Give:

    i the modal salary   **ii** the median salary   **iii** the mean salary.

b The management suggested a pay rise of 6% for all employees. The shopfloor workers suggested a pay rise of £1500 for all employees.

    i One of the suggestions would cause problems for the firm. Which one is that and why?

    ii What difference would each suggestion make to the modal, median and mean salaries?

AU 9 Mr Brennan, a caring maths teacher, told each student their test mark and only gave the test statistics to the whole class. He gave the class the modal mark, the median mark and the mean mark.

a Which average would tell a student whether they were in the top half or the bottom half of the class?

b Which average tells the students nothing really?

c Which average allows a student to gauge how well they have done compared with everyone else?

FM 10 Three players were hoping to be chosen for the basketball team.

The following table shows their scores in the last few games they played.

Tom	16, 10, 12, 10, 13, 8, 10
David	16, 8, 15, 25, 8
Mohaned	15, 2, 15, 3, 5

The teacher said they would be chosen by their best average score.

Which average would each boy want to be chosen by?

PS 11 **a** Find five numbers that have **both** the properties below:

- a range of 5
- a mean of 5.

b Find five numbers that have **all** the properties below:

- a range of 5
- a median of 5
- a mean of 5.

AU 12 What is the average pay at a factory with 10 employees?

The boss said: "£43 295"
A worker said: "£18 210"

They were both correct.
Explain how this can be.

PS 13 A list of nine numbers has a mean of 7.6. What number must be added to the list to give a new mean of 8?

PS 14 A dance group of 17 teenagers had a mean weight of 44.5 kg. To enter a competition there needed to be 18 teenagers with an average weight of 44.4 kg or less. What is the maximum weight that the eighteenth person must be?

6.6 Frequency tables

This section will show you how to:
- revise finding the mode and median from a frequency table
- learn how to calculate the mean from a frequency table

Key word
frequency table

When a lot of information has been gathered, it is often convenient to put it together in a **frequency table**. From this table you can then find the values of the three averages and the range.

EXAMPLE 11

A survey was done on the number of people in each car leaving the Meadowhall Shopping Centre, in Sheffield. The results are summarised in the table below.

Number of people in each car	1	2	3	4	5	6
Frequency	45	198	121	76	52	13

For the number of people in a car, calculate:

  a   the mode   **b**   the median   **c**   the mean.

a   The modal number of people in a car is easy to spot. It is the number with the largest frequency, which is 198. Hence, the modal number of people in a car is 2.

b   The median number of people in a car is found by working out where the middle of the set of numbers is located. First, add up frequencies to get the total number of cars surveyed, which comes to 505. Next, calculate the middle position.

$$(505 + 1) \div 2 = 253$$

Now add the frequencies across the table to find which group contains the 253rd item. The 243rd item is the end of the group with 2 in a car. Therefore, the 253rd item must be in the group with 3 in a car. Hence, the median number of people in a car is 3.

c   To calculate the mean number of people in a car, multiply the number of people in the car by the frequency. This is best done in an extra column. Add these to find the total number of people and divide by the total frequency (the number of cars surveyed).

Number in car	Frequency	Number in these cars
1	45	$1 \times 45 = 45$
2	198	$2 \times 198 = 396$
3	121	$3 \times 121 = 363$
4	76	$4 \times 76 = 304$
5	52	$5 \times 52 = 260$
6	13	$6 \times 13 = 78$
Totals	505	1446

Hence, the mean number of people in a car is $1446 \div 505 = 2.9$ (to 1 decimal place).

Using your calculator

The previous example can also be done by using the statistical mode that is available on some calculators. However, not all calculators are the same, so you will have either to read your instruction manual or experiment with the statistical keys on your calculator.

You may find one labelled:

    DATA or M+ or Σ+ or $\bar{x}$, where $\bar{x}$ is printed in blue.

Try the following key strokes:

    1 × 4 5 DATA   2 × 1 9 8 DATA … 6 × 1 3 DATA $\bar{x}$

EXERCISE 6F

D

1 Find **i** the mode, **ii** the median and **iii** the mean from each frequency table below.

a A survey of the shoe sizes of all the Year 10 boys in a school gave these results.

Shoe size	4	5	6	7	8	9	10
Number of students	12	30	34	35	23	8	3

b A survey of the number of eggs laid by hens over a period of one week gave these results.

Number of eggs	0	1	2	3	4	5	6
Frequency	6	8	15	35	48	37	12

c This is a record of the number of babies born each week over one year in a small maternity unit.

Number of babies	0	1	2	3	4	5	6	7	8	9	10	11	12	13	14
Frequency	1	1	1	2	2	2	3	5	9	8	6	4	5	2	1

d A school did a survey on how many times in a week students arrived late at school. These are the findings.

Number of times late	0	1	2	3	4	5
Frequency	481	34	23	15	3	4

2 A survey of the number of children in each family of a school's intake gave these results.

Number of children	1	2	3	4	5
Frequency	214	328	97	26	3

a Assuming each child at the school is shown in the data, how many children are at the school?

b Calculate the mean number of children in a family.

c How many families have this mean number of children?

FM **d** How many families would consider themselves average from this survey?

FM **3** A dentist kept records of how many teeth he extracted from his patients.

In 1989 he extracted 598 teeth from 271 patients.

In 1999 he extracted 332 teeth from 196 patients.

In 2009 he extracted 374 teeth from 288 patients.

a Calculate the average number of teeth taken from each patient in each year.

AU **b** Explain why you think the average number of teeth extracted falls each year.

4 One hundred cases of apples delivered to a supermarket were inspected and the numbers of bad apples were recorded.

Bad apples	0	1	2	3	4	5	6	7	8	9
Frequency	52	29	9	3	2	1	3	0	0	1

Give:

a the modal number of bad apples per case

b the mean number of bad apples per case.

5 Two dice are thrown together 60 times. The sums of the scores are shown below.

Score	2	3	4	5	6	7	8	9	10	11	12
Frequency	1	2	6	9	12	15	6	5	2	1	1

Find: **a** the modal score **b** the median score **c** the mean score.

6 During a one-month period, the number of days off taken by 100 workers in a factory were noted as follows.

Number of days off	0	1	2	3	4
Number of workers	35	42	16	4	3

Calculate:

a the modal number of days off

b the median number of days off

c the mean number of days off.

7 Two friends often played golf together. They recorded their scores for each hole over the last five games to compare who was more consistent and who was the better player. Their results were summarised in the following table.

No. of shots to hole ball	1	2	3	4	5	6	7	8	9
Roger	0	0	0	14	37	27	12	0	0
Brian	5	12	15	18	14	8	8	8	2

a What is the modal score for each player?

b What is the range of scores for each player?

c What is the median score for each player?

d What is the mean score for each player?

AU **e** Which player is the more consistent and why?

AU **f** Who would you say is the better player and why?

D

PS 8 A tea stain on a newspaper removed four numbers from the following frequency table of goals scored in 40 league football matches one weekend.

Goals	0	1	2		5
Frequency	4	6	9		3

The mean number of goals scored is 2.4.

What could the missing four numbers be?

AU 9 Talera made day trips to Manchester frequently during a year.

The table shows how many days in a week she travelled.

Days	0	1	2	3	4	5
Frequency	17	2	4	13	15	1

Explain how you would find the median number of days Talera travelled in a week to Manchester.

6.7 Grouped data

This section will show you how to:
- identify the modal class
- calculate an estimate of the mean from a grouped table

Key words
estimated
grouped data
mean
modal class

Sometimes the information you are given is grouped in some way (called **grouped data**), as in Example 12, which shows the range of weekly pocket money given to Year 12 students in a particular class.

Normally, grouped tables use continuous data, which is data that can have any value within a range of values, for example, height, weight, time, area and capacity. In these situations, the **mean** can only be **estimated** as you do not have all the information.

Discrete data is data that consists of separate numbers, for example, goals scored, marks in a test, number of children and shoe sizes.

In both cases, when using a grouped table to estimate the mean, first find the midpoint of the interval by adding the two end-values and then dividing by two.

EXAMPLE 12

Pocket money, p (£)	$0 < p \leqslant 1$	$1 < p \leqslant 2$	$2 < p \leqslant 3$	$3 < p \leqslant 4$	$4 < p \leqslant 5$
No. of students	2	5	5	9	15

a Write down the **modal class**.

b Calculate an estimate of the mean weekly pocket money.

a The modal class is easy to pick out, since it is simply the one with the largest frequency. Here the modal class is £4 to £5.

b To estimate the mean, assume that each person in each class has the 'midpoint' amount, then build up the following table.

To find the midpoint value, the two end-values are added together and then divided by two.

Pocket money, p (£)	Frequency (f)	Midpoint (m)	$f \times m$
$0 < p \leqslant 1$	2	0.50	1.00
$1 < p \leqslant 2$	5	1.50	7.50
$2 < p \leqslant 3$	5	2.50	12.50
$3 < p \leqslant 4$	9	3.50	31.50
$4 < p \leqslant 5$	15	4.50	67.50
Totals	36		120

The estimated mean will be £120 ÷ 36 = £3.33 (rounded to the nearest penny).

Note the notation for the classes:

$0 < p \leqslant 1$ means any amount above 0p up to and including £1.

$1 < p \leqslant 2$ means any amount above £1 up to and including £2, and so on.

If you had written 0.01–1.00, 1.01–2.00 and so on for the groups, then the midpoints would have been 0.505, 1.505 and so on. This would not have had a significant effect on the final answer as it is only an estimate.

Note that you **cannot** find the **median** from a grouped table as you do not know the actual values.

You also **cannot** find the **range** but you can say what limits there are. In the table above the smallest possible value for pocket money in the first group is 1p (this is unlikely but it cannot be 0 as the range is $0 < p \leqslant 1$) and the largest is £1. In the last group the smallest possible value is £4.01 and the largest is £5. This means the range must be between £5 – 1p = £4.99 and £4.01 – £1 = £3.01.

EXERCISE 6G

1 For each table of values given below, find:

   i the modal group

   ii an estimate for the mean.

HINTS AND TIPS

When you copy the tables, draw them vertically as in Example 12.

a

x	$0 < x \leqslant 10$	$10 < x \leqslant 20$	$20 < x \leqslant 30$	$30 < x \leqslant 40$	$40 < x \leqslant 50$
Frequency	4	6	11	17	9

b

y	$0 < y \leqslant 100$	$100 < y \leqslant 200$	$200 < y \leqslant 300$	$300 < y \leqslant 400$	$400 < y \leqslant 500$	$500 < x \leqslant 600$
Frequency	95	56	32	21	9	3

c

z	$0 < z \leqslant 5$	$5 < z \leqslant 10$	$10 < z \leqslant 15$	$15 < z \leqslant 20$
Frequency	16	27	19	13

d

Weeks	1–3	4–6	7–9	10–12	13–15
Frequency	5	8	14	10	7

2 Jason brought 100 pebbles back from the beach and weighed them all, recording each weight to the nearest gram. His results are summarised in the table below.

Weight, w (g)	$40 < w \leqslant 60$	$60 < w \leqslant 80$	$80 < w \leqslant 100$
Frequency	5	9	22

Weight, w (g)	$100 < w \leqslant 120$	$120 < w \leqslant 140$	$140 < w \leqslant 160$
Frequency	27	26	11

Find:

a the modal weight of the pebbles

b an estimate of the total weight of all the pebbles

c an estimate of the mean weight of the pebbles.

3 A gardener measured the heights of all his daffodils to the nearest centimetre and summarised his results as follows.

Height (cm)	10–14	15–18	19–22	23–26	27–40
Frequency	21	57	65	52	12

a How many daffodils did the gardener have?

b What is the modal height of the daffodils?

c What is the estimated mean height of the daffodils?

FM 4 A survey was created to see how quickly the AA attended calls that were not on a motorway. The following table summarises the results.

Time (min)	1–15	16–30	31–45	46–60	61–75	76–90	91–105
Frequency	2	23	48	31	27	18	11

a How many calls were used in the survey?

b Estimate the mean time taken per call.

c Which average would the AA use for the average call-out time?

d What percentage of calls do the AA get to within the hour?

5 One hundred light bulbs were tested by their manufacturer to see whether the average life-span of the manufacturer's bulbs was over 200 hours. The following table summarises the results.

Life span, h (hours)	$150 < h \leqslant 175$	$175 < h \leqslant 200$	$200 < h \leqslant 225$	$225 < h \leqslant 250$	$250 < h \leqslant 275$
Frequency	24	45	18	10	3

a What is the modal length of time a bulb lasts?

b What percentage of bulbs last longer than 200 hours?

c Estimate the mean life-span of the light bulbs.

d Do you think the test shows that the average life-span is over 200 hours? Fully explain your answer.

FM 6
AU Three supermarkets each claimed to have the lowest average price increase over the year. The following table summarises their price increases.

Price increase (p)	1–5	6–10	11–15	16–20	21–25	26–30	31–35
Soundbuy	4	10	14	23	19	8	2
Springfields	5	11	12	19	25	9	6
Setco	3	8	15	31	21	7	3

Using their average price increases, make a comparison of the supermarkets and write a report on which supermarket, in your opinion, has the lowest price increases over the year. Do not forget to justify your answers.

FM 7
AU
The table shows the distances run, over a month, by an athlete who is training for a marathon.

Distance, d (miles)	$0 < d \leqslant 5$	$5 < d \leqslant 10$	$10 < d \leqslant 15$	$15 < d \leqslant 20$	$20 < d \leqslant 25$
Frequency	3	8	13	5	2

a A marathon is 26.2 miles. It is recommended that an athlete's daily average mileage should be at least a third of the distance of the race for which they are training. Is this athlete doing enough training?

b The athlete records the times of some runs and calculates that her average pace for all runs is $6\frac{1}{2}$ minutes to a mile. Explain why she is wrong to expect a finishing time for the marathon of $26.2 \times 6\frac{1}{2}$ minutes ≈ 170 minutes.

c The runner claims that the difference in length between her shortest and longest run is 21 miles. Could this be correct? Explain your answer.

PS 8 The table shows the points scored in a general-knowledge competition by all the players.

Points	0–9	10–19	20–29	30–39	40–49
Frequency	8	5	10	5	2

Helen noticed that two numbers were the wrong way round and that this made a difference of 1.7 to the arithmetic mean.

Which two numbers were the wrong way round?

AU 9 The profit made each week by a charity shop is shown in the table below.

Profit	£0–£500	£501–£1000	£1001–£1500	£1501–£2000
Frequency	15	26	8	3

Explain how you would estimate the mean profit made each week.

AU 10 The table shows the number of members of 100 football clubs.

Members	20–29	30–39	40–49	50–59	60–69
Frequency	16	34	27	18	5

a Roger claims that the median number of members is 39.5.

Is he correct? Explain your answer.

b He also says that the range of the number of members is 34.

Could he be correct? Explain your answer.

Frequency polygons

This section will show you how to:

- draw frequency polygons for discrete and continuous data

Key words

continuous data
discrete data
frequency polygon

To help people understand it, statistical information is often presented in pictorial or diagrammatic form, which includes the pie chart, the line graph, the bar chart and the stem-and-leaf diagram. These were covered in Chapter 5. Another method of showing data is by **frequency polygons**.

Frequency polygons can be used to represent both ungrouped data and grouped data, as shown in Example 13 and Example 14 respectively and are appropriate for both **discrete data** and **continuous data**.

Frequency polygons show the shapes of distributions and can be used to compare distributions.

EXAMPLE 13

No. of children	0	1	2	3	4	5
Frequency	12	23	36	28	16	11

This is the frequency polygon for the ungrouped data in the table.

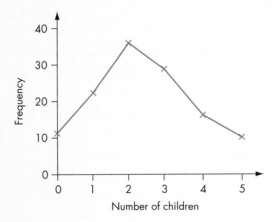

Note:

- The coordinates are plotted from the ordered pairs in the table.

- The polygon is completed by joining up the plotted points with straight lines.

EXAMPLE 14

Weight, w (kg)	$0 < w \leqslant 5$	$5 < w \leqslant 10$	$10 < w \leqslant 15$
Frequency	4	13	25

Weight, w (kg)	$15 < w \leqslant 20$	$20 < w \leqslant 25$	$25 < w \leqslant 30$
Frequency	32	17	9

This is the frequency polygon for the grouped data in the table.

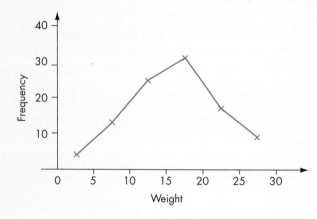

Note:

- The midpoint of each group is used, just as it was in estimating the mean.

- The ordered pairs of midpoints with frequency are plotted, namely:

    (2.5, 4), (7.5, 13), (12.5, 25), (17.5, 32), (22.5, 17), (27.5, 9)

- The polygon should be left like this. Any lines you draw before and after this have no meaning.

If you only have a frequency polygon you can work out the mean from the information on the graph.

EXAMPLE 15

The frequency polygon shows the lengths of 50 courgettes.

Work out the mean length.

The points are plotted at the midpoints so the mean is

$(7 \times 92.5 + 10 \times 97.5 + 16 \times 102.5 + 12 \times 107.5 + 5 \times 112.5) \div 50$

$= 102.3$ mm

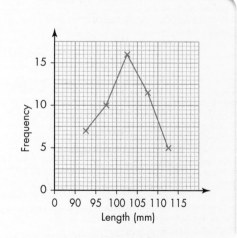

EXERCISE 6H

1 The following table shows how many students were absent from one particular class throughout the year.

Students absent	1	2	3	4	5
Frequency	48	32	12	3	1

a Draw a frequency polygon to illustrate the data.

b Estimate the mean number of absences each lesson.

2 The table below shows the number of goals scored by a hockey team in one season.

Goals	1	2	3	4	5
Frequency	3	9	7	5	2

a Draw the frequency polygon for this data.

b Estimate the mean number of goals scored per game this season.

3 After a spelling test, all the results were collated for girls and boys as below.

Number correct	1–4	5–8	9–12	13–16	17–20
Boys	3	7	21	26	15
Girls	4	8	17	23	20

a Draw frequency polygons to illustrate the differences between the boys' scores and the girls' scores.

b Estimate the mean score for boys and girls separately, and comment on the results.

> **HINTS AND TIPS**
>
> The highest point of the frequency polygon is the modal value.

4 A doctor was concerned at the length of time her patients had to wait to see her when they came to the morning surgery. The survey she did gave her the following results.

Time, m (min)	$0 < m \leq 10$	$10 < m \leq 20$	$20 < m \leq 30$
Monday	5	8	17
Tuesday	9	8	16
Wednesday	7	6	18

Time, m (min)	$30 < m \leq 40$	$40 < m \leq 50$	$50 < m \leq 60$
Monday	9	7	4
Tuesday	3	2	1
Wednesday	2	1	1

a Using the same pair of axes, draw a frequency polygon for each day.

b What is the average amount of time spent waiting each day?

c Why might the average times for each day be different?

5 The frequency polygon shows the amounts of money spent in a corner shop by the first 40 customers one morning.

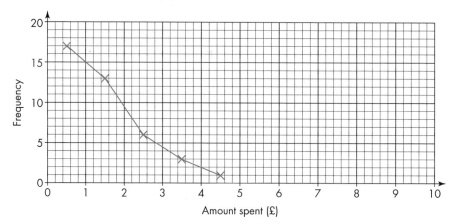

Amount spent (£)

a i Use the frequency polygon to complete the table for the amounts spent by the first 40 customers.

Amount spent, m (£)	$0 < m \leqslant 1$	$1 < m \leqslant 2$	$2 < m \leqslant 3$	$3 < m \leqslant 4$	$4 < m \leqslant 5$
Frequency					

ii Work out the mean amount of money spent by these 40 customers.

b Mid-morning another 40 customers visit the shop and the shopkeeper records the amounts they spend. The table below shows the data.

Amount spent, m (£)	$0 < m \leqslant 2$	$2 < m \leqslant 4$	$4 < m \leqslant 6$	$6 < m \leqslant 8$	$8 < m \leqslant 10$
Frequency	3	5	18	10	4

i Copy the graph above and draw the frequency polygon to show this data.

ii Calculate the mean amount spent by the 40 mid-morning customers.

c Comment on the differences between the frequency polygons and the average amounts spent by the different groups of customers.

6 The frequency polygon shows the ages of 50 staff in a school.

a Draw up a grouped table to show the data.

b Calculate an estimate of the mean age.

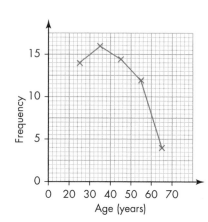

Age (years)

PS 7 The frequency polygon shows the lengths of time that students spent on homework one weekend.

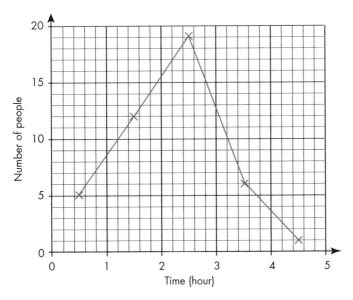

Calculate an estimate of the mean time spent on homework by the students.

AU 8 The frequency polygon shows the times that a number of people waited at a Post Office before being served one morning.

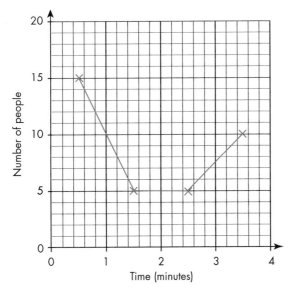

Julie said: "Most people spent 30 seconds waiting."

Explain why this might be wrong.

GRADE BOOSTER

G You can find the mode and median from a list of data

F You can find the range of a set of data and find the mean of a small set of data

E You can find the median and range from a stem-and-leaf diagram

D You can find the mean from a frequency table of discrete data and also draw a frequency polygon for such data

C You can find an estimate of the mean from a grouped table of continuous data and draw a frequency polygon for continuous data

What you should know now

● How to find the range, mode, median and mean of sets of discrete data

● Which average to use in different situations

● How to find the modal class and an estimated mean for continuous data

● How to draw frequency polygons for discrete and continuous data

1 The table shows how many children there were in each family of form 7J.

Number of children	Frequency
1	5
2	11
3	5
4	2
5	2

a   How many children were in the form?

b   What is the modal number of children per family?

c   What is the median number of children per family?

d   What is the mean number of children per family?

2 Find: a the mode   b the median of:

6, 6, 6, 8, 9, 10, 11, 12, 13

3 The marks of ten people in a maths test are shown.

10   15   12   13   9   20   16   11   4   15

Work out the range of these marks.

4 The temperature, in degrees Celsius, at midday at a holiday camp on six summer days was recorded:

20   16   24   29   20   17

Work out the mean temperature at midday for these six days.

5 The number of points scored by the Tigers in the last 10 rugby matches is listed.

38   16   18   76   32
16   16   40   60   42

a   Write down the mode of these scores.   (1)

b   Calculate the mean of these scores.   (3)

c   Calculate the range of these scores.   (1)

(Total 5 marks)

AQA, June 2007, Module 1 Foundation, Question 2

6 Calculate the mean of these numbers.

34   27   38   27   45   17   (3)

(Total 3 marks)

AQA, June 2008, Paper 2 Foundation, Question 12

7 The table shows the ages of 40 people in a village.

Age, x (years)	Frequency
$0 < x \leqslant 20$	4
$20 < x \leqslant 40$	12
$40 < x \leqslant 60$	16
$60 < x \leqslant 80$	6
$80 < x \leqslant 100$	2

a   How many people are more than 60 years old?   (1)

b   Write down the modal class for the ages of the people.   (1)

c   Draw a frequency polygon to represent this data.   (2)

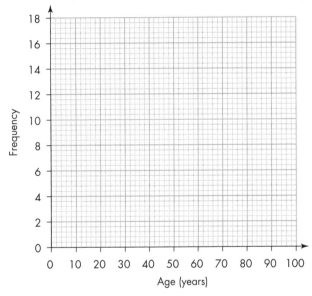

(Total 4 marks)

AQA, November 2008, Paper 1 Foundation, Question 22

8 a   Work out:

  i   the mean   ii   the range of:

  61, 63, 61, 86, 78, 75, 80, 68, 84 and 84.

b   Fred wants to plant a conifer hedge. At the local garden centre he looks at 10 plants from two different varieties of conifer.

All the plants have been growing for six months.

The Sprucy Pine plants have a mean height of 74 cm and a range of 25 cm.

The Evergreen plants have a mean height of 52 cm and a range of 5 cm.

i Give one reason why Fred might decide to plant a hedge of Sprucy Pine trees.

ii Give one reason why Fred might decide to plant a hedge of Evergreen trees.

9 The stem-and leaf-diagram shows the number of packages 15 drivers delivered.

Key 3 | 5 means 35 packages

```
3 | 5  7
4 | 1  3  8  8
5 | 0  2  5  6  7  9
6 | 6  9
7 | 2
```

a What is the range of the packets delivered?

b What is the median of the packets delivered?

c What is the mode of the packets delivered?

10 A rounders coach records the number of rounders the players in her squad scored in a season.

All the players scored at least once.

She shows the data in a stem-and-leaf diagram.

Key | 2 | 7 represents 27 rounders scored

```
0 | 1  1  2  7
1 | 2  5  5
2 | 3  7
3 | 6
4 | 0
5 | 0  9
```

a What is the range of the data? (1)

b How many players are there in the squad? (1)

c What is the median number of rounders scored? (1)

d Calculate the mean number of rounders scored. (3)

(Total 6 marks)

AQA, June 2006, Paper 2 Foundation, Question 21

11 The stem-and-leaf diagram shows the marks of 15 students in a Science test.

Key | 2 | 8 represents a mark of 28

```
1 | 0
2 | 8  8  9  9
3 | 1  2  3  7  8  9
4 | 5  8  9
5 | 4
```

a What is the range of the marks? (1)

b What is the median mark? (1)

c Explain why the median is a suitable average to use. (1)

(Total 3 marks)

AQA, May 2008, Paper 1 Foundation, Question 22

12 The number of goals scored in 15 hockey matches is shown in the table.

Number of goals	Number of matches
1	2
3	1
5	5
6	3
9	4

Calculate the mean number of goals scored. (3)

(Total 3 marks)

AQA, June 2005, Paper 2 Foundation, Question 23

13 The numbers of people in 50 cars are recorded.

Number of people	Frequency
1	24
2	13
3	8
4	4
5	1

Calculate the mean number of people per car.

14 The table shows the distances travelled to work by 40 office workers.

Distance travelled, d (km)	Frequency
$0 < d \leqslant 2$	10
$2 < d \leqslant 4$	16
$4 < d \leqslant 6$	8
$6 < d \leqslant 8$	5
$8 < d \leqslant 10$	1

Calculate an estimate of the mean distance travelled to work by these office workers.

Worked Examination Questions

1 The weights, in kilograms, of a rowing boat crew are:

91, 81, 89, 91, 91, 85, 89, 38

    a Work out:

        i the modal weight **ii** the median weight **iii** the range of the weights **iv** their mean weight.

AU **b** Which of the averages best describes the data? Explain your answer.

a **i** The modal weight is 91 kg.

> Look for the weight that occurs most frequently.
> This is worth 1 mark.

    ii The median weight is 89 kg.

> Arrange the weights in order of size: 38, 81, 85, 89, 89, 91, 91, 91. The middle two are 89. This worth 1 mark.

    iii The range is 53 kg.

> Highest value – lowest value = 91 – 38. This is worth 1 mark.

    iv The mean weight =
655 ÷ 8 = 81.875

> Add up all the weights and divide the total by the number of weights (8). You get 1 mark for method and 1 mark for accuracy.

(5 marks)

b The mean as it is the only average that takes into account all the weights.

> The correct answer is worth 1 mark.

(1 mark)   (**Total:** 6 marks)

2 The mean speed of each member of a cycling club over a long-distance race was recorded and a frequency polygon was drawn.

PS Work out an estimate of the mean speed for the whole club.

Create a grouped frequency table.

Speed, s (mph)	Frequency, f	Midpoint, m	f × m
5–10	12	7.5	90
10–15	23	12.5	287.5
15–20	34	17.5	595
20–25	24	22.5	540
25–30	5	27.5	137.5
30–35	2	32.5	65
	100		1715

> The table must include the midpoint values, the frequency and f × m.
>
> You get 1 mark for giving the frequencies and showing a total.
>
> You get 1 mark for attempting to work out f × m and showing a total.

An estimate of the mean is 1715 ÷ 100 = 17.15 mph

> You get 1 mark for dividing the total f × m by the total f and 1 mark for the correct answer.

(**Total:** 4 marks)

Averages are used to compare data and make statements about sets of data. They are used every day for a wide variety of purposes, from describing the weather to analysing the economy. In this activity averages will be applied to a sporting event.

A fishing competition

Kath's dad ran a fishing competition on the river Avon during the summer.

Kath kept an accurate record of the data collected during the competition.

This table shows a summary of Kath's records, collected from all of the anglers in the competition, for the first four weeks of July.

	Week 1	Week 2	Week 3	Week 4	Week 5
Mean number of fish caught	12.1	12.3	12.2	11.8	
Mean time spent fishing (hrs)	5.6	6.1	5.8	5.4	
Mean weight of fish caught (g)	1576	1728	1635	1437	
Mean length of longest fish caught (cm)	21.7	20.6	21.6	21.9	

In the last week of July, Kath again collected data from the anglers. She did not have time to add this data to her table.

The following tables show all the data that she collected in Week 5.

Number of fish caught	Frequency
0 – 5	6
6 – 10	11
11 – 15	8
16 – 20	5

Time spent fishing (hrs)	Frequency
0 – 4	2
4 hrs 1 min – 5	14
5 hrs 1 min – 6	6
6 hrs 1 min – 7	8

Weight of fish caught (g)	Frequency
0 – 500	1
501 – 1000	8
1001 – 1500	18
1501 – 2000	3

Longest fish caught (cm)	Frequency
0 – 10	2
11 – 15	6
16 – 20	12
21 – 25	10

Your task

Kath must do a presentation at the end of the month to summarise the fishing competition. Help her to write her presentation.

The presentation must include the following:

- The data for Week 5 inserted into the main table
- A graph to represent the data for all five weeks
- Statements to compare the five weeks of the competition
- A description of the 'average angler'.

Getting started

Start by thinking about how averages are calculated. What do the mean, median, mode and range show when applied to sets of data? How do they apply to frequency tables?

What are the mean, median, mode and range for this set of data?

3, 4, 8, 3, 2, 4, 5, 3, 4, 6, 8, 4, 2, 9, 1

Now think about the averages that you will need in your presentation and how these averages are best represented. Use your ideas in your presentation.

Why this chapter matters

Chance is a part of everyday life. Judgements are frequently made based on probability. For example,
- there is an 80% chance that United will win the game tomorrow
- there is a 40% chance of rain tomorrow
- she has a 50–50 chance of having a baby girl
- there is a 10% chance of the bus being on time tonight.

Certain probabilities are given to certain events, although two people might give different probabilities to those same events because of their different views. For example, one person might not agree that there is an 80% chance of United winning the game. They might well say that there is only a 70% chance of United winning tomorrow. A lot depends on what that person believes or has experienced.

Chance may be taken into account for lots of different events, from the lottery to tomorrow's weather. Probability is a branch of mathematics that describes the chance of outcomes.

Probability originated from the study of games of chance, such as tossing a dice or spinning a roulette wheel.

Mathematicians in the 16th and 17th centuries started to think about the mathematics of chance in games. Probability theory, as a branch of mathematics, developed in the 17th century when French gamblers asked mathematicians Blaise Pascal and Pierre de Fermat for help in their gambling.

Now, in the 21st century, probability theory is used to control the flow of traffic through road systems (above) or the running of telephone exchanges (right), and to look at patterns of the spread of infections.

There are many other everyday applications and as you work through this chapter you will see how frequently the language of probability is used.

Chapter

7

Probability: Probability and events

This chapter will show you …

G how to use the the language of probability

F to **C** how to work out the probability of outcomes of events, using either theoretical models or experimental models

C how to predict outcomes, using theoretical models, and compare experimental and theoretical data

Visual overview

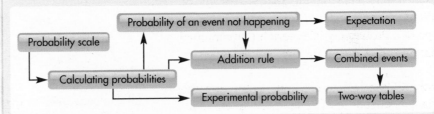

What you should already know

- How to add, subtract and cancel fractions **(KS3 level 4, GCSE grade F)**
- That outcomes of events cannot always be predicted and that the laws of chance apply to everyday events **(KS3 level 4, GCSE grade F)**
- How to list all the outcomes of an event in a systematic manner **(KS3 level 5, GCSE grade E)**

Quick check

1 Cancel the following fractions.

   a $\frac{6}{8}$ **b** $\frac{6}{36}$ **c** $\frac{3}{12}$ **d** $\frac{8}{10}$ **e** $\frac{6}{9}$ **f** $\frac{5}{20}$

2 Calculate the following.

   a $\frac{1}{8} + \frac{3}{8}$ **b** $\frac{5}{12} + \frac{3}{12}$ **c** $\frac{5}{36} + \frac{3}{36}$ **d** $\frac{2}{9} + \frac{1}{6}$ **e** $\frac{3}{5} + \frac{3}{20}$

3 Frank likes to wear brightly coloured hats and socks.

He has two hats, one is green and the other is yellow.
He has three pairs of socks, which are red, purple and pink.

Write down all the six possible combinations of hats and socks Frank could wear.

For example, he could wear a green hat and red socks.

This section will show you how to:
- use the probability scale and the basic language of probability

Key words
certain
chance
event
impossible
likely
outcome
probability
probability scale
unlikely

Almost daily, you hear somebody talking about the probability of whether this or that will happen. They usually use words such as '**chance**', 'likelihood' or 'risk' rather than 'probability'. For example:

"What is the likelihood of rain tomorrow?"
"What chance does she have of winning the 100 metre sprint"
"Is there a risk that his company will go bankrupt?"

You can give a value to the chance of any of these **outcomes** or **events** happening – and millions of others, as well. This value is called the **probability**.

It is true that some things are certain to happen and that some things cannot happen; that is, the chance of something happening can be anywhere between **impossible** and **certain**. This situation is represented on a sliding scale called the **probability scale**, as shown below.

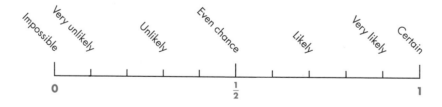

Note: All probabilities lie somewhere in the range of **0** to **1**.

An outcome or an event that cannot happen (is impossible) has a probability of 0.
For example, the probability that pigs will fly is 0.

An outcome or an event that is certain to happen has a probability of 1.
For example, the probability that the sun will rise tomorrow is 1.

FM Functional Maths **AU** (AO2) Assessing Understanding **PS** (AO3) Problem Solving

EXAMPLE 1

Put arrows on the probability scale to show the probability of each of the outcomes of these events.

a You will get a head when throwing a coin.

b You will get a six when throwing a dice.

c You will have maths homework this week.

a This outcome is an even chance. (Commonly described as a fifty-fifty chance.)

b This outcome is fairly **unlikely**.

c This outcome is **likely**.

The arrows show the approximate probabilities on the probability scale.

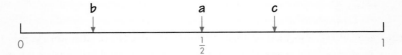

EXERCISE 7A

1 State whether each of the following events is impossible, very unlikely, unlikely, even chance, likely, very likely or certain.

a Picking out a Heart from a well-shuffled pack of cards.

b Christmas Day being on the 25th December.

c Someone in your class is left-handed.

d You will live to be 100.

e A score of seven is obtained when throwing a dice.

f You will watch some TV this evening.

g A new-born baby will be a girl.

2 Draw a probability scale and put an arrow to show the approximate probability of each of the following events happening.

a The next car you see will have been made in Europe.

b A person in your class will have been born in the 20th century.

c It will rain tomorrow.

d In the next Olympic Games, someone will run the 1500 m race in 3 minutes.

e During this week, you will have chips with a meal.

G

F

3 Draw a probability scale and mark an arrow to show the approximate probability of each event.

    a The next person to come into the room will be male.

    b The person sitting next to you in mathematics is over 16 years old.

    c Someone in the class will have mobile phone.

4 Give two events of your own for which you think the probability of an outcome is as follows

    a impossible   **b** very unlikely   **c** unlikely

    d evens   **e** likely   **f** very likely

    g certain.

5 In August, Janine and her family are going on holiday to Corsica, a French island off the south coast of France. She wonders about the chance of various events happening.

For each of the following, state whether the answer is likely to be:

    impossible, very unlikely, unlikely, even chance, likely, very likely, certain.

    a It being sunny most days.

    b The aeroplane taking off smoothly.

    c Her ears popping during the landing (they usually do).

    d Hearing most people speak English on the plane.

    e Hearing someone speak French in the resort they are going to.

    f It raining in France when they arrive.

    g Being able to wear her bikini while on holiday.

    h The sea being warm when she swims.

    i Her becoming the President of France.

    j Her meeting her future husband while there.

    k Her getting sunburnt if she doesn't put sun cream on but lies in the sun all day.

    l Seeing the cost of meals in pounds in restaurants.

AU 6 "I have bought five lottery tickets this week, so I have a good chance of winning."

Explain what is wrong with this statement.

This section will show you how to:
- calculate the probability of outcomes of events

Key words

equally likely

event

outcome

probability fraction

random

In question 2 of Exercise 7A, you may have had difficulty in knowing exactly where to put some of the arrows on the probability scale. It would have been easier for you if each result of the **event** could have been given a value, from 0 to 1, to represent the probability for that result.

For some events, this can be done by first finding all the possible results, or **outcomes**, for a particular event. For example, when you throw a coin there are two **equally likely** outcomes: heads or tails. If you want to calculate the probability of getting a head, there is only one outcome that is possible. So, you can say that there is a 1 in 2, or 1 out of 2, chance of getting a head. This is usually given as a **probability fraction**, namely $\frac{1}{2}$. So, you would write the event as:

$P(\text{head}) = \frac{1}{2}$

Probabilities can also be written as decimals or percentages, so that:

$P(\text{head}) = \frac{1}{2}$ or 0.5 or 50%

It is more usual to give probabilities as fractions in GCSE examinations but you will frequently come across probabilities given as percentages, for example, in the weather forecasts on TV.

The probability of an outcome is defined as:

$$P(\text{event}) = \frac{\text{number of ways the outcome can happen}}{\text{total number of possible outcomes}}$$

This definition always leads to a fraction, which should be cancelled to its simplest form.

Another probability term you will meet is at **random**. This means that the outcome cannot be predicted or affected by anyone.

EXAMPLE 2

A bag contains five red balls and three blue balls. A ball is taken out at random.

What is the probability that it is:

a red **b** blue **c** green?

Use the formula

$$P(\text{event}) = \frac{\text{number of ways the event can happen}}{\text{total number of possible outcomes}}$$

to work out these probabilities.

a There are five red balls out of a total of eight, so $P(\text{red}) = \frac{5}{8}$

b There are three blue balls out of a total of eight, so $P(\text{blue}) = \frac{3}{8}$

c There are no green balls, so this event is impossible: $P(\text{green}) = 0$

EXAMPLE 3

The spinner shown here is spun and the score on the side on which it lands is recorded.

What is the probability that the score is:

a 2
b odd
c less than 5?

a There are two 2s out of six sides, so $P(2) = \frac{2}{6} = \frac{1}{3}$

b There are four odd numbers, so $P(\text{odd}) = \frac{4}{6} = \frac{2}{3}$

c All of the numbers are less than 5, so this is a certain event.

$P(\text{less than 5}) = 1$

EXAMPLE 4

Bernice is always early, just on time or late for work.

The probability that she is early is 0.1, the probability she is just on time is 0.5.

What is the probability that she is late?

As all the possibilities are covered – that is 'early', 'on time' and 'late' – the total probability is 1. So,

$P(\text{early}) + P(\text{on time}) = 0.1 + 0.5 = 0.6$

So, the probability of Bernice being late is $1 - 0.6 = 0.4$.

EXERCISE 7B

1 What is the probability of each of the following events?

a Throwing a 2 with a fair, six-sided dice.

b Throwing a 6 with a fair, six-sided dice.

c Tossing a fair coin and getting a tail.

d Drawing a Queen from a pack of cards.

e Drawing a Heart from a pack of cards.

f Drawing a black card from a pack of cards.

g Throwing a 2 or a 6 with a fair, six-sided dice.

h Drawing a black Queen from a pack of cards.

i Drawing an Ace from a pack of cards.

j Throwing a 7 with a fair, six-sided dice.

HINTS AND TIPS

If an event is impossible, just write the probability as 0, not as a fraction such as $\frac{0}{6}$. If it is certain, write the probability as 1, not as a fraction such as $\frac{6}{6}$.

HINTS AND TIPS

Remember to cancel the fractions if possible.

2 What is the probability of each of the following events?

a Throwing an even number with a fair, six-sided dice.

b Throwing a prime number with a fair, six-sided dice.

c Getting a Heart or a Club from a pack of cards.

d Drawing the King of Hearts from a pack of cards.

e Drawing a picture card or an Ace from a pack of cards.

f Drawing the seven of Diamonds from a pack of cards.

3 A bag contains only blue balls. If I take one out at random, what is the probability of each of these outcomes?

a I get a black ball.

b I get a blue ball.

4 Number cards with the numbers 1 to 10 inclusive are placed in a hat. Bob takes a number card out of the bag without looking. What is the probability that he draws:

a the number 7

b an even number

c a number greater than 6

d a number less than 3

e a number between 3 and 8?

5 A bag contains one blue ball, one pink ball and one black ball. Craig takes a ball from the bag without looking. What is the probability that he takes out:

a the blue ball

b the pink ball

c a ball that is not black?

HINTS AND TIPS

A ball that is not black must be pink or blue.

F

6 A pencil case contains six red pens and five blue pens. Geoff takes out a pen without looking at what it is. What is the probability that he takes out:

a a red pen **b** a blue pen **c** a pen that is not blue?

7 A bag contains 50 balls. 10 are green, 15 are red and the rest are white. Gemma takes a ball from the bag at random. What is the probability that she takes:

a a green ball **b** a white ball

c a ball that is not white **d** a ball that is green or white?

8 A box contains seven bags of cheese and onion crisps, two bags of beef crisps and six bags of plain crisps. Iklil takes out a bag of crisps at random. What is the probability that he gets:

a a bag of cheese and onion crisps **b** a bag of beef crisps

c a bag of crisps that are not cheese and onion **d** a bag of prawn cracker crisps

e a bag of crisps that is either plain or beef?

9 In a Christmas raffle, 2500 tickets are sold. One family has 50 tickets. What is the probability that that family wins the first prize?

E

10 Ashley, Bianca, Charles, Debbie and Eliza are in the same class. Their teacher wants two students to do a special job.

a Write down all the possible combinations of two people, for example, Ashley and Bianca, Ashley and Charles. (There are 10 combinations altogether).

b How many pairs give two boys?

c What is the probability of choosing two boys?

d How many pairs give a boy and a girl?

e What is the probability of choosing a boy and a girl?

f What is the probability of choosing two girls?

> **HINTS AND TIPS**
>
> Try to be systematic when writing out all the pairs.

11 In a sale at the supermarket, there is a box of 10 unlabelled tins. On the side it says: 4 tins of Creamed Rice and 6 tins of Chicken Soup. Mitesh buys this box. When he gets home he wants to have a lunch of chicken soup followed by creamed rice.

a What is the smallest number of tins he could open to get his lunch?

b What is the largest number of tins he could open to get his lunch?

c The first tin he opens is soup. What is the chance that the second tin he opens is:

i soup

ii rice?

12 What is the probability of each of the following events?

a Drawing a Jack from a pack of cards.

b Drawing a 10 from a pack of cards.

c Drawing a red card from a pack of cards.

d Drawing a 10 or a Jack from a pack of cards.

e Drawing a Jack or a red card from a pack of cards.

f Drawing a red Jack from a pack of cards.

13 A bag contains 25 coloured balls. 12 are red, 7 are blue and the rest are green. Martin takes a ball at random from the bag.

a Find:

i P(he takes a red)

ii P(he takes a blue)

iii P(he takes a green).

b Add together the three probabilities. What do you notice?

c Explain your answer to part **b**.

14 The weather tomorrow will be sunny, cloudy or raining.

If P(sunny) = 40%, P(cloudy) = 25%, what is P(raining)?

15 At morning break, Priya has a choice of coffee, tea or hot chocolate.

If P(she chooses coffee) = 0.3 and P(she chooses hot chocolate) = 0.2, what is P(she chooses tea)?

PS 16 The following information is known about the classes at Bradway School.

Year	Y1		Y2		Y3		Y4		Y5		Y6	
Class	P	Q	R	S	T	U	W	X	Y	Z	K	L
Girls	7	8	8	10	10	10	9	11	8	12	14	15
Boys	9	10	9	10	12	13	11	12	10	8	16	17

A class representative is chosen at random from each class.

Which class has the best chance of choosing a boy as the representative?

AU 17 The teacher chooses, at random, a student to ring the school bell.

Tom says: "It's even chances that the teacher chooses a boy or a girl."

Explain why Tom might not be correct.

This section will show you how to:
- calculate the probability of an outcome of an event not happening when you know the probability of the outcome happening

Key word

outcome

In some questions in Exercise 7B, you were asked for the probability of something *not* happening. For example, in question 5 you were asked for the probability of picking a ball that is *not* black. You could answer this because you knew how many balls were in the bag. However, sometimes you do not have this type of information.

The probability of throwing a six on a fair, six-sided dice is $P(6) = \dfrac{1}{6}$.

There are five **outcomes** that are not sixes: 1, 2, 3, 4, 5.

So, the probability of *not* throwing a six on a dice is:

$$P(\text{not a 6}) = \dfrac{5}{6}$$

Notice that:

$$P(6) = \dfrac{1}{6} \quad \text{and} \quad P(\text{not a 6}) = \dfrac{5}{6}$$

So,

$$P(6) + P(\text{not a 6}) = 1$$

If you know that $P(6) = \dfrac{1}{6}$, then $P(\text{not a 6})$ is:

$$1 - \dfrac{1}{6} = \dfrac{5}{6}$$

So, if you know P(outcome happening), then:

$$P(\text{outcome not happening}) = 1 - P(\text{outcome happening})$$

EXAMPLE 5

What is the probability of not picking an Ace from a pack of cards?

First, find the probability of picking an Ace:

$$P(\text{picking an ace from a pack of cards}) = \tfrac{4}{52} = \tfrac{1}{13}$$

Therefore:

$$P(\text{not picking an ace from a pack of cards}) = 1 - \tfrac{1}{13} = \tfrac{12}{13}$$

EXERCISE 7C

1 **a** The probability of winning a prize in a raffle is $\frac{1}{20}$. What is the probability of not winning a prize in the raffle?

b The probability that snow will fall during the Christmas holidays is 45%. What is the probability that it will not snow?

c The probability that Paddy wins a game of chess is 0.7 and the probability that he draws the game is 0.1. What is the probability that he loses the game?

2 Mary picks a card from a pack of well-shuffled playing cards.

Find the probability that she picks:

a **i** a picture card   **ii** a card that is not a picture

b **i** a Club   **ii** not a Club

c **i** an Ace or a King   **ii** neither an Ace nor a King.

3 The following letter cards are put into a bag.

a Steve takes a letter card at random.

   i What is the probability he takes a letter A?

   ii What is the probability he does not take a letter A?

b Richard picks an M and keeps it. Sue now takes a letter from those remaining.

   i What is the probability she takes a letter A?

   ii What is the probability she does not take a letter A?

FM 4 The starting point in a board game is:

Start	Owens Park	Take a chance	Curry Mile	Oxford Road	Pay £500 in tax	Salford Quays	Exchange Quays	Station	Old Trafford	Rest area	The Lowry	Trafford Park

You roll a single dice and move, from the start, the number of places shown by the dice.

What is the probability of *not* landing on:

a a brown square

b the station

c a coloured square?

E

PS **5** Freddie and Taryn are playing a board game. On the next turn Freddie will go to jail if he rolls an even number. Taryn will go to jail if she rolls a 5 or a 6.

Who has the better chance of *not* going to jail on the next turn?

AU **6** Hamzah is told: "The chance of your winning this game is 0.3."

Hamzah says: "So I have a chance of 0.7 of losing."

Explain why Hamzah might be wrong.

7.4 Addition rule for events

This section will show you how to:
- work out the probability of two outcomes of events such as P(A) or P(B)

Key words
event
mutually exclusive

You have used this rule already but it has not yet been formally defined.

Mutually exclusive events are ones that cannot happen at the same time, such as throwing an odd number and an even number on a roll of a dice.

When two events are mutually exclusive, you can work out the probability of either of them occurring by adding up the separate probabilities. Mutually exclusive events are events for which, when one occurs, it does not have any effect on the probability of other events.

EXAMPLE 6

A bag contains 12 red balls, 8 green balls, 5 blue balls and 15 black balls. A ball is drawn at random. What is the probability that it is the following:

    a red   **b** black   **c** red or black   **d** not green?

a $P(\text{red}) = \frac{12}{40} = \frac{3}{10}$

b $P(\text{black}) = \frac{15}{40} = \frac{3}{8}$

c $P(\text{red or black}) = P(\text{red}) + P(\text{black}) = \frac{3}{10} + \frac{3}{8} = \frac{27}{40}$

d $P(\text{not green}) = \frac{32}{40} = \frac{4}{5}$

EXERCISE 7D

1 Iqbal throws an ordinary dice. What is the probability that he throws:

a a 2   **b** a 5   **c** a 2 or a 5?

2 Jennifer draws a card from a pack of cards. What is the probability that she draws:

a a Heart   **b** a Club   **c** a Heart or a Club?

3 A letter is chosen at random from the letters in the word PROBABILITY. What is the probability that the letter will be:

a B   **b** a vowel   **c** B or a vowel?

4 A bag contains 10 white balls, 12 black balls and 8 red balls. A ball is drawn at random from the bag. What is the probability that it will be:

a white   **b** black

c black or white   **d** not red

e not red or black?

> **HINTS AND TIPS**
>
> You can only add fractions with the same denominator.

5 At the local School Fayre the tombola stall gives out a prize if you draw from the drum a numbered ticket that ends in 0 or 5. There are 300 tickets in the drum altogether and the probability of getting a winning ticket is 0.4.

a What is the probability of getting a losing ticket?

b How many winning tickets are there in the drum?

6 John needs his calculator for his mathematics lesson. It is always in his pocket, bag or locker. The probability it is in his pocket is 0.35 and the probability it is in his bag is 0.45. What is the probability that:

a he will have the calculator for the lesson

b his calculator is in his locker?

7 Aneesa has 20 unlabelled CDs, 12 of which are rock, 5 are pop and 3 are classical. She picks a CD at random. What is the probability that it will be:

a rock or pop

b pop or classical

c not pop?

AU 8 The probability that it rains on Monday is 0.5. The probability that it rains on Tuesday is 0.5 and the probability that it rains on Wednesday is 0.5. Kelly argues that it is certain to rain on Monday, Tuesday or Wednesday because 0.5 + 0.5 + 0.5 = 1.5, which is bigger than 1 so it is a certain event. Explain why she is wrong.

FM 9 In a TV game show, contestants throw darts at the dartboard shown.

The angle at the centre of each black sector is 15°.

If a dart lands in a black sector the contestant loses.

Any dart missing the board is rethrown.

What is the probability that a contestant throwing a dart at random does not lose?

PS 10 There are 45 patients sitting in the hospital waiting room.

8 patients are waiting for Dr Speed.
12 patients are waiting for Dr Mayne.
9 patients are waiting for Dr Kildare.
10 patients are waiting for Dr Pattell.
6 patients are waiting for Dr Stone.

A patient suddenly has to go home.

What is the probability that the patient who left was due to see Dr Speed?

AU 11 The probability of it snowing on any one day in February is $\frac{1}{4}$.

One year, there was no snow for the first 14 days.

Ciara said: "The chance of it snowing on any day in the rest of February must now be $\frac{1}{2}$."

Explain why Ciara is wrong.

AU 12
PS At morning break, Pauline has a choice of coffee, tea or hot chocolate.
She also has a choice of a ginger biscuit, a rich tea biscuit or a doughnut.

The probabilities that she chooses each drink and snack are:

Drink	Coffee (C)	Tea (T)	Hot chocolate (H)
Probability	0.2	0.5	0.3

Snack	Ginger biscuit (G)	Rich tea biscuit (R)	Doughnut (D)
Probability	0.3	0.1	0.6

a Leon says that the probability that Pauline has coffee and a ginger biscuit is 0.5. Explain why Leon is wrong.

b There are nine possible combinations of drink and snack. Two of these are coffee and a ginger biscuit (C, G), coffee and rich tea biscuit (C, R).

Write down the other seven combinations.

c Leon now says 'I was wrong before. As there are nine possibilities the probability of Pauline having coffee and a ginger biscuit is $\frac{1}{9}$.'

Explain why Leon is wrong again.

d In fact the probability that Pauline chooses coffee and a ginger biscuit is $0.2 \times 0.3 = 0.06$, and the probability that she chooses coffee and a rich tea biscuit is $0.2 \times 0.1 = 0.02$.

i Work out the other seven probabilities.

ii Add up all nine probabilities. Explain the result.

Experimental probability

This section will show you how to:
- calculate experimental probabilities and relative frequencies from experiments
- recognise different methods for estimating probabilities

Key words
bias
equally likely
experimental data
experimental probability
historical data
relative frequency
trials

ACTIVITY

Heads or tails?

Toss a coin 10 times and record the results like this.

H	T	H	H	T	T	H	T	H	H

Record how many heads you obtained.

Now repeat the above so that altogether you toss the coin 50 times. Record your results and count how many heads you obtained.

Now toss the coin another 50 times and once again record your results and count the heads.

It helps if you work with a partner. First, your partner records while you toss the coin. Then you swap over and record, while your partner tosses the coin. Add the number of heads you obtained to the number your partner obtained.

Now find three more people to do the same activity and add together the number of heads that all five of you obtained.

Now find five more people and add their results to the previous total.

Combine as many results together as possible.

You should now be able to fill in a table like the one on the next page. The first column is the number of times coins were tossed. The second column is the number of heads obtained. The third column is the number in the second column divided by the number in the first column.

The results below are from a group who did the same experiment.

Number of tosses	Number of heads	Number of heads / Number of tosses
10	6	0.6
50	24	0.48
100	47	0.47
200	92	0.46
500	237	0.474
1000	488	0.488
2000	960	0.48
5000	2482	0.4964

If you drew a graph of these results, plotting the first column against the last column, it would look like this.

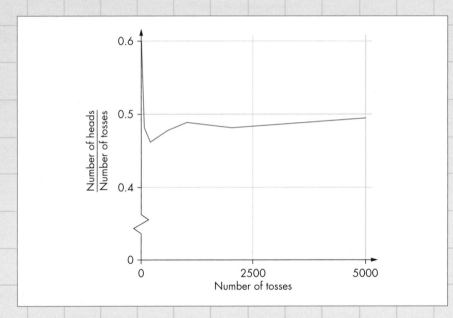

Your results should look very similar.

What happens to the value of $\dfrac{\text{number of heads}}{\text{number of tosses}}$ as the total number of tosses increases?

You should find that it gets closer and closer to 0.5.

The value of 'number of heads ÷ number of tosses' is called an **experimental probability**. As the number of **trials**, or experiments, increases, the value of the experimental probability gets closer to the true or theoretical probability.

Experimental probability is also known as the **relative frequency** of an event.
The relative frequency of an event is an estimate for the theoretical probability. It is given by:

$$\text{relative frequency of an outcome or event} = \frac{\text{frequency of the outcome or event}}{\text{total number of trials}}$$

EXAMPLE 7

The frequency table shows the speeds of 160 vehicles that pass a radar speed check on a dual carriageway.

Speed (mph)	20–29	30–39	40–49	50–59	60–69	70+
Frequency	14	23	28	35	52	8

a What is the experimental probability that a car is travelling faster than 70 mph?

b If 500 vehicles pass the speed check, estimate how many will be travelling faster than 70 mph.

a The experimental probability is the relative frequency, which is $\frac{8}{160} = \frac{1}{20}$.

b The number of vehicles travelling faster than 70 mph will be $\frac{1}{20}$ of 500.

That is:

$$500 \div 20 = 25$$

Finding probabilities

There are three ways in which the probability of an event can be found.

- **First method** If you can work out the theoretical probability of an outcome or event – for example, drawing a King from a pack of cards – this is called using **equally likely** outcomes.

- **Second method** Some probabilities, such as people buying a certain brand of dog food, cannot be calculated using equally likely outcomes. To find the probabilities for such an event, you can perform an experiment such as the one in the Activity on pages 213–214, or conduct a survey. This is called collecting **experimental data**. The more data you collect, the better the estimate is.

- **Third method** The probabilities of some events, such as an earthquake occurring in Japan, cannot be found by either of the above methods. One of the things you can do is to look at data collected over a long period of time and make an estimate (sometimes called a 'best guess') at the chance of the event happening. This is called looking at **historical data**.

EXAMPLE 8

Which method (A, B or C) would you use to estimate the probabilities for the events **a** to **e**?

> A: Use equally likely outcomes
>
> B: Conduct a survey or collect data
>
> C: Look at historical data

a Someone in your class will go abroad for a holiday this year.

b You will win the National Lottery.

c Your bus home will be late.

d It will snow on Christmas Day.

e You will pick a red seven from a pack of cards.

a You would have to ask all the members of your class what they intended to do for their holidays this year. You would therefore conduct a survey, Method B.

b The odds on winning are about 14 million to 1, so this is an equally likely outcome, Method A.

c If you catch the bus every day, you can collect data over several weeks. This would be Method C.

d If you check whether it snowed on Christmas Day for the last few years, you would be able to make a good estimate of the probability. This would be Method C.

e There are 2 red sevens out of 52 cards, so the probability of picking one can be calculated:

$$P(\text{red seven}) = \tfrac{2}{52} = \tfrac{1}{26}$$

This is Method A.

EXERCISE 7E

1 Which of these methods would you use to estimate or state the probabilities for each of the events **a** to **h**?

Method A: Use equally likely outcomes

Method B: Conduct a survey or experiment

Method C: Look at historical data

a How people will vote in the next election.

b A drawing pin dropped on a desk will land point up.

c A Premier League team will win the FA Cup.

d You will win a school raffle.

e The next car to drive down the road will be red.

f You will throw a 'double six' with two dice.

g Someone in your class likes classical music.

h A person picked at random from your school will be a vegetarian.

2 Naseer throws a fair, six-sided dice and records the number of sixes that he gets after various numbers of throws. The table shows his results.

Number of throws	10	50	100	200	500	1000	2000
Number of sixes	2	4	10	21	74	163	329

a Calculate the experimental probability of scoring a 6 at each stage that Naseer recorded his results.

b How many ways can a dice land?

c How many of these ways give a 6?

d What is the theoretical probability of throwing a 6 with a dice?

e If Naseer threw the dice a total of 6000 times, how many sixes would you expect him to get?

3 Marie made a five-sided spinner, like the one shown in the diagram. She used it to play a board game with her friend Sarah.

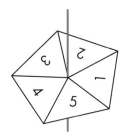

The girls thought that the spinner was not very fair as it seemed to land on some numbers more than others. They threw the spinner 200 times and recorded the results. The results are shown in the table.

Side spinner lands on	1	2	3	4	5
Number of times	19	27	32	53	69

a Work out the experimental probability of each number.

b How many times would you expect each number to occur if the spinner is fair?

c Do you think that the spinner is fair? Give a reason for your answer.

4 A sampling bottle contains 20 balls. The balls are either black or white. (A sampling bottle is a sealed bottle with a clear plastic tube at one end into which one of the balls can be tipped.) Kenny conducts an experiment to see how many black balls are in the bottle. He takes various numbers of samples and records how many of them showed a black ball.

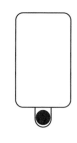

The results are shown in the table.

Number of samples	Number of black balls	Experimental probability
10	2	
100	25	
200	76	
500	210	
1000	385	
5000	1987	

a Copy the table and complete it by calculating the experimental probability of getting a black ball at each stage.

b Using this information, how many black balls do you think there are in the bottle?

5 Use a set of number cards from 1 to 10 (or make your own set) and work with a partner. Take turns to choose a card and keep a record each time of what card you get. Shuffle the cards each time and repeat the experiment 60 times. Put your results in a copy of this table.

Score	1	2	3	4	5	6	7	8	9	10
Total										

a How many times would you expect to get each number?

b Do you think you and your partner conducted this experiment fairly?

c Explain your answer to part **b**.

6 A four-sided dice has faces numbered 1, 2, 3 and 4. The 'score' is the face on which it lands. Five students throw the dice to see if it is biased. They each throw it a different number of times. Their results are shown in the table.

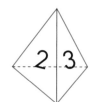

Student	Total number of throws	Score			
		1	2	3	4
Alfred	20	7	6	3	4
Brian	50	19	16	8	7
Caryl	250	102	76	42	30
Deema	80	25	25	12	18
Emma	150	61	46	26	17

   a Which student will have the most reliable set of results? Why?

   b Add up all the score columns and work out the relative frequency of each score. Give your answers to 2 decimal places.

   c Is the dice biased? Explain your answer.

7 If you were about to choose a card from a pack of yellow cards numbered from 1 to 10, what would be the chance of each of the events **a** to **i** occurring? Read each of these statements and describe the probability with a word or phrase chosen from 'impossible', 'not likely', '50–50 chance', 'quite likely', or 'certain'.

   a The next card chosen will be a 4.

   b The next card chosen will be pink.

   c The next card chosen will be a seven.

   d The next card chosen will be a number less than 11.

   e The next card chosen will be a number bigger than 11.

   f The next card chosen will be an even number.

   g The next card chosen will be a number more than 5.

   h The next card chosen will be a multiple of 1.

   i The next card chosen will be a prime number.

PS 8 Andrew made an eight-sided spinner.

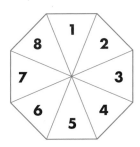

He tested it to see if it was fair.

He spun the spinner and recorded the results.

Unfortunately his little sister spilt something over his results table, so he could not see the middle part.

Number spinner lands on	1	2	3			6	7	8
Frequency	18	19	22			19	20	22

Assuming the spinner was a fair one, try to complete the missing parts of the table for Andrew.

FM **9** At a computer factory, tests were carried out to see how many faulty computer chips were produced in one week.

	Monday	Tuesday	Wednesday	Thursday	Friday
Sample	850	630	1055	896	450
Number faulty	10	7	12	11	4

On which day was it most likely that the highest number of faulty computer chips were produced?

AU **10** Steve tossed a coin 1000 times to see how many heads he got.

He said: "If this is a fair coin, I should get 500 heads."

Explain why he is wrong.

ACTIVITY

Biased spinner

You need a piece of stiff card, a cocktail stick and some sticky tack.

You may find that it is easier to work in pairs.

Make a copy of this hexagon on the card and push the cocktail stick through its centre to make a six-sided spinner. The size of the hexagon does not really matter, but it does need to be *accurately* drawn.

Stick a small piece of tack underneath one of the numbers. You now have a **biased** spinner.

Spin it 100 times and record your results in a frequency table.

Estimate the experimental probability of getting each number.

How can you tell that your spinner is biased?

Put some tack underneath a different number and see whether your partner can predict the number towards which the spinner is biased.

Combined events

> **This section will show you how to:**
> ● work out the probabilities for two events occurring at the same time

> **Key words**
> probability space diagram
> sample space diagram

There are many situations where two events occur together. Four examples are given below.

Throwing two dice

Imagine that two dice, one red and one blue, are thrown. The red dice can land with any one of six scores: 1, 2, 3, 4, 5 or 6. The blue dice can also land with any one of six scores. This gives a total of 36 possible combinations. These are shown in the left-hand diagram below, where combinations are given as (2, 3) and so on. The first number is the score on the blue dice and the second number is the score on the red dice.

The combination (2, 3) gives a total of 5. The total scores for all the combinations are shown in the diagram on the right-hand side. Diagrams that show all the outcomes of combined events are called **sample space diagrams** or **probability space diagrams**.

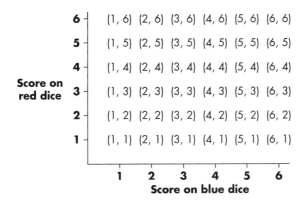

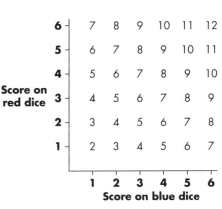

From the diagram on the right, you can see that there are two ways to get a score of 3. This gives a probability of scoring 3 as:

$$P(3) = \frac{2}{36} = \frac{1}{18}$$

From the diagram on the left, you can see that there are six ways to get a 'double'. This gives a probability of scoring a double as:

$$P(\text{double}) = \frac{6}{36} = \frac{1}{6}$$

Throwing coins

Throwing one coin
There are two equally likely outcomes, head or tail:

Throwing two coins together
There are four equally likely outcomes:

Hence:

$$P(2 \text{ heads}) = \frac{1}{4}$$

$$P(\text{head and tail}) = 2 \text{ ways out of } 4 = \frac{2}{4} = \frac{1}{2}$$

Dice and coins

Throwing a dice and a coin

Outcome on coin	H	(1, H)	(2, H)	(3, H)	(4, H)	(5, H)	(6, H)
	T	(1, T)	(2, T)	(3, T)	(4, T)	(5, T)	(6, T)
		1	2	3	4	5	6

Score on dice

Hence:

$$P(\text{head and an even number}) = 3 \text{ ways out of } 12 = \frac{3}{12} = \frac{1}{4}$$

EXERCISE 7F

1 To answer these questions, use the diagram on page 221 for all the possible scores when two fair dice are thrown together.

a What is the most likely score?

b Which two scores are least likely?

c Write down the probabilities of throwing all the scores from 2 to 12.

d What is the probability of a score that is:

i bigger than 10

ii between 3 and 7

iii even

iv a square number

v a prime number

vi a triangular number?

2 Use the diagram on page 221 that shows the outcomes when two fair, six-sided dice are thrown together as coordinates. What is the probability that:

a the score is an even 'double'

b at least one of the dice shows 2

c the score on one dice is twice the score on the other dice

d at least one of the dice shows a multiple of 3?

3 Use the diagram on page 221 that shows the outcomes when two fair, six-sided dice are thrown together as coordinates. What is the probability that:

a both dice show a 6

b at least one of the dice will show a 6

c exactly one dice shows a 6?

4 The diagram shows the scores for the event 'the difference between the scores when two fair, six-sided dice are thrown'. Copy and complete the diagram.

For the event described above, what is the probability of a difference of:

a 1   **b** 0

c 4   **d** 6

e an odd number?

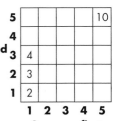

Score on second dice						
6	5	4			1	0
5	4	3				1
4	3					
3	2					
2	1					
1	0					
	1	**2**	**3**	**4**	**5**	**6**

Score on first dice

5 When two fair coins are thrown together, what is the probability of:

a two heads   **b** a head and a tail

c at least one tail   **d** no tails?

Use the diagram of the outcomes when two coins are thrown together, on page 222.

6 Two five-sided spinners are spun together and the total score of the faces that they land on is worked out. Copy and complete the probability space diagram shown.

a What is the most likely score?

b When two five-sided spinners are spun together, what is the probability that:

    i the total score is 5

    ii the total score is an even number

    iii the score is a 'double'

    iv the total score is less than 7?

Score on second spinner					
5					10
4					
3	4				
2	3				
1	2				
	1	**2**	**3**	**4**	**5**

Score on first spinner

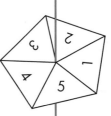

PS 7 Two eight-sided dice showing the numbers 1 to 8 were thrown at the same time.

What is the probability that the product of the two dice is an even square number?

AU 8 Isaac rolls two dice and multiplies both numbers to give their product. He wants to know the probability of rolling two dice that will give him a product between 19 and 35.

Explain why a probability space diagram will help him.

FM 9 Nic went to a garden centre to buy some roses.

She found they came in six different colours – white, red, orange, yellow, pink and copper.

She also found they came in five different sizes – dwarf, small, medium, large climbing and rambling.

a   Draw a probability space diagram to show all the options.

b   She buys a random rose for Auntie Janet. Auntie Janet only likes red and pink roses and she does not like climbing or rambling roses.

What is the probability that Nic has bought for Auntie Janet a rose:

i   that she likes

ii   that she does not like?

PS 10 Mrs Roberts asked: "What is the probability of rolling dice and getting a total of 10 or less. You must choose from impossible, very unlikely, unlikely, even chance, likely, very likely, or certain."

Evie replied: "It depends on how many dice I use."

For how many dice is each of the possible choices the answer?

7.7 Expectation

This section will show you how to:	Key word
• predict the likely number of successful events, given the number of trials and the probability of any one outcome	expect

When you know the probability of an outcome of an event, you can predict how many times you would expect that outcome to happen in a certain number of trials.

Note that this is what you **expect**. It is not necessarily what is going to happen. If what you expected always happened, life would be very dull and boring, and the National Lottery would be a waste of time!

EXAMPLE 9

A bag contains 20 balls, 9 of which are black, 6 white and 5 yellow. A ball is drawn at random from the bag, its colour is noted and then it is put back in the bag. This is repeated 500 times.

    a How many times would you expect a black ball to be drawn?

    b How many times would you expect a yellow ball to be drawn?

    c How many times would you expect a black or a yellow ball to be drawn?

a $P(\text{black ball}) = \dfrac{9}{20}$

Expected number of black balls $= \dfrac{9}{20} \times 500 = 225$

b $P(\text{yellow ball}) = \dfrac{5}{20} = \dfrac{1}{4}$

Expected number of yellow balls $= \dfrac{1}{4} \times 500 = 125$

c Expected number of black or yellow balls $= 225 + 125 = 350$

EXERCISE 7G

1 **a** What is the probability of throwing a 6 with an ordinary dice?

   b I throw an ordinary dice 150 times. How many times can I expect to get a score of 6?

2 **a** What is the probability of tossing a head with a coin?

   b I toss a coin 2000 times. How many times can I expect to get a head?

3 **a** A card is taken at random from a pack of cards. What is the probability that it is:

    i a black card   **ii** a King   **iii** a Heart   **iv** the King of Hearts?

   b I draw a card from a pack of cards and replace it. I do this 520 times. How many times would I expect to get:

    i a black card   **ii** a King   **iii** a Heart   **iv** the King of Hearts?

4 The ball in a roulette wheel can land in one of 37 spaces that are marked with numbers from 0 to 36 inclusive. I always bet on the same number, 13.

   a What is the probability of the ball landing in 13?

   b If I play all evening and there are exactly 185 spins of the wheel in that time, how many times could I expect to win?

5 In a bag there are 30 balls, 15 of which are red, 5 yellow, 5 green, and 5 blue. A ball is taken out at random and then replaced. This is done 300 times. How many times would I expect to get:

a a red ball

b a yellow or blue ball

c a ball that is not blue

d a pink ball?

6 The experiment described in question 5 is carried out 1000 times. Approximately how many times would you expect to get:

a a green ball

b a ball that is not blue?

7 A sampling bottle (as described in question 4 of Exercise 7E) contains red and white balls. It is known that the probability of getting a red ball is 0.3. If 1500 samples are taken, how many of them would you expect to give a white ball?

8 Josie said, "When I throw a dice, I expect to get a score of 3.5."

"Impossible," said Paul, "You can't score 3.5 with a dice."
"Do this and I'll prove it," said Josie.

a An ordinary dice is thrown 60 times. Fill in the table for the expected number of times each score will occur.

Score						
Expected occurrences						

b Now work out the average score that is expected over 60 throws.

c There is an easy way to get an answer of 3.5 for the expected average score. Can you see what it is?

FM 9 The probabilities of some cloud types being seen on any day are given below.

Cumulus	0.3
Stratocumulus	0.25
Stratus	0.15
Altocumulus	0.11
Cirrus	0.05
Cirrcocumulus	0.02
Nimbostratus	0.005
Cumulonimbus	0.004

a What is the probability of *not* seeing one of the above clouds in the sky?

b On how many days of the year would you expect to see altocumulus clouds in the sky?

PS 10 Every evening Anne and Chris cut a pack of cards to see who washes up.

If they cut a King or a Jack, Chris washes up.

If they cut a Queen, Anne washes up.

Otherwise, they wash up together.

In a year of 365 days, how many days would you expect them to wash up together?

AU 11 A market gardener is supplied with tomato plant seedlings and knows that the probability that any plant will develop a disease is 0.003.

How will she find out how many of the tomato plants she should expect to develop a disease?

7.8 Two-way tables

This section will show you how to:
- read two-way tables and use them to do probability and other mathematics

Key word
two-way table

A **two-way table** is a table that links together two variables. For example, the following table shows how many boys and girls there are in a form and whether they are left- or right-handed.

	Boys	Girls
Left-handed	2	4
Right-handed	10	13

This table shows the colour and make of cars in the school car park.

	Red	Blue	White
Ford	2	4	1
Vauxhall	0	1	2
Toyota	3	3	4
Peugeot	2	0	3

One variable is shown in the rows of the table and the other variable is shown in the columns of the table.

EXAMPLE 10

Use the first two-way table on the previous page to answer the following.

    a How many left-handed boys are there in the form?

    b How many girls are there in the form, in total?

    c How many students are there in the form altogether?

    d How many students altogether are right-handed?

    e What is the probability that a student selected at random from the form is:

        i a left-handed boy   **ii** right-handed?

a 2 boys	Read this value from where the 'Boys' column and the 'Left-handed' row meet.
b 17 girls	Add up the 'Girls' column.
c 29 students	Add up all the numbers in the table.
d 23	Add up the 'Right-handed' row.
e **i** P (left-handed boy) = $\frac{2}{29}$	Use the answers to parts **a** and **c**.
ii P (right-handed) = $\frac{23}{29}$	Use the answers to parts **c** and **d**.

EXAMPLE 11

Use the second two-way table on the previous page to answer the following.

    a How many cars were in the car park altogether?

    b How many red cars were in the car park?

    c What percentage of the cars in the car park were red?

    d How many cars in the car park were white?

    e What percentage of the white cars were Vauxhalls?

a 25	Add up all the numbers in the table.
b 7	Add up the 'Red' column.
c 28%	7 out of 25 is the same as 28 out of 100.
d 10	Add up the 'White' column.
e 20%	2 out of 10 is 20%.

EXERCISE 7H

1 The following table shows the top five clubs in the top division of the English Football League at the end of the season for the years 1965, 1975, 1985, 1995 and 2005.

		Year				
		1965	**1975**	**1985**	**1995**	**2005**
Position	**1st**	Man Utd	Derby	Everton	Blackburn	Chelsea
	2nd	Leeds	Liverpool	Liverpool	Man Utd	Arsenal
	3rd	Chelsea	Ipswich	Tottenham	Notts Forest	Man Utd
	4th	Everton	Everton	Man Utd	Liverpool	Everton
	5th	Notts Forest	Stoke	Southampton	Leeds	Liverpool

a Which team was in fourth place in 1975?

b Which three teams are in the top five for four of the five years?

c Which team finished three places lower in 1995 than in 1965?

2 Here is a display of 10 cards.

a Complete the two-way table.

		Shaded	Unshaded
Shape	**Circles**		
	Triangles		

b One of the cards is picked at random. What is the probability it shows either a shaded triangle or an unshaded circle?

3 The two-way table shows the number of doors and the number of windows in each room in a primary school.

		Number of doors		
		1	**2**	**3**
Number of windows	**1**	5	4	2
	2	4	5	4
	3	0	4	6
	4	1	3	2

a How many rooms are there in the school altogether?

b How many rooms have two doors?

c What percentage of the rooms in the school have two doors?

d What percentage of the rooms that have one door also have two windows?

e How many rooms have the same number of windows as doors?

4 Three cards are lettered A, B and C. Three discs are numbered 4, 5 and 6.

| A | B | C | 4 | 5 | 6 |

One card and one disc are chosen at random.

If the card shows A, 1 is deducted from the score on the disc.
If the card shows B, the score on the disc stays the same.
If the card shows C, 1 is added to the score on the disc.

a Copy and complete the table to show all the possible scores.

		Number on disc		
		4	**5**	**6**
	A	3		
Letter on card	**B**	4		
	C	5		

b What is the probability of getting a score that is an even number?

c In a different game the probability of getting a total that is even is $\frac{2}{3}$.
What is the probability of getting a total that is an odd number?

5 The two-way table shows the ages and sexes of a sample of 50 students in a school.

		Age (years)					
		11	**12**	**13**	**14**	**15**	**16**
Sex	**Boys**	4	3	6	2	5	4
	Girls	2	5	3	6	4	6

a How many students are aged 13 years or less?

b What percentage of the students in the table are 16?

c A student from the table is selected at random. What is the probability that the student will be 14 years of age? Give your answer as a fraction in its lowest form.

d There are 1000 students in the school. Use the table to estimate how many boys are in the school altogether.

6 The two-way table shows the numbers of adults and the numbers of cars in 50 houses in one street.

		Number of adults			
		1	**2**	**3**	**4**
	0	2	1	0	0
Number of cars	**1**	3	13	3	1
	2	0	10	6	4
	3	0	1	4	2

a How many houses have exactly two adults and two cars?

b How many houses altogether have three cars?

c What percentage of the houses have three cars?

d What percentage of the houses with just one car have three adults living in the house?

7 Jane has two four-sided spinners.
Spinner A has the numbers 1 to 4 on it and
Spinner B has the numbers 5 to 8 on it.

Both spinners are spun together.

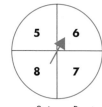

Spinner A   Spinner B

The two-way table shows all the ways the two
spinners can land.

Some of the total scores are filled in.

		Score on Spinner A			
		1	**2**	**3**	**4**
Score on Spinner B	**5**	6	7		
	6	7			
	7				
	8				

a Copy and complete the table to show all the possible total scores.

b How many of the total scores are 9?

c When the two spinners are spun together, what is the probability that the total score
will be:

i 9

ii 8

iii a prime number?

8 The table shows information about the number of items in Zara's wardrobe.

		Type of item		
		Shoes (pairs)	**Trousers**	**T-shirts**
Colour	**Blue**	6	5	2
	Black	12	9	13
	Red	2	2	0

a How many pairs of blue shoes does Zara have?

b How many pairs of trousers does Zara have?

c How many black items does Zara have?

d If a T-shirt is chosen at random from all the T-shirts, what is the probability that it will
be a black T-shirt?

D

9 Zoe throws a fair coin and rolls a fair dice.

If the coin shows a head, she records the score on the dice.
If the coin shows tails, she doubles the number on the dice.

a Copy and complete the two-way table to show Zoe's possible scores.

		Number on dice					
		1	**2**	**3**	**4**	**5**	**6**
Coin	**Head**	1	2				
	Tail	2	4				

b How many of the scores are square numbers?

c What is the probability of getting a score that is a square number?

C

AU 10 A gardener plants some sunflower seeds in a greenhouse and some in the garden. After they have fully grown, he measures the diameter of the sunflower heads. The table shows his results.

		Greenhouse	Garden
Diameter	**Mean diameter**	16.8 cm	14.5 cm
	Range of diameter	3.2 cm	1.8 cm

a The gardener, who wants to enter competitions, says, "The sunflowers from the greenhouse are better."

Using the data in the table, give a reason to justify this statement.

b The gardener's wife, who does flower arranging, says, "The sunflowers from the garden are better."

Using the data in the table, give a reason to justify this statement.

AU 11 Reyki plants some tomato plants in her greenhouse, while her husband Daniel plants some in the garden.

After the summer they compared their tomatoes.

		Garden	Greenhouse
Diameter	**Mean diameter**	1.8 cm	4.2 cm
	Mean number of tomatoes per plant	24.2	13.3

Use the data in the table to explain who had the better crop of tomatoes.

PS 12 Two hexagonal spinners are spun.

Spinner A is numbered 3, 5, 7, 9, 11 and 13.
Spinner B is numbered 4, 5, 6, 7, 8 and 9.

What is the probability that when the two spinners are spun, the result of multiplying two numbers together will give a product greater than 40?

13 Here are two fair spinners.

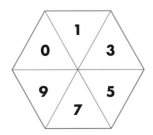 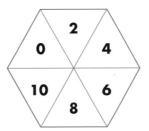

The spinners are spun.

The two numbers obtained are added together.

a Draw a probability sample space diagram.

b What is the most likely score?

c What is the probability of getting a total of 12?

d What is the probability of getting a total of 11 or more?

e What is the probability of getting a total that is an odd number?

GRADE BOOSTER

G You can understand basic terms such as 'certain', 'impossible', 'likely'

F You can understand that the probability scale runs from 0 to 1 and can calculate the probability of events

E You can list all outcomes of two independent events such as tossing a coin and throwing a dice, and calculate probabilities from lists or tables

E You can calculate the probability of an outcome not happening if you know the probability of it happening

D You can understand that the total probability of all possible outcomes in a paticular situation is 1

C You can predict the expected number of successes from a given number of trials if the probability of one success is known

C You can calculate relative frequency from experimental evidence and compare this with the theoretical probability

What you should know now

- How to use the probability scale and estimate the likelihood of outcomes of events depending on their position on the scale

- How to calculate theoretical probabilities from different situations

- How to calculate relative frequency and understand that the reliability of experimental results depends on the number of experiments carried out

1 Toni has ten coloured cards.

Eight cards are blue and two are red.

Toni picks a card at random.

Choose a word from this list to describe each of the following events.

> Impossible   unlikely   evens   likely   certain

a   **i**   The card picked is blue.   (1)

  ii   The card picked is yellow.   (1)

  iii   The card picked is blue or red.   (1)

b   Jay has a different set of ten coloured cards.

He has an even chance of picking a blue card.

How many blue cards are there in this set?   (1)

(Total 4 marks)

AQA, June 2008, Module 1 Foundation, Question 5

2 The following number cards are placed in a bag.

> 1   2   3   4   5
>
> 6   7   8   9

A card is taken out at random.

Find the probability that the number on the card is:

a   5   (1)

b   an even number   (1)

c   a number greater than 10   (1)

(Total 3 marks)

AQA, May 2008, Paper 1 Foundation, Question 10

3 Pupils have a choice of two bus routes to go to school. Data is collected for the journey times over one week. Here are the results.

	Mean (minutes)	Range (minutes)
Route A	14.6	20
Route B	19.2	5

a   Mark says, "It is better to use Route A."
Using the data given in the table, give a reason to justify his statement.

b   Bev says, "It is better to use Route B."
Using the data given in the table, give a reason to justify her statement.

4 A survey is to be carried out on how teenagers prefer to buy their music.

They buy their music from CDs (C) or from downloads (D).

A pilot survey of ten teenagers is carried out first.

Boy	C	Girl	C
Girl	D	Boy	D
Girl	D	Girl	D
Boy	C	Boy	C
Boy	D	Girl	D

a   Construct a two-way table to show these results.   (3)

b   In the full survey, the probability of a teenager preferring CDs is 0.3

What is the probability of a teenager **not** preferring CDs?   (1)

(Total 4 marks)

AQA, November 2008, Paper 2 Foundation, Question 16

5 A bag contains blue, red and green cards only.

One card is taken at random from the bag.

The table shows the probabilities of taking a blue card and a red card.

Colour	Blue	Red	Green
Probability	0.3	0.5	

a   What is the probability of taking a yellow card from the bag?   (1)

b   What is the probability of taking a card that is **not** blue from the bag?   (1)

c   Complete the table to show the probability of taking a green card from the bag.   (1)

(Total 3 marks)

AQA, June 2006, Paper 1, Intermediate, Question 7

6 Jenny has a fair spinner.
The spinner has eight equal sections.
One is red (R), two are white (W) and the rest
are yellow (Y).

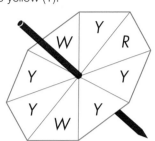

Jenny spins the spinner once.

a Mark the probability scale with the
correct letter for the probability of the
spinner landing on each colour. (3)

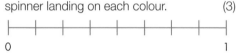

0   1

b Write down the probability that the
spinner lands on blue. (1)

c Write down the probability that the
spinner does **not** land on red. (1)

d Jenny says that whenever she spins this
spinner eight times it will land on white
exactly twice.

Is Jenny correct?

Explain your answer. (1)

(Total 6 marks)

AQA, March 2008, Module 1 Foundation, Question 7

7 A fair six-sided dice
and a fair coin are
thrown at the same
time. This shows the
outcome 1H or
(1, head).

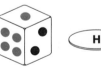

a Complete the list of all the possible
outcomes.

b What is the probability of getting a head and
an even number?

c What is the probability of getting a tail *or* an
odd number *or* both?

8 Jacob has 3 red counters and 7 blue counters.
Tony has 10 red counters.
Emily has only blue counters.

a Jacob puts his counters into a bag.
What is the probability of choosing a
red counter from the bag? (1)

b Tony adds his counters to the bag.
What is the probability of choosing a
red counter now? (2)

c Emily adds her counters to the bag.
The probability of choosing a red counter
now is $\frac{1}{2}$.
How many blue counters did Emily have?
(2)

(Total 5 marks)

AQA, November 2008, Paper 1 Foundation, Question 12

9 A triangular spinner has
sections coloured white (W),
green (G) and blue (B).
The spinner is spun 20 times
and the colour it lands on
each time is recorded.

W W B G G W B
G G W G B G B
G W G B G B

a Copy and complete the relative frequency
table.

Colour	White (W)	Green (G)	Blue (B)
Relative frequency			

b The table below shows the relative
frequencies after this spinner has been
spun 100 times.

Colour	White (W)	Green (G)	Blue (B)
Relative frequency	$\frac{21}{100}$	$\frac{52}{100}$	$\frac{27}{100}$

Which of the two relative frequencies for
white gives the better estimate of the
probability of the spinner landing on white?
Give a reason for your answer.

Worked Examination Questions

1 Simon has a bag containing blue, green, red, yellow and white marbles.

a Complete the table to show the probability of each colour being chosen at random.

b Which colour of marble is most likely to be chosen at random?

c Calculate the probability that a marble chosen at random is blue or white.

Colour of marble	Probability
Blue	0.3
Green	0.2
Red	0.15
Yellow	
White	0.1

a 0.25

2 marks

The probabilities in the table should add up to 1 so,
$$0.3 + 0.2 + 0.15 + 0.1 + \textbf{?} = 1 \qquad 0.75 + \textbf{?} = 1$$
This calculation gets you 1 method mark. Using the calculation, the missing probability is 0.25. This answer gets you 1 mark.

b Blue marble

1 mark

The blue marble is most likely as it has the largest probability of being chosen. The correct answer is worth 1 mark.

c 0.4

2 marks

Total: 5 marks

The word 'or' means you add probabilities of separate events.
The calculation P(blue or white) = P(blue) + P(white) = 0.3 + 0.1 = 0.4 is worth 1 method mark and the correct answer is worth 1 mark.

FM **2** In a raffle 400 tickets have been sold. There is only one prize.

Mr Raza buys 5 tickets for himself and sells another 40.
Mrs Raza buys 10 tickets for herself and sells another 50.
Mrs Hewes buys 8 tickets for herself and sells just 12 others.

a What is the probability of:

  i Mr Raza winning the raffle

  ii Mr Raza selling the winning ticket

  iii Mr Raza either winning the raffle or selling the winning ticket?

b What is the probability of either Mr or Mrs Raza selling the winning ticket?

c What is the probability of Mrs Hewes not winning the lottery?

a **i** $\dfrac{5}{400}$

You get 1 mark for the correct answer.

ii $\dfrac{40}{400}$

You get 1 mark for the correct answer.

iii $\dfrac{(5 + 40)}{400} = \dfrac{45}{400}$ *4 marks*

You get 1 method mark for writing out the combined probability. You also get 1 accuracy mark for expressing this as a number out of 400.

b $\dfrac{(40 + 50)}{400} = \dfrac{90}{400}$ *2 marks*

You get 1 method mark for writing out the combined probability. You also get 1 accuracy mark for expressing this as a number out of 400.

c $1 - \dfrac{8}{400} = \dfrac{392}{400}$ *2 marks*

You get 1 method mark for subtracting from 1. You also get 1 mark for the final answer.

Total: 8 marks

Joe had a stall at the local fair and wanted to make a reasonable profit from the game below.

In this game, the player rolls two balls down the sloping board and wins a prize if they land in slots that total more than seven.

Joe wants to know how much he should charge for each go and what the price should be. He would also like to know how much profit he is likely to make.

1 3 5 3 1

Getting started

Practise calculating probabilities using the spinner and questions below.

- What is the probability of spinning the spinner and getting:
  - a one
  - a five
  - a two
  - a number other than five?

  Give your answer as a fraction and as a decimal.

- If you spun the spinner 20 times, how many times would you expect to get:
  - a five
  - not five
  - an odd number?

- If you spun the spinner 100 times, how many times would you expect to get:
  - a two
  - not a two
  - a prime number?

Now, think about which probabilities you must calculate, in order to help Joe, and to design your own profitable game.

Your task

For this task you can work individually or in pairs.

1 Write a report for Joe which includes:

● a diagram to show the probability of each outcome

● the probability of at least three different outcomes

● the probability of winning

● at least three different ways of setting up the game, showing the cost of one go, the value of the prize and the expected profit for varying numbers of people playing the game.

Based on this information, advise Joe how he should set up the game. Justify your decision.

2 Design your own fairground game. Describe the rules for winning, show the probability of winning using a diagram, and give costings and the projected profit.

Explain why you think your game should be used at the next local fair.

Why this chapter matters

This chapter extends the idea of statistical representation (which you first met in Chapter 5) by introducing pie charts and scatter diagrams.

Pie charts

The pie chart first appeared in 1801 in a publication called *The Statistical Breviary* by William Playfair. Do you remember him? He was one of the first to use bar charts, too.

William Playfair used graphical representations of quantitative data, such as bar charts and pie charts, because he believed that "making an appeal to the eye when trying to show data is the best and easiest method of giving any message that might be wanted to show through such diagrams".

He used circles in interesting ways to represent quantitative relationships, varying their sizes and subdividing them into slices to create circular charts – or 'pie' charts.

The term 'pie chart' was not actually used until years later and it is not the only food metaphor that has been used to describe it. The French referred to it as a camembert – a soft, round cheese!

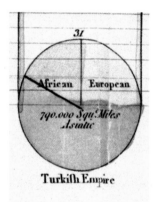
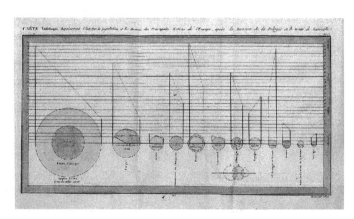

He was said to have been amused at the image of the pie chart (above left), showing a smile, and also liked the use of the pie chart above right, which is now seldom used as it's not clear which area is which.

Scatter diagrams

The word 'scatter' comes to us from Scandinavian influences in the 12th century, but we didn't see any scatter diagrams until one appeared in 1924 in a document from a university in what is now Pakistan. Apparently, they were one of the first establishments to use the technique of plotting points from two sources to see if any connections could be seen between the two.

Scatter diagrams were not used very much until the great energy debate in the late 1960s, when prices and sales of both gas and electricity were being studied. At that time, there was pressure for people to use more electricity, as it was thought to be an infinite power source, whereas gas would seemingly run out one day soon.

We now use both pie charts and scatter diagrams every day, for example, in business presentations, social studies and polls.

Statistics: Pie charts, scatter diagrams and surveys

1 Pie charts

2 Scatter diagrams

3 Surveys

4 The data-handling cycle

5 Other uses of statistics

This chapter will show you ...

- **E** how to draw and interpret pie charts
- **D** how to design a survey sheet and questionnaire
- **C** how to draw scatter diagrams and lines of best fit
- **C** how to interpret scatter diagrams and the different types of correlation
- **C** some of the common features of social statistics
- **C** how to describe the data-handling cycle

Visual overview

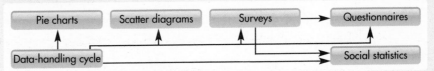

What you should already know

- How to draw and interpret pictograms, bar charts and line graphs **(KS3 level 3, GCSE grade G)**
- How to draw and measure angles **(KS3 level 4, GCSE grade F)**
- How to plot coordinates **(KS3 level 4, GCSE grade G)**

Quick check

1 The bar chart shows how many boys and girls are in five Year 7 forms.

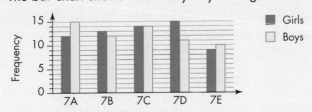

   a How many pupils are in 7A?

   b How many boys altogether are in the five forms?

2 Draw an angle of 72°.

3 Three points, A, B and C, are shown on the coordinate grid.

   What are the coordinates of A, B and C?

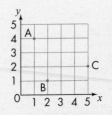

Pie charts

This section will show you how to:
- draw pie charts

Key words
angle
pie chart
sector

Pictograms, bar charts and line graphs (see Chapter 5) are easy to draw but they can be difficult to interpret when there is a big difference between the frequencies or there are only a few categories. In these cases, it is often more convenient to illustrate the data on a **pie chart**.

In a pie chart, the whole of the data is represented by a circle (the 'pie') and each category of it is represented by a **sector** of the circle (a 'slice of the pie'). The **angle** of each sector is proportional to the frequency of the category it represents.

So, a pie chart cannot show individual frequencies, like a bar chart can, for example. It can only show proportions.

Sometimes the pie chart will be marked off in equal sections rather than angles. In these cases, the numbers are always easy to work with.

EXAMPLE 1

20 people were surveyed about their preferred drink. Their replies are shown in the table.

Drink	Tea	Coffee	Milk	Pop
Frequency	6	7	4	3

Show the results on the pie chart given.

You can see that the pie chart has 10 equally-spaced divisions.

As there are 20 people, each division is worth two people. So the sector for tea will have three of these divisions. In the same way, coffee will have $3\frac{1}{2}$ divisions, milk will have 2 divisions and pop will have $1\frac{1}{2}$ divisions.

The finished pie chart will look like the one in the diagram.

Note:

- You should always label the sectors of the chart (use shading and a separate key if there is not enough space to write on the chart).

- Give your chart a title.

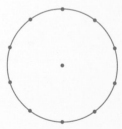

Preferred drinks

FM Functional Maths **AU** (AO2) Assessing Understanding **PS** (AO3) Problem Solving

EXAMPLE 2

In a survey on holidays, 120 people were asked to state which type of transport they used on their last holiday. This table shows the results of the survey. Draw a pie chart to illustrate the data.

Type of transport	Train	Coach	Car	Ship	Plane
Frequency	24	12	59	11	14

You need to find the angle for the fraction of 360° that represents each type of transport. This is usually done in a table, as shown below.

Type of transport	Frequency	Calculation	Angle
Train	24	$\frac{24}{120} \times 360° = 72°$	72°
Coach	12	$\frac{12}{120} \times 360° = 36°$	36°
Car	59	$\frac{59}{120} \times 360° = 177°$	177°
Ship	11	$\frac{11}{120} \times 360° = 33°$	33°
Plane	14	$\frac{14}{120} \times 360° = 42°$	42°
Totals	120		360°

Draw the pie chart, using the calculated angle for each sector.

Note:

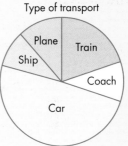

Type of transport

- Use the frequency total (120 in this case) to calculate each fraction.

- Check that the sum of all the angles is 360°.

- Label each sector.

- The angles or frequencies do not have to be shown on the pie chart.

EXERCISE 8A

1 Copy the basic pie chart on the right and draw a pie chart to show each of the following sets of data.

a The favourite pets of 10 children.

Pet	Dog	Cat	Rabbit
Frequency	4	5	1

b The makes of cars of 20 teachers.

Make of car	Ford	Toyota	Vauxhall	Nissan	Peugeot
Frequency	4	5	2	3	6

c The newspaper read by 40 office workers.

Newspaper	*Sun*	*Mirror*	*Guardian*	*The Times*
Frequency	14	8	6	12

2 Draw a pie chart to represent each of the following sets of data.

a The number of children in 40 families.

No. of children	0	1	2	3	4
Frequency	4	10	14	9	3

b The favourite soap-opera of 60 students.

Programme	*Home and Away*	*Neighbours*	*Coronation Street*	*Eastenders*	*Emmerdale*
Frequency	15	18	10	13	4

c How 90 students get to school.

Journey to school	Walk	Car	Bus	Cycle
Frequency	42	13	25	10

3 Mariam asked 24 of her friends which sport they preferred to play. Her data is shown in this frequency table.

Sport	Rugby	Football	Tennis	Squash	Basketball
Frequency	4	11	3	1	5

Illustrate her data on a pie chart.

AU 4 Andy wrote down the number of lessons he had per week in each subject on his school timetable.

Mathematics 5   English 5   Science 8   Languages 6
Humanities 6   Arts 4   Games 2

a How many lessons did Andy have on his timetable?

b Draw a pie chart to show the data.

c Draw a bar chart to show the data.

d Which diagram better illustrates the data? Give a reason for your answer.

AU 5 In the run up to an election, 720 people were asked in a poll which political party they would vote for. The results are given in the table.

Conservative	248
Labour	264
Liberal-Democrat	152
Green Party	56

a Draw a pie chart to illustrate the data.

b Why do you think pie charts are used to show this sort of information during elections?

6 This pie chart shows the proportions of the different shoe sizes worn by 144 pupils in Year 11 in a London school.

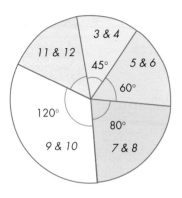

a What is the angle of the sector representing shoe sizes 11 and 12?

b How many pupils had a shoe size of 11 or 12?

c What percentage of pupils wore the modal size?

AU 7 The table below shows the numbers of candidates, at each grade, taking music examinations in Strings and Brass.

	Grades					Total number of candidates
	3	**4**	**5**	**6**	**7**	
Strings	300	980	1050	600	70	3000
Brass	250	360	300	120	70	1100

a Draw a pie chart to represent each of the two examinations.

b Compare the pie charts to decide which group of candidates, Strings or Brass, did better overall. Give reasons to justify your answer.

PS 8 In a survey, a rail company asked passengers whether their service had improved.

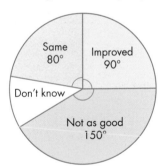

What is the probability that a person picked at random from this survey answered "Don't know"?

AU 9 You have been asked to draw a pie chart representing the different ways in which students come to school one morning.

What data would you collect to do this?

This section will show you how to:
- draw, interpret and use scatter diagrams

Key words
correlation
line of best fit
negative correlation
no correlation
positive correlation
scatter diagram
variable

A **scatter diagram** (also called a scattergraph or scattergram) is a method of comparing two **variables** by plotting their corresponding values on a graph. These values are usually taken from a table.

In other words, the variables are treated just like a set of (x, y) coordinates. This is shown in the scatter diagram that follows, in which the marks scored in an English test are plotted against the marks scored in a mathematics test.

This graph shows **positive correlation**. This means that pupils who get high marks in mathematics tests also tend to get high marks in English tests.

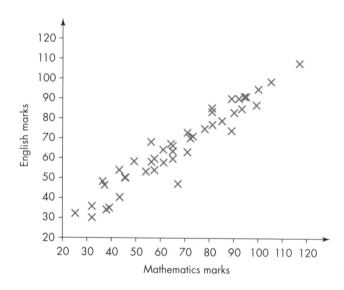

Correlation

There are different types of **correlation**. Here are three statements that may or may not be true.

- The taller people are, the wider their arm span is.
- The older a car is, the lower its value will be.
- The distance you live from your place of work will affect how much you earn.

These relationships could be tested by collecting data and plotting the data on a scatter diagram. For example, the first statement may give a scatter diagram like the first one below.

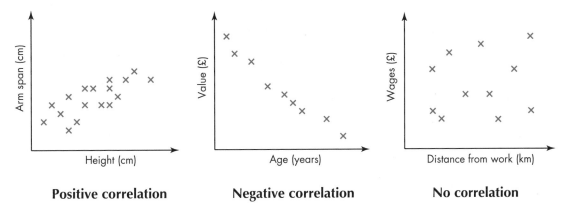

Positive correlation   **Negative correlation**   **No correlation**

This first diagram has **positive correlation** because, as one quantity increases, so does the other. From such a scatter diagram, you could say that the taller someone is, the wider their arm span.

Testing the second statement may give a scatter diagram like the middle one above. This has **negative correlation** because, as one quantity increases, the other quantity decreases. From such a scatter diagram, you could say that, as a car gets older, its value decreases.

Testing the third statement may give a scatter diagram like the one on the right, above. This scatter diagram has **no correlation**. There is no relationship between the distance a person lives from their work and how much they earn.

EXAMPLE 3

The graphs below show the relationship between the temperature and the amount of ice-cream sold, and that between the age of people and the amount of ice-cream they eat.

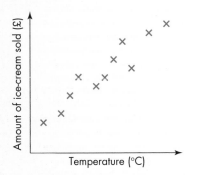
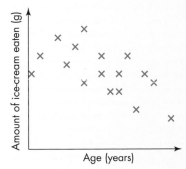

a   Comment on the correlation of each graph.

b   What does each graph tell you?

The first graph has positive correlation and tells us that, as the temperature increases, the amount of ice-cream sold increases.

The second graph has negative correlation and tells us that, as people get older, they eat less ice-cream.

Line of best fit

A **line of best fit** is a straight line that goes between all the points on a scatter diagram, passing as close as possible to all of them. You should try to have the same number of points on both sides of the line. Because you are drawing this line by eye, examiners make a generous allowance around the correct answer. The line of best fit for the scatter diagram at the start of this section is shown below, left.

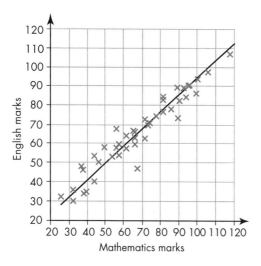
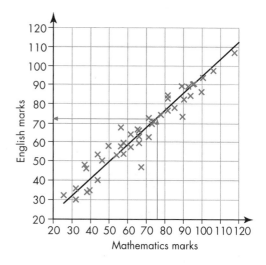

The line of best fit can be used to answer questions such as: "A girl took the mathematics test and scored 75 marks but was ill for the English test. How many marks was she likely to have scored?"

The answer is found by drawing a line up from 75 on the mathematics axis to the line of best fit and then drawing a line across to the English axis as shown in the graph above, right. This gives 73, which is the mark she is likely to have scored in the English test.

EXERCISE 8B

1 Describe the correlation of each of these four graphs.

a

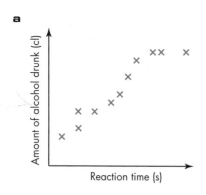

b

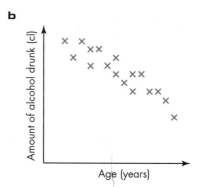

c

d

2 Write in words what each graph in question 1 tells you.

3 The table below shows the results of a science experiment in which a ball is rolled along a desk top. The speed of the ball is measured at various points.

Distance from start (cm)	10	20	30	40	50	60	70	80
Speed (cm/s)	18	16	13	10	7	5	3	0

a Plot the data on a scatter diagram.

b Draw the line of best fit.

c If the ball's speed had been measured at 5 cm from the start, what is it likely to have been?

d Estimate how far from the start the ball was when its speed was 12 cm/s.

HINTS AND TIPS

Often in exams axes are given and most, if not all, of the points are plotted.

4 The heights, in centimetres, of 20 mothers and their 15-year-old daughters were measured. These are the results.

Mother	153	162	147	183	174	169	152	164	186	178
Daughter	145	155	142	167	167	151	145	152	163	168
Mother	175	173	158	168	181	173	166	162	180	156
Daughter	172	167	160	154	170	164	156	150	160	152

a Plot these results on a scatter diagram. Take the *x*-axis for the mothers' heights from 140 to 200. Take the *y*-axis for the daughters' heights from 140 to 200.

b Is it true that the tall mothers have tall daughters?

C

FM 5 The table below shows the marks for ten students in their mathematics and geography examinations.

Student	Anna	Becky	Cath	Dema	Emma	Fatima	Greta	Hannah	Imogen	Sitara
Maths	57	65	34	87	42	35	59	61	25	35
Geog	45	61	30	78	41	36	35	57	23	34

a Plot the data on a scatter diagram. Take the x-axis for the mathematics scores and the y-axis for the geography scores.

b Draw the line of best fit.

c One of the students was ill when she took the geography examination. Which student was it most likely to be?

d If another student, Kate, was absent for the geography examination but scored 75 in mathematics, what mark would you expect her to have scored in geography?

e If another student, Lina, was absent for the mathematics examination but scored 65 in geography, what mark would you expect her to have scored in mathematics?

FM 6 A form teacher carried out a survey of 20 students from his class and asked them to say how many hours per week they spent playing sport and how many hours per week they spent watching TV. This table shows the results of the survey.

Student	1	2	3	4	5	6	7	8	9	10
Hours playing sport	12	3	5	15	11	0	9	7	6	12
Hours watching TV	18	26	24	16	19	27	12	13	17	14

Student	11	12	13	14	15	16	17	18	19	20
Hours playing sport	12	10	7	6	7	3	1	2	0	12
Hours watching TV	22	16	18	22	12	28	18	20	25	13

a Plot these results on a scatter diagram. Take the x-axis as the number of hours playing sport and the y-axis as the number of hours watching TV.

AU b If you knew that another student from the form watched 8 hours of TV a week, would you be able to predict how long they spent playing sport? Explain why.

FM 7 The table shows the times taken and distances travelled by a taxi driver in 10 journeys on one day.

Distance (km)	1.6	8.3	5.2	6.6	4.8	7.2	3.9	5.8	8.8	5.4
Time (minutes)	3	17	11	13	9	15	8	11	16	10

a Draw a scatter diagram of this information, with time on the horizontal axis.

b Draw a line of best fit on your diagram.

c If a taxi journey takes 5 minutes, how far, in kilometres, would you expect the journey to have been?

d How much time would you expect a journey of 4 km to take?

PS **8** Omar records the time taken, in hours, and the average speed, in miles per hour (mph), for several different journeys.

Time (h)	0.5	0.8	1.1	1.3	1.6	1.75	2	2.4	2.6
Speed (mph)	42	38	27	30	22	23	21	9	8

Estimate the average speed for a journey of 90 minutes.

AU **9** Describe what you would expect the scatter graph to look like if someone said that it showed negative correlation.

8.3 Surveys

This section will show you how to:	Key words
● conduct surveys ● ask good questions in order to collect reliable and valid data	data-collection sheet leading question questionnaire response survey

A **survey** is an organised way of asking a lot of people a few, well-constructed questions, or of making a lot of observations in an experiment, in order to reach a conclusion about something. Surveys are used to test out people's opinions or to test a hypothesis.

Simple data-collection sheet

If you need to collect some data to analyse, you will have to design a simple **data-collection sheet**.

Look at this example: "Where do you want to go for the Year 10 trip at the end of term – Blackpool, Alton Towers, The Great Western Show or London?"

You would put this question on the same day to a lot of Year 10 students and enter their answers straight onto a data-collection sheet, as below.

Place	Tally	Frequency
Blackpool	卌 卌 卌 卌 III	23
Alton Towers	卌 卌 卌 卌 卌 卌 卌 卌 卌 I	46
The Great Western Show	卌 卌 IIII	14
London	卌 卌 卌 卌 II	22

Notice how plenty of space is left for the tally marks and how the tallies are 'gated' in groups of five to make counting easier when the survey is complete.

This is a good, simple data-collection sheet because:

- only one question is asked ("Where do you want to go?")
- all the possible venues are listed
- the answer from each interviewee can be easily and quickly tallied, and the next interviewee questioned.

Notice too that, since the question listed specific places, they must all appear on the data collection sheet. You would lose marks in an examination if you just asked the open question: "Where do you want to go?"

Data sometimes needs to be collected to obtain **responses** for two different categories. The data-collection sheet is then in the form of a simple two-way table.

EXAMPLE 4

The head of a school wants to find out how long his students spend doing homework in a week. He carries out a survey on 60 students. He uses the two-way table to show the result.

	0–5 hours	0–10 hours	10–20 hours	More than 20 hours
Year 7				

This is not a good table as the categories overlap. A student who does 10 hours' work a week could tick any of two columns. Response categories should not overlap and there should be only one possible place to put a tick.

A better table would be:

	0 up to 5 hours	More than 5 and up to 10 hours	More than 10 and up to 15 hours	More than 15 hours
Year 7	JHT II	JHT		
Year 8	JHT	JHT II		
Year 9	III	JHT II	II	
Year 10	III	JHT	III	I
Year 11	II	IIII	IIII	II

This gives a more accurate picture of the amount of homework done in each year group.

Using your computer

Once the data has been collected for your survey, it can be put into a computer database. This allows the data to be stored and amended or updated at a later date if necessary.

From the database, suitable statistical diagrams can easily be drawn within the software and averages calculated for you. Your results can then be published in, for example, the school magazine.

EXERCISE 8C

FM 1 "People like the supermarket to open on Sundays."

    a To see whether this statement is true, design a data-collection sheet that will allow you to capture data while standing outside a supermarket.

    b Does it matter on which day you collect data outside the supermarket?

2 The school tuck shop wanted to know which types of chocolate it should order to sell – plain, milk, fruit and nut, wholenut or white chocolate.

    a Design a data-collection sheet that you could use to ask the pupils in your school which of these chocolate types are their favourite.

HINTS AND TIPS

Include space for tallies.

    b Invent the first 30 entries on the chart.

3 What type of television programme do people in your age group watch the most? Is it crime, romance, comedy, documentary, sport or something else? Design a data-collection sheet to be used in a survey of your age group.

4 On what do people of your age tend to spend their money? Is it sport, magazines, clubs, cinema, sweets, clothes or something else? Design a data-collection sheet to be used in a survey of your age group.

5 Design two-way tables to show the following. Invent about 40 entries for each one.

HINTS AND TIPS

Make sure all possible responses are covered.

    a How students in different year groups travel to school in the morning.

    b The type of programme that different age groups prefer to watch on TV.

    c The favourite sport of boys and girls.

    d How much time students in different year groups spend on the computer in the evening.

FM 6 Carlos wanted to find out who eats healthy food.
He decided to investigate the hypothesis:

    "Boys are less likely to eat healthy food than girls are."

    a Design a data-capture form that Carlos could use to help him do this.

    b Carlos records information from a sample of 40 boys and 25 girls. He finds that 17 boys and 15 girls eat healthy food. Based on this sample, is the hypothesis correct? Explain your answer.

AU 7 Show how you would find out what kind of tariffs your classmates use on their mobile phones.

AU 8 You have been asked to find out which shops the parents of the students at your school like to use. When creating a data-collection sheet, what two things must you include?

Questionnaires

When you are putting together a **questionnaire**, you must think very carefully about the sorts of question you are going to ask, to put together a clear, easy-to-use questionnaire.

Here are five rules that you should *always* follow.

- Never ask a **leading question** designed to get a particular response.

- Never ask a personal, irrelevant question.

- Keep each question as simple as possible.

- Include questions that will get a response from whomever is asked.

- Make sure the categories for the responses do not overlap and keep the number of choices to a reasonable number (six at the most).

The following questions are *badly constructed* and should *never* appear in any questionnaire.

✘ *What is your age?* This is personal. Many people will not want to answer. It is always better to give a range of ages such as:

☐ Under 15 ☐ 16–20 ☐ 21–30 ☐ 31–40 ☐ Over 40

✘ *Slaughtering animals for food is cruel to the poor defenceless animals. Don't you agree?* This is a leading question, designed to get a 'yes'. It is better ask an impersonal question such as:

Are you a vegetarian? ☐ Yes ☐ No

✘ *Do you go to discos when abroad?* This can be answered only by those who have been abroad. It is better to ask a starter question, with a follow-up question such as:

Have you been abroad for a holiday? ☐ Yes ☐ No

If 'Yes', did you go to a disco whilst you were away? ☐ Yes ☐ No

✘ *When you first get up in a morning and decide to have some sort of breakfast that might be made by somebody else, do you feel obliged to eat it all or not?* This question is too complicated. It is better to ask a series of shorter questions such as:

What time do you get up for school? ☐ Before 7 ☐ Between 7 and 8 ☐ After 8

Do you have breakfast every day? ☐ Yes ☐ No

If 'No', on how many schooldays do you have breakfast? ☐ 0 ☐ 1 ☐ 2 ☐ 3 ☐ 4 ☐ 5

A questionnaire is usually put together to test a hypothesis or a statement. For example: "People buy cheaper milk from the supermarket as they don't mind not getting it on their doorstep. They'd rather go out to buy it."

A questionnaire designed to test whether this statement is true or not should include these questions:

✓ *Do you have milk delivered to your doorstep?*
✓ *Do you buy cheaper milk from the supermarket?*
✓ *Would you buy your milk only from the supermarket?*

Once the data from these questions has been collected, it can be looked at to see whether or not the majority of people hold views that agree with the statement.

EXERCISE 8D

FM 1 These are questions from a questionnaire on healthy eating.

> **a** *Fast food is bad for you. Don't you agree?*
>
> ☐ Strongly agree   ☐ Agree   ☐ Don't know
>
> Give two criticisms of the question.
>
> **b** *Do you eat fast food?*   ☐ Yes   ☐ No
>
> *If 'Yes', how many times on average per week do you eat fast food?*
>
> ☐ Once or less   ☐ 2 or 3 times   ☐ 4 or 5 times   ☐ More than 5 times
>
> Give two reasons why this is a good question.

2 This is a question from a survey on pocket money:

> *How much pocket money do you get each week?*
>
> ☐ £0–£2   ☐ £0–£5   ☐ £5–£10   ☐ £10 or more
>
> **a** Give a reason why this is not a good question.

AU b Rewrite the question to make it a good question.

3 Design a questionnaire to test the following statement.

> *People under sixteen do not know what is meant by all the jargon used in the business news on TV, but the over-twenties do.*

> **HINTS AND TIPS**
>
> Keep questions simple with clear response categories and no overlapping.

4 *The under-twenties feel quite at ease with computers, while the over-forties would rather not bother with them. The twenty-to-forties always try to look good with computers.*

Design a questionnaire to test this statement.

5 Design a questionnaire to test the following hypothesis.

> *The older you get, the less sleep you need.*

PS 6 Design a questionnaire to test the hypothesis:

> "People with back problems do not sit properly."

The data-handling cycle

This section will show you how:

● use the data-handling cycle to test a hypothesis

Key words

bias

hypothesis

population

primary data

sample

secondary data

The data-handling cycle

Testing out a **hypothesis** involves a cycle of planning, collecting data, evaluating the significance of the data and then interpreting the results, which may or may not show the hypothesis to be true. This cycle often leads to a refinement of the problem, which starts the cycle all over again.

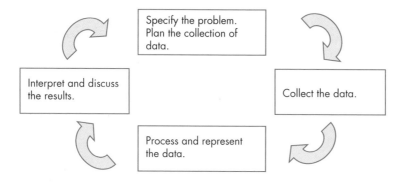

There are four parts to the data-handling cycle.

1   State the hypothesis, which is the idea being tested, outlining the problem and planning what needs to be done.

2   Plan the data collection and collect the data. Record the data collected clearly.

3   Choose the best way to process and represent the data. This will normally mean calculating averages (mean, median, mode) and measures of spread, then representing data in suitable diagrams.

4   Interpret the data and make conclusions.

Then the hypothesis can be refined or changes made to the data collected, for example a different type of data can be collected or the same data can be collected in a different way. In this way, the data-handling cycle helps to improve reliability in the collection and interpretation of data.

EXAMPLE 5

A gardener grows tomatoes, both in a greenhouse and outside.

He wants to investigate the following hypothesis:

"Tomato plants grown inside the greenhouse produce more tomatoes than those grown outside."

Describe the data-handling cycle that may be applied to this problem.

Plan the data collection. Consider 10 tomato plants grown in the greenhouse, and 10 plants grown outside. Count the tomatoes on each plant.

Collect the data. Record the numbers of tomatoes collected from the plants between June and September. Only count those that are 'fit for purpose'.

Choose the best way to process and represent the data. Calculate the mean number collected per plant, as well as the range.

Interpret the data and make conclusions. Look at the statistics. What do they show? Is there a clear conclusion or do you need to alter the hypothesis in any way? Discuss the results, refine the method and continue the cycle.

As you see, in describing the data-handling cycle, you must refer to each of the four parts.

Data Collection

Data that you collect yourself is called **primary data**. You control it, in terms of accuracy and amount.

Data collected by someone else is called **secondary data**. Generally, there is a lot of this type of data available on the internet or in newspapers. This provides a huge volume of data but you have to rely on the sources being reliable, for accuracy.

EXERCISE 8E

Use the data-handling cycle to describe how you would test each of the following hypotheses. In each case state whether you would use primary or secondary data.

1 August is the hottest month of the year.

2 Boys are better than girls at estimating distances.

3 More men go to football matches than women.

4 Tennis is watched by more women than men.

5 The more revision you do, the better your exam results.

6 The older you are, the more likely you are to shop at a department store.

C

Other uses of statistics

This section will show you how:

- statistics are used in everyday life and what information the government needs about the population

Key words

margin of error

national census

polls

retail price index

social statistics

time series

This section will explain about **social statistics** and introduce some of the more common ones in daily use.

In daily life, many situations occur in which statistical techniques are used to produce data. The results of surveys appear in newspapers every day. There are many on-line **polls** and phone-ins that give people the chance to vote, such as in reality TV shows.

Results for these are usually given as a percentage with a **margin of error**, which is a measure of how accurate the information is.

Some common social statistics in daily use are briefly described below.

General index of retail prices

This is also know as the **retail price index** (RPI) and it measures how much the daily cost of living increases (or decreases). One year is chosen as the base year and given an index number, usually 100. The corresponding costs in subsequent years are compared to this and given a number proportional to the base year, such as 103.

Note: The numbers do not represent actual values but just compare current prices to those in the base year.

Time series

Like the RPI, a **time series** measures changes in a quantity over time. Unlike the RPI, though, the actual values of the quantity are used. A time series might track, for example, how the exchange rate between the pound and the dollar changes over time.

National census

A **national census** is a survey of all people and households in a country. Data about categories such as age, gender, religion and employment status is collected to enable governments to plan where to allocate future resources. In Britain a national census is taken every 10 years. The most recent census was in 2001.

EXERCISE 8F

D

1 In 2004 the cost of a litre of petrol was 78p. Using 2004 as a base year, the price index of petrol for each of the next five years is shown in this table.

Year	2004	2005	2006	2007	2008	2009
Index	100	103	108	109	112	120
Price	78p					

Work out the price of petrol in each subsequent year.

Give your answers to 1 decimal place.

2 The following is taken from the UK government statistics website.

In mid-2004 the UK was home to 59.8 million people, of which 50.1 million lived in England. The average age was 38.6 years, an increase on 1971 when it was 34.1 years. In mid-2004 approximately one in five people in the UK were aged under 16 and one in six people were aged 65 or over.

Use this extract to answer the following questions about the UK in 2004.

a How many of the population of the UK *did not* live in England?

b By how much had the average age increased since 1971?

c Approximately how many of the population were aged under 16?

d Approximately how many of the population were aged over 65?

3 The graph shows the exchange rate for the dollar against the pound for each month in one year.

a What was the exchange rate in January?

b Between which two consecutive months did the exchange rate fall most?

c Explain why you could not use the graph to predict the exchange rate in the January following this year.

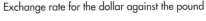

Exchange rate for the dollar against the pound

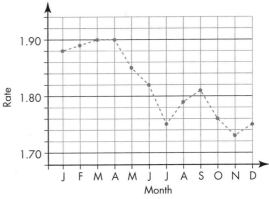

4 The general index of retail prices started in January 1987, when it was given a base number of 100. In January 2006 the index number was 194.1.

If the 'standard weekly shopping basket' cost £38.50 in January 1987, how much would it have cost in January 2006?

FM **5** The time series shows car production in Britain from November 2008 to November 2009.

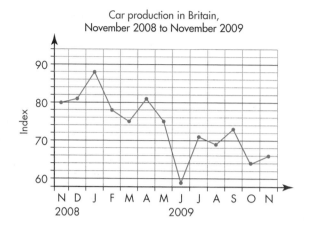

Car production in Britain,
November 2008 to November 2009

a Why was there a sharp drop in production in June 2009?

b The average production over the first three months shown was 172 000 cars.

i Work out an approximate value for the average production over the last three months shown.

ii The base month for the index is January 2005 when the index was 100. What was the approximate production in January 2005?

AU **6** The retail price index measures how much the daily cost of living increases or decreases. If 2008 is given a base index number of 100, then 2009 is given 98. What does this mean?

PS **7** On one day in 2009 Alex spent £51 in a supermarket.

She knew that the price index over the last three years was:

2007	2008	2009
100	103	102

How much would she have paid in the supermarket for the same goods in 2008?

GRADE BOOSTER

F You can interpret a simple pie chart

E You can draw a pie chart

E You can recognise the different types of correlation

D You can design a data-collection sheet

C You can use a line of best fit and use it to make predictions

C You can interpret a scatter diagram

C You can design and criticise questions for questionnaires

C You can describe the data-handling cycle

What you should know now

- How to read and draw pie charts
- How to plot scatter diagrams, recognise correlation, draw lines of best fit and use them to predict values
- How to design questionnaires and know how to ask suitable questions

1 **a** The nationalities of 45 people on a coach were recorded.

Destination	Number of students
French	9
Spanish	12
Italian	6
Greek	10
American	8

Draw a clearly labelled pie chart to represent this information.

b What percentage of the 45 people were French?

2 The table shows the type and number of CDs that Roger owns.

Type	Number
Rock	18
Pop	12
Classical	6

Draw a pie chart to represent this information. (3)

(Total 3 marks)

AQA, June 2007, Module 1 Intermediate, Question 6

3 The pie chart shows the sports played by 60 students during their games lesson.

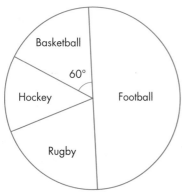

a How many students play football? (1)

b How many students play hockey or rugby? (3)

(Total 4 marks)

AQA, May 2009, Paper 1 Foundation, Question 3

4 The pie chart shows the results of a survey on pets owned by year 7 pupils.

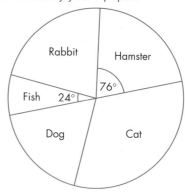

a What fraction of the total number of pets is fish?
Give your answer in its lowest terms.

b The total number of pets is 270.

i Calculate how many of the pets are hamsters.

ii There are 84 cats. *Calculate* the angle at the centre of the sector for cats.

5 Louise wanted to find out the number of hours of television watched last Sunday.

This is her question and response section.

> Question: How many hours of television did you watch last Sunday?
> Response: Tick a box
>
> 1 to 3 hours ☐   4 to 6 hours ☐
> 6 to 8 hours ☐
> more than 8 hours ☐

Write down **two** criticisms of the response section. (2)

(Total 2 marks)

AQA, June 2008, Module 1 Foundation, Question 8(b)

6 A toy shop sells paddling pools.

The table shows the number sold each month.

Month	April	May	June	July	Aug	Sept	Oct
Number of paddling pools	4	5	9	12	7	4	3

C   D   E

a Draw a time-series graph for this data. (2)

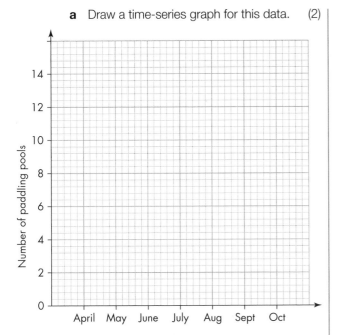

Number of paddling pools

April May June July Aug Sept Oct

b Describe the sales pattern shown by the graph. (1)

(Total 3 marks)

AQA, November 2007, Module 1 Foundation, Question 3

7 Here is part of a railway timetable.

	Departure Times			
Newcastle	0840	0935	1040	1122
York	0943	1034	1144	1225
Leeds	1010	–	1210	–
Derby	1124	1157	1324	1355
Birmingham	1215	1315	1415	1515

a A train leaves Newcastle at 1040.
How long is the journey to Birmingham for this train?
Give your answer in hours and minutes. (3)

b The 1225 train from York takes 1 hour 30 minutes to reach Derby.
The distance from York to Derby is 96 miles.
Calculate the average speed of the train in miles per hour. (3)

(Total 6 marks)

AQA, June 2007, Paper 2 Intermediate, Question 7

8 The table shows the time taken and distance travelled by a taxi driver for 10 journeys one day.

Time (min)	Distance (km)
3	1.7
17	8.3
11	5.1
13	6.7
9	4.7
15	7.3
8	3.8
11	5.7
16	8.7
10	5.3

a Plot on a grid, a scatter diagram with time, on the horizontal axis, from 0 to 20, and distance, on the vertical axis, from 0 to 10.

b Draw a line of best fit on your diagram.

c A taxi journey takes 4 minutes. How many kilometres is the journey?

d A taxi journey is 10 kilometres. How many minutes will it take?

9 Dan and Doris are doing a survey on the type of music people buy.

a This is one question from Dan's survey.

> Classical music is just for snobbish people.
> Don't you agree?
> Tick (✔) a box.
> Strongly agree ☐   Agree ☐
> Don't know ☐

Give two criticisms of Dan's question.

b This is a question from Doris' survey.

> Do you buys CDs?   ☐ Yes   No ☐
> If yes, how many CDs do you buy on average each month?
>   ☐ 2 or less ☐ 3 or 4 ☐ 5 or 6
>   ☐ More than 6

Give two reasons why this is a good question.

Worked Examination Questions

1 The scatter diagram shows the relationship between the total mileage of a car and its value as a percentage of its original value.

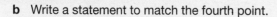

a Which of the four points, A, B, C or D, represents each of the statements below?

Alf: I have a rare car. It has done a lot of miles but it is still worth a lot of money.

Belinda: My car is quite new. It hasn't done many miles.

Charles: My car hasn't done many miles but it is really old and rusty.

b Write a statement to match the fourth point.

c What does the graph tell you about the relationship between the mileage of a car and the percentage of its original value?

d Draw scatter diagrams to show the relationship between:

  i the amount of petrol used and the distance driven

  ii the value of a car and the age of the driver.

---

a Alf is represented by point D.
Belinda is represented by point A.
Charles is represented by point B.

(3 marks)

> Read both axes. The horizontal axis is total mileage and the vertical axis is percentage of original value. So, Alf would be to the right of the horizontal axis and to the top of the vertical axis. Use similar reasoning for the other people. You get 1 mark for each correct person linked to a point.

b 'My car has done a lot of miles and isn't worth very much.'

(1 mark)

> The fourth point, C, is a car that has high mileage with low value.
> Any statement that says something like this answer given would get the 1 mark available.

c The more mileage a car has done, the less is its value.

(1 mark)

> The graph basically shows weak negative correlation, so as one variable increases, the other decreases.
> Using this principle to give the correct answer earns you 1 mark.

d i   **ii**

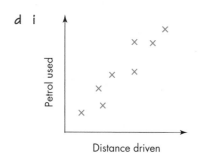

> The first diagram shows positive correlation, as the more miles are driven, the more petrol is used.
> The second diagram shows no correlation as there is no relationship.
> You earn 1 mark for each correct diagram.

(2 marks)

(**Total:** 7 marks)

Worked Examination Questions

AU **2** The table below shows the number of learners at each grade for two practice driving tests, Theory and Practical.

	Grades					
	Excellent	Very good	Good	Pass	Fail	Total number of learners
Theory	208	888	1032	696	56	2880
Practical	240	351	291	108	90	1080

a Represent each of the two practice tests in a pie chart.

b By comparing the pie charts, on which test, Theory or Practical, do you think learners did better overall? Give reasons to justify your answer.

a

	Theory		Practical	
Grade	Frequency	Angle	Frequency	Angle
Excellent	208	$360° \times 208 \div 2880 = 26°$	240	$360° \times 240 \div 1080 = 80°$
Very good	888	$360° \times 888 \div 2880 = 111°$	351	$360° \times 351 \div 1080 = 117°$
Good	1032	$360° \times 1032 \div 2880 = 129°$	291	$360° \times 291 \div 1080 = 97°$
Pass	696	$360° \times 696 \div 2880 = 87°$	108	$360° \times 108 \div 1080 = 36°$
Fail	56	$360° \times 56 \div 2880 = 7°$	90	$360° \times 90 \div 1080 = 30°$

> You will earn 1 mark for showing in at least five places the correct process of $360° \times$ frequency $\div$ total frequency.

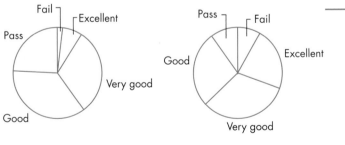

Theory

Practical

> 3 accuracy marks are available for the correct angles calculated. You will lose a mark for each incorrect one, to a minimum of 0.
> Also available are: 1 method mark for drawing two separate pie charts.
> 1 method mark for correctly labelling both charts.
> 1 accuracy mark for each chart being correctly drawn.
> Note that each angle can be up to 2° out for these marks to be given.

(7 marks)

b A greater proportion of learners got "Good" or better on the practical, but learners did better in the theory test as a much smaller proportion failed.

So, I would say the learners did better overall in the practical test.

> You earn 1 mark for stating one comparison correctly.

> You earn 1 mark for giving either of the tests as better overall but only with a justification as here.

(2 marks)

(**Total:** 9 marks)

Riding stables must carefully manage the welfare of their horses, including housing them in stables of the correct size and feeding them the correct amount of food for their weight and intended workload. Mr Owen owns a riding stable and wishes to understand his horses' needs, his customers and how he might go about gathering the right information to help him successfully expand his business.

Getting started

In pairs, consider the following points to help you in planning Mr Owen's expansion of his riding stables.

- There are several different elements to consider when running a riding stable: buying or breeding horses, looking after the horses (including feeding and cleaning), running and training the horses and running classes for different types of students.

- How would you find out if there is correlation between girth, weight and height? How could Mr Owen use this information to predict the body weight of horses of different girths? How useful would this information be to Mr Owen?

- How could you graphically represent the record that Mr Owen kept last summer of the different abilities of his customers? How could he use this information to help in planning his expansion?

- If Mr Owen's customers were asked what they wanted most from the stables, how could you collect, represent and interpret this information?

Your task

Mr Owen needs to work out how much feed to give his horses. He owns six horses, as detailed below. Working in pairs or individually, use the information on the six horses, the Bodyweight calculator and the Feed chart to find the best way to calculate the amount of feed each horse needs.

Feed chart

Body weight of horse (kg)	Weight of feed (kg) at different levels of work	
	Medium	Hard
300	2.4	3.0
350	2.8	3.5
400	3.2	4.0
450	3.6	4.5
500	4.0	5.0
Extra feed per 50 kg	300 g	400 g

Your task

Mr Owen also wants to understand the different abilities and numbers of riders who come to his riding stable, as he wishes to expand his business next year. He keeps a record of his students and the workload they place on the horses during one week of the summer holidays (see Riders table below). How would Mr Owen use this information to make sure he buys the right type of new horses to suit his riders?

Mr Owen is also aware that different riders look for different facilities at the stables. Help him to work out how he can decide which new facilities different riders would value the most.

Help Mr Owen to plan his expansion, using surveys and diagrams.

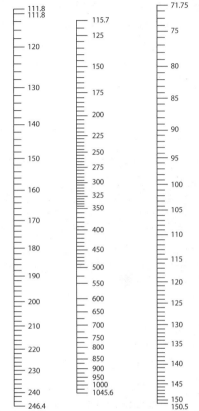

Bodyweight calculator

Girth (cm) Weight (kg) Length (cm)

Using the bodyweight calculator

Place a ruler from your measurement for girth line to your measurement for the length line. The point at which the ruler crosses the weight line is the reading for the approximate weight of the horse. Note that the ruler will cross the weight line at an angle.

Riders	Ability/work	Total
Children	Medium	45
Female novice	Medium	20
Female experienced	Hard	61
Male novice	Medium	15
Male experienced	Hard	29

Horse:	Summer	Sally	Skip	Simon	Barney	Teddy
Girth:	220 cm	190 cm	200 cm	180 cm	160 cm	190 cm
Length:	142 cm	95 cm	114 cm	124 cm	110 cm	140 cm
Height: hands and inches	17 h 2 in	14 h 3 in	16 h 0 in	15 h 3 in	15 h 1 in	16 h 2 in
Work:	Medium	Hard	Hard	Medium	Medium	Hard

A pattern is an arrangement of repeated uniform parts. You see patterns every day in clothes, art and home furnishings. Patterns can also occur in numbers.

There are many mathematical problems that can be solved using patterns in numbers. Some numbers have fascinating features.

Here is a pattern.

$3 + 5 = 8$ (5 miles $\approx$ 8 km)

$5 + 8 = 13$ (8 miles $\approx$ 13 km)

$8 + 13 = 21$ (13 miles $\approx$ 21 km)

Approximately how many kilometres are there in 21 miles?

Note: $\approx$ means 'approximately equal to'.

In the boxes are some more patterns. Can you work out the next line of each pattern?

Now look at these numbers and see why they are special.

$4096 = (4 + 0^9)^6$

$81 = (8 + 1)^2$

Some patterns have special names.
Can you pair up these patterns and the names?

4, 8, 12, 16, …	Prime numbers
1, 4, 9, 16, …	Multiples (of 4)
2, 3, 5, 7, …	Cube numbers
1, 8, 27, 64, …	Square numbers

You will look at these in more detail in this chapter.

Below are four sets of numbers. Think about which number links together all the other numbers in each set. (The mathematics that you cover in 9.2 'Factors of whole numbers' will help you to work this out!)

10, 5, 2, 1

18, 9, 6, 3, 2, 1

25, 5, 1

32, 16, 8, 4, 2, 1

$5^2 = 5 \times 5 = 25$

$50^2 = 50 \times 50 = 2500$

$500^2 = 500 \times 500 = 250\,000$

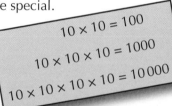

$10 \times 10 = 100$

$10 \times 10 \times 10 = 1000$

$10 \times 10 \times 10 \times 10 = 10\,000$

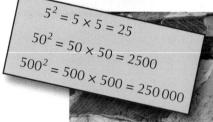

$4^2 = 16$

$34^2 = 1156$

$334^2 = 111\,556$

$1 \times 1 = 1$

$11 \times 11 = 121$

$111 \times 111 = 12\,321$

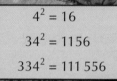

$1 \times 1 = 1$

$2 \times 2 = 1 + 3$

$3 \times 3 = 1 + 3 + 5$

$4 \times 4 = 1 + 3 + 5 + 7$

$1089 \times 9 = 9801$

$10\,989 \times 9 = 98\,901$

$109\,989 \times 9 = 989\,901$

Number: Number properties

This chapter will show you ...

- **G** the meaning of multiples
- **G** the meaning of factors
- **F** how to work out squares and square roots
- **E** the meaning of prime numbers
- **E** how to work out powers
- **C** how to break a number down into its prime factors
- **C** how to work out the least common multiple of two numbers
- **C** how to work out the highest common factor of two numbers

Visual overview

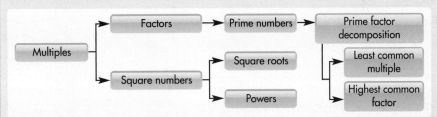

What you should already know

- Multiplication tables up to 10 × 10 **(KS3 level 4, GCSE grade G)**

Quick check

Write down the answers to the following.

1 a 2 × 3	**b** 4 × 3	**c** 5 × 3	
d 6 × 3	**e** 7 × 3	**f** 8 × 3	
2 a 2 × 4	**b** 4 × 4	**c** 5 × 4	
d 6 × 4	**e** 7 × 4	**f** 8 × 4	
3 a 2 × 5	**b** 9 × 5	**c** 5 × 5	
d 6 × 5	**e** 7 × 5	**f** 8 × 5	
4 a 2 × 6	**b** 9 × 6	**c** 8 × 8	
d 6 × 6	**e** 7 × 9	**f** 8 × 6	
5 a 2 × 7	**b** 9 × 7	**c** 8 × 9	
d 6 × 7	**e** 7 × 7	**f** 8 × 7	

Multiples of whole numbers

This section will show you how to:
- find multiples of whole numbers
- recognise multiples of numbers

Key words
multiple
multiplication table
times table

When you multiply any whole number by another whole number, the answer is called a **multiple** of either of those numbers.

For example, 5 × 7 = 35, which means that 35 is a multiple of 5 and it is also a multiple of 7. Here are some other multiples of 5 and 7:

multiples of 5 are   5   10   15   20   25   30   35   …

multiples of 7 are   7   14   21   28   35   42   …

Multiples are the answers that appear in **multiplication tables**. These are also called **times tables**.

×	2	3	4	5	6
2	4	6	8	10	12
3	6	9	12	15	18
4	8	12	16	20	24
5	10	15	20	25	30
6	12	18	24	30	36

For example, 12 is a multiple of 2, 3, 4 and 6 as well as a multiple of 1 and 12.

Recognising multiples

You can recognise the multiples of 2, 3, 4, 5, 6 and 9 in the following ways.

- Multiples of 2 always end in an even number or 0. For example:

    12   34   96   1938   370

- Multiples of 3 are always made up of digits that add up to a multiple of 3. For example:

    15   because   1 + 5 = 6   which is 2 × **3**

    72   because   7 + 2 = 9   which is 3 × **3**

    201   because   2 + 0 + 1 = 3   which is 1 × **3**

- Multiples of 4 always give an even number when divided by 2. For example:

    64   because   64 ÷ 2 = 32   which is even

    212   because   212 ÷ 2 = 106   which is even

    500   because   500 ÷ 2 = 250   which is even

HINTS AND TIPS

Another check is to look at the last two digits of the number. If they give a multiple of 4, the whole numbers is a multiple of 4.

FM Functional Maths   AU (AO2) Assessing Understanding   PS (AO3) Problem Solving

- Multiples of 5 always end in 5 or 0. For example:

    35   60   155   300

- Multiples of 6 are multiples of 2 and multiples of 3. For example:

    42   because it is even   and $4 + 2 = 6$ which is $2 \times$ **3**

    54   because it is even   and $5 + 4 = 9$ which is $3 \times$ **3**

- Multiples of 9 are always made up of digits that add up to a multiple of 9. For example,

    63   because $6 + 3 = 9$ which is $1 \times$ **9**

    738   because $7 + 3 + 8 = 18$ which is $2 \times$ **9**

You can find out whether numbers are multiples of 7 and 8 by using your calculator. For example, to find out whether 341 is a multiple of 7, you have to see whether 341 gives a whole number when it is divided by 7. You therefore key

$$ \boxed{3} \ \boxed{4} \ \boxed{1} \ \boxed{\div} \ \boxed{7} \ \boxed{=} $$

The answer is 48.714 286, which is a decimal number, not a whole number. So, 341 is *not* a multiple of 7.

ACTIVITY

Grid locked

You need eight copies of this 10 × 10 grid.

1	2	3	4	5	6	7	8	9	10
11	12	13	14	15	16	17	18	19	20
21	22	23	24	25	26	27	28	29	30
31	32	33	34	35	36	37	38	39	40
41	42	43	44	45	46	47	48	49	50
51	52	53	54	55	56	57	58	59	60
61	62	63	64	65	66	67	68	69	70
71	72	73	74	75	76	77	78	79	80
81	82	83	84	85	86	87	88	89	90
91	92	93	94	95	96	97	98	99	100

Take one of the grids and shade in all the multiples of 2. You should find that they make a neat pattern.

Do the same thing for the multiples of 3, 4, … up to 9, using a fresh 10 × 10 grid for each number.

Next, draw a grid which is 9 squares wide and write the numbers from 1 to 100 in the grid, like this:

1	2	3	4	5	6	7	8	9
10	11	12	13	14	15	16	17	18
1		21		3	2			27

Make seven more copies of this grid. Then shade in the multiples of 2, 3, … up to 9, using a fresh grid for each number.

Write out the numbers from 1 to 100 on grids of different widths and shade in the multiples of 2, 3, … up to 9, as before.

Describe the patterns that you get.

EXERCISE 9A

1 Write out the first five multiples of:

    a 3   **b** 7   **c** 9   **d** 11   **e** 16

Remember: the first multiple is the number itself.

2 From the numbers below, write down those that are:

    a multiples of 2   **b** multiples of 3

    c multiples of 5   **d** multiples of 9.

111	254	255	108	73
68	162	711	615	98
37	812	102	75	270

> **HINTS AND TIPS**
>
> Remember the rules on pages 270–271.

3 Use your calculator to see which of the numbers below are:

    a multiples of 4   **b** multiples of 7   **c** multiples of 6.

72	135	102	161	197
132	78	91	216	514
312	168	75	144	294

> **HINTS AND TIPS**
>
> There is no point testing odd numbers for multiples of even numbers such as 4 and 6.

PS 4 Find the biggest number that is smaller than 100 and that is:

a a multiple of 2   b a multiple of 3

c a multiple of 4   d a multiple of 5

e a multiple of 7   f a multiple of 6.

PS 5 Find the smallest number that is bigger than 1000 and that is:

a a multiple of 6

b a multiple of 8

c a multiple of 9.

FM 6 **AU** Vishal is packing eggs into boxes of six. He has 50 eggs.
Will all the boxes be full?
Give a reason for your answer.

FM 7 A party of 20 people are getting into taxis. Each taxi holds the same number of passengers. If all the taxis fill up, how many people could be in each taxi? Give two possible answers.

8 Here is a list of numbers.

     6   8   12   15   18   28

a From the list, write down a multiple of 9.

b From the list, write down a multiple of 7.

c From the list, write down a multiple of both 3 and 5.

PS 9 Find the lowest even number that is a multiple of 11 and a multiple of 3.

PS 10 How many numbers between 1 and 100 inclusive are multiples of both 6 and 9?
List the numbers.

PS 11 The number 24 is in the following times tables: 1, 2, 3, 4, 6, 8, 12 and 24.

That is a total of eight times tables.

a In which times tables is the number 10?

b In which times tables is the number 30?

c In which times table is the number 100?

d Which number less than 100 is in the most times tables?

Factors of whole numbers

This section will show you how to:
- identify the factors of a number

A **factor** of a whole number is any whole number that divides into it exactly. So:

the factors of 20 are   1   2   4   5   10   20

the factors of 12 are   1   2   3   4   6   12

This is where it is important to know your multiplication tables.

Factor facts

Remember these facts.

- 1 is always a factor and so is the number itself.

- When you have found one factor, there is always another factor that goes with it – unless the factor is multiplied by itself to give the number. For example, look at the number 20:

  $1 \times 20 = 20$ so 1 and 20 are both factors of 20

  $2 \times 10 = 20$ so 2 and 10 are both factors of 20

  $4 \times 5 = 20$ so 4 and 5 are both factors of 20.

  These are called **factor pairs**.

You may need to use your calculator to find the factors of large numbers.

EXAMPLE 1

Find the factors of 32.

Look for the factor pairs of 32. These are:

   $1 \times 32 = 32$ $2 \times 16 = 32$ $4 \times 8 = 32$

So, the factors of 32 are 1, 2, 4, 8, 16, 32.

EXAMPLE 2

Find the factors of 36.

Look for the factor pairs of 36. These are:

   $1 \times 36 = 36$ $2 \times 18 = 36$ $3 \times 12 = 36$ $4 \times 9 = 36$ $6 \times 6 = 36$

6 is a repeated factor which is counted only once.

So, the factors of 36 are 1, 2, 3, 4, 6, 9, 12, 18, 36.

EXERCISE 9B

1 What are the factors of each of these numbers?

    a 10   **b** 28   **c** 18   **d** 17   **e** 25

    f 40   **g** 30   **h** 45   **i** 24   **j** 16

2 How many different ways can 24 chocolate bars be packed into boxes so that there are exactly the same number of bars in each box?

3 Use your calculator to find the factors of each of these numbers.

    a 120   **b** 150   **c** 144   **d** 180

    e 169   **f** 108   **g** 196   **h** 153

    i 198   **j** 199

> **HINTS AND TIPS**
>
> Remember that once you find one factor this will give you another, unless it is a repeated factor such as 5 × 5.

4 What is the biggest factor that is less than 100 for each of these numbers?

    a 110   **b** 201   **c** 145   **d** 117

    e 130   **f** 240   **g** 160   **h** 210

    i 162   **j** 250

5 Find the largest common factor for each of the following pairs of numbers. (Do not include 1.)

    a 2 and 4   **b** 6 and 10   **c** 9 and 12

    d 15 and 25   **e** 9 and 15   **f** 12 and 21

    g 14 and 21   **h** 25 and 30   **i** 30 and 50

    j 55 and 77

> **HINTS AND TIPS**
>
> Look for the largest number that has both numbers in its multiplication table.

FM 6 A designer is making a box for 12 Christmas decorations.

The decorations are to be packed in rows.

How many decorations must be put in each row to make the top of the box a flat, square shape?

AU 7 Here are five numbers.

    18   21   27   32   36

Use factors to explain why 32 could be the odd one out.

PS 8 Find the highest odd number that is a factor of 40 and a factor of 60.

Prime numbers

This section will show you how to:
● identify prime numbers

Key word
prime number

What are the factors of 2, 3, 5, 7, 11 and 13?

Notice that each of these numbers has only two factors: itself and 1. They are all examples of **prime numbers**.

So, a prime number is a whole number that has only two factors: itself and 1.

Note: 1 is *not* a prime number, since it has only one factor – itself.

The prime numbers up to 50 are:

2, 3, 5, 7, 11, 13, 17, 19, 23, 29, 31, 37, 41, 43, 47

You will need to know these for your GCSE examination.

ACTIVITY

Prime search

You need a 10 × 10 grid.

Cross out 1.

Leave 2 and cross out the rest of the multiples of 2.

Leave 3 and cross out the rest of the multiples of 3. Some of them will already have been crossed out.

Leave 5 and cross out the rest of the multiples of 5. Some of them will already have been crossed out.

Leave 7 and cross out the rest of the multiples of 7. All but three of them will already have been crossed out.

1	2	3	4	5	6	7	8	9	10
11	12	13	14	15	16	17	18	19	20
21	22	23	24	25	26	27	28	29	30
31	32	33	34	35	36	37	38	39	40
41	42	43	44	45	46	47	48	49	50
51	52	53	54	55	56	57	58	59	60
61	62	63	64	65	66	67	68	69	70
71	72	73	74	75	76	77	78	79	80
81	82	83	84	85	86	87	88	89	90
91	92	93	94	95	96	97	98	99	100

The numbers left are prime numbers.

The activity is known as the Sieve of Eratosthenes. (Eratosthenes, a Greek scholar, lived from about 275BC to 194BC.)

EXERCISE 9C

1 Write down the prime numbers between 20 and 30.

2 Write down the only prime number between 90 and 100.

AU 3 Using the rules for recognising multiples, decide which of these numbers are **not** prime numbers.

462   108   848   365   711

PS 4 When three different prime numbers are multiplied together the answer is 105.

What are the three prime numbers?

FM 5 A shopkeeper has 31 identical soap bars.

He is trying to arrange the bars on a shelf in rows, each with the same number of bars.

Is it possible?

Explain your answer.

9.4 Square numbers

This section will show you how to:	Key words
● identify square numbers	square
● use a calculator to find the square of a number	square numbers

What is the next number in this sequence?

1, 4, 9, 16, 25, …

Write each number as:

1 × 1, 2 × 2, 3 × 3, 4 × 4, 5 × 5, …

These factors can be represented by **square** patterns of dots:

1×1 2×2 3×3 4×4 5×5

From these patterns, you can see that the next pair of factors must be $6 \times 6 = 36$, therefore 36 is the next number in the sequence.

Because they form square patterns, the numbers 1, 4, 9, 16, 25, 36, … are called **square numbers**.

When you multiply any number by itself, the answer is called the *square of the number* or the *number squared*. This is because the answer is a square number. For example:

the square of 5 (or 5 squared) is $5 \times 5 = 25$

the square of 6 (or 6 squared) is $6 \times 6 = 36$

There is a short way to write the square of any number. For example:

5 squared (5×5) can be written as 5^2

13 squared (13×13) can be written as 13^2

So, the sequence of square numbers, 1, 4, 9, 16, 25, 36, …, can be written as:

$1^2,$ $2^2,$ $3^2,$ $4^2,$ $5^2,$ $6^2,$ …

You are expected to know the square numbers up to 15×15 (= 225) for the GCSE examination.

EXERCISE 9D

1 The square number pattern starts:

    1   4   9   16   25   …

Copy and continue the pattern above until you have written down the first 20 square numbers. You may use your calculator for this.

PS 2 Work out the answer to each of these number sentences.

    $1 + 3 =$

    $1 + 3 + 5 =$

    $1 + 3 + 5 + 7 =$

Look carefully at the pattern of the three number sentences. Then write down the next three number sentences in the pattern and work them out.

AU **3** Draw one counter.

Now add more counters to your picture to make the next square number.

a How many extra counters did you add?

Now add more counters to your picture to make the next square number.

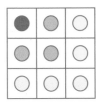

b How many extra counters did you add?

c Without drawing, how many more counters will you need to make the next square number?

d Describe the pattern of counters you are adding.

4 Write down the answer to each of the following. You will need to use your calculator. Look for the x^2 key.

a 23^2 **b** 57^2

c 77^2 **d** 123^2

e 152^2 **f** 3.2^2

g 9.5^2 **h** 23.8^2

i $(-4)^2$ **j** $(-12)^2$

5 **a** Write down the value of 13^2.

b Write down the value of 14^2.

c Estimate the value of 13.2^2.

PS **6** 4 and 81 are square numbers with a sum of 85.

Find two different square numbers with a sum of 85.

7 Find the next three numbers in each of these number patterns. (They are all based on square numbers.) You may use your calculator.

	1	4	9	16	25	36	49	64	81
a	2	5	10	17	26	37	...	...	...
b	2	8	18	32	50	72	...	...	...
c	3	6	11	18	27	38	...	...	...
d	0	3	8	15	24	35	...	...	...
e	101	104	109	116	125	136	...	...	...

> **HINTS AND TIPS**
>
> Look for the connection with the square numbers on the top line.

8 a Work out each of the following. You may use your calculator.

$$3^2 + 4^2 \quad \text{and} \quad 5^2$$
$$5^2 + 12^2 \quad \text{and} \quad 13^2$$
$$7^2 + 24^2 \quad \text{and} \quad 25^2$$
$$9^2 + 40^2 \quad \text{and} \quad 41^2$$
$$11^2 + 60^2 \quad \text{and} \quad 61^2$$

b Describe what you notice about your answers to part **a**.

9 Jasper's bill for his internet is £12 each month for 12 months.

How much does he pay for the whole year?

FM 10 A builder is using flagstones to lay a patio. He thinks that he will need 15 rows, each with 15 flagstones in them. However, he did not allow for the gaps between the flagstones and finds that he only needs 14 rows of each with 14 flagstones in them.

How many flagstones does he have left?

The following exercise will give you some practice on multiples, factors, square numbers and prime numbers.

EXERCISE 9E

1 Write out the first five multiples of each number.

    a 6   **b** 13   **c** 8   **d** 20   **e** 18

Remember: the first multiple is the number itself.

2 Write down the square numbers up to 100.

3 What are the factors of these numbers?

    a 12   **b** 20   **c** 9   **d** 32   **e** 24

    f 38   **g** 13   **h** 42   **i** 45   **j** 36

4 Write out the first three numbers that are multiples of both of the numbers shown.

    a 3 and 4   **b** 4 and 5   **c** 3 and 5   **d** 6 and 9   **e** 5 and 7

AU 5 In question 3, every number had an even number of factors except parts **c** and **j**. What sort of numbers are 9 and 36?

AU 6 In question 3, part **g**, there were only two factors. Why?

7 Write down the prime numbers up to 20.

AU 8 Copy these number sentences and write out the *next four* sentences in the pattern.

$$1 = 1$$
$$1 + 3 = 4$$
$$1 + 3 + 5 = 9$$
$$1 + 3 + 5 + 7 = 16$$

AU 9 Here are four numbers.

14   16   35   49

Copy and complete the table by putting each of the numbers in the correct box.

	Square number	Factor of 70
Even number		
Multiple of 7		

AU 10 Arrange these four number cards to make a square number.

| 1 | 4 | 6 | 7 |

PS 11 If hot-dog sausages are sold in packs of 10 and hot-dog buns are sold in packs of eight, how many of each must you buy to have complete hot dogs with no extra sausages or buns?

PS 12 Rover barks every 8 seconds and Spot barks every 12 seconds. If both dogs bark together, how many seconds will it be before they both bark together again?

PS 13 A bell chimes every 6 seconds. Another bell chimes every 5 seconds. If they both chime together, how many seconds will it be before they both chime together again?

PS 14 Fred runs round a running track in 4 minutes. Debbie runs round in 3 minutes.

If they both start together on the line at the end of the finishing straight, when will they both be on the same line together again?

How many laps will Debbie have run? How many laps will Fred have run?

D

15 From this box, choose one number that fits each of these descriptions.

    a a multiple of 3 and a multiple of 4

    b a square number and an odd number

    c a factor of 24 and a factor of 18

    d a prime number and a factor of 39

    e an odd factor of 30 and a multiple of 3

    f a number with 4 factors and a multiple of 2 and 7

    g a number with 5 factors exactly

    h a multiple of 5 and a factor of 20

    i an even number and a factor of 36 and a multiple of 9

    j a prime number that is one more than a square number

    k written in order, the four factors of this number make a number pattern in which each number is twice the one before

    l an odd number that is a multiple of 7

12	13	21
8		15
	17	
9		18
10		6
14	16	

AU 16 The following numbers are described as triangular numbers.

        1, 3, 6, 10, 15

    a Investigate why they are called triangular numbers.

    b Write down the next five triangular numbers.

9.5 Square roots

This section will show you how to:
- find a square root of a square number
- use a calculator to find the square roots of any number

Key word
square root

The **square root** of a given number is a number that, when multiplied by itself, produces the given number.

For example, the square root of 9 is 3, since $3 \times 3 = 9$.

Numbers also have a negative square root, since -3×-3 also equals 9.

A square root is represented by the symbol $\sqrt{}$. For example, $\sqrt{16} = 4$.

EXERCISE 9F

1 Write down the positive square root of each of these numbers.

a 4	**b** 25	**c** 49	**d** 1	**e** 81
f 100	**g** 64	**h** 9	**i** 36	**j** 16
k 121	**l** 144	**m** 400	**n** 900	**o** 169

2 Write down both possible values of each of these square roots.

| **a** $\sqrt{25}$ | **b** $\sqrt{36}$ | **c** $\sqrt{100}$ | **d** $\sqrt{49}$ | **e** $\sqrt{64}$ |
| **f** $\sqrt{16}$ | **g** $\sqrt{9}$ | **h** $\sqrt{81}$ | **i** $\sqrt{1}$ | **j** $\sqrt{144}$ |

3 Write down the value of each of these. You need only give positive square roots. You will need to use your calculator for some of them. Look for the key.

a 9^2	**b** $\sqrt{1600}$	**c** 10^2	**d** $\sqrt{196}$	**e** 6^2
f $\sqrt{225}$	**g** 7^2	**h** $\sqrt{144}$	**i** 5^2	**j** $\sqrt{441}$
k 11^2	**l** $\sqrt{256}$	**m** 8^2	**n** $\sqrt{289}$	**o** 21^2

4 Write down the positive value of each of the following. You will need to use your calculator.

| **a** $\sqrt{576}$ | **b** $\sqrt{961}$ | **c** $\sqrt{2025}$ | **d** $\sqrt{1600}$ | **e** $\sqrt{4489}$ |
| **f** $\sqrt{10\,201}$ | **g** $\sqrt{12.96}$ | **h** $\sqrt{42.25}$ | **i** $\sqrt{193.21}$ | **j** $\sqrt{492.84}$ |

AU 5 Put these in order, starting with the smallest value.

3^2 $\sqrt{90}$ $\sqrt{50}$ 4^2

AU 6 Between which two consecutive whole numbers does the square root of 20 lie?

PS 7 Use these number cards to make this calculation correct.

$$\sqrt{\square\square\square} = \square\square$$

FM 8 A square wall in a kitchen is being tiled.
Altogether it needs 225 square tiles.
How many tiles are there in each row?

This section will show you how to:
- use powers

Powers are a convenient way of writing repetitive multiplications. (Powers are also called **indices** – singular, index.)

The power that you will use most often is 2, which has the special name **square**. The only other power with a special name is 3, which is called **cube**.

You are expected to know the cubes of numbers, $1^3 = 1$, $2^3 = 8$, $3^3 = 27$, $4^3 = 64$, $5^3 = 125$ and $10^3 = 1000$, for the GCSE examination. **Remember** that in your Unit 2 GCSE examination you will not be allowed to use your calculator to work out powers.

EXAMPLE 3

a What is the value of:

   i 7 squared   **ii** 5 cubed?

b Write each of these numbers out in full.

   i 4^6 **ii** 6^4 **iii** 7^3 **iv** 12^2

c Write the following multiplications as powers.

   i $3 \times 3 \times 3 \times 3 \times 3 \times 3 \times 3 \times 3$ **ii** $13 \times 13 \times 13 \times 13 \times 13$

   iii $7 \times 7 \times 7 \times 7$ **iv** $5 \times 5 \times 5 \times 5 \times 5 \times 5 \times 5$

a The value of 7 squared is $7^2 = 7 \times 7 = 49$

   The value of 5 cubed is $5^3 = 5 \times 5 \times 5 = 125$

b **i** $4^6 = 4 \times 4 \times 4 \times 4 \times 4 \times 4$

   ii $6^4 = 6 \times 6 \times 6 \times 6$

   iii $7^3 = 7 \times 7 \times 7$

   iv $12^2 = 12 \times 12$

c **i** $3 \times 3 \times 3 \times 3 \times 3 \times 3 \times 3 \times 3 = 3^8$

   ii $13 \times 13 \times 13 \times 13 \times 13 = 13^5$

   iii $7 \times 7 \times 7 \times 7 = 7^4$

   iv $5 \times 5 \times 5 \times 5 \times 5 \times 5 \times 5 = 5^7$

Working out powers on your calculator

How would you work out the value of 5^7 on a calculator?

You could key it in as $5 \times 5 \times 5 \times 5 \times 5 \times 5 \times 5 =$. But as you key it in, you may miss a number or press a wrong key. If your calculator has one, you could use the power key, $\boxed{x^\blacksquare}$.

Insert the number 5, then press $\boxed{x^\blacksquare}$ and insert the number 7. The answer displayed is 78125, so

$$5^7 = 78\,125$$

Make sure you know where to find the power key on your calculator. It may be an INV or SHIFT function.

Try using your calculator to work out 3^4, 7^8, 23^4 and 72^3.

Check that you get 81, 5 764 801, 279 841 and 373 248.

EXERCISE 9G

1 Use your calculator to work out the value of each of the following.

a 3^3	**b** 5^3	**c** 6^3	**d** 12^3	**e** 2^4
f 4^4	**g** 5^4	**h** 2^5	**i** 3^7	**j** 2^{10}

2 Work out the values of the following powers of 10.

a 10^2	**b** 10^3	**c** 10^4	**d** 10^5	**e** 10^6

f Describe what you notice about your answers.

g Now write down the value of each of these.

    i 10^8 **ii** 10^{10} **iii** 10^{15}

3 Rewrite each of these, using index notation. You do not have to work them out yet.

a $2 \times 2 \times 2 \times 2$

b $3 \times 3 \times 3 \times 3 \times 3$

c 7×7

d $5 \times 5 \times 5$

e $10 \times 10 \times 10 \times 10 \times 10 \times 10 \times 10$ **f** $6 \times 6 \times 6 \times 6$

g $4 \times 4 \times 4 \times 4$

h $1 \times 1 \times 1 \times 1 \times 1 \times 1 \times 1$

i $0.5 \times 0.5 \times 0.5 \times 0.5$

j $100 \times 100 \times 100$

> **HINTS AND TIPS**
>
> When working out a power, make sure you multiply the number by itself and not by the power. A very common error is to write, for example, $2^3 = 6$ instead of $2^3 = 2 \times 2 \times 2 = 8$.

4 Write the following out in full. You do not have to work them out yet.

a 3^4	**b** 9^3	**c** 6^2	**d** 10^5	**e** 2^{10}
f 8^6	**g** 0.1^3	**h** 2.5^2	**i** 0.7^3	**j** 1000^2

5 Using the power key on your calculator (or another method), work out the values of the power terms in question 3.

6 Using the power key on your calculator (or another method), work out the values of the power terms in question 4.

PS **7** Write the answer to question 3, part **j** as a power of 10.

PS **8** Write the answer to question 4, part **j** as a power of 10.

> **HINTS AND TIPS**
>
> Use the answer you found for question 2f to help you.

9 Copy this pattern of powers of 2 and continue it for another five terms.

2^2 2^3 2^4 ...   .

4   8   16   ...   .

10 Copy the pattern of powers of 10 and fill in the previous five and the next five terms.

...   . 10^2 10^3 ...   .

...   .   100   1000   ...   .

FM **11** A storage container is a cube.
The length of the container is 5 m.
To work out the volume of a cube, use the formula

volume = (length of edge)^3

Work out the total storage space in the container.

AU **12** Write each number as a power of a different number.
The first one has been done for you.

a $32 = 2^5$

b 100

c 8

d 25

AU **13** Marie says that as $3^4 = 81$, 6^2 must also equal 81.

Explain why Marie is wrong.

AU **14** Find the value of the letters that makes the following true.

a $3^4 = x^2$ **b** $2^6 = y^2$

c $2^6 = z^3$ **d** $8^2 = w^3$

e $100^3 = s^2$ **f** 1 million $= r^2$

Multiplying and dividing by powers of 10

This section will show you how to:
- multiply and divide by powers of 10

Key words

power

product

Question 10 of the previous exercise uses **powers** of 10, which you have already seen are special.

When you write a million in figures, how many zeros does it have? What is a million as a power of 10? This table shows some of the pattern of the powers of 10.

Number	0.001	0.01	0.1	1	10	100	1000	10 000	100 000
Powers	10^{-3}	10^{-2}	10^{-1}	10^{0}	10^{1}	10^{2}	10^{3}	10^{4}	10^{5}

What pattern is there in the top row?

What pattern is there in the powers in the bottom row?

Multiplication

In the first part of this section, you will look at multiplications. Multiplication calculations are also called **products**. For example, the product of 5 and 7 is the same as $5 \times 7 = 35$.

The easiest number to multiply by is zero, because any number multiplied by zero gives zero.

The next easiest number to multiply by is one, because any number multiplied by one stays the same.

After that it is a matter of opinion, but it is generally accepted that multiplying by 10 is simple. Try these on your calculator.

    a 7×10 **b** 7.34×10 **c** 43×10

    d 0.678×10 **e** 0.007×10 **f** 34.5×10

Can you see the rule for multiplying by 10? You may have learned that when you multiply a number by 10, you add a zero to the number. This is **only** true when you start with a whole number. It is **not true** for a decimal. The rule is:

- Every time you multiply a number by 10, move the digits in the number one place to the left.

Check to make sure that this happened in examples **a** to **f** above.

It is almost as easy to multiply by 100. Try these on your calculator.

    a 7×100 **b** 7.34×100 **c** 43×100

    d 0.678×100 **e** 0.007×100 **f** 34.5×100

This time you should find that the digits move two places to the left.

You can write 100, 1000, 10 000 as powers of 10. For example,

$$100 = 10 \times 10 = 10^2$$
$$1000 = 10 \times 10 \times 10 = 10^3$$
$$10\,000 = 10 \times 10 \times 10 \times 10 = 10^4$$

You should know the connection between the number of zeros and the power of 10. Try these on your calculator. Look for the connection between the calculation and the answer.

a 12.3×10 **b** 3.45×1000 **c** 3.45×10^3

d $0.075 \times 10\,000$ **e** 2.045×10^2 **f** 6.78×1000

g 25.67×10^4 **h** 34.21×100 **i** $0.032\,4 \times 10^4$

Division

Can you find a similar connection for division by multiples of 10? Try these on your calculator. Look for the connection between the calculation and the answer.

a $12.3 \div 10$ **b** $3.45 \div 1000$ **c** $3.45 \div 10^3$

d $0.075 \div 100$ **e** $2.045 \div 10^2$ **f** $6.78 \div 1000$

g $25.67 \div 10^4$ **h** $34.21 \div 100$ **i** $0.032\,4 \div 10^4$

You can use this principle to multiply multiples of 10, 100 and so on. You use this method in estimation. You should have the skill to do this mentally so that you can check that your answers to calculations are about right. (Approximation of calculations is covered on pages 352–356.)

Use a calculator to work out these multiplications.

a $200 \times 300 =$ **b** $100 \times 40 =$ **c** $2000 \times 3000 =$

d $200 \times 50 =$ **e** $200 \times 5000 =$ **f** $300 \times 40 =$

Can you see a way of doing them without using a calculator or pencil and paper? Dividing is almost as simple. Use a calculator to do these divisions.

a $400 \div 20 =$ **b** $200 \div 50 =$ **c** $1000 \div 200 =$

d $300 \div 30 =$ **e** $250 \div 50 =$ **f** $30\,000 \div 600 =$

Once again, there is an easy way of doing these 'in your head'. Look at these examples.

$300 \times 4000 = 1\,200\,000$ $5000 \div 200 = 25$ $200 \times 50 = 10\,000$

$60 \times 5000 = 300\,000$ $400 \div 20 = 20$ $30\,000 \div 600 = 500$

In 200×3000, for example, you multiply the non-zero digits ($2 \times 3 = 6$) and then write the total number of zeros in both numbers at the end, to give $600\,000$.

$$200 \times 3000 = 2 \times 100 \times 3 \times 1000 = 6 \times 100\,000 = 600\,000$$

For division, you divide the non-zero digits and then cancel the zeros. For example:

$$400\,000 \div 80 = \frac{400\,000}{80} = \frac{{}^{5}\cancel{400\,000}}{{}_{1}\cancel{80}} = 5000$$

EXERCISE 9H

1 Write down the value of each product.

    a 3.1×10 **b** 3.1×100 **c** 3.1×1000 **d** $3.1 \times 10\,000$

2 Write down the value of each product.

    a 6.5×10 **b** 6.5×10^2 **c** 6.5×10^3 **d** 6.5×10^4

3 In questions 1 and 2 there is a connection between the multipliers. What is the connection? (It isn't that the first number is the same.)

4 This list of answers came from a set of questions very similar to those in questions 1 and 2. Write down what the questions must have been, using numbers written out in full and powers of 10. (There is a slight catch!)

    a 73   **b** 730   **c** 7300   **d** 730\,000

5 Write down the value of each of the following.

    a $3.1 \div 10$ **b** $3.1 \div 100$ **c** $3.1 \div 1000$ **d** $3.1 \div 10\,000$

6 Write down the value of each of the following.

    a $6.5 \div 10$ **b** $6.5 \div 10^2$ **c** $6.5 \div 10^3$ **d** $6.5 \div 10^4$

7 In questions 5 and 6 there is a connection between the divisors. What is it?

8 This list of answers came from a set of questions very similar to those in questions 5 and 6. Write down what the questions must have been, using numbers written out in full and powers of 10.

    a 0.73   **b** 0.073   **c** 0.0073   **d** 0.000073

9 Without using a calculator, write down the answers to these.

    a 2.5×100 **b** 3.45×10 **c** 4.67×1000

    d 34.6×10 **e** 20.789×10 **f** 56.78×1000

    g 2.46×10^2 **h** 0.076×10 **i** 0.076×10^3

    j 0.897×10^5 **k** 0.865×1000 **l** 100.5×10^2

    m 0.999×10^6 **n** 234.56×10^2 **o** 98.7654×10^3

    p 43.23×10^6 **q** 78.679×10^2 **r** 203.67×10^1

    s 76.43×10 **t** 34.578×10^5 **u** $0.003\,4578 \times 10^5$

D

D

10 Without using a calculator, write down the answers to these.

HINTS AND TIPS

Even though you are really moving digits left or right, you may think of it as if the decimal point moves right or left.

a $2.5 \div 100$
b $3.45 \div 10$

c $4.67 \div 1000$
d $34.6 \div 10$

e $20.789 \div 100$
f $56.78 \div 1000$

g $2.46 \div 10^2$
h $0.076 \div 10$

i $0.076 \div 10^3$
j $0.897 \div 10^5$

k $0.865 \div 1000$
l $100.5 \div 10^2$
m $0.999 \div 10^6$

n $234.56 \div 10^2$
o $98.7654 \div 10^3$
p $43.23 \div 10^6$

q $78.679 \div 10^2$
r $203.67 \div 10^1$
s $76.43 \div 10$

11 Without using a calculator, write down the answers to these.

a 200×300
b 30×4000
c 50×200

d 60×700
e 70×300
f 10×30

g 3×50
h 200×7
i 200×500

j 100×2000
k 20×1400
l 30×30

m $(20)^2$
n $(20)^3$
o $(400)^2$

p 30×150
q 40×200
r 50×5000

12 Without using a calculator, write down the answers to these.

a $2000 \div 400$
b $3000 \div 60$
c $5000 \div 200$

d $6000 \div 200$
e $2100 \div 300$
f $9000 \div 30$

g $300 \div 50$
h $2100 \div 70$
i $2000 \div 500$

j $10\,000 \div 2000$
k $2800 \div 1400$
l $3000 \div 30$

m $2000 \div 50$
n $80\,000 \div 400$
o $400 \div 20$

p $3000 \div 150$
q $400 \div 200$
r $5000 \div 5000$

s $4000 \div 250$
t $300 \div 2$
u $6000 \div 500$

v $30\,000 \div 2000$
w $2000 \times 40 \div 2000$
x $200 \times 20 \div 800$

y $200 \times 6000 \div 30\,000$
z $20 \times 80 \times 600 \div 3000$

AU 13 You are given that $16 \times 34 = 544$.

a Write down the value of 160×340.
b What is $544\,000 \div 34$?

PS 14 Write the following calculations in order, starting with the one that gives the smallest answer.

5000×4000 600×8000 $200\,000 \times 700$ $30 \times 90\,000$

FM 15 In 2009 there were £20 notes to the value of £28 000 million in circulation. How many £20 notes is this?

Prime factors, LCM and HCF

This section will show you how to:
- identify prime factors
- identify the least common multiple (LCM) of two numbers
- identify the highest common factor (HCF) of two numbers

Key words

factor tree

highest common factor

index notation

least common multiple

prime factor

product

product of prime factors

Start with a number, such as 110, and find two numbers that, when multiplied together, give that number, for example, 2×55. Are they both prime? No, 55 isn't. So take 55 and repeat the operation, to get 5×11. Are these both prime? Yes. So,

$110 = 2 \times 5 \times 11$

The **prime factors** of 110 are 2, 5 and 11.

This method is not very logical and you need to know your multiplication tables well to use it. There are, however, two methods that you can use to make sure you do not miss any of the prime factors.

EXAMPLE 4

Find the prime factors of 24.

Divide 24 by any prime number that goes into it. (2 is an obvious choice.)

Now divide the answer (12) by a prime number. As 12 is even, again 2 is the obvious choice.

2	24
2	12
3	6
	2

Repeat this process until you finally have a prime number as the answer.

So, written as a **product of its prime factors**, $24 = 2 \times 2 \times 2 \times 3$.

A quicker and neater way to write this answer is to use **index notation**, expressing the answer using powers. (Powers are dealt with on pages 284–286.)

In index notation, as a product of its prime factors, $24 = 2^3 \times 3$.

EXAMPLE 5

Find the prime factors of 96.

As a product of prime factors, 96 is $2 \times 2 \times 2 \times 2 \times 2 \times 3 = 2^5 \times 3$.

2	96
2	48
2	24
2	12
2	6
	3

The method shown below is called a **factor tree**.

You start by splitting the number into a **product** of two factors. Then you split these factors, and carry on splitting, until you reach prime numbers.

EXAMPLE 6

Find the prime factors of 76.

Stop splitting the factors here because 2, 2 and 19 are all prime numbers.

So, as a product of prime factors, 76 is $2 \times 2 \times 19 = 2^2 \times 19$.

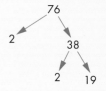

EXAMPLE 7

Find the prime factors of 420.

You can work it upside down, to make an upright tree.

So, as a product of prime factors:

$$420 = 2 \times 5 \times 2 \times 3 \times 7 = 2^2 \times 3 \times 5 \times 7$$

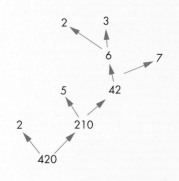

EXAMPLE 8

50 written as the product of prime factors is 2×5^2.

Write the following numbers as products of prime factors in index notation.

a 150   b 500   c 200

a This is 3×50. So, $150 = 2 \times 3 \times 5^2$

b This is 10×50. So, $500 = 2^2 \times 5^3$.

c This is 4×50. So, $200 = 2^3 \times 5^2$.

EXERCISE 9I

1 Copy and complete these factor trees.

a

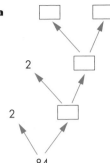

$84 = 2 \times 2 \ldots \ldots$

b

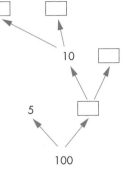

$100 = 5 \times 2 \ldots \ldots$

c

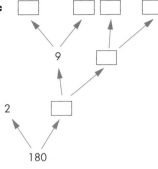

$180 = 2 \ldots \ldots \ldots \ldots$

d

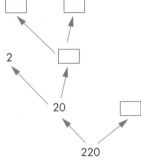

$220 = 2 \ldots \ldots \ldots$

e

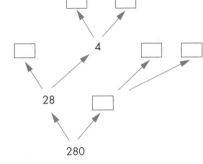

$280 = \ldots \ldots \ldots \ldots \ldots$

f

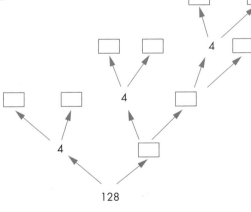

$128 = \ldots \ldots \ldots \ldots \ldots \ldots \ldots$

g

2

50

$50 = \ldots \ldots \ldots$

h

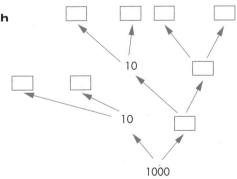

$1000 = \ldots \ldots \ldots \ldots \ldots \ldots$

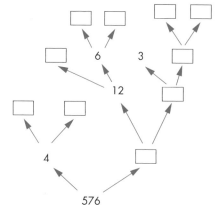

i

576 = ...

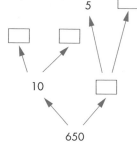

j

650 = ...

2 Use index notation to rewrite your answers to question 1, parts **a** to **j**.
For example:

$$100 = 2 \times 2 \times 5 \times 5 = 2^2 \times 5^2$$

and $\quad 540 = 2 \times 2 \times 3 \times 3 \times 3 \times 5 = 2^2 \times 3^3 \times 5$

3 Write the numbers from 1 to 50 as products of their prime factors. Use index notation. For example:

$1 = 1 \qquad 2 = 2 \qquad 3 = 3$

$4 = 2^2 \qquad 5 = 5 \qquad 6 = 2 \times 3 \qquad ...$

HINTS AND TIPS

Use your previous answers to help you. For example, $9 = 3^2$ so as $18 = 2 \times 9$, $18 = 2 \times 3^2$.

4 **a** What is special about the numbers 2, 4, 8, 16, 32, ...?

b What are the next two terms in this series?

c What are the next three terms in the series 3, 9, 27, ...?

d Continue the series 4, 16, 64, ..., for three more terms.

e Rewrite all the series in parts **a**, **c** and **d** in index notation. For example, the first series is:

$$2^1, 2^2, 2^3, 2^4, 2^5, 2^6, 2^7, ...$$

AU 5 **a** Express 60 as a product of prime factors.

b Write your answer to part **a** in index form.

c Use your answer to part **b** to write 120, 240 and 480 as a product of prime factors in index form.

PS 6 $1001 = 7 \times 11 \times 13$

$1001^2 = 1\,002\,001$

$1001^3 = 1\,003\,003\,001$

   a Write $1\,002\,001$ as a product of prime factors, in index form.

   b Write $1\,003\,003\,001$ as a product of prime factors, in index form.

   c Write $100\,110$ as a product of prime factors, in index form.

 FM 7 Harriet wants to share £40 between three of her grandchildren. Explain why it is not possible for them to get equal shares.

Least common multiple

The **least common multiple** (or *lowest common multiple*), or LCM of two numbers is the smallest number that appears in the multiplication tables of both numbers.

For example, the LCM of 3 and 5 is 15, the LCM of 2 and 7 is 14 and the LCM of 6 and 9 is 18.

There are two ways of working out the LCM.

EXAMPLE 9

Find the LCM of 18 and 24.

Write out the 18 times table: 18, 36, 54, ⑦②, 90, 108, …

Write out the 24 times table: 24, 48, ⑦②, 96, 120, …

Numbers that appear in both tables are *common multiples*. You can see that 72 is the smallest (least) number that appears in both tables, so it is the least common multiple.

EXAMPLE 10

Find the LCM of 42 and 63.

Write 42 in prime factor form: $42 = 2 \times 3 \times 7$

Write 63 in prime factor form: $63 = 3^2 \times 7$

Write down the smallest number, in prime factor form (that includes all the prime factors of both 42 and 63).

     $2 \times 3^2 \times 7$ (This includes $2 \times 3 \times 7$ and $3^2 \times 7$.)

Then work it out:

     $2 \times 3^2 \times 7 = 2 \times 9 \times 7 = 18 \times 7 = 126$

Highest common factor

The **highest common factor** or HCF of two numbers is the biggest number that divides exactly into both of them.

For example, the HCF of 24 and 18 is 6, the HCF of 45 and 36 is 9 and the HCF of 15 and 22 is 1.

EXAMPLE 11

Find the HCF of 28 and 16.

Write out the factors of 28: $\{1, 2, (4), 7, 14, 28\}$

Write out the factors of 16: $\{1, 2, (4), 8, 16\}$

Numbers that appear in both sets of factors are *common factors*. You can see that 4 is the biggest (highest) number that appears in both lists, so it is the highest common factor.

EXAMPLE 12

a Find the HCF of 48 and 120.

b Write 48 and 120 as products of prime factors.

c What connection is there between the answers to **a** and **b**?

a Write out the factors of 48 and 120.

$48 = \{1, 2, 3, 4, 6, 8, 12, 16, 24, 48\}$

$120 = \{1, 2, 3, 4, 5, 6, 8, 10, 12, 15, 20, 24, 30, 40, 60, 120\}$

So, the HCF is 24.

b $48 = 2 \times 2 \times 2 \times 2 \times 3 = 2^4 \times 3$

$120 = 2 \times 2 \times 2 \times 3 \times 5 = 2^3 \times 3 \times 5$

c 48 and 120 are connected by the number 24. 24 is $2 \times 2 \times 2 \times 3 = 2^3 \times 3$ as the product of prime factors, which is in both the product of prime factors of 48 and 120.

EXERCISE 9J

1 Find the LCM of each pair of numbers.

    a 4 and 5   **b** 7 and 8   **c** 2 and 3   **d** 4 and 7

    e 2 and 5   **f** 3 and 5   **g** 3 and 8   **h** 5 and 6

2 What connection is there between the LCMs and the pairs of numbers in question 1?

3 Find the LCM of each pair of numbers.

    a 4 and 8   **b** 6 and 9   **c** 4 and 6   **d** 10 and 15

AU 4 Does the connection you found in question 2 still work for the numbers in question 3? If not, can you explain why not?

5 Find the LCM of each pair of numbers.

    a 24 and 56   **b** 21 and 35   **c** 12 and 28   **d** 28 and 42

    e 12 and 32   **f** 18 and 27   **g** 15 and 25   **h** 16 and 36

FM 6 Cheese slices are in packs of eight.
Bread rolls are in packs of six.

What is the smallest number of each pack that needs to be bought to have the same number of cheese slices and bread rolls?

7 Find the HCF of each pair of numbers.

    a 24 and 56   **b** 21 and 35   **c** 12 and 28   **d** 28 and 42

    e 12 and 32   **f** 18 and 27   **g** 15 and 25   **h** 16 and 36

    i 42 and 27   **j** 48 and 64   **k** 25 and 35   **l** 36 and 54

PS 8 In prime factor form $1250 = 2 \times 5^4$ and $525 = 3 \times 5^2 \times 7$.

    a Which of these are common multiples of 1250 and 525?

      i $2 \times 3 \times 5^3 \times 7$ **ii** $2^3 \times 3 \times 5^4 \times 7^2$ **iii** $2 \times 3 \times 5^4 \times 7$ **iv** $2 \times 3 \times 5 \times 7$

    b Which of these are common factors of 1250 and 525?

      i 2×3 **ii** 2×5 **iii** 5^2 **iv** $2 \times 3 \times 5 \times 7$

PS 9 The HCF of two numbers is 6.

The LCM of the same two numbers is 72.

What are the numbers?

Rules for multiplying and dividing powers

This section will show you how to:

● use rules for multiplying and dividing powers

Key word

power

Look what happens when you multiply numbers that are written as **powers** of the same number or variable (letter).

For example:

$$3^3 \times 3^5 = (3 \times 3 \times 3) \times (3 \times 3 \times 3 \times 3 \times 3)$$
$$= 3^8$$

$$a^2 \times a^3 = (a \times a) \times (a \times a \times a)$$
$$= a^5$$

Can you see the rule? You can find these products just by *adding* the powers.
For example,

$$2^3 \times 2^4 \times 2^5 = 2^{12}$$

$$a^3 \times a^4 = a^{3+4} = a^7$$

Now look what happens when you divide numbers that are written as powers of the same number or letter (variable).

For example,

$$7^6 \div 7 = (7 \times 7 \times 7 \times 7 \times 7 \times 7) \div (7)$$
$$= 7 \times 7 \times 7 \times 7 \times 7$$
$$= 7^5$$

$$a^5 \div a^2 = (a \times a \times a \times a \times a) \div (a \times a)$$
$$= a \times a \times a$$
$$= a^3$$

Can you see the rule? You can do these divisions just by *subtracting* the powers.
For example,

$$a^4 \div a^3 = a^{4-3}$$
$$= a^1$$
$$= a$$

$$b^7 \div b^4 = b^3$$

EXERCISE 9K

1 Write these as single powers of 5.

a $5^2 \times 5^2$ **b** $5^4 \times 5^6$ **c** $5^2 \times 5^3$ **d** 5×5^2 **e** $5^6 \times 5^9$

f 5×5^8 **g** $5^2 \times 5^4$ **h** $5^6 \times 5^3$ **i** $5^2 \times 5^6$

2 Simplify these (write them as single powers of x).

a $x^2 \times x^6$ **b** $x^5 \times x^4$ **c** $x^6 \times x^2$ **d** $x^3 \times x^2$ **e** $x^6 \times x^6$

f $x^5 \times x^8$ **g** $x^7 \times x^4$ **h** $x^2 \times x^8$ **i** $x^{12} \times x^4$

3 Write these as single powers of 6.

a $6^5 \div 6^2$ **b** $6^7 \div 6^2$ **c** $6^3 \div 6^2$ **d** $6^4 \div 6^4$ **e** $6^5 \div 6^4$

f $6^5 \div 6^2$ **g** $6^4 \div 6^2$ **h** $6^4 \div 6^3$ **i** $6^5 \div 6^3$

4 Simplify these (write them as single powers of x).

a $x^7 \div x^3$ **b** $x^8 \div x^3$ **c** $x^4 \div x$ **d** $x^6 \div x^3$ **e** $x^{10} \div x^4$

f $x^6 \div x$ **g** $x^8 \div x^6$ **h** $x^8 \div x^2$ **i** $x^{12} \div x^3$

AU 5   **a** Write down the value of $216 \div 216$.

      b Write $6^3 \div 6^3$ as a single power of 6.

      c $6^3 = 216$

      Use parts **a** and **b** to write down the value of 6^0.

AU 6   **a** Write down the value of $625 \div 625$.

      b Write $5^4 \div 5^4$ as a single power of 5.

      c $5^4 = 625$

      Use parts **a** and **b** to write down the value of 5^0.

AU 7   What do you notice about your answers to questions **5** and **6**?

AU 8 $4^a \times 4^b = 4^7$

      Write down one pair of possible values for a and b.

PS 9   **a** A common error is to write $x^a + x^a = x^{2a}$.

      Find two whole numbers for a and x for which this is true.

      b Another common error is to write $x^a \times x^b = x^{ab}$.

      Find a whole number for x for which this is true.

> **HINTS AND TIPS**
>
> There is only one possible answer, and both a and x are less than 5.

> **HINTS AND TIPS**
>
> There is only one possible answer

GRADE BOOSTER

G You can recognise multiples of the first ten whole numbers

G You can find factors of numbers less than 100

G You can recognise the square numbers up to 100

F You can write down any square number up to $15 \times 15 = 225$

F You can find the square root of any number, using a calculator

E You can write down the cubes of 1, 2, 3, 4, 5 and 10

E You can calculate simple powers of whole numbers

E You can recognise two-digit prime numbers

D You can multiply and divide by powers of 10

D You can multiply and divide numbers that are multiples of 10

C You can work out the prime factors of numbers

C You can work out the LCM and HCF of two numbers

C You can simplify multiplications and divisions of powers

What you should know now

- What multiples are
- How to find the factors of any whole number
- What a prime number is
- What square numbers are
- What square roots are
- How to find powers of numbers
- How to write numbers in prime factor form
- How to find the LCM and HCF of any pair of numbers

1 Here is a list of numbers.

3   7   12   16   19   30   44

a Which number in this list is a multiple of 5?

b Which three numbers in this list are factors of 132?

(Total 3 marks)

AQA, June 2005, Module 5, Paper 2 Foundation, Question 6

2 Here is a list of numbers

1 2 3 4 5 6 7 8 9 10
11 12 13 14 15 16 17 18 19 20
21 22 23 24 25 26 27 28 29 30
31 32 33 34 35 36 37 38 39 40
41 42 43 44 45 46 47 48 49 50

a From the list write down:
  i a square number   **ii** a cube number
  iii a multiple of seven   **iv** a prime number.

b From the list write down:
  i a square number between 40 and 50
  ii an even prime number
  iii a number that is a multiple of five and a multiple of nine.

3 **a** Write down the first five multiples of seven.

b Write down the factors of 14.

c Write down a square number between 10 and 20.

d Write down a prime number between 10 and 20.

e Write down the cube of three.

4 Here are three number cards.

Using these three cards it is possible to make six different three-digit numbers, for example, 348 and 384.

a Write down all six three-digit numbers.
  348,   384, ... , ... , ... , ...

b One of the numbers is a multiple of eight. Which is it?

c None of the numbers is a multiple of five. Explain how you can tell this is true without doing any calculations.

5 Here are six number cards.

a Which of the numbers are multiples of three?

b Which of the numbers are factors of nine?

c Which of the numbers are prime numbers?

d Which of the numbers are square numbers?

e Which number is a cube number?

f Use the numbers to complete this magic square so that each row, column and diagonal add up to 18.

		5
2	6	

6 **a** Work out 3^3.

b Give an example of a cube number that does not divide exactly by three.

(Total 2 marks)

AQA, June 2005, Module 3 Foundation, Question 16

7 Here is a list of numbers.

22   8   48   6   10   25   36   21

a From this list write down
  i the two numbers that add up to 70   (1)
  ii the multiple of 7   (1)
  iii the two factors of 24   (2)
  iv the even square number   (1)
  v the cube number.   (1)

b Work out the largest answer that can be obtained when two numbers from the list are multiplied together.   (2)

(Total 8 marks)

AQA, March 2008, Module 3 Foundation, Question 1

8 **a** Write down the value of: **i** 2^3 **ii** 3^3.

b Complete the number pattern below.

1^2 $= 1 = 1^3$

$(1 + 2)^2$ $= 9 = 1^3 + 2^3$

$(1 + 2 + 3)^2$ $= 36 = 1^3 + 2^3 + 3^3$

$(1 + 2 + \ldots\ldots + \ldots\ldots)^2 = \ldots\ldots = 1^3 + 2^3 + \ldots\ldots + \ldots\ldots$

9 Simplify:

a $c \times c \times c \times c$

b $d^3 \times d^2$

c $\dfrac{e}{e^8}$

10 **a** Write 28 as the product of its prime factors.

b Find the lowest common multiple (LCM) of 28 and 42.

11 Tom, Sam and Matt are counting drum beats.

Tom hits a snare drum every 2 beats.

Sam hits a kettle drum every 5 beats.

Matt hits a bass drum every 8 beats.

Tom, Sam and Matt start by hitting their drums at the same time. How many beats is it before Tom, Sam and Matt next hit their drums at the same time?

12 **a** Work out the value of $5^7 \div 5^4$.

b a and b are prime numbers.

$ab^3 = 54$

Find the values of a and b.

c Find the highest common factor (HCF) of 54 and 135.

13 Use these number cards to make each of the following.

Each card can only be used once throughout all parts of the question.

a A two-digit multiple of 7

b The HCF of 20 and 35

c A two-digit prime number

14 **a** Write 64 as a power of 2.

b Explain how you can tell that 640 000 has only two prime factors.

15 Small pies are sold in packs of 4

Bread sticks are sold in packs of 10

What is the least number of each pack that needs to be bought to have the same number of pies and bread sticks?

Worked Examination Questions

1 **a** Write 24 as a product of prime factors.

   b Find the least common multiple (LCM) of 24 and 32.

   c Find the highest common factor (HCF) of 32 and 48.

a $2^3 \times 3$

2 marks

> Split 24 into products until there are only prime numbers. The calculation $24 = 2 \times 12 = 2 \times 2 \times 6 = 2 \times 2 \times 2 \times 3$ will earn 1 method mark.

> Write the answer in index form to get 1 mark for accuracy.

b 24, 48, 72, 96, 120, ...

   32, 64, 96, 128, ...

   So the LCM of 24 and 32 is 96.

2 marks

> Write out the multiples of 24 and 32 until there is a common multiple. This will get you 1 method mark. Then pick out the smallest (least), value in both (common) lists (multiples). This will get you 1 mark for accuracy.

c Factors of 32 = {1, 2, 4, 8, ⑯ 32}

   Factors of 48 = {1, 2, 3, 4, 6, 8, 12, ⑯ 24, 48}

   So the HCF of 32 and 48 is 16.

2 marks

> Write out the factors of 32 and 48. This will get you 1 method mark.
>
> Then pick out the largest (highest) value in both (common) lists (factors). This will get you 1 mark for accuracy.

Total: 6 marks

---

2 A PE teacher is organising 20 students into equal-sized teams for a competition. How many can she have in each team?

   2, 4, 5 or 10

Total: 2 marks

> By identifying at least three factors of 20 you will get 1 method mark. Although 1 and 20 are factors they cannot form part of the final answer as this is not addressing the team requirement. You will get 1 mark for accuracy for showing this in your final answer.

PS **3** Give a reason why each of the following could be the odd one out.

   123   144   169

   123 because it is not a square number

   144 because it is not odd

   169 because it is not a multiple of 3

Total: 3 marks

> Answer the whole question by giving a reason for each number being the odd one out and not just identifying one of the numbers as the odd one out. Each answer is for any valid reason, so there could be other solutions. For each reason you will earn 1 mark.

Today, many people living in towns and cities do not have their own gardens. Allotments give these people the opportunity to enjoy gardening regardless of not having their own garden. Allotments are also increasingly popular as a way of producing home-grown cheap fruit and vegetables. You have just started renting an allotment so that can grow your own fruit and vegetables. The allotment is divided into rows for planting. The whole plot is 3 m wide and each row is 5 m long.

Your task

Design the plant layout for the allotment using the information that you will gather from the tables. Consider as many different arrangements as possible.

You must explain your choices, stating the assumptions that you have made.

Getting started

Before you begin your main task, you may find it useful to fill in a copy of the following table using the fact box opposite to help you.

Vegetable	Distance between plants (cm)	Number of vegetables per row
Potatoes	30 cm	
Carrots	10 cm	
Broad beans	10 cm	
Onions	10 cm	
Cucumber	30 cm	
Lettuce	20 cm	

Facts

This table shows how much distance is needed between plants and between rows for the key vegetables in your allotment.

Vegetable	Distance between plants (cm)	Distance between rows (cm)
Potatoes	30 cm	50 cm
Carrots	10 cm	20 cm
Broad beans	10 cm	30 cm
Onions	10 cm	20 cm
Cucumber	30 cm	60 cm
Lettuce	20 cm	30 cm

Handy hints

You may find these rules helpful when planning your allotment:

- use one type of vegetable for each complete row
- do not have more than two rows of the same vegetable
- if different plants are next to each other, make sure that the largest necessary distance between rows is left between them
- make sure that vegetables are not planted too near to the edge of the allotment
- use graph paper to represent the allotment
- use a code to represent each plant.

Here is an example for you to discuss.

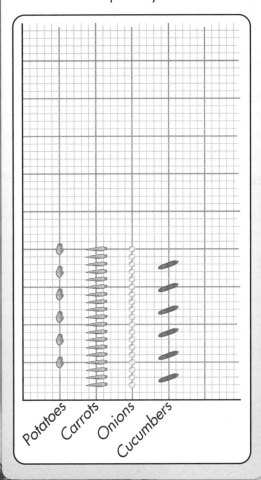

Potatoes Carrots Onions Cucumbers

Why this chapter matters

> **If you were asked to circle one of these to describe mathematics, which would it be?**
>
> Art   Science   Sport   Language
>
> **In fact, you could circle them all.**

Art

Mathematics is important in art. The *Mona Lisa*, probably the most famous painting in the world, uses the proportions of the 'golden ratio' (approximately 1.618) as shown by the red rectangles marked on this copy of the painting. This 'golden ratio' is supposed to be particularly attractive to the human eye.

Science

Obviously, you cannot do much science without using mathematics. In 1962, a *Mariner* space probe went off course and had to be destroyed because someone had used a wrong symbol in a mathematical formula that was part of its programming.

Sport

Is mathematics a sport? There are national and international competitions each year that use mathematics. For example, there is a world Suduko championship each year and university students compete in the annual 'Mathematics Olympiad'.

Language

But perhaps the most important description in the list above is mathematics as language. As we saw in Chapter 1, mathematics is the only universal language. If you write the equation $3x = 9$, it will be understood by people in all countries.

Algebra is the way that the language of mathematics is expressed.

Algebra comes from the Arabic *al-jabr* which means something similar to 'completion'. It was used in a book written in 820AD by a Persian mathematician called al-Khwarizmi.

The use of symbols then developed until the middle of the 17th century, when René Descartes developed what is regarded as the basis of the algebra we use today.

Algebra: Basic algebra

1. The language of algebra

2. Simplifying expressions

3. Expanding brackets

4. Factorisation

5. Substitution

This chapter will show you ...

- **F** how to substitute numbers into expressions and formulae
- **F** how to use letters to represent numbers
- **F** how to form simple algebraic expressions
- **E** how to simplify expressions by collecting like terms
- **D** how to factorise expressions
- **D** how to express simple rules in algebraic form

Visual overview

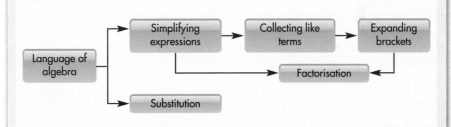

What you should already know

- The **BIDMAS/BODMAS** rule, which gives the order in which you must do the operations of arithmetic when they occur together (KS3 level 5, GCSE grade F)

Quick check

1 Write the answer to each expression.

  a $(5 - 1) \times 2$

  b $5 - (1 \times 2)$

2 Work out $(7 - 5) \times (5 + 4 - 2)$.

3 **a** Put brackets in the calculation to make the answer 40.

    $2 + 3 + 5 \times 4$

  b Put brackets in the calculation to make the answer 34.

    $2 + 3 + 5 \times 4$

This section will show you how to:

- use letters, numbers and mathematical symbols to write algebraic expressions and formulae

Key words

equation
expression
formula
solve
symbol
term
variable

Algebra is based on the idea that if something works with numbers, it will work with letters. The main difference is that when you work only with numbers, the answer is also a number. When you work with letters, you get an **expression** as the answer.

Algebra follows the same rules as arithmetic, and uses the same **symbols** (+, −, × and ÷). Below are seven important algebraic rules.

- Write '4 more than x' as $4 + x$ or $x + 4$.

- Write '6 less than p' or 'p minus 6' as $p - 6$.

- Write '4 times y' as $4 \times y$ or $y \times 4$ or $4y$. The last one of these is the neatest way to write it.

- Write 'b divided by 2' as $b \div 2$ or $\dfrac{b}{2}$.

- When a number and a letter or a letter and a letter appear together, there is a hidden multiplication sign between them. So, $7x$ means $7 \times x$ and ab means $a \times b$.

- Always write '$1 \times x$' as x.

- Write 't times t' as $t \times t$ or t^2.

Here are some algebraic words that you need to know.

Variable: This is what the letters used to represent numbers are called. These letters can take on any value, so they are said to 'vary'.

Expression: This is any combination of letters and numbers. For example, $2x + 4y$ and $\dfrac{p - 6}{5}$ are expressions.

Equation: An equation contains an equals sign and at least one variable. The important fact is that a value can be found for the variable. This is called **solving** the equation. You will learn more about equations in chapter 12.

Formula: These are like equations in that they contain an equals sign, but there is more than one variable and they are rules for working out amounts such as area or the cost of taxi fares.

For example, $V = x^3$, $A = \frac{1}{2}bh$ and $C = 3 + 4m$ are all formulae.

Term: These are the separate parts of expressions, equations or formula.

For example, in $3x + 2y - 7$, there are three terms: $3x$, $+2y$ and -7.

Identity: An identity is similar to an equation, but is true for all values of the variable(s). Instead of the usual equals (=) sign, ≡ is used. For example, $2x \equiv 7x - 5x$.

EXAMPLE 1

What is the area of each of these rectangles?

a 4 cm by 6 cm   **b** 4 cm by w cm   **c** l cm by w cm

The rule for working out the area of a rectangle is:

     area = length × width

So, the area of rectangle **a** is $4 \times 6 = 24 \text{ cm}^2$

The area of rectangle **b** is $4 \times w = 4w \text{ cm}^2$

The area of rectangle **c** is $l \times w = lw \text{ cm}^2$

Now, if A represents the area of rectangle **c**:

     $A = lw$

This is an example of a rule expressed algebraically.

EXAMPLE 2

What is the perimeter of each of these rectangles?

a 6 cm by 4 cm   **b** 4 cm by w cm   **c** l cm by w cm

The rule for working out the perimeter of a rectangle is:

     perimeter = twice the longer side + twice the shorter side

So, the perimeter of rectangle **a** is $2 \times 6 + 2 \times 4 = 20 \text{ cm}$

The perimeter of rectangle **b** is $2 \times 4 + 2 \times w = 8 + 2w \text{ cm}$

The perimeter of rectangle **c** is $2 \times l + 2 \times w = 2l + 2w \text{ cm}$

Now, let P represent the perimeter of rectangle **c**, so:

     $P = 2l + 2w$

which is another example of a rule expressed algebraically.

Expressions such as $A = lw$ and $P = 2l + 2w$ are **formulae**.

As the two examples above show, a formula states the connection between two or more quantities, each of which is represented by a different letter.

In a formula, the letters are replaced by numbers when a calculation has to be made. This is called *substitution* and is explained on page 326.

EXAMPLE 3

Say if the following are expressions (E), equations (Q) or formula (F).

     a $x - 5 = 7$ **b** $P = 4x$ **c** $2x - 3y$

a is an **equation** (Q) as it can be solved to give $x = 12$.

b is a **formula** (F). This is the formula for the perimeter of a square with a side of x.

c is an **expression** (E) with two terms.

EXERCISE 10A

F

1 Write down the algebraic expression for:

    a 2 more than x **b** 6 less than x

    c k more than x **d** x minus t

    e x added to 3   **f** d added to m

    g y taken away from b **h** p added to t added to w

    i 8 multiplied by x **j** h multiplied by j

    k x divided by 4   **l** 2 divided by x

    m y divided by t **n** w multiplied by t

    o a multiplied by a **p** g multiplied by itself.

2 Here are four squares.

i   **ii**   **iii**   **iv**

    a Work out the area and perimeter of each square.

    b Copy and complete these rules.

       i The perimeter, P, of a square of side s centimetres is P = ...

       ii The area, A, of a square of side s centimetres is A = ...

3 Asha, Bernice and Charu are three sisters. Bernice is x years old. Asha is three years older than Bernice. Charu is four years younger than Bernice.

    a How old is Asha?

    b How old is Charu?

4 An approximation method of converting from degrees Celsius to degrees Fahrenheit is given by this rule:

    Multiply by 2 and add 30.

Using C to stand for degrees Celsius and F to stand for degrees Fahrenheit, complete this formula.

    F = ...

5 Cows have four legs. Which of these formulae connects the number of legs (*L*) and the number of cows (*C*)?

   a $C = 4L$

   b $L = C + 4$

   c $L = 4C$

   d $L + C = 4$

6 There are 3 feet in a yard. The rule $F = 3Y$ connects the number of feet (*F*) and the number of yards (*Y*). Write down rules, using the letters shown, to connect:

   a the number of centimetres (*C*) in metres (*M*)

   b the number of inches (*N*) in feet (*F*)

   c the number of wheels (*W*) on cars (*C*)

   d the number of heads (*H*) on people (*P*).

> **HINTS AND TIPS**
>
> Check your formula with a numerical example. In 4 yards there are 12 feet, so, if $F = 3Y$ is correct, then $12 = 3 \times 4$, which is true.

7 **a** Anne has three bags of marbles. Each bag contains *n* marbles. How many marbles does she have altogether?

   b Bea gives her another three marbles. How many marbles does Anne have now?

   c Anne puts one of her new marbles in each bag. How many marbles are there now in each bag?

   d Anne takes two marbles out of each bag. How many marbles are there now in each bag?

8 Simon has *n* cubes.

- Rob has twice as many cubes as Simon.
- Tom has two more than Simon.
- Vic has three fewer than Simon.
- Will has three more than Rob.

How many cubes does each person have?

> **HINTS AND TIPS**
>
> Remember that you do not have to write down a multiplication sign between numbers and letters, or letters and letters.

E

9 **a** John has been drawing squares and writing down the area and the perimeter of each of them. He has drawn three squares. Finish his work by writing down the missing areas and perimeters.

$P = 4n$
$A = n^2$

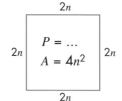

$P = \ldots$
$A = 4n^2$

$P = 12n$
$A = \ldots$

b Write down the area and the perimeter of this partly-covered square.

10 **a** I go shopping with £10 and spend £6. How much do I have left?

b I go shopping with £10 and spend £x. How much do I have left?

c I go shopping with £y and spend £x. How much do I have left?

d I go shopping with £$3x$ and spend £x. How much do I have left?

11 Give the total cost of:

a five pens at 15p each

b x pens at 15p each

c four pens at Ap each

d y pens at Ap each.

12 A boy went shopping with £A. He spent £B. How much did he have left?

13 Five ties cost £A. What is the cost of one tie?

PS **14** **a** My dad is 72 and I am T years old. How old shall we each be in x years' time?

b My mum is 64 years old. In two years' time she will be twice as old as I am. What age am I now?

15 I am twice as old as my son. I am T years old.

a How old is my son?

b How old will my son be in four years' time?

c How old was I x years ago?

16 What is the perimeter of each of these figures?

a $2x$

Square

b $4m$

Equilateral triangle

c $3t$

Regular hexagon

17 Write down the number of marbles each student ends up with.

Student	Action	Marbles
Andrea	Start with three bags each containing n marbles and give away one marble from each bag	
Bert	Start with three bags each containing n marbles and give away one marble from one bag	
Colin	Start with three bags each containing n marbles and give away two marbles from each bag	
Davina	Start with three bags each containing n marbles and give away n marbles from each bag	
Emma	Start with three bags each containing n marbles and give away n marbles from one bag	
Florinda	Start with three bags each containing n marbles and give away m marbles from each bag	

AU 18 The answer to $3 \times 4m$ is $12m$.

Write down two **different** expressions for which the answer is $12m$.

AU 19 Three expressions for the perimeter of a rectangle with length l and width w are:

$P = l + w + l + w$

$P = 2l + 2w$

$P = 2(l + w)$

> **HINTS AND TIPS**
>
> Just pick some easy numbers for l and w.

Show, using a numerical example, that they all give the same result.

PS 20 My sister is three years older than I am.

The sum of our ages is 29.

How old am I?

> **HINTS AND TIPS**
>
> If I am x years old, work out how old my sister is in terms of x and use this to set up a simple equation.

PS 21 Ali has 65p and Heidi has 95p. How much should Heidi give to Ali so they both have the same amount?

22 Say if the following are expressions (E), equations (Q) or formula (F).

a $2x - 5$

b $s = \sqrt{A}$

c $2x - 3 = 1$

Simplifying expressions

This section will show you how to:
- simplify algebraic expressions by multiplying terms
- simplify algebraic expressions by collecting like terms

Key words
coefficient
like terms
simplify

Simplifying an algebraic expression means making it neater and, usually, shorter by combining its terms where possible.

Multiplying expressions

When you multiply algebraic expressions, first you multiply the numbers, then the letters.

EXAMPLE 4

Simplify:

a $2 \times t$ **b** $m \times t$ **c** $2t \times 5$ **d** $3y \times 2m$

The convention is to write the number first then the letters, but if there is no number just put the letters in alphabetical order. The number in front of the letter is called the **coefficient**.

a $2 \times t = 2t$ **b** $m \times t = mt$ **c** $2t \times 5 = 10t$ **d** $3y \times 2m = 6my$

In an examination you will not be penalised for writing $2ba$ instead of $2ab$, but you will be penalised if you write $ab2$ as this can be confused with powers, so *always* write the number first.

EXAMPLE 5

Simplify:

a $t \times t$ **b** $3t \times 2t$ **c** $3t^2 \times 4t$ **d** $2t^3 \times 4t^2$

Multiply the same variables, using powers. The indices are added together.

a $t \times t = t^2$ (Remember: $t = t^1$)   **b** $3t \times 2t = 6t^2$

c $3t^2 \times 4t = 12t^3$ **d** $2t^3 \times 4t^2 = 8t^5$

EXERCISE 10B

1 Simplify the following expressions.

a $2 \times 3t$ **b** $5y \times 3$ **c** $2w \times 4$

d $5b \times b$ **e** $2w \times w$ **f** $4p \times 2p$

g $3t \times 2t$ **h** $5t \times 3t$ **i** $m \times 2t$

j $5t \times q$ **k** $n \times 6m$ **l** $3t \times 2q$

m $5h \times 2k$ **n** $3p \times 7r$

> **HINTS AND TIPS**
>
> Remember to multiply numbers and add indices.

AU 2 **a** Which of the following expressions are equivalent?

$2m \times 6n$ $4m \times 3n$ $2m \times 6m$ $3m \times 4n$

b The expressions $2x$ and x^2 are the same for only two values of x. What are these values?

PS 3 A square and a rectangle have the same area.

The rectangle has sides $2x$ cm and $8x$ cm.

What is the length of a side of the square?

4 Simplify the following expressions.

a $y^2 \times y$ **b** $3m \times m^2$ **c** $4t^2 \times t$

d $3n \times 2n^2$ **e** $t^2 \times t^2$ **f** $h^3 \times h^2$

g $3n^2 \times 4n^3$ **h** $3a^4 \times 2a^3$ **i** $k^5 \times 4k^2$

j $-t^2 \times -t$ **k** $-4d^2 \times -3d$ **l** $-3p^4 \times -5p^2$

m $3mp \times p$ **n** $3mn \times 2m$ **o** $4mp \times 2mp$

FM 5 There are 2000 students at Highville school. One student starts a rumour by telling it to two other students. The next day, those two students each tell the rumour to two other students who have not heard it already. The next day, those four students each tell the rumour to two other students who have not heard it before, and so on. How many days will it be before the whole school has heard the rumour?

> **HINTS AND TIPS**
>
> Fill in a table like this.
>
> | Day | 1 | 2 | 3 | 4 |
> |---|---|---|---|---|
> | Number told | 2 | 4 | 8 | 16 |
> | Total who know | 3 | 7 | 15 | 31 |
>
> In an examination there will always be space to the right of the table to draw in two columns – one for the mid-point and the other for the mid-point frequency.

Collecting like terms

Like terms are those that are multiples of the same variable or of the same combination of variables. For example, a, $3a$, $9a$, $\frac{1}{4}a$ and $-5a$ are all like terms.

So are $2xy$, $7xy$ and $-5xy$, and so are $6x^2$, x^2 and $-3x^2$.

Collecting like terms generally involves two steps.

- Collect like terms into groups.

- Then combine the like terms in each group.

Only like terms can be added or subtracted to simplify an expression. For example,

$a + 3a + 9a - 5a$	simplifies to	$8a$
$2xy + 7xy - 5xy$	simplifies to	$4xy$

Note that the variable does not change. All you have to do is combine the coefficients.

For example,

$$6x^2 + x^2 - 3x^2 = (6 + 1 - 3)x^2 = 4x^2$$

But an expression such as $4p + 8t + 5x - 9$ cannot be simplified, because $4p$, $8t$, $5x$ and 9 are *not like terms*, which *cannot* be combined.

EXAMPLE 6

Simplify the expression:

$$7x^2 + 3y - 6z + 2x^2 + 3z - y + w + 9$$

Write out the expression:

$$7x^2 + 3y - 6z + 2x^2 + 3z - y + w + 9$$

Then collect like terms:

$$\boxed{7x^2 + 2x^2} \;\; \boxed{+3y - y} \;\; \boxed{-6z + 3z} \;\; \boxed{+ w} \;\; \boxed{+ 9}$$

Then combine them:

$$9x^2 \quad + \quad 2y \quad - \quad 3z \quad + w \; + 9$$

So, the expression in its simplest form is:

$$9x^2 + 2y - 3z + w + 9$$

EXERCISE 10C

1 Joseph is given £t, John has £3 more than Joseph, and Joy has £$2t$.

  a How much more money has Joy than Joseph?

  b How much do the three of them have altogether?

2 Write down an expression for the perimeter of each of these shapes.

a

b

c

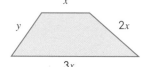

3 Write each of these expressions in a shorter form.

a $a + a + a + a + a$

b $c + c + c + c + c + c$

c $4e + 5e$

d $f + 2f + 3f$

e $5j + j - 2j$

f $9q - 3q - 3q$

g $3r - 3r$

h $2w + 4w - 7w$

i $5x^2 + 6x^2 - 7x^2 + 2x^2$

j $8y^2 + 5y^2 - 7y^2 - y^2$

k $2z^2 - 2z^2 + 3z^2 - 3z^2$

HINTS AND TIPS

The term a has a coefficient of 1, i.e. $a = 1a$, but you do not need to write the 1.

4 Simplify each of the following expressions.

a $3x + 4x$

b $5t - 2t$

c $-2x - 3x$

d $-k - 4k$

e $m^2 + 2m^2 - m^2$

f $2y^2 + 3y^2 - 5y^2$

HINTS AND TIPS

Remember that only **like** terms can be added or subtracted.
If all the terms cancel out, just write 0 rather than $0x^2$, for example.

5 Simplify each of the following expressions.

a $5x + 8 + 2x - 3$

b $7 - 2x - 1 + 7x$

c $4p + 2t + p - 2t$

d $8 + x + 4x - 2$

e $3 + 2t + p - t + 2 + 4p$

f $5w - 2k - 2w - 3k + 5w$

g $a + b + c + d - a - b - d$

h $9k - y - 5y - k + 10$

6 Simplify these expressions. (Be careful – two of them will not simplify.)

a $c + d + d + d + c$

b $2d + 2e + 3d$

c $f + 3g + 4h$

d $5u - 4v + u + v$

e $4m - 5n + 3m - 2n$

f $3k + 2m + 5p$

g $2v - 5w + 5w$

h $2w + 4y - 7y$

i $5x^2 + 6x^2 - 7y + 2y$

j $8y^2 + 5z - 7z - 9y^2$

k $2z^2 - 2x^2 + 3x^2 - 3z^2$

7 Find the perimeter of each of these shapes, giving it in its simplest form.

a

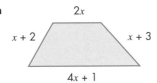

b

c

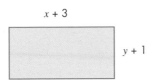

AU 8 $3x + 5y + 2x - y = 5x + 4y$

Write down two other **different** expressions which are equal to $5x + 4y$.

AU 9 Find the missing terms to make these equations true.

a $4x + 5y + \ldots\ldots\ldots - \ldots\ldots\ldots = 6x + 3y$

b $3a - 6b - \ldots\ldots\ldots + \ldots\ldots\ldots = 2a + b$

PS 10 ABCDEF is an L-shape.

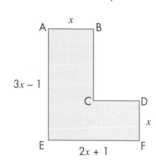

$AB = DF = x$

$AE = 3x - 1$ and $EF = 2x + 1$

> **HINTS AND TIPS**
>
> Make sure your explanation uses expressions. Do not try to explain in words alone.

a Explain why the length $BC = 2x - 1$.

b Find the perimeter of the shape in terms of x.

c If $x = 2.5$ cm, what is the perimeter of the shape?

FM 11 Sean wants to measure the size of a rectangular lawn but he does not have a tape measure. Instead he measures the length and width using his pace and his shoe length. He finds that the length is four paces plus a shoe length and the width is two paces and two shoe lengths. He writes this as $4p + s$ and $2p + 2s$.

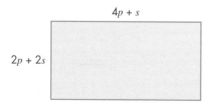

> **HINTS AND TIPS**
>
> Convert 1 m to 100 cm, then convert the answer back to metres.

a Work out the perimeter in terms of p and s.

b Later he finds that his pace is 1 m and his shoe length is 25 cm. What is the actual perimeter of the lawn? Give your answer in metres.

AU 12 A teacher asks her class to work out the perimeter of this L shape.

Tia says: 'There is information missing so you cannot work out the perimeter.'

Maria says: 'The perimeter is $4x - 1 + 4x - 1 + 3x + 2 + 3x + 2$.'

Who is correct?

Explain your answer.

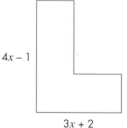

Expanding brackets

This section will show you how to:
- expand brackets such as $2(x - 3)$
- expand and simplify brackets

Key words
expand
multiply out
simplify

Expanding

In mathematics, the term '**expand**' usually means '**multiply out**'. For example, expressions such as $3(y + 2)$ and $4y^2(2y + 3)$ can be expanded by multiplying them out.

Remember that there is an invisible multiplication sign between the outside number and the opening bracket. So $3(y + 2)$ is really $3 \times (y + 2)$, and $4y^2(2y + 3)$ is really $4y^2 \times (2y + 3)$.

You expand by multiplying *everything inside* the brackets by what is outside the brackets.

EXAMPLE 7

Expand $3(y + 2)$.

$3(y + 2) = 3 \times (y + 2) = 3 \times y + 3 \times 2 = 3y + 6$

EXAMPLE 8

Expand $4y^2(2y + 3)$.

$4y^2(2y + 3) = 4y^2 \times (2y + 3) = 4y^2 \times 2y + 4y^2 \times 3 = 8y^3 + 12y^2$

Look at these next examples of expansion, which show how each term inside the brackets has been multiplied by the term outside the brackets.

$2(m + 3) = 2m + 6$

$3(2t + 5) = 6t + 15$

$m(p + 7) = mp + 7m$

$x(x - 6) = x^2 - 6x$

$4t(t + 2) = 4t^2 + 8t$

$y(y^2 - 4x) = y^3 - 4xy$

$3x^2(4x + 5) = 12x^3 + 15x^2$

$3(2 + 3x) = 6 + 9x$

$2x(3 - 4x) = 6x - 8x^2$

$3t(2 + 5t - p) = 6t + 15t^2 - 3pt$

EXERCISE 10D

1 Expand these expressions.

    a $2(3 + m)$ **b** $5(2 + l)$ **c** $3(4 - y)$ **d** $4(5 + 2k)$

    e $4(3d - 2n)$ **f** $t(t + 3)$ **g** $m(m + 5)$ **h** $k(k - 3)$

    i $g(3g + 2)$ **j** $y(5y - 1)$ **k** $p(5 - 3p)$ **l** $3m(m + 4)$

    m $3t(5 - 4t)$ **n** $3d(2d + 4e)$ **o** $2y(3y + 4k)$ **p** $5m(3m - 2p)$

2 Expand these expressions.

    a $y(y^2 + 5)$ **b** $h(h^3 + 7)$ **c** $k(k^2 - 5)$ **d** $3t(t^2 + 4)$

    e $3d(5d^2 - d^3)$ **f** $3w(2w^2 + t)$ **g** $5a(3a^2 - 2b)$ **h** $3p(4p^3 - 5m)$

    i $m^2(5 + 4m)$ **j** $t^3(t + 2t^2)$ **k** $g^2(5t - 4g^2)$ **l** $3t^2(5t + m)$

FM 3 The local supermarket is offering £1 off a large tin of biscuits. Morris wants five tins.

    a If the original price of one tin is £t, which of the expressions below represents how much it will cost Morris to buy five tins?

        $5(t - 1)$ $5t - 1$ $t - 5$ $5t - 5$

    b Morris has £20 to spend. If each tin is £4.50, will he have enough money for five tins? Show your working to justify your answer.

AU 4 Dylan wrote the following.

    $3(5x - 4) = 8x - 4$

    Dylan has made two mistakes.

    Explain the mistakes that Dylan has made.

> **HINTS AND TIPS**
>
> It is not enough just to give the right answer. You must try to explain, for example, why Dylan wrote $8x$ and what he should really have written if this is wrong.

PS 5 The expansion $2(x + 3) = 2x + 6$ can be shown by this diagram.

            x 3

	x	3
2	$2x$	6

    a What expansion is shown by this diagram?

3	$6y$	9

    b Write down an expansion that can be shown by this diagram.

$12z$	8

Expand and simplify

This usually means that you need to expand more than one set of brackets and **simplify** the resulting expressions.

You will often be asked to expand and simplify expressions.

EXAMPLE 9

Expand and simplify $3(4 + m) + 2(5 + 2m)$.

$3(4 + m) + 2(5 + 2m) = 12 + 3m + 10 + 4m = 22 + 7m$

EXAMPLE 10

Expand and simplify $3t(5t + 4) - 2t(3t - 5)$.

$3t(5t + 4) - 2t(3t - 5) = 15t^2 + 12t - 6t^2 + 10t = 9t^2 + 22t$

Notice that multiplying $-2t$ by -5 gives an answer of $+10t$.

EXAMPLE 11

Expand and simplify $4a(2b - 3f) - 3b(a + 2f)$.

$4a(2b - 3f) - 3b(a + 2f) = 8ab - 12af - 3ab - 6bf = 5ab - 12af - 6bf$

EXERCISE 10E

1 Simplify these expressions.

   a $4t + 3t$ **b** $2y + y$ **c** $3d + 2d + 4d$

   d $5e - 2e$ **e** $4p - p$ **f** $3t - t$

   g $2t^2 + 3t^2$ **h** $3ab + 2ab$ **i** $7a^2d - 4a^2d$

2 Expand and simplify these expressions.

   a $3(4 + t) + 2(5 + t)$ **b** $5(3 + 2k) + 3(2 + 3k)$

   c $4(1 + 3m) + 2(3 + 2m)$ **d** $2(5 + 4y) + 3(2 + 3y)$

   e $4(3 + 2f) + 2(5 - 3f)$ **f** $5(1 + 3g) + 3(3 - 4g)$

   g $3(2 + 5t) + 4(1 - t)$ **h** $4(3 + 3w) + 2(5 - 4w)$

> **HINTS AND TIPS**
>
> Expand the expression before trying to collect like terms. If you try to expand and collect at the same time you will probably make a mistake.

3 Expand and simplify these expressions.

a $4(3 + 2h) - 2(5 + 3h)$ **b** $5(3g + 4) - 3(2g + 5)$

c $3(4y + 5) - 2(3y + 2)$ **d** $3(5t + 2) - 2(4t + 5)$

e $5(5k + 2) - 2(4k - 3)$ **f** $4(4e + 3) - 2(5e - 4)$

g $3(5m - 2) - 2(4m - 5)$ **h** $2(6t - 1) - 3(3t - 4)$

> **HINTS AND TIPS**
>
> Be careful with minus signs. They are causes of the most common errors students make in examinations. Remember $-2 \times -4 = 8$ but $-2 \times 5 = -10$. You will learn more about multiplying and dividing with negative numbers in Chapter 3.

4 Expand and simplify these expressions.

a $m(4 + p) + p(3 + m)$ **b** $k(3 + 2h) + h(4 + 3k)$

c $t(2 + 3n) + n(3 + 4t)$ **d** $p(2q + 3) + q(4p + 7)$

e $3h(2 + 3j) + 2j(2h + 3)$ **f** $2y(3t + 4) + 3t(2 + 5y)$

g $4r(3 + 4p) + 3p(8 - r)$ **h** $5k(3m + 4) - 2m(3 - 2k)$

FM 5 A two-carriage train has f first-class seats and $2s$ standard-class seats.

A three-carriage train has $2f$ first-class seats and $3s$ standard-class seats.

On a weekday, five two-carriage trains and two three-carriage trains travel from Hull to Liverpool.

a Write down an expression for the total number of first-class and standard-class seats available during the day.

b On average on any day, half of the first-class seats are used. Each first-class seat costs £60.

On average on any day, three-quarters of the standard-class seats are used. Each standard-class seat costs £40.

How much money does the rail company earn in an average day on this route? Give your answer in terms of f and s.

c $f = 15$ and $s = 80$. It costs the rail company £30 000 per day to operate this route. How much profit do they make on an average day?

AU 6 Fill in whole-number values so that the following expansion is true.

$$3(\ldots\ldots x + \ldots\ldots y) + 2(\ldots\ldots x + \ldots\ldots y) = 11x + 17y$$

> **HINTS AND TIPS**
>
> There is more than one answer. You don't have to give them all.

PS 7 A rectangle with sides 5 and $3x + 2$ has a smaller rectangle with sides 3 and $2x - 1$ cut from it.

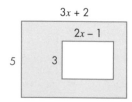

> **HINTS AND TIPS**
>
> Write out the expression for the difference of the two answers and then work it out.

Work out the remaining area.

10.4 Factorisation

This section will show you how to:
- 'reverse' the process of expanding brackets by taking out a common factor from each term in an expression

Key words
factor
factorisation

Factorisation is the opposite of expansion. It puts an expression into brackets.

To factorise an expression, look for the common **factors** in every term of the expression. Follow through the examples below to see how this works.

EXAMPLE 12

Factorise each expression. **a** $6t + 9m$ **b** $6my + 4py$
  c $8kp + 4k - 12km$ **d** $8kp + 4kt - 12km$

a The common factor is 3, so $6t + 9m = 3(2t + 3m)$

b The common factor is $2y$, so $6my + 4py = 2y(3m + 2p)$

c The common factor is $4k$, so $8kp + 4k - 12km = 4k(2p + 1 - 3m)$

d The common factor is $4k$, so $8kp + 4kt - 12km = 4k(2p + t - 3m)$

Notice that if you multiply out each answer you will get the expressions you started with.

This diagram may help you to see the difference and the connection between expansion and factorisation.

Note: When the whole term is the common factor, as in part **c**, then you are left with 1, not 0, inside the brackets.

Expanding

$3(2t + 3m) = 6t + 9m$

Factorising

EXERCISE 10F

1 Factorise the following expressions. The first three have been started for you.

a $6m + 12t = 6(\quad)$ **b** $9t + 3p = 3(\quad)$ **c** $8m + 12k = 4(\quad)$

d $4r + 8t$ **e** $mn + 3m$ **f** $5g^2 + 3g$

g $4w - 6t$ **h** $8p - 6k$ **i** $16h - 10k$

j $2mp + 2mk$ **k** $4bc + 2bk$ **l** $6ab + 4ac$

m $3y^2 + 2y$ **n** $4t^2 - 3t$ **o** $4d^2 - 2d$

p $3m^2 - 3mp$

HINTS AND TIPS

First look for a common factor of the numbers and then look for common factors of the letters.

2 Factorise the following expressions.

a $6p^2 + 9pt$

b $8pt + 6mp$

c $8ab - 4bc$

d $12a^2 - 8ab$

e $9mt - 6pt$

f $16at^2 + 12at$

g $5b^2c - 10bc$

h $8abc + 6bed$

i $4a^2 + 6a + 8$

j $6ab + 9bc + 3bd$

k $5t^2 + 4t + at$

l $6mt^2 - 3mt + 9m^2t$

m $8ab^2 + 2ab - 4a^2b$

n $10pt^2 + 15pt + 5p^2t$

3 Factorise the following expressions where possible. List those that cannot be factorised.

a $7m - 6t$

b $5m + 2mp$

c $t^2 - 7t$

d $8pt + 5ab$

e $4m^2 - 6mp$

f $a^2 + b$

g $4a^2 - 5ab$

h $3ab + 4cd$

i $5ab - 3b^2c$

FM 4 Three friends have a meal together. They each have a main meal costing £6.75 and a dessert costing £3.25.

Chris says that the bill in pounds, will be $3 \times 6.75 + 3 \times 3.25$.

Mary says that she has an easier way to work out the bill as $3 \times (6.75 + 3.25)$.

a Explain why Chris and Mary's methods both give the correct answer.

b Explain why Mary's method is better.

c What is the total bill?

AU 5 Three students are asked to factorise the expression $12m - 8$.

These are their answers.

Aidan	Bella	Craig
$2(6m - 4)$	$4(3m - 2)$	$4m\left(3 - \dfrac{2}{m}\right)$

All the answers are factorised correctly, but only one is the normally accepted answer.

a Which student gave the answer that is normally accepted as correct?

b Explain why the other two students' answers are not normally accepted as correct answers.

PS 6 Explain why $5m + 6p$ cannot be factorised.

ACTIVITY

Algebra dominoes

This is an activity for two people.

You need some card to make a set of algebra dominoes like those below.

$4 \times n$	t^2		$2b$	$2 - t$		$\dfrac{12n}{2}$	$0.5n$		$5w$	$b + b$

$3t - 2$	$3 \times 2y$		$5 + y$	$n + 2 + n + 3$		$\dfrac{4t + 2n}{2}$	$t \times t$		$5b - 3b$	$6n$

$6y$	$t - 2$		$2a + 2$	$2t + 2 - 3t$		$y + 5$	$7n - n$		$3n + 3n$	$4t - 2 - t$

b^2	$\dfrac{1}{2}n$		$t + 3 - 2$	$2n - 1$		$t + 5$	$b \times 2$		$10w \div 2$	$n + n + n + n$

$2t + n$	$4n$		$n + 2 + n - 3$	$2n + 5$		$\dfrac{n}{2}$	$2(a + 1)$		$n \div 2$	$n \times 4$

Turn the dominoes over and shuffle them. Deal five dominoes to each player.

One player starts by putting down a domino.

The other player may put down a domino that matches either end of the domino on the table. For example, if one player has put down the domino with $6n$ at one end, the other player could put down a domino that has an expression equal in value, such as the domino with $3n + 3n$ because $3n + 3n = 6n$. Otherwise, this player must pick up a domino from the spares.

The first player follows, playing a domino or picking one up, and so on, in turn.

The winner is the first player who has no dominoes.

Make up your own set of algebra dominoes.

Substitution

This section will show you how to:
- substitute numbers for letters in formulae and evaluate the resulting numerical expression
- use a calculator to evaluate numerical expressions

Key words
brackets
calculator
formula
substitution

One of the most important features of algebra is the use of expressions and **formulae**, and the **substitution** of real numbers into them.

The value of an expression, such as $3x + 2$, changes when different values of x are substituted into it. For example, the expression $3x + 2$ has the value:

5 when $x = 1$ 14 when $x = 4$

and so on. A formula expresses the value of one variable as the others in the formula change. For example, the formula for the area, A, of a triangle of base b and height h is:

$$A = \frac{b \times h}{2}$$

When $b = 4$ and $h = 8$:

$$A = \frac{4 \times 8}{2} = 16$$

EXAMPLE 13

The formula for the area of a trapezium is:

$$A = \frac{(a + b)h}{2}$$

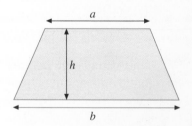

Find the area of the trapezium when $a = 5$, $b = 9$ and $h = 3$.

$$A = \frac{(5 + 9) \times 3}{2} = \frac{14 \times 3}{2} = 21$$

Always substitute the numbers for the letters before trying to work out the value of the expression. You are less likely to make a mistake this way. It is also useful to write **brackets** around each number, especially with negative numbers.

EXERCISE 10G

1 Find the value of $3x + 2$ when:

   a $x = 2$ **b** $x = 5$ **c** $x = 10$

2 Find the value of $4k - 1$ when:

   a $k = 1$ **b** $k = 3$ **c** $k = 11$

3 Find the value of $5 + 2t$ when:

   a $t = 2$ **b** $t = 5$ **c** $t = 12$

4 Evaluate $15 - 2f$ when: **a** $f = 3$ **b** $f = 5$ **c** $f = 8$

5 Evaluate $5m + 3$ when: **a** $m = 2$ **b** $m = 6$ **c** $m = 15$

6 Evaluate $3d - 2$ when: **a** $d = 4$ **b** $d = 5$ **c** $d = 20$

> **HINTS AND TIPS**
>
> It helps to put the numbers in brackets.
> $3(2) + 2 = 6 + 2 = 8$
> $3(5) + 2 = 15 + 2 = 17$
> etc …

FM 7 A taxi company uses the following rule to calculate their fares.

    Fare = £2.50 plus 50p per kilometre.

   a How much is the fare for a journey of 3 km?

   b Farook pays £9.00 for a taxi ride. How far was the journey?

   c Maisy knows that her house is 5 miles from town. She has £5.50 left in her purse after a night out. Has she got enough for a taxi ride home?

AU 8 Kaz knows that x, y and z have the values 2, 8 and 11, but she does not know which variable has which value.

   a What is the maximum value that the expression $2x + 6y - 3z$ could be?

   b What is the minimum value that the expression $5x - 2y + 3z$ could be?

> **HINTS AND TIPS**
>
> You could just try all combinations, but if you think for a moment you will find that the $6y$ term must give the largest number. This will give you a clue to the other terms.

PS 9 The formula for the area, A, of a rectangle with length l and width w is $A = lw$.

The formula for the area, T, of a triangle with base b and height h is $T = \frac{1}{2}bh$.

Find values of l, w, b and h so that $A = T$.

10 Find the value of $\dfrac{8 \times 4h}{5}$ when: **a** $h = 5$ **b** $h = 10$ **c** $h = 25$

11 Find the value of $\dfrac{25 - 3p}{2}$ when: **a** $p = 4$ **b** $p = 8$ **c** $p = 10$

12 Evaluate $\dfrac{x}{3}$ when: **a** $x = 6$ **b** $x = 24$ **c** $x = -30$

13 Evaluate $\dfrac{A}{4}$ when: **a** $A = 12$ **b** $A = 10$ **c** $A = -20$

14 Find the value of $\dfrac{12}{y}$ when: **a** $y = 2$ **b** $y = 4$ **c** $y = 6$

15 Find the value of $\dfrac{24}{x}$ when: **a** $x = 2$ **b** $x = 3$ **c** $x = 16$

FM 16 A holiday cottage costs £150 per day to rent.

A group of friends decide to rent the cottage for seven days.

a Which formula represents the cost of the rental for each person if there are n people in the group? Assume that they share the cost equally.

$$\dfrac{150}{n} \qquad \dfrac{150}{7n} \qquad \dfrac{1050}{n} \qquad \dfrac{150n}{n}$$

> **HINTS AND TIPS**
>
> To check your choice in part **a**, make up some numbers and try them in the formula. For example, take $n = 5$.

b Eventually 10 people go on the holiday. When they get the bill, they find that there is a discount for a seven-day rental.

After the discount, they each find it cost them £12.50 less than they expected.

How much does a 7-day rental cost?

AU 17 **a** p is an odd number and q is an even number.

Say if each of these expressions is odd or even.

i $p + q$ **ii** $p^2 + q$ **iii** $2p + q$ **iv** $p^2 + q^2$

b x, y and z are all odd numbers.

Write an expression, using x, y and z, so that the value of the expression is always even.

> **HINTS AND TIPS**
>
> There are many answers for **b** and **a** should give you a clue.

PS 18 A formula for the cost of delivery, in pounds, of orders from a do-it-yourself warehouse is:

$$D = 2M - \dfrac{C}{5}$$

where D is the cost of the delivery, M is the distance in miles from the store and C is the cost of the goods to be delivered.

> **HINTS AND TIPS**
>
> Note: a rebate is a refund of some of the money that someone has already paid for goods or services.

a How much does the delivery cost when $M = 30$ and $C = 200$?

b Bob buys goods worth £300 and lives 10 miles from the store.

i The formula gives the cost of delivery as a negative value. What is this value?

ii Explain why Bob will not get a rebate from the store.

c Maya buys goods worth £400. She calculates that her cost of delivery will be zero. What is the greatest distance that Maya could live from the store?

GRADE BOOSTER

F You can use a formula expressed in words

F You can substitute numbers into expressions and use letters to write a simple algebraic expression

E You can simplify expressions by collecting like terms

D You can use letters to write more complicated expressions, expand expressions with brackets and factorise simple expressions

C You can expand and simplify expressions with brackets and factorise expressions

What you should know now

- How to simplify a variety of algebraic expressions by multiplying, collecting like terms and expanding brackets

- How to factorise expressions by removing common factors

- How to substitute into expressions, using positive or negative whole numbers and decimals

1 Simplify each expression.

   a $p + 5p - 2p$

   b $3q \times 4r$

   c $7t - 10t$

2 **a** Simplify: $5a + 2b - a + 5b$

   b Expand: $5(p + 2q - 3r)$

3 **a** Matt buys 10 boxes of apple juice at 24 pence each.

     i Calculate the total cost.

     ii He pays with a £10 note.
       How much change will he receive?

4 Graham is y years old.

   Harriet is 5 years older than Graham.

   a Write down an expression for Harriet's age.

   b Jane is half as old as Harriet.
     Write down an expression for Jane's age.

5 **a** Simplify $7x + 8x - 2x$ (1)

   b Use the formula $H = 5P + 3L$

     to find P when $H = 26$ and $L = 2$ (3)

               (Total 4 marks)

   AQA, November 2008, Paper 2 Foundation, Question 13

6 A golf ball is travelling towards a hole.

   The distance of the ball from the hole, s feet, after time t seconds, is given by

   $s = t^2 - 6t + 9$

   a The ball drops into the hole after 3 seconds.
     By working out s when $t = 3$, show that this is correct.   (3)

               (Total 3 marks)

   AQA, June 2008, Paper 1 Foundation, Question 19(a)

7 **a** Find the value of a^3 when $a = 4$.

   b Find the value of $5x + 3y$ when $x = -2$ and $y = 4$.

   c There are p seats in a standard class coach and q seats in a first class coach. A train has five standard class coaches and two first class coaches.

     Write down an expression in terms of p and q for the total number of seats in the train.

---

8 $d = 3e + 2h^2$

   Calculate the value of d when $e = 3.7$ and $h = 2$.

9 **a** Expand and simplify this expression.
     $2(x + 3) + 5(x + 2)$

   b Expand and simplify this expression.
     $(4x + y) - (2x - y)$

10 **a** Multiply out $4(x - 3)$ (1)

   b Factorise $x^2 + 5x$ (1)

               (Total 2 marks)

   AQA, June 2007, Paper 2 Foundation, Question 22

11 Shapes are made from quarter circles and rectangles. For example

   The area of a quarter circle is Q cm^2.
   The area of a rectangle is R cm^2.
   This shape  has an area of 2Q + R cm^2.

   a Write down the area of this shape in terms of Q and R.   (1)

   b This shape  has an area of
     R – Q cm^2.
     Write down the area of this shape in terms of Q and R.   (2)

               (Total 3 marks)

   AQA, June 2009, Paper 2 Foundation, Question 20

12 **a** Expand $6(x - 7)$ (1)

   b Expand and simplify
     $x(2x + 3) - 4(x^2 - 1)$ (2)

               (Total 3 marks)

   AQA, November 2008, Paper 2 Foundation, Question 24

C   D   E   F

Worked Examination Questions

1 Factorise completely:

$4x^2 - 8xy$

$4x^2 - 8xy = 4x \times x - 4x \times 2y$

$\qquad = 4x(x - 2y)$

(Total: 2 marks)

> Note the words 'Factorise completely'. This is a clue that there is more than one common factor. Look for a common factor of 4 and 8, e.g. 4. Look for a common factor of x^2 and xy, e.g. x.

> Split up the terms, using the common factors.

> Write as a factorised expression.

> The correct answer gets 2 marks (1 for accuracy and 1 for method). A partial factorisation such as $4(x^2 - 2xy)$ or $2x(2x - 4y)$ would get 1 mark.

(AU) **2** A rectangle has a length of $2x + 4$ and width of $x + 2$.

   a Show that the perimeter can be written as $6(x + 2)$.

   b Mark says that the perimeter must always be an even number.

Find a value of x that proves that Mark is wrong.

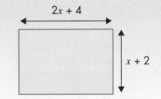

a Perimeter $= 2 \times (2x + 4) + 2 \times (x + 2)$

$\qquad = 2 \times 2(x + 2) + 2(x + 2)$

$\qquad = 4(x + 2) + 2(x + 2)$

$\qquad = 6(x + 2)$

> Write down an expression for the perimeter. This will get you 1 method mark.

> Take out the common factor.

An alternative is

$2x + 4 + 2x + 4 + x + 2 + x + 2 = 6x + 12$

$\qquad\qquad\qquad\qquad 6x + 12 = 6(x + 2)$

> Collect the like terms. These final two steps will get you 1 mark.

(2 marks)

b $6(x + 2) = 15$

$\qquad x + 2 = 2.5$

$\qquad\quad x = 0.5$

(1 mark)

> Pick an odd value for the perimeter, say 15. Any value that works will be worth 1 mark.

> There are many answers. Any value that makes the value inside the brackets 'something and a half', such as $x = 1.5$ or $x = 2.5$ will work.

(Total: 3 marks)

Many people go walking each weekend. It is good exercise and can be a very enjoyable pastime.

When walkers set out they often try to estimate the length of time the walk will take. There are many factors that could influence this, but one rule that can help in estimating how long the walk will take is Naismith's Rule.

Naismith's rule

Naismith's rule is a rule of thumb that you can use when planning a walk, by calculating how long it will take. The rule was devised by William Naismith, a Scottish mountaineer, in 1892.

The basic rule is:

Allow 1 hour for every 3 miles (5 km) forward, plus $\frac{1}{2}$ hour for every 1000 feet (300 m) of ascent.

Getting started

Before you begin your main task, you may find it useful to fill in the following table to practise using Naismith's Rule.

Can you use algebra to display the rule?

Day	Distance (km)	Height (m)	Time (m)
1	16	250	
2	18	0	
3	11	340	
4	13	100	
5	14	120	

Now, in small groups think about:

- What kind of things influence the speed at which you walk?
- Do different types of routes make people walk at different rates?
- If there is a large group of people will they all walk at the same rate?

Use all the ideas you have just discussed as you move on to your main task.

Your task

You are going to compare data to see if Naismith's rule is still a useful way to work out how much time to allow for different walks.

The table on the right shows the actual times taken by a school group as they did five different walks in five days. Use this information to work out the following:

1 If the group had started at the same times and had the same breaks, how long would the group have taken each day, according to Naismith's rule?

2 Do you think Naismith's rule is still valid today? Explain your reasons.

3 If your friend was going to climb Ben Nevis, setting out at 11.30 am, would you advise them to do the walk? You will need to research the distance and climb details of the pathway up Ben Nevis, in order to advise them fully.

Day	Distance (km)	Height (m)	Time (minutes)	Time (hours/ minutes)	Start	Breaks	Finish
1	16	250	255	4 h 15 m	10.00 am	2 h	4.15 pm
2	18	0	270	4 h 30 m	10.00 am	1 h 30 m	4.00 pm
3	11	340	199	3 h 19 m	09.30 am	2 h 30 m	3.19 pm
4	13	100	195	3 h 15 m	10.30 am	2 h 30 m	4.15 pm
5	14	120	222	3 h 42 m	10.30 am	2 h 30 m	4.42 pm

Why this chapter matters

Most jobs will require you to use some mathematics on a day-to-day basis. Being competent in all your number skills will therefore help you to be more successful in your job.

The mathematics used in the world of work will range from simple mental arithmetic calculations such as addition, subtraction, multiplication and division, to more complex calculations involving calculators, negative numbers and approximation. It will be up to you to select the mathematics that you need to carry out your job. Understanding essential mathematical techniques and how to apply these to a real-life context will make this much easier.

Jobs using mathematics

How many jobs can you think of that require some mathematics?

Here are a few ideas.

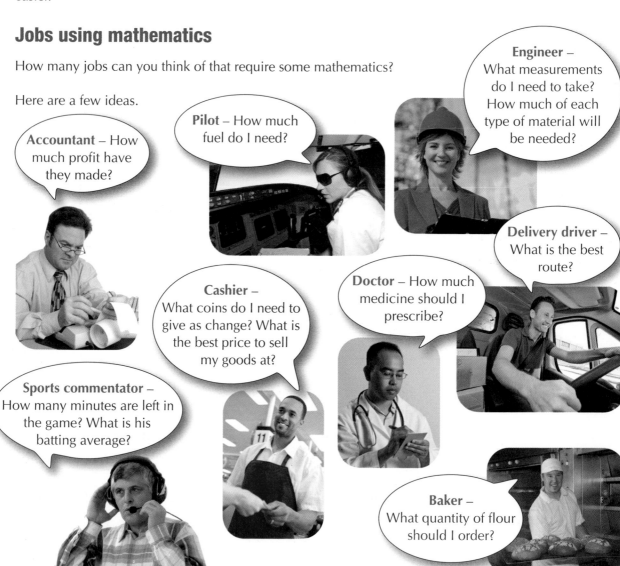

If you already have a career in mind that you would like to do, think of the questions you will need to ask to carry out your job successfully and the mathematics you will require to find the answers to those questions.

Number: Further number skills

1. Long multiplication

2. Long division

3. Arithmetic with decimal numbers

4. Multiplying and dividing with negative numbers

5. Approximation of calculations

This chapter will show you ...

- **F** a reminder of the ways you can multiply a three-digit number by a two-digit number
- **F** a reminder of long division
- **E** how to calculate with decimal numbers
- **E** how to multiply and divide negative numbers
- **C** how to use decimal places and significant figures to make approximations
- **C** sensible rounding methods

Visual overview

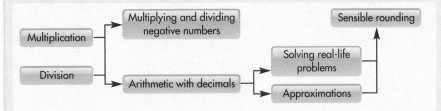

What you should already know

- Multiplication tables up to 10×10 **(KS3 level 4, GCSE grade G)**
- How to simplify fractions **(KS3 level 5, GCSE grade G)**

Quick check

1. Write down the first five multiples of 6.
2. Write down the first five multiples of 8.
3. Write down a number that is both a multiple of 3 and a multiple of 5.
4. Write down the smallest number that is a multiple of 4 and a multiple of 5.
5. Write down the smallest number that is a multiple of 4 and a multiple of 6.
6. Simplify the following fractions.

   a $\frac{8}{10}$ **b** $\frac{5}{20}$ **c** $\frac{4}{16}$ **d** $\frac{32}{100}$ **e** $\frac{36}{100}$ **f** $\frac{16}{24}$ **g** $\frac{16}{50}$

This section will show you how to:

- multiply a three-digit number (e.g. 358) by a two-digit number (e.g. 74) using
  - the grid method (or box method)
  - the column method (or traditional method)
  - the partition method

When you are asked to do long multiplication on the GCSE non-calculator paper, you will be expected to use an appropriate method. The three most common are:

- The **grid method** (or box method), see Example 1 below.

- The **column method** (or traditional method), see Example 2 below.

- The **partition method**, see Example 3 below.

EXAMPLE 1

Work out 243 × 68 without using a calculator.

Using the grid method split the two numbers into hundreds, tens and units and write them in a grid like the one below. Multiply all the pairs of numbers.

×	200	40	3
60	12000	2400	180
8	1600	320	24

Add the separate answers to find the total.

```
  12000
   2400
    180
   1600
    320
     24
  16524        So, 243 × 68 = 16524
   1 1
```

Note the use of carry marks to help with the calculation. Always try to write carried marks much smaller than the other numbers, so that you don't confuse them with the main calculation.

EXAMPLE 2

Work out 357 × 24 without using a calculator.

There are several different ways to do long multiplication, but the following is perhaps the method that is most commonly used. This is the column method.

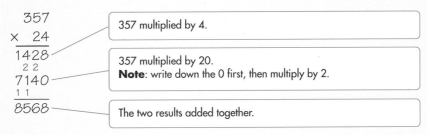

So, 357 × 24 = 8568

EXAMPLE 3

Work out 358 × 74 by the partition method.

Set out a grid as shown.

- Put the larger number along the top and the smaller number down the right-hand side.

- Multiply each possible pair in the grid, putting the numbers into each half as shown.

- Add up the numbers in each diagonal. If a total is larger than nine (in this example there is a total of 14), split the number and put the 1 in the next column on the left ready to be added in that diagonal.

- When you have completed the totalling, the number you are left with is the answer to the multiplication.

So, 358 × 74 = 26 492

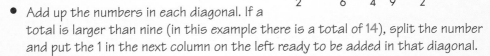

EXERCISE 11A

1. Use your preferred method to calculate the following without using a calculator.

a 357 × 34	**b** 724 × 63	**c** 714 × 42	**d** 898 × 23
e 958 × 54	**f** 676 × 37	**g** 239 × 81	**h** 437 × 29
i 539 × 37	**j** 477 × 55	**k** 371 × 85	**l** 843 × 93
m 507 × 34	**n** 810 × 54	**o** 905 × 73	**p** 1435 × 72
q 2504 × 56	**r** 4037 × 23	**s** 8009 × 65	**t** 2070 × 38

F

2 There are 48 cans of soup in a crate. A supermarket had a delivery of 125 crates of soup. The supermarket shelves will hold a total of 2500 cans. How many cans will be in the store room?

FM 3 Greystones Primary School has 12 classes, each of which has 26 students. The school hall will hold 250 students. Can all the students fit in the hall for an assembly?

FM 4 Suhail walks to school each day, there and back. The distance to school is 450 m. Suhail claims he walks over a marathon in distance, to and from school, in a school term of 64 days. A marathon is 42.1 km.

Is he correct?

5 On one page of a newspaper there are seven columns. In each column there are 172 lines, and in each line there are 50 letters. The newspaper has the equivalent of 20 pages of print, excluding photographs and adverts. Are there more than a million letters in the paper?

6 A tank of water was emptied into casks. Each cask held 81 litres. 71 casks were filled and there were 68 litres left over. How much water was there in the tank to start with?

FM 7 Joy was going to do a sponsored walk to raise money for the Macmillan Nurses. She managed to get 18 people to sponsor her, each for 35p per kilometre. She walked a total of 48 km. Did Joy reach her target of £400?

11.2 Long division

This section will show you how to:	Key words
• divide, without a calculator, a three-digit or four-digit number by a two-digit number, e.g. $840 \div 24$	long division remainder

There are several different ways of doing **long division**. It is acceptable to use any of them, provided it gives the correct answer and you can show all your working clearly. Two methods are shown in this book. Example 4 shows the *Italian method*, sometimes called the *DMSB* method (Divide, Multiply, Subtract and Bring down). It is the most commonly used way of doing long division.

Example 5 shows a method of repeated subtraction, which is sometimes called the *chunking method*.

EXAMPLE 4

Work out 840 ÷ 24.

It is a good idea to jot down the appropriate times table before you start the long division. In this case, it will be the 24 times table.

1	2	3	4	5	6	7	8	9
24	48	72	96	120	144	168	192	216

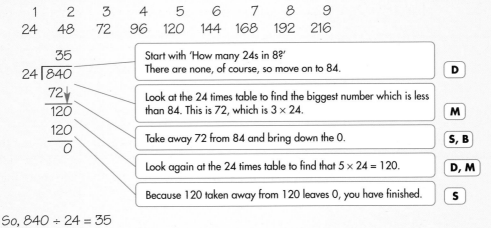

$$\begin{array}{r} 35 \\ 24\overline{)840} \\ 72\downarrow \\ \overline{120} \\ 120 \\ \overline{0} \end{array}$$

Start with 'How many 24s in 8?'
There are none, of course, so move on to 84.   **D**

Look at the 24 times table to find the biggest number which is less than 84. This is 72, which is 3 × 24.   **M**

Take away 72 from 84 and bring down the 0.   **S, B**

Look again at the 24 times table to find that 5 × 24 = 120.   **D, M**

Because 120 taken away from 120 leaves 0, you have finished.   **S**

So, 840 ÷ 24 = 35

You may do a division as a short division, without writing down all the numbers. It will look like this:

$$24\overline{)8\ 4^{12}0}\ \ \frac{3\ 5}{}$$

Notice how the **remainder** from 84 is placed in front of the 0 to make it 120.

EXAMPLE 5

Work out 1655 ÷ 35.

Jot down some of the multiples of 35 that may be useful.

$1 \times 35 = 35$ $2 \times 35 = 70$ $5 \times 35 = 175$ $10 \times 35 = 350$ $20 \times 35 = 700$

$$\begin{array}{r} 1655 \\ -\ \ 700 \\ \hline 955 \\ -\ \ 700 \\ \hline 255 \\ -\ \ 175 \\ \hline 80 \\ -\ \ \ 70 \\ \hline 10 \end{array}$$

20×35 ⟷ From 1655, subtract a large multiple of 35, such as 20 × 35 = 700.

20×35 ⟷ From 955, subtract a large multiple of 35, such as 20 × 35 = 700.

5×35 ⟷ From 255, subtract a multiple of 35, such as 5 × 35 = 175.

2×35 ⟷ From 80, subtract a multiple of 35, such as 2 × 35 = 70.

47

Once the remainder of 10 has been found, you cannot subtract any more multiples of 35. Add up the multiples to see how many times 35 has been subtracted.

So, 1655 ÷ 35 = 47, remainder 10

Sometimes, as here, you will not need a whole multiplication table, and so you could jot down only those parts of the table that you will need. But, don't forget, you are going to have to work *without* a calculator, so you do need all the help you can get.

EXAMPLE 6

Naseema is organising a coach trip for 640 people. Each coach will carry 46 people. How many coaches are needed?

You need to divide the number of people (640) by the number of people in a coach (46).

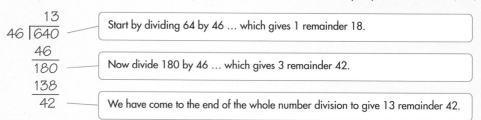

$$\begin{array}{r} 13 \\ 46\overline{)640} \\ \underline{46} \\ 180 \\ \underline{138} \\ 42 \end{array}$$

Start by dividing 64 by 46 ... which gives 1 remainder 18.

Now divide 180 by 46 ... which gives 3 remainder 42.

We have come to the end of the whole number division to give 13 remainder 42.

This tells Naseema that 14 coaches are needed to take all 640 passengers.
(There will be 46 − 42 = 4 spare seats)

EXERCISE 11B

1 Solve the following by long division.

a 525 ÷ 21	**b** 480 ÷ 32	**c** 925 ÷ 25	**d** 645 ÷ 15
e 621 ÷ 23	**f** 576 ÷ 12	**g** 1643 ÷ 31	**h** 728 ÷ 14
i 832 ÷ 26	**j** 2394 ÷ 42	**k** 829 ÷ 22	**l** 780 ÷ 31
m 895 ÷ 26	**n** 873 ÷ 16	**o** 875 ÷ 24	**p** 225 ÷ 13
q 759 ÷ 33	**r** 1478 ÷ 24	**s** 756 ÷ 18	**t** 1163 ÷ 43

2 3600 supporters of Barnsley Football Club want to go to an away game by coach. Each coach can hold 53 passengers. How many coaches will they need altogether?

3 How many stamps costing 26p each can I buy for £10?

FM 4 Kirsty is collecting a set of 40 porcelain animals. Each animal costs 45p. Each month she spends up to £5 of her pocket money on these animals. How many months will it take her to buy the full set?

FM 5 Amina wanted to save up to see a concert. The cost of a ticket was £25. She was paid 75p per hour to mind her little sister. For how many hours would Amina have to mind her sister to be able to afford the ticket?

AU 6 The magazine *Teen Dance* costs £2.20 in a newsagent. It costs £21 to get the magazine on a yearly subscription. How much cheaper is the magazine each month if it is bought by subscription?

Arithmetic with decimal numbers

This section will show you how to:

- identify the information that a decimal number shows
- round a decimal number
- identify decimal places
- add and subtract two decimal numbers
- multiply and divide a decimal number by a whole number less than 10
- multiply a decimal number by a two-digit number
- multiply a decimal number by another decimal number

Key words

decimal fraction
decimal place
decimal point
digit
evaluate
round

The number system is extended by using decimal numbers to represent fractions.

The **decimal point** separates the **decimal fraction** from the whole-number part.

For example, the number 25.374 means:

Tens	Units		Tenths	Hundredths	Thousandths
10	1		$\frac{1}{10}$	$\frac{1}{100}$	$\frac{1}{1000}$
2	**5**	**.**	**3**	**7**	**4**

You already use decimal notation to express amounts of money. For example:

£32.67   means $3 \times £10$
$2 \times £1$
$6 \times £0.10$ (10 pence)
$7 \times £0.01$ (1 penny)

Decimal places

When a number is written in decimal form, the **digits** to the right of the decimal point are called **decimal places**. For example:

79.4 is written 'with one decimal place'

6.83 is written 'with two decimal places'

0.526 is written 'with three decimal places'.

To **round** a decimal number to a particular number of decimal places, take these steps:

- Count along the decimal places from the decimal point and look at the first digit to be removed.

- When the value of this digit is less than five, just remove the unwanted places.

● When the value of this digit is five or more, add 1 onto the digit in the last decimal place then remove the unwanted places.

Here are some examples.

5.852 rounds to 5.85 to two decimal places

7.156 rounds to 7.16 to two decimal places

0.274 rounds to 0.3 to one decimal place

15.3518 rounds to 15.4 to one decimal place

EXERCISE 11C

1 Round each of the following numbers to one decimal place.

a 4.83	**b** 3.79	**c** 2.16	**d** 8.25
e 3.673	**f** 46.935	**g** 23.883	**h** 9.549
i 11.08	**j** 33.509	**k** 7.054	**l** 46.807
m 0.057	**n** 0.109	**o** 0.599	**p** 64.99
q 213.86	**r** 76.07	**s** 455.177	**t** 50.999

HINTS AND TIPS

Just look at the value of the digit in the second decimal place.

2 Round each of the following numbers to two decimal places.

a 5.783	**b** 2.358	**c** 0.977	**d** 33.085	**e** 6.007
f 23.5652	**g** 91.7895	**h** 7.995	**i** 2.3076	**j** 23.9158
k 5.9999	**l** 1.0075	**m** 3.5137	**n** 96.508	**o** 0.009
p 0.065	**q** 7.8091	**r** 569.897	**s** 300.004	**t** 0.0099

3 Round each of the following to the number of decimal places (dp) indicated.

a 4.568 (1 dp)	**b** 0.0832 (2 dp)	**c** 45.715 93 (3 dp)
d 94.8531 (2 dp)	**e** 602.099 (1 dp)	**f** 671.7629 (2 dp)
g 7.1124 (1 dp)	**h** 6.903 54 (3 dp)	**i** 13.7809 (2 dp)
j 0.075 11 (1 dp)	**k** 4.001 84 (3 dp)	**l** 59.983 (1 dp)
m 11.9854 (2 dp)	**n** 899.995 85 (3 dp)	**o** 0.0699 (1 dp)
p 0.009 87 (2 dp)	**q** 6.0708 (1 dp)	**r** 78.392 5 (3 dp)
s 199.9999 (2 dp)	**t** 5.0907 (1 dp)	

4 Round each of the following to the nearest whole number.

a 8.7	**b** 9.2	**c** 2.7	**d** 6.5	**e** 3.28
f 7.82	**g** 3.19	**h** 7.55	**i** 6.172	**j** 3.961
k 7.388	**l** 1.514	**m** 46.78	**n** 23.19	**o** 96.45
p 32.77	**q** 153.9	**r** 342.5	**s** 704.19	**t** 909.5

FM **5** Belinda puts the following items in her shopping basket: bread (£1.09), meat (£6.99), cheese (£3.91) and butter (£1.13).

By rounding each price to the nearest pound, work out an estimate of the total cost of the items.

AU **6** Which of the following are correct roundings of the number 3.456?

3   3.0   3.4   3.40   3.45   3.46   3.47   3.5   3.50

PS **7** When a number is rounded to three decimal places the answer is 4.728

Which of these could be the number?

4.71   4.7275   4.7282   4.73

Adding and subtracting with decimals

When you are working with decimals, you must *always* set out your work carefully.

Make sure that the decimal points are in line underneath the first point and each digit is in its correct place or column.

Then you can add or subtract just as you have done before. The decimal point of the answer will be placed directly underneath the other decimal points.

EXAMPLE 7

Work out 4.72 + 13.53.

$$
\begin{array}{r}
4.72 \\
+\ 13.53 \\
\hline
18.25 \\
\hline
{\scriptstyle 1}
\end{array}
$$

So, 4.72 + 13.53 = 18.25

Notice how to deal with 7 + 5 = 12, the 1 carrying forward into the next column.

EXAMPLE 8

Work out 7.3 − 1.5.

$$
\begin{array}{r}
{}^{6}\!\!\not{7}.{}^{1}3 \\
-\ 1.5 \\
\hline
5.8
\end{array}
$$

So, 7.3 − 1.5 = 5.8

Notice how to deal with the fact that you cannot take 5 from 3. You have to take one of the units from 7, replace the 7 with a 6 and make the 3 into 13.

Hidden decimal point

Whole numbers are usually written without decimal points. Sometimes you *do* need to show the decimal point in a whole number (see Example 9), in which case it is placed at the right-hand side of the number, followed by a zero.

EXAMPLE 9

Work out 4.2 + 8 + 12.9.

$$\begin{array}{r} 4.2 \\ 8.0 \\ + 12.9 \\ \hline 25.1 \\ \hline {\scriptstyle 1\ 1} \end{array}$$

So, 4.2 + 8 + 12.9 = 25.1

EXERCISE 11D

1 Work out each of these.

a 47.3 + 2.5	**b** 16.7 + 4.6	**c** 43.5 + 4.8
d 28.5 + 4.8	**e** 1.26 + 4.73	**f** 2.25 + 5.83
g 83.5 + 6.7	**h** 8.3 + 12.9	**i** 3.65 + 8.5
j 7.38 + 5.7	**k** 7.3 + 5.96	**l** 6.5 + 17.86

> **HINTS AND TIPS**
>
> When the numbers to be added or subtracted do not have the same number of decimal places, put in extra zeros, for example:
>
> $$\begin{array}{r} 3.65 \\ + 8.50 \\ \hline \end{array} \qquad \begin{array}{r} 8.25 \\ - 4.50 \\ \hline \end{array}$$

2 Work out each of these.

a 3.8 – 2.4	**b** 4.3 – 2.5	**c** 7.6 – 2.8
d 8.7 – 4.9	**e** 8.25 – 4.5	**f** 19.7 – 13.8
g 9.4 – 5.7	**h** 8.62 – 4.85	**i** 8 – 4.3
j 9 – 7.6	**k** 15 – 3.2	**l** 24 – 8.7

3 **Evaluate** each of the following. (Take care – they are a mixture.)

a 23.8 + 6.9	**b** 8.3 – 1.7	**c** 9 – 5.2	**d** 12.9 + 3.8
e 17.4 – 5.6	**f** 23.4 + 6.8	**g** 35 + 8.3	**h** 9.54 – 2.81
i 34.8 + 3.15	**j** 8.1 – 3.4	**k** 12.5 – 8.7	**l** 198.5 + 12

AU 4 Viki has £4.75 in her purse after buying a watch for £11.99.

a How much did she have in her purse before she bought the watch?

b She then goes home by bus. After paying her bus fare she has £3.35 left in her purse. How much was the bus fare?

FM **5** Pipes are sold in 5.3 m lengths.

Will three pipes be enough to make this arrangement (excluding the corner pieces)? Justify your answer.

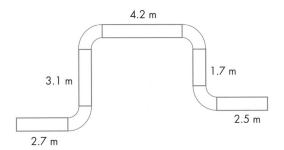

AU **6** Copy and complete the following.

a 12.5 + ... = 17.8   **b** 31.6 + ... = 38.3   **c** 7.16 + ... = 9.21

d ...... + 4.2 = 6.1   **e** ...... + 10.21 = 15.16   **f** ...... + 27.54 = 31.25

AU **7** Copy and complete the following.

a 13.2 − ...... = 11.6   **b** 81.4 − ...... = 38.7   **c** 7.51 − ...... = 3.22

d ...... − 3.1 = 9.7   **e** ...... − 14.6 = 7.8   **f** ...... − 17.32 = 34.65

PS **8** Mark went shopping. He went into three shops and bought one item from each shop.

In total he spent £43.97.

Music Store		Clothes Store		Book store	
CDs:	£5.98	Shirt:	£12.50	Magazine:	£2.25
DVDs:	£7.99	Jeans	£32.00	Pen:	£3.98

What did he buy?

Multiplying and dividing decimals by single-digit numbers

You can carry out these operations in exactly the same way as with whole numbers, as long as you remember to put each digit in its correct column.

Again, the decimal point is kept in line underneath or above the first point.

EXAMPLE 10

Work out 4.5 × 3.

$$
\begin{array}{r}
4.5 \\
\times \quad 3 \\
\hline
13.5 \\
\end{array}
$$
  1

So, 4.5 × 3 = 13.5

EXAMPLE 11

Work out 8.25 ÷ 5.

$$\begin{array}{r} 1.\,6\,5 \\ 5\,\overline{\smash{)}\,8.^3 2^2 5} \end{array}$$

So, 8.25 ÷ 5 = 1.65

EXAMPLE 12

Work out 5.7 ÷ 2.

$$\begin{array}{r} 2.\,8\,5 \\ 2\,\overline{\smash{)}\,5.^1 7^1 0} \end{array}$$

So, 5.7 ÷ 2 = 2.85

HINTS AND TIPS

We add a 0 after the 5.7 in order to continue dividing.
We do not use remainders with decimal places.

EXERCISE 11E

1 Evaluate each of these.

a 2.4×3	**b** 3.8×2	**c** 4.7×4	**d** 5.3×7
e 6.5×5	**f** 3.6×8	**g** 2.5×4	**h** 9.2×6
i 12.3×5	**j** 24.4×7	**k** 13.6×6	**l** 19.3×5

2 Evaluate each of these.

a 2.34×4	**b** 3.45×3	**c** 5.17×5	**d** 4.26×3
e 0.26×7	**f** 0.82×4	**g** 0.56×5	**h** 0.92×6
i 6.03×7	**j** 7.02×8	**k** 2.55×3	**l** 8.16×6

3 Evaluate each of these.

a $3.6 \div 2$	**b** $5.6 \div 4$	**c** $4.2 \div 3$	**d** $8.4 \div 7$
e $4.26 \div 2$	**f** $3.45 \div 5$	**g** $8.37 \div 3$	**h** $9.68 \div 8$
i $7.56 \div 4$	**j** $5.43 \div 3$	**k** $1.32 \div 4$	**l** $7.6 \div 4$

4 Evaluate each of these.

HINTS AND TIPS

Remember to keep the decimal points in line.

    a 3.5 ÷ 2   **b** 6.4 ÷ 5   **c** 7.4 ÷ 4   **d** 7.3 ÷ 2

    e 8.3 ÷ 5   **f** 5.8 ÷ 4   **g** 7.1 ÷ 5   **h** 9.2 ÷ 8

    i 6.7 ÷ 2   **j** 4.9 ÷ 5   **k** 9.2 ÷ 4   **l** 7.3 ÷ 5

5 Evaluate each of these.

    a 7.56 ÷ 4   **b** 4.53 ÷ 3   **c** 1.32 ÷ 5   **d** 8.53 ÷ 2

    e 2.448 ÷ 2   **f** 1.274 ÷ 7   **g** 0.837 ÷ 9   **h** 16.336 ÷ 8

    i 9.54 ÷ 5   **j** 14 ÷ 5   **k** 17 ÷ 4   **l** 37 ÷ 2

FM **6** Soup is sold in packs of five for £3.25 and packs of eight for £5. Which is the cheaper way of buying soup?

FM **7** **AU** **a** Mike took his wife and four children to a theme park. The tickets were £13.25 for each adult and £5.85 for each child. How much did all the tickets cost Mike?

    b While in the park, the children wanted ice creams.

    Ice creams cost £1.60 each for large ones or £1.20 each for small ones.
    Their mother only has £5.

    Which size should she buy? Give a reason for your answer.

PS **8** Mary was laying a path through her garden. She bought nine paving stones, each 1.35 m long. She wanted the path to run straight down the garden, which is 10 m long. Has Mary bought too many paving stones? Show all your working.

Long multiplication with decimals

As before, you must put each digit in its correct column and keep the decimal point in line.

EXAMPLE 13

Evaluate 4.27 × 34.

$$
\begin{array}{r}
4.27 \\
\times \quad 34 \\
\hline
17.08 \\
{\scriptstyle 1\,2} \\
128.10 \\
{\scriptstyle 2} \\
\hline
145.18 \\
{\scriptstyle 1}
\end{array}
$$

So, 4.27 × 34 = 145.18

EXERCISE 11F

1 Evaluate each of these.

a 3.72×24 **b** 5.63×53 **c** 1.27×52 **d** 4.54×37

e 67.2×35 **f** 12.4×26 **g** 62.1×18 **h** 81.3×55

i 5.67×82 **j** 0.73×35 **k** 23.8×44 **l** 99.5×19

2 Find the total cost of each of the following purchases.

a 18 ties at £12.45 each

b 25 shirts at £8.95 each

c 13 pairs of tights at £2.30 a pair

> **HINTS AND TIPS**
>
> When the answer is an amount of money in pounds, you must write it with two decimal places. Writing £224.1 will lose you a mark. It should be £224.10.

PS 3 Theo says that he can change multiplications into easier multiplications with the same answer by doubling one number and halving the other number.

For example to work out 8.4×12 he does 16.8×6

Use his method to work out 2.5×14.

FM 4 A party of 24 scouts and their leader went into a zoo. The cost of a ticket for each scout was £2.15 and the cost of a ticket for the leader was £2.60. What was the total cost of entering the zoo?

FM 5 **a** A market gardener bought 35 trays of seedlings. Each tray cost £3.45.
AU   What was the total cost of the trays of seedlings?

b There were 20 seedlings on each tray which are sold at 85p each. How much profit did the market gardener make per tray?

Multiplying two decimal numbers together

Follow these steps to multiply one decimal number by another decimal number.

- First, complete the whole calculation as if the decimal points were not there.

- Then, count the total number of decimal places in the two decimal numbers. This gives the number of decimal places in the answer.

EXAMPLE 14

Evaluate 3.42 × 2.7.

Ignoring the decimal points gives the following calculation:

```
     342
  ×   27
    2394
      2 1
    6840
    9234
      1 1
```

Now, 3.42 has two decimal places (.42) and 2.7 has one decimal place (.7). So, the total number of decimal places in the answer is three.

So, 3.42 × 2.7 = 9.234

EXERCISE 11G

1 Evaluate each of these.

a 2.4 × 0.2   **b** 7.3 × 0.4   **c** 5.6 × 0.2   **d** 0.3 × 0.4

e 0.14 × 0.2   **f** 0.3 × 0.3   **g** 0.24 × 0.8   **h** 5.82 × 0.52

i 5.8 × 1.23   **j** 5.6 × 9.1   **k** 0.875 × 3.5   **l** 9.12 × 5.1

FM 2 Jerome is making a jacket. He has £30 to spend and needs 3.4 m of cloth. The cloth is £8.75 per metre.

Can Jerome afford the cloth?

3 For each of the following:

i estimate the answer by first rounding each number to the nearest whole number

ii calculate the exact answer, and then calculate the difference between this and your answers to part **i**.

a 4.8 × 7.3   **b** 2.4 × 7.6   **c** 15.3 × 3.9   **d** 20.1 × 8.6

e 4.35 × 2.8   **f** 8.13 × 3.2   **g** 7.82 × 5.2   **h** 19.8 × 7.1

4 a Use any method to work out 26 × 22

b Use your answer to part **a** to work out:

i 2.6 × 2.2

ii 1.3 × 1.1

iii 2.6 × 8.8.

Multiplying and dividing with negative numbers

This section will show you how to:
- multiply and divide with negative numbers

Key word
negative

The rules for multiplying and dividing with **negative** numbers are very easy.

- When the signs of the numbers are the *same*, the answer is *positive*.
- When the signs of the numbers are *different*, the answer is *negative*.

Here are some examples.

$$2 \times 4 = 8 \qquad 12 \div -3 = -4 \qquad -2 \times -3 = 6 \qquad -12 \div -3 = 4$$

A common error is to confuse, for example, -3^2 and $(-3)^2$.

$$-3^2 = -3 \times 3 = -9$$

but,

$$(-3)^2 = -3 \times -3 = +9$$

So, this means that if a variable is introduced, for example, $a = -5$, the calculation would be as follows:

$$a^2 = -5 \times -5 = +25$$

EXAMPLE 15

$a = -2$ and $b = -6$

Work out

a a^2 **b** $a^2 + b^2$ **c** $b^2 - a^2$ **d** $(a - b)^2$

a a^2 $= -2 \times -2 = +4$

b $a^2 + b^2$ $= +4 + -6 \times -6 = 4 + 36 = 40$

c $b^2 - a^2$ $= 36 - 4 = 32$

d $(a - b)$ $= (-2 - -6)^2 = (-2 + 6)^2 = (4)^2 = 16$

EXERCISE 11H

1 Write down the answers to the following.

a -3×5	**b** -2×7	**c** -4×6	**d** -2×-3	**e** -7×-2
f $-12 \div -6$	**g** $-16 \div 8$	**h** $24 \div -3$	**i** $16 \div -4$	**j** $-6 \div -2$
k 4×-6	**l** 5×-2	**m** 6×-3	**n** -2×-8	**o** -9×-4
p $24 \div -6$	**q** $12 \div -1$	**r** $-36 \div 9$	**s** $-14 \div -2$	**t** $100 \div 4$
u -2×-9	**v** $32 \div -4$	**w** 5×-9	**x** $-21 \div -7$	**y** -5×8

2 Write down the answers to the following.

a $-3 + -6$	**b** -2×-8	**c** $2 + -5$	**d** 8×-4	**e** $-36 \div -2$
f -3×-6	**g** $-3 - -9$	**h** $48 \div -12$	**i** -5×-4	**j** $7 - -9$
k $-40 \div -5$	**l** $-40 + -8$	**m** $4 - -9$	**n** $5 - 18$	**o** $72 \div -9$
p $-7 - -7$	**q** $8 - -8$	**r** 6×-7	**s** $-6 \div -1$	**t** $-5 \div -5$
u $-9 - 5$	**v** $4 - -2$	**w** $4 \div -1$	**x** $-7 \div -1$	**y** -4×0

3 What number do you multiply by -3 to get the following?

a 6   **b** -90 **c** -45 **d** 81   **e** 21

4 What number do you divide -36 by to get the following?

a -9 **b** 4   **c** 12   **d** -6 **e** 9

5 Evaluate the following.

a $-6 + (4 - 7)$ **b** $-3 - (-9 - -3)$ **c** $8 + (2 - 9)$

6 Evaluate the following.

a $4 \times (-8 \div -2)$ **b** $-8 - (3 \times -2)$ **c** $-1 \times (8 - -4)$

7 What do you get if you divide -48 by the following?

a -2 **b** -8 **c** 12   **d** 24

AU 8 Write down six different multiplications that give the answer -12.

AU 9 Write down six different divisions that give the answer -4.

10 Find the answers to the following.

a -3×-7	**b** $3 + -7$	**c** $-4 \div -2$	**d** $-7 - 9$	**e** $-12 \div -6$
f $-12 - -7$	**g** 5×-7	**h** $-8 + -9$	**i** $-4 + -8$	**j** $-3 + 9$
k -5×-9	**l** $-16 \div 8$	**m** $-8 - -8$	**n** $6 \div -6$	**o** $-4 + -3$
p -9×4	**q** $-36 \div -4$	**r** -4×-8	**s** $-1 - -1$	**t** $2 - 67$

AU 11 **a** Work out 6×-2

b The average temperature drops by 2 °C every day for six days. How much has the temperature dropped altogether?

c The temperature drops by 6 °C for each of the next three days. Write down the calculation to work out the total drop in temperature over these three days.

PS 12 Put these calculation in order from lowest to highest.

-5×4 $-20 \div 2$ $-16 \div -4$ 3×-6

13 $x = -2$, $y = -3$ and $z = -4$. Work out

a x^2 **b** $y^2 + z^2$ **c** $z^2 - x^2$ **d** $(x - y)^2$

D

Approximation of calculations

This section will show you how to:
- identify significant figures
- round to one significant figure
- approximate the result before multiplying two numbers together
- approximate the result before dividing two numbers
- round a calculation, at the end of a problem, to give what is considered to be a sensible answer

Key words
approximate
round
significant figure

Rounding to significant figures

You will often use **significant figures** when you want to **approximate** a number with quite a few digits in it.

The following table illustrates some numbers written to one, two and three significant figures (sf).

One sf	8	50	200	90 000	0.000 07	0.003	0.4
Two sf	67	4.8	0.76	45 000	730	0.006 7	0.40
Three sf	312	65.9	40.3	0.0761	7.05	0.003 01	0.400

In the GCSE examination you usually only have to **round** numbers to one significant figure.

The steps taken to round a number to one significant figure are very similar to those used for decimal places.

- From the left, find the second digit. If the original number is less than one, start counting from the first non-zero digit.
- When the value of the second digit is less than five, leave the first digit as it is.
- When the value of the second digit is equal to or greater than five, add 1 to the first digit.
- Put in enough zeros at the end to keep the number the right size.

For example, the following tables show some numbers rounded to one significant figure.

Number	Rounded to 1 sf
78	80
32	30
0.69	0.7
1.89	2
998	1000
0.432	0.4

Number	Rounded to 1 sf
45 281	50 000
568	600
8054	8000
7.837	8
99.8	100
0.078	0.08

EXERCISE 11I

1 Round each of the following numbers to 1 significant figure.

a 46 313	**b** 57 123	**c** 30 569	**d** 94 558	**e** 85 299
f 54.26	**g** 85.18	**h** 27.09	**i** 96.432	**j** 167.77
k 0.5388	**l** 0.2823	**m** 0.005 84	**n** 0.047 85	**o** 0.000 876
p 9.9	**q** 89.5	**r** 90.78	**s** 199	**t** 999.99

2 Round each of the following numbers to 1 significant figure.

a 56 147	**b** 26 813	**c** 79 611	**d** 30 578	**e** 14 009
f 5876	**g** 1065	**h** 847	**i** 109	**j** 638.7
k 1.689	**l** 4.0854	**m** 2.658	**n** 8.0089	**o** 41.564
p 0.8006	**q** 0.458	**r** 0.0658	**s** 0.9996	**t** 0.009 82

3 Write down the smallest and the greatest numbers of sweets that can be found in each of these jars.

a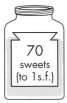
70 sweets (to 1s.f.)

b
100 sweets (to 1s.f.)

c
1000 sweets (to 1s.f.)

4 Write down the smallest and the greatest numbers of people that might live in these towns.

Elsecar   population 800 (to one significant figure)

Hoyland   population 1000 (to one significant figure)

Barnsley   population 200 000 (to one significant figure)

PS 5 A joiner estimates that he has 20 pieces of skirting board in stock. He is correct to one significant figure. He uses three pieces and now has 10 left to one significant figure.

How many could he have had to start with?
Work out all possible answers.

AU 6 There are 500 fish in a pond to one significant figure.

What is the least possible number of fish that could be taken from the pond so that there are 400 fish in the pond to one significant figure?

Approximation of calculations

How would you approximate the value of a calculation? What would you actually do when you try to approximate an answer to a problem?

For example, what is the approximate answer to 35.1×6.58?

To find the approximate answer, you simply round each number to 1 significant figure, then complete the calculation. So in this case, the approximation is:

$35.1 \times 6.58 \approx 40 \times 7 = 280$

Note the symbol $\approx$ which means 'approximately equal to'.

For the division $89.1 \div 2.98$, the approximate answer is $90 \div 3 = 30$.

Sometimes when dividing it can be sensible to round to 2 sf instead of 1 sf. For example,

$24.3 \div 3.87$ using $24 \div 4$ gives an approximate answer of 6

whereas

$24.3 \div 3.87$ using $20 \div 4$ gives an approximate answer of 5.

Both of these answers would be acceptable in the GCSE examination as they are both sensible answers, but generally rounding to one significant figure is easier.

A quick approximation is always a great help in any calculation since it often stops you giving a silly answer.

EXERCISE 11J

D

1 Find approximate answers to the following.

    a 5435×7.31 **b** 5280×3.211 **c** $63.24 \times 3.514 \times 4.2$

    d 3508×2.79 **e** $72.1 \times 3.225 \times 5.23$ **f** $470 \times 7.85 \times 0.99$

    g $354 \div 79.8$ **h** $36.8 \div 1.876$ **i** $5974 \div 5.29$

Check your answers on a calculator to see how close you were.

2 Find the approximate monthly pay of the following people whose annual salaries are given.

    a Paul £35 200   **b** Michael £25 600

    c Jennifer £18 125   **d** Ross £8420

3 Find the approximate annual pay of the following people who earn:

    a Kevin £270 a week   **b** Malcolm £1528 a month   **c** David £347 a week

AU 4 A farmer bought 2713 kg of seed at a cost of £7.34 per kg. Find the approximate total cost of this seed.

5 By rounding, find an approximate answer to each of the following.

a $\dfrac{573 + 783}{107}$ b $\dfrac{783 - 572}{24}$ c $\dfrac{352 + 657}{999}$ d $\dfrac{1123 - 689}{354}$

e $\dfrac{589 + 773}{658 - 351}$ f $\dfrac{793 - 569}{998 - 667}$ g $\dfrac{354 + 656}{997 - 656}$ h $\dfrac{1124 - 661}{355 + 570}$

i $\dfrac{28.3 \times 19.5}{97.4}$ j $\dfrac{78.3 \times 22.6}{3.69}$ k $\dfrac{3.52 \times 7.95}{15.9}$ l $\dfrac{11.78 \times 77.8}{39.4}$

6 Find the approximate answer to each of the following.

   a $208 \div 0.378$ b $96 \div 0.48$ c $53.9 \div 0.58$

   d $14.74 \div 0.285$ e $28.7 \div 0.621$ f $406.9 \div 0.783$

Check your answers on a calculator to see how close you were.

7 A litre of paint will cover an area of about 8.7 m². Approximately how many litre cans will I need to buy to paint a room with a total surface area of 73 m²?

8 By rounding, find the approximate answer to each of the following.

a $\dfrac{84.7 + 12.6}{0.483}$ b $\dfrac{32.8 \times 71.4}{0.812}$ c $\dfrac{34.9 - 27.9}{0.691}$ d $\dfrac{12.7 \times 38.9}{0.42}$

FM 9 It took me 6 hours and 40 minutes to drive from Sheffield to Bude, a distance of 295 miles. My car uses petrol at the rate of about 32 miles per gallon. The petrol cost £3.51 per gallon.

   a Approximately how many miles did I travel each hour?

   b Approximately how many gallons of petrol did I use in going from Sheffield to Bude?

   c What was the approximate cost of all the petrol for my journey to Bude and back again?

PS 10 Kirsty arranges for magazines to be put into envelopes. She sorts out 178 magazines between 10.00 am and 1.00 pm. Approximately how many magazines will she be able to sort in a week in which she works for 17 hours?

11 An athlete runs 3.75 km every day. Approximately how far does he run in:

   a a week   b a month   c a year?

AU 12 1 kg = 1000 g

A box full of magazines weighs 8 kg. One magazine weighs about 15 g. Approximately how many magazines are there in the box?

13 An apple weighs about 280 grams.

   a What is the approximate weight of a bag containing a dozen apples?

   b Approximately how many apples will there be in a sack weighing 50 kg?

Sensible rounding

Sensible rounding is simply writing or saying answers to questions which have a real-life context so that the answer makes sense and is the sort of thing someone might say in a normal conversation.

For example:

The distance from Rotherham to Sheffield is 9 miles is a sensible statement.

The distance from Rotherham to Sheffield is 8.7864 miles is not sensible.

6 tins of paint is sensible.

5.91 tins of paint is not sensible.

As a general rule if it sounds sensible it will be acceptable.

EXERCISE 11K

1 Round each of the following to give sensible answers.

    a I am 1.7359 m tall.

    b It took me 5 minutes 44.83 seconds to mend the television.

    c My kitten weighs 237.97 g.

    d The correct temperature at which to drink Earl Grey tea is 82.739 °C.

    e The distance from Wath to Sheffield is 15.528 miles.

    f The area of the floor is 13.673 m².

FM 2 Rewrite the following article using sensible amounts.

It was a hot day, the temperature was 81.699 °F and still rising. I had now walked 5.3289 km in just over 113.98 minutes. But I didn't care since I knew that the 43 275 people watching the race were cheering me on. I won by clipping 6.2 seconds off the record time. This was the 67th time the race had taken place since records first began in 1788. Well, next year I will only have 15 practice walks beforehand as I strive to beat the record by at least another 4.9 seconds.

AU 3 A lorry load of scrap metal weighs 39.715 tonnes.
It is worth £20.35 per tonne.

Approximately how much is the load worth?

PS 4 The accurate temperature is 18.2 °C.
David rounds the temperature to the nearest 5 °C.
David says the temperature is about 20 °C.

How much would the temperature rise for David to say that the temperature is about 25 °C?

GRADE BOOSTER

F You can multiply a three-digit number by a two-digit number without using a calculator

F You can divide a three- or four-digit number by a two-digit number

F You can solve real problems involving multiplication and division

F You can round decimal numbers to a specific number of places

E You can evaluate calculations involving decimal numbers

E You can round numbers to one significant figure

E You can multiply and divide negative numbers

D You can estimate the approximate value of a calculation before calculating

C You can give sensible answers to real-life questions

What you should know now

- How to do long multiplication
- How to do long division
- How to perform calculations with decimal numbers
- How to round to a specific number of decimal places
- How to round to a specific number of significant figures
- How to multiply and divide with negative numbers
- How to make estimates by suitable rounding

1 **a** Kim buys 4 birthday cards at £1.55 each.
What change does she get from £10? (2)

b Each week Kim receives pocket money.
She gets £5.50 each week plus £3.75 for every hour she helps in the garden.
One week she helps for 3 hours in the garden.
Work out her total pocket money for that week. (2)

(Total 4 marks)

AQA, June 2007, Paper 2 Foundation, Question 8

2 Josh is buying as many batteries as he can for £10.
The batteries cost £1.29 each.

a How many can he buy? (1)

b How much change does he get from a £10 note? (2)

(Total 3 marks)

AQA, June 2006, Paper 2 Foundation, Question 11

3 Tom works from 1.45 pm to 5.30 pm every weekday.

a How long does Tom work each day in hours and minutes? (2)

b On Saturday Tom works $6\frac{1}{2}$ hours.
He is paid £5.40 per hour.
How much is Tom paid for Saturday's work? (2)

(Total 4 marks)

AQA, March 2005, Module 3 Foundation, Question 4

4 A coach costs £345 to hire.

There are 55 seats on the coach.

Work out a sensible seat price assuming at least 45 seats are sold.

5 **a** Put these numbers in order of size.
Start with the largest number.
0.786   0.09   0.8 (1)

b Write 0.786 to 2 decimal places. (1)

c Convert $\frac{3}{8}$ to a decimal. (2)

d Work out 0.1×0.7 (1)

(Total 5 marks)

AQA, November 2006, Module 3 Foundation, Question 15

6 Work out

a $5^2 \times 2^3$ (2)

b $\frac{7}{8} - \frac{1}{2}$ (2)

(Total 4 marks)

AQA, November 2006, Module 3 Foundation, Question 16

7 **a** Work out 3^3 (1)

b Give an example of a cube number that does **not** divide exactly by three. (1)

(Total 2 marks)

AQA, June 2005, Module 3 Foundation, Question 16

8 Three pupils use calculators to work out

$$\frac{32.7 + 14.3}{1.28 - 0.49}$$

Arnie gets 43.4, Bert gets 36.2 and Chuck gets 59.5. Use approximations to show which one of them is correct.

9 Work out $3\frac{2}{5} - 1\frac{2}{3}$

10 Use approximations to estimate the value of

$$\sqrt{\frac{323\,407}{0.48}}$$

11 Each term of a sequence is formed by multiplying the previous term by –2 and then subtracting 1. The first three terms are

2, –5, 9 …

a Write down the next two terms of the sequence.

b A later term in the sequence is 119. What was the previous term?

C   D   E   F

Worked Examination Questions

FM **1** In a **survey** the number of visitors to a website was recorded daily. Altogether it was visited 30 million times. Each day it was visited 600 000 times.

Based on this information, for how many days did the survey last?

You need to find the number of days using the following calculation:
   total times visited ÷ number of visits a day
You get 1 method mark for showing the calculation.

$$30\ 000\ 000 \div 600\ 000 = \frac{30\ 000\ 000}{600\ 000}$$

You can cancel the five zeros on the top and the bottom.

$$= \frac{300}{6} = 50 \text{ days}$$

Total: 2 marks

Check that your final answer is sensible. You get 1 accuracy mark for the correct answer of 50 days.

PS **AU** **2** A theatre has 400 tickets available each night for a show on Friday and Saturday nights.
The manager of the theatre wants to raise £1500 from ticket sales each night.
She expects to sell all the tickets for Saturday but only three-quarters of the tickets for Friday.
If the ticket price is the same for both days, how much should she charge?

$\frac{3}{4} \times 400 = 300$

You get 1 method mark for working out that she sells $\frac{3}{4}$ of 400 tickets on Friday.

$300 + 400 = 700$ tickets altogether sold

£3000 needed

You get 1 mark for realising that £3000 (£1500 × 2) needs to raised.

$3000 \div 700 = 4.28$

Round up to ensure a profit,
so for example £4.50 or £5 per ticket

For attempting to work out the exact amount per seat (3000 ÷ 700 or £4.28) you get 1 method mark.

Total: 4 marks

Give a sensible price (e.g. to nearest 10p or with a built-in profit margin) to get 1 mark for accuracy.

Healthy eating and regular exercise form part of a balanced lifestyle. Health clubs and gyms are a popular way to keep fit. Exercise machines in gyms often show how many calories are burnt off during a workout.

This activity investigates the relationship between calorie intake and burn-off rates.

Remember
We must not burn off all the calories that we consume: the body needs calories as energy.

Getting started

Before you begin your main task, use the information given on these pages to work out:

● the weight category for each person

● the calories they take in at breakfast and the amount they burn off through exercise.

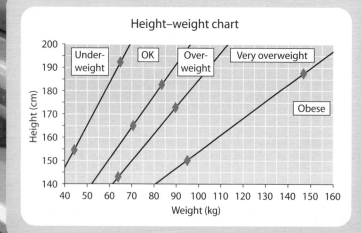

Height–weight chart

Facts	
Calories per 100 g	
Apple	46
Bacon	440
Banana	76
Bread	246
Butter	740
Cornflakes	370
Eggs	148
Porridge	368
Sausages	186
Yoghurt	62
Apple juice (100 ml)	41
Orange juice (100 ml)	36
Semi-skimmed milk (100 ml)	48
Skimmed milk (100 ml)	34
Sugar (1 teaspoonful)	20
Tea or coffee (black)	0

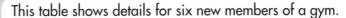

This table shows details for six new members of a gym.

Person	Height & weight	Breakfast	Exercise machine
Lynn	height 162 cm weight 60 kg	150 g toast 20 g butter 250 ml orange juice	cross-trainer (9 cal/min) for 15 minutes
Jess	height 168 cm weight 82 kg	50 g bacon 200 g sausages 50 g eggs tea with 40 ml semi-skimmed milk	walking (6 cal/min) for 30 minutes
Andy	height 180 cm weight 75 kg	100 g apple 100 g banana 150 g yoghurt 200 ml apple juice	running (8 cal/min) for 20 minutes
Dave	height 192 cm weight 95 kg	50 g bacon 150 g bread 20 g butter 200 ml semi-skimmed milk	exercise bike (7 cal/min) for 20 minutes
Pete	height 175 cm weight 60 kg	30 g cornflakes 300 ml semi-skimmed milk tea with 40 ml skimmed milk 2 teaspoons sugar	step machine (9 cal/min) for 15 minutes
Ola	height 165 cm weight 45 kg	75 g porridge 300 ml semi-skimmed milk black coffee 1 teaspoon sugar	rowing (8 cal/min for 20 minutes

Your task

Design a healthy breakfast and then look at how long it would take to burn off the calories contained in this breakfast on each exercise machine.

Use these points to help you in your task:

- Think about the different breakfast options that you find in a canteen, at home or in a cafe.
- Try to calculate the calories in some of these breakfast options.
- Now think about how much exercise you should do to burn off these calories.

The first equation ever written, using a modern equals sign, was:

14.꙾ℯ.———.15.ℊ=====71.ℊ.

It was written by Robert Recorde in 1557.
In today's notation this is $14\sqrt{x} + 15 = 71$.
The solution is $x = 16$.
Three of the most important equations in the world are shown on this page.

Why does the Moon keep orbiting the Earth and not fly off into space?

This is explained by Newton's law of universal gravitation, which describes the gravitational attraction between two bodies:

$$F = G \times \frac{m_1 \times m_2}{r^2}$$

where F is the force between the bodies, G is the gravitational constant, m_1 and m_2 are the masses of the two bodies and r is the distance between them.

Why don't planes fall out of the sky?

This is explained by Bernoulli's principle, which states that as the speed of a fluid increases, its pressure decreases. This is what causes the pressure differential between the top and bottom of an aircraft wing, as shown in the diagram on the left.

In its simplest form, the equation can be written as:

$$p + q = p_0$$

where p = static pressure, q = dynamic pressure and p_0 is the total pressure.

How can a couple of kilograms of plutonium have enough energy to wipe out a city?

This is explained by Einstein's theory of special relativity, which states that the speed of light is the same for all observers, even if one of them is moving at half the speed of light. It also connects mass and energy in the equation:

$$E = mc^2$$

where E is the energy, m is the mass and c is the speed of light. As the speed of light is nearly 300 000 kilometres per second, the amount of energy in a small mass is huge. If this can be released, it can be used for good (as in nuclear power stations) or harm (as in nuclear bombs).

Algebra: Equations and inequalities

1 Solving simple linear equations

2 Solving equations with brackets

3 Equations with the variable on both sides

4 Rearranging formulae

5 Solving linear inequalities

This chapter will show you ...

- to **F** to **E** how to solve linear equations with the variable on one side only
- **C** how to solve linear equations with the variable on both sides
- **C** how to rearrange simple formulae
- **C** how to solve simple linear inequalities

Visual overview

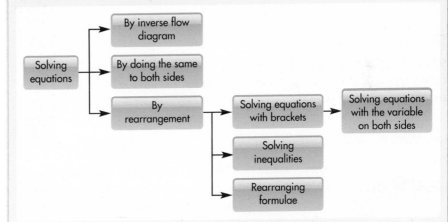

What you should already know

- The basic language of algebra (KS3 level 5, GCSE grade C)
- How to expand brackets and collect like terms (KS3 level 6, GCSE grade D)
- That addition and subtraction are opposite (inverse) operations (KS3 level 4, GCSE grade F)
- That multiplication and division are opposite (inverse) operations (KS3 level 4, GCSE grade F)

Quick check

1 **a** Simplify $5x + 3x - 2x$.   **b** Expand $4(3x - 1)$.

   c Expand and simplify $2(3x - 1) + 3(4x + 3)$.

2 What number can go in the box to make the calculation true?

   a $13 + \square = 9$ **b** $4 \times \square = 10$

This section will show you how to:

- solve a variety of simple linear equations, such as $3x - 1 = 11$, where the variable only appears on one side
- use inverse operations and inverse flow charts
- solve equations by doing the same on both sides
- deal with negative numbers
- solve equations by rearrangement

Key words

do the same to both sides
equation
inverse flow diagram
inverse operations
rearrangement
solution
variable

A teacher gave these instructions to her class.

What algebraic expression represents the teacher's statement? (See Chapter 10.)

- Think of a number.
- Double it.
- Add 3.

This is what two of her students said.

Can you work out Kim's answer and the number that Freda started with?

Kim's answer will be
$2 \times 5 + 3 = 13$.

My final answer was 10.

Freda's answer can be set up as an **equation**.

An equation is formed when an expression is put equal to a number or another expression. You are expected to deal with equations that have only one **variable** or letter.

The **solution** to an equation is the value of the variable that makes the equation true.
For example, the equation for Freda's answer is

$$2x + 3 = 10$$

where x represents Freda's number.

The value of x that makes this true is $x = 3\frac{1}{2}$.

I chose the number 5.

Freda

Kim

FM Functional Maths **AU** (AO2) Assessing Understanding **PS** (AO3) Problem Solving

To solve an equation, you have to 'undo' it. That is, you have to reverse the processes that set up the equation in the first place.

Freda did two things. First she multiplied by 2 and then she added 3. The reverse process is *first* to subtract 3 and *then* to divide by 2. So, to solve:

$$2x + 3 = 10$$

Subtract 3 $\qquad 2x + 3 - 3 = 10 - 3$

$$2x = 7$$

Divide by 2 $\qquad \dfrac{2x}{2} = \dfrac{7}{2}$

$$x = 3\dfrac{1}{2}$$

The problem is knowing how an equation is set up in the first place, so that you can undo it in the right order.

There are four ways to solve equations:

- **inverse operations**
- **inverse flow diagrams**
- **'doing the same to both sides'**
- **rearrangement**.

They are all essentially the same. You will have to decide which method you prefer, although you should know how to use all four.

There is one rule about equations that you should *always* follow.

Check that your answer works in the original equation.

For example, to check the answer to Freda's equation, put $x = 3\frac{1}{2}$ into Freda's equation. This gives:

$$2 \times 3\tfrac{1}{2} + 3 = 7 + 3 = 10$$

which is correct.

Inverse operations

One way to solve equations is to use **inverse operations**. The opposite or inverse operation to addition is subtraction (and vice versa) and the opposite or inverse operation to multiplication is division (and vice versa).

That means you can 'undo' the four basic operations by using the inverse operation.

EXAMPLE 1

Solve these equations.

a $w + 7 = 9$ **b** $x - 8 = 10$ **c** $2y = 8$ **d** $\dfrac{z}{5} = 3$

a The opposite operation to $+ 7$ is $- 7$, so the solution is $9 - 7 = 2$.

Check: $2 + 7 = 9$

b The opposite operation to $- 8$ is $+ 8$, so the solution is $10 + 8 = 18$.

Check: $18 - 8 = 10$

c $2y$ means $2 \times y$. The opposite operation to $\times 2$ is $\div 2$, so the solution is $8 \div 2 = 4$.

Check: $2 \times 4 = 8$

d $\dfrac{z}{5}$ means $z \div 5$. The opposite operation to $\div 5$ is $\times 5$, so the solution is $3 \times 5 = 15$.

Check: $15 \div 5 = 3$

EXERCISE 12A

1 Solve the following equations by applying the inverse of the operation on the left-hand side to the right-hand side.

a $x + 6 = 10$ **b** $w - 5 = 9$

c $y + 3 = 8$ **d** $p - 9 = 1$

e $2x = 10$ **f** $3x = 18$

g $\dfrac{z}{3} = 8$ **h** $4x = 10$

i $\dfrac{q}{4} = 1$ **j** $x + 9 = 10$

k $r - 7 = 21$ **l** $\dfrac{s}{6} = 2$

> **HINTS AND TIPS**
>
> **Remember** to perform the inverse operation on the number on the right-hand side.

PS 2 The solution to the equation $5x = 20$ is $x = 4$.

Write down two different equations for which the solution is 4.

AU 3 Here are three equations.

a $x + 6 = 12$

b $x - 1 = 5$

c $x + 5 = 9$

Give a reason why each one could be the odd one out.

> **HINTS AND TIPS**
>
> Solve the equations to give you a clue and look for similarities.

4 Set up an equation to represent the following. Use x for the variable.

My sister is 3 years older than I am. She is 17 years old. How old am I?

5 Set up an equation to represent the following. Use y for the variable.

Six apples cost £1.80. How much is one apple?

Inverse flow diagrams

Another way to solve simple linear equations is to use inverse flow diagrams.

This flow diagram represents the instructions that their teacher gave to Kim and Freda.

$$\longrightarrow \boxed{\times 2} \longrightarrow \boxed{+ 3} \longrightarrow$$

The **inverse flow diagram** looks like this.

$$\longleftarrow \boxed{\div 2} \longleftarrow \boxed{- 3} \longleftarrow$$

Running Freda's answer through this gives:

$$\overset{3\frac{1}{2}}{\longleftarrow} \boxed{\div 2} \overset{7}{\longleftarrow} \boxed{- 3} \overset{10}{\longleftarrow}$$

So, Freda started with $3\frac{1}{2}$ to get an answer of 10.

EXAMPLE 2

Use an inverse flow diagram to solve the following equation.

$3x - 4 = 11$

Flow diagram:

$$\longrightarrow \boxed{\times 3} \longrightarrow \boxed{- 4} \longrightarrow$$

Inverse flow diagram:

$$\longleftarrow \boxed{\div 3} \longleftarrow \boxed{+ 4} \longleftarrow$$

Put through the value on the right-hand side of the equals sign.

$$\overset{5}{\longleftarrow} \boxed{\div 3} \overset{15}{\longleftarrow} \boxed{+ 4} \overset{11}{\longleftarrow}$$

So, the answer is $x = 5$.

Checking the answer gives:

$3 \times 5 - 4 = 11$

which is correct.

EXERCISE 12B

1 Use inverse flow diagrams to solve each of the following equations. Remember to check that each answer works for its original equation.

a $3x + 5 = 11$ **b** $3x - 13 = 26$

c $3x - 7 = 32$ **d** $4y - 19 = 5$

e $3a + 8 = 11$ **f** $2x + 8 = 14$

g $2y + 6 = 18$ **h** $8x + 4 = 12$

i $2x - 10 = 8$ **j** $\dfrac{x}{5} + 2 = 3$

k $\dfrac{t}{3} - 4 = 2$ **l** $\dfrac{y}{4} + 1 = 7$

m $\dfrac{k}{2} - 6 = 3$ **n** $\dfrac{h}{8} - 4 = 1$ **o** $\dfrac{w}{6} + 1 = 4$

p $\dfrac{x}{4} + 5 = 7$ **q** $\dfrac{y}{2} - 3 = 5$ **r** $\dfrac{f}{5} + 2 = 8$

> **HINTS AND TIPS**
>
> **Remember** the rules of BIDMAS/BODMAS.
> So $3x + 5$ means do $x \times 3$ first then $+5$ in the flow diagram. Then do the opposite (inverse) operations in the inverse flow diagram.

PS 2 The diagram shows a two-step number machine.

Find a value for the input that gives the same value for the output.

AU 3 A man buys two apples and gets 46p change from £1.

He wants to know the cost of each apple.

By setting up a flow diagram (or otherwise) work out the cost of one apple.

Doing the same to both sides

You need to know how to solve equations by performing the same operation on both sides of the equals sign.

Mary had two bags of marbles, each of which contained the same number of marbles, and five spare marbles.

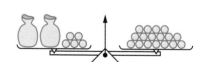

She put them on scales and balanced them with 17 single marbles.

How many marbles were there in each bag?

If x is the number of marbles in each bag, then the equation representing Mary's balanced scales is:

$$2x + 5 = 17$$

Take five marbles from each pan:

$$2x + 5 - 5 = 17 - 5$$
$$2x = 12$$

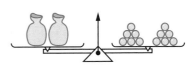

Now halve the number of marbles on each pan.

That is, divide both sides by 2:

$$\frac{2x}{2} = \frac{12}{2}$$

$$x = 6$$

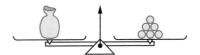

Checking the answer gives $2 \times 6 + 5 = 17$, which is correct.

EXAMPLE 3

Solve each of these equations by 'doing the same to both sides'.

a $3x - 5 = 16$ **b** $\dfrac{x}{2} + 2 = 10$

Add 5 to both sides.

$$3x - 5 + 5 = 16 + 5$$

$$3x = 21$$

Divide both sides by 3.
$$\frac{3x}{3} = \frac{21}{3}$$

$$x = 7$$

Checking the answer gives:

$$3 \times 7 - 5 = 16$$

which is correct.

Subtract 2 from both sides.

$$\frac{x}{2} + 2 - 2 = 10 - 2$$

$$\frac{x}{2} = 8$$

Multiply both sides by 2.
$$\frac{x}{2} \times 2 = 8 \times 2$$

$$x = 16$$

Checking the answer gives:

$$16 \div 2 + 2 = 10$$

which is correct.

Dealing with negative numbers

The solution to an equation may be a negative number. You need to know that when a negative number is multiplied or divided by a positive number, then the answer is also a negative number. For example:

$$-3 \times 4 = -12 \quad \text{and} \quad -10 \div 5 = -2$$

Check these on your calculator.

EXERCISE 12C

1 Solve each of the following equations by 'doing the same to both sides'. Remember to check that each answer works for its original equation.

a $x + 4 = 60$

b $3y - 2 = 4$

HINTS AND TIPS

Be careful with negative numbers.

c $3x - 7 = 11$

d $5y + 3 = 18$

e $7 + 3t = 19$

f $5 + 4f = 15$

g $3 + 6k = 24$

h $4x + 7 = 17$

i $5m - 3 = 17$

j $\dfrac{w}{3} - 5 = 2$

k $\dfrac{x}{8} + 3 = 12$

l $\dfrac{m}{7} - 3 = 5$

m $\dfrac{x}{5} + 3 = 3$

n $\dfrac{h}{7} + 2 = 1$

o $\dfrac{w}{3} + 10 = 4$

p $\dfrac{x}{3} - 5 = 7$

q $\dfrac{y}{2} - 13 = 5$

r $\dfrac{f}{6} - 2 = 8$

AU 2
PS

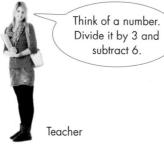

Teacher

Think of a number. Divide it by 3 and subtract 6.

My answer is –1.

My starting number is 6.

Mandy

Andy

a What answer did Andy get?

b What number did Mandy start with?

AU 3 The solution of the equation $4x + 17 = 9$ is $x = -2$.

Make up two more different equations of the form $ax + b = c$ where a, b and c are positive whole numbers, for which the answer is also –2.

AU 4 A teacher asked her class to solve the equation $2x - 1 = 7$.

Amanda wrote:

$$2x - 1 = 7$$
$$2x - 1 - 1 = 7 - 1$$
$$2x = 6$$
$$2x - 2 = 6 - 2$$
$$x = 4$$

Betsy wrote:

$$2x - 1 = 7$$
$$2x - 1 + 1 = 7 + 1$$
$$2x = 8$$
$$2x \div 2 = 8 \div 2$$
$$x = 4$$

When the teacher read out the correct answer of 4, both students ticked their work as correct.

a Which student used the correct method?

b Explain the mistakes the other student made.

ACTIVITY

Balancing with unknowns

Suppose you want to solve an equation such as:

$2x + 3 = x + 4$

You can imagine it as a balancing problem with marbles.

2 bags + 3 marbles = 1 bag + 4 marbles

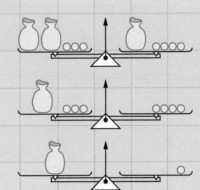

Take one bag from each side.

Take three marbles from each side.

There must be one marble in the bag.

This means that $x = 1$.

Checking the answer gives $2 \times \mathbf{1} + 3 = \mathbf{1} + 4$, which is correct.

Set up each of the following problems as a 'balancing picture' and solve it by 'doing the same to both sides'. Remember to check that each answer works. The first two problems include the pictures to start you off.

1 $2x + 6 = 3x + 1$

2 $4x + 2 = x + 8$

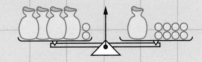

3 $5x + 1 = 3x + 11$

5 $3x + 8 = 2x + 10$

7 $2x + 12 = 5x + 6$

4 $x + 9 = 2x + 7$

6 $5x + 7 = 3x + 21$

8 $3x + 6 = x + 9$

(Some of the marbles could be broken in half!)

9 Explain why there is no answer to this problem:

$x + 3 = x + 4$

10 One of the bags of marbles on the left-hand pan has had three marbles taken out.

Try to draw the pictures to solve this problem:

$4x - 3 = 2x + 5$

Rearrangement

Solving equations by rearrangement is the most efficient method and the one used throughout the rest of this chapter. The terms of the equation are rearranged until the variable is on its own – usually on the left-hand side of the equals sign.

EXAMPLE 4

Solve $4x + 3 = 23$.

Move the 3 to give: $\qquad\qquad\qquad\qquad\qquad 4x = 23 - 3 = 20$

Now divide both sides by 4 to give: $\qquad\qquad x = \dfrac{20}{4} = 5$

So, the solution is $x = 5$.

EXAMPLE 5

Solve $\dfrac{y - 4}{5} = 3$.

Move the 5 to give: $\qquad\qquad\qquad\qquad y - 4 = 3 \times 5 = 15$

Now move the 4 to give: $\qquad\qquad\qquad y = 15 + 4 = 19$

So, the solution is $y = 19$.

EXERCISE 12D

1 Solve each of the following equations. Remember to check that each answer works for its original equation.

a $2x + 4 = 6$

b $2t + 7 = 13$

c $3x + 10 = 16$

d $4y + 15 = 23$

e $2x - 8 = 10$

f $4t - 3 = 17$

g $5x - 6 = 24$

h $7 - x = 3$

i $12 - 3y = 6$

j $2k + 8 = 4$

k $\dfrac{x}{3} + 7 = 15$

l $\dfrac{t}{5} + 3 = 5$

m $\dfrac{w}{3} - 5 = 2$

n $\dfrac{x}{8} + 3 = 12$

o $\dfrac{m}{7} - 3 = 5$

> **HINTS AND TIPS**
>
> When a variable changes sides of the equals sign, it also changes signs, that is, plus becomes minus and vice versa, multiply becomes divide and vice versa. This is sometimes called 'Change sides, change signs'.

AU **2** A teacher read out the following to her class:
PS

> "I am thinking of a number. I subtract 5 from it and then divide the result by 4. The answer is 7. What number did I think of to start with?"

a What was the number the teacher thought of?

b Bryn misunderstood the instructions and got the operations the wrong way round. What number did Bryn think the teacher started with?

3 Solve each of the following equations. Remember to check that each answer works for its original equation.

a $\dfrac{k + 1}{2} = 3$
b $\dfrac{h - 4}{8} = 3$
c $\dfrac{w + 1}{6} = 1$

d $\dfrac{x + 5}{4} = 10$
e $\dfrac{y - 3}{6} = 5$
f $\dfrac{f + 2}{5} = 5$

FM **4** At a conference, doughnuts are delivered for the mid-morning break. The waiter takes five off the tray before taking them to the delegates. There are 10 delegates and they each get two doughnuts.

How many doughnuts were delivered?

> **HINTS AND TIPS**
>
> Begin by associating a letter with 'doughnuts'. Then use algebra to work out your answer.

12.2 Solving equations with brackets

This section will show you how to:
- solve equations that include brackets

Key words
expand
inverse operations

When an equation contains brackets, you must first **expand** or multiply out the brackets and then solve the equation by using one of the previous methods. This example uses **inverse operations**.

EXAMPLE 6

Solve $5(x + 3) = 25$.

First multiply out the brackets: $5x + 15 = 25$

Rearrange. $5x + 15 - 15 = 25 - 15 = 10$

Divide by 5. $\dfrac{5x}{5} = \dfrac{10}{5}$

$x = 2$

EXAMPLE 7

Solve $3(2x - 7) = 15$.

Multiply out the brackets: $6x - 21 = 15$

Add 21 to both sides. $\qquad 6x = 36$

Divide both sides by 6. $\qquad x = 6$

EXERCISE 12E

1 Solve each of the following equations. Some of the answers may be decimals or negative numbers. Remember to check that each answer works for its original equation. Use your calculator if necessary.

a $2(x + 5) = 16$

b $5(x - 3) = 20$

c $3(t + 1) = 18$

d $4(2x + 5) = 44$

e $2(3y - 5) = 14$

f $5(4x + 3) = 135$

g $4(3t - 2) = 88$

h $6(2t + 5) = 42$

i $2(3x + 1) = 11$

j $4(5y - 2) = 42$

k $6(3k + 5) = 39$

l $5(2x + 3) = 27$

m $5(2x - 1) = -45$

n $7(3y + 5) = -7$

> **HINTS AND TIPS**
>
> Once the brackets have been expanded the equations are the same sort as those you have already been dealing with. Remember to multiply everything inside the brackets by what is outside.

AU 2 Fill in values for a, b and c so that the answer to this equation is $x = 4$.

$a(bx + 3) = c$

PS 3 My son is x years old. In five years' time I will be twice his age and both our ages will be multiples of 10. The sum of our ages will be between 50 and 100.

How old am I now?

> **HINTS AND TIPS**
>
> Set up an equation and put it equal to 60, 70, 80, etc. Solve the equation and see if the answer fits the conditions.

PS 4 A rectangle with sides 4 cm and $3x + 1$ cm has a smaller rectangle with sides 2 cm and $2x - 1$ cm cut from it. The remaining area is 32 cm^2.

What is the value of x?

$3x + 1$ cm

$2x - 1$ cm

4 cm $\qquad$ 2 cm

12.3 Equations with the variable on both sides

> **This section will show you how to:**
> - solve equations where the variable appears on both sides of the equation
>
> **Key word**
> variable

When a letter or **variable** appears on both sides of an equation, it is best to use the 'do the same to both sides' method of solution and collect all the terms containing the variable on the left-hand side of the equation. If there are more of the variable on the right-hand side, it is easier to turn the equation round. When an equation contains brackets, they must be multiplied out first.

EXAMPLE 8

Solve $5x + 4 = 3x + 10$.

There are more xs on the left-hand side, so you do not need to turn the equation round.

Subtract $3x$ from both sides.	$2x + 4 = 10$
Subtract 4 from both sides.	$2x = 6$
Divide both sides by 2.	$x = 3$

EXAMPLE 9

Solve $2x + 3 = 6x - 5$.

There are more xs on the right-hand side, so turn the equation round.

	$6x - 5 = 2x + 3$
Subtract $2x$ from both sides.	$4x - 5 = 3$
Add 5 to both sides.	$4x = 8$
Divide both sides by 4.	$x = 2$

EXAMPLE 10

Solve $3(2x + 5) + x = 2(2 - x) + 2$.

Multiply out both brackets.	$6x + 15 + x = 4 - 2x + 2$
Simplify both sides.	$7x + 15 = 6 - 2x$

There are more xs on the left-hand side, so you do not need to turn the equation round.

Add $2x$ to both sides.	$9x + 15 = 6$
Subtract 15 from both sides.	$9x = -9$
Divide both sides by 9.	$x = -1$

D

EXERCISE 12F

1 Solve each of the following equations.

a $2x + 3 = x + 5$ **b** $5y + 4 = 3y + 6$

c $4a - 3 = 3a + 4$ **d** $5t + 3 = 2t + 15$

e $7p - 5 = 3p + 3$ **f** $6k + 5 = 2k + 1$

g $2t - 7 = 4t - 3$ **h** $2p - 1 = 9 - 3p$

PS 2

I am thinking of a number. I multiply it by 3 and subtract 2.

I am thinking of a number. I multiply it by 2 and add 5.

Terry and June find that they both thought of the same number and both got the same final answer.

What number did they think of?

C

3 Solve each of the following equations.

a $2(d + 3) = d + 12$ **b** $5(x - 2) = 3(x + 4)$ **c** $3(2y + 3) = 5(2y + 1)$

d $3(h - 6) = 2(5 - 2h)$ **e** $4(3b - 1) + 6 = 5(2b + 4)$

f $2(5c + 2) - 2c = 3(2c + 3) + 7$

PS 4 Wilson has eight coins, all of the same value, as well as seven pennies.

Chloe has 11 coins of the same value as those that Wilson has and she also has five pennies.

Wilson says, "If you give me one of your coins and four pennies, we will each have the same amount of money."

What is the value of the coins that Wilson and Chloe have?

AU 5 Explain why the equation $3(2x + 1) = 2(3x + 5)$ cannot be solved.

AU 6 Explain why there are an infinite number of solutions to the equation

$2(6x + 9) = 3(4x + 6)$.

HINTS AND TIPS

Remember the rule 'Change sides, change signs'. Show all your working on this type of question. Rearrange before you simplify. If you try to rearrange and simplify at the same time, you will probably get it wrong.

HINTS AND TIPS

Set up an expression for each of them. Put them equal and solve the equation.

HINTS AND TIPS

Call the coin x and set up the expressions, e.g. Wilson has $8x + 7$. Then take one x and 4 from Chloe's expression and add one x and 4 to Wilson's. Then put the expressions equal and solve.

HINTS AND TIPS

Expand the brackets and collect terms on one side as usual. Explain what happens.

Rearranging formulae

This section will show you how to:

- rearrange formulae, using the same methods as for solving equations

Key words

expression

rearrange

subject

transpose

variable

The **subject** of a formula is the **variable** (letter) in the formula that stands on its own, usually on the left-hand side of the 'equals' sign. For example, x is the subject of each of the following.

$$x = 5t + 4 \qquad x = 4(2y - 7) \qquad x = \frac{1}{t}$$

If you need to change the existing subject to a different variable, you have to **rearrange** (**transpose**) the formula to get that variable on the left-hand side.

You do this by using the same rule as for solving equations, that is, move the terms concerned from one side of the 'equals' sign to the other.

The main difference is that when you solve an equation each step gives a numerical value. When you rearrange a formula each step gives an algebraic **expression**.

EXAMPLE 11

Make m the subject of $T = m - 3$.

Move the 3 so that the m is on its own. $\qquad T + 3 = m$

Reverse the formula. $\qquad m = T + 3$

EXAMPLE 12

From the formula $P = 4t$, express t in terms of P.

(This is another common way of asking you to make t the subject.)

Divide both sides by 4. $\qquad \dfrac{P}{4} = \dfrac{4t}{4}$

Reverse the formula. $\qquad t = \dfrac{P}{4}$

EXAMPLE 13

From the formula $C = 2m + 3$, make m the subject.

Move the 3 so that the $2m$ is on its own. $C - 3 = 2m$

Divide both sides by 2. $\dfrac{C - 3}{2} = \dfrac{2m}{2}$

Reverse the formula. $m = \dfrac{C - 3}{2}$

EXERCISE 12G

1 $T = 3k$ Make k the subject.

2 $P = m + 7$ Make m the subject.

3 $X = y - 1$ Express y in terms of X.

4 $Q = \dfrac{p}{3}$ Express p in terms of Q.

5 $p = m + t$ **a** Make m the subject.
                      b Make t the subject.

6 $t = 2k + 7$ Express k in terms of t.

7 $g = \dfrac{m}{v}$ Make m the subject.

8 $t = m^2$ Make m the subject.

9 $C = 2\pi r$ Make r the subject.

10 $A = bh$ Make b the subject.

11 $P = 2l + 2w$ Make l the subject.

12 $m = p^2 + 2$ Make p the subject.

> **HINTS AND TIPS**
>
> **Remember** about inverse operations and the rule 'Change sides, change signs'.

FM 13 Kieran notices that the price of five cream buns is 75p more than the price of nine mince pies.

Let the price of a cream bun be x pence and the price of a mince pie be y pence.

a Express the cost of one mince pie, y, in terms of the price of a cream bun, x.

b If the price of a cream bun is 60p, how much is a mince pie?

> **HINTS AND TIPS**
>
> Set up a formula using the first sentence of information, then rearrange it.

PS 14 Distance, speed and time are connected by the formula:

distance = speed × time

A delivery driver drove 126 km in 1 hour and 45 minutes.

On the return journey he was held up at road works, so his average speed decreased by 9 km per hour.

How long was he held up at the road works?

> **HINTS AND TIPS**
>
> Work out the average speed for the first journey, then work out the average speed for the return journey.

15 The formula for converting degrees Celsius to degrees Fahrenheit is $C = \dfrac{5}{9}(F - 32)$.

    a   Show that when $F = -40$, C is also equal to -40.

    b   Find the value of C when $F = 68$.

    c   Use this flow diagram to establish the formula for converting degrees Fahrenheit to degrees Celsius.

$$°F \longrightarrow \boxed{-32} \longrightarrow \boxed{\times\ 5} \longrightarrow \boxed{\div\ 9} \longrightarrow °C$$

12.5   Solving linear inequalities

This section will show you how to:
- solve a simple linear inequality

Key words
inclusive inequality
integer
linear inequality
number line
strict inequality

Inequalities behave similarly to equations, which you have already met. In the case of **linear inequalities**, you can use the same rules to solve them as you use for linear equations. There are four inequality signs, < which means 'less than', > which means 'greater than', ≤ which means 'less than or equal to' and ≥ which means 'greater than or equal to'. Be careful. Never replace the inequality sign with an equals sign or you will get the wrong answer and could end up getting no marks in an exam.

EXAMPLE 14

Solve $2x + 3 < 14$.

This is rewritten as:

$$2x < 14 - 3$$

that is $2x < 11$.

Divide both sides by 2. $\dfrac{2x}{2} < \dfrac{11}{2}$

$$\Rightarrow \quad x < 5.5$$

This means that x can take any value below 5.5 but it *cannot* take the value 5.5.

     < and > are called **strict inequalities**.

Note: The inequality sign used in the problem is the sign to give in the answer.

EXAMPLE 15

Solve $\dfrac{x}{2} + 4 \geqslant 13$.

Solve just like an equation but leave the inequality sign in place of the equals sign.

Subtract 4 from both sides. $\quad \dfrac{x}{2} \geqslant 9$

Multiply both sides by 2. $\qquad x \geqslant 18$

This means that x can take any value above 18 and including 18.

$\quad \leqslant$ and $\geqslant$ are called **inclusive inequalities**.

EXERCISE 12H

1 Solve the following linear inequalities.

a $x + 4 < 7$ **b** $t - 3 > 5$ **c** $p + 2 \geqslant 12$

d $2x - 3 < 7$ **e** $4y + 5 \leqslant 17$ **f** $3t - 4 > 11$

g $\dfrac{x}{2} + 4 < 7$ **h** $\dfrac{y}{5} + 3 \leqslant 6$ **i** $\dfrac{t}{3} - 2 \geqslant 4$

j $3(x - 2) < 15$ **k** $5(2x + 1) \leqslant 35$ **l** $2(4t - 3) \geqslant 34$

2 Write down the largest value of x that satisfies each of the following.

a $x - 3 \leqslant 5$, where x is a positive integer.

b $x + 2 < 9$, where x is a positive even integer.

c $3x - 11 < 40$, where x is a square number.

d $5x - 8 \leqslant 15$, where x is a positive odd number.

e $2x + 1 < 19$, where x is a positive prime number.

3 Write down the smallest value of x that satisfies each of the following.

a $x - 2 \geqslant 9$, where x is a positive integer.

b $x - 2 > 13$, where x is a positive even integer.

c $2x - 11 \geqslant 19$, where x is a square number.

d $3x + 7 \geqslant 15$, where x is a positive odd number.

e $4x - 1 > 23$, where x is a positive prime number.

FM 4 Ahmed went to town with £20 to buy two CDs. His return bus fare was £3. The CDs were the same price as each other. When he got home he still had some money in his pocket. What was the most each CD could cost?

> **HINTS AND TIPS**
>
> Set up an inequality and solve it.

AU 5 **a** Explain why you cannot make a triangle with three sticks of length 3 cm, 4 cm and 8 cm.

b Three side of a triangle are x, $x + 2$ and 10 cm.
x is a whole number.
What is the smallest value x can take?

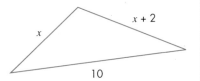

PS 6 These five cards have inequalities and equations marked on them.

| $x > 0$ | $x < 3$ | $x \geqslant 4$ | $x = 2$ | $x = 6$ |

The cards are shuffled and then turned over, one at a time.

If two consecutive cards have solutions with any numbers in common, then a point is scored.

If their solutions do not have any numbers in common, then a point is deducted.

a When the cards are laid out in the order below, the first two score –1 because $x = 6$ and $x < 3$ have no numbers in common.

| $x = 6$ | $x < 3$ | $x > 0$ | $x = 2$ | $x \geqslant 4$ |

Explain why the total for this combination scores 0.

b Now the cards are laid out in this order. What does this combination score?

| $x > 0$ | $x = 6$ | $x \geqslant 4$ | $x = 2$ | $x < 3$ |

c Arrange the five cards to give a maximum score of 4.

| | | | | |

The number line

The solution to a linear inequality can be shown on the **number line** by using the following conventions.

 $x \leqslant$ $x \geqslant$  $x <$  $x >$

A strict inequality *does not* include the boundary point but an inclusive inequality *does* include the boundary point.

Below are five examples.

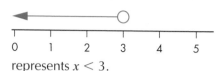

represents $x < 3$.

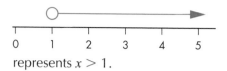

represents $x > 1$.

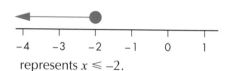

represents $x \leqslant -2$.

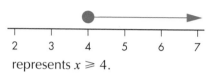

represents $x \geqslant 4$.

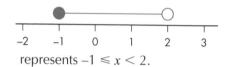

represents $-1 \leqslant x < 2$.

This is a 'between' inequality. It can be written as $x \geqslant -1$ and $x < 2$ but the notation $-1 \leqslant x < 2$ is much neater.

EXAMPLE 16

a Write down the inequality shown by this diagram.

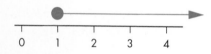

b i Solve the inequality $2x + 3 < 11$. **ii** Mark the solution to **b** on a number line.

c Write down the integers that satisfy both the inequality in **a** and the inequality in **b**.

a The inequality shown is $x \geqslant 1$.

b i $2x + 3 < 11 \Rightarrow 2x < 8 \Rightarrow x < 4$

ii

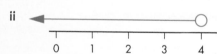

c The integers that satisfy both inequalities are 1, 2 and 3.

EXERCISE 12I

1 Write down the inequality that is represented by each diagram below.

a

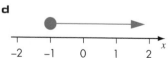

b

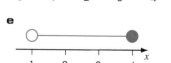

c

d

e

f

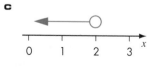

2 Draw diagrams to illustrate the following.

a $x \leqslant 3$ **b** $x > -2$ **c** $x \geqslant 0$ **d** $x < 5$

e $x \geqslant -1$ **f** $2 < x \leqslant 5$ **g** $-1 \leqslant x \leqslant 3$ **h** $-3 < x < 4$

3 Solve the following inequalities and illustrate their solutions on number lines.

a $x + 4 \geqslant 8$ **b** $x + 5 < 3$ **c** $x - 1 \leqslant 2$ **d** $x - 4 > -1$

e $2x > 8$ **f** $3x \leqslant 15$ **g** $4x + 3 < 9$ **h** $\dfrac{x}{2} + 3 \leqslant 2$

i $\dfrac{x}{5} - 2 > 8$ **j** $2x - 1 \leqslant 4$ **k** $\dfrac{x + 2}{3} > 4$ **l** $\dfrac{x - 1}{4} < 3$

AU 4 Copy the number line below twice. On your copies draw two inequalities so that only the integers {–1, 0, 1, 2} are common to both inequalities.

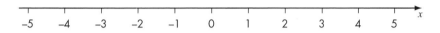

FM 5 Max went to the supermarket with £1.20. He wanted to buy three apples costing x pence each and a chocolate bar costing 54p. When he got to the till, he found he didn't have enough money.

Max took one of the apples back and paid for two apples and the chocolate bar. He counted his change and found he had enough money to buy a 16p chew.

a Explain why $3x + 54 > 120$ and solve the inequality.

b Explain why $2x + 54 \leqslant 104$ and solve the inequality.

c Show the solution to both of these inequalities on a number line.

d What is the possible price of an apple?

PS 6 Here are four inequalities and two sets of integers.

Group them into two sets of three.

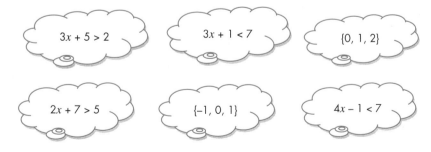

$3x + 5 > 2$

$3x + 1 < 7$

{0, 1, 2}

$2x + 7 > 5$

{–1, 0, 1}

$4x - 1 < 7$

GRADE BOOSTER

F You can solve equations such as $4x = 12$ and $x - 8 = 3$

E You can solve equations such as $3x + 2 = 7$ or $\dfrac{x}{3} - 7 = 1$

D You can solve equations such as $\dfrac{x - 2}{3} = 6$ or $3x + 7 = x - 6$

C You can solve equations such as $3(x - 4) = 5x + 8$

C You can solve inequalities such as $3x + 2 < 5$

C You can rearrange simple formulae

What you should know now

- How to solve a variety of linear equations using rearrangement or 'doing the same thing to both sides'
- How to rearrange simple formulae
- How to solve simple inequalities

1 Solve these equations.

   a $4x = 20$

   b $5x - 1 = 9$

   c $3 + x = 9$

   d $4x + 3 = 2x + 13$

2

The number I thought of was 15.

Jason — My answer is 3.

Teacher — Think of a number double it and subtract 7.

Zara

   a What answer did Zara get?

   b What was the number Jason thought of?

3 An orange costs z pence. A lemon costs 4 pence more than an orange.

   a Write down an expression, in terms of z, for the cost of one lemon.

   b Write down an expression, in terms of z, for the total cost of three oranges and one lemon.

   c The total cost of three oranges and one lemon is 60 pence.

     Form an equation in terms of z and solve it to find the cost of one orange.

4 **a** Solve these equations.

     i $2x = 9$

     ii $3x - 8 = 13$

     iii $6x + 9 = x + 24$

   b Simplify these expressions.

     i $5q + 6q + 2q$

     ii $5n + 4p + 2n - p$

5 The length of a rectangle is 10.5 cm. The perimeter of the rectangle is 28 cm.

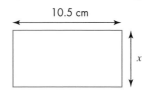

10.5 cm

x

   a Using x to represent the length, set up an equation for the information above.

   b Solve the equation to find the width of the rectangle.

6 Solve the following equations.

   a $x + 3 = 10$ (1)

   b $2x = 10$ (1)

   c $3x - 8 = 10$ (2)

   d $5(x + 4) = 10$ (3)

   e $11 + \dfrac{x}{3} = 15$ (2)

                    (Total 9 marks)

AQA, November 2008, Paper 1 Foundation, Question 15

7 Solve the following equations.

   a $x + 3 = 8$ (1)

   b $3y + 4 = 16$ (2)

   c $2(3z - 1) = 13$ (3)

                    (Total 6 marks)

AQA, June 2008, Paper 1 Foundation, Question 18

8 **a** Factorise $6x - 10$ (1)

   b Solve the equation $4y + 3 = 8$ (2)

   c Solve the equation $2(t + 5) = 8$ (3)

   d List all the integer solutions of the inequality

             $-6 \leqslant 3n < 5$ (3)

                    (Total 9 marks)

AQA, November 2008, Paper 2 Foundation, Question 12

9 **a** Solve the equation $7x - 3 = 60$ (2)

b y is an odd integer.

Is each statement below true or false? (3)

$7y - 3$ is never odd

$7y - 3$ is never prime

$7y - 3$ is never a multiple of 7

c Write down one integer which satisfies the inequality $7w > 63$ (1)

(Total 6 marks)

AQA, June 2009, Paper 1 Foundation, Question 10

10 Solve the equations

a $7x - 9 = 3x + 5$ (3)

b $7(y - 9) = 3y + 5$ (3)

(Total 6 marks)

AQA, June 2009, Paper 2 Foundation, Question 22

11 **a** Factorise $x^2 + 4x$ (1)

b Solve the inequality $7y < 3y + 6$ (2)

c Make r the subject of the formula $p = 3 + 2r$ (2)

(Total 5 marks)

AQA, June 2005, Paper 1 Intermediate, Question 16

12 Make t the subject of the formula:

$$u = \frac{t}{3}$$

13 ABC is a triangle with sides, given in centimetres, of x, $2x + 1$ and $3x - 3$.

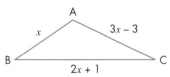

The perimeter of the triangle is 22 cm. Find the value of x.

14 **a** Rearrange the formula:

$C = 6r$

to make r the subject.

b Rearrange the formula:

$A = 3r^2$

to make r the subject.

15 **a** Solve the inequality $3x + 2 \leq 8$ (2)

b Write down all the integer values of x satisfying this inequality $-4 \leq 2x < 4$ (2)

(Total 4 marks)

AQA, June 2009, Paper 1 Foundation, Question 21

 16 **a** Solve the inequality $3(x - 2) \leq 9$ (3)

b The inequality $x \leq 3$ is shown on the number line below.

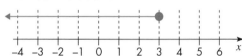

Draw another inequality on the number line so that only the following integers satisfy both inequalities

$\{-2, -1, 0, 1, 2, 3\}$ (1)

(Total 4 marks)

AQA, November 2006, Paper 2 Higher, Question 4

Worked Examination Questions

 1 In the table below, the letters a, b, c and d represent different numbers. The total of each row is given at the side of the table.

a	a	a	a	32
a	a	b	b	36
a	a	b	c	33
a	b	c	d	31

Find the values of a, b, c and d.

$a = 8$ ——————
$b = 10$ ——————
$c = 7$
$d = 6$

> Look for clues in the question. The first row is all a so $4a = 32$, so $a = 8$

> Use $a = 8$ in the second row to work out b and so on.

> Each correct answer is worth 1 mark.

Total: 4 marks

FM **2** Mark set off for town with a £20 note and £1.50 in change.
His bus fare was 50p.
He bought three CDs for the same price each and a bottle of pop for 98p.
He then came home on the bus, paying 50p for his fare.
Set up an inequality using this information and taking x as the price of a CD.
Work out the most Mark could have paid for each CD.

$3x + 198 < 2150$ ——————
$3x < 1952$ ——————
$x < 650.667$
The most Mark could have paid was £6.50. ——————

Total: 4 marks

> You get 1 method mark and 1 accuracy mark for setting up an equation to show that three CDs plus what Mark spent must be less than what he set off with.

> You get 1 mark for accurately solving the inequality.

> You get 1 accuracy mark for taking the next integer value below the inequality as the answer.

AU **3** The solution of the equation $5x + 3 = 3x + 7$ is $x = 2$.

Write down a different equation of the form $ax + b = cx + d$ for which the solution is also $x = 2$.

$6 \times 2 + b = 3 \times 2 + d$ ——————
$12 + 7 = 6 + 13$ ——————
So $6x + 7 = 3x + 13$ has a solution of $x = 2$. ——————
However, there are many other possible answers.

Total: 4 marks

> Start with a value for a and c, say 6 and 3 and work out 6×2 on the left and 3×2 on the right. This is worth 2 marks.

> Add values to both sides to get the same total. This is worth 1 mark.

> You get 1 mark for writing down the equation.

Buildings and bridges have to have incredible strength and be able to withstand different weather conditions. Many buildings use the triangle as the basis of their design. Triangles have interesting properties that can be represented using algebra.

Look at the buildings in the photographs.

How many triangles can you see? What kind of triangles can you spot? Why do you think so many buildings use triangles in their design?

Getting started

You have the following straight pieces of wood.

4 m   4 m   4 m

6 m   6 m

9 m

13 m

- What combination can you use to make an equilateral triangular frame?
- What combination can you use to make an isosceles triangular frame?
- What combinations will not make a triangle?

Handy hints

You might find that tables are a useful way to record your results. For example:

Right-angled triangles

a	b	c	a^2	b^2	c^2
6	8	10	36	64	100

Your task

You are going to investigate the relationship between angles and side length in different types of triangle.

Start by constructing several triangles, as described below:

- Draw three triangles, each with one side of 8 cm and one of 6 cm. Use compasses to mark off the lengths.
- Draw one right-angled triangle, one obtuse-angled triangle and one acute-angled triangle. In each case measure the third side.
- Repeat another four times with two other starting lengths.
- Label the two sides you started with a and b and the side you measured c.

Now investigate the relationship between a^2, b^2 and c^2 and whether the angle is a right-angle, obtuse or acute.

Explain your findings by writing down mathematical rules such as these:

- When a triangle with sides a, b and c is right-angled then …
- When a triangle with sides a, b and c is obtuse-angled then …
- When a triangle with sides a, b and c is acute-angled then …

Resources required

- Compasses
- Ruler

Line graphs are used in many media, including newspapers and the textbooks of most of the subjects that you learn in school.

Graphs show the relationship between two variables. Often one of these variables is time and the graph shows how the other variable changes over time.

For example, the graph shown top right illustrates how the exchange rate between the dollar and the pound changed over five months in 2009.

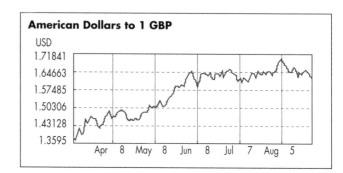

The earliest line graphs, such as the one shown on the right, appeared in the book *A Commercial and Political Atlas*, written in 1786 by William Playfair, who also used bar charts and pie charts for the first time. Playfair argued that charts and graphs communicated information to an audience better than tables of data. Do you think this is true?

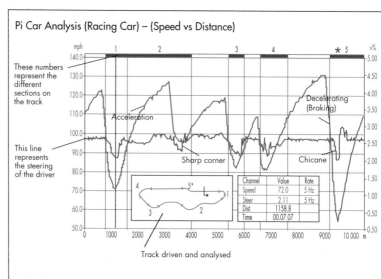

A line graph showing imports and exports to and from Denmark and Norway by William Playfair.

The graph shown below right illustrates all the data from a racing car going round a circuit. Engineers can use this to fine-tune parts of the car to give the best performance. It perfectly illustrates that graphs give a visual representation of how variables change and can be used to compare data in a way that looking at lists of data cannot.

Think about instances in school and everyday life where a line graph would help you to communicate information more effectively.

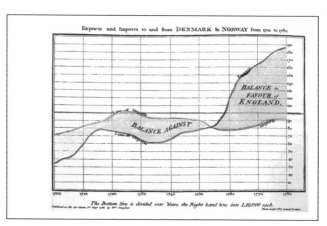

13 Algebra: Graphs

1 Conversion graphs

2 Travel graphs

3 Flow diagrams and graphs

4 Linear graphs

This chapter will show you ...

F how to read information from a conversion graph

to **E** **D** how to read information from a travel graph

to **E** **D** how to draw a straight-line graph from its equation

Visual overview

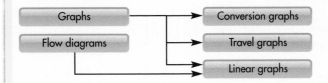

Graphs → Conversion graphs

Flow diagrams → Travel graphs

→ Linear graphs

What you should already know

- How to plot coordinates in the first quadrant **(KS3 level 3, GCSE grade G)**
- How speed, distance and time are related (from Chapter 9) **(KS3 level 6, GCSE grade D)**
- How to substitute numbers into a formula (from Chapter 7) **(KS3 level 5, GCSE grade E)**
- How to use a flow diagram to set up an expression (from Chapter 13) **(KS3 level 5, GCSE grade E)**
- How to read and estimate from scales **(KS3 level 5, GCSE grade E)**

Quick check

Write down the coordinates of the following points.

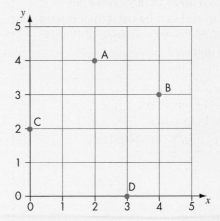

Conversion graphs

This section will show you how to:
- convert from one unit to another unit by using a graph

Key words
conversion graph
estimate
scales

Look at Examples 1 and 2, and make sure that you can understand the conversions. You need to be able to read these types of graph by finding a value on one axis and following it through to the other axis. Make sure you understand the **scales** on the axes to help you **estimate** the answers.

EXAMPLE 1

This is a **conversion graph** between litres and gallons.

a How many litres are there in 5 gallons?

b How many gallons are there in 15 litres?

From the graph you can see that:

a 5 gallons are approximately equivalent to 23 litres.

b 15 litres are approximately equivalent to $3\frac{1}{4}$ gallons.

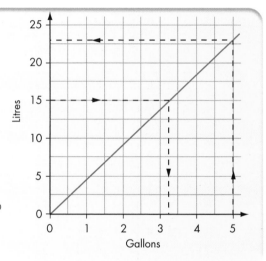

EXAMPLE 2

This is a graph of the charges made for units of electricity used in the home.

a How much will a customer who uses 500 units of electricity be charged?

b How many units of electricity will a customer who is charged £20 have used?

From the graph you can see that:

a A customer who uses 500 units of electricity will be charged £45.

b A customer who is charged £20 will have used about 150 units.

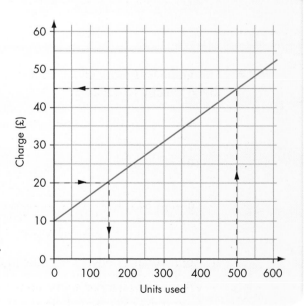

FM Functional Maths   AU (AO2) Assessing Understanding   PS (AO3) Problem Solving

EXERCISE 13A

FM **1** This is a conversion graph between kilograms (kg) and pounds (lb).

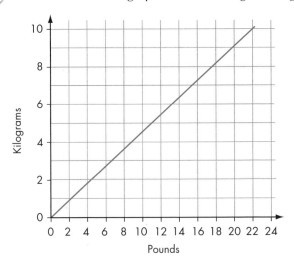

a Use the graph to make an approximate conversion of:

  i 18 lb to kilograms

  ii 5 lb to kilograms

  iii 4 kg to pounds

  iv 10 kg to pounds.

b Approximately how many pounds are equivalent to 1 kg?

c Explain how you could use the graph to convert 48 lb to kilograms.

FM **2** This is a conversion graph between inches (in) and centimetres (cm).

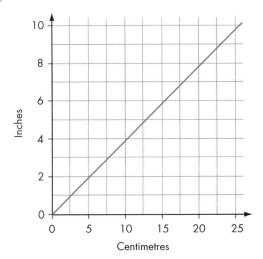

a Use the graph to make an approximate conversion of:

  i 4 in to centimetres

  ii 9 in to centimetres

  iii 5 cm to inches

  iv 22 cm to inches.

b Approximately how many centimetres are equivalent to 1 in?

c Explain how you could use the graph to convert 18 into centimetres.

FM **3** This graph was produced to show the approximate equivalence of the British pound (£) to the Singapore dollar ($).

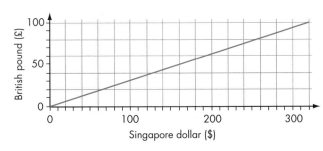

a Use the graph to make an approximate conversion of:

  i £100 to Singapore dollars

  ii £30 to Singapore dollars

  iii $150 to British pounds

  iv $250 to British pounds.

b Approximately how many Singapore dollars are equivalent to £1?

AU **c** What would happen to the conversion line on the graph if the pound became weaker against the Singapore dollar?

4 A hire firm hired out industrial blow heaters. They used the following graph to approximate what the charges would be.

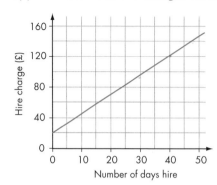

a Use the graph to find the approximate charge for hiring a heater for:

   i 40 days

   ii 25 days.

b Use the graph to find out how many days' hire you would get for a cost of:

   i £100

   ii £140.

5 A conference centre had the following chart on the office wall so that the staff could see the approximate cost of a conference, based on the number of people attending it.

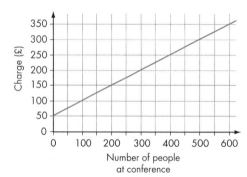

a Use the graph to find the approximate charge for:

   i 100 people

   ii 550 people.

b Use the graph to estimate how many people can attend a conference at the centre for a cost of:

   i £300

   ii £175.

6 At a small shop, the manager marked all goods at the pre-VAT prices and the sales assistant had to use the following chart to convert these marked prices to selling prices.

a Use the chart to find the selling price of goods marked:

   i £60

   ii £25.

b What was the marked price if you bought something for:

   i £100

   ii £45?

7 Granny McAllister still finds it hard to think in degrees Celsius. So she always uses the following conversion graph to help her to understand the weather forecast.

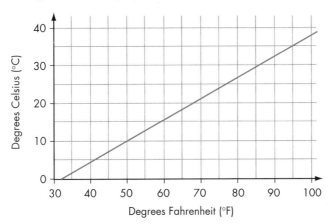

a Use the graph to make an approximate conversion of:

i 35 °C to Fahrenheit

ii 20 °C to Fahrenheit

iii 50 °F to Celsius

iv 90 °F to Celsius.

b Water freezes at 0 °C. What temperature is this in Fahrenheit?

FM 8 Tea is sold at a school fete between 1.00 pm and 2.30 pm. The numbers of cups of tea that had been sold were noted at half-hour intervals.

Time	1.00	1.30	2.00	2.30	3.00	3.30
No. of cups of tea sold	0	24	48	72	96	120

a Draw a graph to illustrate this information. Use a scale from 1 to 4 hours on the horizontal time axis, and from 1 to 120 on the vertical axis for numbers of cups of tea sold.

b Use your graph to estimate when the 60th cup of tea was sold.

FM 9 I lost my fuel bill, but while talking to my friends I found out that:

Bill, who had used 850 units, was charged £57.50
Wendy, who had used 320 units, was charged £31
Rhanni, who had used 540 units, was charged £42.

a Plot the given information and draw a straight-line graph. Use a scale from 0 to 900 on the horizontal units axis, and from £0 to £60 on the vertical cost axis.

b Use your graph to find what I will be charged for 700 units.

E

AU 10 The graph shows the number of passengers arriving in Exeter each day on a particular train that is due at 0815 in December 2009.

The first of December was a Tuesday. Sundays are marked with red lines.

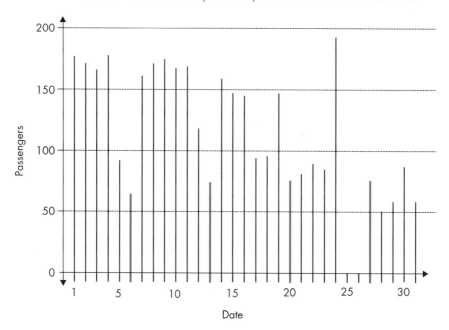

Date

a No passengers used the train on the 25th and 26th. Why was this?

b One of the schools in Exeter closed for Christmas on 16th December. What evidence is there on the graph to support this?

c There was a steady increase in passengers using the train on Saturday through the month and a large number using the train on the 24th. What reason can you give for this?

C

PS 11
AU Leon is travelling from Paris to Calais.

When he sets off he has enough fuel to drive about 100 miles.

Sometime into the journey he sees this sign.

Does he have enough fuel to get to Calais or will he have to visit a petrol station?

Justify your answer.

Calais 125 km

Paris 75 km

PS 12 Two taxi companies use these rules for calculating fares:

CabCo: £2.50 basic charge and £0.75 per kilometre

YellaCabs: £2.00 basic charge and £0.80 per kilometre

This map shows the distances, in kilometres, that three friends, Anya (A), Bettina (B) and Calista (C) live from a restaurant (R) and from each other.

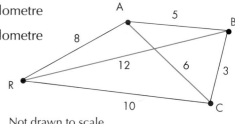

Not drawn to scale

You may find a copy of the grid below useful in answering the following question.

a If they each take an individual cab home, which company should they each choose?

b Work out the cheapest way they can travel home if two, or all three, share a cab.

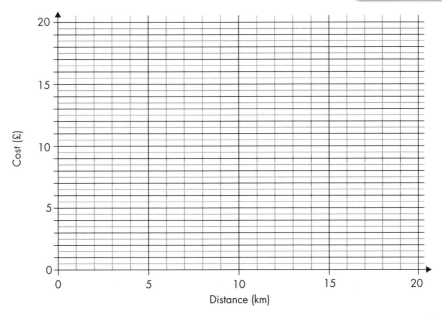

13.2 **Travel graphs**

This section will show you how to:
- read information from a travel graph
- find an average speed from a travel graph

Key words
average speed
distance–time graph
travel graph

As the name suggests, a **travel graph** gives information about how someone or something has travelled over a given time period. It is also called a **distance–time graph**.

A travel graph is read in a similar way to the conversion graphs you have just done. But you can also find the **average speed** from a distance–time graph by using the formula:

$$\text{average speed} = \frac{\text{total distance travelled}}{\text{total time taken}}$$

EXAMPLE 3

The distance–time graph below represents a car journey from Barnsley to Nottingham, a distance of 50 km, and back again.

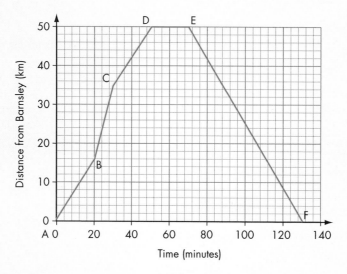

a What can you say about points B, C and D?

b What can you say about the journey from D to F?

c Work out the average speed for each of the five stages of the journey.

From the graph:

a B: After 20 minutes the car was 16 km away from Barnsley.

C: After 30 minutes the car was 35 km away from Barnsley.

D: After 50 minutes the car was 50 km away from Barnsley, so at Nottingham.

b D–F: The car stayed at Nottingham for 20 minutes, and then took 60 minutes for the return journey.

c The average speeds over the five stages of the journey are worked out as follows.

A to B represents 16 km in 20 minutes.

20 minutes is $\frac{1}{3}$ of an hour, so we need to multiply by 3 to give distance/hour. Multiplying both numbers by 3 gives 48 km in 60 minutes, which is 48 km/h.

B to C represents 19 km in 10 minutes.

Multiplying both numbers by 6 gives 114 km in 60 minutes, which is 114 km/h.

C to D represents 15 km in 20 minutes.

Multiplying both numbers by 3 gives 45 km in 60 minutes, which is 45 km/h.

D to E represents a stop: no further distance travelled.

E to F represents the return journey of 50 km in 60 minutes, which is 50 km/h.

So, the return journey was at an average speed of 50 km/h.

You always work out the distance travelled in 1 hour to get the speed in kilometres per hour (km/h) or miles per hour (mph or miles/h).

EXERCISE 13B

FM 1 Paul was travelling in his car to a meeting. This distance–time graph illustrates his journey.

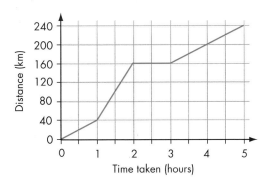

> **HINTS AND TIPS**
>
> Read the question carefully. Paul set off at 7 o'clock in the morning and the graph shows the time after this.

a How long after he set off did he

  i stop for his break

  ii set off after his break

  iii get to his meeting place?

b At what average speed was he travelling:

  i over the first hour

  ii over the second hour

  iii for the last part of his journey?

> **HINTS AND TIPS**
>
> If part of a journey takes 30 minutes, for example, just double the distance to get the average speed per hour.

c The meeting was scheduled to start at 10.30 am.

  What is the latest time he should have left home?

2 A small bus set off from Leeds to pick up Mike and his family. It then went on to pick up Mike's parents and grandparents. It then travelled further, dropping them all off at a hotel. The bus then went on a further 10 km to pick up another party and took them back to Leeds. This distance–time graph illustrates the journey.

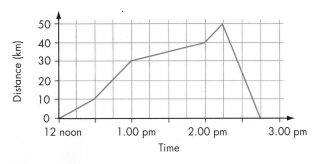

a How far from Leeds did Mike's parents and grandparents live?

b How far from Leeds is the hotel at which they all stayed?

c What was the average speed of the bus on its way back to Leeds?

D

3 James was travelling to Cornwall on his holidays. This distance–time graph illustrates his journey.

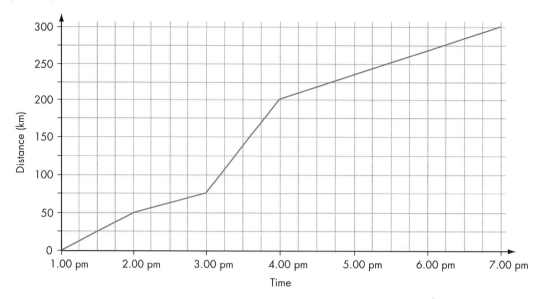

a His greatest speed was on the motorway.

   i How far did he travel along the motorway?

   ii What was his average speed on the motorway?

b **i** When did he travel most slowly?

   ii What was his lowest average speed?

> **HINTS AND TIPS**
>
> **Remember** that the graph is made up of straight lines, as it shows average speed for each section of the journey. In reality, speed is rarely constant – except sometimes on motorways.

PS 4 Azam and Jafar were having a race. The distance–time graph below illustrates the distances covered.

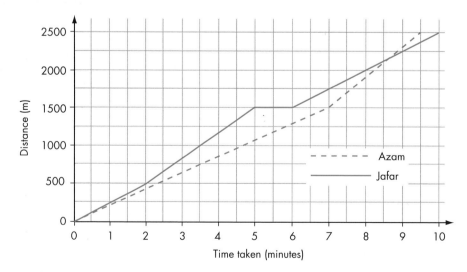

Write a commentary to describe the race.

FM 5 Three friends, Patrick, Araf and Sean, ran a 1000 metres race. The race is illustrated on the distance–time graph below.

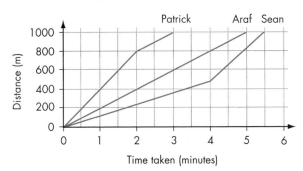

The school newspaper gave the following report of Patrick's race:

'Patrick took an early lead, running the first 800 metres in 2 minutes. He then slowed down a lot and ran the last 200 metres in 1 minute, to finish first in a total time of 3 minutes.'

a Describe the races of Araf and Sean in a similar way.

b **i** What is the average speed of Patrick in kilometres per hour?

ii What is the average speed of Araf in kilometres per hour?

iii What is the average speed of Sean in kilometres per hour?

AU 6 A walker sets off at 9.00 am from point P to walk along a trail at a steady pace of 6 km per hour.

90 minutes later, a cyclist sets off from P on the same trail at a steady pace of 15 km per hour.

At what time did the cyclist overtake the walker?

You may use a graph to help you solve this question.

> **HINTS AND TIPS**
>
> This question can be done by many methods, but drawing a distance–time graph is the easiest.

D

PS **7** Three school friends all set off from school at the same time, 3.45 pm. They all lived 12 km away from the school. The distance–time graph below illustrates their journeys.

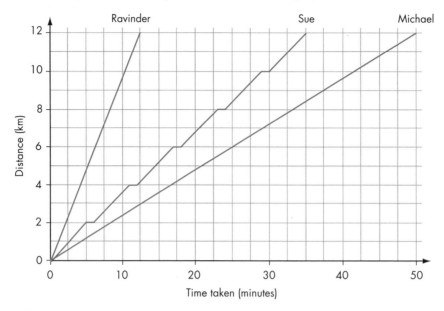

One of them went by bus, one cycled and one was taken by car.

a i Explain how you know that Sue used the bus.

ii Who went by car?

b At what time did each friend get home?

c i When the bus was moving, it covered 2 kilometres in 5 minutes. What is this speed in kilometres per hour?

ii Overall, the bus covered 12 kilometres in 35 minutes. What is this speed in kilometres per hour?

iii How many stops did the bus make before Sue got home?

This section will show you how to:
- find the equations of horizontal and vertical lines
- use flow diagrams to draw graphs

Key words

equation of a line
flow diagram
function
input value
line segment
negative coordinates
output value
x-value
y-value

Plotting negative coordinates

A set of axes can form four sectors called quadrants, but so far, all the points you have read or plotted on graphs have been coordinates in the first quadrant. The grid below shows you how to read and plot coordinates in all four quadrants and how to find the equations of vertical and horizontal lines. This involves using **negative coordinates**.

The coordinates of a point are given in the form (x, y), where x is the number along the x-axis and y is the number up the y-axis.

The coordinates of the four points on the grid are:

    A(2, 3)   B(–1, 2)   C(–3, –4)   D(1, –3)

The x-coordinate of all the points on line X are 3.
So you can say the **equation of line** X is $x = 3$.

The y-coordinate of all the points on line Y are –2.
So you can say the equation of line Y is $y = -2$.

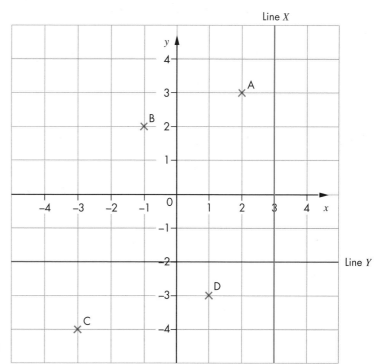

Note: The equation of the x-axis is $y = 0$ and the equation of the y-axis is $x = 0$.

Flow diagrams

One way of drawing a graph is to obtain a set of coordinates from an equation by means of a **flow diagram**. These coordinates are then plotted and the graph is drawn.

In its simplest form, a flow diagram consists of a single box, which may be thought of as containing a mathematical operation, called a **function**. A set of numbers fed into one side of the box is changed by the operation into another set, which comes out from the opposite side of the box. For example, the box shown below represents the operation of multiplying by 3.

Input — 0, 1, 2, 3, 4 → $\boxed{\times 3}$ → Output — 0, 3, 6, 9, 12

The numbers that are fed into the box are called **input values** and the numbers that come out are called **output values**.

The input and output values can be arranged in a table.

x	0	1	2	3	4
y	0	3	6	9	12

The input values are called **x-values** and the output values are called **y-values**. These form a set of coordinates that can be *plotted on a graph.* In this case, the coordinates are (0, 0), (1, 3), (2, 6), (3, 9) and (4, 12).

Most functions consist of more than one operation, so the flow diagrams consist of more than one box. In such cases, you need to match the *first* input values to the *last* output values. The values produced in the middle operations are just working numbers and can be missed out.

0, 1, 2, 3, 4 → $\boxed{\times 2}$ → 0, 2, 4, 6, 8 → $\boxed{+ 3}$ → 3, 5, 7, 9, 11

So, for the two-box flow diagram the table looks like this.

x	0	1	2	3	4
y	3	5	7	9	11

This gives the coordinates (0, 3), (1, 5), (2, 7), (3, 9) and (4, 11).

The two flow diagrams above represent respectively the equation $y = 3x$ and the equation $y = 2x + 3$, as shown below.

x → $\boxed{\times 3}$ → $3x$ 　　　　 x → $\boxed{\times 2}$ → $2x$ → $\boxed{+ 3}$ → $2x + 3$

$y = 3x$ 　　　　　　　　　　$y = 2x + 3$

It is now an easy step to plot the coordinates for each equation on a set of axes, to produce the graphs of $y = 3x$ and $y = 2x + 3$, as shown below.

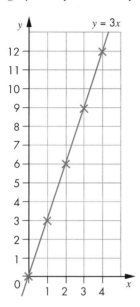

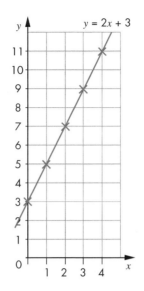

Remember:
Always label graphs.

Note: The line drawn is a **line segment**, as it is only part of an infinitely long line. You will not be penalised if you extend the line beyond the given range of values.

One of the practical problems in graph work is deciding the range of values for the axes. In examinations this is not usually a problem as the axes are drawn for you. Throughout this section, diagrams like the one below will show you the range for your axes for each question. These diagrams are not necessarily drawn to scale.

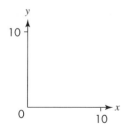

This particular diagram means draw the x-axis (horizontal axis) from 0 to 10 and the y-axis (vertical axis) from 0 to 10. You can use any type of graph or squared paper to draw your axes.

Note that the *scale* on each axis need *not always be the same*.

EXAMPLE 4

Use the flow diagram below to draw the graph of $y = 4x - 1$.

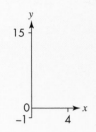

Now enter the values in a table.

x	0	1	2	3	4
y					

The table becomes:

x	0	1	2	3	4
y	−1	3	7	11	15

So, the coordinates are:

$(0, -1), (1, 3), (2, 7), (3, 11), (4, 15)$

Plot these points and join them up to obtain the graph shown on the right.

This is the graph of $y = 4x - 1$.

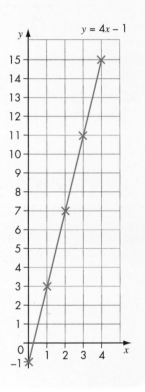

Always label your graphs. In an examination, you may need to draw more than one graph on the same axes. If you do not label your graphs you may lose marks.

EXERCISE 13C

1

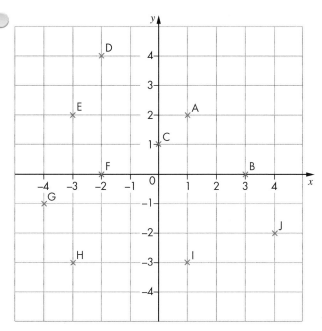

a Write down the coordinates of all the points A to J on the grid.

b Write down the coordinates of the midpoint of the line joining:

   i A and B   **ii** H and I   **iii** D and J.

c Write down the equations of the lines labelled 1 to 4 on the grid.

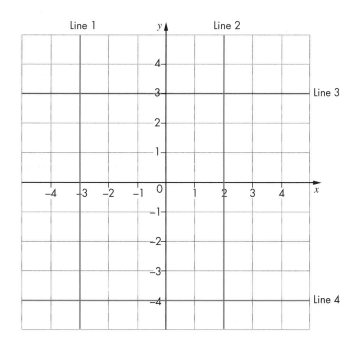

d Write down the equation of the line that is exactly halfway between:

   i line 1 and line 2   **ii** line 3 and line 4.

2 Draw the graph of $y = x + 2$.

x	0	1	2	3	4
y					

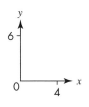

3 Draw the graph of $y = 2x - 2$.

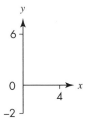

x	0	1	2	3	4
y					

4 Draw the graph of $y = \dfrac{x}{3} + 1$.

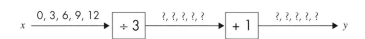

x	0	3	6	9	12
y					

5 Draw the graph of $y = \dfrac{x}{2} - 4$.

x	0	2	4	6	8
y					

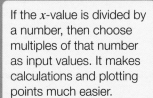

HINTS AND TIPS

If the x-value is divided by a number, then choose multiples of that number as input values. It makes calculations and plotting points much easier.

6 **a** Draw the graphs of $y = 2x$ and $y = x + 6$ on the same grid.

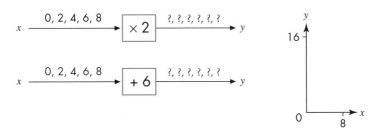

b At which point do the lines intersect?

7 **a** Draw the graphs of $y = x - 3$ and $y = 2x - 6$ on the same grid.

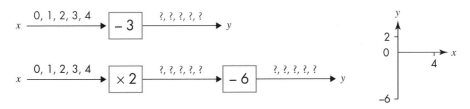

b At which point do the lines intersect?

8 Draw the graph of $y = 5x - 1$. Choose your own inputs and axes.

FM **9** A tea shop sells two types of afternoon tea: a cream tea which costs £3.50 and a high tea which costs £5.00.

To work out the cost of different combinations of teas, they use a wall chart or a flow diagram.

a Use the flow chart to work out the cost of three cream teas and two high teas.

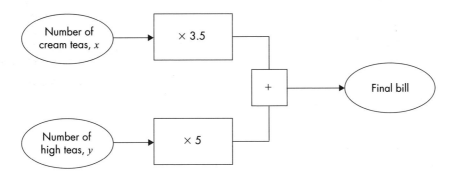

D

b The wall chart is partially filled in.

Use the flow diagram to complete the chart.

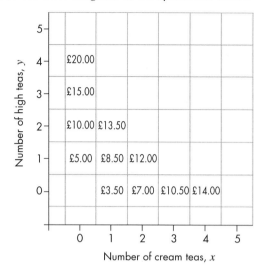

c A party paid £30.50. Can you say for sure what their order was?

AU 10 A teacher reads out the following 'think of a number' problem:

'I am thinking of a number: I multiply it by 3 and add 1.'

a Represent this using a flow diagram.

b If the input is x and the output is y, write down a relationship between x and y.

c Draw a graph for x-values from 0 to 5.

d Explain how you could use the graph to find the number the teacher thought of if the final answer was 13.

PS 11 This flow diagram connects two variables X and Y.

This graph connects the variable Y and X.

Fill in the missing values on the Y-axis.

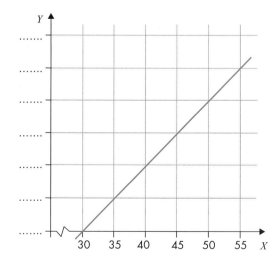

Linear graphs

This section will show you how to:
- draw linear graphs without using flow diagrams
- find the gradient of a straight line
- use the gradient to draw a straight line

Key words
gradient
linear graphs
slope

This chapter is concerned with drawing straight-line graphs. These graphs are usually referred to as **linear graphs**.

The minimum number of points needed to draw a linear graph is two but it is better to plot three or more because that gives at least one point to act as a check. There is no rule about how many points to plot but here are some tips for drawing graphs.

- Use a sharp pencil and mark each point with an accurate cross.

- Position your eyes directly over the graph. If you look from the side, you will not be able to line up your ruler accurately.

Drawing graphs by finding points

This method is a bit quicker and does not need flow diagrams. However, if you prefer flow diagrams, use them.

Follow through Example 5 to see how this method works.

EXAMPLE 5

Draw the graph of $y = 4x - 5$ for values of x from 0 to 5. This is usually written as $0 \leqslant x \leqslant 5$.

Choose three values for x: these should be the highest and lowest x-values and one in between.

Work out the y-values by substituting the x-values into the equation.

Keep a record of your calculations in a table, as shown below.

x	0	3	5
y			

When $x = 0$, $y = 4(0) - 5 = -5$
This gives the point $(0, -5)$.

When $x = 3$, $y = 4(3) - 5 = 7$
This gives the point $(3, 7)$.

When $x = 5$, $y = 4(5) - 5 = 15$
This gives the point $(5, 15)$.

Hence your table is:

x	0	3	5
y	−5	7	15

You now have to decide the extent (range) of the axes. You can find this out by looking at the coordinates that you have so far.

The smallest x-value is 0, the largest is 5.
The smallest y-value is −5, the largest is 15.

Now draw the axes, plot the points and complete the graph.

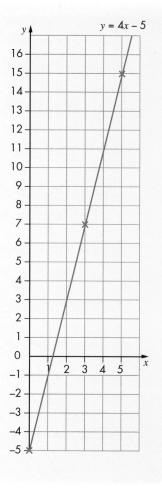

$y = 4x - 5$

It is nearly always a good idea to choose 0 as one of the x-values. In an examination, the range for the x-values will usually be given and the axes will already be drawn.

EXERCISE 13D

Read through these hints before drawing the following linear graphs.

- Use the highest and lowest values of x given in the range.

- Do not pick x-values that are too close together, such as 1 and 2. Try to space them out so that you can draw a more accurate graph.

- Always label your graph with its equation. This is particularly important when you are drawing two graphs on the same set of axes.

- If you want to use a flow diagram, use one.

- Create a table of values. You will often have to complete these in your examinations.

1 Draw the graph of $y = 3x + 4$ for x-values from 0 to 5 ($0 \leq x \leq 5$).

2 Draw the graph of $y = 2x - 5$ for $0 \leq x \leq 5$.

3 Draw the graph of $y = \dfrac{x}{2} - 3$ for $0 \leq x \leq 10$.

4 Draw the graph of $y = 3x + 5$ for $-3 \leq x \leq 3$.

5 Draw the graph of $y = \dfrac{x}{3} + 4$ for $-6 \leq x \leq 6$.

6 **a** On the same set of axes, draw the graphs of $y = 3x - 2$ and $y = 2x + 1$ for $0 \leq x \leq 5$.

   b At which point do the two lines intersect?

7 **a** On the same axes, draw the graphs of $y = 4x - 5$ and $y = 2x + 3$ for $0 \leq x \leq 5$.

   b At which point do the two lines intersect?

8 **a** On the same axes, draw the graphs of $y = \dfrac{x}{3} - 1$ and $y = \dfrac{x}{2} - 2$ for $0 \leq x \leq 12$.

   b At which point do the two lines intersect?

9 **a** On the same axes, draw the graphs of $y = 3x + 1$ and $y = 3x - 2$ for $0 \leq x \leq 4$.

   b Do the two lines intersect? If not, why not?

10 **a** Copy and complete the table to draw the graph of $x + y = 5$ for $0 \leq x \leq 5$.

x	0	1	2	3	4	5
y	5		3		1	

   b Now draw the graph of $x + y = 7$ for $0 \leq x \leq 7$.

11 Ian the electrician used this formula to work out how much to charge for a job:

   $C = 25 + 30H$

   where C is the charge and H is how long the job takes.

   John the electrician uses this formula:

   $C = 35 + 27.5H$

   a On a copy of the grid, draw lines to represent these formulae.

   FM **b** For what length of job do Ian and John charge the same amount?

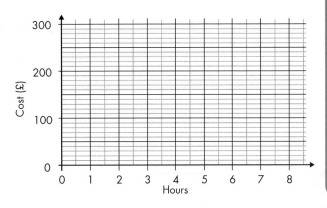

AU 12 **a** Draw the graphs $y = 4$, $y = x$ and $x = 1$ on a copy of the grid on the right.

b What is the area of the triangle formed by the three lines?

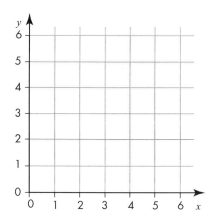

PS 13 The two graphs below show y against x and y against z.

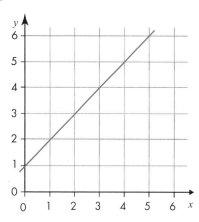 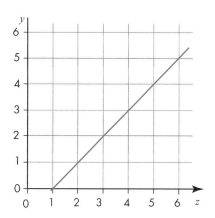

On a copy of the blank grid, show the graph of x against z.

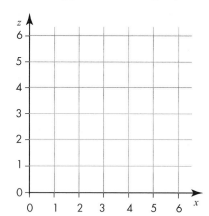

HINTS AND TIPS

When $x = 1$, $y = 2$ and when $y = 2$, $z = 3$.
So, plot coordinates for $x = 1$, $z = 3$.

Gradient

The **slope** of a line is called its **gradient**. The steeper the slope of the line, the larger the value of the gradient.

The gradient of the line shown here can be measured by drawing, as large as possible, a right-angled triangle which has part of the line as its hypotenuse (sloping side). The gradient is then given by:

$$\text{gradient} = \frac{\text{distance measured up}}{\text{distance measured along}}$$

$$= \frac{\text{difference on } y\text{-axis}}{\text{difference on } x\text{-axis}}$$

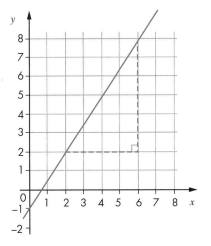

For example, to measure the steepness of the line in the first diagram, below, you first draw a right-angled triangle that has part of this line as its hypotenuse. It does not matter where you draw the triangle but it makes the calculations much easier if you choose a sensible place. This usually means using existing grid lines, so that you avoid fractional values. See the second and third diagrams below.

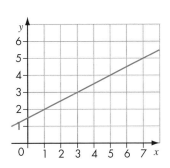

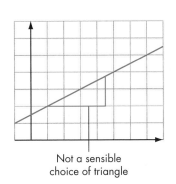

Not a sensible choice of triangle

A sensible choice of triangle

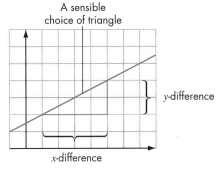

y-difference

x-difference

After you have drawn the triangle, measure (or count) how many squares there are on the vertical side. This is the difference between the *y*-coordinates. In this case, it is 2.

Then measure (or count) how many squares there are on the horizontal side. This is the difference between the *x*-coordinates. In the case above, this is 4.

To work out the gradient, you make the following calculation.

$$\text{gradient} = \frac{\text{difference of the } y\text{-coordinates}}{\text{difference of the } x\text{-coordinates}}$$

$$= \frac{2}{4} = \frac{1}{2} \text{ or } 0.5$$

Note that the value of the gradient is not affected by where the triangle is drawn. As you are calculating the ratio of two sides of the triangle, the gradient will always be the same wherever you draw the triangle.

Remember: Take care when finding the differences between the coordinates of the two points. Choose one point as the first and the other as the second, and subtract in the *same order* each time to find the difference. When a line slopes *down from right to left* (/) the gradient is always positive, but when a line slopes *down from left to right* (\) the gradient is always negative, so you must make sure there is a minus sign in front of the fraction.

EXAMPLE 6

Find the gradient of each of these lines.

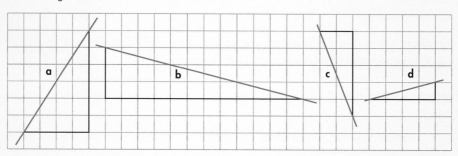

In each case, a sensible choice of triangle has already been made.

a y-difference = 6, x-difference = 4   Gradient = $6 \div 4 = \dfrac{3}{2} = 1.5$

b y-difference = 3, x-difference = 12   Line slopes down from left to right,

so gradient = $-(3 \div 12) = -\dfrac{1}{4} = -0.25$

c y-difference = 5, x-difference = 2   Line slopes down from left to right,

so gradient = $-(5 \div 2) = -\dfrac{5}{2} = -2.5$

d y-difference = 1, x-difference = 4   Gradient = $1 \div 4 = \dfrac{1}{4} = 0.25$

Drawing a line with a certain gradient

To draw a line with a certain gradient, you need to 'reverse' the process described above. Use the given gradient to draw the right-angled triangle first. For example, take a gradient of 2.

Start at a convenient point (A in the diagrams opposite). A gradient of 2 means for an x-step of 1 the y-step must be 2 (because 2 is the fraction $\frac{2}{1}$). So, move one square across and two squares up, and mark a dot.

Repeat this as many times as you like and draw the line. You can also move one square back and two squares down, which gives the same gradient, as the third diagram shows.

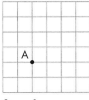

Stage 1

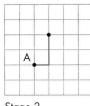

Stage 2

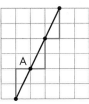

Stage 3

Remember: For a positive gradient you move across (left to right) and then *up*. For a negative gradient you move across (left to right) and then *down*.

EXAMPLE 7

Draw lines with these gradients. **a** $\frac{1}{3}$ **b** -3 **c** $-\frac{1}{4}$

a This is a fractional gradient which has a *y*-step of 1 and an *x*-step of 3. Move three squares across and one square up every time.

b This is a negative gradient, so for every one square across, move three squares down.

c This is also a negative gradient and it is a fraction. So for every four squares across, move one square down.

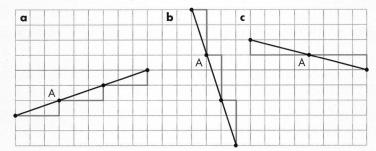

D

EXERCISE 13E

FM 1 Ravi was ill in hospital.

This is his temperature chart for the two weeks he was in hospital.

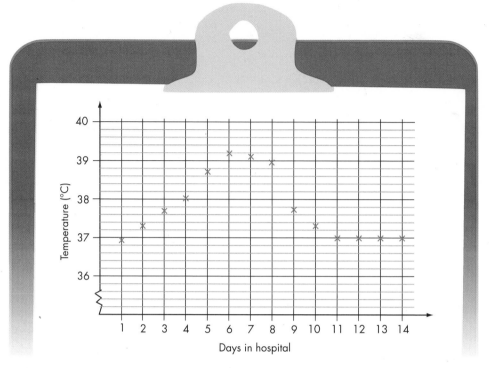

a What was Ravi's highest temperature?

b Between which days did Ravi's temperature increase the most? Explain how you can tell.

c Between which days did Ravi's temperature fall the most? Explain how you can tell.

d When Ravi's temperature went over 38.5 °C he was put on an antibiotic drip.

   i On what day did Ravi go on the drip?

   ii How many days did it take for the antibiotics to work before Ravi's temperature started to come down?

e Once a patient's temperature returns to normal for four days, they are allowed home. What is the normal body temperature?

2 Find the gradient of each of these lines.

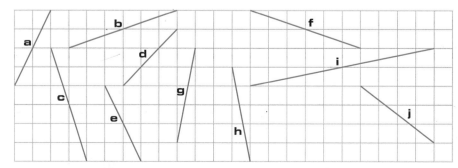

C

3 Find the gradient of each of these lines. What is special about these lines?

a

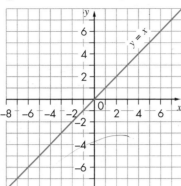

b

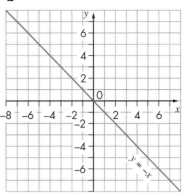

4 Draw lines with these gradients.

a 4   **b** $\dfrac{2}{3}$ **c** –2   **d** $-\dfrac{4}{5}$ **e** 6   **f** –6

AU 5 Students in a class were asked to predict the y-value for an x-value of 10 for this line.

Rob says 'The gradient is 1, so the line is $y = x + 2$. When $x = 10$, $y = 12$.'

Rob is wrong.

Explain why and work out the correct y-value.

FM 6
PS
The Health and Safety regulations for vent pipes from gas appliances state that the minimum height depends on the pitch (gradient) of the roof.

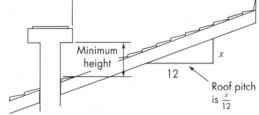

This is the rule:

Minimum height = 1 metre or twice the pitch in metres, whichever is greatest

a What is the minimum height of a roof with a pitch of 2?

b What is the minimum height of a roof with a pitch of 0.5?

c What is the minimum height for these two roofs?

i

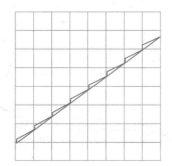

ii

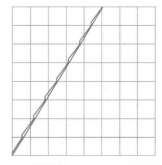

GRADE BOOSTER

F You can read off values from a conversion graph

E You can plot points in all four quadrants

E You can read off distances and times from a travel graph

E You can draw a linear graph given a table of values to complete

D You can find an average speed from a travel graph

D You can draw a linear graph without being given a table of values

What you should know now

- How to use conversion graphs
- How to use travel graphs to find distances, times and speeds
- How to draw a linear graph

1 This is a conversion graph for gallons and litres.

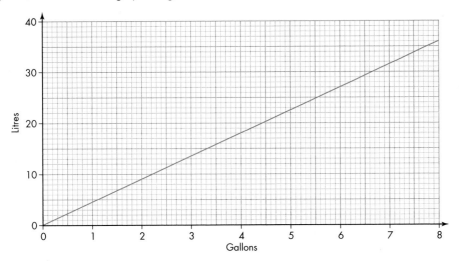

Litres (vertical axis)
Gallons (horizontal axis)

a Use the graph to convert:

  i 4 gallons to litres

  ii 30 litres to gallons. (2)

b It is known that 50 gallons is approximately 225 litres.

  Explain how you can use the graph to show this. (1)

(Total 3 marks)

AQA, June 2005, Paper 1 Foundation, Question 2

2 a Show that the value of x is 6. (1)

Input

3 → +27 → ÷5 → Output x

b Calculate the value of y. (2)

Input

4 → +y → ×2 → Output 22

(Total 3 marks)

AQA, November 2007, Paper 1 Intermediate, Question 2

3 Here is a rule to work out the cost to hire a carpet cleaner.

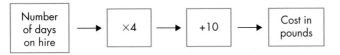

Number of days on hire → ×4 → +10 → Cost in pounds

a How much does it cost to hire the carpet cleaner for five days? (2)

b Cath hires a carpet cleaner and pays £38.

For how many days does she hire the carpet cleaner? (2)

(Total 4 marks)

AQA, June 2007, Paper 1 Foundation, Question 9

4 The points A and B are shown on the grid.

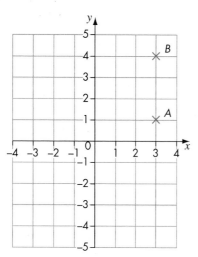

a Write down the coordinates of A and B. (2)

b Plot the points C (–2, 4) and D (–2, 2). (2)

c Join the points ABCD.

What is the name of the shape ABCD? (1)

(Total 5 marks)

AQA, November 2008, Paper 2 Foundation, Question 6

5 a Complete the table of values for
$y = 2x + 3$ (1)

x	–3	–2	–1	0	1	2
y		–1	1	3	5	7

b On a grid like the one below draw the graph of $y = 2x + 3$ for values of x from –3 to 2 (2)

c Use your graph to solve $2x + 3 = 0$

Explain how you obtained your answer. (2)

(Total 5 marks)

AQA, June 2009, Paper 1 Foundation, Question 17

6

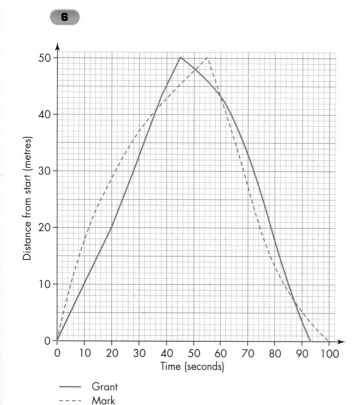

— Grant
- - - Mark

Grant and Mark race each other over two lengths of a 50 metre swimming pool.

a Who won the race? (1)

b What was the winning time? (1)

c What was Grant's average speed during the first 30 seconds of the race? (2)

d i Who was swimming faster at 60 seconds? (1)

ii How can you tell from the graph? (1)

(Total 6 marks)

AQA, November 2007, Paper 2 Intermediate, Question 10

Worked Examination Questions

(FM) **1** The graph shows the increase in rail fares as a percentage of the fares in 1997 since the railways were privatised in 1997.

    a In what year did first class fares double in price from 1997?

    b Approximately how much would a first class fare that cost £100 in 1997 cost in 2010?

    c During which period did first class fares rise the most? How can you tell?

    d An unregulated standard class fare cost £35 in 2008. Approximately how much would this fare have been in 1997?

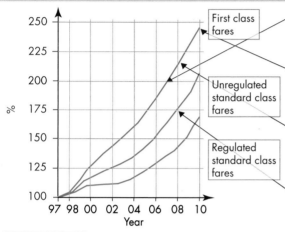

a 2007.

Read when the fares were 200%. This is worth 1 mark.

b £223.

Read the percentage increase in 2010. The correct answer is worth 1 mark.

c 2005–2010:

This is the steepest part of the graph. The correct answer is worth 1 mark.

d £20.

Unregulated fares have gone up by 75%. 75% of £20 is £15. The correct answer is worth 1 mark.

Total: 5 marks

(PS) **2** This graph shows the conversion between two variables x and y.

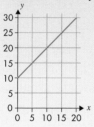

This graph shows the conversions between two variables y and z.

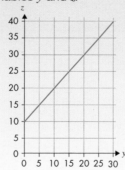

On the graph below, draw the conversion between x and z.

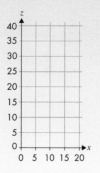

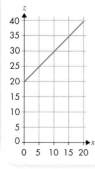

When $x = 0$, $y = 10$ and when $y = 10$, $z = 20$

When $x = 20$, $y = 30$ and when $y = 30$, $z = 40$

Connect at least two x-values to y-values. The obvious choices are 0 and 20 as these are the limits for x. This is worth 1 method mark and 1 accuracy mark.

Draw a line joining the pairs of x- and z-values, i.e. (0, 20) to (20, 40). This is worth 1 accuracy mark.

Total: 3 marks

A group of friends are going on a holiday to France. They have decided to go on motorbikes and have asked you to join them as a pillion passenger. The ferry will take your group to Boulogne and the destination is Perpignan.

Planning your motorbike trip will involve a range of mathematics, much of which can be represented on graphs.

Your task

The following task will require you to work in groups of 2–3.

Using all the information that you gather from these pages and your own knowledge, investigate the key mathematical elements of your motorbike trip.

You must draw at least one conversion graph and try to use as many different mathematical methods as possible.

Getting started

Start by thinking about the mathematics that you use when you go on holiday. Here are a few questions to get you going.

● What information do you need before you travel?
● How many euros (€) are there in one British pound (£)?
● What differences might you find when you travel abroad?
● What are the differences between metric and imperial units of measure? (It may help to list the conversion facts that you know.)
● After approximately how long would you need to stop to rest when travelling?

Handy hints

There are a number of measures and units in France that will need converting when you get there. Two of the most noticeable are:

● **Currency:** in France the currency is in euros
● **Distances**: in France, distances are measured in kilometres, and hence speeds are in kilometres per hour.

1 Euro = £0.90

1 gallon ≈ 4 litres

1 mile ≈ 1.6 km

A motorbike fuel tank holds 3 gallons and travels about 45 miles per gallon.

The cost of petrol in France is 1.2 per litre.

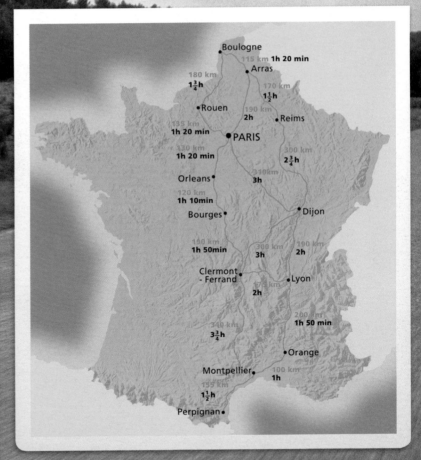

Why this chapter matters

We have already seen that patterns appear in numbers – prime numbers, square numbers and multiples all form patterns. Number patterns are not only of mathematical value – they also make the study of nature and geometric patterns a little more intriguing.

There are many mathematical patterns that appear in nature. The most famous of these is probably the Fibonacci series:

1   1   2   3   5   8   13   21   …

This is formed by adding the two previous terms to get the next term.

The sequence was discovered in 1202 by the Italian Leonardo Fibonacci (c1170–1250), when he was investigating the breeding patterns of rabbits!

Since then, the pattern has been found in many other places in nature. The spirals found in a nautilus shell and in the seed heads of a sunflower plant also follow the Fibonacci series.

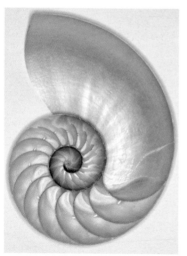 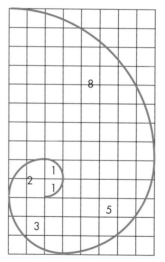 

Fractals form another kind of pattern.

Fractals are geometric patterns that are continuously repeated on a smaller scale.

A good example of a fractal is this: start with an equilateral triangle and draw an equilateral triangle, a third the size of the original, on the middle of each side. Keep on repeating this and we get an increasingly complex-looking shape.

The final pattern shown here is called the Koch snowflake. It is named after the Swedish mathematician Helge von Koch (1870–1924).

Fractals are commonly found in nature, a good example being the complex patterns found in plants, such as the fern above right.

Do you know of any other numerical or geometric patterns that you have come across in everyday life?

Chapter

14 Algebra: Patterns

1 Patterns in number

2 Number sequences

3 The *n*th term of a sequence

4 General rules from given patterns

This chapter will show you ...

- **E** some of the common sequences of numbers
- **E** how to recognise rules for sequences
- **E** how to express the rule for a sequence in words
- **D** how to work out a sequence, given a formula for the *n*th term
- **C** how to express the rule for a sequence algebraically

Visual overview

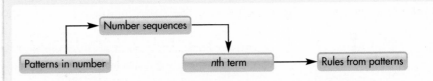

What you should already know

- Basic algebra and how to use letters for numbers (**KS3 level 4, GCSE grade F**)
- How to substitute numbers into algebraic expressions (**KS3 level 5, GCSE grade E**)
- How to solve simple linear equations (**KS3 level 5, GCSE grade E**)

Quick check

1 Angela is x years old. Write down expressions for the ages of the following people, in terms of x.

  a Angela's brother Bill, who is three years older than her.

  b Angela's mother Carol, who is twice as old as Angela.

  c Angela's father Dick, whose age is the sum of Angela's age and Bill's age.

2 Work out the value of the expression $2n + 3$ for:

  a $n = 1$

  b $n = 2$

  c $n = 3$.

Patterns in number

This section will show you how to:

- recognise patterns in number sequences

Key words

pattern

sequence

Look at these number **patterns**.

$0 \times 9 + 1 = 1$
$1 \times 9 + 2 = 11$
$12 \times 9 + 3 = 111$
$123 \times 9 + 4 = 1111$
$1234 \times 9 + 5 = 11111$

$1 \times 8 + 1 = 9$
$12 \times 8 + 2 = 98$
$123 \times 8 + 3 = 987$
$1234 \times 8 + 4 = 9876$
$12345 \times 8 + 5 = 98765$

$1 \times 3 \times 37 = 111$
$2 \times 3 \times 37 = 222$
$3 \times 3 \times 37 = 333$
$4 \times 3 \times 37 = 444$

$7 \times 7 = 49$
$67 \times 67 = 4489$
$667 \times 667 = 444889$
$6667 \times 6667 = 44448889$

Check that the patterns you see there are correct and then try to continue each pattern without using a calculator. The numbers form a **sequence**. Check them with a calculator afterwards.

Spotting patterns is an important part of mathematics. It helps you to see rules for making calculations.

EXERCISE 14A

In questions 1 to 10, look for the pattern and then write the next two lines. Check your answers with a calculator afterwards.

You might find that some of the answers are too big to fit in a calculator display. This is one of the reasons why spotting patterns is important.

AU 1

$1 \times 1 = 1$
$11 \times 11 = 121$
$111 \times 111 = 12321$
$1111 \times 1111 = 1234321$

AU 2

$9 \times 9 = 81$
$99 \times 99 = 9801$
$999 \times 999 = 998001$
$9999 \times 9999 = 99980001$

> **HINTS AND TIPS**
>
> Look for symmetries in the number patterns.

FM Functional Maths   **AU** (AO2) Assessing Understanding   **PS** (AO3) Problem Solving

AU 3
$3 \times 4 = 3^2 + 3$
$4 \times 5 = 4^2 + 4$
$5 \times 6 = 5^2 + 5$
$6 \times 7 = 6^2 + 6$

AU 4
$10 \times 11 = 110$
$20 \times 21 = 420$
$30 \times 31 = 930$
$40 \times 41 = 1640$

HINTS AND TIPS

Think of the numbers as 1 10, 4 20, 9 30, 16 40 …

AU 5
$1 = 1 = 1^2$
$1 + 2 + 1 = 4 = 2^2$
$1 + 2 + 3 + 2 + 1 = 9 = 3^2$
$1 + 2 + 3 + 4 + 3 + 2 + 1 = 16 = 4^2$

AU 6
$1 = 1 = 1^3$
$3 + 5 = 8 = 2^3$
$7 + 9 + 11 = 27 = 3^3$
$13 + 15 + 17 + 19 = 64 = 4^3$

AU 7
$1 = 1$
$1 + 1 = 2$
$1 + 2 + 1 = 4$
$1 + 3 + 3 + 1 = 8$
$1 + 4 + 6 + 4 + 1 = 16$
$1 + 5 + 10 + 10 + 5 + 1 = 32$

AU 8
$12\ 345\ 679 \times 9 = 111\ 111\ 111$
$12\ 345\ 679 \times 18 = 222\ 222\ 222$
$12\ 345\ 679 \times 27 = 333\ 333\ 333$
$12\ 345\ 679 \times 36 = 444\ 444\ 444$

AU 9
$1^3 = 1^2 = 1$
$1^3 + 2^3 = (1 + 2)^2 = 9$
$1^3 + 2^3 + 3^3 = (1 + 2 + 3)^2 = 36$

HINTS AND TIPS

$4 + 5 = 9 = 3^2$
$12 + 13 = 25 = 5^2$
$24 + 25 = 49 = 7^2$

AU 10
$3^2 + 4^2 = 5^2$
$10^2 + 11^2 + 12^2 = 13^2 + 14^2$
$21^2 + 22^2 + 23^2 + 24^2 = 25^2 + 26^2 + 27^2$

From your observations on the number patterns in questions 1 to 10, answer questions 11 to 19 without using a calculator.

HINTS AND TIPS

Look for clues in the patterns from questions 1 to 10, for example, $1111 \times 1111 = 1234321$. This is four 1s times four 1s, so what will it be for nine 1s times nine 1s?

PS 11 $111\ 111\ 111 \times 111\ 111\ 111 =$

PS 12 $999\ 999\ 999 \times 999\ 999\ 999 =$

PS 13 $12 \times 13 =$

PS 14 $90 \times 91 =$

PS 15 $1 + 2 + 3 + 4 + 5 + 6 + 7 + 8 + 9 + 8 + 7 + 6 + 5 + 4 + 3 + 2 + 1 =$

PS 16 $57 + 59 + 61 + 63 + 65 + 67 + 69 + 71 =$

PS 17 $1 + 9 + 36 + 84 + 126 + 126 + 84 + 36 + 9 + 1 =$

PS 18 $12\ 345\ 679 \times 81 =$

PS 19 $1^3 + 2^3 + 3^3 + 4^3 + 5^3 + 6^3 + 7^3 + 8^3 + 9^3 =$

PS 20 The letters of the alphabet are written as the pattern:

ABBCCCDDDDEEEEEFFFFFFGGGGGGG …

so that the number of times each letter is written matches its place in the alphabet.

So, for example, as J is the 10th letter in the alphabet, there will be 10 Js in the list.

When the pattern gets to the 26th Z, it repeats.

What letter will be the 1000th in the list?

> **HINTS AND TIPS**
>
> Work out how many letters there are in the sequence from ABB … to … ZZZ, then work out how many of these sequences are needed to get past 1000.

14.2 Number sequences

This section will show you how to:
- recognise how number sequences are building up

Key words

consecutive

difference

sequence

term

term-to-term

A number **sequence** is an ordered set of numbers with a rule for finding every number in the sequence. The rule that takes you from one number to the next could be a simple addition or multiplication, but often it is more tricky than that. So you need to look *very* carefully at the pattern of a sequence.

Each number in a sequence is called a **term** and is in a certain position in the sequence.

Look at these sequences and their rules.

3, 6, 12, 24, … doubling the previous term each time … 48, 96, …

2, 5, 8, 11, … adding 3 to the previous term each time … 14, 17, …

1, 10, 100, 1000, … multiplying the previous term by 10 each time … 10 000, 100 000

1, 8, 15, 22, … adding 7 to the previous term each time … 29, 36, …

These are all quite straightforward once you have looked for the link from one term to the next (**consecutive** terms). Sequences like this may be called **term-to-term** sequences.

Differences

For some sequences you need to look at the **differences** between consecutive terms to determine the pattern.

EXAMPLE 1

Find the next two terms of the sequence 1, 3, 6, 10, 15, … .

Looking at the differences between consecutive terms:

```
1     3     6     10     15
   ↑     ↑     ↑     ↑
   2     3     4     5
```

> This is a special sequence of numbers. Do you recognise it? You will meet it again, later in the chapter.

So the sequence continues as follows.

```
1     3     6     10     15     21     28
   ↑     ↑     ↑     ↑
   2     3     4     5   ⌊ +6 ⌋⌊ +7 ⌋
```

So the next two terms are 21 and 28.

The differences usually form a number sequence of their own, so you need to find the *sequence of the differences* before you can expand the original sequence.

EXERCISE 14B

AU 1 Look at the following number sequences. Write down the next three terms in each and explain how each sequence is formed.

   a 1, 3, 5, 7, …   **b** 2, 4, 6, 8, …

   c 5, 10, 20, 40, …   **d** 1, 3, 9, 27, …

   e 4, 10, 16, 22, …   **f** 3, 8, 13, 18, …

   g 2, 20, 200, 2000, …   **h** 7, 10, 13, 16, …

   i 10, 19, 28, 37, …   **j** 5, 15, 45, 135, …

   k 2, 6, 10, 14, …   **l** 1, 5, 25, 125, …

2 By considering the differences in the following sequences, write down the next two terms in each case.

   a 1, 2, 4, 7, 11, …   **b** 1, 2, 5, 10, 17, …

   c 1, 3, 7, 13, 21, …   **d** 1, 4, 10, 19, 31, …

   e 1, 9, 25, 49, 81, …   **f** 1, 2, 7, 32, 157, …

   g 1, 3, 23, 223, 2223, …   **h** 1, 2, 4, 5, 7, 8, 10, …

   i 2, 3, 5, 9, 17, …   **j** 3, 8, 18, 33, 53, …

F

E

E

3 Look at the sequences below. Find the rule for each sequence and write down its next three terms.

a 3, 6, 12, 24, …   **b** 3, 9, 15, 21, 27, …

c 128, 64, 32, 16, 8, …   **d** 50, 47, 44, 41, …

e 2, 5, 10, 17, 26, …   **f** 5, 6, 8, 11, 15, 20, …

g 5, 7, 8, 10, 11, 13, …   **h** 4, 7, 10, 13, 16, …

i 1, 3, 6, 10, 15, 21, …   **j** 1, 2, 3, 4, …

k 100, 20, 4, 0.8, …   **l** 1, 0.5, 0.25, 0.125, …

D

AU **4** Look carefully at each number sequence below. Find the next two numbers in the sequence and try to explain the pattern.

a 1, 1, 2, 3, 5, 8, 13, …

b 1, 4, 9, 16, 25, 36, …

c 3, 4, 7, 11, 18, 29, …

d 1, 8, 27, 64, 125, …

> **HINTS AND TIPS**
>
> These patterns do not go up by the same value each time so you will need to find another connection between the terms.

5 Triangular numbers are found as follows.

1   3   6   10

Find the next four triangular numbers.

6 Hexagonal numbers are found as follows.

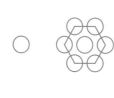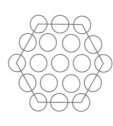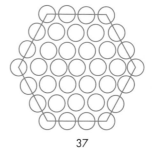

1   7   19   37

Find the next three hexagonal numbers.

AU 7 On the first day of Christmas my true love sent to me:

> a partridge in a pear tree

On the second day of Christmas my true love sent to me:

> two turtle doves
> and a partridge in a pear tree

and so on until …

On the twelfth day of Christmas my true love sent to me:

> twelve drummers drumming
> eleven pipers piping
> ten lords a-leaping
> nine ladies dancing
> eight maids a-milking
> seven swans a-swimming
> six geese a-laying
> five golden rings
> four calling birds
> three French hens
> two turtle doves
> and a partridge in a pear tree.

How many presents were given in total on the twelve days of Christmas?

Work out the pattern for the number of presents each day and find the total number of presents after each day. Describe any patterns that you spot.

PS 8 The first term that these two sequences have in common is 17:

> 8, 11, 14, 17, 20, ...
>
> 1, 5, 9, 13, 17, ...

What are the next two terms that the two sequences have in common?

AU 9 Two sequences are:

> 2, 5, 8, 11, 14, ...
>
> 3, 6, 9, 12, 15, ...

Will the two sequences ever have a term in common? Yes or no?
Justify your answer.

FM 10 The sequence 1, 1, 2, 3, 5, 8, 13, 21, 34, … can be used to give an approximate conversion of miles to kilometres.

For example, 5 miles ≈ 8 kilometres, 8 miles ≈ 13 kilometres, and so on.

a Convert 55 miles to kilometres

b Convert 68 kilometres to miles.

The *n*th term of a sequence

This section will show you how to:
- recognise how number sequences are built up
- generate sequences, given the *n*th term
- find an algebraic rule for the *n*th term of a sequence

Key words
coefficient
consecutive
difference
linear sequence
*n*th term

Finding the rule

When using a number sequence, you sometimes need to know, say, its 50th term, or even a higher term in the sequence. To do so, you need to find the rule that produces the sequence in its general form.

It may be helpful to look at the problem backwards. That is, take a rule and see how it produces a sequence. The rule is given for the general term, which is called the **nth term**.

EXAMPLE 2

A sequence is formed by the rule $3n + 1$, where $n = 1, 2, 3, 4, 5, 6, ...$ Write down the first five terms of the sequence.

Substituting $n = 1, 2, 3, 4, 5$ in turn:

$(3 \times 1 + 1), (3 \times 2 + 1), (3 \times 3 + 1), (3 \times 4 + 1), (3 \times 5 + 1), ...$

$\qquad$ 4 $\qquad$ 7 $\qquad$ 10 $\qquad$ 13 $\qquad$ 16

So the sequence is 4, 7, 10, 13, 16, ...

Notice that in Example 2 the **difference** between each term and the next is always 3, which is the **coefficient** of *n* (the number attached to *n*). Also, the constant term is the difference between the first term and the coefficient, that is, $4 - 3 = 1$.

EXAMPLE 3

The *n*th term of a sequence is $4n - 3$. Write down the first five terms of the sequence.

Substituting $n = 1, 2, 3, 4, 5$ in turn:

$(4 \times 1 - 3), (4 \times 2 - 3), (4 \times 3 - 3), (4 \times 4 - 3), (4 \times 5 - 3)$

$\qquad$ 1 $\qquad$ 5 $\qquad$ 9 $\qquad$ 13 $\qquad$ 17

So the sequence is 1, 5, 9, 13, 17, ...

Notice that in Example 3 the difference between each term and the next is always 4, which is the coefficient of *n*.

Also, the constant term is the difference between the first term and the coefficient, that is, $1 - 4 = -3$.

EXERCISE 14C

1 Use each of the following rules to write down the first five terms of a sequence.

    a $2n + 1$ for $n = 1, 2, 3, 4, 5$ **b** $3n - 2$ for $n = 1, 2, 3, 4, 5$

    c $5n + 2$ for $n = 1, 2, 3, 4, 5$ **d** n^2 for $n = 1, 2, 3, 4, 5$

    e $n^2 + 3$ for $n = 1, 2, 3, 4, 5$

2 Write down the first five terms of the sequence that has as its nth term:

    a $n + 3$ **b** $3n - 1$ **c** $5n - 2$

    d $n^2 - 1$ **e** $4n + 5$.

> **HINTS AND TIPS**
>
> Substitute numbers into the expressions until you can see how the sequence works.

3 The first two terms of the sequence of fractions $\dfrac{n - 1}{n + 1}$ are:

$$n = 1: \quad \frac{1 - 1}{1 + 1} = \frac{0}{2} = 0 \qquad n = 2: \quad \frac{2 - 1}{2 + 1} = \frac{1}{3}$$

Work out the next five terms of the sequence.

4 A sequence is formed by the rule $\frac{1}{2} \times n \times (n + 1)$ for $n = 1, 2, 3, 4, \ldots$.

    The first term is given by $n = 1$: $\frac{1}{2} \times 1 \times (1 + 1) = 1$

    The second term is given by $n = 2$: $\frac{1}{2} \times 2 \times (2 + 1) = 3$

    a Work out the next five terms of this sequence.

    b This is a well-known sequence you have met before. What is it?

FM 5 A haulage company uses this formula to calculate the cost of transporting n pallets.

    For $n \leqslant 5$, the cost will be £$(40n + 50)$

    For $6 \leqslant n \leqslant 10$, the cost will be £$(40n + 25)$

    For $n \geqslant 11$, the cost will be £$40n$

    a How much will the company charge to transport 7 pallets?

    b How much will the company charge to transport 15 pallets?

    c A company is charged £170 for transporting pallets. How many pallets did they transport?

    d Another haulage company uses the formula £$50n$ to calculate the cost for transporting n pallets.

    At what value of n do the two companies charge the same amount?

PS **6** The formula for working out a series of fractions is $\dfrac{2n+1}{3n+1}$.

   a Work out the first three fractions in the series.

   b **i** Work out the value of the fraction as a decimal when $n = 1\,000\,000$.

   ii What fraction is equivalent to this decimal?

   iii How can you tell this from the original formula?

AU **7** The nth term of a sequence is $3n + 7$.
The nth term of another sequence is $4n - 2$.

These two series have several terms in common but only one term that is common and has the same position in the sequence.

Without writing out the sequences, show how you can tell, using the expressions for the nth term, that this is the 9th term.

8 5! means factorial 5, which is $5 \times 4 \times 3 \times 2 \times 1 = 120$.

   7! means $7 \times 6 \times 5 \times 4 \times 3 \times 2 \times 1 = 5040$.

   a Calculate 2!, 3!, 4! and 6!.

   b If your calculator has a factorial button, check that it gives the same answers as you get for part **a**. What is the largest factorial you can work out with your calculator before you get an error?

Finding the nth term of a linear sequence

In a **linear sequence** the *difference* between one term and the next is always the same.

For example:

   2, 5, 8, 11, 14, … difference of 3

The nth term of this sequence is given by $3n - 1$.

Here is another linear sequence.

   5, 7, 9, 11, 13, … difference of 2

The nth term of this sequence is given by $2n + 3$.

So, you can see that the nth term of a linear sequence is *always* of the form $An + b$, where:

● A, the coefficient of n, is the difference between each term and the next term (**consecutive** terms)

● b is the difference between the first term and A.

EXAMPLE 4

Find the nth term of the sequence 5, 7, 9, 11, 13, ...

The difference between consecutive terms is 2. So the first part of the nth term is $2n$.

Subtract the difference, 2, from the first term, 5, which gives $5 - 2 = 3$.

So the nth term is given by $2n + 3$. (You can test it by substituting $n = 1, 2, 3, 4, ...$.)

EXAMPLE 5

Find the nth term of the sequence 3, 7, 11, 15, 19, ...

The difference between consecutive terms is 4. So the first part of the nth term is $4n$.

Subtract the difference, 4, from the first term, 3, which gives $3 - 4 = -1$.

So the nth term is given by $4n - 1$.

EXAMPLE 6

From the sequence 5, 12, 19, 26, 33, ... , find:

a the nth term   **b** the 50th term.

a The difference between consecutive terms is 7. So the first part of the nth term is $7n$.

Subtract the difference, 7, from the first term, 5, which gives $5 - 7 = -2$.

So the nth term is given by $7n - 2$.

b The 50th term is found by substituting $n = 50$ into the rule, $7n - 2$.

50th term $= 7 \times 50 - 2 = 350 - 2$
$= 348$

EXERCISE 14D

1 Find the next two terms and the nth term in each of these linear sequences.

a 3, 5, 7, 9, 11, ...

b 5, 9, 13, 17, 21, ...

c 8, 13, 18, 23, 28, ...

d 2, 8, 14, 20, 26, ...

e 5, 8, 11, 14, 17, ...

f 2, 9, 16, 23, 30, ...

g 1, 5, 9, 13, 17, ...

h 3, 7, 11, 15, 19, ...

i 2, 5, 8, 11, 14, ...

j 2, 12, 22, 32, ...

k 8, 12, 16, 20, ...

l 4, 9, 14, 19, 24, ...

HINTS AND TIPS

Remember to look at the differences and the first term.

2 Find the *n*th term and the 50th term in each of these linear sequences.

a 4, 7, 10, 13, 16, …   b 7, 9, 11, 13, 15, …   c 3, 8, 13, 18, 23, …

d 1, 5, 9, 13, 17, …   e 2, 10, 18, 26, …   f 5, 6, 7, 8, 9, …

g 6, 11, 16, 21, 26, …   h 3, 11, 19, 27, 35, …   i 1, 4, 7, 10, 13, …

j 21, 24, 27, 30, 33, …   k 12, 19, 26, 33, 40, …   l 1, 9, 17, 25, 33, …

3 For each sequence **a** to **j**, find:

i the *n*th term   ii the 100th term.

a 5, 9, 13, 17, 21, …   b 3, 5, 7, 9, 11, 13, …   c 4, 7, 10, 13, 16, …

d 8, 10, 12, 14, 16, …   e 9, 13, 17, 21, …   f 6, 11, 16, 21, …

g 0, 3, 6, 9, 12, …   h 2, 8, 14, 20, 26, …   i 7, 15, 23, 31, …

j 25, 27, 29, 31, …

FM 4 An online CD retail company uses the following price chart. The company charges a standard basic price for a single CD, including postage and packing.

n	1	2	3	4	5	6	7	8	9	10	11	12	13	14	15
Charge (£)	10	18	26	34	42	49	57	65	73	81	88	96	104	112	120

a Using the charges for 1 to 5 CDs, work out an expression for the *n*th term.

b Using the charges for 6 to 10 CDs, work out an expression for the *n*th term.

c Using the charges for 11 to 15 CDs, work out an expression for the *n*th term.

d What is the basic charge for a CD?

PS 5 Look at this series of fractions.

$$\frac{31}{109}, \frac{33}{110}, \frac{35}{111}, \frac{37}{112}, \frac{39}{113}, \dots$$

a Explain why the *n*th term of the numerators is $2n + 29$.

b Write down the *n*th term of the denominators.

c Explain why the terms of the series will eventually get very close to 1.

d Which term of the series has a value equal to 1?

AU 6 The square numbers are 1, 4, 9, 16, 25, … .

a Continue the sequence for another five terms.

b The *n*th term of this sequence is n^2. Give the *n*th term of these sequences.

i 2, 5, 10, 17, 26, …   ii 2, 8, 18, 32, 50 …   iii 0, 3, 8, 15, 24, …

General rules from given patterns

This section will show you how to:
- find the nth term from practical problems
- recognise some special sequences and how they are built up

Many problem-solving situations that you are likely to meet involve number sequences. So you do need to be able to formulate general rules from given number patterns.

EXAMPLE 7

The diagram shows a pattern of squares building up.

a How many squares will there be in the nth pattern?

b What is the largest pattern number you can make with 200 squares?

a

Pattern number	1	2	3	4	5
Number of squares	1	3	5	7	9

Looking at the difference between consecutive patterns, you should see it is always 2 squares. So, use $2n$. Subtract the difference, 2, from the first number, which gives $1 - 2 = -1$. So the number of squares in the nth pattern is $2n - 1$.

b $2n - 1 = 200$

$2n = 201$

$n = 100.5$

So, 200 squares will make up to the 100th pattern.

There are some number sequences that occur frequently. It is useful to know these as they are very likely to occur in examinations.

Even numbers: The even numbers are 2, 4, 6, 8, 10, 12, … . The nth term of this sequence is $2n$.

Odd numbers: The odd numbers are 1, 3, 5, 7, 9, 11, … . The nth term of this sequence is $2n - 1$.

Square numbers: The square numbers are 1, 4, 9, 16, 25, 36, … . The nth term of this sequence is n^2.

Triangular numbers: The triangular numbers are 1, 3, 6, 10, 15, 21, … . The nth term of this sequence is $\frac{1}{2}n(n + 1)$.

Powers of 2: The powers of 2 are 2, 4, 8, 16, 32, 64, … . The nth term of this sequence is 2^n.

Powers of 10: The powers of 10 are 10, 100, 1000, 10 000, 100 000, 1 000 000, … . The nth term of this sequence is 10^n.

Prime numbers: The first 20 prime numbers are 2, 3, 5, 7, 11, 13, 17, 19, 23, 29, 31, 37, 41, 43, 47, 53, 59, 61, 67, 71.

A prime number is a number that has only two factors, 1 and itself.

There is no pattern to the prime numbers so they do not have an nth term.

Remember: There is only one even prime number, and that is 2.

EXERCISE 14E

1 A pattern of squares is built up from matchsticks as shown.

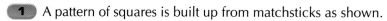

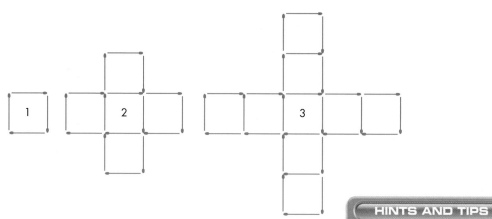

a Draw the fourth diagram.

b How many squares are there in the *n*th diagram?

c How many squares are there in the 25th diagram?

d With 200 squares, which is the biggest diagram that could be made?

HINTS AND TIPS

Write out the number sequences to help you see the patterns.

2 A pattern of triangles is built up from matchsticks.

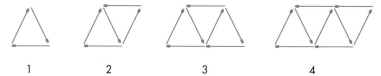

1   2   3   4

a Draw the fifth set of triangles in this pattern.

b How many matchsticks are needed for the *n*th set of triangles?

c How many matchsticks are needed to make the 60th set of triangles?

d If there are only 100 matchsticks, which is the largest set of triangles that could be made?

AU 3 A conference centre had tables each of which could sit six people. When put together, the tables could seat people as shown.

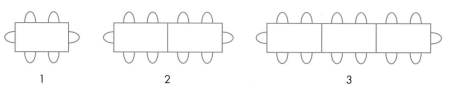

1   2   3

a How many people could be seated at four tables?

b How many people could be seated at *n* tables put together in this way?

c At a conference, 50 people wished to use the tables in this way. How many tables would they need?

4 Regular pentagons of side length 1 cm are joined together to make a pattern as shown.

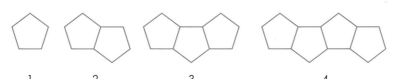

Copy this pattern and write down the perimeter of each shape.

a What is the perimeter of patterns like this made from:

i 6 pentagons **ii** n pentagons **iii** 50 pentagons?

b What is the largest number of pentagons that can be put together like this to have a perimeter less than 1000 cm?

FM 5 Lampposts are put at the end of every 100 m stretch of a motorway, as shown.

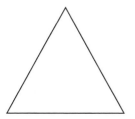 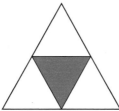 

a How many lampposts are needed for:

i 900 m of this motorway **ii** 8 km of this motorway?

b The contractor building the M99 motorway has ordered 1598 lampposts. How long is the M99?

PS 6 Draw an equilateral triangle.

Mark the midpoints of each side and draw and shade in the equilateral triangle formed by joining these points.

Repeat this with the three unshaded triangles remaining.

Keep on doing this with the unshaded triangles that are left.

The pattern is called a Sierpinski triangle and is one of the earliest examples of a fractal type pattern.

The shaded areas in each triangle are $\frac{1}{4}, \frac{7}{16}, \frac{37}{64}, \frac{175}{256}$.

It is very difficult to work out an nth term for this series of fractions.

Use your calculator to work out the **unshaded** area, e.g. $\frac{3}{4}, \frac{9}{16}$ ...

You should be able to write down a formula for the nth term of this pattern.

Pick a large value for n.

Will the shaded area ever cover all of the original triangle?

AU 7 Thom is building three different patterns with matches.

He builds the patterns in steps.

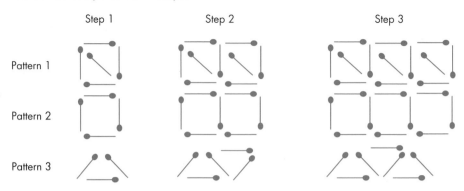

Step 1 Step 2 Step 3

Pattern 1

Pattern 2

Pattern 3

Thom has five boxes of matches which are labelled 'Average contents 42 matches'.

Will Thom have enough matches to get to step 20 with all these patterns together?

Show your working.

8 a The powers of 2 are 2, 4, 8, 16, 32, ...

What is the nth term of this sequence?

b A supermarket sells four different-sized bottles of water.

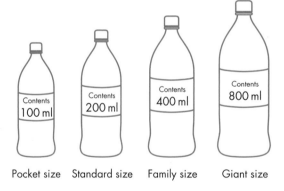

Contents 100 ml   Contents 200 ml   Contents 400 ml   Contents 800 ml

Pocket size   Standard size   Family size   Giant size

i Describe the number pattern that the contents follow.

ii The supermarket introduces a super giant size, which is the next sized bottle in the pattern. How much water is there in this bottle?

9 The powers of 10 are 10^1, 10^2, 10^3, 10^4, 10^5, ...

This gives the sequence 10, 100, 1000, 10 000, 100 000, ...

The nth term is given by 10^n.

a Describe the connection between the number of zeros in each term and the power of the term.

b If $10^n = 1\,000\,000$, what is the value of n?

10 The number p is odd and the number q is even. State if the following are odd or even.

a $p + 1$ **b** $q + 1$ **c** $p + q$

GRADE BOOSTER

F You can give the next term in a sequence and describe how the pattern is building up

E You can find any term in a number sequence and recognise patterns in number calculations

D You can substitute numbers into an nth term rule

D You can understand how odd and even numbers interact in addition, subtraction and multiplication problems

C You can give the nth term of a linear sequence

What you should know now

- How to recognise a number pattern and explain how the pattern is made
- How to recognise a linear sequence and find its nth term

1 a Write down the next two terms in the sequence.

31, 27, 23, 19 (2)

b What is the rule for continuing the sequence? (1)

c Jane says that the sequence will eventually include –3.

Explain why Jane is wrong. (1)

(Total 4 marks)

AQA, June 2009, Paper 2 Foundation, Question 13

2 a Write down the next two numbers in the following sequences.

i 60 54 48 42 36 ....

ii 1 2 4 8 16 .... (4)

b Another sequence begins

1 3 7 15 31

Explain the rule for continuing this sequence. (1)

(Total 5 marks)

AQA, June 2008, Paper 1 Foundation, Question 9

3 A pattern is formed from squares.

| Pattern 1 | Pattern 2 | Pattern 3 | Pattern 4 |

a Draw Pattern 4. (1)

b Find the number of squares in Pattern 6. (1)

(Total 2 marks)

AQA, June 2008, Paper 2 Foundation, Question 4

4 The first ten prime numbers are 2, 3, 5, 7, 11, 13, 17, 19, 23, 29.

P is a prime number.
Q is an odd number.

State whether each of the following is always odd, always even or could be either odd or even.

a $P(Q + 1)$

b $Q - P$

5 The nth term of a sequence is given by the expression

$n^2 + 5$

Write down the first **three** terms of the sequence. (2)

(Total 2 marks)

AQA, November 2008, Paper 2 Foundation, Question 19

6 a A sequence of numbers starts

9 7 5 3 ....

Write down the next two numbers in this sequence. (2)

b A different sequence uses this rule.

Add the last two numbers then halve the result

i The sequence of numbers starts

12 4 8 6 ....

Work out the next two numbers in this sequence. (2)

ii Jenna says that the rule to find the next number in this sequence could also be:

"Find the mean of the last two numbers."

Is Jenna right?

Explain your answer. (1)

(Total 5 marks)

AQA, June 2007, Paper 1 Foundation, Question 9

7 a A sequence has nth term $4n + 1$.

i Write down the first three terms of this sequence. (2)

ii Toms says that 2006 is a term in this sequence.

Explain why he is wrong. (1)

b A different sequence has nth term

$(n + 3)^2 - 9$

Show that the first term of this sequence is 7. (1)

(Total 4 marks)

AQA, November 2006, Paper 1 Intermediate, Question 8

C D E F

8 p and q are odd numbers.

a Is $p + q$ an odd number, an even number or could it be either? (1)

b Is pq an odd number, an even number or could it be either? (1)

(Total 2 marks)

AQA, June 2005, Paper 1 Foundation, Question 24

9 Here is a number pattern.

Line 1 $\qquad 1 = \dfrac{1 \times 2}{2}$

Line 2 $\qquad 1 + 2 = \dfrac{2 \times 3}{2}$

Line 3 $\qquad 1 + 2 + 3 = \dfrac{3 \times 4}{2}$

Line 4 $\qquad 1 + 2 + 3 + 4 = \dfrac{4 \times 5}{2}$

Line 5 $\qquad 1 + 2 + 3 + 4 + 5 =$

a Complete line 5 of the pattern. (1)

b Write down line 6 of the pattern. (1)

c Use the pattern to find the sum of the whole numbers from 1 to 24.
You **must** show your working. (2)

(Total 4 marks)

AQA, June 2007, Paper 2 Intermediate, Question 2

10 Consecutive patterns are put together.

Pattern 1 and 2   Pattern 2 and 3   Pattern 3 and 4

a The numbers of counters in the combined patterns form the sequence:

4, 9, 16, ...

How many counters will be in the next combined pattern in the sequence?

b What type of numbers are 4, 9, 16, ... ?

c How many counters will be in the combined pattern formed by patterns 9 and 10?

11 Martin says that the square of any number is always bigger than the number. Give an example to show that Martin is wrong.

12 It is known that n is an integer.

a Explain why $2n + 1$ is always an odd number for all values of n.

b Explain why n^2 could be either odd or even.

13 Here are the nth terms of three sequences.

Sequence 1 nth term $4n + 1$
Sequence 2 nth term $3n + 3$
Sequence 3 nth term $3n - 1$

For each sequence state whether the numbers in the sequence are

A   Always multiples of 3
S   Sometimes multiples of 3
N   Never multiples of 3 (3)

(Total 3 marks)

AQA, November 2006, Paper 2 Intermediate, Question 13

14 a Write down the next term for each of the following sequences.
Give the rule for each sequence.

i 7, 13, 19, 25, ... (2)

ii 11, 8, 5, 2, ... (2)

b Find the nth term of this sequence.
6, 10, 14, 18, ... (2)

(Total 6 marks)

AQA, November 2008, Paper 1 Foundation, Question 13

Worked Examination Questions

PS **1 a** Matches are used to make patterns.

  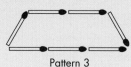 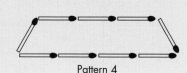

Pattern 1   Pattern 2   Pattern 3   Pattern 4

    i How many matches would be needed for the 10th pattern?

    ii How many matches would be needed for the nth pattern?

b The patterns are used to make a sequence of shapes.

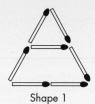 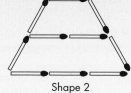 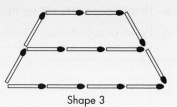

Shape 1   Shape 2   Shape 3

The number of matches needed to make these shapes is

    7, 10, 13, 16, ….

    i How many matches are needed for the nth shape?

    ii What shape number could be made with 64 matches?

a i The number of matches needed is 21.

   ii $2n + 1$

(2 marks)

> The number of matches needed is 3, 5, 7, 9, … which is going up by 2 each time.
> Continuing the sequence for 10 terms gives 3, 5, 7, 9, 11, 13, 15, 17, 19, 21.
> You get 1 mark for the correct answer.

b i $3n + 4$

   ii 20th shape

(4 marks)

(**Total:** 6 marks)

> The sequence goes up by 2 each time and the first term is 3, so the nth term is $2n + 1$.
> You get you 1 mark for the correct answer.

> The sequence goes up by 3 each time and the first term is 7 so the nth term is $3n + 4$. ($3n$ on its own would get 1 method mark. The full answer gets you 1 method mark and 1 mark for accuracy.)

> $3n + 4 = 64$, then $3n = 60$, so $n = 20$.
> (Setting up the equation $3n + 4 = 64$ gets you 1 method mark and the answer of 20 gets 1 mark for accuracy.)

Worked Examination Questions

2 Tom is building fences, using posts and rails.

Stage 1
2 posts, 3 rows

Stage 2
3 posts, 6 rows

Stage 3
4 posts, 9 rows

    a How many rails will there be in a fence with 6 posts?

    b How many posts will be needed for a fence with 27 rails?

    c Posts cost £12 and rails costs £5.
       Write down a formula for the cost of a fence with n posts.

a 15 rails

(1 mark)

b 10 posts

(1 mark)

c £$(27n - 15)$

(2 marks)

(**Total:** 4 marks)

> This answer can be found by 'counting on', i.e.
> 5 posts, 12 rails
> 6 posts, 15 rails.
> This gets you 1 mark.

> This could be found by 'counting on' but it is better to find a rule. The number of rails is in the 3 times table and is the multiple that is 1 less than the number of posts.
> $27 = 9 \times 3$, so number of posts is $9 + 1$.
> This gets you 1 mark.

> It is very important that once a formula is found, it is checked. This is a fundamental part of functional maths. So take one of the given examples at the start of the question:
>   Stage 2 uses 3 posts and 6 rails, for which the cost is $3 \times 12 + 6 \times 5 = £66$.
> The formula gives $27 \times 3 - 15 = 81 - 15 = 66$.

> Once the formula is found in part (b) it is a matter of putting the costs and the nth terms together.
> Cost $= 12n + 3 \times 5 \times (n - 1)$
> You get 1 method mark for the equation.
> You get 1 accuracy mark for simplifying the answer.

 3 Here are formulae for the nth terms of three sequences.

    Formula 1: $4n + 1$
    Formula 2: $5n - 2$
    Formula 3: $5n + 10$

    Say if the sequences generated by the nth terms always (A) give multiples of 5, never (N) give multiples of 5 or sometimes (S) give multiples of 5.

Formula 1: Sometimes (S)

Formula 2: Never (N)

Formula 3: Always (A)

(**Total:** 3 marks)

> Substitute $n = 1, 2, 3$, etc. until you can be sure of the sequences.
> These are:
>   5, 9, 13, 17, 21, 25, 29, …
>   3, 8, 13, 18, 23, 28, …
>   15, 20, 25, 30, 35, 40, …
> (You get 1 mark for each part.)

Some sets of square numbers have a special connection. For example:

$$3^2 + 4^2 = 5^2$$

The sets (3, 4, 5) is called a Pythagorean triple. (In Book 2, Chapter 14 you will learn about Pythagoras' theorem, which is connected with right-angled triangles. Pythagorean triples, however, were well known before Pythagoras himself!)

Pythagorean triples were used by ancient people in the construction of great monuments such as Stonehenge and the Egyptian pyramids. They are an excellent example of how we can use patterns.

Getting started

Many patterns, including Pythagorean triples, can be found, using diagrams.

1 Working in pairs, start with the smallest odd number and, going up in consecutive odd numbers, draw diagrams to represent the numbers. Extend your diagrams using a rule.

Have a look at what another group has done. Have they found the same rule as yours? Is there more than one way to represent odd numbers diagrammatically?

Getting started (continued)

2   Represent a square number diagrammatically – the clue is in the name.

One representation of odd numbers can be used to show how consecutive odd numbers add together to make square numbers. See if you can find this and show it in a diagram of 3^2.

3   Use the pattern from the diagrams to complete this sequence:

$$1 \qquad\qquad = 1^2 = 1$$
$$1 + 3 \qquad\quad = 2^2 = 4$$
$$1 + 3 + 5 \quad\; = ... = ...$$
$$1 + 3 + 5 + 7 = ... = ...$$
$$\qquad\qquad\qquad = ... = ...$$

Look for connections between the last odd number and the square number.

Use these connections to fill in the missing numbers in this sequence:

$$1 + 3 + 5 + ... + 19 = ... = ...$$
$$1 + 3 + 5 + ... + ... = 12^2 = 144$$
$$1 + 3 + 5 + ... + 99 = ... = ...$$
$$1 + 3 + 5 + ... + ... = 200^2 = 40\,000$$

Your task

It is your task to use diagrams to find patterns, and make and test generalisations.

1   Draw accurate diagrams to show that (3, 4, 5) is a Pythagorean triple and that it is true that $3^2 + 4^2 = 5^2$.

2   Show, using a diagram, that (5, 12, 13) is a Pythagorean triple.

3   What is the next Pythagorean triple?

4   Use this method to find at least three more Pythagorean triples.

(Use a calculator to check that you are right)

Extension

Use the internet to find out about Pythagoras, his theorem and the Platonic Formula.

PITAGORA

Answers to Chapter 1

1.1 Adding with grids

Exercise 1A

1 a
1	3	7	11
9	2	8	19
6	5	4	15
16	10	19	45

b
0	6	7	13
8	1	4	13
9	5	3	17
17	12	14	43

c
0	8	7	15
1	6	2	9
9	3	4	16
10	17	13	40

d
2	4	6	12
3	5	7	15
8	9	1	18
13	18	14	45

e
5	9	3	17
6	1	8	15
2	7	4	13
13	17	15	45

f
0	8	3	11
7	2	4	13
1	6	5	12
8	16	12	36

g
9	4	8	21
7	0	5	12
1	6	3	10
17	10	16	43

h
0	8	6	14
7	1	4	12
5	9	2	16
12	18	12	42

i
1	8	7	16
6	2	5	13
0	9	3	12
7	19	15	41

2 a Yes (£33) with £1 left over **b** 23

3 a 7 and 11
b 31
c 7 + 11 + 12 = 30 (largest two odds and one even gives larger total than largest three evens)

4 Possible answer: 4, 6, 8

5 a
1	7	8	16
0	3	6	9
5	4	2	11
6	14	16	36

b
1	2	3	6
6	5	4	15
7	8	9	24
14	15	16	45

c
9	3	6	18
4	0	5	9
1	2	8	11
14	5	19	38

d
9	1	6	16
2	7	4	13
8	5	0	13
19	13	10	42

e
2	9	6	17
4	1	3	8
5	0	8	13
11	10	17	38

f
1	7	8	16
6	2	4	12
5	9	3	17
12	18	15	45

g
0	2	1	3
9	6	7	22
8	4	5	17
17	12	13	42

h
1	0	3	4
8	7	4	19
9	6	5	20
18	13	12	43

i
1	5	4	10
6	2	3	11
8	7	0	15
15	14	7	36

6 Possible answer: 9, 11, 16

7 Possible answer: 11 and 13

1.2 Multiplication tables check

Exercise 1B

1 a 20 **b** 21 **c** 24 **d** 15 **e** 16 **f** 12
g 10 **h** 42 **i** 24 **j** 18 **k** 30 **l** 28
m 18 **n** 56 **o** 25 **p** 45 **q** 27 **r** 30
s 49 **t** 24 **u** 36 **v** 35 **w** 32 **x** 36
y 48 **z** £48 × 2 = £96, yes

2 a 5 **b** 4 **c** 6 **d** 6 **e** 5 **f** 4
g 7 **h** 6 **i** 2 **j** 3 **k** 7 **l** 8
m 9 **n** 5 **o** 8 **p** 9 **q** 4 **r** 7
s 7 **t** 9 **u** 5 **v** 4 **w** 5 **x** 7
y 6 **z** £6 per hour, 10 hours

3 a 12 **b** 15 **c** 21 **d** 13 **e** 8 **f** 7
g 14 **h** 3 **i** 30 **j** 6 **k** 35 **l** 5
m 16 **n** 7 **o** 16 **p** 15 **q** 27 **r** 6
s 15 **t** 24 **u** 40 **v** 6 **w** 17 **x** 72
y 46 **z** Ahmed is paid more (£33) than Ben (£32)

4 a 86 **b** 56 **c** 358 + 6

5 a 30 **b** 50 **c** 80 **d** 100 **e** 120 **f** 180
g 240 **h** 400 **i** 700 **j** 900 **k** 1000 **l** 1400
m 2400 **n** 7200 **o** 10 000 **p** 2 **q** 7 **r** 9
s 17 **t** 30 **u** 3 **v** 8 **w** 12 **x** 29
y 50

6 a 8 (3 × 8) **b** 900 (900 ÷ 10)

7 For example: 4 × 5 = 20 and 5 × 6 = 30

8 For example: 3 × 4 × 5 = 60 = 10 × 6 and 5 × 6 × 7 = 210 = 35 × 6

1.3 Order of operations and BIDMAS/BODMAS

Exercise 1C

1 a 11 **b** 6 **c** 10 **d** 12 **e** 11 **f** 13
g 11 **h** 12 **i** 12 **j** 4 **k** 13 **l** 3

2 a 16 **b** 2 **c** 10 **d** 10 **e** 6 **f** 18
g 6 **h** 15 **i** 9 **j** 12 **k** 3 **l** 8

3 b 3 + (2 × 4) = 11   **c** (9 ÷ 3) − 2 = 1
d 9 − (4 ÷ 2) = 7   **e** (5 × 2) + 3 = 13
f 5 + (2 × 3) = 11   **g** (10 ÷ 5) − 2 = 0
h 10 − (4 ÷ 2) = 8   **i** (4 × 6) − 7 = 17
j 7 + (4 × 6) = 31   **k** (6 ÷ 3) ÷ 7 = 9
l 7 + (6 ÷ 2) = 10

4 a 38 **b** 48 **c** 3 **d** 2 **e** 5 **f** 14
g 10 **h** 2 **i** 5 **j** 19 **k** 15 **l** 2
m 20 **n** 19 **o** 54 **p** 7 **q** 2 **r** 7
s 7 **t** 38 **u** 42 **v** 10 **w** 2 **x** 10
y 10 **z** 24

5 a (4 + 1) **b** No brackets needed
c (2 + 1) **d** No brackets needed
e (4 + 4) **f** (16 − 4)
g No brackets needed **h** No brackets needed
i (20 − 10) **j** No brackets needed
k (5 + 5) **l** (4 + 2)
m (15 − 5) **n** (7 − 2)
o (3 + 3) **p** No brackets needed
q No brackets needed **r** (8 − 2)

6 a 8 **b** 6 **c** 6 **d** 13 **e** 11 **f** 9
g 12 **h** 8 **i** 15 **j** 16 **k** 1 **l** 7

7 No, correct answer is 5 + 42 = 47

8 a $2 + 3 \times 4 = 14$
   b $8 - 4 \div 4 = 7$ (correct)
   c $6 + 3 \times 2 = 12$ (correct)
   d $7 - 1 \times 5 = 2$
   e $2 \times 7 + 2 = 16$ (correct)
   f $9 - 3 \times 3 = 0$

9 a $2 \times 3 + 5 = 11$
   b $2 \times (3 + 5) = 16$
   c $2 + 3 \times 5 = 17$
   d $5 - (3 - 2) = 4$
   e $5 \times 3 - 2 = 13$
   f $5 \times 3 \times 2 = 30$

10 $4 + 5 \times 3 = 19$
   $(4 + 5) \times 3 = 27$. So $4 + 5 \times 3$ is smaller

11 $(5 - 2) \times 6 = 18$

12 $10 \div (5 - 3) = 4$

13 $10 - 3 \times 1.5$ and $10 - 1.5 - 1.5 - 1.5$

1.4 Place value and ordering numbers

Exercise 1D

1 a 40   **b** 5 units   **c** 100   **d** 90   **e** 80   **f** 9 units
   g 80   **h** 500   **i** 0   **j** 5000   **k** 0   **l** 4 units
   m 300   **n** 90   **o** 80 000

2 a Forty-three, two hundred
   b One hundred and thirty-six; four thousand and ninety-nine
   c Two hundred and seventy-one; ten thousand, seven hundred and forty-four

3 a Five million, six hundred thousand
   b Four million, seventy-five thousand, two hundred
   c Three million, seven thousand, nine hundred and fifty
   d Two million, seven hundred and eighty-two

4 a 8 200 058   **b** 9 406 107   **c** 1 000 502
   d 2 076 040

5 a 9, 15, 21, 23, 48, 54, 56, 85
   b 25, 62, 86, 151, 219, 310, 400, 501
   c 97, 357, 368, 740, 888, 2053, 4366

6 a 95, 89, 73, 52, 34, 25, 23, 7
   b 700, 401, 174, 117, 80, 65, 18, 2
   c 6227, 3928, 2034, 762, 480, 395, 89, 59

7 a Larger   **b** Larger   **c** Smaller
   d Larger   **e** Larger   **f** Smaller
   g Larger   **h** Smaller   **i** Smaller

8 a Number 4 (£128 250)
   b Number 1 (£129 100)
   c £850

9 a 368, 386, 638, 683, 836, 863
   b 368
   c 863

10 408, 480, 804, 840

11 33, 35, 38, 53, 55, 58, 83, 85, 88

12 7045 or 7405

13 a $973 + 85 = 1058$ or
     $975 + 83 = 1058$ or
     $985 + 73 = 1058$ or
     $983 + 75 = 1058$
   b $357 - 98 = 259$

1.5 Rounding

Exercise 1E

1 a 20   **b** 60   **c** 80   **d** 50   **e** 100   **f** 20
   g 90   **h** 70   **i** 10   **j** 30   **k** 30   **l** 50
   m 80   **n** 50   **o** 90   **p** 40   **q** 70   **r** 20
   s 100   **t** 110

2 a 200   **b** 600   **c** 800   **d** 500   **e** 1000   **f** 100
   g 600   **h** 400   **i** 1000   **j** 1100   **k** 300   **l** 500
   m 800   **n** 500   **o** 900   **p** 400   **q** 700   **r** 800
   s 1000   **t** 1100

3 a 1   **b** 2   **c** 1   **d** 1   **e** 3   **f** 2
   g 3   **h** 2   **i** 1   **j** 1   **k** 3   **l** 2
   m 74   **n** 126   **o** 184

4 a 2000   **b** 6000   **c** 8000   **d** 5000   **e** 10 000   **f** 1000
   g 6000   **h** 3000   **i** 9000   **j** 2000   **k** 3000   **l** 5000
   m 8000   **n** 5000   **o** 9000   **p** 4000   **q** 7000   **r** 8000
   s 1000   **t** 2000

5 a 230   **b** 570   **c** 720   **d** 520   **e** 910   **f** 230
   g 880   **h** 630   **i** 110   **j** 300   **k** 280   **l** 540
   m 770   **n** 500   **o** 940   **p** 380   **q** 630   **r** 350
   s 1010   **t** 1070

6 a True   **b** False   **c** True   **d** True   **e** True   **f** False

7 Welcome to Swinton population 1400 (to the nearest 100)

8 a Man Utd v West Brom
   b Blackburn v Fulham
   c 40 000, 19 000, 42 000, 26 000, 40 000, 68 000, 35 000, 25 000, 20 000
   d 39 600, 19 000, 42 100, 26 100, 40 400, 67 800, 34 800, 25 500, 20 200

9 a 35 min   **b** 55 min   **c** 15 min
   d 50 min   **e** 10 min   **f** 15 min
   g 45 min   **h** 35 min   **i** 5 min
   j 0 min

10 a 375
   b 25 (350 to 374 inclusive)

11 A number between 75 and 84 inclusive added to a number between 45 and 54 inclusive with a total not equal to 130, for example $79 + 49 = 128$

1.6 Adding and subtracting numbers with up to four digits

Exercise 1F

1 a 713   **b** 151   **c** 6381
   d 968   **e** 622   **f** 1315
   g 8260   **h** 818   **i** 451
   j 852

2 a 646   **b** 826   **c** 3818
   d 755   **e** 2596   **f** 891
   g 350   **h** 2766   **i** 8858
   j 841   **k** 6831   **l** 7016
   m 1003   **n** 4450   **o** 9944

3 **a** 450 **b** 563 **c** 482
  d 414 **e** 285 **f** 486
  g 244 **h** 284 **i** 333
  j 216 **k** 2892 **l** 4417
  m 3767 **n** 4087 **o** 1828

4 **a** 128 **b** 29 **c** 334
  d 178 **e** 277 **f** 285
  g 335 **h** 399 **i** 4032
  j 4765 **k** 3795 **l** 5437

5 **a** 558 miles **b** 254 miles

6 252

7 **a** 6, 7 **b** 4, 7 **c** 4, 8
  d 7, 4, 9 **e** 6, 9, 7 **f** 6, 2, 7
  g 2, 6, 6 **h** 4, 5, 9 **i** 4, 8, 8
  j 4, 4, 9, 8

8 Units digit should be 6 (from 14 − 8)

9 **a** 3, 5 **b** 8, 3 **c** 5, 8
  d 8, 5, 4 **e** 6, 7, 5 **f** 1, 2, 1
  g 2, 7, 7 **h** 5, 5, 6 **i** 8, 3, 8
  j 1, 8, 8, 9

10 For example: 181 − 27 = 154

1.7 Multiplying and dividing by single-digit numbers

Exercise 1G

1 **a** 56 **b** 65 **c** 51
  d 38 **e** 108 **f** 115
  g 204 **h** 294 **i** 212
  j 425 **k** 150 **l** 800
  m 960 **n** 1360 **o** 1518

2 **a** 294 **b** 370 **c** 288
  d 832 **e** 2163 **f** 2520
  g 1644 **h** 3215 **i** 3000
  j 2652 **k** 3696 **l** 1880
  m 54 387 **n** 21 935 **o** 48 888

3 **a** 219 **b** 317 **c** 315
  d 106 **e** 99 **f** 121
  g 252 **h** 141 **i** 144
  j 86 **k** 63 **l** 2909
  m 416 **n** 251 **o** 1284

4 **a** 705 miles **b** £3525

5 **a** 47 miles
  b Three numbers with a total of 125. First number must be less than 50. second number less than first number, third number less than second number, for example 48, 42 and 35.

6 **a** 119 **b** 96 **c** 144
  d 210 **e** 210

7 **a** 13 **b** 37 weeks **c** 43 m
  d 36 **e** 45

8 **a** 152 + 190 = 324
  b (10 × 190) + 76 = 1976
  c (100 × 38) + 190 = 3990

Examination questions

1 **a** **i** 63 507 **ii** 64 000
  b **i** Ten thousand, seven hundred and eighty **ii** 10 800

2 **a** **i** 2379 **ii** 9732
  b 3 × 9 = 27
  c 0

3 **a** 43 550
  b 43 649

4 **a** True, multiplication works both ways/Both sides equal 288
  b False, it does matter which way you do a division, 36 ÷ 9 = 4, 9 ÷ 36 = 0.25
  c True, because 6 + 5 = 11, so 6 × 3 + 5 × 3 = 18 + 15 = 33 = 11 × 3

5 7760 metres

6 **a** £1505
  b 19 people

7 **a** 10 000
  b One thousand and ten
  c 3000
  d 800
  e 4337

8 **a** Intermediate
  b Thirty thousand, three hundred and thirty-eight
  c 30 000

9 **a** 15 380
  b 15 400

10 **a** $(2 \times 3)^2 + 6 = 42$ **b** $2 \times (3^2 + 6) = 30$

11 **a** Adam has done 5 × 2 instead of 5^2.
    Bekki has added 3 to 5 first, instead of doing the power first.
  b 26

Answers to Chapter 2

2.1 Recognise a fraction of a shape

Exercise 2A

1 a $\frac{1}{4}$ **b** $\frac{1}{3}$ **c** $\frac{5}{8}$ **d** $\frac{7}{12}$ **e** $\frac{4}{9}$

f $\frac{3}{10}$ **g** $\frac{3}{8}$ **h** $\frac{15}{16}$ **i** $\frac{5}{12}$ **j** $\frac{7}{18}$

k $\frac{4}{8}=\frac{1}{2}$ **l** $\frac{4}{12}=\frac{1}{3}$ **m** $\frac{6}{9}=\frac{2}{3}$

n $\frac{6}{10}=\frac{3}{5}$ **o** $\frac{4}{8}=\frac{1}{2}$ **p** $\frac{5}{64}$

2 Check students' diagrams.

3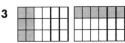

4 a g **b** i **c** neither **d** e
e neither **f** m **g** k **h** e

5 Fraction B is not $\frac{1}{3}$. Fraction C does not have a numerator of 4.

6 $\frac{1}{2}$

2.2 Adding and subtracting simple fractions

Exercise 2B

1 a $\frac{3}{4}$ **b** $\frac{4}{8}=\frac{1}{2}$ **c** $\frac{3}{5}$ **d** $\frac{8}{10}=\frac{4}{5}$

e $\frac{2}{3}$ **f** $\frac{5}{7}$ **g** $\frac{7}{9}$ **h** $\frac{5}{6}$ **i** $\frac{4}{5}$

j $\frac{7}{8}$ **k** $\frac{5}{10}=\frac{1}{2}$ **l** $\frac{5}{7}$ **m** $\frac{4}{5}$

n $\frac{5}{6}$ **o** $\frac{5}{9}$ **p** $\frac{7}{11}$

2 a $\frac{2}{4}=\frac{1}{2}$ **b** $\frac{3}{5}$ **c** $\frac{3}{8}$ **d** $\frac{3}{10}$

e $\frac{1}{3}$ **f** $\frac{4}{6}=\frac{2}{3}$ **g** $\frac{3}{7}$ **h** $\frac{5}{9}$

i $\frac{1}{5}$ **j** $\frac{3}{7}$ **k** $\frac{3}{9}=\frac{1}{3}$ **l** $\frac{6}{10}=\frac{3}{5}$

m $\frac{3}{6}=\frac{1}{2}$ **n** $\frac{2}{8}=\frac{1}{4}$ **o** $\frac{2}{11}$

p $\frac{4}{10}=\frac{2}{5}$

3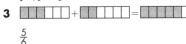
$\frac{5}{6}$

4 a ▢ **b** ▢

c i $\frac{3}{4}$ **ii** $\frac{1}{4}$

5 a ▭ **b** ▭

c i $\frac{6}{10}=\frac{3}{5}$ **ii** $\frac{8}{10}=\frac{4}{5}$

iii $\frac{7}{10}$

6 Start with five-fifths, remove four-fifths, put back two-fifths so $\frac{5}{5}-\frac{4}{5}+\frac{2}{5}=\frac{3}{5}$

7 $\frac{1}{6}$ (40 out of the 240 seats)

8 $\frac{1}{8}$ (4 of the 32 students)

9 a No, would sell 18 snacks per journey, i.e. 36 for two journeys

b $\frac{18}{30}$ or $\frac{3}{5}$

2.3 Recognise equivalent fractions, using diagrams

Exercise 2C

1 a $\frac{4}{24}$ **b** $\frac{8}{24}$ **c** $\frac{3}{24}$ **d** $\frac{16}{24}$ **e** $\frac{20}{24}$

f $\frac{18}{24}$ **g** $\frac{9}{24}$ **h** $\frac{15}{24}$ **i** $\frac{21}{24}$ **j** $\frac{12}{24}$

2 a $\frac{11}{24}$ **b** $\frac{9}{24}$ **c** $\frac{7}{24}$ **d** $\frac{19}{24}$ **e** $\frac{23}{24}$

f $\frac{23}{24}$ **g** $\frac{21}{24}$ **h** $\frac{22}{24}$ **i** $\frac{19}{24}$ **j** $\frac{23}{24}$

3 a $\frac{5}{20}$ **b** $\frac{4}{20}$ **c** $\frac{15}{20}$ **d** $\frac{16}{20}$ **e** $\frac{2}{20}$

f $\frac{10}{20}$ **g** $\frac{12}{20}$ **h** $\frac{8}{20}$ **i** $\frac{14}{20}$ **j** $\frac{6}{20}$

4 a $\frac{9}{20}$ **b** $\frac{14}{20}$ **c** $\frac{11}{20}$ **d** $\frac{19}{20}$ **e** $\frac{19}{20}$

5 a $\frac{2}{6}$ **b** $\frac{2}{3}$ **c** none **d** $\frac{6}{8}$

6 a $\frac{4}{10}, \frac{8}{20}, \frac{10}{25}$ **b** for example $\frac{12}{30}$

7 a

×	2	3	4	5
3	6	9	12	15
4	8	12	16	20

b $\frac{6}{8}, \frac{9}{12}, \frac{12}{16}, \frac{15}{20}$

8 a $\frac{1}{12}$

b i $\frac{7}{12}$ **ii** $\frac{9}{12}$ (or $\frac{3}{4}$) **iii** $\frac{11}{12}$

iv $\frac{9}{12}$ (or $\frac{3}{4}$) **v** $\frac{7}{12}$

2.4 Equivalent fractions and simplifying fractions by cancelling

Exercise 2D

1 a $\frac{8}{20}$ **b** $\frac{3}{12}$ **c** $\frac{15}{40}$ **d** $\frac{12}{15}$ **e** $\frac{15}{18}$

f $\frac{12}{28}$ **g** × 2, $\frac{6}{20}$ **h** × 3, $\frac{3}{9}$

i × 4, $\frac{12}{20}$ **j** × 6, $\frac{12}{18}$

k $\times 3$, $\frac{9}{12}$ **l** $\times 5$, $\frac{25}{40}$

m $\times 2$, $\frac{14}{20}$ **n** $\times 4$, $\frac{4}{24}$ **o** $\times 5$, $\frac{15}{40}$

2 a $\frac{1}{2} = \frac{2}{4} = \frac{3}{6} = \frac{4}{8} = \frac{5}{10} = \frac{6}{12}$

b $\frac{1}{3} = \frac{2}{6} = \frac{3}{9} = \frac{4}{12} = \frac{5}{15} = \frac{6}{18}$

c $\frac{3}{4} = \frac{6}{8} = \frac{9}{12} = \frac{12}{16} = \frac{15}{20} = \frac{18}{24}$

d $\frac{2}{5} = \frac{4}{10} = \frac{6}{15} = \frac{8}{20} = \frac{10}{25} = \frac{12}{30}$

e $\frac{3}{7} = \frac{6}{14} = \frac{9}{21} = \frac{12}{28} = \frac{15}{35} = \frac{18}{42}$

3 a $\frac{2}{3}$ **b** $\frac{4}{5}$ **c** $\frac{5}{7}$ **d** $\div 6$, $\frac{2}{3}$

e $25 \div 4$, $\frac{3}{5}$ **f** $\div 3$, $\frac{7}{10}$

4 a 32 **b** $\frac{1}{2}$ **c** $\frac{5}{6}$

5 a $\frac{2}{3}$ **b** $\frac{1}{3}$ **c** $\frac{2}{3}$ **d** $\frac{3}{4}$ **e** $\frac{1}{3}$

f $\frac{1}{2}$ **g** $\frac{7}{8}$ **h** $\frac{4}{5}$ **i** $\frac{1}{2}$ **j** $\frac{1}{4}$

k $\frac{4}{5}$ **l** $\frac{5}{7}$ **m** $\frac{5}{7}$ **n** $\frac{2}{3}$ **o** $\frac{2}{5}$

p $\frac{2}{5}$ **q** $\frac{1}{3}$ **r** $\frac{7}{10}$ **s** $\frac{1}{4}$

t $\frac{3}{2} = 1\frac{1}{2}$ **u** $\frac{2}{3}$ **v** $\frac{2}{3}$ **w** $\frac{3}{4}$

x $\frac{3}{2} = 1\frac{1}{2}$ **y** $\frac{7}{2} = 3\frac{1}{2}$

6 a $\frac{1}{2}, \frac{2}{3}, \frac{5}{6}$ **b** $\frac{1}{2}, \frac{5}{8}, \frac{3}{4}$ **c** $\frac{2}{5}, \frac{1}{2}, \frac{7}{10}$

d $\frac{7}{12}, \frac{2}{3}, \frac{3}{4}$ **e** $\frac{1}{6}, \frac{1}{4}, \frac{1}{3}$ **f** $\frac{3}{4}, \frac{4}{5}, \frac{9}{10}$

g $\frac{7}{10}, \frac{4}{5}, \frac{5}{6}$ **h** $\frac{3}{10}, \frac{1}{3}, \frac{2}{5}$

7 a $\frac{1}{3} + \frac{1}{4} = \frac{4}{12} + \frac{3}{12} = \frac{7}{12}$

Explanations may involve ruling out other combinations.

b $\frac{1}{2}$ as the smallest denominator is

the biggest unit fraction.
Diagrams may be used but must be based on equal sized area.

8 a $\frac{1}{5}$ **b** $\frac{1}{77}$

9 a $\frac{3}{8}$ **b** $\frac{1}{2}$ **c** $\frac{5}{16}$

2.5 Improper fractions and mixed numbers

Exercise 2E

1 a $2\frac{1}{3}$ **b** $2\frac{2}{3}$ **c** $2\frac{1}{4}$ **d** $1\frac{3}{7}$ **e** $2\frac{2}{5}$

f $1\frac{2}{5}$ **g** $2\frac{2}{3}$ **h** $3\frac{3}{4}$ **i** $3\frac{1}{3}$ **j** $2\frac{1}{7}$

k $2\frac{5}{6}$ **l** $3\frac{3}{5}$ **m** $4\frac{3}{4}$ **n** $3\frac{1}{7}$ **o** $1\frac{3}{11}$

p $1\frac{1}{11}$ **q** $5\frac{3}{7}$ **r** $2\frac{5}{7}$ **s** $5\frac{5}{7}$ **t** $8\frac{2}{5}$

u $2\frac{1}{10}$ **v** $2\frac{1}{2}$ **w** $1\frac{2}{3}$ **x** $3\frac{1}{8}$ **y** $2\frac{3}{10}$

z $2\frac{1}{11}$

2 a $\frac{10}{3}$ **b** $\frac{35}{6}$ **c** $\frac{9}{5}$ **d** $\frac{37}{7}$ **e** $\frac{41}{10}$

f $\frac{17}{3}$ **g** $\frac{5}{2}$ **h** $\frac{13}{4}$ **i** $\frac{43}{6}$ **j** $\frac{29}{8}$

k $\frac{19}{3}$ **l** $\frac{89}{9}$ **m** $\frac{59}{5}$ **n** $\frac{16}{5}$ **o** $\frac{35}{8}$

p $\frac{28}{9}$ **q** $\frac{26}{5}$ **r** $\frac{11}{4}$ **s** $\frac{30}{7}$ **t** $\frac{49}{6}$

u $\frac{26}{9}$ **v** $\frac{37}{6}$ **w** $\frac{61}{5}$ **x** $\frac{13}{8}$ **y** $\frac{71}{10}$

z $\frac{73}{9}$

3 Students check their own answers.

4 $\frac{27}{4} = 6\frac{3}{4}$, $\frac{31}{5} = 6\frac{1}{5}$, $\frac{13}{2} = 6\frac{1}{2}$, so $\frac{27}{4}$ is

the biggest since $\frac{1}{5}$ is less than $\frac{1}{2}$

and $\frac{3}{4}$ is greater than $\frac{1}{2}$

5 Any mixed number which is between
7.7272... and 7.9. For example $7\frac{4}{5}$

6 Any mixed number which is between
5.8181... and 5.875. For example $5\frac{16}{19}$

Note that adding the numerators of two fractions and then adding the denominators always gives an answer in between the two fractions.

7 $\frac{9}{4}$ or $\frac{25}{9}$

2.6 Adding and subtracting fractions with the same denominator

Exercise 2F

1 a $\frac{5}{7}$ **b** $\frac{7}{9}$ **c** $\frac{4}{5}$ **d** $\frac{6}{7}$ **e** $\frac{7}{11}$

f $\frac{7}{9}$ **g** $\frac{10}{13}$ **h** $\frac{10}{11}$

2 a $\frac{3}{7}$ **b** $\frac{1}{9}$ **c** $\frac{4}{11}$ **d** $\frac{7}{13}$ **e** $\frac{4}{7}$

f $\frac{1}{5}$ **g** $\frac{4}{9}$ **h** $\frac{3}{11}$

3 a $\frac{6}{8} = \frac{3}{4}$ **b** $\frac{4}{10} = \frac{2}{5}$ **c** $\frac{6}{9} = \frac{2}{3}$

d $\frac{2}{4} = \frac{1}{2}$ **e** $\frac{6}{10} = \frac{3}{5}$ **f** $\frac{6}{12} = \frac{1}{2}$

g $\frac{8}{16} = \frac{1}{2}$ **h** $\frac{10}{16} = \frac{5}{8}$

4 a $\frac{4}{8} = \frac{1}{2}$ **b** $\frac{4}{10} = \frac{2}{5}$ **c** $\frac{4}{6} = \frac{2}{3}$

d $\frac{8}{10} = \frac{4}{5}$ **e** $\frac{6}{12} = \frac{1}{2}$ **f** $\frac{2}{8} = \frac{1}{4}$

g $\frac{2}{16} = \frac{1}{8}$ **h** $\frac{6}{18} = \frac{1}{3}$

5 a $\frac{12}{10} = \frac{6}{5} = 1\frac{1}{5}$ **b** $\frac{9}{8} = 1\frac{1}{8}$

c $\frac{9}{8} = 1\frac{1}{8}$ **d** $\frac{13}{8} = 1\frac{5}{8}$

e $\frac{11}{8} = 1\frac{3}{8}$ **f** $\frac{7}{6} = 1\frac{1}{6}$

g $\frac{9}{6} = \frac{3}{2} = 1\frac{1}{2}$ **h** $\frac{5}{4} = 1\frac{1}{4}$

6 a $\frac{10}{8} = \frac{5}{4} = 1\frac{1}{4}$ **b** $\frac{6}{4} = \frac{3}{2} = 1\frac{1}{2}$

c $\frac{5}{5} = 1$ **d** $\frac{16}{10} = \frac{8}{5} = 1\frac{3}{5}$

e $\frac{10}{8} = \frac{5}{4} = 1\frac{1}{4}$ **f** $\frac{22}{16} = \frac{11}{8} = 1\frac{3}{8}$

g $\frac{16}{12} = \frac{8}{6} = \frac{4}{3} = 1\frac{1}{3}$

h $\frac{18}{16} = \frac{9}{8} = 1\frac{1}{8}$

7 a $\frac{5}{8}$ **b** $\frac{5}{10} = \frac{1}{2}$ **c** $\frac{1}{4}$ **d** $\frac{3}{8}$

e $\frac{1}{4}$ **f** $\frac{3}{8}$ **g** $\frac{4}{10} = \frac{2}{5}$ **h** $\frac{5}{16}$

8 $\frac{1}{8}$

9 Ayesha

10 $\frac{4}{6} = \frac{2}{3}$

11 $\frac{3}{8}$

12 $\frac{2}{5}$

13 $\frac{3}{8}$

14 $\frac{4}{11}$

15 $\frac{1}{6}$

16 $\frac{5}{8}$

17 Paul, as $\frac{2}{3}$ is bigger than $\frac{5}{8}$

2.7   Finding a fraction of a quantity

Exercise 2G

1 a 18 **b** 10 **c** 18 **d** 28
e 15 **f** 18 **g** 48 **h** 45

2 a £1800 **b** 128 g **c** 160 kg
d £116 **e** 65 litres **f** 90 min
g 292 days **h** 21 h **i** 18 h
j 2370 miles

3 a $\frac{5}{8}$ of 40 = 25 **b** $\frac{3}{4}$ of 280 = 210

c $\frac{4}{5}$ of 70 = 56 **d** $\frac{5}{6}$ of 72 = 60

e $\frac{3}{5}$ of 95 = 57 **f** $\frac{3}{4}$ of 340 = 255

4 £6080

5 £31 500

6 13 080

7 52 kg

8 a 856 **b** 187 675

9 a £50 **b** £550

10 a 180 g **b** 900 g

11 a £120 **b** £240

12 Lion Autos

13 Offer B

2.8   Multiplying and dividing fractions

Exercise 2H

1 a $\frac{1}{6}$ **b** $\frac{1}{20}$ **c** $\frac{2}{9}$ **d** $\frac{1}{6}$ **e** $\frac{1}{4}$ **f** $\frac{2}{5}$

g $\frac{1}{2}$ **h** $\frac{1}{2}$ **i** $\frac{3}{14}$ **j** $\frac{35}{48}$ **k** $\frac{8}{15}$ **l** $\frac{21}{32}$

2 a 25 sheep **b** $\frac{1}{6}$

3 562 500

4 6 No one, they all got $\frac{1}{4}$

5 a $\frac{3}{4}$ **b** $1\frac{2}{5}$ **c** $1\frac{1}{15}$ **d** $1\frac{1}{14}$ **e** 4 **f** 4

g 5 **h** $1\frac{5}{7}$

6 18

7 a $2\frac{2}{15}$ **b** 38 **c** $1\frac{7}{8}$ **d** $\frac{9}{32}$

2.9   One quantity as a fraction of another

Exercise 2I

1 a $\frac{1}{3}$ **b** $\frac{1}{5}$ **c** $\frac{2}{5}$ **d** $\frac{5}{24}$ **e** $\frac{2}{5}$

f $\frac{1}{6}$ **g** $\frac{2}{7}$ **h** $\frac{1}{3}$

2 $\frac{3}{5}$

3 $\frac{12}{31}$

4 $\frac{7}{12}$

5 Jon saves $\frac{30}{90} = \frac{1}{3}$

Matt saves $\frac{35}{100}$ which is greater than $\frac{1}{3}$, so Matt saves the greater proportion of his earnings.

6 $\frac{13}{20} = \frac{65}{100}, \frac{16}{25} = \frac{64}{100}$, so first mark is better.

2.10   Rational numbers and reciprocals

Exercise 2J

1 a 0.5   **b** 0.$\dot{3}$ **c** 0.25
d 0.2   **e** 0.1$\dot{6}$ **f** 0.142 85$\dot{7}$
g 0.125   **h** 0.$\dot{1}$ **i** 0.$\dot{1}$
j 0.076 923

2 a i 0.571428571428571428571428...
   ii 0.714285714285714285714285
   iii 0.857142857142857142857142
b The recurring digits are all in the same sequence but they start in a different place each time.

3 a i 0.$\dot{4}$ **ii** 0.$\dot{2}$ **iii** 0.$\dot{1}$
b Halve the answers to get 1 ÷ 20 = 0.05 and 1 ÷ 20 = 0.05 and 1 ÷ 40 = 0.025

4 0.$\dot{1}$, 0.$\dot{2}$, 0.$\dot{3}$, 0.$\dot{4}$, 0.$\dot{5}$, 0.$\dot{6}$, 0.$\dot{7}$, 0.$\dot{8}$
The recurring digit is the numerator of the fraction.

5 0.0$\dot{9}$, 0.1$\dot{8}$, 0.2$\dot{7}$, 0.3$\dot{6}$, 0.4$\dot{5}$, 0.5$\dot{4}$, 0.6$\dot{3}$, 0.7$\dot{2}$, 0.8$\dot{1}$, 0.9$\dot{0}$
The recurring digits follow the nine times table.

6 $\frac{9}{22}$ = 0.40$\dot{9}$, $\frac{3}{7}$ = 0.$\dot{4}$28 57$\dot{1}$,

$\frac{16}{37}$ = 0.$\dot{4}$3$\dot{2}$, $\frac{4}{9}$ = 0.$\dot{4}$,

$\frac{5}{11}$ = 0.$\dot{4}$$\dot{5}$, $\frac{6}{13}$ = 0.$\dot{4}$61 53$\dot{8}$,

7 $\frac{7}{24}$ = $\frac{35}{120}$, $\frac{3}{10}$ = $\frac{36}{120}$, $\frac{19}{60}$ = $\frac{38}{120}$,

$\frac{2}{5}$ = $\frac{48}{120}$, $\frac{5}{12}$ = $\frac{50}{120}$

8 a $\frac{1}{8}$ **b** $\frac{17}{50}$ **c** $\frac{29}{40}$ **d** $\frac{5}{16}$

e $\frac{89}{100}$ **f** $\frac{1}{20}$ **g** 2$\frac{7}{20}$ **h** $\frac{7}{32}$

9 a 0.08$\dot{3}$ **b** 0.0625   **c** 0.05
d 0.04   **e** 0.02

10 a $\frac{4}{3}$ = 1$\frac{1}{3}$ **b** $\frac{6}{5}$ = 1$\frac{1}{5}$

c $\frac{5}{2}$ = 2$\frac{1}{2}$ **d** $\frac{10}{7}$ = 1$\frac{3}{7}$

e $\frac{20}{11}$ = 1$\frac{9}{11}$ **f** $\frac{15}{4}$ = 3$\frac{3}{4}$

11 a 0.75, 1.$\dot{3}$ **b** 0.8$\dot{3}$, 1.2
c 0.4, 2.5   **d** 0.7, 1.428 57$\dot{1}$
e 0.55, 1.8$\dot{1}$ **f** 0.2$\dot{6}$ 3.75

12 The answer is always 1.

13 1 ÷ 0 is infinite so there is no finite answer.

14 a 10 **b** 2
c The reciprocal of a reciprocal is always the original number.

15 The reciprocal of x is greater than the reciprocal of y.
For example, reciprocal of 2 is 0.5, reciprocal of 10 is 0.1.

Examination questions

1 $\frac{3}{10}$

2 a $\frac{2}{5}$ **b** 6 squares shaded **c** $\frac{8}{9}$ and $\frac{22}{32}$

3 $\frac{1}{5}$, $\frac{1}{3}$, $\frac{7}{10}$

4 77 acres

5 $\frac{1}{2}$

6 172 grams

7 £4.80

8 27 kg

9 a 70
b Cannot have half of an odd number for a whole number answer (175 ÷ 2 = 87.5)
c 1400

10 a 12   **b** $\frac{2}{3}$ of 40 is not a whole number

11 a $\frac{11}{35}$ **b** 1$\frac{11}{35}$

12 $\frac{1}{8}$

13 3$\frac{7}{8}$

14 660 grams

15 Smaller. The amount added ($\frac{1}{5}$ of the original) is smaller than the amount later taken away ($\frac{1}{5}$ of 1$\frac{1}{5}$ of the original)
e.g. 100 × 1$\frac{1}{5}$ = 120, 120 × $\frac{4}{5}$ = 96, 96 < 100

16 a i $\frac{1}{5}$ or 0.2   **ii** $\frac{5}{4}$ or 1$\frac{1}{4}$ or 1.25
b i 0.5555 ... or 0.$\dot{5}$ **ii** 0.6666 ... or 0.$\dot{6}$

17 a 0.8   **b** Any example such as the reciprocal of $\frac{1}{2}$

Answers to Chapter 3

3.1   Introduction to negative numbers

Activity

1 a 860 feet   **b** 725 feet   **c** 75 feet
d 475 feet   **e** 1100 feet   **f** 575 feet
g 425 feet   **h** 310 feet   **i** 700 feet
j 1010 feet

2 480 feet

3 1180 feet

4 Closed gate/Collapsed tunnel and Dead Man's seam/C seam

5 910 feet

6 Dead Man's seam/D seam and B seam/C seam

7 Collapsed tunnel/North gate

3.1 Introduction to negative numbers

Exercise 3A

1 **a** 0 °C **b** 5 °C **c** −2 °C
 d −5 °C **e** −1 °C

2 **a** 11 degrees **b** 9 degrees

3 8 degrees

4

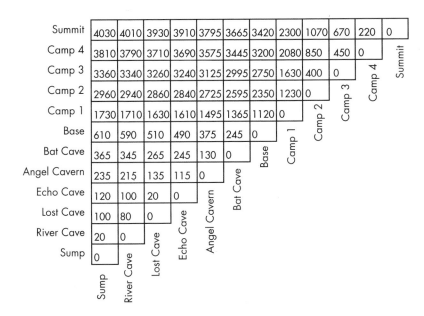

	Sump	River Cave	Lost Cave	Echo Cave	Angel Cavern	Bat Cave	Base	Camp 1	Camp 2	Camp 3	Camp 4	Summit
Summit	4030	4010	3930	3910	3795	3665	3420	2300	1070	670	220	0
Camp 4	3810	3790	3710	3690	3575	3445	3200	2080	850	450	0	
Camp 3	3360	3340	3260	3240	3125	2995	2750	1630	400	0		
Camp 2	2960	2940	2860	2840	2725	2595	2350	1230	0			
Camp 1	1730	1710	1630	1610	1495	1365	1120	0				
Base	610	590	510	490	375	245	0					
Bat Cave	365	345	265	245	130	0						
Angel Cavern	235	215	135	115	0							
Echo Cave	120	100	20	0								
Lost Cave	100	80	0									
River Cave	20	0										
Sump	0											

3.2 Everyday use of negative numbers

Exercise 3B

1 −£5

2 −£9

3 Profit

4 −200 m

5 −50 m

6 Above

7 −3 h

8 −5 h

9 After

10 −2 °C

11 −8 °C

12 Above

13 −70 km

14 −200 km

15 North

16 +5 m

17 −5 mph

18 −2

19 **a** You owe the bank £89.72.
 b You are paying money out of the account.
 c You are paying money into the account.

20 **a** −11 °C **b** 6 degrees

21 **a** −8 **b** 7 **c** 15

22 9 days

23 1.54am

3.3 The number line

Exercise 3C

1 Many different answers to each part

2 Many different answers to each part

3 **a** Is smaller than **b** is bigger than **c** Is smaller than
d Is smaller than **e** is bigger than **f** Is smaller than
g Is smaller than **h** is bigger than **i** is bigger than
j Is smaller than **k** Is smaller than **l** is bigger than

4 **a** Is smaller than **b** Is smaller than **c** Is smaller than
d is bigger than **e** Is smaller than **f** Is smaller than

5 **a** < **b** > **c** < **d** < **e** < **f** >
g < **h** > **i** > **j** > **k** < **l** <
m > **n** > **o** < **p** >

6 **a**

-5	-4	-3	-2	-1	0	1	2	3	4	5

b

-25	-20	-15	-10	-5	0	5	10	15	20	25

c

-10	-8	-6	-4	-2	0	2	4	6	8	10

d

-50	-40	-30	-20	-10	0	10	20	30	40	50

e

-15	-12	-9	-6	-3	0	3	6	9	12	15

f

-20	-16	-12	-8	-4	0	4	8	12	16	20

g

$-2\frac{1}{2}$	-2	$-1\frac{1}{2}$	-1	$-\frac{1}{2}$	0	$\frac{1}{2}$	1	$1\frac{1}{2}$	2	$2\frac{1}{2}$

h

-100	-80	-60	-40	-20	0	20	40	60	80	100

i

-250	-200	-150	-100	-50	0	50	100	150	200	250

7 6 °C   −2 °C   −4 °C   2 °C

8

$-4\frac{1}{2}$					$-\frac{1}{4}$				$+3\frac{3}{4}$			
-6	-5	-4	-3	-2	-1	0	1	2	3	4	5	6

3.4 Arithmetic with negative numbers

Exercise 3D

1 **a** −2° **b** −3° **c** −2° **d** −3° **e** −2° **f** −3°
g 3 **h** 3 **i** −1 **j** −1 **k** 2 **l** −3
m −4 **n** −6 **o** −6 **p** −1 **q** −5 **r** −4
s 4 **t** −1 **u** −5 **v** −4 **w** −5 **x** −5

2 **a** −4 **b** −4 **c** −10 **d** 2 **e** 8 **f** −5
g 2 **h** 5 **i** −7 **j** −12 **k** 13 **l** 25
m −32 **n** −30 **o** −5 **p** −8 **q** −12 **r** 10
s −36 **t** −14 **u** 41 **v** 12 **w** −40 **x** −101

3 **a** 6 **b** −5 **c** 6 **d** −1 **e** −2 **f** −6
g −6 **h** −2 **i** 3 **j** 0 **k** −7 **l** −6
m 8 **n** 1 **o** −9 **p** −9 **q** −5 **r** −80
s −7 **t** −1 **u** −47

4 Students' own check

5 **a** 7 degrees **b** −6 °C

6 **a** 2 − 8
b 2 + 5 − 8 or 2 + 4 − 7 or 8 − 4 − 5 or 8 − 2 − 7
or 5 − 4 − 2
c 2 − 5 − 7 − 8 **d** 2 + 5 − 4 − 7 − 8

7 500 ft

Exercise 3E

1 **a** 6 **b** 7 **c** 8 **d** 6 **e** 8 **f** 10
g 2 **h** −3 **i** 1 **j** 2 **k** −1 **l** −7
m 2 **n** −3 **o** 1 **p** −5 **q** 3 **r** −4
s −3 **t** −8 **u** −10 **v** −9 **w** −4 **x** −9

2 **a** −8 **b** −10 **c** −11 **d** −3 **e** 2 **f** −5
g 1 **h** 4 **i** 7 **j** −8 **k** −5 **l** −11
m 11 **n** 6 **o** 8 **p** 8 **q** −2 **r** −1
s −9 **t** −5 **u** 5 **v** −9 **w** 8 **x** 0

3 **a** 3 °C **b** 0 °C **c** −3 °C **d** −5 °C **e** −11 °C

4 **a** 10 degrees Celsius **b** 7 degrees Celsius
c 9 degrees Celsius

5 −9, −6, −5, −1, 1, 2, 3, 8

6 **a** −3 **b** −4 **c** −2 **d** −7 **e** −14 **f** −6
g −12 **h** −10 **i** 4 **j** −4 **k** 14 **l** 11
m −4 **n** −1 **o** −10 **p** −5 **q** −3 **r** 5
s −4 **t** −8

7 **a** 2 **b** −3 **c** −5 **d** −7 **e** −10 **f** −20

8 **a** 2 **b** 4 **c** −1 **d** −5 **e** −11 **f** 8

9 **a** 13 **b** 2 **c** 5 **d** 4 **e** 11 **f** −2

10 **a** −10 **b** −5 **c** −2 **d** 4 **e** 7 **f** −4

11 Check student's answers

12 Check student's answers

13 **a** −5 **b** 6 **c** 0 **d** 2 **e** 13 **f** 0
g −6 **h** −2 **i** 212 **j** 5 **k** 3 **l** 3
m −67 **n** 7 **o** 25

14 **a** −1, 0, 1, 2, 3 **b** −6, −5, −4, −3, −2
c −3, −2, −1, 0, 1 **d** −8, −7, −6, −5, −4
e −9, −8, −7, −6, −5 **f** 3, 4, 5, 6, 7
g −12, −11, −10, −9, −8 **h** −16, −15, −14, −13, −12
i −2, −1, 0, 1, 2, 3; −4, −3, −2, −1, 0, 1
j −12, −11, −10, −9, −8, −7; −14, −13, −12, −11, −10, −9
k −2, −1, 0, 1, 2, 3; 0, 1, 2, 3, 4, 5
l −8, −7, −6, −5, −4, −3, −2; −5, −4, −3, −2, −1, 0, 1
m −10, −9, −8, −7, −6, −5, −4; −1, 0, 1, 2, 3, 4, 5
n 3, 4, 5, 6, 7, 8, 9; −5, −4, −3, −2, −1, 0, 1

15 **a** −4 **b** 3 **c** 4 **d** −6 **e** 7 **f** 2
g 7 **h** −6 **i** −7 **j** 0 **k** 0 **l** −6
m −7 **n** −9 **o** 4 **p** 0 **q** 5 **r** 0
s 10 **t** −5 **u** 3 **v** −3 **w** −9 **x** 0
y −3 **z** −3

16 **a** +6 + +5 = 11 **b** +6 + −9 = −3
c +6 − −9 = 15 **d** +6 − +5 = 1

17 a +5 + +7 − −9 = +21   **b** +5 + −9 − +7 = −11
   c +7 + −7, +4 + −4

18 It may not come on as the thermometer inaccuracy might be between 0° and 2° or 2° and 4°

19 − 1 and 6

Exercise 3F

1 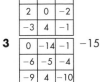 −12

4
2	−12	1
−4	−3	−2
−7	6	−8
−9

2 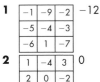 0

5
−3	−6	−9
−12	−6	0
−3	−6	−9
−18

3
0	−14	−1
−6	−5	−4
−9	4	−10
−15

6
−2	−18	−1
−6	−7	−8
−13	4	−12
−21

7
−4	−12	−5
−8	−7	−6
−9	−2	−10
−21

10
−8	−1	−3	−14
−8	−9	−7	−2
−11	−6	−4	−5
1	−10	−12	−5
−26

8
2	1	−3
−5	0	5
3	−1	−2
0

9
−2	−10	−3
−6	−5	−4
−7	0	−8
−15

11
−7	5	2	−16
−6	−8	−5	3
−11	−3	0	−2
8	−10	−13	−1
−16

Examination questions

1 a 2580   **b** 295   **c** −4

2 a −9 °C   **b** 5 degrees   **c** −4 °C

3 a Aberdeen   **b** 6 degrees   **c** Bristol, Leeds
   d Aberdeen, 18 degrees

4
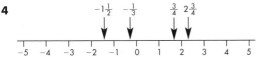

5 a −5 °C, −1 °C, 2 °C   **b** 7 degrees

6 a 8 degrees   **b** −7 °C

7 a −2 °C   **b** 6 °C

8 a i −15 °C   **ii** 12 °C   **b** −6 °C

9 a 2 °C   **b** −7 °C   **c** −3 °C

10 a 28 degrees
   b i Any value above −58 °C
     ii Any value below −86 °C but above −273 °C

Answers to Chapter 4

4.1 Equivalent percentages, fractions and decimals

Exercise 4A

1 a $\frac{2}{25}$ **b** $\frac{1}{2}$ **c** $\frac{1}{4}$ **d** $\frac{7}{20}$ **e** $\frac{9}{10}$ **f** $\frac{3}{4}$

2 a 0.27   **b** 0.85   **c** 0.13   **d** 0.06   **e** 0.8   **f** 0.32

3 a $\frac{3}{25}$ **b** $\frac{2}{5}$ **c** $\frac{9}{20}$ **d** $\frac{17}{25}$ **e** $\frac{1}{4}$ **f** $\frac{5}{8}$

4 a 29%   **b** 55%   **c** 3%   **d** 16%   **e** 60%   **f** 125%

5 a 28%   **b** 30%   **c** 95%   **d** 34%   **e** 27.5%   **f** 87.5%

6 a 0.6   **b** 0.075   **c** 0.76   **d** 0.3125   **e** 0.05   **f** 0.125

7 150

8 none

9 20

10 a 77%   **b** 39%   **c** 63%

11 27%

12 61.5%

13 a 50%   **b** 20%   **c** 80%

14 12.5%, 25%, 37.5%, 50%, 75%

15 a 20%   **b** 25%   **c** 75%   **d** 45%   **e** 14%   **f** 50%
   g 60%   **h** 17.5%   **i** 55%   **j** 130%

16 a 33.3%   **b** 16.7%   **c** 66.7%   **d** 83.3%   **e** 28.6%   **f** 78.3%
   g 68.9%   **h** 88.9%   **i** 81.1%   **j** 20.9%

17 a 7%   **b** 80%   **c** 66%   **d** 25%   **e** 54.5%   **f** 82%
   g 30%   **h** 89.1%   **i** 120%   **j** 278%

18 a $\frac{3}{5}$ **b** 0.6   **c** 60%

19 a 63%, 83%, 39%, 62%, 77%   **b** English

20 6.7%

21 25.5%

22 34%, 0.34, $\frac{17}{50}$; 85%, 0.85, $\frac{17}{20}$; 7.5%, 0.075, $\frac{3}{40}$

23 $\frac{9}{10}$ or 90%

4.2 Calculating a percentage of a quantity

Exercise 4B

1 a 0.88   **b** 0.3   **c** 0.25   **d** 0.08   **e** 1.15

2 a 78%   **b** 40%   **c** 75%   **d** 5%   **e** 110%

3 **a** £45 **b** £6.30 **c** 128.8 kg
d 1.125 kg **e** 1.08 h **f** 37.8 cm
g £0.12 **h** 2.94 m **i** £7.60
j 33.88 min **k** 136 kg **l** £162

4 48

5 £2410

6 **a** 86% **b** 215

7 8520

8 287

9 Each team: 54 000, referees: 900, other teams: 9000 (100 to each, FA: 18 000, celebrities: 8100

10 990

11 Mon: 816, Tue: 833, Wed: 850, Thu: 799, Fri: 748

12 **a** £3.25 **b** 2.21 kg **c** £562.80
d £6.51 **e** 42.93 m **f** £24

13 480 cm^3 nitrogen, 120 cm^3 oxygen

14 13

15 £270

16 More this year as it was 3% of a higher amount than last year.

4.3 Increasing or decreasing quantities by a percentage

Exercise 4C

1 **a** 1.1 **b** 1.03 **c** 1.2 **d** 1.07 **e** 1.12

2 **a** £62.40 **b** 12.96 kg **c** 472.5 g
d 599.5 m **e** £38.08 **f** £90
g 391 kg **h** 824.1 cm **i** 253.5 g
j £143.50 **k** 736 m **l** £30.24

3 £29 425

4 1 690 200

5 **a** Bob: £17 325, Anne: £18 165, Jean: £20 475, Brian: £26 565
b 5% of different amounts is not a fixed amount. The more pay to start with, the more the increase (5%) will be.

6 £83.05

7 193 800

8 575 g
9 918

10 60

11 TV: £287.88, microwave: £84.60, CD: £135.13, stereo: £34.66

12 £20

Exercise 4D

1 **a** 0.92 **b** 0.85 **c** 0.75 **d** 0.91 **e** 0.88

2 **a** £9.40 **b** 23 kg **c** 212.4 g
d 339.5 m **e** £4.90 **f** 39.6 m
g 731 m **h** 83.52 g **i** 360 cm
j 117 min **k** 81.7 kg **l** £37.70

3 £5525

4 **a** 52.8 kg **b** 66 kg **c** 45.76 kg

5 Mr Speed: £176, Mrs Speed: £297.50, James: £341, John: £562.50

6 448

7 705

8 £18 975

9 **a** 66.5 mph **b** 73.5 mph

10 £16.72, £22.88

11 **a** 524.8 units
b Less gas since 18% of the smaller amount of 524.8 units (94.464 units) is less than 18% of 640 units (115.2 units). I use 619.264 units now.

12 TV £222.31, DVD player £169.20

13 10% off £50 is £45, 10% off £45 is £40.50; 20% off £50 is £40

4.4 Expressing one quantity as a percentage of another

Exercise 4E

1 **a** 25% **b** 60.6% **c** 46.3% **d** 12.5% **e** 41.7% **f** 60%
g 20.8% **h** 10% **i** 1.9% **j** 8.3% **k** 45.5% **l** 10.5%

2 32%

3 6.5%

4 33.7%

5 **a** 49.2% **b** 64.5% **c** 10.6%

6 17.9%

7 4.9%

8 90.5%

9 **a** Brit Com: 20.9%, USA: 26.5%, France: 10.3%, Other 42.3%
b Total 100%, all imports
10 Calum 41.7%, Stacey 42.9%, Stacey has greater percentage increase.

11 Takings £144.94, cost wholesale £108. Percentage profit = 34.2%, so not achieved target.

Exercise 4F

1 a 0.6, 60%   **b** $\frac{7}{10}$, 70%   **c** $\frac{11}{20}$, 0.55

2 a £10.20   **b** 48 kg   **c** £1.26

3 a 56%   **b** 68%   **c** 37.5%

4 a 276   **b** 3204

5 a 20%   **b** 30%   **c** £13.20

6 a £6400   **b** £5440

7 a 70.4 kg   **b** iii

4.5   Ratio

Exercise 4G

1 a 1 : 3   **b** 3 : 4   **c** 2 : 3   **d** 2 : 3   **e** 2 : 5   **f** 2 : 5
g 5 : 8   **h** 25 : 6   **i** 3 : 2   **j** 8 : 3   **k** 7 : 3   **l** 5 : 2
m 1 : 6   **n** 3 : 8   **o** 5 : 3   **p** 4 : 5

2 a 1 : 3   **b** 3 : 2   **c** 5 : 12   **d** 8 : 1   **e** 17 : 15   **f** 25 : 7
g 4 : 1   **h** 5 : 6   **i** 1 : 24   **j** 48 : 1   **k** 5 : 2   **l** 3 : 14
m 2 : 1   **n** 3 : 10   **o** 31 : 200   **p** 5 : 8

3 $\frac{7}{10}$

4 $\frac{10}{25} = \frac{2}{5}$

5 a $\frac{2}{5}$ **b** $\frac{3}{5}$

6 a $\frac{7}{10}$ **b** $\frac{3}{10}$

7 Amy $\frac{3}{5}$, Katie $\frac{2}{5}$

8 Fruit crush $\frac{5}{32}$, lemonade $\frac{27}{32}$

9 $13\frac{1}{2}$ litres

10 a $\frac{1}{2}$ **b** $\frac{7}{20}$ **c** $\frac{3}{20}$

11 James $\frac{1}{2}$, John $\frac{3}{10}$, Joseph $\frac{1}{5}$

12 sugar $\frac{5}{22}$, flour $\frac{3}{11}$, margarine $\frac{2}{11}$, fruit $\frac{7}{22}$

13 3 : 1

14 1 : 4

Exercise 4H

1 a 160 g, 240 g   **b** 80 kg, 200 kg   **c** 150, 350
d 950 m, 50 m   **e** 175 min, 125 min
f £20, £30, £50   **g** £36, £60, £144
h 50 g, 250 g, 300 g   **i** £1.40, £2, £1.60
j 120 kg, 72 kg, 8 kg

2 a 175   **b** 30%

3 a 40%   **b** 300 kg

4 21

5 a Mott: no, Wright: yes, Brennan: no, Smith: no, Kaye: yes
b For example: W26, H30; W31, H38; W33, H37

6 a 1 : 400 000   **b** 1 : 125 000   **c** 1 : 250 000
d 1 : 25 000   **e** 1 : 20 000   **f** 1 : 40 000
g 1 : 62 500   **h** 1 : 10 000   **i** 1 : 60 000

7 a 1 : 1 000 000   **b** 47 km   **c** 8 mm

8 a 1 : 250 000   **b** 2 km   **c** 4.8 cm

9 a 1 : 20 000   **b** 0.54 km   **c** 40 cm

10 a 1 : 1.6   **b** 1 : 3.25   **c** 1 : 1.125
d 1 : 1.44   **e** 1 : 5.4   **f** 1 : 1.5
g 1 : 4.8   **h** 1 : 42   **i** 1 : 1.25

Exercise 4I

1 a 3 : 2   **b** 32   **c** 80

2 1000 g

3 10 125

4 a 14 min   **b** 75 min

5 a 11 pages   **b** 32%

6 Kevin £2040, John £2720

7 a lemonade 20 litres, ginger 0.5 litres
b This one, one-thirteenth is greater than one-fiftieth.

8 100

9 40 cc

Examination questions

1 50%, $\frac{7}{10}$, 0.03

2 a i 0.4375   **ii** 0.27   **b** 0.095, $\frac{6}{10}$, 65%, 0.7

3 a £30   **b** £220

4 $\frac{3}{5}$ of £25 = £15 so is larger than 40% of £30 which is £12

5 £20

6 £141

7 50%

8 a £495   **b** £594

9 65 824

10 a £120   **b i** 220   **ii** 54p   **c** 1%

11 20% off £300 = £240, 10% off 240 = £216, 30% off 300 = £210

12 a 0.6   **b** £55.48   **c** 72%

Answers to Chapter 5

5.1   Frequency diagrams

Exercise 5A

1 a

Goals	0	1	2	3
Frequency	6	8	4	2

b 1 goal   **c** 22

2 a

Temperature (°C)	14–16	17–19	20–22	23–25	26–28
Frequency	5	10	8	5	2

b 17–19 °C
c Getting warmer in the first half and then getting cooler towards the end.

3 a Observation   **b** Sampling   **c** Observation
d Sampling   **e** Observation   **f** Experiment

4 a

Score	1	2	3	4	5	6
Frequency	5	6	6	6	3	4

b 30   **c** Yes, frequencies are similar.

5 a

Height (cm)	151–155	156–160	161–165	166–170	171–175	176–180	181–185	186–190
Frequency	2	5	5	7	5	4	3	1

b 166–170 cm   **c** Student's survey results.

6 various answers such as 1–10, 11–20, etc.
or 1–20, 21–40, 41–60

7 The ages 20 and 25 are in two different groups.

8 Student's survey results and frequency tables.

5.2   Statistical diagrams

Exercise 5B

1

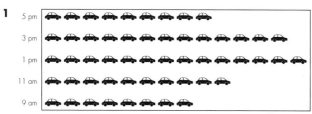

Key ⬗ = 5 cars

2

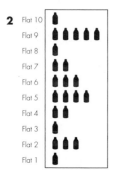

Key ▮ = 1 pint

3 a May 9 h, Jun 11 h, Jul 12 h, Aug 11 h, Sep 10 h
b July   **c** Visual impact, easy to understand.

4 a Simon   **b** £165
c Difficult to show fractions of a symbol.

5 a i 12   **ii** 6   **iii** 13
b Check students' pictograms.   **c** 63

6 Use a key of 17 students to one symbol.

7 There would be too many symbols to show.

8 a–c Student's pictograms.

9 The second teddy bear is much bigger than twice the size of the small teddy.

5.3   Bar charts

Exercise 5C

1 a Swimming   **b** 74
c For example: limited facilities
d No. It may not include people who are not fit.

2 a

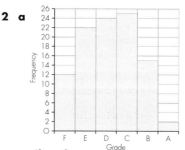

b $\frac{40}{100} = \frac{2}{5}$ **c** Easier to read the exact frequency.

3 a

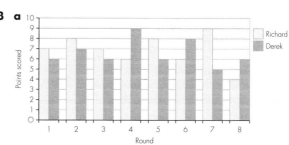

b Richard got more points overall, but Derek was more consistent.

4 a

Time (min)	1–10	11–20	21–30	31–40	41–50	51–60
Frequency	4	7	5	5	7	2

b

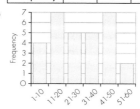

c Some live close to the school. Some live a good distance away and probably travel to school by bus.

5 a

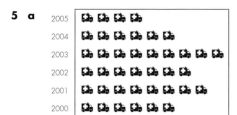

2005
2004
2003
2002
2001
2000

Key 🚚 = 1 accident

b

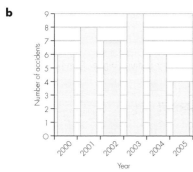

c Use the pictogram because an appropriate symbol makes more impact.

6 Yes. If you double the minimum temperature each time, it is very close to the maximum temperature.

7 The graphs do not start at zero.

8 Student's survey results and pictograms and bar charts.

9 Student's frequency tables and dual bar chart.

10 a 3   **b** 5   **c** 9
d The number of boys absent increases during the week but the number of girls absent decreases.

5.4 Line graphs

Exercise 5D

1 a Tuesday, 52p   **b** 2p   **c** Friday   **d** £90

2 a

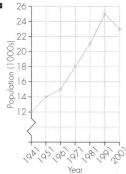

b about 16 500
c 1981 and 1991
d No; do not know the reason why the population started to decrease after 1991

3 a

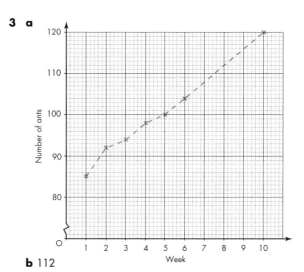

b 112

4 a

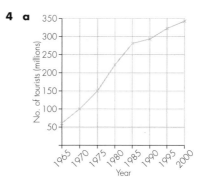

b About 410 million
c 1975 and 1980
d Student's explanation of trend.

5 a

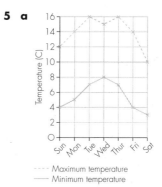

- - - - Maximum temperature
———— Minimum temperature

b 7 °C and 10 °C

6 From a graph, about 1040 g

7 All the temperatures were presumably higher than 20 degrees.

5.5 Stem-and-leaf diagrams

Exercise 5E

1 a 17 s   **b** 22 s   **c** 21 s

2 a 57   **b** 55   **c** 56   **d** 48
e Boys did better, because their marks are higher.

3 a 2 8 9
3 4 5 6 8 8 9
4 1 1 3 3 3 8 8
Key 4|3 represents 43 cm
b 48 cm   **c** 43 cm   **d** 20 cm

4 a 0 2 8 9 9 9
1 2 3 7 7 8
2 0 1 2 3
Key 1|2 represents 12 messages
b 23   **c** 9

5 All the data start with a 5 and there are only two digits.

Examination questions

1 a Correct tallies and frequencies -7,10,13
b Child
c 8 + 10 or 18 adults
15 (children) 18 adults
He is not correct

2 a Concert   **b** £200   **c** £75   **d** £50

3 a All 3 days completed
Wed 10, 16
Thurs 15, 12
Fri 14, 11
b No. On Wednesday orange juice was more popular.

4 a Both bars drawn 1, 10   **b** Corn Flakes
c Oven Chips   2 × 2.5 = 5

5 a 12   **b** $5\frac{1}{2}$ or 5.5   **c** 1   **d** 20 − 8 = 12

6 a 14   **b** Thursday
c 15 + 8 = 23   **d** 10 + 9 + 20 + 12 + 8 = 59
e No. On Wednesday more adults attend than children

7 a Week 3
b 14 students
c Valid reason, e.g. exam next week, last class

8 a Vertical scale does not start from zero
The horizontal scale is not linear
No £ sign or labelling on Sales or title or what it is about

9 a £15   **b** 2001−2

Answers to Chapter 6

6.1   The mode

Exercise 6A

1 a 4   **b** 48   **c** −1   **d** $\frac{1}{4}$ **e** no mode   **f** 3.21

2 a red   **b** sun   **c** β   **d** ★

3 a 32   **b** 6   **c** no
d no; boys generally take larger shoe sizes

4 a 5   **b** no; more than half the form got a higher mark

5 a
b 70   **c** 24
d cannot tell; know only that 9 households had between 0 and 4 e-mails
e 10–14

6 The mode will be the most popular item or brand sold in a shop.

7 a 28   **b i** brown   **ii** blue   **iii** brown
c Both students had blue eyes.

8 a May lose count.
b Put in a table, or arrange in order   **c** 4

6.2   The median

Exercise 6B

1 a 5   **b** 33   **c** $7\frac{1}{2}$ **d** 24   **e** $8\frac{1}{2}$ **f** 0
g 5.25

2 a £2.20   **b** £2.25   **c** median, because it is the central value

3 a 5   **b i** 15   **ii** 215   **iii** 10   **iv** 10

4 a 13, Ella   **b** 162 cm, Pat   **c** 40 kg, Elisa
d Ella, because she is closest to the 3 medians

5 a 12   **b** 13

6 a 21   **b** 16
c

Mark	12	13	14	15	16	17	18
Frequency	1	3	4	3	6	3	1

d 15

7 Answers will vary

8 a 22 s   **b** 25 s

9 a 56   **b** 48   **c** 49   **d** 45.5
e Boys have higher average and highest score.

10 12, 14, 14, 16, 20, 22, 24

11 2 | 4
3 | 8 8 9
4 | 1 2 5 7 7 7 8
5 | 0 3 5 8
6 | 0 3 4 4 8 9
7 | 1 3 5
8 | 9

key: 2 | 4 = 24 median = 53

12 a Possible answer: 11, 15, 21, 21 (one below or equal to 12 and three above or equal)
b Any four numbers higher than or equal to 12, and any two lower or equal
c Eight, all 4 or under

13 A median of £8 does not take into account the huge value of the £3000 so is in no way representative.

6.3 The mean

Exercise 6C

1 a 6   **b** 24   **c** 45   **d** 1.57   **e** 2

2 a 55.1   **b** 324.7   **c** 58.5   **d** 44.9   **e** 2.3

3 a 61   **b** 60   **c** 59   **d** Brian   **e** 2

4 42 min

5 a £200   **b** £260   **c** £278
d Median, because the extreme value of £480 is not taken into account

6 a 35   **b** 36

7 a 6
b 16; all the numbers and the mean are 10 more than those in part a
c i 56   **ii** 106   **iii** 7

8 Possible answers: Speed – Kath, James, John, Joseph; Roberts – Frank, James, Helen, Evie. Other answers are possible.

9 36

10 24

6.4 The range

Exercise 6D

1 a 7   **b** 26   **c** 5   **d** 2.4   **e** 7

2 a 5°, 3°, 2°, 7°, 3°
b Variable weather over England

3 a £31, £28, £33   **b** £8, £14, £4
c Not particularly consistent

4 a 82 and 83   **b** 20 and 12
c Fay, because her scores are more consistent

5 a 5 min and 4 min   **b** 9 min and 13 min
c Number 50, because times are more consistent

6 a Issac, Oliver, Andrew, Chloe, Lilla, Billy and Isambard
b 70 cm to 92 cm

7 a Teachers because they have a high mean and students could not have a range of 20.
b Year 11 students as the mean is 15–16 and the range is 1.

6.5 Which average to use

Exercise 6E

1 a i 29   **ii** 28   **iii** 27.1   **b** 14

2 a i Mode 3, median 4, mean 5   **ii** 6, 7, $7\frac{1}{2}$ **iii** 4, 6, 8
b i Mean: balanced data   **ii** Mode: 6 appears five times
iii Median: 28 is an extreme value

3 a Mode 73, median 76, mean 80
b The mean, because it is the highest average

4 a 150   **b** 20

5 a i 6   **ii** 16   **iii** 26   **iv** 56   **v** 96
b Units are the same
c i 136   **ii** 576   **iii** 435   **iv** 856
d i 5.6   **ii** 15.6   **iii** 25.6   **iv** 55.6   **v** 95.6

6 a Mean   **b** Median   **c** Mode
d Median   **e** Mode   **f** Mean

7 No. Mode is 31, median is 31, and mean is $31\frac{1}{2}$

8 a i £20 000   **ii** £28 000   **iii** £34 000
b i The 6% rise, because it gives a greater increase in salary for the higher paid employees.
ii 6% increase: £21 200, £29 680, £36 040;
+£1500: £21 500, £29 500, £35 500

9 a Median   **b** Mode   **c** Mean

10 Tom mean, David median, Mohaned mode

11 Possible answers: **a** 1, 6, 6, 6, 6   **b** 2, 5, 5, 6, 7

12 Boss chose the mean while worker chose the mode.

13 11.6

14 42.7 kg

6.6 Frequency tables

Exercise 6F

1 a i 7   **ii** 6   **iii** 6.4   **b i** 4   **ii** 4   **iii** 3.7
c i 8   **ii** 8.5   **iii** 8.2   **d i** 0   **ii** 0   **iii** 0.3

2 a 668   **b** 1.9   **c** 0   **d** 328

3 a 2.2, 1.7, 1.3   **b** Better dental care

4 a 0   **b** 0.96

5 a 7   **b** 6.5   **c** 6.5

6 a 1   **b** 1   **c** 0.98

7 a Roger 5, Brian 4   **b** Roger 3, Brian 8
c Roger 5, Brian 4   **d** Roger 5.4, Brian 4.5
e Roger, because he has the smaller range
f Brian, because he has the better mean

8 Possible answers: 3, 4, 15, 3 or 3, 4, 7, 9 …

9 Add up the weeks to see she travelled in 52 weeks of the year, the median is in the 26th and 27th week. Looking at the weeks in order, the 23rd entry is the end of 2 days in a week so the median must be in the 3 days in a week.

6.7　Grouped data

Exercise 6G

1 **a i** $30 < x \leq 40$ **ii** 29.5 **b i** $0 < y \leq 100$ **ii** 158.3
　c i $5 < z \leq 10$ **ii** 9.43 **d i** 7–9 **ii** 8.4 weeks

2 **a** $100 < w \leq 120$ g **b** 10 860 g **c** 108.6 g

3 **a** 207 **b** 19–22 cm **c** 20.3 cm

4 **a** 160 **b** 52.6 min **c** modal group **d** 65%

5 **a** $175 < h \leq 200$ **b** 31% **c** 193.25 **d** No

6 Average price increases: Soundbuy 17.7p, Springfields 18.7p, Setco 18.2p

7 **a** Yes average distance is 11.7 miles per day.
　b Because shorter runs will be completed faster, which will affect the average.
　c Yes because the shortest could be 1 mile and the longest 25 miles.

8 The first 5 and the 10 are the wrong way round.

9 Find the midpoint of each group, multiply that by the frequency and add those products. Divide that total by the total frequency.

10 **a** As we do not know what numbers are in each group, we cannot say what the median is.
　b Yes. The lowest number could be, for example, 28, and the highest could be 52, giving a range of 34.

6.8　Frequency polygons

Exercise 6H

1 **a** 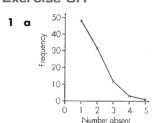 **b** 1.72

2 **a** 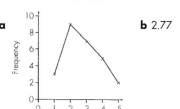 **b** 2.77

3 **a**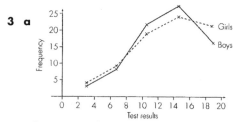
b boys 12.9, girls 13.1

4 **a**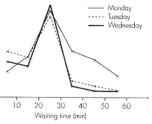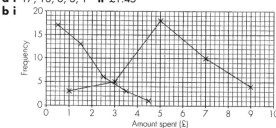
b Mon 28.4, Tue 20.9, Wed 21.3
c There are more people on a Monday as they became ill over the weekend.

5 **a i** 17, 13, 6, 3, 1 **ii** £1.45
b i

(graph)

ii £5.35
c There is a much higher mean, first group of people just want a paper or a few sweets. Later people are buying food for the day.

6 **a**

Age, x	$20 < x \leq 30$	$30 < x \leq 40$	$40 < x \leq 50$	$50 < x \leq 60$	$60 < x \leq 70$
Frequency	14	16	14	12	4

b 41

7 2.17 hours

8 That is the middle value of the time group 0 to 1 minute, it would be very unusual for most of them to be exactly in the middle at 30 seconds.

Examination questions

1 **a** 25 **b** 2 **c** 2 **d** 2.4

2 **a** 6 **b** 9

3 16 **4** 21 °C **5 a** 16 **b** 35.4 **c** 60

6 31.3 or answer that rounds to 31.3

7 **a** 8 **b** $40 < x \leq 60$
c Points plotted at (10, 2), (30, 12), (50, 16), (70, 6), (90, 2) and a line connecting these points.

8 **a i** 74 **ii** 25
b i They are quick growing **ii** They are of even height

9 **a** 37 **b** 52 **c** 48

10 **a** 58 **b** 13 **c** 15
d $288 \div 13 = 22.2$

11 **a** 44 **b** 33
c Not affected by particularly low (or high) mark

12 1 **13** 1.9 **14** 3.55 km

Answers to Chapter 7

7.1 Probability scale

Exercise 7A

1 **a** unlikely   **b** certain   **c** likely
   d very unlikely   **e** impossible   **f** very likely
   g evens

2

3

4 Student to provide own answers.

5 **a** very likely   **b** very likely   **c** very likely
   d very likely   **e** certain   **f** very unlikely
   g certain or very likely   **h** very likely
   i impossible   **j** unlikely   **k** certain
   l very unlikely

6 As there is so little chance of winning the lottery with one ticket, even though having five tickets increases the chances fivefold, winning is still very unlikely.

7.2 Calculating probabilities

Exercise 7B

1 **a** $\frac{1}{6}$ **b** $\frac{1}{6}$ **c** $\frac{1}{2}$ **d** $\frac{1}{13}$ **e** $\frac{1}{4}$ **f** $\frac{1}{2}$
   g $\frac{1}{3}$ **h** $\frac{1}{26}$ **i** $\frac{1}{13}$ **j** 0

2 **a** $\frac{1}{2}$ **b** $\frac{1}{2}$ **c** $\frac{1}{2}$ **d** $\frac{1}{52}$ **e** $\frac{4}{13}$ **f** $\frac{1}{52}$

3 **a** 0 **b** 1

4 **a** $\frac{1}{10}$ **b** $\frac{1}{2}$ **c** $\frac{2}{5}$ **d** $\frac{1}{5}$ **e** $\frac{2}{5}$

5 **a** $\frac{1}{3}$ **b** $\frac{1}{3}$ **c** $\frac{2}{3}$

6 **a** $\frac{6}{11}$ **b** $\frac{5}{11}$ **c** $\frac{6}{11}$

7 **a** $\frac{1}{5}$ **b** $\frac{1}{2}$ **c** $\frac{1}{2}$ **d** $\frac{7}{10}$

8 **a** $\frac{7}{15}$ **b** $\frac{2}{15}$ **c** $\frac{8}{15}$ **d** 0 **e** $\frac{8}{15}$

9 $\frac{1}{50}$

10 **a** AB, AC, AD, AE, BC, BD, BE, CD, CE, DE
   b 1 **c** $\frac{1}{10}$ **d** 6 **e** $\frac{3}{5}$ **f** $\frac{3}{10}$

11 **a** 2 **b** 7 **c i** $\frac{5}{9}$ **ii** $\frac{4}{9}$

12 **a** $\frac{1}{13}$ **b** $\frac{1}{13}$ **c** $\frac{1}{2}$ **d** $\frac{2}{13}$ **e** $\frac{7}{13}$ **f** $\frac{1}{26}$

13 **a i** $\frac{12}{25}$ **ii** $\frac{7}{25}$ **iii** $\frac{6}{25}$
   b They add up to 1.
   c All possible outcomes are mentioned.

14 35%

15 0.5

16 Class U

17 There might not be the same number of boys as girls in the class.

7.3 Probability that an outcome of an event will not happen

Exercise 7C

1 **a** $\frac{19}{20}$ **b** 55%   **c** 0.2

2 **a i** $\frac{3}{13}$ **ii** $\frac{10}{13}$ **b i** $\frac{1}{4}$ **ii** $\frac{3}{4}$
   c i $\frac{2}{13}$ **ii** $\frac{11}{13}$

3 **a i** $\frac{1}{4}$ **ii** $\frac{3}{4}$ **b i** $\frac{3}{11}$ **ii** $\frac{8}{11}$

4 **a** $\frac{1}{2}$ **b** 1 **c** $\frac{1}{3}$

5 Taryn

6 Because it might be possible for the game to end in a draw.

7.4 Addition rule for events

Exercise 7D

1 **a** $\frac{1}{6}$ **b** $\frac{1}{6}$ **c** $\frac{1}{3}$

2 **a** $\frac{1}{4}$ **b** $\frac{1}{4}$ **c** $\frac{1}{2}$

3 **a** $\frac{2}{11}$ **b** $\frac{4}{11}$ **c** $\frac{6}{11}$

4 **a** $\frac{1}{3}$ **b** $\frac{2}{5}$ **c** $\frac{11}{15}$ **d** $\frac{11}{15}$ **e** $\frac{1}{3}$

5 **a** 0.6   **b** 120

6 **a** 0.8   **b** 0.2

7 **a** $\frac{17}{20}$ **b** $\frac{2}{5}$ **c** $\frac{3}{4}$

8 Because these are three separate events. Also, probability cannot exceed 1.

9 $\frac{3}{4}$

10 $\frac{8}{45}$

11 The probability for each day stays the same, at $\frac{1}{4}$.

12 a The choices of drink and snack are not connected.
  b (C, D), (T, G), (T, R), (T, D), (H, G), (H, R), (H, D)
  c A possibility is not the same as a probability.
    Nine possibilities do not mean a probability of $\frac{1}{9}$.
  d i (C, D) = 0.12, (T, G) = 0.15, (T, R) = 0.05,
    (T, D) = 0.3, (H, G) = 0.09, (H, R) = 0.03, (H, D) = 0.18
    ii The total is 1 as this covers all the possibilities.

7.5   Experimental probability

Exercise 7E

1 a B   **b** B   **c** C   **d** A   **e** B   **f** A
  g B   **h** B

2 a 0.2, 0.08, 0.1, 0.105, 0.148, 0.163, 0.1645
  b 6   **c** 1   **d** $\frac{1}{6}$ **e** 1000

3 a 0.095, 0.135, 0.16, 0.265, 0.345
  b 40   **c** No; all numbers should be close to 40.

4 a 0.2, 0.25, 0.38, 0.42, 0.385, 0.3974   **b** 8

5 a 6   **b, c** Student to provide own answers.

6 a Caryl, threw the greatest number of times.
  b 0.39, 0.31, 0.17, 0.14
  c Yes; all answers should be close to 0.25.

7 a not likely   **b** impossible   **c** not likely
  d certain   **e** impossible   **f** 50–50 chance
  g 50–50 chance   **h** certain   **i** quite likely

8 The missing top numbers are 4 and 5, the bottom two numbers
  are both likely to be close to 20.

9 Thursday

10 Although he might expect the probability to be close to $\frac{1}{2}$, giving
  500 heads, the actual number of heads is unlikely to
  be exactly 500, but should be close to it.

7.6   Combined events

Exercise 7F

1 a 7   **b** 2 and 12

  c $\frac{1}{36}, \frac{1}{18}, \frac{1}{12}, \frac{1}{9}, \frac{5}{36}, \frac{1}{6}, \frac{5}{36}, \frac{1}{9}, \frac{1}{12}, \frac{1}{18}, \frac{1}{36}$

  d i $\frac{1}{12}$ **ii** $\frac{1}{3}$ **iii** $\frac{1}{2}$ **iv** $\frac{7}{36}$ **v** $\frac{5}{12}$ **vi** $\frac{5}{18}$

2 a $\frac{1}{12}$ **b** $\frac{11}{36}$ **c** $\frac{1}{6}$ **d** $\frac{5}{9}$

3 a $\frac{1}{36}$ **b** $\frac{11}{36}$ **c** $\frac{5}{18}$

4

Score on second dice						
6	5	4	3	2	1	0
5	4	3	2	1	0	1
4	3	2	1	0	1	2
3	2	1	0	1	2	3
2	1	0	1	2	3	4
1	0	1	2	3	4	5
	1	2	3	4	5	6

Score on first dice

  a $\frac{5}{18}$ **b** $\frac{1}{6}$ **c** $\frac{1}{9}$ **d** 0   **e** $\frac{1}{2}$

5 a $\frac{1}{4}$ **b** $\frac{1}{2}$ **c** $\frac{3}{4}$ **d** $\frac{1}{4}$

6

Score on second spinner					
5	6	7	8	9	10
4	5	6	7	8	9
3	4	5	6	7	8
2	3	4	5	6	7
1	2	3	4	5	6
	1	2	3	4	5

Score on first spinner

  a 6   **b i** $\frac{4}{25}$ **ii** $\frac{13}{25}$ **iii** $\frac{1}{5}$ **iv** $\frac{3}{5}$

7 $\frac{8}{64} = \frac{1}{8}$

8 It will show all the possible products.

9 a

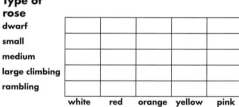

Type of rose / **Colour of rose**
(dwarf, small, medium, large climbing, rambling)
(white, red, orange, yellow, pink, copper)

  b i $\frac{6}{30} = \frac{1}{5}$ **ii** $\frac{4}{5}$

10 impossible: no dice; very unlikely: 5 or more dice; unlikely:
  4 dice; evens: not possible; likely: 3 dice; very likely: 2 dice;
  certain: 1 dice

7.7   Expectation

Exercise 7G

1 a $\frac{1}{6}$ **b** 25

2 a $\frac{1}{2}$ **b** 1000

3 a i $\frac{1}{2}$ **ii** $\frac{1}{13}$ **iii** $\frac{1}{4}$ **iv** $\frac{1}{52}$

  b i 260   **ii** 40   **iii** 130   **iv** 10

4 a $\frac{1}{37}$ **b** 5

5 a 150   **b** 100   **c** 250   **d** 0

6 a 167   **b** 833

7 1050

8 a 10, 10, 10, 10, 10, 10   **b** 3.5
c Find the average of the scores (21 ÷ 6)

9 a 0.111   **b** 40

10 281 days

11 Multiply the number of plants by 0.003.

7.8   Two-way tables

Exercise 7H

1 a Everton   **b** Man Utd, Everton, Liverpool   **c** Leeds

2 a

		Shaded	Unshaded
Shape	Circle	3	3
	Triangle	2	2

b $\frac{1}{2}$

3 a 40   **b** 16   **c** 40%   **d** 40%   **e** 16

4 a

		No. on disc		
		4	**5**	**6**
Letter on card	**A**	3	4	5
	B	4	5	6
	C	5	6	7

b $\frac{4}{9}$ **c** $\frac{1}{3}$

5 a 23   **b** 20%   **c** $\frac{4}{25}$ **d** 480

6 a 10   **b** 7   **c** 14%   **d** 15%

7 a

		Spinner A			
		1	**2**	**3**	**4**
Spinner B	**5**	6	7	8	9
	6	7	8	9	10
	7	8	9	10	11
	8	9	10	11	12

b 4   **c i** $\frac{1}{4}$ **ii** $\frac{3}{16}$ **iii** $\frac{1}{4}$

8 a 6   **b** 16   **c** 34   **d** $\frac{13}{15}$

9 a

		Number on dice					
		1	**2**	**3**	**4**	**5**	**6**
Coin	**H**	1	2	3	4	5	6
	T	2	4	6	8	10	12

b 2 (1 and 4)   **c** $\frac{1}{4}$

10 a Those from the greenhouse have a larger mean diameter.
b Those from the garden have a smaller range, so are more consistent.

11 Either Reyki, because she had bigger tomatoes, or Daniel, because he had more tomatoes.

12 $\frac{22}{36} = \frac{11}{18}$

13 a

Score on second spinner	10	10	11	13	15	17	19
	8	8	9	11	13	15	17
	6	6	7	9	11	13	15
	4	4	5	7	9	11	13
	2	2	3	5	7	9	11
	0	0	1	3	5	7	9
		0	1	3	5	7	9

Score on first spinner

b 9   **c** 0   **d** $\frac{15}{36} = \frac{5}{12}$ **e** $\frac{30}{36} = \frac{5}{6}$

Examination questions

1 a i Likely   **ii** Impossible   **iii** Certain
b 5

2 a $\frac{1}{9}$ **b** $\frac{4}{9}$ **c** 0

3 a Shorter mean time
b Small range, so more consistent

4 a

	C	D
Boy	3	2
Girl	1	4

b 0.7

5 a 0   **b** 0.7   **c** 0.2

6 a R $\left(\frac{1}{8}\right)$ W $\left(\frac{2}{8}\right)$ Y $\left(\frac{5}{8}\right)$ **b** 0   **c** $\frac{7}{8}$
d No, because the spinner can land on any of the 3 colours each time it is spun

7 a 1H, 1T, 2H, 2T, 3H, 3T, 4H, 4T, 5H, 5T, 6H, 6T
b $\frac{1}{4}$ **c** $\frac{3}{4}$

8 a $\frac{3}{10}$ **b** $\frac{13}{20}$ **c** 6

9 a W $\frac{1}{4}$, G $\frac{9}{20}$, B $\frac{3}{10}$ **b** Second, as there are more trials

Answers to Chapter 8

8.1 Pie charts

Exercise 8A

1 a
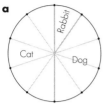

b
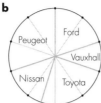

c

2 Pie charts with following angles:
 a 36°, 90°, 126°, 81°, 27°
 b 90°, 108°, 60°, 78°, 24°
 c 168°, 52°, 100°, 40°

3 Pie charts with these angles: 60°, 165°, 45°, 15°, 75°

4 a 36
 b Pie charts with these angles: 50°, 50°, 80°, 60°, 60°, 40°, 20°
 c Student's bar chart.
 d Bar chart, because easier to make comparisons.

5 a Pie charts with these angles: 124°, 132°, 76°, 28°
 b Split of total data seen at a glance.

6 a 55° **b** 22 **c** $33\frac{1}{3}$%

7 a Pie charts with these angles:
 Strings: 36°, 118°, 126°, 72°, 8°
 Brass: 82°, 118°, 98°, 39°, 23°
 Overall, the strings candidates did better, as a smaller proportion failed. A higher proportion of Brass candidates scored very good or excellent.

8 $\frac{1}{9}$

9 Choose a class in the school at random and ask each student how they get to school most mornings.

8.2 Scatter diagrams

Exercise 8B

1 a Positive correlation **b** Negative correlation
 c No correlation **d** Positive correlation

2 a A person's reaction time increases as more alcohol is consumed.
 b As people get older, they consume less alcohol.
 c No relationship between temperature and speed of cars on M1.
 d As people get older, they have more money in the bank.

3 a, b Student's scatter diagram and line of best fit.
 c about 20 cm/s **d** about 35 cm

4 a Student's scatter diagram.
 b Yes, usually (good correlation).

5 a, b Student's scatter diagram and line of best fit.
 c Greta **d** about 70 **e** about 72

6 a Student's scatter diagram.
 b no, because there is no correlation.

7 a, b Student's scatter diagram and line of best fit.
 c about 2.4 km **d** 8 minutes

8 23 mph

9 Points showing a line of best fit sloping down from top left to bottom right.

8.3 Surveys

Exercise 8C

1–5 Student's own answers.

6 a The form should look something like this.
 Question: Which of the following foods would you normally eat for your main meal of the day?

Name	Sex	Chips	Beef burgers	Vegetables	Pizza	Fish

 b Yes, it looks correct as a greater proportion of girls ate healthy food.

7 The data-collection sheet should look something like this.
 Question: What kind of tariff do you use on your mobile phone?

Name	Pay as you go		Contract	
	200 or more free texts	Under 200 free texts	200 or more free texts	Under 200 free texts

 Various data-collection sheets would achieve the purpose; the student's answer will be accepted, provided he or she has offered some choices that can distinguish one tariff from another.

8 Examples are: shops names, year of student, tally space, frequency.

Exercise 8D

1 a Leading question, not enough responses.
 b Simple 'yes' and 'no' response, with a follow-up question, responses cover all options and have a reasonable number of choices.

2 a Overlapping responses.
 b ☐ £0–£2 ☐ over £2 up to £5
    ☐ over £5 up to £10 ☐ over £10

3–5 Students to provide own questionnaires.

6 A possible solution is:

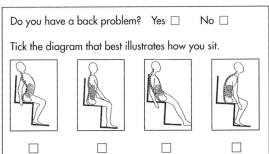

Do you have a back problem?   Yes ☐   No ☐

Tick the diagram that best illustrates how you sit.

☐   ☐   ☐   ☐

8.4   The data-handling cycle

Exercise 8E

1 Secondary data. Student to give own description of the data-handling cycle.

2 Primary data. Student to give own description of the data-handling cycle.

3 Primary or secondary. Student to give own description of the data-handling cycle.

4 Primary or secondary. Student to give own description of the data-handling cycle.

5 Primary. Student to give own description of the data-handling cycle.

6 Primary. Student to give own description of the data-handling cycle.

8.5   Other uses of statistics

Exercise 8F

1 Price: 78p, 80.3p, 84.2p, 85p, 87.4p, 93.6p

2 a 9.7 million   **b** 4.5 years   **c** 12 million
   d 10 million

3 a £1 = $1.88
   b Greatest drop was from June to July.
   c There is no trend in the data so you cannot tell if it will go up or down.

4 £74.73

5 a Holiday month
   b i 138–144 thousand   **ii** 200–210 thousand

6 The general cost of living in 2009 dropped to 98% of that in 2008.

7 £51.50

Examination questions

1 a pie chart drawn with angles at following degrees:
     French =72°, Spanish = 96°, Italian =48°, Greek =80°, American =64°
   b 20%

2 pie chart drawn with correct angles: 180° or 120° or 60° seen or implied
   Exactly 3 sectors correct ± 2°
   Correctly labelled

3 a 30
   b 20

4 a $\frac{1}{15}$ **b i** 57   **ii** 112°

5 No box for less than 1
   4–6 and 6–8 overlap

6 a Their numbers plotted on months and joined with "straight" lines or dotted lines
   b Increases until July then decreases/Increases in summer then decreases

7 a 3 h 35 m
   b 64

8 a Points plotted on graph. Time labelled on the X axis and distance on the Y axis
   b Line of best fit diagonally down from right to left.
   c Answer dependent on students graph
   d Answer dependent on students graph

9 a Leading question; categories not specific
   b Straightforward replies; categories clear

Answers to Chapter 9

9.1   Multiples of whole numbers

Exercise 9A

1 **a** 3, 6, 9, 12, 15   **b** 7, 14, 21, 28, 35
    c 9, 18, 27, 36, 45   **d** 11, 22, 33, 44, 55
    e 16, 32, 48, 64, 80

2 **a** 254, 108, 68, 162, 98, 812, 102, 270
    b 111, 255, 108, 162, 711, 615, 102, 75, 270
    c 255, 615, 75, 270   **d** 108, 162, 711, 270

3 **a** 72, 132, 216, 312, 168, 144
    b 161, 91, 168, 294
    c 72, 102, 132, 78, 216, 312, 168, 144, 294

4 **a** 98   **b** 99   **c** 96   **d** 95   **e** 98   **f** 96

5 **a** 1002   **b** 1008   **c** 1008

6 No, 50 is not a multiple of 6.

7 4 or 5 (as 2, 10 and 20 are not realistic answers)

8 **a** 18   **b** 28   **c** 15

9 66

10 5 numbers: 18, 36, 54, 72, 90

11 **a** 1, 2, 5, 10
    b 1, 3, 5, 6, 10, 15, 50
    c 1, 2, 4, 5, 10, 20, 50, 100
    d For example, 60, 72, 84, 96

9.2   Factors of whole numbers

Exercise 9B

1 **a** 1, 2, 5, 10   **b** 1, 2, 4, 7, 14, 28
    c 1, 2, 3, 6, 9, 18   **d** 1, 17
    e 1, 5, 25   **f** 1, 2, 4, 5, 8, 10, 20, 40
    g 1, 2, 3, 5, 6, 10, 15, 30   **h** 1, 3, 5, 9, 15, 45
    i 1, 2, 3, 4, 6, 8, 12, 24   **j** 1, 2, 4, 8, 16

2 8 ways (1, 2, 3, 4, 6, 8, 12, 24 per box)

3 **a** 1, 2, 3, 4, 5, 6, 8, 10, 12, 15, 20, 24, 30, 40, 60, 120
    b 1, 2, 3, 5, 6, 10, 15, 25, 30, 50, 75, 150
    c 1, 2, 3, 4, 6, 8, 9, 12, 16, 18, 24, 36, 48, 72, 144
    d 1, 2, 3, 4, 5, 6, 9, 10, 12, 15, 18, 20, 30, 36, 45, 60, 90, 180
    e 1, 13, 169
    f 1, 2, 3, 4, 6, 9, 12, 18, 27, 36, 54, 108
    g 1, 2, 4, 7, 14, 28, 49, 98, 196
    h 1, 3, 9, 17, 51, 153
    i 1, 2, 3, 6, 9, 11, 18, 22, 33, 66, 99, 198
    j 1, 199

4 **a** 55   **b** 67   **c** 29   **d** 39   **e** 65   **f** 80
    g 80   **h** 70   **i** 81   **j** 50

5 **a** 2   **b** 2   **c** 3   **d** 5   **e** 3   **f** 3
    g 7   **h** 5   **i** 10   **j** 11

6 4 rows of 3 or 3 rows of 4.

7 It does not have a factor of 3.

8 5

9.3   Prime numbers

Exercise 9C

1 23 and 29

2 97

3 All these numbers are not prime.

4 3, 5, 7

5 Only if all 31 bars are in a single row, as 31 is a prime number and its only factors are 1 and 31.

9.4   Square numbers

Exercise 9D

1 36, 49, 64, 81, 100, 121, 144, 169, 196, 225, 256, 289, 324, 361, 400

2 4, 9, 16, 25, 36, 49

3 **a** 3   **b** 5   **c** 7   **d** Odd numbers

4 **a** 529   **b** 3249   **c** 5929   **d** 15 129   **e** 23 104
    f 10.24   **g** 90.25   **h** 566.44   **i** 16   **j** 144

5 **a** 169
    b 196
    c answer between 169 and 196 (exact answer is 174.24)

6 36 and 49

7 **a** 50, 65, 82   **b** 98, 128, 162   **c** 51, 66, 83
    d 48, 63, 80   **e** 149, 164, 181

8 **a** 25, 169, 625, 1681, 3721
    b Answers in each row are the same

9 £144

10 29

Exercise 9E

1 **a** 6, 12, 18, 24, 30   **b** 13, 26, 39, 52, 65
    c 8, 16, 24, 32, 40   **d** 20, 40, 60, 80, 100
    e 18, 36, 54, 72, 90

2 1, 4, 9, 16, 25, 36, 49, 64, 81, 100

3 **a** 1, 2, 3, 4, 6, 12   **b** 1, 2, 4, 5, 10, 20
     c 1, 3, 9   **d** 1, 2, 4, 8, 16, 32
     e 1, 2, 3, 4, 6, 8, 12, 24   **f** 1, 2, 19, 38
     g 1, 13   **h** 1, 2, 3, 6, 7, 14, 21, 42
     i 1, 3, 5, 9, 15, 45   **j** 1, 2, 3, 4, 6, 9, 12, 18, 36

4 **a** 12, 24, 36   **b** 20, 40, 60   **c** 15, 30, 45
     d 18, 36, 54   **e** 35, 70, 105

5 Square numbers

6 13 is a prime number

7 2, 3, 5, 7, 11, 13, 17, 19

8 $1 + 3 + 5 + 7 + 9 = 25$
     $1 + 3 + 5 + 7 + 9 + 11 = 36$
     $1 + 3 + 5 + 7 + 9 + 11 + 13 = 49$
     $1 + 3 + 5 + 7 + 9 + 11 + 13 + 15 = 64$

9

	Square number	Factor of 70
Even number	16	14
Multiple of 7	49	35

10 4761 (69^2)

11 4 packs of sausages, 5 packs of buns

12 24 seconds

13 30 seconds

14 12 minutes; Debbie: 4 and Fred: 3

15 **a** 12   **b** 9   **c** 6   **d** 13   **e** 15   **f** 14
     g 16   **h** 10   **i** 18   **j** 17   **k** 8   **l** 21

16 **b** 21, 28, 36, 45, 55

9.5   Square roots

Exercise 9F

1 **a** 2   **b** 5   **c** 7   **d** 1   **e** 9   **f** 10
     g 8   **h** 3   **i** 6   **j** 4   **k** 11   **l** 12
     m 20   **n** 30   **o** 13

2 **a** +5, −5   **b** +6, −6   **c** +10, −10
     d +7, −7   **e** +8, −8   **f** +4, −4
     g +3, −3   **h** +9, −9   **i** +1, −1
     j +12, −12

3 **a** 81   **b** 40   **c** 100   **d** 14   **e** 36   **f** 15
     g 49   **h** 12   **i** 25   **j** 21   **k** 121   **l** 16
     m 64   **n** 17   **o** 441

4 **a** 24   **b** 31   **c** 45   **d** 40   **e** 67   **f** 101
     g 3.6   **h** 6.5   **i** 13.9   **j** 22.2

5 $\sqrt{50}$, $3^2\sqrt{90}$, 4^2

6 4 and 5

7 $\sqrt{324} = 18$

8 15 tiles

9.6   Powers

Exercise 9G

1 **a** 27   **b** 125   **c** 216   **d** 1728   **e** 16   **f** 256
     g 625   **h** 32   **i** 2187   **j** 1024

2 **a** 100   **b** 1000   **c** 10 000   **d** 100 000   **e** 1 000 000
     f The power is the same as the number of zeros
     g **i** 100 000 000   **ii** 10 000 000 000
     iii 1 000 000 000 000 000

3 **a** 2^4 **b** 3^5 **c** 7^2 **d** 5^3 **e** 10^7 **f** 6^4
     g 4^4 **h** 1^7 **i** 0.5^4 **j** 100^3

4 **a** $3 \times 3 \times 3 \times 3$ **b** $9 \times 9 \times 9$ **c** 6×6
     d $10 \times 10 \times 10 \times 10 \times 10$
     e $2 \times 2 \times 2 \times 2 \times 2 \times 2 \times 2 \times 2 \times 2 \times 2$
     f $8 \times 8 \times 8 \times 8 \times 8 \times 8$ **g** $0.1 \times 0.1 \times 0.1$
     h 2.5×2.5 **i** $0.7 \times 0.7 \times 0.7$ **j** 1000×1000

5 **a** 16   **b** 243   **c** 49   **d** 125   **e** 10 000 000
     f 1296   **g** 256   **h** 1   **i** 0.0625   **j** 1 000 000

6 **a** 81   **b** 729   **c** 36   **d** 100 000   **e** 1024
     f 262 144   **g** 0.001   **h** 6.25   **i** 0.343   **j** 1 000 000

7 10^6

8 10^6

9 4, 8, 16, 32, 64, 128, 256, 512

10 0.001, 0.01, 0.1, 1, 10, 100, 1000, 10 000, 100 000,
     1 000 000, 10 000 000, 100 000 000

11 125 m^3

12 **a** answer given   **b** 10^2 **c** 2^3 **d** 5^2

13 $6^2 = 36$ or $81 = 9^2$

14 **a** $x = 9$ **b** $y = 8$ **c** $z = 4$
     d w = 4   **e** $s = 1000$ **f** $r = 1000$

9.7   Multiplying and dividing by powers of 10

Exercise 9H

1 **a** 31   **b** 310   **c** 3100   **d** 31 000

2 **a** 65   **b** 650   **c** 6500   **d** 65 000

3 Factors of 10 are the same, e.g. $100 = 10^2$

4 **a** 7.3×10 **b** 7.3×10^2 **c** 7.3×10^3
     d 7.3×10^5

5 **a** 0.31   **b** 0.031   **c** 0.0031
     d 0.00031

6 **a** 0.65   **b** 0.065   **c** 0.0065
     d 0.00065

7 Factors of 10 are the same, e.g. $1000 = 10^3$

8 **a** $7.3 \div 10$ **b** $7.3 \div 10^2$ **c** $7.3 \div 10^3$
     d $7.3 \div 10^5$

9 a 250 **b** 34.5 **c** 4670
  d 346 **e** 207.89 **f** 56 780
  g 246 **h** 0.76 **i** 76
  j 89 700 **k** 865 **l** 10 050
  m 999 000 **n** 23 456 **o** 98 765.4
  p 43 230 000 **q** 7867.9 **r** 2036.7
  s 764.3 **t** 3 457 800 **u** 345.78

10 a 0.025 **b** 0.345 **c** 0.004 67
  d 3.46 **e** 0.207 89 **f** 0.056 78
  g 0.0246 **h** 0.0076 **i** 0.000 076
  j 0.000 008 97 **k** 0.000 865 **l** 1.005
  m 0.000 000 999 **n** 2.3456 **o** 0.098 765 4
  p 0.000 043 23 **q** 0.786 79 **r** 20.367
  s 7.643

11 a 60 000 **b** 120 000 **c** 10 000
  d 42 000 **e** 21 000 **f** 300
  g 150 **h** 1400 **i** 100 000
  j 200 000 **k** 28 000 **l** 900
  m 400 **n** 8000 **o** 160 000
  p 4500 **q** 8000 **r** 250 000

12 a 5 **b** 50 **c** 25 **d** 30 **e** 7 **f** 300
  g 6 **h** 30 **i** 4 **j** 5 **k** 2 **l** 100
  m 40 **n** 200 **o** 20 **p** 20 **q** 2 **r** 1
  s 16 **t** 150 **u** 12 **v** 15 **w** 40 **x** 5
  y 40 **z** 320

13 a 54 400 **b** 16 000

14 $30 \times 90\,000 = 2\,700\,000$
  $600 \times 8000 = 4\,800\,000$
  $5000 \times 4000 = 20\,000\,000$
  $200\,000 \times 700 = 140\,000\,000$

15 1400 million

9.8 Prime factors, LCM and HCF

Exercise 9I

1 a $84 = 2 \times 2 \times 3 \times 7$ **b** $100 = 2 \times 2 \times 5 \times 5$
  c $180 = 2 \times 2 \times 3 \times 3 \times 5$ **d** $220 = 2 \times 2 \times 5 \times 11$
  e $280 = 2 \times 2 \times 2 \times 5 \times 7$
  f $128 = 2 \times 2 \times 2 \times 2 \times 2 \times 2 \times 2$
  g $50 = 2 \times 5 \times 5$ **h** $1000 = 2 \times 2 \times 2 \times 5 \times 5 \times 5$
  i $576 = 2 \times 2 \times 2 \times 2 \times 2 \times 2 \times 3 \times 3$
  j $650 = 2 \times 5 \times 5 \times 13$

2 a $2^2 \times 3 \times 7$ **b** $2^2 \times 5^2$ **c** $2^2 \times 3^2 \times 5$
  d $2^2 \times 5 \times 11$ **e** $2^3 \times 5 \times 7$ **f** 2^7
  g 2×5^2 **h** $2^3 \times 5^3$ **i** $2^6 \times 3^2$
  j $2 \times 5^2 \times 13$

3 $1, 2, 3, 2^2, 5, 2 \times 3, 7, 2^3, 3^2, 2 \times 5, 11, 2^2 \times 3, 13, 2 \times 7,$
  $3 \times 5, 2^4, 17, 2 \times 3^2, 19, 2^2 \times 5, 3 \times 7, 2 \times 11, 23, 2^3 \times 3,$
  $5^2, 2 \times 13, 3^3, 2^2 \times 7, 29, 2 \times 3 \times 5, 31, 2^5, 3 \times 11, 2 \times 17,$
  $5 \times 7, 2^2 \times 3^2, 37, 2 \times 19, 3 \times 13, 2^3 \times 5, 41, 2 \times 3 \times 7,$
  $43, 2^2 \times 11, 3^2 \times 5, 2 \times 23, 47, 2^4 \times 3, 7^2, 2 \times 5^2$

4 a Each is double the previous number
  b 64, 128
  c 81, 243, 729
  d 256, 1024, 4096
  e $3, 3^2, 3^3, 3^4, 3^5, 3^6, \ldots; 4, 4^2, 4^3, 4^4, 4^5, \ldots$

5 a $2 \times 2 \times 3 \times 5$
  b $2^2 \times 3 \times 5$
  c $120 = 2^3 \times 3 \times 5, 240 = 2^4 \times 3 \times 5, 480 = 2^5 \times 3 \times 5$

6 a $7^2 \times 11^2 \times 13^2$
  b $7^3 \times 11^3 \times 13^3$
  c $7^{10} \times 11^{10} \times 13^{10}$

7 Because 3 is not a factor of 40 so it does not divide exactly

Exercise 9J

1 a 20 **b** 56 **c** 6 **d** 28 **e** 10 **f** 15
  g 24 **h** 30

2 It is their product

3 a 8 **b** 18 **c** 12 **d** 30

4 No. Because the numbers in each part have common factors

5 a 168 **b** 105 **c** 84 **d** 84 **e** 96 **f** 54
  g 75 **h** 144

6 3 packs of cheese slices and 4 packs of bread rolls

7 a 8 **b** 7 **c** 4 **d** 14 **e** 4 **f** 9
  g 5 **h** 4 **i** 3 **j** 16 **k** 5 **l** 9

8 a i no **ii** yes **iii** yes **iv** no
  b i no **ii** no **iii** yes **iv** no

9 18 and 24

9.9 Rules for multiplying and dividing powers

Exercise 9K

1 a 5^4 **b** 5^{10} **c** 5^5 **d** 5^3 **e** 5^{15} **f** 5^9
  g 5^6 **h** 5^9 **i** 5^8

2 a x^8 **b** x^9 **c** x^8 **d** x^5 **e** x^{12} **f** x^{13}
  g x^{11} **h** x^{10} **i** x^{16}

3 a 6^3 **b** 6^5 **c** 6^1 **d** 6^0 **e** 6^1 **f** 6^3
  g 6^2 **h** 6^1 **i** 6^2

4 a x^4 **b** x^5 **c** x^3 **d** x^3 **e** x^6 **f** x^5
  g x^2 **h** x^6 **i** x^9

5 a 1 **b** 6^0 **c** 1

6 a 1 **b** 5^0 **c** 1

7 Answers for power 0 are always 1.

8 Two values with a sum of 7, for example $a = 5$ and $b = 2$

9 a $a = 1$ and $x = 2$
  b $x = 1$

Examination questions

1 a 30 **b** 3, 12, 44

2 a i 1, 4, 9, 16, 25, 36 or 49
  ii 1, 8 or 27
  iii 7, 14, 21, 28, 35, 42 or 49
  iv 2, 3, 5, 7, 11, 13, 17, 19, 23, 29, 31, 37, 41, 43 or 47
 b i 49 **ii** 2 **iii** 45

3 a 7, 14, 21, 28, 35   **b** 1, 2, 7, 14
 c 16 **d** 11, 13, 17 or 19   **e** 27

4 a 438, 483, 834, 843   **b** 384
 c Multiples of 5 end in 0 or 5, none of these numbers does

5 a 3, 9 **b** 3, 9 **c** 3, 7 **d** 4, 9 **e** 8
 f 9, 4, (5), (2), (6), 10, 7, 8, 3

6 a 27   **b** e.g. 1, 8, 64 or 125

7 a i 22 and 48 **ii** 21 **iii** 8 and 6 **iv** 36 **v** 8
 b 1728

8 a i 8 **ii** 27   **b** 3, 4, 100, 3^3, 4^3

9 a c^4 **b** d^5 **c** $1/e^7$

10 a $2^2 \times 7$ **b** 84

11 40 beats

12 a 5^3 **b** $a = 2, b = 3$ **c** 27

13 a 14, 21, 42
 b 5
 c 23, 43, 13, 31

14 a 2^6
 b 640 000 = 64 × 10 000; 64 has one prime factor (2) and 10 000 has one other prime factor (5).

15 2 packs of bread sticks, 5 packs of small pies.

Answers to Chapter 10

10.1 The language of algebra

Exercise 10A

1 a $x + 2$ **b** $x - 6$ **c** $k + x$ **d** $x - t$ **e** $x + 3$
 f $d + m$ **g** $b - y$ **h** $p + t + w$ **i** $8x$
 j hj **k** $x \div 4$ or $\dfrac{x}{4}$ **l** $2 \div x$ or $\dfrac{2}{x}$
 m $y \div t$ or $\dfrac{y}{t}$ **n** wt **o** a^2 **p** g^2

2 a i $P = 4, A = 1$ **b i** $P = 4s$ cm
  ii $P = 4x, A = x^2$ **ii** $A = s^2$ cm^2
  iii $P = 12, A = 9$
  iv $P = 4t, A = t^2$

3 a $x + 3$ yr   **b** $x - 4$ yr

4 $F = 2C + 30$

5 Rule **c**

6 a $C = 100M$ **b** $N = 12F$ **c** $W = 4C$ **d** $H = P$

7 a $3n$ **b** $3n + 3$ **c** $n + 1$ **d** $n - 1$

8 Rob: $2n$, Tom: $n + 2$, Vic: $n - 3$, Will: $2n + 3$

9 a $P = 8n, A = 9n^2$ **b** $P = 24n, A = 36n^2$

10 a £4   **b** £$(10 - x)$ **c** £$(y - x)$ **d** £$2x$

11 a 75p **b** $15x$ p **c** $4A$ p **d** Ay p

12 £$(A - B)$

13 £$A \div 5$ or $\dfrac{£A}{5}$

14 a Dad: $(72 + x)$ yr, me: $(T + x)$ yr   **b** 31

15 a $T \div 2$ or $\dfrac{T}{2}$ **b** $T \div 2 + 4$ or $\dfrac{T}{2} + 4$ **c** $T - x$

16 a $8x$ **b** $12m$ **c** $18t$

17 Andrea: $3n - 3$, Bert: $3n - 1$, Colin: $3n - 6$ or $3(n - 2)$, Davina: 0, Emma: $3n - n = 2n$. Florinda: $3n - 3m$

18 For example, $2 \times 6m$, $1 \times 12m$, $6m + 6m$, etc

19 Any values picked for l and w and substituted into the formulae to give the same answers

20 13

21 15p

22 a expression   **b** formula   **c** equation

10.2 Simplifying expressions

Exercise 10B

1 a $6t$ **b** $15y$ **c** $8w$ **d** $5b^2$ **e** $2w^2$ **f** $8p^2$
 g $6t^2$ **h** $15t^2$ **i** $2mt$ **j** $5qt$ **k** $6mn$ **l** $6qt$
 m $10hk$ **n** $21pr$

2 a All except $2m \times 6m$
 b 2 and 0

3 $4x$ cm

4 a y^3 **b** $3m^3$ **c** $4t^3$ **d** $6n^3$ **e** t^4 **f** h^5
 g $12n^5$ **h** $6a^7$ **i** $4k^7$ **j** t^3 **k** $12d^3$ **l** $15p^6$
 m $3mp^2$ **n** $6m^2n$ **o** $8m^2p^2$

5 The number of people who get told the rumour doubles each day ie 2, 4, 8, 16, 32, 64, 128, 256, 512, 1024, 2048, but the number who know the rumour is 3, 7, 15, 31, 63, 127, 255, 511, 1023, 2047 so by the 10th day everyone in the school would know, plus 47 other people!

Exercise 10C

1 a £t **b** £$(4t + 3)$

2 a $10x + 2y$ **b** $7x + y$ **c** $6x + y$

3 a $5a$ **b** $6c$ **c** $9e$ **d** $6f$ **e** $4j$ **f** $3q$
g 0 **h** $-w$ **i** $6x^2$ **j** $5y^2$ **k** 0

4 a $7x$ **b** $3t$ **c** $-5x$ **d** $-5k$ **e** $2m^2$ **f** 0

5 a $7x + 5$ **b** $5x + 6$ **c** $5p$
d $5x + 6$ **e** $5p + t + 5$ **f** $8w - 5k$
g c **h** $8k - 6y + 10$

6 a $2c - 3d$ **b** $5d - 2e$ **c** $f + 3g + 4h$
d $6u - 3v$ **e** $7m - 7n$ **f** $3k + 2m + 5p$
g $2v$ **h** $2w - 3y$ **i** $11x^2 - 5y$
j $-y^2 - 2z$ **k** $x^2 - z^2$

7 a $8x + 6$ **b** $3x + 16$ **c** $2x + 2y + 8$

8 Any acceptable answers, e.g. $x + 4x + 2y + 2y$ or $6x - x + 6y - 2y$

9 a $2x$ and $2y$ **b** a and $7b$

10 a $3x - 1 - x$ **b** $10x$ **c** 25 cm

11 a $12p + 6s$ **b** 13 m and 50 cm

12 Maria is correct, as the two short horizontal lengths are equal to the bottom length and the two short vertical lengths are equal to the side length.

10.3 Expanding brackets

Exercise 10D

1 a $6 + 2m$ **b** $10 + 5l$ **c** $12 - 3y$

d $20 + 8k$ **e** $12d - 8n$ **f** $t^2 + 3t$

g $m^2 + 5m$ **h** $k^2 - 3k$ **i** $3g^2 + 2g$

j $5y^2 - y$ **k** $5p - 3p^2$ **l** $3m^2 + 12m$

m $15t - 12t^2$ **n** $6d^2 + 12de$ **o** $6y^2 + 8ky$

p $15m^2 - 10mp$

2 a $y^3 + 5y$ **b** $h^4 + 7h$ **c** $k^3 - 5k$
d $3t^3 + 12t$ **e** $15d^3 - 3d^4$ **f** $6w^3 + 3tw$
g $15a^3 - 10ab$ **h** $12p^4 - 15mp$ **i** $5m^2 + 4m^3$
j $t^4 + 2t^5$ **k** $5g^2t - 4g^4$ **l** $15t^3 + 3mt^2$

3 a $5(t - 1)$ and $5t - 5$
b Yes as $5(t - 1)$ when $t = 4.50$ is $5 \times 3.50 = £17.50$

4 He has worked out 3×5 as 8 instead of 15 and he has not multiplied the second term by 3. Answer should be $15x - 12$.

5 a $3(2y + 3)$
b $2(6z + 4)$ or $4(3z + 2)$

Exercise 10E

1 a $7t$ **b** $3y$ **c** $9d$ **d** $3e$ **e** $3p$ **f** $2t$
g $5t^2$ **h** $5ab$ **i** $3a^2d$

2 a $22 + 5t$ **b** $21 + 19k$ **c** $10 + 16m$
d $16 + 17y$ **e** $22 + 2f$ **f** $14 + 3g$
g $10 + 11t$ **h** $22 + 4w$

3 a $2 + 2h$ **b** $9g + 5$ **c** $6y + 11$
d $7t - 4$ **e** $17k + 16$ **f** $6e + 20$
g $7m + 4$ **h** $3t + 10$

4 a $4m + 3p + 2mp$ **b** $3k + 4h + 5hk$ **c** $3n + 2t + 7nt$
d $3p + 7q + 6pq$ **e** $6h + 6j + 13hj$ **f** $6t + 8y + 21ty$
g $24p + 12r + 13pr$ **h** $20k - 6m + 19km$

5 a $5(f + 2s) + 2(2f + 3s) = 9f + 16s$
b £$(270f + 480s)$ **c** $42\,450 - 30\,000 = £12\,450$

6 for x-coefficients 3 and 1 or 1 and 4; For y-coefficients 5 and 1 or 3 and 4 or 1 and 7

7 $5(3x + 2) - 3(2x - 1) = 9x + 13$

10.4 Factorisation

Exercise 10F

1 a $6(m + 2t)$ **b** $3(3t + p)$ **c** $4(2m + 3k)$
d $4(r + 2t)$ **e** $m(n + 3)$ **f** $g(5g + 3)$
g $2(2w - 3t)$ **h** $2(4p - 3k)$ **i** $2(8h - 5k)$
j $2m(p + k)$ **k** $2b(2c + k)$ **l** $2a(3b + 2c)$
m $y(3y + 2)$ **n** $t(4t - 3)$ **o** $2d(2d - 1)$
p $3m(m - p)$

2 a $3p(2p + 3t)$ **b** $2p(4t + 3m)$ **c** $4b(2a - c)$
d $4a(3a - 2b)$ **e** $3t(3m - 2p)$ **f** $4at(4t + 3)$
g $5bc(b - 2)$ **h** $2b(4ac + 3ed)$ **i** $2(2a^2 + 3a + 4)$
j $3b(2a + 3c + d)$ **k** $t(5t + 4 + a)$
l $3mt(2t - 1 + 3m)$ **m** $2ab(4b + 1 - 2a)$
n $5pt(2t + 3 + p)$

3 a Not possible **b** $m(5 + 2p)$ **c** $t(t - 7)$
d Not possible **e** $2m(2m - 3p)$ **f** Not possible
g $a(4a - 5b)$ **h** Not possible **i** $b(5a - 3bc)$

4 a Mary has taken out a common factor
b Because the bracket adds up to £10
c £30

5 Bella. Aidan has not taken out the largest possible common factor. Craig has taken m out of both terms but there isn't an m in the second term.

6 There are no common factors.

10.5 Substitution

Exercise 10G

1 a 8 **b** 17 **c** 32

2 a 3 **b** 11 **c** 43

3 a 9 **b** 15 **c** 29

4 a 9 **b** 5 **c** -1

5 a 13 **b** 33 **c** 78

6 a 10 **b** 13 **c** 58

7 a £4 **b** 13 km
c No, 5 miles is 8 km so fare would be £6.50

8 a $2 \times 8 + 6 \times 11 - 3 \times 2 = 76$
b $5 \times 2 - 2 \times 11 + 3 \times 8 = 12$

9 Any values such that $lw = \frac{1}{2}bh$ or $bh = 2lw$

10 a 32 **b** 64 **c** 160

11 a 6.5 **b** 0.5 **c** −2.5

12 a 2 **b** 8 **c** −10

13 a 3 **b** 2.5 **c** −5

14 a 6 **b** 3 **c** 2

15 a 12 **b** 8 **c** $1\frac{1}{2}$

16 a $\dfrac{1050}{n}$ **b** £925

17 a i odd
ii odd
iii even
iv odd
b Any valid expression such as $xy + z$

18 a £20
b i −£40
ii Delivery cost will be zero.
c 40 miles

Examination questions

1 a $4p$ **b** $12qr$ **c** $-3t$

2 a $4a + 7b$
b $5p + 10q - 15r$

3 a i £2.40 **ii** £7.60

4 a $y + 5$ **b** $1-2\,(\,y + 5)$

5 a $13x$ **b** 4

6 a $s = (3)^2 - 6(3) + 9 = 9 - 18 + 9 = 0$

7 a 64 **b** 2 **c** $5p + 2q$

8 19.1

9 a $7x + 16$
b $2x + 2y$ or $2(x + y)$

10 a $4x - 12$
b $x(x + 5)$

11 a $4Q + 3R$
b $2R - 4Q$

12 a $6x - 42$
b $-2x^2 + 3x + 4$

Answers to Chapter 11

11.1 Long multiplication

Exercise 11A

1 a 12 138 **b** 45 612 **c** 29 988
d 20 654 **e** 51 732 **f** 25 012
g 19 359 **h** 12 673 **i** 19 943
j 26 235 **k** 31 535 **l** 78 399
m 17 238 **n** 43 740 **o** 66 065
p 103 320 **q** 140 224 **r** 92 851
s 520 585 **t** 78 660

2 3500

3 No, 62 pupils cannot get in

4 Yes, he walks 57.6 km

5 Yes, 1 204 000 letters

6 5819 litres

7 Yes, she raised £302.40

11.2 Long division

Exercise 11B

1 a 25 **b** 15 **c** 37
d 43 **e** 27 **f** 48
g 53 **h** 52 **i** 32
j 57 **k** 37 rem 15 **l** 25 rem 5
m 34 rem 11 **n** 54 rem 9 **o** 36 rem 11
p 17 rem 4 **q** 23 **r** 61 rem 14
s 42 **t** 27 rem 2

2 68

3 38

4 4 months

5 34 h

6 £1.75

11.3 Arithmetic with decimal numbers

Exercise 11C

1 a 4.8 **b** 3.8 **c** 2.2 **d** 8.3 **e** 3.7 **f** 46.9
g 23.9 **h** 9.5 **i** 11.1 **j** 33.5 **k** 7.1 **l** 46.8
m 0.1 **n** 0.1 **o** 0.6 **p** 65.0 **q** 213.9 **r** 76.1
s 455.2 **t** 51.0

2 a 5.78 **b** 2.36 **c** 0.98 **d** 33.09 **e** 6.01 **f** 23.57
g 91.79 **h** 8.00 **i** 2.31 **j** 23.92 **k** 6.00 **l** 1.01
m 3.51 **n** 96.51 **o** 0.01 **p** 0.07 **q** 7.81
r 569.90 **s** 300.00 **t** 0.01

3 a 4.6 **b** 0.08 **c** 45.716 **d** 94.85 **e** 602.1
f 671.76 **g** 7.1 **h** 6.904 **i** 13.78 **j** 0.1 **k** 4.002
l 60.0 **m** 11.99 **n** 899.996 **o** 0.1 **p** 0.01
q 6.1 **r** 78.393 **s** 200.00 **t** 5.1

4 a 9 **b** 9 **c** 3 **d** 7 **e** 3 **f** 8
g 3 **h** 8 **i** 6 **j** 4 **k** 7 **l** 2
m 47 **n** 23 **o** 96 **p** 33 **q** 154 **r** 343
s 704 **t** 910

5 £1 + £7 + £4 + £1 = £13

6 3, 3.46, 3.5

7 4.7275 or 4.7282

Exercise 11D

1 a 49.8 **b** 21.3 **c** 48.3 **d** 33.3 **e** 5.99 **f** 8.08
g 90.2 **h** 21.2 **i** 12.15 **j** 13.08 **k** 13.26 **l** 24.36

2 a 1.4 **b** 1.8 **c** 4.8 **d** 3.8 **e** 3.75 **f** 5.9
g 3.7 **h** 3.77 **i** 3.7 **j** 1.4 **k** 11.8 **l** 15.3

3 a 30.7 **b** 6.6 **c** 3.8 **d** 16.7 **e** 11.8 **f** 30.2
g 43.3 **h** 6.73 **i** 37.95 **j** 4.7 **k** 3.8 **l** 210.5

4 a £16.74 **b** £1.40

5 2.7 m + 2.5 m = 5.2 m (one pipe)
3.1 m + 1.7 m = 4.8 m (second pipe)
4.2 m (third pipe). Three pipes needed.

6 a 5.3 **b** 6.7 **c** 2.05 **d** 1.9 **e** 4.95 **f** 3.71

7 a 1.6 **b** 42.7 **c** 4.29 **d** 12.8 **e** 22.4 **f** 51.97

8 DVD, shirt and pen

Exercise 11E

1 a 7.2 **b** 7.6 **c** 18.8 **d** 37.1 **e** 32.5 **f** 28.8
g 10.0 **h** 55.2 **i** 61.5 **j** 170.8 **k** 81.6 **l** 96.5

2 a 9.36 **b** 10.35 **c** 25.85 **d** 12.78 **e** 1.82 **f** 3.28
g 2.80 **h** 5.52 **i** 42.21 **j** 56.16 **k** 7.65 **l** 48.96

3 a 1.8 **b** 1.4 **c** 1.4 **d** 1.2 **e** 2.13 **f** 0.69
g 2.79 **h** 1.21 **i** 1.89 **j** 1.81 **k** 0.33 **l** 1.9

4 a 1.75 **b** 1.28 **c** 1.85 **d** 3.65 **e** 1.66 **f** 1.45
g 1.42 **h** 1.15 **i** 3.35 **j** 0.98 **k** 2.3 **l** 1.46

5 a 1.89 **b** 1.51 **c** 0.264 **d** 4.265 **e** 1.224 **f** 0.182
g 0.093 **h** 2.042 **i** 1.908 **j** 2.8 **k** 4.25 **l** 18.5

6 Pack of 8 at £0.625 each

7 a £49.90
b Small, so that all four children can have an ice cream
(cost £4.80)

8 Yes. She only needed 8 paving stones.

Exercise 11F

1 a 89.28 **b** 298.39 **c** 66.04
d 167.98 **e** 2352.0 **f** 322.4
g 1117.8 **h** 4471.5 **i** 464.94
j 25.55 **k** 1047.2 **l** 1890.5

2 a £224.10 **b** £223.75 **c** £29.90

3 5 × 7 = 35

4 £54.20

5 a £120.75 **b** £17 − £3.45 = £13.55

Exercise 11G

1 a 0.48 **b** 2.92 **c** 1.12
d 0.12 **e** 0.028 **f** 0.09
g 0.192 **h** 3.0264 **i** 7.134
j 50.96 **k** 3.0625 **l** 46.512

2 Yes, with 25p left over.

3 a 35, 35.04, 0.04 **b** 16, 18.24, 2.24
c 60, 59.67, 0.33 **d** 180, 172.86, 7.14
e 12, 12.18, 0.18 **f** 24, 26.016, 2.016
g 40, 40.664, 0.664 **h** 140, 140.58, 0.58

4 a 572 **b i** 5.72 **ii** 1.43 **iii** 22.88

11.4 Multiplying and dividing with negative numbers

Exercise 11H

1 a −15 **b** −14 **c** −24 **d** 6 **e** 14 **f** 2
g −2 **h** −8 **i** −4 **j** 3 **k** −24 **l** −10
m −18 **n** 16 **o** 36 **p** −4 **q** −12 **r** −4
s 7 **t** 25 **u** 18 **v** −8 **w** −45 **x** 3
y −40

2 a −9 **b** 16 **c** −3 **d** −32 **e** 18 **f** 18
g 6 **h** −4 **i** 20 **j** 16 **k** 8 **l** −48
m 13 **n** −13 **o** −8 **p** 0 **q** 16 **r** −42
s 6 **t** 1 **u** −14 **v** 6 **w** −4 **x** 7
y 0

3 a −2 **b** 30 **c** 15 **d** −27 **e** −7

4 a 4 **b** −9 **c** −3 **d** 6 **e** −4

5 a −9 **b** 3 **c** 1

6 a 16 **b** −2 **c** −12

7 a 24 **b** 6 **c** −4 **d** −2

8 For example: 1 × (−12), −1 × 12, 2 × (−6), 6 × (−2),
3 × (−4), 4 × (−3)

9 For example: 4 ÷ (−1), 8 ÷ (−2), 12 ÷ (−3), 16 ÷ (−4),
20 ÷ (−5), 24 ÷ (−6)

10 a 21   **b** −4   **c** 2   **d** −16   **e** 2   **f** −5
    g −35   **h** −17   **i** −12   **j** 6   **k** 45   **l** −2
    m 0   **n** −1   **o** −7   **p** −36   **q** 9   **r** 32
    s 0   **t** −65

11 a −12   **b** 12 degrees   **c** 3×-6

12 $-5 \times 4, 3 \times -6, -20 \div 2, -16 \div -4$

13 a 4   **b** 13   **c** 10   **d** 1

11.5   Approximation of calculations

Exercise 11I

1 a 50 000   **b** 60 000   **c** 30 000
   d 90 000   **e** 90 000   **f** 50
   g 90   **h** 30   **i** 100
   j 200   **k** 0.5   **l** 0.3
   m 0.006   **n** 0.05   **o** 0.0009
   p 10   **q** 90   **r** 90
   s 200   **t** 1000

2 a 60 000   **b** 30 000   **c** 80 000
   d 30 000   **e** 10 000   **f** 6000
   g 1000   **h** 800   **i** 100
   j 600   **k** 2   **l** 4
   m 3   **n** 8   **o** 40
   p 0.8   **q** 0.5   **r** 0.07
   s 1   **t** 0.01

3 a 65, 74   **b** 95, 149   **c** 950, 1499

4 Elsecar 750, 849; Hoyland 950, 1499;
   Barnsley 150 000, 249 999

5 15, 16 or 17

6 1, because there could be 450 then 449

Exercise 11J

1 a 35 000   **b** 15 000   **c** 960
   d 12 000   **e** 1050   **f** 4000
   g 4   **h** 20   **i** 1200

2 a £3000   **b** £2000   **c** £1500
   d £700

3 a £15 000   **b** £18 000   **c** £18 000

4 £21 000

5 a 14   **b** 10   **c** 1.1   **d** 1   **e** 5   **f** $\frac{2}{3}$

   g 3 or 4   **h** $\frac{1}{2}$ **i** 6   **j** 400   **k** 2   **l** 20

6 a 500   **b** 200   **c** 90   **d** 50   **e** 50   **f** 500

7 8

8 a 200   **b** 2800   **c** 10   **d** 1000

9 a 40   **b** 10   **c** £70

10 1000 or 1200

11 a 28 km   **b** 120 km   **c** 1440 km

12 400

13 a 3 kg   **b** 200

Exercise 11K

1 a 1.7 m   **b** 6 min   **c** 240 g
   d 80 °C   **e** 16 miles   **f** 14 m²

2 82 °F, 5.3 km, 110 min, 43 000 people, 6.2 s, 67th, 1788,
   15, 5 s

3 $40 \times £20 = £800$

4 $22.5 \,°C − 18.2 \,°C = 4.3 \,°C$

Examination questions

1 a £3.80   **b** £16.75

2 a 7   **b** £0.97

3 a 3 hours 45 minutes
   b £35.10

4 £7.75 or £8.00

5 a 0.08, 0.786, 0.09   **b** 0.79
   c 0.375   **d** 0.07

6 a 200   **b** $\frac{3}{8}$

7 a 27   **b** 1 or 8 or 64 or 125 or 1000 or ...

8 Chuck $(30 + 14) \div (1.3 − 0.5) = 44 \div 0.8 = 55$

9 $1\frac{11}{15}$

10 800

11 a −19, 37   **b** −60

Answers to Chapter 12

12.1 Solving simple linear equations

Exercise 12A

1 **a** $x = 4$ **b** $w = 14$ **c** $y = 5$
   d $p = 10$ **e** $x = 5$ **f** $x = 6$
   g $z = 24$ **h** $x = 2.5$ **i** $q = 4$
   j $x = 1$ **k** $r = 28$ **l** $s = 12$

2 Any valid equation such as $4x = 16$ or $x + 3 = 7$

3 **a** Because it only has even numbers.
   b Because it has a minus sign.
   c Because the answer is not 6.

4 $x + 3 = 17, x = 14$

5 $6y = 180, y = 30, 30p$

Exercise 12B

1 **a** $\leftarrow \div 3 \leftarrow -5 \leftarrow, x = 2$ **b** $\leftarrow \div 3 \leftarrow + 13 \leftarrow, x = 13$
   c $\leftarrow \div 3 \leftarrow + 7 \leftarrow, x = 13$ **d** $\leftarrow \div 4 \leftarrow + 19 \leftarrow, y = 6$
   e $\leftarrow \div 3 \leftarrow -8, a = 1$ **f** $\leftarrow \div 2 \leftarrow -8 \leftarrow, x = 3$
   g $\leftarrow \div 2 \leftarrow -6 \leftarrow, y = 6$ **h** $\leftarrow \div 8 \leftarrow -4 \leftarrow, x = 1$
   i $\leftarrow \div 2 \leftarrow + 10 \leftarrow, x = 9$ **j** $\leftarrow \times 5 \leftarrow -2 \leftarrow, x = 5$
   k $\leftarrow \times 3 \leftarrow + 4 \leftarrow, t = 18$ **l** $\leftarrow \times 4 \leftarrow -1 \leftarrow, y = 24$
   m $\leftarrow \times 2 \leftarrow + 6 \leftarrow, k = 18$ **n** $\leftarrow \times 8 \leftarrow + 4 \leftarrow, h = 40$
   o $\leftarrow \times 6 \leftarrow -1 \leftarrow, w = 18$ **p** $\leftarrow \times 4 \leftarrow -5 \leftarrow, x = 8$
   q $\leftarrow \times 2 \leftarrow + 3 \leftarrow, y = 16$ **r** $\leftarrow \times 5 \leftarrow -2 \leftarrow, f = 30$

2 2

3 27p

Exercise 12C

1 **a** 56 **b** 2 **c** $6\frac{1}{}$
   d 3 **e** 4 **f** $2\frac{1}{2}$
   g $3\frac{1}{2}$ **h** $2\frac{1}{2}$ **i** 4
   j 21 **k** 72 **l** 56
   m 0 **n** -7 **o** -18
   p 36 **q** 36 **r** 60

2 **a** -4
   b 15

3 Any valid equation such as
   $3x + 8 = 2, 6x + 20 = 8$

4 **a** Betsy
   b Second line: Amanda subtracts 1 instead of adding 1; fourth
   line: Amanda subtracts 2 instead of dividing by 2.

Exercise 12D

1 **a** 1 **b** 3 **c** 2
   d 2 **e** 9 **f** 5
   g 6 **h** 4 **i** 2
   j -2 **k** 24 **l** 10
   m 21 **n** 72 **o** 56

2 **a** 33 **b** 48

3 **a** 5 **b** 28 **c** 5
   d 35 **e** 33 **f** 23

4 25

12.2 Solving equations with brackets

Exercise 12E

1 **a** 3 **b** 7 **c** 5
   d 3 **e** 4 **f** 6
   g 8 **h** 1 **i** 1.5
   j 2.5 **k** 0.5 **l** 1.2
   m -4 **n** -2

2 Any values that work, e.g. $a = 2$, $b = 3$ and $c = 30$

3 55

4 3.25

12.3 Equations with the variable on both sides

Exercise 12F

1 **a** 2 **b** 1 **c** 7
   d 4 **e** 2 **f** -1
   g -2 **h** 2

2 $3x - 2 = 2x + 5, x = 7$

3 **a** 6 **b** 11 **c** 1
   d 4 **e** 9 **f** 6

4 $8x + 7 + x + 5 = 11x$
   $+ 5 - x - 5, x = 12$

5 $6x + 3 = 6x + 10$,
   $6x - 6x = 10 - 3, 0 = 7$ which is obviously false. Both sides
   have $6x$, which cancels out.

6 When both sides are expanded you get $12x + 18 = 12x + 18$
   so no matter what value is put in for x it will work.

12.4 Rearranging formulae

Exercise 12G

1 $k = \frac{T}{3}$

2 $m = P - 7$

3 $y = X + 1$

4 $p = 3Q$

5 **a** $m = p - t$ **b** $t = p - m$

6 $k = \frac{t - 7}{2}$

7 $m = gv$

8 $m = \sqrt{t}$

9 $r = \frac{C}{2\pi}$

10 $b = \frac{A}{h}$

11 $I = \frac{P - 2w}{2}$

12 $p = \sqrt{m - 2}$

13 a $5x = 9y + 75, y = \frac{5x - 75}{9}$
b 25p

14 Average speed on first journey
= 72 k/h. Return 63 k/h,
taking 2 hours. Held up for 15 min.

15 a $-40 - 32 = -72, -72 \div 9 = -8, 5 \times -8 = -40$
b $68 - 32 = 36, 36 \div 9 = 4, 4 \times 5 = 20$
c $F = \frac{9}{5} C + 32$

12.5 Solving linear inequalities

Exercise 12H

1 a $x < 3$ **b** $t > 8$ **c** $p \geqslant 10$ **d** $x < 5$ **e** $y \leqslant 3$ **f** $t > 5$
g $x < 6$ **h** $y \leqslant 15$ **i** $t \geqslant 18$ **j** $x < 7$ **k** $x \leqslant 3$ **l** $t \geqslant 5$

2 a 8 **b** 6 **c** 16 **d** 3 **e** 7

3 a 11 **b** 16 **c** 16 **d** 3 **e** 7

4 $2x + 3 < 20, x < 8.50$ so the most was £8.49

5 a Because $3 + 4 = 7$ which is less than the third side 8
b $x + x + 2 > 10, 2x + 2 > 10, 2x > 8, x > 4$, so smallest value of x is 5.

6 a $x = 6$ and $x < 3$ scores -1 (nothing in common), $x < 3$ and $x > 0$ scores $+1$ (1 in common, for example), $x > 0$ and $x = 2$ scores $+1$ (2 in common), $x = 2$ and $x \geqslant 4$ scores -1 (nothing in common), $-1 + 1 + 1 - 1 = 0$
b $x > 0$ and $x = 6$ scores $+1$ (6 in common), $x = 6$ and $x \geqslant 4$ scores $+1$ (6 in common), $x \geqslant 4$ and $x = 2$ scores -1 (nothing in common), $x = 2$ and $x < 3$ scores $+1$ (2 in common). $+1 +1 - 1 + 1 = 2$
c Any acceptable combination for example:
$x = 2, x < 3, x > 0, x \geqslant 4, x = 6$

Exercise 12I

1 a $x > 1$ **b** $x \leqslant 3$ **c** $x < 2$
d $x \geqslant -1$ **e** $x \leqslant -1$ **f** $1 < x \leqslant 4$
g $-2 < x < 4$

2 a $x \leqslant 3$ **b** $x > -2$

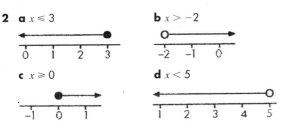

c $x \geqslant 0$ **d** $x < 5$

e $x \geqslant -1$ **f** $2 < x \leqslant 5$

g $-1 \leqslant x \leqslant 3$ **h** $-3 < x < 4$

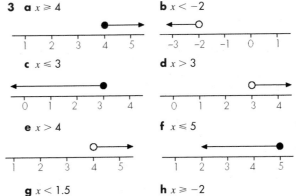

3 a $x \geqslant 4$ **b** $x < -2$

c $x \leqslant 3$ **d** $x > 3$

e $x > 4$ **f** $x \leqslant 5$

g $x < 1.5$ **h** $x \geqslant -2$

i $x > 50$ **j** $x \leqslant 2.5$

k $x > 10$ **l** $x < 13$

4 Any two inequalities that overlap only on the integers -1, 0, 1 and 2; for example $x \geqslant -1$ and $x < 3$

5 a Because 3 apples plus the chocolate bar cost more than £1.20, $x > 22$
b Because 2 apples plus the chocolate bar left Max with at least 16p change, $x \leqslant 25$

c
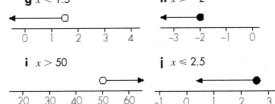

d Apples could cost 23p, 24p or 25p.

6 Set 1: $3x + 5 > 2, \{0, 1, 2\}, 4x - 1 < 7$
Set 2: $3x + 1 < 7, \{-1, 0, 1\}, 2x + 7 \geqslant 5$

Examination questions

1 a 5 **b** 2 **c** 6 **d** 5

2 a 11 **b** 5

3 a $z + 4$ (pence)
b $4z + 4$ (pence)
c $4z + 4 = 60$ 14p

4 a i 4.5 **ii** 7 **iii** 3
b i $13q$ **ii** $7n + 3p$

5 a $2(x + 10.5) = 28$
   b 3.5 cm

6 a 7   **b** 5   **c** 6   **d** -2 **e** 12

7 a 5   **b** 4   **c** 2.5

8 a $2(3x - 5)$
   b 1.25
   c -1
   d $-2, -1, 0, 1$

9 a 9
   b False, False, True
   c 10 or any integer greater than 10

10 a 3.5   **b** 17

11 a $x(x + 4)$
   b $y < 1.5$ **c** $r = \dfrac{p - 3}{2}$

12 $t = 3u$

13 4

14 a $r = \dfrac{C}{6}$

   b $r = \sqrt{(A/3)}$

15 a $x \leqslant 2$
   b $-2, 1, 0, 1$

16 Left Boundary:
   $-3 \leqslant$ open circle < -2 or $-3 \leqslant$ closed circle < -2
   Right Boundary:
   Closed circle on 3 or line beyond 3 with any termination
   (e.g. arrow, circle, nothing)

Answers to Chapter 13

13.1 Conversion graphs

Exercise 13A

1 a i $8\frac{1}{4}$ kg   **ii** $2\frac{1}{4}$ kg   **iii** 9 lb   **iv** 22 lb
   b 2.2 lb
   c Read off the value for 12.6 (5.4 kg) and multiply this by 4 (21.6 kg)

2 a i 10 cm   **ii** 23 cm   **iii** 2 in   **iv** $8\frac{3}{4}$ in
   b $2\frac{1}{2}$ cm
   c Read off the value for 9 in (23 cm) and multiply this by 2 (46 cm)

3 a i $320   **ii** $100   **iii** £45   **iv** £78
   b $3.20
   c It would become less steep.

4 a i £120   **ii** £82
   b i 32   **ii** 48

5 a i £100   **ii** £325
   b i 500   **ii** 250

6 a i £70   **ii** £29
   b i £85   **ii** £38

7 a i 95 °F   **ii** 68 °F   **iii** 10 °C   **iv** 32 °C
   b 32 °F

8 a Check student's graph   **b** 2.15 pm

9 a Check student's graph   **b** £50

10 a No trains on Christmas day and Boxing day
   b Sudden drop in passenger numbers
   c Increased shopping and last-minute present buying

11 No as 100 miles is about 160 km. He has travelled 75 km and has 125 km to go which is a total of 200 miles.

12 a Anya: CabCo £8.50, YellaCabs £8.40, so YellaCabs is best
   Bettina: CabCo £11.50, YellaCabs £11.60, so CabCo is best
   Calista: CabCo £10, YellaCabs £10, so either
   b If they shared a cab, the shortest distance is 16 km, which would cost £14.50 with CabCo and £14.80 with Yellacabs.

13.2 Travel graphs

Exercise 13B

1 a i 2 h   **ii** 3 h   **iii** 5 h
   b i 40 km/h   **ii** 120 km/h   **iii** 40 km/h
   c 6.30 am

2 a 30 km
   b 40 km
   c 100 km/h

3 a i 125 km   **ii** 125 km/h
   b i Between 2 and 3 pm   **ii** 25 km/h

4 Jafar started the race quickly and covered the first 1500 metres in 5 minutes. He then took a break for a minute and then finished the race at a slower pace taking 10 minutes overall. Azam started the race at a slower pace, taking 7 minutes to run 1500 metres. He then sped up and finished the race in a total of $9\frac{1}{2}$ minutes, beating Jafar.

5 a Araf ran the race at a constant pace, taking 5 minutes to cover the 1000 metres. Sean started slowly, covering the first 500 metres in 4 minutes. He then went faster, covering the last 500 metres in $1\frac{1}{2}$ minutes, giving a total time of $5\frac{1}{2}$ minutes for the race.
   b i 20 km/h   **ii** 12 km/h   **iii** 10.9 km/h

6 There are three methods for doing this question.
   This table shows the first, which is writing down the distances covered each hour.

Time	9 am	9:30	10:00	10.30	11.00	11.30	12.00	12.30
Walker	0	3	6	9	12	15	18	21
Cyclist	0	0	0	0	7.5	15	22.5	30

The second method is algebra:
Walker takes T hours until overtaken,
so $T = \dfrac{D}{6}$; Cyclist takes $T - 1.5$ to overtake, so $T - 1.5 = \dfrac{D}{15}$.
Rearranging gives $15T - 22.5 = 6T$, $9T = 22.5$, $T = 2.5$

The third method is a graph:

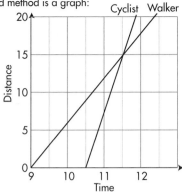

All methods give the same answer of 11:30 when the cyclist overtakes the walker.

7 **a i** Because it stopped several times   **ii** Ravinder
  b Ravinder at 3.55 pm or 3.58 pm, Sue at 4.20 pm, Michael at 4.35 pm
  c i 24 km/h   **ii** 20.6 km/h   **iii** 5

13.3 Flow diagrams and graphs

Exercise 13C

1 **a** A(1, 2), B(3, 0), C(0, 1), D(−2, 4), E(−3, 2), F(−2, 0), G(−4, −1), H(−3, −3), I(1, −3), J(4, −2)
  b i (2, 1)   **ii** (−1, −3)   **iii** (1, 1)
  c $x = -3, x = 2, y = 3, y = -4$
  d i $x = -\frac{1}{2}$ **ii** $y = -\frac{1}{2}$

2 Values of y: 2, 3, 4, 5, 6

3 Values of y: −2, 0, 2, 4, 6

4 Values of y: 1, 2, 3, 4, 5

5 Values of y: −4, −3, −2, −1, 0

6 **a** Values of y: 0, 4, 8, 12, 16 and 6, 8, 10, 12, 14
  b (6, 12)

7 **a** Values of y: −3, −2, −1, 0, 1 and −6, −4, −2, 0, 2
  b (3, 0)

8 Points could be (0, −1), (1, 4), (2, 9), (3, 14), (4, 19), (5, 24), etc

9 **a** £20.50
  b £25.00, £28.50, £32.00, £35.50, £39.00, £42.50;
(£20.00), £23.50, £27.00, £30.50, £34.00, £37.50;
(£15.00), £18.50, £22.00, £25.50, £29.00, £32.50;
(£10.00), (£13.50), £17.00, £20.50, £24.00, £27.50;
(£5.00), (£8.50), (£12.00), £15.50, £19.00, £22.50;
(£0.00), (£3.50), (£7.00), (£10.50), (£14.00), £17.50
  c Yes, they had 3 cream teas and 4 high teas.

10 **a**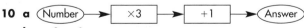

  b $y = 3x + 1$
  c Graph from (0, 1) to (5, 16)
  d Read from 13 on the y-axis across to the graph and down to the x-axis. This should give a value of 4.

11 0, 8, 16, 24, 32, 40, 48

13.4 Linear graphs

Exercise 13D

1 Extreme points are (0, 4), (5, 19)

2 Extreme points are (0, −5), (5, 5)

3 Extreme points are (0, −3), (10, 2)

4 Extreme points are (−3, −4), (3, 14)

5 Extreme points are (−6, 2), (6, 6)

6 **a** Extreme points are (0, −2), (5, 13) and (0, 1), (5, 11)
  b (3, 7)

7 **a** Extreme points are (0, −5), (5, 15) and (0, 3), (5, 13)
  b (4, 11)

8 **a** Extreme points are (0, −1), (12, 3) and (0, −2), (12, 4)
  b (6, 1)

9 **a** Extreme points are (0, 1), (4, 13) and (0, −2), (4, 10)
  b Do not cross because they are parallel

10 **a** Values of y: 5, 4, 3, 2, 1, 0. Extreme points are (0, 5), (5, 0)
  b Extreme points are (0, 7), (7, 0)

11 **a** Graph from (0, 25) to (8, 265) for Ian and graph from (0, 35) to (8, 255) for John.
  b 4 hours

12 **a** Horizontal line through 4, vertical line through 1 and line from origin to (6, 6).
  b 4.5 units squared

13 Graph passing through (x, z) (0, 2), (1, 3), (2, 4), (3, 5), (4, 6)

Exercise 13E

1 **a** 39.2 °C   **b** Days 4 and 5, steepest line
  c Days 8 and 9, steepest line   **d i** Day 5   **ii** 2 **e** 37 °C

2 **a** 2   **b** $\frac{1}{3}$ **c** −3   **d** 1   **e** −2
  f $-\frac{1}{3}$ **g** 5   **h** −5   **i** $\frac{1}{5}$ **j** $-\frac{3}{4}$

3 **a** 1
  b −1
  They are perpendicular and symmetrical about the axes.

4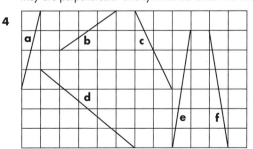

5 Rob has misread the scales. The gradient is actually 2. The line is $y = 2x + 2$. When $x = 10$, $y = 22$. **6** **a** 4 m   **b** 1 m
  c i 1.375 m   **ii** 3.2 m

6 **a** 4 m   **b** 1 m   **c i** 1.375 m   **ii** 3.2 m

Examination questions

1 a i 18   **ii** 6.7
  b Convert 5 gallons and multiply answer by 10

2 a 6   **b** 7

3 a £30   **b** 7 days

4 a A(3, 1); B(3, 4)   **b** Points plotted at $(-2, 2)$
  c Trapezium

5 a -3
  b Points of x and y values in the table plotted correctly on graph.
  c $x = -1.5$, read where the graph crosses the x axis

6 a Grant   **b** 93 sec   **c** 68m/min
  d i Mark   **ii** Steeper line

Answers to Chapter 14

14.1 Patterns in number

Exercise 14A

1 $11111 \times 11111 = 123454321$,
    $111111 \times 111111 = 12345654321$

2 $99999 \times 99999 = 9999800001$,
    $999999 \times 999999 = 999998000001$

3 $7 \times 8 = 7^2 + 7$, $8 \times 9 = 8^2 + 8$

4 $50 \times 51 = 2550$, $60 \times 61 = 3660$

5 $1 + 2 + 3 + 4 + 5 + 4 + 3 + 2 + 1 = 25 = 5^2$,
    $1 + 2 + 3 + 4 + 5 + 6 + 5 + 4 + 3 + 2 + 1 = 36 = 6^2$

6 $21 + 23 + 25 + 27 + 29 = 125 = 5^3$,
    $31 + 33 + 35 + 37 + 39 + 41 = 216 = 6^3$

7 $1 + 6 + 15 + 20 + 15 + 6 + 1 = 64$,
    $1 + 7 + 21 + 35 + 35 + 21 + 7 + 1 = 128$

8 $12\,345\,679 \times 45 = 555\,555\,555$,
    $12\,345\,679 \times 54 = 666\,666\,666$

9 $1^3 + 2^3 + 3^3 + 4^3 = (1 + 2 + 3 + 4)^2 = 100$,
    $1^3 + 2^3 + 3^3 + 4^3 + 5^3 = (1 + 2 + 3 + 4 + 5)^2 = 225$

10 $36^2 + 37^2 + 38^2 + 39^2 + 40^2 = 41^2 + 42^2 + 43^2 + 44^2$,
    $55^2 + 56^2 + 57^2 + 58^2 + 59^2 + 60^2 = 61^2 + 62^2 + 63^2 + 64^2 + 65^2$

11 12345678987654321

12 999999998000000001

13 $12^2 + 12$

14   8190

15 $81 = 9^2$

16 $512 = 8^3$

17   512

18   999 999 999

19 $(1 + 2 + 3 + 4 + 5 + 6 + 7 + 8 + 9)^2 = 2025$

20   X. There are 351 $(1 + 2 + ... + 25 + 26)$ letters from A to Z.
    $3 \times 351 = 1053$. $1053 - 26 = 1027$, $1027 - 25 = 1002$, so,
    as Z and Y are eliminated, the 1000th letter must be X.

14.2 Number sequences

Exercise 14B

1 a 9, 11, 13: add 2
  b 10, 12, 14: add 2
  c 80, 160, 320: double
  d 81, 243, 729: multiply by 3
  e 28, 34, 40: add 6
  f 23, 28, 33: add 5
  g 20 000, 200 000, 2 000 000: multiply by 10
  h 19, 22, 25: add 3
  i 46, 55, 64: add 9
  j 405, 1215, 3645: multiply by 3
  k 18, 22, 26: add 4
  l 625, 3125, 15 625: multiply by 5

2 a 16, 22   **b** 26, 37   **c** 31, 43
  d 46, 64   **e** 121, 169   **f** 782, 3907
  g 22 223, 222 223 **h** 11, 13   **i** 33, 65
  j 78, 108

3 a 48, 96, 192   **b** 33, 39, 45   **c** 4, 2, 1
  d 38, 35, 32   **e** 37, 50, 65   **f** 26, 33, 41
  g 14, 16, 17   **h** 19, 22, 25   **i** 28, 36, 45
  j 5, 6, 7   **k** 0.16, 0.032, 0.0064
  l 0.0625, 0.031 25, 0.015 625

4 a 21, 34: add previous 2 terms
  b 49, 64: next square number
  c 47, 76: add previous 2 terms
  d 216, 343: cube numbers

5   15, 21, 28, 36

6   61, 91, 127

7   364: Daily totals are 1, 3, 6, 10, 15, 21, 28, 36, 45, 55, 66,
    78 (these are the triangle numbers). Cumulative totals are: 1, 4,
    10, 20, 35, 56, 84, 120, 165, 220, 286, 364.

8   29, 41

9   No, they both increase by the same number (3).

10 a 89 km
   b 42 miles

14.3 The nth term of a sequence

Exercise 14C

1 a 3, 5, 7, 9, 11   **b** 1, 4, 7, 10, 13
  c 7, 12, 17, 22, 27   **d** 1, 4, 9, 16, 25
  e 4, 7, 12, 19, 28

2 a 4, 5, 6, 7, 8   **b** 2, 5, 8, 11, 14
  c 3, 8, 13, 18, 23   **d** 0, 3, 8, 15, 24
  e 9, 13, 17, 21, 25

3 $\frac{2}{4}, \frac{3}{5}, \frac{4}{6}, \frac{5}{7}, \frac{6}{8}$

4 a 6, 10, 15, 21, 28   **b** Triangular numbers

5 a £305   **b** £600
  c 3   **d** 5

6 a $\frac{3}{4}, \frac{5}{7}, \frac{7}{10}$

  b i 0.6666667778   **ii** $\frac{2}{3}$

  iii ignore the constant term (1) and just cancel the ns,
    i.e. $\frac{2n+1}{3n+1} \approx \frac{2n}{3n} = \frac{2}{3}$

7 Write $3n + 7 = 4n - 2$ and solve for n.

8 a 2, 6, 24, 720
  b 69! (but this does depend on the calculator)

Exercise 14D

1 a 13, 15, $2n + 1$ **b** 25, 29, $4n + 1$ **c** 33, 38, $5n + 3$
  d 32, 38, $6n - 4$ **e** 20, 23, $3n + 2$ **f** 37, 44, $7n - 5$
  g 21, 25, $4n - 3$ **h** 23, 27, $4n - 1$ **i** 17, 20, $3n - 1$
  j 42, 52, $10n - 8$ **k** 24, 28, $4n + 4$ **l** 29, 34, $5n - 1$

2 a $3n + 1$, 151   **b** $2n + 5$, 105   **c** $5n - 2$, 248
  d $4n - 3$, 197   **e** $8n - 6$, 394   **f** $n + 4$, 54
  g $5n + 1$, 251   **h** $8n - 5$, 395   **i** $3n - 2$, 148
  j $3n + 18$, 168   **k** $7n + 5$, 355   **l** $8n - 7$, 393

3 a i $4n + 1$ **ii** 401   **b i** $2n + 1$ **ii** 201
  c i $3n + 1$ **ii** 301   **d i** $2n + 6$ **ii** 206
  e i $4n + 5$ **ii** 405   **f i** $5n + 1$ **ii** 501
  g i $3n - 3$ **ii** 297   **h i** $6n - 4$ **ii** 596
  i i $8n - 1$ **ii** 799   **j i** $2n + 23$ **ii** 223

4 a $8n + 2$ **b** $8n + 1$
  c $8n$ **d** £8

5 a 31, 33, 35, ... goes up in 2s, so the nth term is $2n \pm a$
    and $2 + 29 = 31$
  b $n + 108$
  c $\frac{2n + 29}{n + 108} \approx \frac{2n}{n} = 2$
  d The 79th term, i.e. when $2n + 29 = n + 108$, $n = 79$

6 a 36, 49, 64, 81, 100
  b i $n^2 + 1$ **ii** $2n^2$ **iii** $n^2 - 1$

14.4   General rules from given patterns

Exercise 14E

1 a appropriate diagram   **b** $4n - 3$
  c 97   **d** 50th diagram

2 a appropriate diagram   **b** $2n + 1$
  c 121   **d** 49th set

3 a 18   **b** $4n + 2$ **c** 12

---

4 a i 20 cm   **ii** $(3n + 2)$ cm   **iii** 152 cm
  b 332

5 a i 20   **ii** 162
  b 79.8 km

6 Formula is $(\frac{3}{4})^n$.
  Picking a large value of n gives an answer of 0 on a calculator,
  so eventually the whole area would be covered.

7 Yes, as the number of matches is 12, 21, 30, 39, ..., which is $9n$
  + 3, so he will need $9 \times 20 + 3 = 183$ matches for the 20th
  step and he has $5 \times 42 = 210$ matches.

8 a 2^n
  b i The quantity doubles   **ii** 1600 ml

9 a They are the same

10 a even   **b** odd   **c** odd

Examination questions

1 a 15, 11
  b Subtract 4
  c Sequence continues 7, 3, −1, −5

2 a i 30, 24   **ii** 32, 64
  b Add 2, 4, 8, 16, etc.

3 a Correct drawing with 7 squares, 4 on top and 3 below
  b 11

4 a Always even
  b Could be either odd or even.

5 6, 9, 14

6 a 1, −1
  b i 7, 6.5   **ii** Yes, as this is the same as $(a + b) \div 2$

7 a i 5, 9, 13   **ii** All numbers are odd
  b $(1 + 3)^2 - 9 = 4^2 - 9 = 16 - 9 = 7$

8 a Even
  b Odd

9 a $\frac{5 \times 6}{2}$

  b $1 + 2 + 3 + 4 + 5 + 6 = \frac{6 \times 7}{2}$

  c $1 + ... + 24 = \frac{24 \times 25}{2} = 300$

10 a i 25
  b square numbers
  c 100

11 The square of any positive fraction less than 1, for example

12 a For any value of n, $2n$ is even, so $2n + 1$ is odd
  b The square of an odd number will be odd, the square of an
    even number will be even

13 S, A, N

14 a i 31, add 6   **ii** −1, subtract 3
  b $4n + 2$

above/below A number greater than/less than another number. For example, 'above average', 'below freezing' (point of water). An object over/under another object.

addition One of the basic operations of arithmetic. The process of combining two or more values to find their total value. Addition is the inverse operation to subtraction.

after/before A number greater than/less than another number. For example '9 is the number after 8', '20 comes before 40'. An event occurring later/earlier than another event.

angle The space (usually measured in degrees [°]) between two intersecting lines or surfaces (planes). The amount of turn needed to move from one line or plane to the other.

appropriate Describes an action, data or information which is relevant to the situation or investigation.

approximate An inexact value that is accurate enough for the current situation.

average A single number that represents or typifies a collection of values. The three commonly used averages are mode, mean, and median.

axis (plural: axes) A fixed line used for reference, along or from which distances or angles are measured. A pair of coordinate axes are shown.

bar chart A diagram where quantities are represented by rectangles of the same width but different, appropriate heights.

below See **above/below**.

bias A survey is biased if it has not been taken from a truly random sample.

brackets The symbols '(' and ')' which are used to separate part of an expression. This may be for clarity or to indicate a part to be worked out individually. When a number or value is placed immediately before an expression or value inside a pair of brackets, the two are to be multiplied together. For example, $6a(5b + c) = 30ab + 6ac$

calculator An electronic device for working out mathematical operations. It is used by pressing keys and the results are shown on the screen.

cancel A fraction can be simplified to an equivalent fraction by dividing the numerator and denominator by a common factor. This is called cancelling.

certain Definite. An event is definitely going to occur. The probability that the event will occur = 1.

chance The likelihood, or probability, of an event occurring.

class A collection of values grouped under one category or range.

class interval The size or spread of the measurement defining a class. For example, heights could be grouped in 1 cm or 10 cm class intervals.

coefficient The number in front of an unknown quantity (the letter) in an algebraic term. For example, in $8x$, 8 is the coefficient of x.

column A vertical list of numbers or values. The vertical parts of a table. A way of arranging numbers to be added or subtracted.

column method (or traditional method) A method of calculating a 'long multiplication' by multiplying the number by the value of each digit of the multiplier and displaying the results in columns before adding them together to find the result.

common unit Express two or more quantities in the same unit, for the purpose of comparison or use in calculations. For example, if one time is given in hours and another in days, they need to be converted to a 'common unit' before they can be compared or used in a calculation.

consecutive Next to each other. For example, Monday and Tuesday are consecutive days, 7 and 8 are consecutive numbers.

consistency A set of data is consistent if all the values are within a small or common range. If a few of the results fall outside this range, the data is not consistent and these 'rogue' results will affect or skew the conclusions drawn from the data.

continuous data Data that can be measured rather than counted, such as weight and height.

conversion graph A graph that can be used to convert from one unit to another. It is drawn by joining two or more points where the equivalence is known. Sometimes, but not always, it will pass through the origin.

correlation One measurement is affected by or affects another. For example, weight and height may correlate, but weight and hair colour do not.

credit When you credit money to an account, you pay money in. If you pay 'using credit' (or with a credit card), you are paying with money you don't have. (Your bank is crediting you – lending you – money to use. This usually has to be paid back with additional interest. If your account is 'in credit', you have money in the account. You have a positive amount of money. (See also **debit**.)

cube The result of raising a number to the power of three. For example, 'two cubed' is written: 2^3, which is $2 \times 2 \times 2 = 8$.

data collection sheet A form or table which is used for recording data collected during a survey.

debit When money is taken from an account, the account is debited with that amount. A debit card can only be used to spend money that you have – the cost is debited from the account. If your account is 'in debit', you have spent more than you had. You now have a negative amount (you owe money to the bank).

decimal Any number using base 10 for the number system. It usually refers to a number written with one or more decimal places.

decimal equivalents A number can be written as decimal, a fraction or a percentage. A fraction or percentage can be converted to a decimal equivalent (a decimal of the same value).

decimal fraction Usually refers to the part of a decimal number after (to the right of) the decimal point, that is, the part less than 1.

decimal place Every digit in a number has a place value (hundreds, tens, ones, etc.). The places after (to the right of) the decimal point have place values of tenths, hundredths, etc. These are called the decimal places.

decimal point The dot used to separate the integer (whole number) place values from the fraction place values (tenths, etc.)

denominator The number under the line in a fraction. It tells you the denomination, name or family of the fraction. For example, a denominator of 3, tells you are thinking about thirds; the whole thing has been divided into three parts. (See also **numerator**.)

difference The result of the subtraction of two numbers; the amount by which one number is greater than another number.

digit A number symbol. Our (decimal or denary) number system uses the digits 0, 1, 2, 3, 4, 5, 6, 7, 8 and 9.

discrete data Data that is counted, rather than measured, such as favourite colour or a measurement that occurs in integer values, such as the number of days.

division One of the basic operations of arithmetic. Division shows the result of sharing. For example, share 12 books among 3 people, they get 4 books each ($12 \div 3 = 4$). It is also used to calculate associated factors. For example, 'How many threes in twelve? ($12 \div 3 = 4$) There are four threes in twelve (or $4 \times 3 = 12$).' It is the inverse operation to multiplication. It can be written using $A \div B$, A/B or $\frac{A}{B}$.

do the same to both sides To keep an equation balanced, you must do the same thing to both sides. If you add something to one side, you must add the same thing to the other side. If you double one side, you must double the other side, etc. If you are manipulating a fraction, you must do the same thing to the numerator and the denominator to keep the value of fraction unchanged. However you can only multiply or divide the numbers. Adding or subtracting will alter the value of the fraction.

dual bar chart This shows two bar charts on one set of axes. It might show the heights of boys and the heights of girls, rather than the heights of all children.

equally likely Two events are described as equally likely if the probabilities of the occurrence of each of the events are equal. For example, when a die is thrown, the outcomes 6 and 2 are equally likely. (They both have a probability of $\frac{1}{6}$.)

equation A number sentence where one side is equal to the other. An equation always contains an equals sign (=).

equation of a line An equation, usually containing two variables (such as x and y), and from which you can plot a line on graph paper. For example, $y = 2x + 3$.

equivalent The same, equal in value. For example, equivalent fractions, equivalent expressions.

equivalent fractions Equivalent fractions are fractions which can be cancelled down to the same value, such as $\frac{10}{20} = \frac{5}{10} = \frac{1}{2}$.

estimate (as a verb) To state or calculate a value close to the actual value by using experience to judge a distance, weight, etc. or by rounding numbers to make the calculation easier. (as a noun) The same as estimation.

evaluate Work out the value of something.

event Something that happens. An event could be the toss of a coin, the throw of a die or a football match.

expand Make bigger. Expanding brackets means you must multiply the terms inside a bracket by the number or letters outside. This will take more room to write, so you have 'expanded' the expression.

experimental data Data gathered from an experiment.

experimental probability The probability found by a series of trials or experiments. It will be an estimate of the true probability.

expression Collection of symbols representing a number. These can include numbers, variables (x, y, etc.), operations (+, ×, etc.), functions (squaring etc.), but there will be no equals sign (=).

extreme values Extreme values in a collection of data are very high and very low values, often noticeable because they are much greater or smaller than the rest of the data.

factor A whole number that divides exactly into a given number.

factor pair A pair of whole numbers whose product make a given number.

factor tree A tree-like diagram used to help find the prime factors of a number.

factorisation Finding one or more factors of a given number.

flow diagram A diagram showing the progression of a calculation or a logical path.

formula (plural: formulae) An equation that enables you to convert or find a measurement from another known measurement or measurements. For example, the conversion formula from the Fahrenheit scale of temperature to the more common Celsius scale is

$$C = \frac{5}{9}(F - 32)$$

where C is the temperature on the Celsius scale and F is the temperature on the Fahrenheit scale.

fraction A fraction means 'part of something'. To give a fraction a name, such as 'fifths' we divide the whole amount into equal parts (in this case five equal parts). A 'proper' fraction represents an amount less than one (The numerator is smaller than the denominator.) Any two numbers or expressions can be written as a fraction, i.e. they are written as a numerator and denominator. (See also **numerator** and **denominator**.)

frequency How often something occurs.

frequency table A table showing values (or classes of values) of a variable alongside the number of times each one has occurred.

frequency polygon A line graph drawn from the information given in a frequency table.

function A function of x is any algebraic expression in which x is the only variable. This is often represented by the function notation $f(x)$ or 'function of x'.

gradient How steep a hill or the line of a graph is. The steeper the slope, the larger the value of the gradient. A horizontal line has a gradient of zero.

greater than (>) Comparing the value of two numbers or quantities. For example, $8 > 4$ states that 8 has a higher value than 4.

grid A table of columns and rows such as those used to add up numbers. Squared or graph paper used for drawing charts and graphs.

grid method (or box method) A method of calculating a 'long multiplication' by arranging the value of each digit in a grid and multiplying them all separately before adding them together to find the result.

grouped data Data from a survey that is grouped into classes.

grouped frequency table A method of tabulating data by grouping it into classes. The frequency of data values that occur within a class is recorded as the frequency of that class.

highest common factor (HCF) When all the factors of two or more numbers are found, some numbers will have factors in common (the same factors). For example, 6 has factors 1, 2, 3 and 6. 9 has factors 1, 3, and 9. They both have the factors 1 and 3. (1 and 3 are common factors.) The greatest of these is 3, so 3 is the highest common factor.

historical data Data cannot always be found by experiment or from a survey. Data collected by other people, sometimes over a long period of time, is called historical data. Weather records would provide historical data.

impossible If something cannot happen, it is said to be impossible. The probability of it happening = 0.

improper fraction An improper fraction is a fraction whose numerator is greater than the denominator. The fraction could be re-written as a mixed number. For example, $\frac{7}{2} = 3$.

inclusive inequality See **linear inequality**.

index (plural: indices) A power. For example, in the expression 3^4, 4 is the index, power or exponent.

index notation A way of writing numbers (particularly factors) using indices. For example, $2700 = 2 \times 2 \times 3 \times 3 \times 3 \times 5 \times 5$. This is written more efficiently as $2^2 \times 3^3 \times 5^2$.

indices see **index**.

inequality An equation shows two numbers or expressions that are equal to each other. A inequality shows two numbers or expressions that are not equal. The symbols $<, \leq, \geq, >$ are used.

input value The number or value that goes into a flow diagram. The value at the start of the flow diagram.

integer A whole number. Integers include all the positive whole numbers, negative whole numbers and zero.

inverse flow diagram A flow diagram to show the reverse operation or series of operations. For example, the inverse of 2 (+ 3) (× 4) → 20 would be 20 (÷ 4) (−3) → 2.

inverse operations Operations that reverse or cancel out the effect of each other. For example addition is the inverse of subtraction, division is the inverse of multiplication.

key A key is shown on a pictogram and stem and leaf diagram to explain what the symbols and numbers mean. A key may also be found on a dual bar chart, to explain what the bars represent.

least common multiple (LCM) Every number has an infinite number of multiples. Two (or more) numbers might have some multiples in common (the same multiples). The smallest of these is called the lowest (or least) common multiple. For example, 6 has multiples of 6, 12, 18, 24, 30, 36, etc. 9 has multiples of 9, 18, 27, 36, 45, etc. They both have multiples of 18 and 36, 18 is the LCM.

less than (<) Comparing the value of two numbers or quantities. Example: 2 < 7 states that 2 is less than 7.

like terms Terms in algebra that are the same apart from their numerical coefficients. For example: $2ax^2$ and $5ax^2$ are a pair of like terms but $5x^2y$ and $7xy^2$ are not. Like terms can be combined by adding together their numerical coefficients so $2ax^2 + 5ax^2 = 7ax^2$.

likely If an event is likely to occur, there is a good chance that it will occur. There is no fixed number for its probability, but it will be between ½ and 1.

line graph A graph constructed by joining a number of points together.

line of best fit When data from an experiment or survey is plotted on graph paper, the points may not lie in an exact straight line or smooth curve. You can draw a line of best fit by looking at all the points and deciding where the line should go. Ideally, there should be as many point above the line as there are below it.

line segment A part of a line.

linear graphs A straight-line graph from an equation such as $y = 3x + 4$.

linear inequality An inequality usually involving one variable not raised to any power, such as $x < 2 + 4x$. A **strict inequality** will use the symbol < or >, an **inclusive inequality** uses the symbol ≤ or ≥.

linear sequence A pattern of numbers where the difference between consecutive terms is always the same.

lowest terms A fraction which is in its simplest form is said to be written in its lowest terms. For example, the fraction $\frac{16}{24}$ may be written in its lowest terms as $\frac{2}{3}$.

mean The mean value of a sample of values is the sum of all the values divided by the number of values in the sample. The mean is often called the average, although there are three different concepts associated with 'average': mean, mode and median.

median The middle value of a sample of data that is arranged in order. For example, the sample 3, 2, 6, 2, 2, 3, 7, 4 may be arranged in order as follows 2, 2, 2, 3, 3, 4, 6, 7. The median is the fourth value, which is 3. If there is an even number of values the median is the mean of the two middle values, for example, 2, 3, 6, 7, 8, 9, has a median of 6.5.

middle value The middle value of a sample of data is needed to find the median of that data. The values must be arranged in order first.

mixed number A number written as a whole number and a fraction. For example, the improper fraction $\frac{5}{2}$ can be written as the mixed number $2\frac{1}{2}$.

modal class If data is arranged in classes, the mode will be a class rather than a specific value. It is called the modal class.

modal value See **mode**.

mode The value that occurs most often in a sample. For example, the mode or modal value of the sample: 2, 2, 3, 3, 3, 3, 4, 5, 5, is 3.

more than (>) See **greater than**.

multiple The multiples of a number are found by multiplying the number by each of 1, 2, 3, ... For example, the multiples of 10 are 10, 20, 30, 40, etc.

multiplication A basic operation of arithmetic. Multiplication is associated with repeated addition. For example: $4 \times 8 = 8 + 8 + 8 + 8 = 32$. Multiplication is the inverse of division.

multiplication tables A grid or tables used to list the multiplication of numbers, often up to 10×10, sometimes up to 12×12.

multiplier The number used to multiply by.

multiply See **multiplication**.

multiply out When brackets have a number or expression in front of them, it is a short way of writing, 'multiply everything inside the brackets by this'. Performing these multiplications is called 'multiplying out'.

mutually exclusive If the occurrence of a certain event means that another event cannot occur, the two events are mutually exclusive. For example, if you miss a bus you cannot also catch the bus.

negative (in maths) Something less than zero. The opposite of positive. (See also **negative number** and **positive**.)

negative coordinates To plot a point on a graph, two coordinates (x and y) are required. If either the x or y values are on the negative part of the number line, they are negative coordinates.

negative correlation If the effect of increasing one measurement is to decrease another, they are said to show negative correlation. For example, the time taken for a certain journey will have negative correlation with the speed of the vehicle. The slope of the line of best fit has a negative gradient.

negative number Describes a number whose value is less than zero. For example, -2, -4, -7.5, are all negative numbers. (See also **positive**.)

no correlation If the points on a scatter graph are random and do not appear to form a straight line, the two measurements show no correlation. One does not affect the other.

nth term The 'general term in a sequence. It describes the rule used to get any term.

number line A continuous line on which all the numbers (whole numbers and fractions) can be shown by points at distances from zero.

numerator The number above the line in a fraction. It tells you the number of parts you have. For example, $\frac{3}{5}$ means you have three of the five parts. (See also **denominator**.)

observation Something that is seen. It can also be the result of a measurement during an experiment or something recorded during a survey.

operation (in maths) an action carried out on two or more numbers. It could be addition, subtraction, multiplication or division.

order Arranged according to a rule. For example ascending order.

ordered data Data or results arranged in ascending or descending order.

outcome The result of an event or trial in a probability experiment, such as the score from a throw of a die.

output value The number or value that comes out of a flow diagram. The value at the end of the flow diagram.

partition method A method of multiplication in a grid where the results of the multiplication of each digit are written and read diagonally before addition.

pattern This could be geometric, where pictures or colours are arranged according to a rule, such as using symmetry. Or it could be numerical where numbers are generated according to an arithmetic rule.

percentage A number written as a fraction with 100 parts. Instead of writing $\overline{100}$, we use the symbol %. So $\frac{50}{100}$ is written as 50%.

percentage change Instead of stating an actual amount by which something has changed you give the percentage change. For example, if the mass of sack of potatoes decreases from 50 kg to 49 kg, the actual change is 1 kg and the percentage change is 2%.

percentage decrease If an actual amount decreases, the percentage change will be a percentage decrease.

percentage increase If an actual amount increases, the percentage change will be a percentage increase.

percentage loss If an amount of money decreases, the percentage change will be a percentage loss.

percentage profit If an amount of money increases, the percentage change will be a percentage profit.

pictograms A pictorial method of representing data on a graph.

pie chart A chart that represents data as slices of a whole 'pie' or circle. The circle is divided into sections. The number of degrees in the angle at the centre of each section represents the frequency.

place value The value of a digit depends upon its place or position in the number.

positive (in maths) Something greater than zero. The opposite of negative (See also **positive number** and **negative**.)

positive correlation If the effect of increasing one measurement is to increase another, they are said to show positive correlation. For example, the time taken for a journey in a certain vehicle will have positive correlation with the distance covered. The slope of the line of best fit has a positive gradient.

positive number Describes a number whose value is greater than zero. The counting numbers are all positive numbers. (See also **negative**.)

power The number of times a number or expression is multiplied by itself. The name given to the symbol to indicate this, such as ^{2}. (See also **index**.)

prime factor A factor of a number that is also a prime number. (See also **prime number**.)

prime number A number whose only factors are 1 and itself. 1 is not a prime number. 2 is the only even prime number.

probability The measure of the possibility of an event occurring.

probability fraction All probabilities lie between 0 and 1. Any probability that is not 0 or 1 is given as a fraction – the probability fraction.

probability scale A line divided at regular intervals. It is usually labelled 'impossible', unlikely, even chance, etc., to show the likelihood of an event occurring. Possible outcomes can then be marked along the scale.

probability space diagram A diagram or table showing all the possible outcomes of an event.

product The result of multiplying two or more numbers or expressions together.

product of prime factors The result of multiplying two or more prime factors together.

profit/loss The gain or loss made from buying and selling.

proper fraction A fraction in which the numerator is smaller than the denominator. For example, the fraction $\frac{2}{3}$ is a proper fraction and the fraction $\frac{3}{2}$ is not.

quantity An measurable amount of something which can be written as a number or a number with appropriate units. For example, the capacity of a bottle.

random Haphazard. A random number is one chosen without following a rule. Choosing items from a bag without looking means they are chosen at random; every item has an equal chance of being chosen.

range The difference between the largest and smallest data values in a given set of data.

ratio The ratio of A to B is a number found by dividing A by B. It is written as A : B. For example, the ratio of 1 m to 1 cm is written as 1 m : 1 cm = 100 : 1. Notice that the two quantities must both be in the same units if they are to be compared in this way.

rational number A rational number is a number that can be written as a fraction, for example, $\frac{1}{4}$ or $\frac{10}{3}$.

raw data Data in the form it was collected. It hasn't been ordered or arranged in any way.

rearrangement To change the arrangement of something. An equation can be rearranged using the rules of algebra to help you solve it. Data can be rearranged to help you analyse it.

reciprocal The reciprocal of any number is 1 divided by the number. The effect of finding the reciprocal of a fraction is to turn it upside down. The reciprocal of 3 is $\frac{1}{3}$, the reciprocal of $\frac{1}{4}$ is 4, the reciprocal of $\frac{10}{3}$ is $\frac{3}{10}$.

recurring decimal A decimal number that repeats forever with a repeating pattern of digits.

relative frequency Also known as experimental probability. It is the ratio of the number of successful events to the number of trials. It is an estimate for the theoretical probability.

representative A number or quantity that is typical of a set of data. A person that is typical of a given group. An average is representative of all the given values.

rounding An approximation for a number that is accurate enough for some specific purpose. The rounded number, which can be rounded up or rounded down, may be used to make arithmetic easier or may be less precise than the unrounded number.

row A horizontal list of numbers or values. The horizontal parts of a table.

sample The part of a population that is considered for statistical analysis. The act of taking a sample within a population is called sampling. There are two factors that need to be considered when sampling from a population:

1. The size of the sample. The sample must be large enough for the results of a statistical analysis to have any significance. 2. The way in which the sampling is done. The sample should be representative of the population.

sample space diagram See **probability space diagram**.

scales A scale on a diagram shows the scale factor used to make the drawing.

scatter diagram A diagram of points plotted of pairs of values of two types of data. The points may fall randomly or they may show some kind of correlation.

sector A region of a circle, like a slice of a pie, bounded by an arc and two radii.

sequence A pattern of numbers which are related by a common difference.

shape Could be a 2-D or 3-D shape. Any drawing or object. In mathematics we usually study simple shapes such as squares, prisms, etc. or compound shapes that can be formed by combining two or three simple shapes, such as an ice-cream cone made by joining a hemisphere to a cone.

sign A symbol used to represent something such as ×, ÷, = and √. The 'sign of a number' means whether it is a positive or negative number.

significant figure The significance of a particular digit in a number is concerned with its relative size in the number. The first (or most) significant figure is the left-most, non-zero digit; its size and place value tell you the approximate value of the complete number. The least significant figure is the right-most digit; it tells you a small detail about the complete number. For example, if we write 78.09 to 3 significant figures we would use the rules of rounding and write 78.1. (See also **approximate**.)

simplest form A fraction cancelled down so it cannot be simplified any further. An expression where the arithmetic is completed so that it cannot be simplified any further.

simplify To make an equation or expression easier to work with or understand by combining like terms or cancelling down. For example: $4a - 2a + 5b + 2b = 2a + 7b$, $\frac{12}{18} = \frac{2}{3}$.

slope See **gradient**.

solution The result of solving a mathematical problem. Solutions are often given in equation form.

solve Finding the value or values of a variable (x) which satisfy the given equation.

spread See **range**.

square The result of multiplying a number by itself. For example, 5^2 or 5 squared is equal to $5 \times 5 = 25$.

strict inequality See **linear equality**.

subject The subject of a formula is the letter on its own on one side of the equals sign. For example, t is the subject of this formula: $t = 3f + 7$.

substitution When a letter in an equation, expression or formula is replaced by a number, we have substituted the number for the letter. For example, if $a = b + 2x$, and we know $b = 9$ and $x = 6$, we can write $a = 9 + 2 \times 6$. So $a = 9 + 12 = 17$.

subtraction One of the basic operations of arithmetic. It finds the difference between two numbers. Subtraction is the inverse operation to addition.

symbol A written mark that has a meaning. All digits are symbols of the numbers they represent. +, <, √ and ° are other mathematical symbols. A pictogram uses symbols to represent amounts.

tally chart A chart with marks made to record each object or event in a certain category or class. The marks are usually grouped in fives to make counting the total easier.

term 1. A part of an expression, equation or formula. Terms are separated by + and – signs.

term 2. A number in a sequence or arrangement in a pattern.

terminating decimal 'Terminating' means 'ending'. A terminating decimal can be written down exactly. $\frac{33}{100}$ can be written as 0.33, but $\frac{3}{10}$ is 0.3333….. with the 3s recurring forever.

term-to-term A sequence of numbers is said to be term-to-term if the rule that determines each next term is the same.

times table See **multiplication table**.

top-heavy A fraction where the numerator is greater than the denominator could be described as top-heavy.

transpose To rearrange a formula.

trends A collection data can be analysed (for example by drawing a time graph) so that any trend or pattern, such as falling profits, may be discovered.

trial An experiment to discover an approximation to the probability of the outcome of an event will consist of many trials where the event takes place and the outcome is recorded.

unlikely An outcome with a low chance of occurring.

unordered data See **raw data**.

variable A quantity that can have many values. These values may be discrete or continuous. They are often represented by x and y in an expression.

x-value The value along the horizontal axis on a graph.

y-value The value along the vertical axis on a graph.

INDEX

William Collins' dream of knowledge for all began with the publication of his first book in 1819. A self-educated mill worker, he not only enriched millions of lives, but also founded a flourishing publishing house. Today, staying true to this spirit, Collins books are packed with inspiration, innovation and practical expertise. They place you at the centre of a world of possibility and give you exactly what you need to explore it.

Collins. Freedom to teach.

Published by Collins
An imprint of HarperCollins*Publishers*
77–85 Fulham Palace Road
Hammersmith
London
W6 8JB

Browse the complete Collins catalogue at
www.collinseducation.com

© HarperCollins*Publishers* Limited 2010

10 9 8 7 6 5 4 3 2 1

ISBN-13 978-0-00-734002-6

Kevin Evans, Keith Gordon, Trevor Senior and Brian Speed assert their moral rights to be identified as the authors of this work

British Library Cataloguing in Publication Data
A Catalogue record for this publication is available from the British Library

Commissioned by Katie Sergeant
Project managed by Alexandra Riley
Edited and proofread by Brian Asbury, Joan Miller, Philippa Boxer, Margaret Shepherd and Karen Westall
Indexing by Michael Forder
Answer check by Amanda Dickson
Photo research by Jane Taylor
Cover design by Angela English
Content design by Nigel Jordan
Typesetting by Gray Publishing
Functional maths and problem-solving pages by EMC Design and Jerry Fowler
Production by Arjen Jansen
Printed and bound by L.E.G.O. S.p.A. Italy

AQA has checked that the content and level of this publication are appropriate for its GCSE Mathematics (4360) specification.

Acknowledgements

The publishers have sought permission from AQA to reproduce questions from past GCSE Mathematics papers.

The publishers wish to thank the following for permission to reproduce photographs. Every effort has been made to trace copyright holders and to obtain their permission for the use of copyright material. The publishers will gladly receive any information enabling them to rectify any error or omission at the first opportunity.

Talking heads throughout © René Mansi/iStockphoto.com; p.6 © Karen Mower/iStockphoto.com, © D.Huss/iStockphoto.com; p.34–35 © Walesonview.com, © zwo5de/iStockphoto.com, © rydrych/iStockphoto.com, © BorisPamikov/iStockphoto.com; p.70–71 Cheshire Regiment/Wikipedia, © Xdrew, © reprorations.com; p.72 © ajb/iStockphoto.com, © Andrew Howe/iStockphoto.com, © fotoIE/iStockphoto.com, © Kiankhoon/iStockphoto.com, © theasis/iStockphoto.com, © Peter van Wagner/iStockphoto.com; p.96–97 © SDbT/iStockphoto.com, © JoeBiafore/iStockphoto.com, © laflor/iStockphoto.com, © dalton00/iStockphoto.com; p.98 © weareadventurers/iStockphoto.com, © Roland Frommknecht/iStockphoto.com, © Compassandcamera/iStockphoto.com, © Eugenio d'Orio/iStockphoto.com, © Steve Stone/iStockphoto.com; p.126 © Viktor Polyacov (Dr), © Jerry Fowler; p.128 William Playfair/Wikimedia Commons, © HultonArchive/iStockphoto.com; p. 156–157 © Roob/iStockphoto.com, © johnwoodcock/iStockphoto.com; p.158 © JenDen 2005/iStockphoto.com, © Domenico Pellegriti/iStockphoto.com; p.196–197 © SpatzPhoto/Alamy; p.198 © iLex/iStockphoto.com, © George Clerk/iStockphoto.com, © Owen Price/iStockphoto.com; p.238–239 © Olivier Meerson, © Jerry Fowler; p.240 William Playfair/Wikimedia Commons; p.266–267 © Robert Terry, © Jerry Fowler; p.268 © John W. DeFeo/iStockphoto.com, © Elena Talberg/iStockphoto.com, © Robert Churchill/iStockphoto.com, © Izabela Habur/iStockphoto.com; p.304–305 © shoobydoooo/iStockphoto.com, © ARTPUPPY/iStockphoto.com, © Daxi/iStockphoto.com; p.306 Leonardo da Vinci/Wikimedia Commons, Chris73/ Wikimedia Commons; p.332–333 © Peter Garbet/iStockphoto.com, © Iztok Grilic/iStockphoto.com, © Chritine Glade/iStockphoto.com, © Anastasia Pelikh/iStockphoto.com; p.334 © Bejan Fatur/iStockphoto.com, © Claudio Baba/iStockphoto.com, © Viktor Kitaykin/iStockphoto.com, © lisafx/iStockphoto.com, © nullplus/iStockphoto.com, © Joas Kotzch/iStockphoto.com, © Sean Locke/iStockphoto.com, © tjerophotography/iStockphoto.com; p.360-361 © Robert Stainforth/Alamy; p.362 © PJ Morley/iStockphoto.com, © Dane Wirtzfeld/iStockphoto.com; p.388–389 © Hhakim/iStockphoto.com, © chrisp0/iStockphoto.com, © roc8jas/iStockphoto.com, © dynasoar/iStockphoto.com, © troyek/iStockphoto.com, © TT/iStockphoto.com; p.390 William Playfair/Wikimedia Commons; p.424–425 © Catherine Karnow/Corbis; p.426 © Rick Szczechowski/iStockphoto.com, © Derek Dammann/iStockphoto.com; p.448–449 © Sculpies/iStockphoto.com, © James Mcquarrie (Dr), © Andrey Konovalikov (Dr), © Christian Delbert (Dr).

With thanks to Samantha Burns, Claire Beckett, Andy Edmonds, Anton Bush (Gloucester High School for Girls), Matthew Pennington (Wirral Grammar School for Girls), James Toyer (The Buckingham School), Gordon Starkey (Brockhill Park Performing Arts College), Laura Radford and Alan Rees (Wolfreton School) and Mark Foster (Sedgefield Community College).